RACIAL AND ETHNIC RELATIONS
SIXTH EDITION

Joe R. Feagin
University of Florida

Clairece Booher Feagin

PRENTICE HALL, UPPER SADDLE RIVER, NEW JERSEY 07458

Library of Congress Cataloging-in-Publication Data

Feagin, Joe R.
    Racial and ethnic relations / Joe R. Feagin, Clairece Booher
Feagin. — 6th ed.
        p.   cm.
    Includes bibliographical references and index.
    ISBN 0–13–674722–1
    1. Minorities—United States.   2. United States—Race relations.
    II. Title.
    E184.A1F38   1999
    305.8′00973—dc21   98-28380
                                                              CIP

Editorial Director: Charlyce Jones Owen
Editor in Chief: Nancy Roberts
Acquisitions Editor: John Chillingworth
Managing Editor: Sharon Chambliss
Marketing Manager: Christopher DeJohn
Project Management and Interior Design: Serena Hoffman
Photo Researcher: Beth Boyd
Illustrator: Maria Piper
Buyer: Mary Ann Gloriande
Cover Art Director: Jayne Conte
Cover Designer: Anthony Gemmellaro
Cover Art: Diana Ong (1993), "Untitled Crowd"

This book was set in 10/12 Palatino by DM Cradle Associates
and was printed and bound by Hamilton Printing Company.
The cover was printed by Phoenix Color Corp.

 © 1999, 1996, 1993, 1989, 1984, 1978 by Prentice-Hall, Inc.
Simon & Schuster/A Viacom Company
Upper Saddle River, New Jersey 07458

Printed in the United States of America

10   9   8   7   6   5   4   3

ISBN 0-13-674722-1

Prentice-Hall International (UK) Limited, *London*
Prentice-Hall of Australia Pty. Limited, *Sydney*
Prentice-Hall Canada Inc., *Toronto*
Prentice-Hall Hispanoamericana, S.A., *Mexico*
Prentice-Hall of India Private Limited, *New Delhi*
Prentice-Hall of Japan, Inc., *Tokyo*
Simon & Schuster Asia Pte. Ltd., *Singapore*
Editora Prentice-Hall do Brasil, Ltda., *Rio de Janeiro*

Contents

Part II: A Nation of Immigrants: An Overview of the Economic and Political Conditions of Selected Racial and Ethnic Groups   65

Preface

Over the last two decades, numerous scholars, journalists, and politicians have argued that there is a "declining significance of race" or an "end to racism" in the United States. They have written or spoken optimistically about the decrease in discrimination and the improving character of racial and ethnic relations in this nation. Over the same period of time, however, the scholarly journals and mass media have been filled with accounts of hate crimes targeting people of color, reports of white supremacist groups, discussions of lawsuits over discrimination in employment and public accommodations, research analyses of widespread housing discrimination, descriptions of riots stemming from police brutality, political controversies over affirmative action and other antidiscrimination programs, and intense debates about the character and impact of the recent immigrants, who are mostly Latino and Asian.

Thus, as we move into the twenty-first century, there is much discussion and argument about racial and ethnic discrimination, oppression, and conflict. Contrary to what some scholars and journalists assert, this debate reflects underlying social, economic, and political realities in the United States. As we move into the twenty-first century, many Americans are well aware of the continuing significance of race, racism, and ethnicity, not only in this country but also in other countries—from the Republic of South Africa to the former Yugoslavia and the former Soviet Union. Racial and ethnic oppression and conflict are extraordinarily important in the modern world and have the potential to tear apart any nation, including a highly industrialized one.

One result of a reinvigorated interest in racial and ethnic matters in many circles is the creation of college and university courses that focus on racial-ethnic divisions or cultural diversity in the United States. We have revised this edition of *Racial and Ethnic Relations* with this continuing interest in U.S. racial and ethnic heritages and conflicts in mind. This book is designed both for sociology and other social science courses titled Racial and Ethnic Relations, Race Relations, Minority Groups, and Minority Relations, and also for various other courses on cultural diversity, multiculturalism, and racial and ethnic groups offered in college, university, and business settings.

One purpose of this book is to provide readers with access to the important literature on racial and ethnic groups in the United States and, to a lesser extent, in other countries around the globe. We have drawn on a broad array of sources, including articles, books, and other data analyses by sociologists, political scientists, social psychologists, anthropologists, historians, economists, investigative journalists, and legal scholars. We have limited space, so we have not been able to deal with all the important racial and ethnic groups in the United States. Instead, we have focused on a modest number of major racial and ethnic groups, preferring to accent depth rather than breadth in analyses. In recent decades, social science analyses have begun to dig deeper into the "what," "why," and "how" of racial and ethnic oppression and conflict. We draw heavily on this ever-growing research.

The introduction to Part I looks briefly at the origins of the racial and ethnic mosaic that is the United States. It serves as an introduction to Chapters 1 and 2, which discuss major concepts and theories in the study of racial and ethnic relations. The introduction to Part II sketches the political and economic history of the United States to provide the context for understanding the adaptation and oppression of certain immigrant groups that, voluntarily or involuntarily, came to U.S. shores. Only one major group, Native Americans, cannot be viewed as relatively recent immigrants; indeed, as the original inhabitants they were the victims of the stream of immigrants from outside North America. The situations and experiences of Native American societies and the various groups that have immigrated to North America are considered in Chapters 3–13. Chapter 14 moves away from the United States to look at patterns of racial and ethnic relations in several other countries around the world: South Africa, Brazil, France, Russia, and Bosnia. Here, we examine how global patterns of racial oppression and conflict have been implemented or fostered by European colonizers and their descendants during the colonial and decolonization periods in the histories of these countries.

This sixth revised edition of *Racial and Ethnic Relations* updates each chapter with new materials and research, such as the research on housing discrimination and segregation discussed in Chapter 8. In several chapters we give expanded attention to new conceptual approaches to racial and ethnic relations. For example, in Chapter 2 and elsewhere, we note the utility of the new segmented assimilation theory in making sense of recent patterns of immigration. We explore, too, how new theorizing about assimilation is forcing deeper probing of the dimensions and variations in adaptation patterns, as well as the sometimes negative consequences of integration into mainstream U.S. culture. In Chapter 2 we have added a new section that attempts to move power–conflict theorizing toward a more comprehensive framework for understanding racial oppression. Where possible in the group chapters, we have given attention to current events and issues, such as the case of Tiger Woods, the first American of African ancestry to win the Masters golf tourney. In addition, in Chapter 13 we deal with the increasingly multiracial and multicultural character of U.S. society. We examine some of the implications of the forecasts by demographers that over the course of the twenty-first century the United States will become a nation whose population majority is composed of Latino, African, Asian, and Native Americans.

In writing this and previous editions of this textbook, we have received useful comments and suggestions from numerous colleagues, students, teachers, correspondents, editors, and reviewers. We are indebted to those whose advice, suggestions, and insights have made this a better book. Among these are Joane Nagel, Howard Winant, Edna Bonacich, Karyn McKinney, Eileen O'Brien, Leslie Inniss, Richard Alba, Yanick St. Jean, Debra Van Ausdale, Robert Parker, Daniel Duarte, Teun Van Dijk, Harriett Romo, Alice Littlefield, Wendy Ng, John R. Sosa, Jaime Martinez, Bud Khleif, Howard Leslie, Larry Horn, Doris Wilkinson, Anthony Orum, James Button, Ward Churchill, Edward Múrguía, S. Dale McLemore, Nestor Rodríguez, Melvin Sikes, Hernan Vera, Gideon Sjoberg, Gilberto Cardenas, Nikitah Imani, David Roth, John Butler, Andrew Greeley, Joseph Lopreato, Graham Kinloch, Eric Woodrum, Lester Hill, Chad Oliver, Marcia A. Herndon, Rogelio Nuñez, Tom Walls, Samuel Heilman, Phylis Cancilla Martinelli, José Limon, Devon Peña, Diana Kendall, Robena Jackson, Mark Chesler, David O'Brien, and Bradley Stewart. We would also like to thank the students of several sociology colleagues, including Professor Yanick St. Jean, for their helpful comments in revising this book. We are also indebted to Pinar Batur-Vanderlippe of Vassar College for revising Chapter 14.

We hope that you find this revised edition informative and intellectually stimulating. We welcome comments, especially in regard to future editions. Please write to us at the Department of Sociology, Box 117330, University of Florida, Gainesville, FL, 32611–2036.

Joe R. Feagin
Clairece Booher Feagin

PART I

The Racial and Ethnic Mosaic

More than two hundred years ago, the new United States severed its colonial ties with Europe. Born in revolution, this new nation was portrayed as centrally dedicated to freedom and equality. Over the next two centuries a vigorous nation would emerge, with great racial and ethnic diversity. Yet the new society had its seamy side. Racial and ethnic oppression and conflict were also imbedded in the founding period and in the history of the new republic. The European immigrants often took the lands of Native Americans by force. By the end of the seventeenth century, the enslavement of Africans and African Americans was fundamental to the economy of the North American colonies, and resistance and revolt by these enslaved Americans were recurring problems for white slaveholders. In succeeding centuries other non-European peoples, such as Chinese, Japanese, and Mexican Americans, would suffer serious yokes of oppression. But non-Europeans were not the only ones to face oppressive conditions. Discrimination against white immigrant groups was part of the sometimes forgotten history of both the pre- and post-revolutionary periods.

In the earliest period the colonial population on the prospering Atlantic coast was predominantly English in its origins and basic social institutions. Because of England's

huge appetite for raw materials and new markets, English authorities encouraged non-English immigration to the colonies. Yet there was popular opposition, verbal and violent, to the long line of new white immigrants. "Foreigners" soon became a negative category for many colonists. "Despite the need for new settlers English colonials had mixed feelings about foreign arrivals. Anglo-Saxon mobs attacked Huguenots in Frenchtown, Rhode Island, and destroyed a Scotch-Irish frontier settlement in Worcester, Massachusetts."[1] In the 1700s, colonies such as Virginia, Pennsylvania, and Rhode Island attempted to restrict non-British immigrants.[2]

The basic documents of the new republic reflect its patterns of racial relations and racial subordination, and some of the republic's first laws were aimed at hampering groups of non-English origin. The otherwise radical Declaration of Independence, prepared mostly by Thomas Jefferson, originally contained language accusing King George of pursuing slavery, of waging "cruel war against human nature itself, violating its most sacred rights of life and liberty in the persons of a distant people who never offended him, captivating them and carrying them into slavery in another hemisphere, or to incur miserable death in the transportation thither."[3] Jefferson further noted that the English king had not attempted to prohibit

1

the slave trade and had encouraged enslaved Africans to "rise in arms" against white colonists. But because of pressure from white slaveholding interests in the South and white slave-trading interests in New England, this critique of slavery was omitted from the final version of the Declaration. Even in this revolutionary period, the doctrines of freedom and equality could not be extended to the African American population, for criticism of King George on the issue of slavery was in fact criticism of the North American social and economic system. Jefferson himself was a major slaveholder whose wealth was tied to an oppressive, slaveholding agricultural system.

The U.S. Constitution explicitly recognized racial subordination in several places. First, as a result of a famous compromise between northern and southern representatives to the Constitutional Convention, Article I originally stipulated that three-fifths of a given state's enslaved population was to be counted among the total in apportioning the state's legislative representation—that is, each enslaved American was officially viewed as three-fifths of a person. Interestingly, in this case southern slaveowners pressed for full inclusion of the enslaved African Americans in the population count, while northern interests were opposed.

In addition, a section was added to Article I permitting the slave trade to continue until 1808. The Constitution also incorporated a fugitive slave provision that required the return of runaways to their owners, a provision opposed by few whites at the time.[4] Neither the statement in the Declaration of Independence that "all men are created equal" nor the Constitution's Bill of Rights was seen as applying to Americans of African descent. Slavery, ironically, would last much longer in the new "democratic" republic than in aristocratic Britain.[5]

African Americans were not the only group to suffer from government action. Numerous other non-English groups continued to find themselves less than equal under the law. Anti-immigrant legislation in the late 1700s and early 1800s included the Alien, Sedition, and Naturalization Acts.[6] Irish, German, and French immigrants were growing in number by the late eighteenth century, and concern with the liberal political sentiments of the new immigrants was great. The Naturalization Act stiffened residency requirements for citizenship from five to fourteen years; the Alien Act gave the president the power to expel foreigners. President John Adams was pressed to issue orders deporting immigrants under the Alien Act and did so in two cases. Shiploads of foreign immigrants left the country out of fear of exclusion.

Inequality in life chances along racial and ethnic lines was a fundamental fact of the new nation's institutions. At first, liberty and justice were for men of British descent only. This situation did not go unchallenged. By the late eighteenth century many Irish and German immigrants had come into the colonies. Indeed, a significant proportion of the 4 million persons enumerated in the first United States census were of non-English origins.

Over the next two centuries, English domination was modified by the ascendance of other northern Europeans. These groups in turn were challenged by southern and eastern European and non-European groups trying to move up in the social, economic, and political systems. Gradually, the new nation became an unprecedented mixing of diverse peoples.

Most in the non-British immigrant groups gradually came to adopt the English language and adjust to English institutions, seen by many as the core society and culture. Most entering groups adapted, to some degree, to the dominant culture and ways. White immigrant groups eventually gained substantial power and status in the process.

In contrast to white immigrants, the voluntary and involuntary immigrants from Africa, Asia, and Latin America, as well as Native Americans, have generally remained subordinate to white Americans in political, cultural, and economic terms. Racial and ethnic diversity, inequality, and oppression were and continue to be part of the foundation of U.S. society. Nonetheless, Americans of color have long challenged their subordinate status, and they continue to do so. If current demographic trends continue, they will become the majority of the U.S. population by the middle of the twenty-first century.

Today, as in the past, issues of immigration, adaptation, inequality, and oppression are at the heart of the sociological study of racial and ethnic relations in the United States. They will continue to be central issues for the foreseeable future. In the two chapters of Part I, we will define basic terms used by social scientists and examine these concepts from a critical perspective. Chapter 1 examines terms such as *race, racism, ethnic group,* and *prejudice*. Chapter 2 reviews major conceptual frameworks, including assimilation theories and power–conflict theories, for interpreting the complex structure and long-term development of racial and ethnic relations in the United States.

CHAPTER 1

Basic Concepts in the Study of Racial and Ethnic Relations

In the 1980s Susie Guillory Phipps, the wife of a white businessperson in Louisiana, went to court to try to get the racial designation on her birth certificate at the Louisiana Bureau of Vital Records changed from "colored" to "white." A 1970 Louisiana "blood" law required that persons with one-thirty-second or more "Negro blood" (ancestry) were to be designated as "colored" on birth records; before 1970 "any traceable amount" of African ancestry had been used to define a person as colored. The white-skinned Phipps was the descendant of an eighteenth-century white plantation owner and an African American slave, and her small amount of African ancestry was enough to get her classified as "colored" on her official Louisiana birth certificate. Because other records supported the designation, Phipps lost her case against the state of Louisiana.[1]

This controversy raises the basic question of how a person comes to be defined as *white* or *black* in U.S. society. It is only under racist assumptions that having one black ancestor makes one black while having one white ancestor does not make one white. If the latter were the law in Louisiana, of course, many *black* residents there—those who have at least one white ancestor (often a slaveholder)—would be classified as *white*! This story illustrates that racial categories are constructed and defined socially and politically, not scientifically.

A logical place to start making sense out of this system of racial definition is with basic terms and concepts. People have often used such terms as *racial groups* and *prejudice* without specifying their meaning. Since these are basic concepts in the study of intergroup relations, we will analyze them in detail.

ISSUES OF RACE AND RACISM

Racial Groups and Hierarchies

Both *racial group* and the more common term *race* have been used in a number of senses in social science and popular writings. *Human race, Jewish race, Negro race*—

4

such terms in the literature suggest a range of meanings. In sixteenth- and early seventeenth-century Europe, the word *race* was used for descendants of a common ancestor, emphasizing kinship linkages rather than physical characteristics such as hair type or skin color. It was only in the late eighteenth century that the term *race* came to mean a category of human beings with distinctive physical characteristics transmitted by descent.[2]

In the 1600s François Bernier was one of the first Europeans to sort human beings into distinct categories. Soon a hierarchy of physically distinct groups (not yet termed *races*) came to be accepted, with white Europeans, not surprisingly, at the top. Africans were relegated by European observers to the bottom, in part because of (black) Africans' color and allegedly "primitive" culture, but also because Africans were often known to Europeans as slaves. Economic and political subordination resulted in a low position in the white classification system.[3]

Immanuel Kant's use of the German phrase for "races of mankind" in the 1770s was one of the first explicit uses of the term in the sense of biologically distinct categories of human beings. In 1795 Johann Blumenbach, a German anatomist, established a racial classification system that became an influential typology. At the top of his racial hierarchy were the Caucasians (Europeans), followed in order by the Mongolians (Asians), the Ethiopians (Africans), the Americans (Native Americans), and the Malays (Polynesians). Blumenbach was the first to use the term *Caucasian*; he felt that the Europeans in the Caucasus mountains of Russia were "the most beautiful race of men." Ever since, Europeans have been called by a term that originally applied only to a small and unrepresentative area of Europe. Blumenbach also chose the term Caucasian because he believed the earliest human beings came from there. (Twentieth-century archaeologists have found the earliest human remains in Africa.)[4]

The concept of race as a biologically distinctive category was developed by northern Europeans who, for much of their histories, had been largely isolated from contact with people who differed from them physically or culturally. Before the development of large sailing ships in the late 1400s, they had little contact with people from Asia, Africa, or the Americas. Soon, however, it was these northern Europeans who established slave systems in the Americas. The slave colonies were legitimated and rationalized by the northern Europeans, including the English, who classified African slaves as a lesser "race." The idea of race was not developed from close scientific observations of all human beings. Rather, "race was, from its inception, a folk classification, a product of popular beliefs about human differences that evolved from the sixteenth through the nineteenth centuries."[5]

From the eighteenth century to the twentieth century, the use of *race* by biologists, physical anthropologists, and other scientists usually drew on this folk classification of race in the sense of biologically distinctive groups. The scientists who used race in this sense reflected their own racial prejudices or those of the general public. Thus, "the scientists themselves undertook efforts to document the existence of the differences that the European cultural worldview demanded and had already created."[6] Basic to this increasingly prevalent view was the

Blumenbach theory of a set number of biologically distinct "races" with differing physical characteristics and the belief that these characteristics were hereditary and thus created a natural hierarchy of groups. By the late nineteenth century, numerous European and U.S. scientists and popular writers were systematically downgrading all peoples not of northern European origin, especially southern Europeans and Jewish Europeans, as inferior "races."[7]

This singling out of people within the human species in terms of a biologized "race" hierarchy is a distinctively European and Euro-American idea. "Indigenous peoples . . . have observed and appreciated cultural diversity as variations on cosmological themes. As a rule, the indigenous worldview encompasses all humanity."[8] In the view of M. Annette Jaimes, indigenous peoples around the globe typically emphasize "building alliances" across a variety of racial and ethnic groups. U.S. examples include the assistance in agricultural techniques given by Native Americans to early European settlers and later to Japanese Americans who were imprisoned during World War II (see Chapter 11) in concentration camps located near reservations in the western United States.[9]

Ideological Racism

The development of ideological racism is rooted in European global expansion that began in earnest in the late 1400s. We can define *ideological racism* specifically as *an ideology that considers a group's unchangeable physical characteristics to be linked in a direct, causal way to psychological or intellectual characteristics and that, on this basis, distinguishes between superior and inferior racial groups.*[10] The "scientific racism" of such European writers as De Gobineau in the mid-nineteenth century was used to justify the spread of European colonialism in Asia, Africa, and the Americas. A long line of racist theorists followed in De Gobineau's footsteps, including the Nazi leader Adolf Hitler. They even applied the ideology of racial inferiority to culturally distinct white European groups, such as Jewish Europeans. In a racist ideology, real or alleged physical characteristics are linked to *cultural* traits that the dominant group considers undesirable or inferior.

Ideological racism has long been common in the United States. For example, in 1935 an influential white University of Virginia professor wrote:

> The size of the brain in the Black Race is below the medium both of the Whites and the Yellow-Browns, frequently with relatively more simple convolutions. The frontal lobes are often low and narrow. The parietal lobes voluminous, the occipital protruding. The psychic activities of the Black Race are a careless, jolly vivacity, emotions and passions of short duration, and a strong and somewhat irrational egoism. Idealism, ambition, and the co-operative faculties are weak. They love amusement and sport but have little initiative and adventurous spirit.[11]

This example of crude ideological racism links physical and personality characteristics. Although this type of racist portrait often passed for science before World War II—and in today's white supremacy organizations (for example, the Ku Klux Klan), some of it still does—it is, in fact, pseudoscience. Ideological racists have simply accepted as true the stereotyped characteristics traditionally applied by whites to African Americans or other people of color.

Modern biologists and anthropologists have demonstrated the wild-eyed irrationality of this racist mythology. The basic tenet of racist thinking is that physical differences such as skin color or nose shape are intrinsically and unalterably tied to meaningful differentials in basic intelligence or "civilization." Yet, in spite of periodic assertions of such a linkage by white supremacy groups and pseudo-scientists, no scientific support for this assumed linkage exists.

Indeed, there is no distinctive biological reality called "race" that can be determined by objective scientific procedures. The social, medical, and physical sciences have demonstrated this fact.[12] Given the constant blending and inter-breeding of human groups over many centuries and into the present, it is impossible to sort human beings into unambiguously distinctive "races" on genetic grounds. There is simply too much overlapping of genetic characteristics across the variety of human populations. Two randomly selected individuals from the world's population would have in common, on average, about 99.8 percent of their genetic material. Most of the genetic variation in regard to human populations "occurs *within* populations, not *between* them."[13] There are genetic differences between geographically scattered human populations, but these differences are slight. The racial importance of the slight dissimilarities is socially, not scientifically, determined.

Human populations singled out as "races" are simply groups with visible differences that Europeans and European Americans have decided to emphasize as important in their social, economic, and political relations. As physiologist Jared Diamond has noted, such racial categorizing is neither objective nor scientific. Indeed, there are *many* different ways of classifying human populations in terms of genetic characteristics: "One such procedure would group Italians and Greeks with most African blacks. It would classify Xhosa—the South African 'black' group to which [South African] President Nelson Mandela belongs—with Swedes rather than Nigerians."[14] What Diamond has in mind are the antimalarial genes that are not found among the light-skinned Swedes or dark-skinned southern African groups like the Xhosas, but are commonly found in northern African groups and among Europeans such as Italians and Greeks. These antimalarial genes may be more important for human beings than those determining skin color variations, yet they are not used by Europeans or Euro-Americans, including pseudoscientists, for their "racial" classifications.[15]

There is only one "human race (Homo sapiens)," to which we all belong. Every human being is in fact distantly *related* to every other human being. The indigenous view of human beings, previously noted, is now accepted by most scientists.[16] Nonetheless, the lack of scientific support has not lessened the popularity of racist ideologies. The scholar Ashley Montagu has noted the extreme danger of ideological racism, a view shaped in part by his observation of the consequence of the German Nazi ideology, according to which there were physically distinct Aryan and Jewish races.[17] That racist ideology lay behind the killing of millions of European Jews (and other Europeans) during the 1930s and 1940s.

Racial Group

Today, social scientists view race not as a given biological reality but as a socially constructed reality. Sociologist Oliver C. Cox, one of the first to underscore this perspective, defined a race as "any people who are distinguished, or consider themselves distinguished, in social relations with other peoples, by their physical characteristics."[18] From the social-definition perspective, characteristics such as skin color have no self-evident meaning; rather, they have *social* meaning. Similarly, a *racial group* has been defined by Pierre van den Berghe as a "human group that defines itself and/or is defined by other groups as different from other groups by virtue of innate and immutable physical characteristics."[19]

A racial group is not something naturally generated as part of the self-evident order of the universe. A person's race is typically determined by and important to certain outsiders, although a group's self-definition can also be important. In this book we will define a *racial group* as a *social group that persons inside or outside the group have decided is important to single out as inferior or superior, typically on the basis of real or alleged physical characteristics subjectively selected.* Racial group distinctions are rooted in ideological racism, which, as we noted previously, links physical characteristics to "inferior" or "superior" cultural and intellectual characteristics.

In the United States, a number of groups would fit this definition. Asian Americans, African Americans, Native Americans ("American Indians"), and Mexican Americans have had their physical characteristics, such as skin color and eye shape, singled out by dominant white Americans as badges of social and racial inferiority. Some groups once defined as racial groups—and as physically and mentally inferior groups at that—are no longer defined that way. In later chapters we will see that Irish and Italian Americans were once defined as inferior "races" (or racial groups) by Anglo-Protestant Americans. Later, the social definition of these European immigrants as a racial group was replaced by an Anglo-Protestant construction of the groups as white *ethnic groups,* a term we will examine shortly.

The examples of Irish and Italian Americans make it clear that racial definitions are not fixed essences that last forever, but instead are temporary constructions that are shaped in social and political struggles in particular times and in particular societies. Racial definitions can change and even disappear.

Why are some physical characteristics, such as skin color, selected as a basis for distinguishing racial groups, whereas other characteristics, such as eye color, seldom are? These questions cannot be answered in biological terms. They require historical and sociological analysis. Such characteristics as skin color are, as Banton has argued, "easily observed and ordered in the mind."[20] They take on particular significance in group interaction. More important than ease of observation is the way in which economic or political subordination and exploitation create a need to identify the powerless group in a certain way. In justifying exploitation, the exploiting group often defines the real (or alleged) physical characteristics singled out to typify the exploited group as inferior racial characteristics.

Technological differences in weaponry and firepower, for example, between European and African peoples facilitated the subordination of Africans as slaves in the English and other European colonies. In turn, the generally darker skin of the Africans and their descendants came to be used by white groups as an indicator of subordinate racial–cultural status. Skin-color characteristics have no inherent meaning; in group interaction they become important because they can be used to classify members of the dominant and subordinate groups.

Knowledge of one's relatives sometimes affects one's assignment to a racial group, particularly for those who lack the emphasized physical characteristics. At various times in many societies, people have been distinguished not only on the basis of their own physical characteristics but also on the basis of a socially determined "rule of descent."[21] For example, in Nazi Germany Adolf Hitler's officials often identified Jewish Germans on the basis of their having one or more Jewish ancestors or relatives.

Ancestry and Multiracial Realities

The socially applied rules of descent have varied greatly from society to society. For example, in some countries there are special categories or designations for mixed-ancestry groups, such as the "Coloreds" for people with African and European ancestry in South Africa. Many Latin American countries recognize two or more mixed-ancestry categories. Mixed-ancestry distinctions have been rare in the United States. In the case of African Americans, interracial blending has, over time, caused dark skin color to become a less reliable characteristic for those making racial distinctions, and the rule of descent has gained more importance as a mechanism of racial identification to perpetuate discrimination. Today, black Americans "evidence an unusually wide range of physical traits. Their skin color extends from ebony to a shade paler than many 'whites.' "[22] (The majority are not *literally* black but rather a shade of brown.)

In many U.S. communities, the social aspect of the defining process becomes obvious when a light-skinned person, say, of one-eighth African ancestry but with none of the physical traits most whites associate with African Americans, is regarded as black because one of his or her ancestors is known to be of African ancestry. Sometimes termed the "one drop of blood" rule, this odd rule of descent is unique to the United States. Indeed, in Caribbean nations such as Jamaica or in many parts of Africa, a person who is one-eighth African in ancestry and seven-eighths European would be considered "white."

Mixed racial ancestry does not fit neatly into the traditional U.S. system of racial categorizing. Today, there are some 2 million children in interracial families in the United States, and more than 1 million interracial marriages occur annually. The existence and experiences of these Americans underscore the social construction of racial identities. Consider the case of Tiger Woods, a talented golfer. In 1997, at the age of 21, Woods became the center of great mass media attention when he won a number of major golf tournaments, including the Masters tourney, where he posted a record score.[23] Woods's racial–ethnic background is quite com-

Golf star Tiger Woods hits his tee shot during a 1996 tournament.

plex. He has described his ancestry as one-eighth white, one-eighth Native American, one-fourth African American, one-fourth Thai, and one-fourth Chinese. However, the mass media have often portrayed Woods as African American. Following his major victories, his father also spoke of him as a black sports star, and Woods presented himself in some early commercials as black. Later Woods accented his mixed ancestry and seemed to some observers to play down his African American identity. After some criticism by African Americans who were proud of his achievements and his African ancestry, Woods issued a statement that he was proud of his African American and other ancestry.[24]

Nonetheless, many in the media have continued to view Woods as a black sports star, and it seems likely that far more Americans see him as African American than as multiracial. After Woods won the Master's tourney, a white golfer, Fuzzy Zoeller, spoke about "that little boy" and joked that he hoped Woods would not pick collard greens and fried chicken, or whatever it is that they eat, for the next Master's championship dinner.[25] This white golfer saw Woods as an African American. He later met with Woods and apologized for his comments.[26]

Since the 1990 census, when nearly 10 million Americans did not check off any of the conventional racial categories, the government has been considering ways to describe what is called the nation's growing multiracial character. In 1997, Congress debated the addition of a "multiracial" category in the U.S. census for the year 2000, a change supported by many Americans of mixed racial–ethnic ancestry. Others suggested that the presence of such a box might reduce the count in other categories, such as "black," which would hurt civil rights enforcement in some areas (although in test surveys only one percent of respondents checked a multiracial option). Congress decided against the creation of a specific multiracial category for the 2000 census. Instead, individuals will be allowed to mark multiple ancestry groups. This debate over the census ancestry categories clearly indicates that racial designations are socially constructed and maintained.[27]

ETHNIC GROUPS

What Is an Ethnic Group?

The term *ethnic group* has been used by social scientists in two different senses, one narrow and one broad. Some definitions of the term are broad enough to include socially defined racial groups. For example, in Milton Gordon's broad definition, an ethnic group is a social group distinguished "by race, religion, or national origin."[28] Like the definition of racial group, this definition contains the notion of set-apartness. But here the distinctive characteristics can be physical or cultural, and language and religion are seen as critical markers or signs of ethnicity even where there is no physical distinctiveness. Sociologist Nathan Glazer has given this inclusive definition of ethnic groups:

> A single family of social identities—a family which, in addition to races and ethnic groups, includes religions (as in Holland), language groups (as in Belgium), and all of which can be included in the most general term, ethnic groups, groups defined by descent, real or mythical, and sharing a common history and experience.[29]

Today, many scholars, such as Thomas Sowell in his *Ethnic America* and Werner Sollors in an introduction to *The Invention of Ethnicity*, still view religious, national–origin, and racial groups as falling under the umbrella term *ethnic group*.[30]

Other scholars prefer a narrower definition of ethnic group, one that omits groups defined substantially in terms of physical characteristics (those called racial groups) and is limited to groups distinguished primarily on the basis of cultural or national–origin characteristics. *Cultural characteristics* include language; *national origin* refers to the country (and national culture) from which the person or his or her ancestors came.

The word *ethnic* comes from the Greek *ethnos*, originally meaning "nation." In its earliest English usage, about 1470 B.P., the word referred to culturally different "heathen" countries or nations (those not Christian or Jewish). Apparently, the first usage of "ethnic group" to denote national origin developed in the period of heavy immigration from southern and eastern European nations to the United States in the early twentieth century. Since the 1930s and 1940s, a number of prominent social scientists have suggested that the narrower definition of ethnic group, more in line with the original Greek meaning of nationality, makes the term more useful.[31]

Social scientist W. Lloyd Warner, who was perhaps the first to use the term *ethnicity*, distinguished between ethnic groups—which he saw as characterized by cultural differences—and racial groups, characterized substantially by physical differences.[32] More recent scholars have also preferred the narrower usage. In van den Berghe's view, for example, ethnic groups are "socially defined but on the basis of cultural criteria."[33]

In this book, the usual meaning of *ethnic group* will be the narrower one—*a group socially distinguished or set apart, by others or by itself, primarily on the basis of cultural or national–origin characteristics.* Such set-apart groups, such as Irish Americans or Italian Americans, usually develop a strong sense of a common cultural heritage and a common ancestry. Some broad social categories, such as the religious category of "Baptists," have been considered by some to be ethnic groups, but in the sense we use the term here they are not. Religious groups that are open to relatively easy conversion are not, strictly speaking, ethnic because ethnicity says something about accepted lines of common descent or origin as well as current cultural characteristics.

Many social analysts who use the broader definition of ethnic group (that is, the one that includes racial groups) argue that the experiences of people defined as "nonwhite" are essentially similar to the experiences of white groups. Some social scientists have argued that in the United States the situations and experiences of non-European groups such as African or Asian Americans are in broad ways similar to those of white immigrants from Europe, especially in regard to the process of gradual integration into the Anglo-Protestant core society. Some analysts further assume that the experiences of both European and non-European groups are adequately explained by the same theoretical framework—typically the conventional assimilationist framework.[34]

In contrast, many analysts who prefer the narrower definition of *ethnic group* as a socially constructed category that differs in important ways from the term *racial group* tend to view the experiences of subordinated racial groups as distinctively different from those of white European ethnic groups.[35] Philomena Essed has argued that much of the public and scholarly use of the umbrella term *ethnic group* for all groups, including racial groups, in the last two decades has had political and racial overtones: "Indeed, the substitution of 'ethnicity' for 'race' as a basis of categorization is accompanied by increasing unwillingness among the dominant group to accept responsibility for the problems of racism."[36] While Essed's point is accurate for much writing that views such groups as African Americans and Mexican Americans as ethnic groups that are no different in their experiences from groups like Italian Americans and Irish Americans, it does not apply to those scholars who prefer the term *ethnic group* because they feel its use indicates that all groups have genuine and significant cultural histories.[37]

In addition, many scholars emphasize the point that all socially constructed racial groups contain subgroups that can be seen as ethnic groups because they have distinctive cultural identities. Examples of this include Italian Americans within the white racial group and Jamaican Americans within the black racial group.

Definitions of *racial group* and *ethnic group* which emphasize their social meaning and construction directly reject the biological determinism that views such groups as self-evident with unchanging physical or intellectual characteristics. People themselves, both outside and inside racial and ethnic groups, determine when certain physical or cultural characteristics are important enough to single out a group for social purposes, whether for good or for ill.

A given social group may be viewed by different outsiders or at different times as a racial or an ethnic group. Indeed, some groups have been defined by the same outsiders on the basis of both physical and cultural criteria. During the 1930s, Jewish Germans, for example, were identified as a "race" in Nazi Germany, in part because of physical characteristics that were alleged to be different from those of other Germans. However, as we noted previously, identification of Jewish Germans for persecution by Nazi bureaucrats and storm troopers was based more on ethnic characteristics—cultural characteristics such as religion or language and genealogical ties to known Jewish ancestors—than on physical characteristics.

In their contacts with early European societies, black Africans seem to have been viewed in ethnic rather than in racial terms. St. Clair Drake's research on early black African contacts with Europeans and lighter-skinned North Africans has shown that in the first centuries of contact, during the Egyptian, Greek, and Roman periods, European outsiders generally attached far greater significance to Africans' culture and nationality than to their physical characteristics. Before the sixteenth century "neither White Racism nor *racial slavery* existed."[38] Similarly, Frank

The United States is a nation of great racial and ethnic diversity.

Snowden has demonstrated that the early encounters between African blacks and Mediterranean whites led to a generally favorable image of African blacks among whites and to friendships and intermarriage—much different from the black–white relations in modern race-conscious societies. While some Europeans in these periods did express negative views of Africans' color, these views never developed into an acute color consciousness linked to an ideological view of Africans as an inferior species with intellectual deficits. Virulent color prejudice in the form of ideological racism emerged only in the modern world, primarily in the imperial expansion into Africa and the Americas by European nations seeking colonies between the 1400s and the 1700s.[39] Historical conditions have shaped whether and how skin color becomes a marker in the processes of exploitation and oppression.

Ancestry is important to the concept of ethnic group whether it is defined in a narrow or a broad sense. Perception of a common ancestry, real or mythical, has been part of outsiders' definitions and of ethnic groups' self-definitions. Sociologist Max Weber saw ethnic groups broadly as "human groups that entertain a subjective belief in their common descent."[40] In addition to a sense of common ancestry, a consciousness of shared experiences and of shared cultural patterns is important in shaping a group's identity.

Recently, a number of social scientists have focused on the ways in which people's constructions and conceptions of their own and others' ethnic identities change over time and from one situation to another. These social constructionists emphasize the importance of studying the "ways in which ethnic boundaries, identities, and cultures are negotiated, defined, and produced through social interaction inside and outside ethnic communities."[41] Drawing on her field research, Mary Waters has shown the options white Americans have with regard to their ethnic identity. A white person of both English and Irish ancestry may choose either ethnic identity, both, or none, preferring in the latter case to identify only as "American."[42] Waters has also documented how Afro-Caribbean immigrants sometimes view themselves as African Americans and sometimes as an ethnic group distinct from native-born blacks within the African American racial group.[43] Nonetheless, Afro-Caribbean Americans have no choice in how they are viewed—as black Americans—by the dominant white group. This fact of American life again reveals the central role that power inequalities play in the social definition of certain human groups as racial groups.

We should note that *racial group* and *ethnic group* are only two of the terms used in research on racial and ethnic relations. Among the other terms are *majority group* and *minority group*.[44] Louis Wirth explicitly defined a minority group in terms of its subordinate position: "A group of people who, because of their physical or cultural characteristics, are singled out from others in the society in which they live for differential and unequal treatment and who therefore regard themselves as objects of collective discrimination."[45]

However, many scholars today consider it more accurate to use a term such as *dominant group* for the majority group and a term like *subordinate group* for a minority group. This usage is appropriate because a majority group in this sense can be numerically a minority, as was once the case with white Europeans in a number of colonial societies. Moreover, some demographic forecasts see the white majority, in population terms, becoming a statistical minority in the United States by the middle of the twenty-first century.

THE MATTER OF CULTURE

Cultural differences between groups are usually at the heart of racial and ethnic relations and conflict. Sociologists and anthropologists generally define *culture* as the shared values, understandings, symbols, and practices of a group of people. The shared symbols are the means by which people "communicate, perpetuate, and develop their knowledge about and attitudes toward life."[46] There are cultural objects (the symbols and practices) as well cultural creators and cultural receivers (the people who create and use the cultural objects).[47]

In Chapter 2 we will observe the importance of culture in the process by which one group adapts to another. We will examine the concept of *dominant culture*, the understandings and symbols created and controlled by a powerful group, as well as the concept of an *immigrant culture*, the understandings and symbols of an immigrant group entering the sphere of the dominant culture. Milton Gordon has argued that new immigrant groups coming into North America after the English have tended to give up much of their own cultural heritage to conform to the dominant Anglo-Protestant core culture: "If there is anything in American life which can be described as an overall American culture which serves as a reference point for immigrants and their children, it can best be described, it seems to us, as the middle-class cultural patterns of, largely, white Protestant, Anglo-Saxon origins, leaving aside for the moment the question of minor reciprocal influences on this culture exercised by the cultures of later entry into the United States."[48]

In subsequent chapters we will also see how some subordinated racial and ethnic groups have drawn on their well-developed cultures to resist discrimination and slavish assimilation to the dominant Anglo-Protestant culture. Some analysts describe these as *cultures of resistance*. The cultural heritage and present cultural understandings of subordinated groups, such as Native Americans or African Americans, have positive historical and current significance. They not only foster a sense of identity and pride but also facilitate the group's survival and enhance its ability to resist oppression. For example, the strong family and kinship values of various Native American societies enabled them to survive in the face of Euro-American invasions of their lands. Moreover, contrary to prevailing white stereotypes about black families, the strong family ties of African Americans have played a central role in creating a sense of pride and identity and have provided crucial support for coping with widespread discrimination from whites.

PREJUDICE AND STEREOTYPES

Another important term in the study of intergroup relations is *prejudice*, which in popular discourse is associated mostly with negative attitudes about members of selected racial and ethnic groups. An understanding of how and why negative attitudes develop is best achieved by first defining *ethnocentrism*, which was long ago described by Sumner as the "view of things in which one's own group is the center of everything, and all others are scaled and rated with reference to it."[49] Individuals who develop *positive ethnocentrism* are characterized by a loyalty to the values, beliefs, and members of their own group. Ethnocentrism often prompts negative views of outgroups through a constant evaluation of outgroups in terms of ingroup values and ways. Such negative views are manifested in prejudices and stereotypes that influence the social, economic, and political interaction among groups.[50]

Prejudice has been defined by Gordon Allport as "thinking ill of others without sufficient warrant."[51] The term comes from the Latin word *praejudicium*, or a judgment made prior to knowledge or experience. In English the word evolved from meaning "hasty judgment" to the present connotation of unfavorable bias based on an unsupported judgment. Although prejudice can theoretically apply to favorable prejudgments, its current usage in both popular speech and social science analysis is almost exclusively negative. Defined more precisely, *prejudice* is, to closely paraphrase Allport, *an antipathy based on a faulty generalization. It may be felt or expressed. It may be directed toward a group as a whole, or toward an individual because he or she is a member of that group.*[52] As used in this text, *prejudice* has both an emotional and a cognitive aspect; it involves a negative feeling or attitude toward the outgroup as well as an inaccurate belief. An example might be "I as a white person hate black and Latino people because black and Latino people always smell worse than whites." The first part of the sentence expresses the negative emotion (the hatred); the last part, an inaccurate generalization. This latter cognitive aspect has been termed a *stereotype—that is, an overgeneralization associated with a racial or ethnic category that goes beyond existing evidence.*

Why do some people stereotype others? Why have Irish Americans been stereotyped as lazy drunkards, African Americans as indolent, Italian Americans as criminals with "Mafia" ties, Asian Americans as "treacherous Orientals"? Such questions encourage us to examine the role that prejudices and stereotypes play in the history and daily lives of individuals and groups. Sociological analysts of stereotyping emphasize group pressures on individuals for conformity or rationalization, while psychological analysts stress individual irrationality or personality defects.

Much research has highlighted the expressive function of prejudice for the individual. Frustration–aggression theories, psychoanalytic theories, and authoritarian personality perspectives focus on the *externalization* function of prejudice—the transfer of an individual's internal psychological problem onto an external object as a solution to that problem. Psychologically oriented interpretations often attribute racial or ethnic prejudice to special emotional problems of "sick" or "abnormal" individuals, such as a deep hatred of their own fathers.[53]

In a classic study of prejudice and personality, *The Authoritarian Personality*, T. W. Adorno and his colleagues argued that people who hate such groups as Jewish Americans or black Americans typically differ from tolerant people in regard to central personality traits—specifically, that they tend to exhibit "authoritarian personalities."[54] Those with authoritarian personalities differ from others in their greater submission to authority, tendency to stereotype, superstition, and great concern for social status. They see the world as sinister and threatening, a view that easily leads to intolerance of outgroups that occupy subordinate positions in the social world around them.

Some scholars have raised serious questions about this stress on the expressive function of prejudice. They have suggested that social *conformity* may be a much more important factor.[55] Most people accept their own social situations as given and hold the prejudices taught at home and at school. Conformity to the prejudices of relatives and friends is a major source of individual prejudice. In this view, most prejudices are not the result of deep psychological pathologies, but rather reflect shared social definitions of outgroups. In such cases prejudice functions as a means of social adjustment. Most of us can think of situations in which we or our acquaintances have adjusted to new racial beliefs while moving from one region or setting to another. As Schermerhorn notes, "prejudice is a product of *situations*," not "a little demon that emerges in people simply because they are depraved."[56]

An additional function of prejudice is to rationalize a subordinate group's powerless position. Herbert Blumer suggested some years ago that prejudice is more than a matter of negative feelings possessed by members of one group for another; it is also "rooted in a sense of group position."[57] The dominant group comes to rationalize its privileged position. Prejudice is deeply rooted in the history of human contacts, but modern prejudices can sometimes be found grouped together in some type of ideological racism. Fully developed racist ideologies, as we have noted, appear to have arisen with European imperialism and colonization of people of color around the world. Modern prejudice, Oliver C. Cox argues, "is a divisive attitude seeking to alienate dominant group sympathy from an 'inferior' race, a whole people, for the purpose of facilitating its exploitation."[58] When peoples are subordinated, as in the cases of the white enslavement of Africans in the American colonies and the restrictive quotas for Jewish Americans in some colleges in the 1920s and 1930s, those in power—here, Anglo-Protestant whites—gradually develop views that rationalize the exploitation and oppression of others.

This tendency to develop a racial ideology that defends privilege persists. In recent years a number of scholars in a variety of disciplines have suggested that the majority of white Americans possess a racial consciousness that consists of not just a few prejudices and stereotypes but a broader structure of racialized thought, a way of organizing and processing information about themselves and people of color. A sense of racial superiority, overt or unconscious, grows out of a process in which whites grow up with power over and separated from people of color. Many racial ideas are formed by the informal and tacit lessons whites learn as children at home and school and as adults as they absorb messages from the mass media and socialize with relatives, coworkers, and friends.[59]

Some members of dominant groups who discriminate are motivated by a desire for economic or political gain. Such people strive to maintain their undeserved privileges, whether or not they rationalize the striving in terms of racial prejudices and stereotypes.[60] Such striving involves a system of racial inequality in which the dominant racial group benefits economically, politically, and psychologically—and acts to maintain its benefits. However, in the everyday world of discrimination, it is likely that the desire to protect privilege will be accompanied by negative views of the group targeted for discrimination.

Images of people of color that are held by dominant white groups today have many similarities with stereotypes of the past, although some changes in white thinking have occurred since the civil rights movement of the 1960s. Recent changes in racial prejudices and stereotypes in the United States have been examined by a number of researchers. David Sears and John McConahay have identified what they term *symbolic* or *modern racism*—that is, white beliefs that serious antiblack discrimination does not exist today and that African Americans are making illegitimate demands for social changes. These social psychologists have found that among whites "old-fashioned racism" favoring rigid segregation and extreme antiblack stereotypes has largely been replaced by this modern racism whose proponents accept modest desegregation but resist the large-scale changes necessary for full racial integration of the society.[61] Similarly, Lawrence Bobo has suggested that whites have an "ideology of bounded racial change." That is, whites' support for changes in discrimination ends when such changes seriously endanger their standard of living. Bobo suggests that many whites display "a loosely coherent set of attitudes and beliefs that, among other things, attributes patterns of black–white inequality to the dispositional shortcomings of black Americans."[62]

Thomas Pettigrew has noted white reactions to the achievements of African Americans in the recent years and has suggested that what he calls the "ultimate attribution error" on the part of whites includes not only blaming black victims for their failures but also discounting black successes by attributing the latter to luck or unfair advantages rather than to intelligence and hard work.[63] While this research on modern racism has mostly examined white attitudes toward black Americans, many of the new concepts can be used to interpret white prejudices and stereotypes directed at other people of color.

DISCRIMINATION

Distinguishing Dimensions

Public discussions of discrimination and of government programs to eradicate it (for example, affirmative action) are often confusing because the important dimensions of racial or ethnic discrimination are not distinguished. As a first step in sorting out the confusion, we suggest the diagram in Figure 1–1. The dimensions of discrimination include (a) motivation, (b) discriminatory actions, (c) effects, (d) the relation between motivation and actions, (e) the relation between actions and effects, (f) the immediate institutional context, and (g) the larger societal context.[64] A given set of discriminatory acts—such as the exclusion of Jewish

American applicants from Ivy League colleges in the 1920s or the exclusion of African American children from all-white public schools until the 1960s—can be looked at in terms of these dimensions. One can ask what the motivation was for this discrimination. Was it prejudice, stereotyping, or another motive? One can also ask what form the exclusionary practices actually took. For example, in the case of segregated public schools in the South, principals refused black children entrance into their buildings. Also of importance are the long-term effects of these discriminatory practices. One effect was the poorer school facilities most black children encountered. Yet these practices were not the actions of isolated white principals. Rather, they were part of an institutionalized pattern of segregated education in the South, the effects of which are still present in U.S. society. Finally, such legalized patterns of school discrimination were part of a larger social context of general racial subordination of black Americans across many institutional areas in the South. Today, as in the past, racial discrimination remains a multi-dimensional problem encompassing all institutional areas of U.S. society.

Research on Prejudice and Discrimination

Much research on discrimination has focused on one type of motivation—prejudice [see (a) in Figure 1–1]. Many analysts emphasize the relation between prejudice and discrimination [(d) in Figure 1–1], viewing prejudice as the critical cause of discriminatory treatment of a singled-out group. Allport suggested that few

FIGURE 1–1   The Dimensions of Discrimination

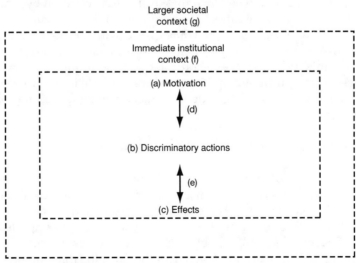

SOURCE: Adapted from Joe R. Feagin, "Affirmative Action in an Era of Reaction," *Consultations on the Affirmative Action Statement of the U.S. Commission on Civil Rights* (Washington, DC: U.S. Government Printing Office, 1982), pp. 44–48.

prejudiced people keep their prejudices entirely to themselves; instead they act out their feelings in various ways.[65] In his classic study *An American Dilemma* (1944), Gunnar Myrdal saw racial prejudice as "the whole complex of valuations and beliefs which are behind discriminatory behavior on the part of white Americans."[66] A few years later Robert K. Merton argued that for some people discrimination is motivated not by their own prejudices but by fear of the prejudices of others in the dominant group.[67]

Some experimental studies by social psychologists have focused on the relationship between prejudice and expressed discrimination. These researchers have examined whether prejudiced people do, in fact, discriminate, and, if so, how that prejudice is linked to discrimination. Such studies have generally found a weak positive correlation between expressed prejudice (for example, on questionnaires) and the measured discriminatory behavior. Knowing how prejudiced a subject is does not necessarily help predict the character of his or her actions. In addition, some experimenters have tried to develop nonobvious measures of discrimination. One such measure involved setting up an experimental situation in which whites encountered a black person (a confederate of the researcher) who needed help making a phone call at a public telephone. The researcher then observed if the racial identity of the person needing help affected the white responses. As we noted previously, public opinion surveys of white attitudes toward blacks have shown a significant decline in certain old-fashioned racist attitudes since the 1940s, and some of these experimental researchers have questioned whether the whites responding to such surveys are actually concealing their racial prejudices. Reviewing laboratory studies that used less obvious measures of discrimination, such as the phone call experiment just mentioned, Faye Crosby and her associates have shown that overt discrimination by whites actually varies with the social situation. It is more likely in anonymous situations than in face-to-face encounters that whites have with blacks they know. The researchers also noted that experimental studies have found much more antiblack discrimination than they should have if the unprejudiced views that many whites express in public opinion surveys were their real views of black Americans. Many whites seem to hide their racial feelings when responding to opinion pollsters.[68]

Defining Institutional and Individual Discrimination

The emphasis on individual prejudice and on bigoted individuals in many traditional assessments of discrimination has led some scholars to accent the institutionalization of discrimination. For example, Stokely Carmichael and Charles Hamilton distinguished the concepts of *individual racism*, exemplified by the actions of white terrorists bombing a black church, and of *institutional racism*, illustrated by accumulating institutional practices that lead to large numbers of black children suffering because of seriously inadequate food and medical facilities in U.S. central cities.[69] Carmichael and Hamilton introduced the concept of institutional racism to the discussion of U.S. racial relations. In their book *Black Power*, these authors move beyond a focus on individual bigots. In their view, institutional racism can involve actions in which dominant group members have "no intention of subordinating others because of color, or are totally unaware of doing so."[70] We should note that the term *racism* is used here for patterns of discrimination that target *racially* subordinated groups, such as African Americans.

In his analysis of racial discrimination and mental health, Pettigrew has distinguished between *direct* and *indirect* racial discrimination, applying the latter term to restrictions in one area (such as screening out job applicants because they do not have a college degree) that are shaped by racial discrimination in another area (historical exclusion of black Americans from many white universities prior to the 1960s).[71]

Recent conceptual work on racial discrimination emphasizes the close relationship between its individual ("micro") and institutional ("macro") dimensions, which must be viewed as two aspects of the same phenomenon. Social psychologist Essed has underscored the "mutual interdependence of the macro and micro dimensions" of racial discrimination. From the macro perspective, racism is "a system of structural inequalities and a historical process." From a micro perspective, racism involves individual discriminators whose specific actions are racist "only when they activate existing structural racial inequalities in the system."[72] The routine actions of discriminators reinforce and are shaped by a hierarchical system of racial dominance and inequality.

Thus, the group context of discriminatory actions is very important. The working definition of *discrimination* we emphasize in this book is as follows: *actions carried out by members of dominant groups, or their representatives, that have a differential and harmful impact on members of subordinate groups.* The dominant and subordinate groups we focus on here are racial and ethnic groups. From this perspective, the most serious discrimination in U.S. society involves the harmful practices taken by members of powerful racial and ethnic groups against those with much less power and fewer resources. Discrimination involves *actions* as well as one or more *discriminators* and one or more *victims*. A further distinction between *intentional* (motivated by prejudice or intent to harm) and *unintentional* (not motivated by prejudice or intent to harm) is useful for identifying different types of discrimination.[73]

Drawing on the two dimensions of scale and intention, we suggest four major types of discrimination. Type A, *isolate discrimination,* is harmful action taken intentionally by a member of a dominant racial or ethnic group against members of a subordinate group, without the support of other members of the dominant group in the immediate social or community context. An example would be a white Anglo police officer who implements anti-Latino hostility by beating up Mexican American prisoners at every opportunity, even though the majority of Anglo officers and department regulations specifically oppose such actions. (If the majority of Anglo officers in that department behaved in this fashion, the beatings would fall under the heading of type C discrimination.) The term *isolate* should not be taken to mean that type A discrimination is rare, for it is indeed commonplace.

Type B, *small-group discrimination,* is harmful action taken intentionally by a small number of dominant-group individuals acting in concert against members of subordinate racial and ethnic groups, without the support of the norms and of most other dominant group members in the immediate social or community context. The bombing of Irish Catholic churches in the 1800s by small groups of British Americans or the burning of crosses at black homes in several U.S. cities in the 1990s by members of white supremacist groups are likely examples.

Type C, *direct institutionalized discrimination,* is organizationally prescribed or community-prescribed action that by intention has a differential and negative impact on members of subordinate racial and ethnic groups. Typically, these actions are not sporadic but are routinely carried out by a large number of dominant-group individuals guided by the legal or informal norms of the immediate organizational or community context. Historical examples include the intentional exclusion, by law, of African Americans and Jewish Americans from certain resi-

Ku Klux Klan members salute in front of a burning cross during a recent rally in Texas.

dential neighborhoods and jobs. Type C discrimination can be seen today in the actions of those white real estate agents and owners who regularly create barriers for black homebuyers seeking homes in white neighborhoods. They are acting in accord with informal norms shared by many whites in their communities.[74]

Type D, *indirect institutionalized discrimination*, consists of dominant-group practices having a harmful impact on members of subordinate racial and ethnic groups even though the organizationally or community-prescribed norms or regulations guiding those actions have been established with no intent to harm. For example, intentional discrimination institutionalized in the schooling of subordinate group members such as black and Latino Americans—resulting in inadequate educations for many of them—has often handicapped their attempts to compete with dominant-group members in the employment sphere, where hiring and promotion standards incorporate educational credentials. In addition, the impact of past discrimination lingers on in the present: Current generations of groups once severely subordinated usually have less inherited wealth and other resources than dominant groups do.

The Sites and Range of Discrimination

Discrimination includes a spatial dimension. For instance, in a white-dominated society, a racially subordinated person's vulnerability to discrimination can vary from the most private to the most public sites. If the latter is in a relatively protected site, such as with friends at home, then the probability of experiencing racial or ethnic hostility and discrimination from dominant-group members is low. In contrast, if that same person—for example, a professor—is in a moderately protected site, such as in a departmental setting within a predominantly white university, the probability of experiencing hostility and discrimination may increase, although the professional status of the professor offers some protection. The probability of hostility and discrimination may increase further as this person moves from work and school settings into such public accommodations as hotels, restaurants, and stores, or into public spaces such as city streets, because the social constraints on discriminatory behavior are weaker there. As we will see in the chapters that follow, those members of subordinate racial and ethnic groups who have ventured the most into settings once reserved for members of dominant groups, either in the past or in the present, are likely to face substantial discrimination and hostility.[75]

In his classic study *The Nature of Prejudice*, Allport notes that discrimination by members of a dominant group against those in a subordinate group ranges from antilocution, or speaking against, to avoidance, to exclusion, to physical attack, and, finally to extermination.[76] For example, a dominant-group member, such as an English American, may try to exclude a Jewish American from her or his university or club. Or a white American may hurl a racist epithet at a Chinese American.

One can also distinguish subtle and covert categories of discrimination from the more blatant forms. *Subtle discrimination* can be defined as unequal and harmful treatment of members of subordinate racial and ethnic groups that is obvious to the victim but not as overt as traditional, "door-slamming" varieties of discrimination. In modern bureaucratic settings such as corporate workplaces, many white employers and employees have internalized inclinations to subtle discriminatory behavior that they consider normal and acceptable. This type of discrimination often goes unnoticed by nondiscriminating members of the dominant group.[77]

For instance, in research on African American managers who have secured entry-level positions in corporations, Ed Jones has found a predisposition among whites, both coworkers and bosses, to assume the best about persons of their own color and the worst about (black) people different from themselves in evaluating job performance. Like Pettigrew's "ultimate attribution error," this critical predisposition, which can be conscious or subconscious, can result in discrimination in promotions that is more subtle than the blatant discrimination of exclusion. The black managers interviewed by Jones and other researchers report that their achievements are often given less attention than their failures, while the failures of comparable white managers are more likely to be excused in terms of situational factors or even overlooked. This negative feedback on a black worker's performance makes it more difficult for her or him to perform successfully in the future.[78]

Covert discrimination, in contrast, is harmful treatment of members of subordinate racial and ethnic groups that is hidden and difficult to document and prove. Covert discrimination includes sabotage and tokenism. For example, in one research study, a black female mail carrier reported that white male coworkers were hiding some of her mail, so that when she returned from her route, there was still mail waiting to be delivered. Because of this sabotage, her white manager blamed her and gave her a less desirable route.[79] African, Asian, and Latino Americans are sometimes hired as "tokens" or "window dressing": they are placed in conspicuous positions just to make an organization look good instead of being evaluated honestly in terms of their abilities for higher-level employment. Some employers hire a few for "front" positions in order to reduce pressures to expand the number of employees from racially or ethnically subordinated groups to more representative proportions. Tokenism can become a barrier to individual and group advancement.

Cumulative and Systemic Discrimination

Various combinations of blatant, covert, and subtle forms of discrimination can coexist in a given organization or community. The patterns of discrimination cutting across political, economic, and social organizations in our society can be termed *systemic discrimination.* One National Council of Churches group portrayed systemic racial discrimination this way: "Both consciously and unconsciously, racism is enforced and maintained by the legal, cultural, religious, educational, economic, political, environmental and military institutions of societies. Racism is more than just a personal attitude; it is the institutionalized form of that attitude."[80] Related to systemic discrimination is the cumulative impact of discrimination on its victims. Particular instances of racial or ethnic discrimination may seem minor to outside observers if considered in isolation. But when blatant actions, such as verbal harassment or physical attack, combine with subtle and covert slights, such as sabotage, the cumulative impact of all this discrimination over months, years, and lifetimes is usually far more than the sum of the individual instances. Racial and ethnic oppression is typically both systemic and cumulative.

Responding to Discrimination

The responses of subordinate-group members to discrimination can range from deference or withdrawal to verbal and physical confrontation to legal action. Even where dominant-group members expect acquiescence in discrimination, some subordinate-group members may not oblige. Victims often fight back, sometimes in organized ways, as was exemplified by the civil rights movement of the 1950s and 1960s, and sometimes by individuals in everyday settings, especially if they are among those subordinate group members with some monetary or legal resources. Discrimination that begins as one-way action may become two-way negotiation, often to the surprise of the discriminators.

Consider this example from research by Joe Feagin and Melvin Sikes, in which a black woman manager in a U.S. corporation describes a meeting with her white boss about her job performance:

> We had a five scale rating, starting with outstanding, then very good, then good, then fair, and then less than satisfactory. I had gone into my evaluation interview anticipating that he would give me a "VG" (very good), feeling that I deserved an "outstanding" and prepared to fight for my outstanding rating. Knowing, you know, my past experience with him, and more his way toward females. But even beyond female, I happened to be the only black in my position within my branch. So the racial issue would also come into play. And he and I had had some very frank discussions about race specifically. About females, but more about race when he and I talked. So I certainly knew that he had a lot of prejudices in terms of blacks. And [he] had some very strong feelings based on his upbringing about the abilities of blacks. He said to me on numerous occasions that he considered me to be an exception, that I certainly was not what he felt the abilities of an average black person [were]. While I was of course appalled and made it perfectly clear to him. . . . But, when I went into the evaluation interview, he gave me glowing comments that cited numerous achievements and accomplishments for me during the year, and then concluded it with, "so I've given you a G." You know, which of course just floored me. . . . [I] maintained my emotions and basically just said, as unemotionally as I possibly could, that I found that unacceptable, I thought it was inconsistent with his remarks in terms of my performance, and I would not accept it. I think I kind of shocked him, because he sort of said, "well I don't know what that means," you know, when I said I wouldn't accept it. I said, I'm not signing the evaluation. And at that point, here again knowing that the best way to deal with most issues is with facts and specifics, I had already come in prepared. . . . I had my list of objectives for the year where I was able to show him that I had achieved every objective and I exceeded all of them. I also had . . . my sales performance: the dollar amount, the products . . . both in total

dollar sales and also a product mix. I sold every product in the line that we offered to our customers. I had exceeded all of my sales objectives. You know, as far as I was concerned, it was outstanding performance.

Then she noted the final result:

So he basically said, "well, we don't have to agree to agree," and that was the end of the session. I got up and left. Fifteen minutes later he called me back in and said, "I've thought about what you said, and you're right, you do have an O." So it's interesting how in fifteen minutes I went from a G to an O. But the interesting point is had I not fought it, had I just accepted it, I would have gotten a G rating for that year, which has many implications.[81]

This example of an attempt at employment discrimination is a common one and illustrates a number of points made in this chapter. Because of certain physical characteristics, this woman was viewed by her white boss as a member of a racial group he stereotypes as generally incapable. He discriminated against her by downplaying her accomplishments with a low evaluation. In this case she did not acquiesce to his negative rating. Because of prior experience with his reportedly racist and sexist attitudes, this woman came to the encounter with some expectation of having to counter his actions. The one-way action that was probably expected by the boss soon became two-way negotiation. This black woman made tactical use of her middle-class resources to win a concession and a changed evaluation.

Over the last two decades there has been an increase in the number of middle-class African Americans and other people of color who have the resources to contest blatant discrimination more directly and, sometimes, successfully. Thus, microlevel discrimination may be the first stage in a two-way encounter. The initial discrimination, the counter, and the discriminator's response, as well as the resources and perceptions of those involved, are important aspects of everyday racism in the United States.

Does "Reverse Discrimination" Exist?

Many neoconservative analysts, both scholars and popular commentators, have written about "reverse discrimination" and "reverse racism" in recent decades. Most of these discussions argue that white Americans suffer seriously from the implementation of affirmative action programs that attempt to redress discrimination against African Americans or members of other subordinate racial groups. During the Ronald Reagan and George Bush administrations in the 1980s and early 1990s, the idea of reverse discrimination was used to legitimate a restructuring of the U.S. Commission on Civil Rights and the U.S. Department of Justice, so that both formerly pro-affirmative-action agencies became opponents of affirmative action programs.

Much of the neoconservative discussion uses the phrase *reverse discrimination* in order to deflect attention from the serious problem of large-scale patterns of institutionalized discrimination still directed by whites against African

Americans and other people of color. As we have seen, racial discrimination, as conceptualized by most scholars of racial and ethnic relations, emphasizes the dominant group–subordinate group context of discrimination. Thus, racial discrimination refers to the actions of members of dominant groups—for example, white Americans—that are taken to harm members of subordinate groups, such as blacks, Latinos, or Native Americans. Historically and today, systemic white discrimination, often called *white racism* when it targets racial groups, is not just a matter of occasional white bigotry but involves the white group's power and resources to enforce white prejudices in discriminatory practices in all major social institutions.

Certainly, individual members of subordinated racial groups can be motivated by their prejudices to take action to harm those in the dominant white group. There is some antiwhite prejudice among people of color. There is also some antiwhite discrimination, but it is relatively uncommon compared with discrimination against people of color. With a modest number of exceptions, members of racially subordinate groups do not have the power or institutional position to express the prejudices they may hold about whites in the form of everyday discrimination. As a rule, African Americans and other people of color do not have the institutional support to inflict substantial and recurring discrimination on whites in such areas as employment, business contracts, college classrooms, department stores, and housing. Indeed, not one member of these racially subordinated groups participates in systemic society-wide discrimination against white Americans, because the possibility does not exist in the United States. Indeed, there is no indication that any currently oppressed group would want to turn the tables and oppress white Americans if they could do so.

Think for a moment about the historical and contemporary patterns of racial discrimination directed by large numbers of whites against just one major group, African Americans. That mistreatment has meant, and still means, widespread blatant and subtle discrimination by whites against blacks in most organizations in all major institutions in U.S. society—in housing, employment, business, education, health services, and the legal system. (See Chapter 8 for details.) For nearly four centuries now, many millions of whites have participated directly in discrimination against millions of blacks. Judging from public opinion polls, at least 80 million whites currently hold some negative stereotypes of African Americans and millions still participate in acts of discrimination. In addition, most whites still watch antiblack discrimination taking place in the United States without actively working personally or politically to stop it. This widespread and systemic discrimination has brought extraordinarily heavy economic and social losses (perhaps trillions in monetary costs alone over nearly 400 years) for African Americans in most institutional sectors of this society.[82]

What would the *reverse* of this centuries-old antiblack discrimination really look like? The reverse of the institutionalized discrimination by whites against blacks would mean reversing the power and resource inequalities for several hundred years. In the past and today, most organizations in major institutional areas such as housing, education, and employment would be run at the top and middle-levels by a disproportionate number of powerful black managers and officials. These powerful black officials would have aimed much racial discrimination at whites, including many years of slavery and legal segregation. As a result, millions of whites would have suffered—and would still suffer—hundreds of billions of dollars in economic losses and lower wages, as well as high rates of unemployment and political disenfranchisement for long periods, widespread housing segregation, inferior school facilities, and violent lynchings. That societal condition would be something one could reasonably call a condition that "reversed the discrimination" against African Americans. It does not now exist, nor has it ever existed.

What is usually termed *reverse discrimination* is something much different from this antiwhite scenario. The usual reference is to affirmative action programs that, for a time or in certain places, have used racial screening criteria to overcome a small amount of the discrimination that targets people of color. Whatever cost a few years of affirmative action have meant for whites (or white men), those costs do not add up to anything close to the total cost that inverting the historical and contemporary patterns of discrimination against people of color would actually entail. Affirmative action plans, as currently set up—and there are far fewer effective plans than most critics suggest[83]—do not make concrete and devastating a widespread antiwhite prejudice on the part of people of color. As established and implemented, affirmative action plans have mostly involved modest remedial efforts (typically designed by white men) to bring token-to-modest numbers of people of color and white women into certain areas of our economic, social, and political institutions where these groups have historically been excluded.

A modest number of white men have indeed paid a price for some affirmative action programs. If affirmative action is successful, it will entail some cost to be paid by those who have benefited most from centuries of racial and gender discrimination. Yet, to compare the scale of white male suffering to the scale of the suffering of people of color or white women from institutionalized discrimination is inappropriate and unrealistic.

Thus, a white man who suffers as an individual from remedial programs such as affirmative action in employment or education suffers in only one area of life (and often only once) and because he is an *exception* to his privileged racial group. A person of color who suffers from racial discrimination usually suffers in all areas of his or her life and primarily because the whole group has been and still is subordinated, not because he or she is an exception.[84]

SUMMARY

In this chapter we have examined the key terms *race, racial group, racism, ethnic group, minority (subordinate) group, majority (dominant) group, prejudice, stereotyping, discrimination, individual* and *institutional discrimination, subtle* and *covert discrimination, systemic* and *cumulative discrimination,* and *reverse discrimination.* These critical concepts loom large in discussions of race and ethnic issues. More than a century of discussion of these concepts lies behind the voyage we have set out on here and in the following chapters. We must carefully think through the meaning of such terms as *race* and *racial group,* because such concepts have themselves been used in the shaping of ethnic and racial relations.

Ideas about race and racial groups have been dangerous for human beings, playing an active role in the triggering, or the convenient rationalizing, of societal processes costing millions of lives. Ideas can and do have an impact. The sharp cutting edge of race, in the context of theorizing about "racial inferiority," can be seen in the enslavement by white Europeans of millions of Africans between the seventeenth and nineteenth centuries and in Nazi actions taken against European Jews in the 1930s and 1940s. Sometimes it is easy to consider words and concepts as harmless abstractions. However, some reflection on both recent and distant Western history exposes the lie in this naive view. The concept may not be "mightier than the sword," to adapt an old cliché, but it is indeed mighty.

CHAPTER 2

Adaptation and Conflict: Racial and Ethnic Relations in Theoretical Perspective

RACIAL AND ETHNIC HIERARCHIES

How do groups that are termed racial groups or ethnic groups develop? How do groups come into contact with one another in the first place? How do they adjust to one another beyond the initial contact? A number of social science theories have been developed to analyze how intergroup contact leads to initial patterns of racial and ethnic interaction and stratification. Various other theories explore the persistence of racial and ethnic patterns. Group domination and stratification, as well as intergroup conflict, are critical issues in these racial and ethnic theories.

Like many other societies, U.S. society is made up of a diversity of racial and ethnic groups. As in the 1790s, so in the present the number of racial and ethnic groups in North America remains impressive, although the exact mix of groups is different. Racial and ethnic diversity is basic in the history of this society.

Yet diversity, as the previously discussed terms *dominant group* and *subordinate group* suggest, has often been linked to a racial and ethnic *hierarchy,* to stratification and substantial inequality among groups. Human beings organize themselves for a number of different reasons—for example, for earning a living, for conducting religious rituals, and for governing. Among the important features of social organization are ranking systems. Such systems rank categories of people, not just individuals. In this and in other societies, several social ranking systems coexist, some systems classifying people by their racial or ethnic group or gender group, others ranking people by their age, disability, or class position. Each ranking system has distinct social categories; rewards, privileges, and power vary with a group's position within the system. Some categories, such as English Americans in the U.S. racial/ethnic system, have generally had much greater power and resources than other categories, such as Native Americans or African Americans. Such power and resource inequality tends to persist from one generation to the next. In racial/ethnic ranking systems, certain ascribed (that is, attributed not achieved) characteristics—such as one group's racial characteristics as perceived by another group—become the criteria for unequal social positions and social rewards.[1]

The image of a ladder will make the concept of racial and ethnic stratification clearer. In Figure 2–1 the positions of five selected racial and ethnic groups at a specific time in U.S. history are diagramed on a ladder. Some groups are higher than others, suggesting that they have greater privileges— social, economic, and political—than the lower groups. A group substantially higher than another on an important dimension is viewed as a dominant group; one substantially lower than another is seen as a subordinate group. The more groups in a society, the more complex the image, with middle groups standing in a relation of dominance to some groups and in a relation of subordination to others.

Consider the United States in 1790, about the time of its founding. For that year one might roughly diagram the five groups in Figure 2–1 in terms of such factors as overall economic or political power, so that the top group would be English Americans, with Scottish Americans a little down the ladder. Farther

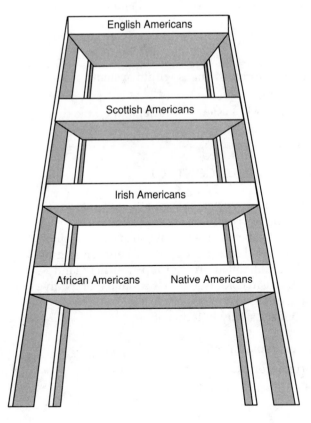

FIGURE 2–1
A Ladder of Dominance: The United States as of 1790

down are the Irish immigrants, a group composed at the time mostly of poor farmers and indentured servants. At the bottom in terms of power and resources would be African Americans, most of whom were in slavery in the South. Those Native American ("Indian") groups and individuals within the boundaries of the new nation—many others were still outside it—were also at the bottom of the racial–ethnic hierarchy in terms of economic and political power and resources. The new nation encompassed a racial–ethnic hierarchy from its beginning.[2]

Some Basic Questions

A number of social science theories have been developed to explain this diversity and stratification and the intergroup adaptation that creates them. In some contexts *theory* means vague speculation; but in the social sciences the term refers to a conceptual framework used to interpret or explain some aspect of our everyday existence. The social theorists Ernest Barth and Donald Noel have summarized some major questions raised in the analysis of racial and ethnic relations:

1. How does one explain the origin and emergence of racial and ethnic diversity and stratification?

2. How does one explain the continuation of racial and ethnic diversity and stratification?

3. How does one interpret internal adaptive changes within systems of racial and ethnic diversity and stratification?

4. How does one explain major changes in systems of racial and ethnic diversity and stratification?[3]

MIGRATION AND GROUP CONTACT

Racial and ethnic relations and stratification systems originate with intergroup contact as different groups, often with no common ancestry, come into each other's spheres of influence. Contact can be between an established or indigenous people and a migrating people (group A → land of group B) or between migrating groups moving into a previously uninhabited area (group A → new land ← group B). The movement of the English colonists into the lands of Native Americans in the 1600s is an example of the first case.

Migration has been viewed by Charles Tilly in terms of:

1. the actual migrating units (for example, families);
2. the situation at the point of origin (for example, the home country);
3. the situation at the destination (for example, a U.S. city);

4.   the socioeconomic and political framework within which the migration occurs (for example, modern capitalism).[4]

Certain precontact factors shape both the migration and the outcome of the contact that results from migration. Push factors include what is happening in the immigrants' home country—high unemployment or intergroup hostilities, for example. Depressed economies or painful religious or political conflicts in sending countries have generated major migrations to the United States. Pull factors also generate migration. Immigrants may be attracted by the portrayal, accurate or inaccurate, of better conditions—such as abundant jobs—at the destination. The outcome of the initial contact is influenced by the resources and characteristics of the migrating group (such as its wealth or language) and of the receiving group (such as its receptiveness to newcomers). Technological assets, such as industrial skills or firepower, have proven an advantage to certain groups. Some argue, for example, that European settlers were able to conquer Native Americans largely because of the latter's less developed weaponry.[5]

Types of Migration

In his pioneering book *Comparative Ethnic Relations*, Schermerhorn suggested four major types of migration that generate racial and ethnic relations. These can be seen as a continuum that ranges from involuntary to completely voluntary migration:

1.   movements of forced labor;

2.   contract-labor movement;

3.   movement of displaced persons and refugees;

4.   voluntary migration.[6]

Movements of forced labor would include the forcible removal of Africans to North America; *contract–labor* transfer includes the migration of indentured Irish servants to the English colonies and of Chinese laborers to western North America. *Displaced persons* include the streams of refugees produced by war, such as Jewish immigrants from Europe in the 1930s and more recently Vietnamese refugees. *Voluntary migration* covers the great migration of southern and eastern European groups to the United States in the early twentieth century and of several Asian groups in the late twentieth century.

The voluntary migration of powerful colonizers, sometimes termed *colonization migration*, often precedes the types just listed. Colonization migration can be seen in the English trading companies whose employees founded the first North American colonies, a development that led to the dispersal or destruction of Native American societies already inhabiting the continent.[7] We will return to this issue of colonialism later.

PATTERNS OF RACIAL AND ETHNIC ADAPTATION

The Initial Contact

What happens once different human groups come into contact as the result of migration? Outcomes vary. In the initial stage, outcomes include:

1.   exclusion or genocidal destruction;
2.   egalitarian symbiosis;
3.   a hierarchy or stratification system.

Genocide is the extermination of one group by another—one outcome of contacts between European settlers and Native Americans on the Atlantic coast of North America. *Egalitarian symbiosis* refers to peaceful coexistence and a rough economic and political equality between two groups. Occasional examples of this outcome can be found in the history of world migrations, but they are rare, especially in North America. Some authors argue that by the early nineteenth century, Scottish Americans were approaching equality with English Americans in many areas. A more common result of migration and contact is stratification. Stanley Lieberson has listed two hierarchies that can result from intergroup contact. *Migrant superordination* occurs when the migrating group imposes its will on indigenous groups, usually through superior weapons and political or military organization. The Native American populations of the United States and Canada were subordinated in this fashion. *Indigenous superordination* occurs when groups immigrating into a new society become subordinate to groups already there, as was the case for Africans forcibly brought to North and South America by Europeans.[8]

Later Adaptation Patterns

Beyond the initial period of contact between two groups, the range of possible outcomes of intergroup contact includes:

1.   continuing genocide;
2.   continuing egalitarian symbiosis;
3.   replacement of stratification by inclusion along conformity lines;
4.   replacement of stratification by inclusion along cultural pluralism lines;
5.   continuing subordination, ranging from moderate to extreme, of a racial or ethnic group.

One type of outcome can be a continuing thrust by the dominant group to exterminate the subordinate group. Attempts by European Americans to annihilate some Native American groups continued until the early twentieth century. Alternatively, an egalitarian symbiosis can continue beyond initial peaceful interaction. Another outcome is for an initial hierarchy, characterized by a sharp inequality of power and resources, to be modified by extensive assimilation of the incoming group into the dominant culture and society. This can take two forms. In the first, inclusion occurs by means of conformity to the dominant group's culture. By surrendering much of its cultural heritage and conforming to the dominant group, the incoming group gains increased acceptance and resource equality. Some have argued that many non-English European immigrant groups, such as Scots and Scandinavians, eventually gained rough equality with the English Americans in this way.

Another possibility is *cultural pluralism*—substantial economic and political assimilation and greater equality along with substantial persistence of subcultural (for example, religious) distinctiveness. In this outcome, substantial assimilation of the immigrant group to the host group is primarily economic and political, with cultural distinctiveness continuing in certain major respects. The interaction of certain white immigrant groups, such as Irish-Catholic Americans, and the host group offers a possible example of this outcome.

A fifth outcome of continuing intergroup contact is persisting, and substantial, racial or ethnic stratification. The extent and inequality of the stratification can vary, but for many non-European groups, such as Native Americans and Mexican Americans, political and economic inequality has remained so great as to constitute what some term a condition of *internal colonialism*. Even in this case, partial acculturation usually occurs in terms of adaptation to the dominant group's culture (for instance, to the English language).

Types of Theories

In the United States, explanatory theories of racial and ethnic relations have been concerned with migration, adaptation, exploitation, stratification, and conflict. Most such theories can be roughly classified as either order theories or power–conflict theories, depending on their principal concerns. *Order theories* tend to accent patterns of inclusion—the orderly integration and assimilation of particular racial and ethnic groups to a dominant culture and society, as in the third and fourth outcomes just described. The central focus is on progressive adaptation to the dominant culture and on stability in intergroup relations. *Power–conflict* theories give more attention to the first and fifth outcomes—genocide and continuing hierarchy—and to the persisting inequality of the power and resource distribution associated with racial or ethnic subordination. In the United States, most assimilation theories are order theories. Internal colonialism theories and class-oriented neo-Marxist viewpoints are power–conflict theories. These broad categories encompass considerable variation, but they do provide a starting point for analysis.

ASSIMILATION AND OTHER ORDER PERSPECTIVES

In the United States, much social theorizing has emphasized assimilation, the more or less orderly adaptation of a migrating group to the ways and institutions of an established host group. Charles Hirschman has noted that "the assimilation perspective, broadly defined, continues to be the primary theoretical framework for sociological research on racial and ethnic inequality." The reason for this dominance, he suggests, is the "lack of convincing alternatives."[9] The English word *assimilate* comes from the Latin *assimulare*, meaning to make similar.

Robert E. Park

Robert E. Park, a major sociological analyst, argued that European out-migration was a major catalyst for societal reorganization around the globe. In his view intergroup contacts regularly go through stages of a *race relations cycle.* Fundamental social forces, such as out-migration, lead to recurring cycles in intergroup history: "The race relations cycle which takes the form, to state it abstractly, of *contacts, competition, accommodation* and *eventual assimilation,* is apparently progressive and irreversible."[10] In the contact stage, migration and exploration bring peoples together, which in turn leads to economic competition and thus to new social organization. Competition and conflict flow from the contacts between host peoples and the migrating groups. Accommodation, a critical condition in the race relations cycle, often takes place rapidly. It involves a migrating group's forced adjustment to a new social situation. Park seems to have viewed accommodation as involving a stabilization of relations, including the possibility of permanent caste systems. Sometimes he spoke of the race relations cycle as inevitably leading from contact to assimilation. At other times, however, he recognized that the assimilation of a migrant group might involve major barriers and take a substantial period of time to complete.

Nonetheless, Park and most scholars working in this tradition have argued that there is a long-term trend toward assimilation of subordinated racial and ethnic groups in modern societies. "Assimilation is a process of interpenetration and fusion in which persons and groups acquire the memories, sentiments, and attitudes of other persons or groups, and, by sharing their experience and history, are incorporated with them in a common cultural life."[11] Even racially subordinate groups are expected to assimilate.[12]

Stages of Assimilation: Milton Gordon

Since Park's pioneering analysis in the 1920s, many U.S. racial and ethnic relations theorists and numerous textbook writers have adopted an assimilationist perspective, although most have departed from Park's framework in a number of important ways. Milton Gordon, author of the influential *Assimilation in American Life,* distinguishes a variety of initial encounters between racial and ethnic groups and an array of possible assimilation outcomes. While Gordon presents three competing images of assimilation—the melting pot, cultural pluralism, and Anglo-conformity—he focuses on Anglo-conformity as the descriptive reality. As we noted in Chapter 1, in Gordon's view immigrant groups entering the United States have given up much of their cultural heritage and conformed substantially to an Anglo-Protestant core culture.[13] For theorists like Gordon, cultural assimila-

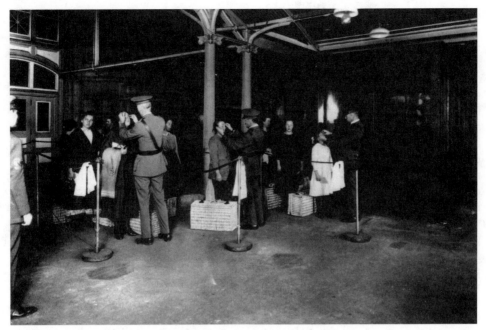

U.S. Immigration officials inspect European immigrants at Ellis Island, New York (1923).

tion is a very important dimension of intergroup adaptation in the United States. This view of assimilation usually emphasizes the way in which new groups must conform to the preexisting Anglo-Protestant culture.

Gordon notes that Anglo-conformity has been substantially achieved for most immigrant groups in the United States, especially in regard to cultural assimilation. Most groups following the early English migration have adapted to the Anglo core culture. Gordon distinguishes seven dimensions of adaptation:

1. *cultural assimilation*: change of cultural patterns to those of the core society;
2. *structural assimilation*: penetration of cliques and associations of the core society at the primary-group level;
3. *marital assimilation*: significant intermarriage;
4. *identification assimilation*: development of a sense of identity linked to the core society;
5. *attitude-receptional assimilation*: absence of prejudice and stereotyping;
6. *behavior-receptional assimilation*: absence of intentional discrimination;
7. *civic assimilation*: absence of value and power conflict.[14]

Whereas Park believed structural assimilation, including new primary-group ties such as intergroup friendships, flowed from cultural assimilation, Gordon stresses that these are separate stages of assimilation and may take place at different rates.

For Gordon, structural assimilation only relates to primary-group cliques and relations. In his view, the movement of a new immigrant group into the *secondary groups* of the host society—that is, into the employing organizations, such as corporations or public bureaucracies, and educational and political institutions—is not a separate type of structural assimilation. This omission of a thorough discussion of this secondary–structural assimilation is a major flaw in Gordon's typology and theory. Looking at U.S. history, one would conclude that admission into the dominant group's secondary groups does not necessarily mean entering the dominant group's friendship cliques. Moreover, the dimension Gordon calls *civic assimilation* is somewhat confusing, since he includes in it "values," which are really part of cultural assimilation, and "power," which is a central aspect of structural assimilation at the secondary-group level.

Gordon's assimilation theory continues to influence researchers. For example, Silvia Pedraza made significant use of Gordon's conceptual framework in her research on Cuban and Mexican immigration, and Richard Alba contrasted his view of the loss of strong ethnic identities among white ethnic Americans with Gordon's idea of identificational assimilation. In an examination of Gordon's seven dimensions of assimilation, J. Allen Williams and Suzanne Ortega examined interviews with a midwestern sample and found that cultural assimilation was not necessarily the first type of assimilation to occur. For example, the Mexican Americans in the sample were less culturally assimilated than African Americans, yet more assimilated structurally. Those of Swiss and Swedish backgrounds ranked about the same on the study's measure of cultural assimilation, but the Swedish Americans were less assimilated structurally. Williams and Ortega concluded that assimilation varies considerably from one group to another and that Gordon's seven types can be grouped into three more general categories of structural, cultural, and receptional assimilation.[15]

In a later book, *Human Nature, Class, and Ethnicity* (1978), Gordon recognized that his assimilation theory neglects power issues and proposed including these in his model. He mentions the different resources available to competing racial groups and refers briefly to black–white conflict, but gives little attention to the impact of economic power, material resource inequalities, or capitalistic economic history on U.S. racial and ethnic relations.[16]

Focused on the millions of white European immigrants and their adjustments, Gordon's model emphasizes *generational* changes within immigrant groups over time. Substantial *acculturation* (cultural assimilation) to the Anglo-Protestant culture has often been completed by the second or third generation for more recent European immigrant groups. The partially acculturated first generation formed protective communities and associations, but the children of those immigrants were considerably more exposed to Anglo-conformity pressures in the mass media and in schools.[17] Gordon suggests that substantial assimilation along civic, behavior-receptional, and attitude-receptional dimensions has occurred for numerous European immigrant groups. Most have also made considerable progress toward equality at the secondary–structural levels of employment and politics, although the dimensions of this assimilation are neither named nor discussed in any detail by Gordon.

For many white, particularly non-Protestant, groups, structural assimilation at the primary-group level is underway, yet far from complete. Gordon suggests that substantially complete cultural assimilation (for example, adoption of the English language) along with substantial structural (primary-group) separation form a characteristic pattern of adaptation for many white ethnic groups. Even these relatively acculturated groups tend to limit their informal friendships and marriage ties either to their immediate ethnic groups or to similar groups that are part of their general religious community. Following Will Herberg, who argued that there are three great community "melting pots" in the United States—Jews, Protestants, and Catholics—Gordon suggests that primary-group ties beyond one's own group are often developed within one's broad socioreligious community.[18]

Gordon recognizes that racial prejudice and discrimination have retarded structural assimilation, but he seems to suggest that non-European Americans, including African Americans, particularly those in the middle class, will eventually be absorbed into the dominant culture and society. In regard to blacks, he argues, optimistically, that the United States has "moved decisively down the road toward implementing the implications of the American creed [of equality and justice] for race relations"—as in employment and housing. The tremendous progress that he perceives black Americans have made has, in his view, created a policy dilemma for the government: Should it adopt a traditional political liberalism that ignores racial groups or a "corporate liberalism" that recognizes group rights along racial lines? Gordon includes under corporate liberalism government programs of affirmative action, which he rejects.[19] The optimism of many assimilation analysts about the eventual implementation of the American creed of equality for black and certain other non-European Americans is problematical, as we will see in Chapter 8.

Some assimilation analysts, notably Gordon and Alba, have argued that the once-prominent ethnic identities, especially of European American groups, are fading over time. Alba suggests that ethnic identity is still of consequence for non-Latino whites but declares that "a new ethnic group is forming—one based on a vague *ancestry* from anywhere on the European continent."[20] In other words, such distinct ethnic identities as English American and Irish American are gradually giving way to a vague identification as "European American." Alba emphasizes this as a trend. Interestingly, research on intermarriages between members of different white ethnic groups has revealed that large proportions of the children of such marriages see themselves as having multiple ethnic identities, while others choose one of their heritages, or simply "American," as their ethnic identity.[21]

Ethnogenesis and Ethnic Pluralism

Some theorists working in the assimilation tradition reject the argument that most European American groups have become substantially assimilated to a generic Anglo-Protestant or Euro-American identity and way of life. A few have explored models of adjustment that depart from Anglo-conformity in the direction of ethnic or cultural pluralism. It was a Jewish American of Polish and Latvian origin who early formulated a perspective called cultural pluralism. Horace Kallen (1882–1974) argued that membership in ethnic–cultural groups was not a membership one could readily abandon. Writing in *The Nation* in 1915, he argued that ethnic groups had a right to exist on their own terms; that is, democracy applied to ethnic groups. He argued against the ruthless Americanization advocated by many white Anglo-Protestant nativists at the time. By the 1920s he had given the name *cultural pluralism* to the view that each ethnic group has the democratic right to retain its own heritage.[22] Kallen's pioneering analysis did not look in detail at the assimilation process, but it did set early precedents for the perspective now called *multiculturalism* (see Chapter 13).

More recent analysts adopting a cultural pluralism perspective accept some Anglo-conformity adjustment as inevitable, if not desirable. In *Beyond the Melting Pot*, Nathan Glazer and Daniel Moynihan agree that the original customs and home-country ways of European immigrants were mostly lost by the third generation. But this did not mean the decline of ethnicity. The European immigrant groups usually remained distinct in terms of name, identity, and, for the most part, primary-group ties.[23]

Andrew Greeley has developed the interesting concept of *ethnogenesis* and applied it to those white immigrant groups set off by nationality and religion. Greeley is critical of the traditional assimilation perspective because it assumes "that the strain toward homogenization in a modern industrial society is so great as to be virtually irresistible."[24] Traditionally, the direction of this assimilation in the United States is assumed to be toward the dominant Anglo-Protestant culture. But, from the ethnogenesis perspective, adaptation has meant more than this one-way conformity. The traditional assimilation model does not explain the persistence of ethnicity in the United States—the emphasis among immigrants on ethnicity as a way of becoming American and, in recent decades, the self-conscious attempts to create ethnic identity and manipulate ethnic symbols.

The complex ethnogenesis model of intergroup adaptation proposed by Greeley is illustrated in Figure 2–2. Greeley suggests, as shown in the left-hand box (host/common/immigrant), that in many cases host and immigrant groups had a somewhat similar *cultural* inheritance. For example, some later European immigrant groups had a cultural background initially similar to that of earlier English settlers. As a result of the interaction of subsequent generations with each other and with descendants of earlier immigrants, in schools and through the influence of the media (symbolized by the long arrows in the center of the figure) the number of cultural traits common to the host and immigrant groups often

FIGURE 2–2   **The Ethnogenesis Perspective**

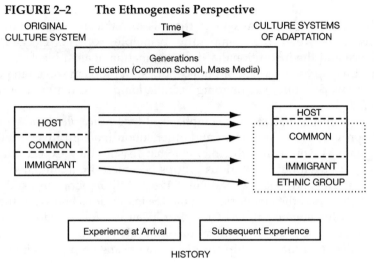

SOURCE: Andrew M. Greeley, *Ethnicity in the United States* (New York: John Wiley, 1974), p. 309.

increased. Yet, as is illustrated in the right-hand boxes, late in the adaptive process certain aspects of the heritage of the home country have remained very important to the character of the immigrant–ethnic group. From this perspective, ethnic groups share traits with the host group and retain major characteristics of their nationalities as well. A modern ethnic group is one part home-country heritage and one part common culture, mixed together in a distinctive way because of a unique history of development within the North American crucible.[25]

A number of research studies have documented the persistence of distinctive white ethnic groups such as Italian Americans and Jewish Americans in U.S. cities, not just in New York and Chicago but in San Francisco, New Orleans, and Tucson as well. William Yancey and his associates have suggested that ethnicity is an "emergent phenomenon"—that its importance varies in cities and that its character and strength depend on the specific historical conditions in which it emerges and grows.[26]

Some Problems with Assimilation Theories

Most assimilation theorists take as their examples of ethnic adaptation white European groups migrating more or less voluntarily to the United States. But what of the adaptation and assimilation of non-European groups beyond the stage of initial contact? Some analysts of assimilation include people of color in their theories, despite the problems that arise from such an inclusion. Some have argued that assimilation, cultural and structural, is the necessary, if long-term, answer to the racial problem in the United States. One prominent analyst of U.S. racial relations, Gunnar Myrdal, argued that as a practical matter it is "to the advantage of American Negroes as individuals and as a group to become assimilated into American culture, to acquire the traits held in esteem by the dominant white Americans."[27] In Myrdal's view there is an ethical contradiction in the United States between the democratic principles of the Declaration of Independence and the institutionalized discrimination against black Americans. For Myrdal this represents a "lag of public morals," a problem solved in principle but still being worked out in an ongoing assimilation process that may or may not be completed.

More optimistic analysts have emphasized *progressive inclusion,* which will eventually provide black Americans and other subordinate groups with full citizenship in fact as well as in principle. For that reason, they expect ethnic and racial conflict to disappear as various groups become fully assimilated into the dominant culture and society. Nathan Glazer, Milton Gordon, and Talcott Parsons have stressed the egalitarianism of U.S. institutions and what they view as the progressive emancipation of non-European groups. Gordon and others have underscored the gradual assimilation of middle-class black Americans over several decades. Full membership for black Americans seems inevitable, notes Parsons, for "the only tolerable solution to the enormous [racial] tensions lies in constituting a single societal community with full membership for all."[28] The importance of racial, as well as ethnic, stratification is expected to decline as powerful, universalistic societal forces wipe out the vestiges of earlier ethnocentric value systems. White immigrants have desired substantial assimilation and have been absorbed. The same is expected to happen eventually for non-European groups.

Assimilation theories have been criticized for having an "establishment" bias. A number of Asian American scholars and leaders have reacted vigorously to the application of the concept of assimilation to Asian Americans, arguing that the very concept originated in a period (1870–1925) of intense attacks by white Americans on Asian immigrants. The term was thus tainted from the beginning by its association with the notion that the only "good groups" were those that could assimilate in Anglo-conformity fashion. In the 1990s several researchers have explored another assumption of traditional assimilationist thinking—the idea that new immigrants both should and do assimilate to the core culture in a linear, one-directional manner. Immigrants must progressively "become American" in order to overcome the inferiority of their old languages, cultures, and societies. This ethnocentric view ignores the fact that the assimilation process can have a negative impact. As Ruben Rumbaut notes, recent research indicates that in certain ways the physical or mental health of immigrant groups *declines* as they become better off economically and more assimilated to the core culture. Over a period of time immigrants gradually adopt the unhealthy diet of most Americans (and many become overweight) and experience certain family and social stresses (for example, teenagers become depressed or suicidal) associated with mainstream American life. The shift from the culture of origin to the core American culture is not necessarily a shift from an inferior to a superior culture, as many native-born Americans might assume.[29]

Unlike Robert Park, who paid substantial attention to the historical and global contexts of migration, many of today's assimilation theorists do not analyze sufficiently the historical background and development of a particular racial or ethnic group within a national or international context. Recently, a few researchers have developed a perspective called "transnationalism." Like traditional assimilation analyses, transnationalism emphasizes the fact that individual migrants tend to migrate along family and friendship networks. But, as Steven Gold states in an analysis of Israeli immigrants to the United States, transnationalism also emphasizes the "large scale economic, political, and legal structures within which immigrants develop their communities and lives." Transnationalism also sees immigration as an "on-going process through which ideas, resources, and people change locations and develop meanings in multiple settings."[30] Immigrants often maintain their interest in the home country, and their attachments may be strong to two or more "homes" at once. Their motivation for immigration can be complex and multifaceted. They seek opportunities in a new country, but maintain strong ties to the old country. This is the case for the Israeli immigrants that Gold studied; even for most of the second generation, their self-identity is still Israeli, not American.

Biosocial Perspectives

Some U.S. theorists, including assimilationists, now hold a biosocial perspective on racial and ethnic relations. The old European and American notion that racial and ethnic groups are deeply rooted in human beings' biological makeup has received renewed attention from a few social scientists and biologists in the United States since the 1970s. In *Human Nature, Class, and Ethnicity*, for example, Gordon suggests that ethnic ties are rooted in the "biological organism of man." Ethnicity is a fundamental part of the physiological as well as the psychological self. Ethnicity "cannot be shed by social mobility, as for instance social class background can, since society insists on its inalienable ascription from cradle to grave." Gordon seems to have in mind the rootedness of intergroup relations, including racial and ethnic relations, in the everyday realities of kinship and other socially constructed group boundaries, not the old racist notion of the unchanging biological character and separateness of racial groups. He goes further, however, emphasizing that human beings tend to be "selfish, narcissistic and perpetually poised on the edge of aggression." And it is these selfish tendencies that lie behind racial and ethnic tensions.[31] Gordon is here adopting a Hobbesian ("dog-eat-dog") view of human nature.

Critics of this biosocial view have suggested that it attributes to fundamental "human nature" what are in reality only modern capitalism's specific individualistic values. That is, under capitalism selfishness and narcissism are *learned* rather than inherent in the human biological makeup. Although decidedly different from the earlier biological theories, the modern biosocial analysis remains problematical. The exact linkages between the deep genetic underpinnings of human nature and concrete racial or ethnic behavior are not spelled out beyond some vague analysis of kin selection and selfish behavior. A more convincing sociobiological analysis might attempt to show more precisely how the "desires" of the human genes are changed, through several specified levels or techniques, into social phenomena such as slavery or language assimilation. As yet, this has not been done.

Another difficulty with the biosocial approach is that in the everyday world, racial and ethnic relations are immediately social rather than biological. As Edna Bonacich has pointed out, many racial and ethnic groups have mixed biological ancestry. Jewish Americans, for example, have a very mixed ancestry: as a group, they share no distinctive biological characteristics. Biologically diverse Italian immigrants from different regions of Italy gained a sense of being Italian American (even Italian) in the United States. The bonds holding Jewish Americans and Italian Americans together were not genetically based or biologically primordial, but rather the result of real *historical* experiences as these groups became established in the United States. Moreover, if ethnicity is primordial in a biological sense, it should always be a prominent force in human affairs. Sometimes ethnicity leads to recurring conflict, as in the case of Jews and Gentiles in the United States; in other cases, as with Scottish and English Americans, it quietly disappears in the ongoing assimilation process. Sentiments based on common ancestry are important, but they are activated primarily in the concrete experiences and histories of specific migrating and host groups.[32]

Emphasizing Migration: Competition Theory

Competition theory is a contemporary example of the exploration of migration issues in the tradition of Robert Park. Park emphasized that ethnic relations grew out of the migration of peoples, which in turn led to competition for scarce resources and then to accommodation and assimilation. Competition theorists have explored the contact and competition parts of this "race relations cycle." Unlike some order-oriented theorists, they do address questions of protest and conflict, although they do not give much attention to power, exploitation, or inequality issues. The *human ecology* tradition in sociological thought draws on the ideas of Park and other ecologists and emphasizes the "struggle of human groups for survival" within their physical environments. This tradition, which highlights demographic trends such as the migration of groups and population concentration in cities, has been adopted by competition analysts researching racial and ethnic groups.[33]

Competition theorists such as Susan Olzak and Joane Nagel view ethnicity broadly as a social phenomenon distinguished by boundaries of language, skin color, and culture. They consider the tradition of human ecology valuable because it emphasizes the stability of ethnic population boundaries over time, as well as the impact of shifts in these boundaries resulting from migration; ethnic group membership often coincides with the creation of a distinctive group niche in the labor force. Competition occurs when two or more ethnic groups attempt to secure the same resources, such as jobs or housing.[34]

According to competition theorists, collective action is fostered by immigration across geographical borders and by the expansion of once-segregated ethnic groups into the same labor and housing markets to which other groups have access. Attacks on immigrant or black workers, for example, increase at the city level when a group moves out of segregated jobs and challenges other groups and not, as one might expect, in cities where ethnic groups are locked into segregation and poverty. Olzak uses empirical data on ethnic and racial violence in the nineteenth century to show that collective action, such as Anglo-Protestant crowds attacking European immigrants entering the United States, increases when immigration expands and recessions occur. The ethnic boundary of the native-born was mobilized against immigrant and black workers "when ethnic competition was activated by a rising supply of low-wage labor and tight labor markets. In this case the ethnic groups that mobilized were not fully assimilated, but had retained aspects of their traditional identity and drew on that for mobilization against other groups."[35] Olzak has further suggested a distinction between social situations of economic decline, which can increase interethnic competition for jobs and other economic goals, and situations of new ethnic integration, in which the social integration of once-segregated societies brings ethnic groups into new job and other economic competition.[36]

Competition theorists have emphasized that economic struggles often accompany political competition, which includes competition among ethnic groups for elected and appointed offices, tax dollars, and other types of political power. Nagel has shown how contenders for political power often organize along ethnic lines and argues that "ethnicity is a convenient basis for political organizers due to the commonality of language and culture and the availability of ethnic organizations with ready-made leadership and membership."[37] Political policies that may favor one group, such as affirmative action programs for African Americans, have created political mobilization among other groups, such as Latinos and Asian Americans, that seek similar programs.

Competition theorists sometimes contrast their analyses with the power–conflict views we will discuss in the next section, perspectives that emphasize the role of capitalism, economic subordination, and institutionalized discrimination. Competition theorists write about a broad range of ethnic conflicts around the globe. When they deal with urban ethnic worlds in the United States, they often write as though institutionalized racism and capitalism-generated exploitation of workers are not major forces in recurring ethnic and racial competition and conflict in U.S. cities. As we have seen, these theorists emphasize migration and population concentration, as well as other demographic factors.

As we will see shortly, a power–conflict theorist might counter this emphasis by noting that the competition theorists are studying markets and interethnic competition in cities without a clear sense of the great inequality that has undergirded urban job and housing markets in the United States for several centuries. Missing from competition theory is a systematic and deep concern with the issues of inequality, power, exploitation, and racial discrimination that are accented by power–conflict theories.

POWER–CONFLICT THEORIES

The last few decades have witnessed the development of major *power–conflict* frameworks explaining U.S. racial and ethnic relations, perspectives that place much greater emphasis on economic stratification and power issues than one finds in assimilation and competition theories. Within this broad category of power–conflict theories are a number of subcategories, including the caste perspective, the internal colonialism viewpoint, and a variety of class-based and neo-Marxist theories.

The Caste School

One early exception to the assimilation perspective was the *caste school of racial relations*, which developed in the 1940s under W. Lloyd Warner and Allison Davis.[38] Focusing on black–white relations in the South, these researchers viewed the position of African Americans as distinctively different from that of other racial and ethnic groups. After the Civil War, a new social system, a caste system, replaced the slavery system of the South. The white and black castes were separated by a total prohibition of intermarriage as well as by economic and social inequality. Warner and his associates were critical of the emphasis in most social science analysis on prejudiced attitudes and feelings. Instead, they emphasized institutionalized discrimination as the foundation of a castelike system of U.S. apartheid.[39]

Early Class Theories of Racial Relations

William E. B. Du Bois, one of the first sociological analysts in the United States, was an African American civil rights activist who had experienced the brutality of racism firsthand. Drawing on Marxist class analysis in many of his writings, Du Bois was perhaps the first major theorist to emphasize that racial oppression and capitalist–class oppression were inextricably tied together in the United States. In his view the interplay of racism and capitalism explained why there has never been real democracy for people in all racial groups in the United States. In a 1948 article titled "Is Man Free?," he argued that both black workers and white workers were prevented from exercising full democratic rights because of the control of a small capitalist class (for example, the owners of workplaces) over the economy and politics. He believed that a democratic U.S. society must include not only equality for African Americans but also full control of workplaces by workers. Du Bois's Marxist ideas are still fresh and provocative but have been ignored in most social science analyses of racial issues.[40]

An early power–conflict analyst who drew on Du Bois and on class analysis was Oliver C. Cox, a scholar whose work has also been neglected, in part because of its Marxist approach. Cox emphasized the role of the capitalist class in racial exploitation; he analyzed the economic dimensions of the forced slave migration from Africa and the oppressiveness of later conditions for African American slaves. Slave trade was "a way of recruiting labor for the purpose of exploiting the great natural resources of America." The color of Africans was not important: They were chosen "simply because they were the best workers to be found for the heavy labor in the mines and plantations across the Atlantic." A search for cheap labor by a profit-oriented capitalist class led to a system of racial subordination. Racial prejudice developed later as an ideology rationalizing this economic subordination of African Americans.[41]

Internal Colonialism

Analysts of internal colonialism prefer to see the racial stratification and the class stratification of U.S. capitalism as separate but related systems of oppression. In social science theories, neither should be reduced to the other. An emphasis on power and resource inequalities across racial lines is at the heart of the internal colonialism model.

The framework of internal colonialism is built in part on the work of analysts of *external colonialism*—the worldwide imperialism of certain capitalist nations, including the United States and European nations.[42] Balandier has noted that Europe's capitalist expansion has affected non-European peoples since the fifteenth century: "Until very recently the greater part of the world's population, not belonging to the white race (if we exclude China and Japan), knew only a status of dependency on one or another of the European colonial powers."[43] External colonialism involves the running of a country's economy and politics by an outside colonial power. Many colonies eventually became independent of their colonizers, such as Britain or France, but continued to have their economies directed by the capitalists and corporations of the former colonial powers. This system of continuing dependency has been called *neocolonialism*. Neocolonialism is common today where there were few white settlers in the colonized country. Colonies that experienced a large in-migration of white settlers often show a different pattern. In such cases external colonialism becomes *internal colonialism* when the control and exploitation of non-European groups in the colonized country passes from whites in the home country to white immigrant groups within the newly independent country.[44]

Non-European groups in the United States can be viewed in terms of internal colonialism. Internal colonialism here emerged out of classical European colonialism and imperialism and took on a life of its own. The origin and initial stabilization of internal colonialism in North America predate the Revolutionary War. The systematic subordination of non-Europeans began with "genocidal attempts by colonizing settlers to uproot native populations and force them into other regions."[45] Native Americans were killed or driven off desirable lands. Enslaved Africans were a cheap source of labor for white plantation owners before and after the Revolution. Later, Asians and Pacific peoples were imported as contract workers or annexed in the expansionist period of U.S. development. Robert Blauner, a colonialism theorist, notes that agriculture in the South often depended on black labor; in the Southwest, Mexican agricultural development was forcibly taken over by European settlers, and later agricultural development was based substantially on cheap Mexican labor coming into what was once northern Mexico.[46]

In exploiting the labor of non-European peoples, who were made slaves or were paid very low wages, white agricultural and industrial capitalists reaped enormous profits. From the internal colonialism perspective, contemporary racial and ethnic inequality is grounded in the economic interests of whites in low-wage labor—the underpinning of capitalistic economic exploitation. Non-European groups were subordinated because of European American desires for labor and land. Internal colonialism theorists have recognized the central role of government support of the exploitation of groups such as Native, African, Latino, and Asian Americans. The colonial and U.S. governments played an important role in legitimating slavery in the seventeenth through the nineteenth centuries and in providing the soldiers who subordinated Native Americans across the nation and Mexicans in the Southwest.

Most internal colonialism theorists are not concerned primarily with white immigrant groups, many of which entered the United States after non-European groups were subordinated. Instead, they wish to analyze the establishment of racial stratification and the control processes that maintain white dominance and ideological racism.[47]

A Neo-Marxist Emphasis on Class

Analysts of racial and ethnic relations have sometimes combined an internal colonialism perspective with an emphasis on class stratification that draws on the Marxist research pioneered by Du Bois and Cox. Mario Barrera suggests that the heart of internal colonialism is an interactive structure of class *and* racial stratification that divides U.S. society. Class, in the economic–exploitation sense of that term, is central in this perspective. Basic to current internal colonialism are four classes that have developed in U.S. capitalism:

1.   *capitalists*: that small group of people who control capital investments and the means of production and who buy the labor of many others;

2.   *managers*: that modest-sized group of people who work as administrators for the capitalists and have been granted control over the work of others;

3.   *petit bourgeoisie*: that small group of merchants who control their own businesses and do most of their work themselves, buying little labor power from others;

4.   *working class*: that huge group of blue-collar and white-collar workers who sell their labor to employers in return for wages and salaries.

The dominant class in the U.S. political–economic system is the capitalist class, which in the workplace subordinates working people in all racial and ethnic groups to its profit and investment needs. It is the capitalists who decide whether and where to create jobs. They are responsible for the flight of capital and jobs from many central cities to the suburbs and overseas.

Barrera argues that each class contains segments that are set off in terms of racial group and ethnicity. Figure 2–3 suggests how this works. Each class is cross-cut by a line of racial segmentation separating those who suffer from institutionalized discrimination, such as black Americans and Mexican Americans, from those who do not. Take the example of the working class. Although black, Latino, and Native American workers may share the same *class* position with white workers in that they are struggling against capitalist employers for better wages and working conditions, they are also in a subordinate position because of structural discrimination along racial lines within that working class. Barrera notes that the dimensions of this discrimination often include lower wages for many subordinate-group workers, as well as their concentration in lower-status occupations. These Americans suffer from both class exploitation (as wage workers) and racial exploitation (as workers of color).[48]

Cultural Resistance and Oppositional Culture

Internal colonialism theorists accent the role of the cultural stereotyping and racist ideologies of dominant groups seeking to subordinate people of color. A racist ideology dominates an internal colonialist society, intellectually dehumanizing the colonized. Stereotyping and prejudice, seen in many traditional assimilation theories as more or less temporary problems, are viewed by colonialism analysts as a way of rationalizing exploitation over a very long period, if not permanently. Attempts are made by the dominant group to envelop subordinate groups in dominant cultural values, traditions, and language—in the case of people of color, to "whiten" their cultures. In a system of internal colonialism, cultural as well as racial markers are used to set off subordinate groups such as Native Americans, Mexican Americans, Japanese Americans, and African Americans from the white Euro-American group.[49]

A number of power–conflict scholars have honed the idea of *oppositional culture* as a basis for understanding the resistance of non-European groups to this dominant Euro-American culture. For example, Bonnie Mitchell and Joe Feagin argue that the oppositional cultures of Americans of color are "distinct from the dominant Euro-American culture, while also reflecting or reacting to elements of

FIGURE 2–3
The Class and Racial Structure of
Internal Colonialism

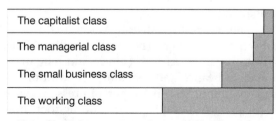

Note: Shaded area represents people of color.

the larger society. . . . In the colonies and later the United States the pressures on non-Europeans for conformity to the Euro-American culture forced minority Americans to become bicultural, to know both the dominant Euro-American culture and their own oppositional culture as well."[50]

In the centuries of intergroup contact before the creation of what is now called the United States, Mexico, and Canada, the area of North America was populated by a diverse mixture of European, African, and Native American cultures. The nation of the United States created in the late 1700s encompassed African enslavement and the genocide of Native Americans. Faced with oppression, these and other victims of white colonialism have drawn on their own cultural resources, as well as their distinctive knowledge of Euro-American culture and society, to resist oppression in every way possible. The cultures of those oppressed by European Americans have not only provided a source of individual, family, and community resistance to racial oppression and colonialism, but have also infused, often in unrecognized ways, some significant elements into the evolving cultural mix that constitutes the core culture of the United States. Thus, the oppositional cultures of colonized groups such as African, Latino, and Native Americans have helped preserve several key elements of U.S. society, including its tradition of civil rights and social justice.[51]

Looking back over U.S. history, several researchers have researched the cultural strategies developed by subordinated groups to resist oppression. In his research on slave systems and other systems of oppression, James Scott has shown that intentional deception is at the heart of much interaction between the powerless and the powerful.[52] For example, enslaved African Americans were not free to speak their minds to white masters, so they spoke or sang among themselves in ways (for example, in religious-spiritual terms) that disguised their criticism of enslavement and white oppression. The backstage discourse of African American slaves and other oppressed groups included openly expressed ideological critiques that could not be discussed publicly because of retaliation. Afro-Christianity was an example of how enslaved African Americans resisted the "ideological hegemony" (attempts to brainwash) of white slavemasters. In public religious services, enslaved African Americans pretended to accept Christian preaching about obedience. However, when and where no whites were present, Afro-Christianity emphasized "themes of deliverance and redemption, Moses and the Promised Land, the Egyptian captivity, and emancipation."[53] For these Americans, the Promised Land meant the North and freedom, and the afterlife was often viewed as a place where their white oppressors would be severely punished.[54]

The religion of African Americans mixed African and European elements from the beginning. The protest-inclined African values prevailed over the European values. African culture and religion were major sources of the inclination to resistance and rebellion. In addition to ideological resistance, enslaved African Americans, like other oppressed peoples elsewhere, used a variety of more open resistance tactics, including foot-dragging at work, running away, and assaulting or killing brutal white overseers and masters.

Anticolonial Nationalism

Ideological resistance has taken a number of different forms in the twentieth century. For example, anticolonial *nationalism* has developed as part of the cultural resistance to European colonialism and its legitimating racist ideology. This is especially true for those people of color who see the strategy of integration as a failure. Pan-Africanism and cultural nationalism are two examples of this resistance to both internal colonialism and liberal solutions for that colonialism.

From the early 1900s to the 1950s, for example, the sociologist W. E. B. Du Bois was not only a key figure in theorizing about racial relations from a Marxist perspective but was also a major exponent of the importance of cultural nationalism. He saw pan-African nationalism as a partial solution for the conditions in which people of African descent found themselves and argued that the pan-African movement "means to us what the Zionist movement must mean to the Jews, the centralization of race effort and the recognition of a racial fount."[55] Over great objections from the U.S. State Department, Du Bois succeeded in putting together the first Pan-African Congress in 1919, which was attended by nearly sixty delegates from fifteen countries. Speaking for the "Negroes of the world," the Congress did not ask for immediate decolonization of Africans and their descendants around the globe but rather for more democratic treatment. The Congress called for the abolition of all forms of slavery and for curtailment of colonial exploitation. The Pan-African Congress was an important step toward uniting people of African descent and was perceived as radical by white European and American leaders.[56] From 1919 to the 1950s, Du Bois worked to promote ideas of pan-Africanism. In his view the liberation of African Americans would be greatly facilitated by a cultural and intellectual coupling to Africa.[57]

The 1920 Harlem Renaissance was a dramatic flowering of writing and arts focused on African American values and traditions. This form of cultural nationalism accented not so much political and economic resistance strategies but resistance in the form of an enhanced cultural identity and a strong sense of peoplehood.[58] Since at least the 1920s a series of African American leaders and organizations, including Marcus Garvey, Malcolm X, and the Nation of Islam, have rejected assimilation and integration philosophies and accented African values, traditions, dress, language, and culture.[59]

Other people of color have drawn on cultural nationalism as a means of resisting Euro-American culture and discrimination. For example, in Chapter 9 we will examine protests by Mexican Americans in New Mexico. The Alianza Federal de Mercedes, founded in the 1960s by Reies Lopez Tijerina, sought to recover lands in New Mexico that had been taken by Anglo-American invaders and to establish a strong Mexican American identity with links to the Mexican heritage. A militant *Chicano* movement, which emphasized Mexican culture and national pride, also emerged among Mexican Americans in a dramatic way in the 1960s and 1970s.

An African American family in African dress celebrates Kwanzaa.

Recent Afrocentric Theories

Building on the work of Du Bois, several social scientists have developed a comprehensive Afrocentric perspective that includes a strong critique of the cultural imperialism of Euro-Americans and the Eurocentric character of the dominant culture. In several books since 1980, sociologist Molefi Kete Asante has broken new ground in the development of this perspective, arguing for the use of the term *Afrocentricity.* Asante underscores and analyzes the fundamental Eurocentric bias in the dominant culture, particularly the elements of that culture that have been absorbed by African Americans. He is critical of the language of much ethnic analysis. "The use of the terms *ethnicity, disadvantaged, minority,* and *ghetto* are antithetical to our political consciousness which is indivisible from the international political struggle against racism. Our American situation has never been defined as 'ethnic' until now when it is beneficial for the oppressor."[60]

Similarly, anthropologist Marimba Ani writes: "European cultural imperialism is the attempt to proselytize, encourage, and project European ideology. . . . European nationalism implies European expansion, that, in turn, mandates European imperialism."[61] Beginning in the 1400s, this imperialism came to encompass most of the globe. This physical invasion was supported by a well-developed theory of white European supremacy, a worldview that attempted to destroy the cultures and self-conceptions of African and African American peoples.

Seen from this critical power–conflict perspective, the Euro-American worldview includes the myth of European cultural and national superiority, a celebration of materialism over cooperative and spiritual values, and a belief in the superiority of the Judeo-Christian religious tradition over other religious traditions. Colonial invaders have sought to convert all conquered peoples to these myths and conceptions. Because of the profound effect this Euro-American view has had on the subordinated peoples, Afrocentric theorists argue that African Americans must direct their "energies toward the recreation of cultural alternatives informed by ancestral visions of a future that celebrates . . . Africaness."[62] The central focus of this is to develop an oppositional cultural viewpoint that is rooted in African values and philosophies.

Criticism of Internal Colonialism Theories

A neocolonial situation is one in which a postcolonial country (for example, an African country) has separated politically from a European colonial power but continues to be dependent on that country. The former colony uses indigenous leaders to help the former colonial power exploit the local population economically. It has a distinct territorial boundary. Joan Moore suggests that this neocolonialism model does not apply very well to subordinate groups in the United States because these groups are not generally confined to a specific bounded territory nor do they contain the exploitative intermediary elite of overseas neocolonialism. This space-centered critique has been repeated by Michael Omi and Howard Winant, who argue that the social and spatial intermixing of all racial groups in the United States casts serious doubt on the internal colonialism argument about territorially bounded colonization.[63]

However, most internal colonialism researchers have recognized the differences between internal colonial and neocolonial oppression. These theorists note that the situations of groups like Mexican Americans or African Americans in the United States are different from those in a newly independent (once colonized) nation still dependent on a European country. In response to the critique, internal colonialism analysts might argue that there are many aspects of colonialism still evident in U.S. racial and ethnic relations and emphasize that non-European groups in the United States (1) are usually residentially segregated, (2) are typically "superexploited" in employment and deficient in other material conditions when compared with white immigrants, (3) are culturally stigmatized, and (4) have had some of their leaders co-opted by whites.

The Split Labor Market View: Another Class-Based Theory

Internal colonialism analysts are sometimes unclear about whether all classes of whites benefit from the colonization of people of color or just the dominant class of capitalist employers. A power–conflict perspective that helps in assessing this question is the *split labor market* view, which treats class in the sense of position in the "means of production." This viewpoint has been defended by Edna Bonacich.

She argues that in U.S. society, dominant-group (white) workers do not share the interests of the top political–economic class, the capitalists. Yet both the employer class and the white part of the working class discriminate against the racially subordinated part of the working class.[64]

Developing a class analysis of racial subordination, Oliver Cox argued that the capitalist class, motivated by a desire for profit and cheap labor, sought African labor for the slave system in the United States. Ever since, this employer class has helped keep African Americans in a subordinate economic position in U.S. society. Similarly, Al Szymanski argued that since employers have not created enough jobs for all those wishing to work, black and white workers are pitted against each other for too few jobs, often to the broad advantage of employers as a class.[65]

In contrast, Bonacich emphasizes that discrimination against black workers by white workers seeking to protect their own privileges, however limited these may be, is very important. Capitalists bring in black and other racially subordinated workers to decrease labor costs, but white workers resist because they fear job displacement or lower wages. For example, over the last century white workers' unions have restricted the access of black workers to many job ladders, thus splitting the labor market and reducing black incomes. Research on unions provides historical evidence for this argument. Thus, Stanley Greenberg concludes that from the 1880s to the 1960s the industrial unions in Alabama "helped forge a labor framework" that created and perpetuated rigidly segregated white and black jobs.[66] In some areas informal segregation persists to the present day. White workers gain and lose from this structural racism. They gain in the short run, because there is less competition for privileged job categories from those who are racially excluded. But white workers lose in the long run because employers can use a cordoned-off sector of lower-wage workers to undercut them.[67]

Middleman Minorities, Ethnic Enclaves, and Segmented Assimilation

Drawing on insights of earlier scholars, Edna Bonacich has explored the in-between position, in terms of power and resources, that certain racial and ethnic groups have occupied in stratified societies. These groups find their economic niche as small-business people positioned between other producers and consumers. Some ethnic and racial groups become small-scale traders and merchants doing jobs that dominant groups are not eager to do. For example, many first-generation Jewish and Japanese Americans, excluded from mainstream employment by white Protestants, became small-scale merchants, tailors, restaurant operators, or gardeners. These groups have held "a distinctive class position that is of special use to the ruling class." They "act as a go-between to this society's more subordinate groups."[68]

Bonacich and John Modell found that Japanese Americans fit what has been termed the "middleman minority" model. Before World War II, Japanese Americans resided in highly organized communities. Their local economies were based on self-employment, including gardening and truck farming, and on other nonindustrial family businesses. The social solidarity of the first generation of Japanese Americans helped them establish successful small businesses. However, they faced hostility from the surrounding society, and in fact were driven into the businesses they developed because they were denied other employment opportunities. By the second generation there was some breakdown in the small-business position of Japanese Americans, for many of that generation moved into professional occupations outside the ethnic niche economy.[69]

Some middleman groups, such as Jewish and Korean American merchants in certain central cities, have become targets of hostility from groups that are less well off, such as poor Latino and African Americans. In addition, strong ingroup bonds can make the middleman group an effective competitor, and even Anglo-Protestant capitalists may become hostile toward an immigrant group that competes too effectively. Thus, in some cities Jewish American business people have been viewed negatively by some better-off Anglo-Protestant merchants, who have the power to discriminate against them, as well as by the poor renters and customers with whom they deal as landlords and merchants. Some scholars of racial and ethnic relations have criticized the application of "middleman minority" theory to Asian Americans, arguing that Korean Americans and Chinese Americans, although substantially involved in trade, have rarely been a *middle* group of entrepreneurs situated between a poor racial/ethnic group and a richer racial/ethnic group. More generally, this middleman perspective does not deal adequately with the movement of large numbers of the middleman group into the dominant group, as has happened for Jewish Americans.

A somewhat similar perspective, *enclave theory,* examines secondary–structural incorporation into the economy, especially the ways in which certain non-European immigrant groups have created social and economic enclaves in cities. Both the middleman and the enclave perspectives give more emphasis to economic inequality and discrimination than assimilation perspectives, and they stress the incorporation of certain groups, such as Asians and Cubans, into the United States through the means of small businesses and specialized "ethnic economies." The major differences between the two viewpoints seem to stem from the examples emphasized. Groups studied by enclave theorists, such as Cuban Americans, have created enclaves that are more than merchant or trading economies—they often include manufacturing enterprises, for example. These economic enclaves may compete directly with established Anglo-Protestant business elites. In contrast, the middleman groups develop trading economies and are likely to fill an economic niche that complements that of established white businesses. In reality, however, there appears to be little difference between the real-world experiences of those described as middleman groups and those described as enclave groups.

An example of the enclave perspective can be seen in the work of Alejandro Portes and Robert Manning, who examined the communities and economies of the Cubans in Miami and the Koreans in Los Angeles, groups that have developed many small businesses that cater to customers inside and outside their own communities. Enclave economies require an immigrant group with entrepreneurial talents, business experience, available capital, and a pool of low-wage labor. These characteristics enabled Cuban Americans in Miami to build a strong enclave economy. These enclaves, unlike the "colonies" of internal colonialism, typically do not relegate newcomers to a permanent position of inferiority. Portes and Manning criticize the internal colonialism and split labor market viewpoints for trying to encompass all subordinate racial and ethnic groups, although they agree that the situations of African Americans, Mexican Americans, and Native Americans can be explained as internal colonialism. Enclave analysts have so far paid insufficient attention to the exploitation that goes on in the enclave economy, such as the exploitation of low-wage immigrant workers by the immigrant (for example, Cuban American) employers. They also neglect the impact of the surrounding political and economic system—in the Cuban and Korean cases, multinational capitalism—which shapes the initial migration as well as the character of the specific enclave economies. In some ways, then, these enclave theorists straddle the fence between the order and power–conflict theories.[70]

In the 1990s some immigration analysts who are concerned with structural barriers that prevent some immigrant groups from assimilating in the manner that might be predicted from a traditional assimilation perspective have developed the concept of *segmented* assimilation. Ruben Rumbaut has underscored the diversity of adaptation experiences of various immigrant groups, calling on immigration researchers to spell out what is "being 'assimilated,' by whom, under what circumstances, and in reference to what sector of American society." Moreover, reviewing the immigration literature, Alejandro Portes and Min Zhou have argued that the outcomes of adaptation by immigrants to U.S. society vary greatly, with some confined to the lower economic rungs of the societal ladder and others experiencing rapid economic development while maintaining much of their traditional culture. The experiences of immigrants include both upward and downward mobility, and thus reflect a variable and segmented assimilation. Why is there such variation? The answers lie in such structural factors as racial discrimination and residential segregation, as well as in the financial and cultural capital that immigrants bring with them. The ability of immigrant families to counter discrimination and other barriers with family or group mobilization of economic and cultural resources can affect their incorporation into the larger society. In discussions of variations in cultural and social capital, the arguments about segmented assimilation overlap to some degree with the ideas of the ethnogenesis theory discussed previously. The main difference lies in the greater attention given by segmentation theorists to major structural barriers such as racial discrimination and entrenched segregation.[71]

Women and Gendered Racism

Most theories of racial and ethnic relations have neglected gender stratification, the hierarchy in which men as a group dominate women as a group in terms of power and resources. In recent years a number of scholars have researched the situations of women within racial and ethnic groups in the United States. Their analyses assess the ways in which male supremacy, or a *patriarchal system*, inter-acts with and operates within a system of racial and ethnic stratification. Discussing racial and ethnic cultures around the globe, Adrienne Rich has defined a patriarchal system as "a familial-social, ideological, political system in which men—by force, direct pressure, or through ritual, tradition, law and language, customs, etiquette, education, and the division of labor—determine what part women shall or shall not play, and in which the female is everywhere subsumed under the male."[72]

Asking whether racism or patriarchy has been the primary source of oppres-sion, social psychologist Philomena Essed examined black women in the United States and the Netherlands. She found racism and sexism interacting regularly. The oppression of black women can thus be seen as *gendered racism*. For example, under slavery African American women were exploited not only for labor but also often as sex objects for some white men. After slavery they were excluded from most job categories available to white men and white women; major employment changes came only with the civil rights movement of the 1960s. Today, racism has many gendered forms. In the U.S. mass media, for example, the white female is the standard for female beauty. Women of color are often stereotyped as matri-archs in female-headed families or as "welfare queens." In the economy they are found disproportionately in lower-paid "female jobs," such as typists or nurse's aides. Some women of color are closely bound in their social relations with those who oppress them in such areas as domestic employment (maids) and other low-paid service work.[73]

In her book *Black Feminist Thought*, Patricia Hill Collins argues that a black-feminist theoretical framework can highlight and analyze critically the negative stereotypes of black women in white society—the stereotypes of the docile mammy, the domineering matriarch, the promiscuous whore, and the irresponsi-ble welfare mother. These severely negative images persist among many whites because they are fostered by the mass media and because they undergird white discrimination against black women in the United States.[74]

Scholars assessing the situations of other women of color, including Native Americans, Asian Americans, and Latinas, have similarly emphasized the cumu-lative and interactive character of racial and gender oppression and the necessity of liberating these women from white stereotypes and discrimination. For exam-ple, Denise Segura has examined labor-force data on Mexican American women and developed the concept of *triple oppression*, the mutually reinforcing and inter-active set of racial, class, and gender forces the cumulative effects of which "place women of color in a subordinate social and economic position relative to men of color and the white population."[75]

The State and Racial Formation

Looking at the important role of governments in creating racial and ethnic desig-nations and institutionalizing discrimination, Michael Omi and Howard Winant have developed an innovative theory of *racial formation*. Racial tensions and oppression, in their view, cannot be explained solely in terms of class or nationalism. Racial and ethnic relations are substantially defined by the actions of governments, ranging from the passing of legislation, such as restrictive immigration laws, to the imprisonment of groups defined as a threat (for example, Japanese Americans in World War II). Although the internal colonialism viewpoint gives some emphasis to the state's role in the exploitation of people of color, it has not developed this argument sufficiently.

Omi and Winant note that the U.S. government has shaped the politics of racial relations: The U.S. Constitution and a lengthy series of laws openly defined racial groups and interracial relationships (for example, slavery) in racist terms. The U.S. Constitution counted each African American slave as three-fifths of a person, and the Naturalization Law of 1790 explicitly declared that only white immigrants could qualify for naturalization. Many non-Europeans, including Africans and Asians, were prevented from becoming citizens. Japanese and other Asian immigrants, for example, were banned by law until the 1950s from becoming citizens. In 1854 the California Supreme Court even ruled that Chinese immigrants should be classified as "Indians"(!), therefore denying them the political rights available to white Americans.[76]

For centuries, the U.S. government officially favored northern European immigrant groups over southern Europeans, such as Italians, and over people from other continents. For example, the Immigration Act of 1924 was used to exclude Asian immigrants and most immigrants from southern and eastern Europe, those whom the Anglo-Protestant political leaders in Congress saw as racially inferior and a threat to their control of the society. Northern European Americans working through the government thereby shaped the subsequent racial and ethnic mix of the United States.

Toward a Comprehensive Theory of Racial Oppression

All the authors reviewed in the last section are grappling with important dimensions of racial oppression in the United States. Drawing on these authors, particularly Du Bois, Cox, and Blauner, and on our own recent work, we here suggest a comprehensive power–conflict theory, one we call a *theory of racial oppression*. As our concrete example, we use the case of white Americans and African Americans. We accent six major themes in the development of racial oppression:

1. *Initiation of Oppression*: At an early point in time, the European colonialists established hierarchical group relations with the peoples they oppressed and exploited for their land and labor. Soon this hierarchy of oppression was explained in racial terms. The subordinated groups were viewed as biologically and culturally inferior "races." This racialized oppression has never been eradicated and remains central to U.S. society to the present day.

2. *Mechanisms of Oppression*: In the past and in the present, racial hierarchies are supported by a range of dominant-group feelings and attitudes, including hostility, contempt, and fear. Although these feelings and prejudices

are important, racial hierarchies are perpetuated primarily by the discriminatory practices carried out by many members of the dominant racial group (in this case, white Americans) against those in subordinate racial groups.

3. *Privileges of Oppression*: Great material and symbolic privileges benefit those in the dominant racial group. Much misery and serious social and economic burdens come to those in subordinate racial groups.

4. *Elite Maintenance of Oppression*: The actions of the white elite have created and maintained organizations, institutions, and ideologies that reflect its vested interest in racial and class hierarchies. Most non-elite whites have accepted the society's racial hierarchy, along with fewer material resources than the elite, because of their access to certain privileges and advantages generally associated with "whiteness."

5. *Rationalization of Oppression*: Once a system of racial oppression and privilege is put in place, it is thoroughly defended and rationalized by a set of racist ideas. An ideology accenting superior and inferior racial groups is created and circulated by those whites in power and is taken for granted and further circulated by many rank-and-file whites.

6. *Resistance to Oppression*: Opposition to this racial oppression is a constant in North American history. African Americans and other Americans of color have a long history of individual and group protest against the reality and burdens of racial oppression.

William E. B. Du Bois, in *The World and Africa* (1946), showed how the great misery and poverty then evident in Europe's African colonies were "a main cause of wealth and luxury in Europe. The results of this poverty were disease, ignorance, and crime. Yet these had to be represented as natural characteristics of backward peoples."[77] Du Bois argued that the history of African colonization has been omitted from mainstream histories of European development, wealth, and affluence. He further argued that any serious understanding of European wealth must *center* on the history of African colonialism, for the economic resources of Africans were taken to help create that wealth.

Similarly, the first step in developing a comprehensive theory of racial oppression in the United States is to put the four-centuries-long white domination of people of color at the center of the analysis. From the beginning, colonialism in North America involved racialized oppression and exploitation: The European colonists built up wealth by taking for themselves the human and other resources of Africans and Native Americans. It has been said that a major task for the residents of the former Communist states of Eastern Europe is to forget the falsified past once taught them and to learn about their actual past. In this process, old heroes become villains and old villains become heroes. This is true for Americans as well. The exclusion or distortion of the full history of racial oppression in the United States in many mainstream accounts and textbooks must be replaced by accurate accounts.

Together with Du Bois, Oliver C. Cox was one of the first to examine the colonial origins of oppression in North America. He showed how capitalism, which was involved in the movement of Europeans overseas, created a situation "favorable for the development of white race prejudice."[78] Modern racial prejudice and racial ideology developed as these colonizers moved from viewing colonized populations as "heathens" to seeing them as racially inferior. Thus colonialism, with its theft of land and labor, created modern racial relations. As Cox views it, modern racial oppression did not arise out of some "abstract, natural, immemorial feeling of mutual antipathy between groups" but rather grew out of "a practical exploitative relationship" that was combined with a rudimentary form of racial prejudice.[79]

The origins of racial hierarchies in the actual experiences of colonialism and exploitation in a particular historical period rather than in innate intergroup hostilities is a second major theme in a comprehensive theory of oppression. "Race" is not an inborn human trait but rather a *way of relating* between individuals and groups. A comprehensive theory of oppression must begin with the real world of everyday experience and the historical relationships between groups of human beings.

Our conceptual framework recognizes the centrality of the history of economic exploitation in North America, which began with the seizure of Native American lands (see Chapter 7) and the enslavement of Africans (see Chapter 8) by violent means. Land and labor obtained by theft formed the economic and social foundation of what became the United States. Most Native Americans were killed or driven out of white areas, while enslaved Africans were forced to become a central part of the economy of new white communities. This genocidal action against Native Americans and the importation, subordination, and exploitation of enslaved Africans set in place the foundation for nearly 400 years of oppression in North America.

By the mid-1600s, the liberty and lives of all Americans of African heritage were controlled by a system of racial oppression. For most, this took the form of legalized slavery. Transplanted and enslaved Africans became a major point of reference for the construction of the colonial economy, polity, legal system, and values, and even white selves. Their subjugation became the model for the treatment of other Americans of color in later periods. The white-male elite among the colonizers reinforced this economy of oppression by legalizing it in the founding laws of the new republic. As we have seen, slavery was upheld in key provisions of the original U.S. Constitution. Wealthy slaveholders such as George Washington and Thomas Jefferson led in the creation of the legal system of the new nation; Americans of color had *no* representation whatsoever in the process. From the beginning, government was used to create and enforce racial oppression.

A third theme in this comprehensive theory is the importance of the power and privilege of those called "whites" and the related misery and burdens of those termed the racial "others." Racial oppression operates from a socially organized set of ideas and practices that deny African Americans and other people of color the privileges, power, opportunities, and rewards that U.S. society offers white

Americans. The racial hierarchy stipulates different resources and life chances for the dominant and subordinate groups. As the dominant group, whites enjoy economic, political, and symbolic advantages. At some level of their consciousness, most whites seem aware of these privileges.[80]

White Americans and black Americans have different group interests because they have had unequal access to "life, liberty, and the pursuit of happiness" and to the material and other resources that shape the quality of everyday life. Whites discriminate against black men, women, and children in order to protect white interests and privileges. For example, many whites' frequent discriminatory actions that restrict the access of African Americans and other Americans of color to better-paying jobs or to certain residential areas outweigh their commitment to the values of racial equality.[81] Today, the majority of low-wage service and unskilled menial jobs in numerous employment sectors are held by African Americans and other people of color; workers in these jobs often service better-off whites, such as employers, managers, and skilled workers. As a result, "these jobs entail a transfer of energies whereby the servers enhance the status of those served."[82]

The other side of white privilege is the set of material and psychological burdens that bear down on African Americans and other people of color. In its everyday operation the racial system dehumanizes those in a subordinated group. The most precious asset of the racial "other," the control over life and liberty, is that which is most taken away. Institutionalized discrimination and inequality constitute the social structure of racial oppression, and its psychological dynamic is individual dehumanization. Our conceptual framework recognizes some degree of variation in these discriminatory burdens depending on the social position and gender of the oppressed individual. For example, black women often face gendered racism—the double burden of suffering discrimination because they are black and because they are female. Historically and in the present, institutionalized oppression has prevented most Americans of color from developing to their full potential.

A fourth aspect of our theory of oppression recognizes the differential role of different class and gender groups among white Americans. The actions of the white elite—originally composed of slaveholders and merchants but later of industrialists and other entrepreneurs—are critical in the creation and maintenance of the racist system at the foundation of U.S. society. As Du Bois and Cox made clear early on, in the process of protecting its top position, this mostly white male elite has worked to create organizations, institutions, and ideologies that substantially incorporate its interests. The elite holds disproportionate power and wealth. When its interests conflict with those of other racial or class groups, the elite works hard to deflect challenges to its dominance.

Racial domination has affected a number of subordinated racial groups because early on the white elite made such domination a central organizing principle of intergroup life in the United States.[83] The discriminatory treatment of non-black subordinated groups has varied, but in every case it is the dominant white group—and within it the ruling elite—that has set the basic terms for this treatment and thus for group development.

In the economic arena, the ruling class has been substantially interested in the exploitation of the land and labor of Americans of color, while the white working and middle classes have been more concerned about job and housing competition with Americans of color. Ordinary whites are important in enforcing racial discrimination in everyday life, since they constitute the majority of whites. Middle-class and working-class whites are responsible for much of the everyday discrimination against African Americans and other people of color, as recent studies of employment and housing discrimination show (see Chapter 8).

A fifth theme in our theory is that once racial oppression is in place, it is thoroughly defended and rationalized. The taking of the land and labor of Americans of color is rooted not only in the laws and founding documents of the larger society but also in a strong ideology accenting the alleged inferiority of those at the bottom of the racial ladder. This ideology is structured by intellectuals and other elite leaders and communicated to the general public in both overt and subtle forms. One way to maintain whites' position in a social hierarchy is to cover the underlying reality with an ideology that defines the subordinated as "inferior" groups who "deserve their place" in society.

Since the 1700s, white intellectuals and other leaders have tried to hide the actual sources of racial and class inequalities. The dominant group created images of itself as racially superior and explained inequality in racist terms. A comprehensive theory of racial oppression must include the role of this rationalization. From the beginning, religious, economic, political, intellectual, and media elites perpetuated negative images of racial outgroups in order to legitimate racial oppression. The often unseen power of the white elite still works through the racist beliefs and images (for example, the black woman as a lazy "welfare queen") perpetuated in the media, schools, workplaces, and churches of the nation.

Racist ideas and their societal underpinning vary somewhat over time, but certain elements have persisted since the seventeenth century. William E. B. Du Bois wrote of the "psychological wage" that white workers receive in a system of oppression. Whites with fewer resources than the white elite accept less because of their access to the privileges of whiteness. For example, when white working people, openly or half-consciously viewing themselves as racially superior, have refused to organize with workers of color against stubborn employers in order to secure better wages, they have received fewer economic resources. They may accept this situation because they have come to prize the privileges of whiteness, although they may only be dimly aware of these privileges because of their commonplace character. Ordinary white Americans suffer in this racialized, class-stratified society, and the dominant ideology, with its stereotypes of Americans of color, makes it harder for most of these whites to understand not only the situation of the racial "others" but also their own societal situation. Most whites do not feel powerful or privileged, especially relative to the white elite, and they are unable to see the real sources of class and racial inequality in the society. Indeed, many whites target Americans of color as bearing primary responsibility for their own or the nation's economic difficulties. And some of these join white supremacist groups, which may engage in terrorism against Americans of color. Whites, too, pay a price for their privilege, for this privilege prevents them from realizing in the society the full meaning of concepts that most of them consider important: fairness, equality, competition, freedom, and justice.

A sixth aspect of a complete theory of racial oppression emphasizes the many countering and resistance strategies developed by members of racially oppressed groups, both individually and collectively. Protest against racial oppression includes not only overt confrontation with members of the dominant group but also the development of an alternative perspective on the everyday world one must live in, a perspective generated over a long period of time by those fighting discrimination and domination. African Americans and other people of color are theorists of their own everyday experience, as they have made clear in a long history of antidiscrimination protest and civil rights movements. Out of their everyday experiences with racism, Americans of color have created countercultures of resistance that are the foundation for individual and group strategies to counter or destroy oppression.

Evidence of a counterculture of resistance can be seen in the black civil rights movement that was so powerful in the 1950s and 1960s. Organized protest against discrimination during this period included economic and bus boycotts, sit-ins, and demonstrations. This black resistance to segregation spurred the creation of civil rights organizations such as the Southern Christian Leadership Conference (SCLC), which was led by Dr. Martin Luther King, Jr. Most demonstrations included large-scale participation by African Americans from all class backgrounds. This organized activism was rooted in a strong local base of churches, clubs, and other organizations that provided money and mobilized people to enable organizations such as the SCLC to achieve success in fighting racism and segregation.[84] During the 1960s this powerful civil rights movement played an important role in persuading the U.S. Congress to pass major civil rights laws.

In summary, then, a racially oppressive society must be comprehended in its totality. All of these dimensions are important to a fully developed framework for understanding modern racial oppression.

SUMMARY

This chapter has reviewed major theories of migration and subsequent patterns of intergroup adaptation. Migration—varying from the movement of conquerors to slave importation to voluntary immigration—creates intergroup contact and thus racial and ethnic relations and conflicts. Adaptation can have different outcomes in the period of initial contact, ranging from extreme genocide to peaceful symbiosis to some type of hierarchy and inequality. Further adaptation may lead to further genocide, to symbiosis, to Anglo-conformity, to some type of cultural pluralism, or to continuing inequality and hierarchy.

Most theories discussed in this chapter fall under the two broad categories of assimilation theories and power–conflict theories. Both types of theories offer insights into the character and development of racial and ethnic relations. Assimilation theories tend to focus on voluntary immigrant groups and emphasize Anglo-conformity or pluralism outcomes. Assimilation analysts have pointed out the different dimensions of intergroup adaptation, such as acculturation and marital assimilation and have accented the role of value consensus in holding a racial and ethnic system together.

In contrast, power–conflict theories focus on involuntary immigration or colonial oppression and thus accent substantial inequality and hierarchy. Power–conflict theories have certain recurring themes:

1. a central concern for racial and ethnic inequalities in economic position, power, and resources;

2. an emphasis on the interrelationship of racial inequalities, the economic institutions of capitalism, and the subordination of women under patriarchal systems;

3. an emphasis on the role of the government in legalizing exploitation and segregation and in defining racial and ethnic relations;

4. an emphasis on resistance to domination by those who are oppressed.

In analyzing U.S. history, power–conflict analysts have emphasized the forced character of much cultural and economic adaptation, particularly for non-European groups, and the role of coercion, segregation, colonization, and institutionalized discrimination in keeping groups such as African, Mexican, and Native Americans on the bottom rungs of the societal racial/ethnic ladder. Power–conflict perspectives have examined the role of government in racial oppression (as in laws barring intermarriage) and have stressed the importance of oppositional cultures in providing the foundations for subordinate group resistance to racial oppression.

Power–conflict theorists have often emphasized the importance of examining racial and ethnic relations in the context of the historical development of capitalism and patriarchy. In the introduction to Part II we will explore the utility of such an approach in evaluating the broad contours of racial and ethnic relations over more than three and one-half centuries of North American history.

PART II

A Nation of Immigrants: An Overview of the Economic and Political Conditions of Selected Racial and Ethnic Groups

In the chapters that follow we examine a number of important racial and ethnic groups in U.S. society. For each we look at aspects of its history and analyze its current situation in terms of the theories of racial–ethnic relations reviewed in Chapter 2. Before examining these groups in detail, we will set them in the historical context of nearly four centuries of North American economic and political development. We accent two important dimensions of this society in our overview: the changing capitalistic economy and the expanding political and governmental framework. Within these broad frameworks, each group has worked out its own cultural and social patterns in the complex nation we call the United States.

IMMIGRATION, THE ECONOMY, AND GOVERNMENT

North American economic development has seen several stages: mercantilism coupled with a plantation-slave economy, competitive industrial capitalism, and multinational capitalism. Economic institutions and developments and related government actions have shaped the character of all waves of

immigration and the subsequent patterns of immigrant adjustment.

Native Americans were the original inhabitants of the land to which the English and subsequent immigrants migrated; many in the indigenous societies lost their lives and lands as a result of the often brutal European invasion and conquest.

Table II–1 briefly lists most of the immigrant groups discussed in this book. Each group entered North America under particular historical circumstances. Many started in slavery, low-wage jobs, small-scale farming, or small businesses. Political and economic conditions at the time of entry were very important. Some groups entered when low-wage jobs were plentiful on farms or in cities; others entered when fewer jobs were available. The extent of racial and ethnic discrimination and oppression has varied considerably. Also important were the economic and other resources brought by the immigrant groups. Those immigrants who came voluntarily and with a little capital, some education, or entrepreneurial experience often had access to better jobs or developed small businesses—opportunities not available to immigrants with less in the way of resources.

TABLE II–1   Selected Immigrant Groups: An Overview

Immigrant Group	Time of Entry	Economic Conditions in North America	Government Conditions and Actions
Phase One: Commercial Capitalism and the Slave Society: 1600–1865			
1. English	1600s–1800s	Mercantilism; land taken from Native Americans; English entrepreneurs and yeoman farmers; commercial capitalism emerges.	English state creates land companies; colonial governments define individualized property and protect property.
2. Africans	1600s–1800s	Enslaved as property; became major source of labor for plantation capitalism.	Colonial governments establish slave codes; U.S. Constitution legitimates slave trade; U.S. government substantially controlled by plantation oligarchy.
3. Irish Catholics	1830s–1860s	Driven out of Ireland by oppression and famine; labor recruited for low-wage jobs in transport, construction.	U.S. government opens up western lands; Irish take urban political machines from British Americans.
Phase Two: Industrial Capitalism: 1865–1920			
4. Chinese	1850s–1870s	Contract labor and low-wage work in mining, railroads, construction; menial service work for white settlers.	Local governments help recruit Chinese labor; later, anti-Chinese laws passed in California; 1882 Exclusion Act.
5. Italians	1880s–1910s	Moved as peasants into industrial capitalism; overseas recruitment for low-wage industrial and construction jobs in the cities.	Government backing for labor recruitment; U.S. treaties with Europe; intervention in European affairs (World War I); incoming numbers reduced by 1924 Immigration Act.
6. Eastern European Jews	1880s–1910s	Industrial capitalism utilized their skilled and unskilled labor; small entrepreneurs re-established themselves; much anti-Semitic discrimination.	Government backing for labor recruitment; U.S. treaties with Europe; incoming numbers reduced by 1924 Immigration Act.
7. Japanese	1880s–1900s	Recruited as agricultural laborers for Hawaii; later migrated to West Coast as laborers; served in domestic work; created small businesses.	Government backing for labor recruiting; U.S. imperialism in Asia; conquest of Philippines and Hawaii; government laws exclude Asians.

TABLE II–1   *(Continued)*

Phase Three: Advanced Industrial (Multinational) Capitalism: 1920s–1990s

8. Mexicans	1910s–1990s	With Asian/European labor cut off, Mexicans recruited for farms and industry; low-wage jobs in new urban industries.	U.S. government provides labor recruitment programs and fosters U.S. agribusiness in Mexico, stimulating out-migration; U.S. Border Patrol monitors immigration; new laws regulate immigration.
9. Puerto Ricans	1940s–1990s	Early farm labor migration; U.S. corporations recruit labor; blue-collar work in service economy.	Conquest of Puerto Rico in 1898; U.S. government-supported agribusiness takes over economy, creates surplus labor, stimulates migration to U.S.
10. Recent Asian and Caribbean Groups	1960s–1990s	Many political and economic refugees; create economic niches; make use of expanding service economy.	U.S. intervention in Asia from 1853 to 1990s; government action in South Korea, Vietnam, Taiwan, Philippines stimulates out-migration; Cubans and Haitians flee political repression.

COMMERCIAL CAPITALISM AND THE SLAVE SOCIETY: 1607–1865

Colonial Society and Slave Labor

The colonial society that grew up on the east coast of North America during the 1600s was tied closely to England and the expansionist policies of the English political and economic elites. The early economic system in these colonies was a combination of state enterprises under the English king and enterprises developed by independent entrepreneurs, including, by the eighteenth century, the slave plantation owners in the South and the merchants in the North. As was the case with other European colonial powers, the objective of English colonization was to secure raw materials and markets for English goods. The first joint-stock companies were formed by merchants under the auspices of James I of England. Employees of the Southern Company settled Jamestown; this was the English colony that bought Africans from a Dutch ship in 1619.

English merchants and entrepreneurs invested capital in the extraction of raw materials for home industries. The colonies served the empire as a source of raw materials and as a dumping ground for the surplus workers and peasants displaced by the expansion of capitalism in Europe. Production for profit was not the only important economic dimension, for the colonies also became home to many English and other northern European immigrants—people displaced from the land in Europe and seeking to become small farmers. In the colonies there were two major modes of production, the household (small-farm) mode and the capitalist (slave plantation and merchant) mode.[1] The North American colonies had so much free land that it was difficult for English entrepreneurs to secure enough European labor, particularly for large-scale agriculture. They tried using white indentured servants, but these immigrants worked off their terms of servitude and went into farming for themselves.

From the 1600s to the mid-1800s, people of African descent were the major source of slave labor for the white merchant and agricultural capitalists in the British colonies. After 1790 the emergence of cotton and sugar as international commodities created a strong demand for enslaved workers on the southern plantations. The number of enslaved African Americans increased from 59,000 in 1714 to 3.9 million in 1860. This forced labor built up profits (capital) not only for further investments in expanding plantations and related business enterprises, but also for depositing in banks, where it could be used or borrowed by the white merchants, shippers, and industrialists of the North and South.

There is some debate over whether the plantation economy was fully capitalist, but Edna Bonacich's evaluation seems accurate:

> Although colonial producers of raw materials came to depend upon coerced labor, their orientation was essentially capitalist. They were involved in the investment of capital in the enterprise whose purpose was the production of commodities for a market, while profits were created by the extraction of surplus from labor by having the slaves work longer hours than was necessary for their own subsistence. The oppression of African Americans, past and present, is rooted in the requirements of early capitalism.[2]

Civil War: The Southern Plantation Oligarchy versus Northern Entrepreneurs

By the late 1700s the slave mode of production was generally profitable; the South was the most prosperous and powerful region in the country from the late 1700s to the 1850s. In the United States southerners owned much of the productive land, much of the agricultural produce for export, many processing mills and other valuable equipment, and the slave laborers. Southerners dominated U.S. politics, as most presidents between Washington and Lincoln were either slaveholders or sympathetic to slavery; for decades few major decisions made by the federal legislative and judicial branches went against the interests of the slaveholding oligarchy. The U.S. Civil War was to a substantial degree a struggle for economic and political power between northern industrialists and small farmers on the one hand and the southern plantation oligarchy on the other. The victory of the North in that war marked the arrival of northern industrialists as the dominant force in the U.S. economy and government.[3]

Immigrant Laborers in the North

During the 1800s in the northern states, the growing industrial working class and the class of small farmers were peopled with immigrants from Ireland, Germany, and Scandinavia. Immigrant labor often became the labor for the growing number of industrial enterprises—the textile mills, railroad shops, and foundries. The pull factors motivating millions of Irish Catholic immigrants to cross the Atlantic after 1820 were the same as those that have attracted immigrants for centuries to a country portrayed by industrial recruiters as the land of opportunity. There were major push factors as well. In Ireland a potato disease created severe food shortages; this crisis plus the political and economic oppression of Ireland by England generated the migration of 1.6 million Irish to the United States over several decades. Many small farmers and artisans from Ireland sold their labor to U.S. employers; they became domestic servants, railroad laborers, miners, and industrial workers in cities.

The arrival of large numbers of white immigrants from northern Europe laid the foundation for new patterns of racial conflict. African Americans became a smaller percentage of urbanites in the North. Free black workers were used by industrial entrepreneurs in the North mostly as low-wage labor, sometimes even as strikebreakers. Using them against white immigrant strikers further increased the hostility of these immigrant workers toward African Americans. By the 1840s free black workers in the North were being forcibly displaced from jobs by the new white immigrants, including Irish American workers. While the Irish immigrants arrived from a country where the English oppressed and stereotyped them as an "inferior race," within a generation in the United States the majority of the Irish had come to see themselves as part of a "superior white race."

Western Expansion: Native Americans and Mexican Americans

Fostered by U.S. governmental decrees and military protection, the great westward expansion in the nineteenth century brought not only Native Americans but also a new group—the Mexicans—into the orbit of exploitation by white European American entrepreneurs, soldiers, and settlers. The racist ideology of the "white man's civilizing responsibility" for non-European groups guided white expansionists and justified for them the taking of Mexican and Native American lands in the West. Expansionists believed the "Mexican race" and the "Indian race" should become subordinate to the "Anglo-Saxon race." The first Mexican citizens, long residents of the Southwest, did not migrate; they and their land were brought into the United States by force as the result of the Mexican-American War in the 1840s.

INDUSTRIAL CAPITALISM: 1865–1920

Industrial Capitalism and Government Expansion Overseas

The Civil War was followed not only by westward expansion but also by an industrial boom. An economy dominated by competitive capitalism, by small and medium-sized businesses, gradually became one that was dominated by large enterprises. The growth of these enterprises was dramatic, and the United States soon surpassed Great Britain in numerous production categories. The proportion of workers engaged in agriculture declined between the 1860s and the 1920s, while the proportion in manufacturing doubled. By the last two decades of the nineteenth century, many corporations were growing dramatically through mergers and acquisitions.

Leading white industrialists expanded corporate investments and activities in numerous countries overseas, often backed by a U.S. government growing in military power. The movement of U.S. Navy ships, as well as merchants and missionaries, into countries such as China, Japan, and the Philippines often disrupted the rural economies of these countries, thereby increasing the surplus of farm workers and shaping out-migration. U.S. military and economic power pressured Asian countries to submit to U.S. influence. Given the often difficult economic conditions in these nations, U.S. labor recruiters enticed many Asian workers to Hawaii and the west coast of the United States. More than 200,000 Chinese laborers came to the United States between 1848 and 1882 to do the hard work in West Coast mining, railroad, and service businesses. After the Chinese were excluded by a racist immigration law, Japanese immigrants were recruited for similar low-wage jobs. Japan sent many thousands of emigrants to Hawaii and to the United States, a migration triggered by western influence and by labor recruiting by U.S. employers.[4]

The U.S. victory in the Spanish-American War of the 1890s resulted in the annexation of Puerto Rico and the Philippines by the expansionist U.S. government and the effective domination of Cuba. When the United States took over Puerto Rico, much of that island was owned by smaller farmers, but soon U.S. companies were controlling much of the production. Puerto Rico, the Philippines, and Cuba would later send large numbers of emigrants to the U.S. mainland.[5]

African Americans: Exclusion from Western Lands

The second half of the nineteenth century was a period of major governmental growth and bureaucratization in the United States. Government action had a major influence on racial and ethnic relations. One of the first actions of Abraham Lincoln and the new Republican legislators in the early 1860s was to pass the Homestead Act, a major wealth-building program for the many white immigrant families seeking land, including the Germans, Scandinavians, and Irish. A European American family wishing to farm was given 160 to 320 acres of land if they would develop it. After the Civil War, the U.S. Land Office ruled that most black Americans were ineligible for these land grants because they were not citizens when the act was passed. Some land was made available in portions of the former slave states, but black families for the most part did not have the opportunity that many white families had to build up the landed wealth.[6]

In the late 1800s and early 1900s, southern black workers were one possible source of labor for northern industries, but the white oligarchy in the South, after a brief postwar Reconstruction period, took back control of the South's economy and state governments and made certain that most of the newly freed African Americans remained in the South as low-wage laborers, tenant farmers, or sharecroppers. There was little distribution of plantation land to the black men and women who had made that land fruitful.

Southern and Eastern European Immigrants

Unable to use southern black labor, or preferring not to use it, northern industrialists turned to Europe. The majority of the 20.7 million immigrants to the United States between 1881 and 1920 were from southern and eastern Europe. Labor shortages and increasing wages for native white workers encouraged U.S. industrialists to seek immigrant labor. A 1910 survey of twenty major manufacturing and mining industries found that six out of every ten workers were foreign-born. Without this immigrant labor, the great industrial expansion of the United States would not have been possible.[7] In some cases these new workers displaced native-born white workers. Anti-immigrant hostility (nativism) among the workers in older European American groups increased as a result.[8]

European Immigrants and Black Americans

Irving Kristol once argued that "The Negro Today Is Like the Immigrant of Yesterday." His argument illustrates the view that the experience of African Americans moving to the industrial cities is not significantly different from that of white immigrant groups, that African Americans should eventually move up economically and socially just as those immigrants did.[9] This argument overlooks important differences between the experiences of white and black immigrants. Group mobility was possible for European immigrants because:

1. Most arrived at a time when urban jobs were generally available, when U.S. capitalism was expanding, and opportunities were relatively abundant.

2. Many had some technical or other skills or a little capital—resources available to few African Americans.

3. Most faced far less severe employment and housing discrimination than black workers.

4. Most found housing, however inadequate, reasonably near the workplace.

5. In key cities, the political system was changing from Anglo-Protestant business dominance to shared power by business

elites and political machines oriented to white immigrant voters.[10]

In the critical periods of European immigration, cities such as New York, Philadelphia, Boston, and Chicago were expanding centers of manufacturing. Blue-collar jobs were frequently available, if not plentiful. In the mid-nineteenth century, Irish and German immigrants were attracted to rural areas and to cities, where most found industrial, service, or government jobs. From 1890 to 1930, southern and eastern Europeans came in large numbers to the cities. One study notes that "the Italian concentration in construction and the Polish in steel were related to the expansion of these industries as the groups arrived."[11] Many workers migrated as a result of labor recruiting by U.S. employers in Europe.

Among the immigrants who arrived in the period between 1880 and 1920 were large numbers of Jewish immigrants fleeing oppression in Europe. Although poverty-stricken, many Jewish immigrants were part of an urban industrial proletariat and came with some experience in skilled trades. One study found that two-thirds of the Jewish immigrants were skilled workers, whereas other southern and eastern European immigrants were primarily peasant farmers or farm workers. When Jewish immigrants entered in large numbers around 1900, the clothing industry was moving to mass production and offered jobs for tailors and seamstresses, as well as unskilled jobs, and there were also chances for small-scale entrepreneurs in a number of areas.

The situation for the African Americans who began to move to the northern cities after 1910 was different. Black workers who migrated from the South had no access to government jobs and were regularly displaced by the new white immigrant groups, who forced them out of job after job, such as construction and transport jobs, and into marginal, low-paying jobs. Stanley Lieberson has explored why southern and eastern European immigrants have done well in

northern cities, compared with black Americans. Among his conclusions are that (1) black migrants were the victims of more severe racial discrimination over a longer period than were white immigrant groups, and (2) economic competition between whites and the growing group of black workers in the urban North led to extensive hostility and institutionalized discrimination by whites.[12]

ADVANCED INDUSTRIAL (MULTINATIONAL) CAPITALISM: 1920s–1990s

Mexican Immigrants

With the industrialization accompanying World War I came a sharp decline in the number of laborers available for agricultural work. The need was filled in part by Mexican labor, recruited with substantial help from the federal government. Mexican laborer and family migrations increased significantly in the 1920s. Agencies in cities such as Los Angeles and San Antonio recruited Mexican workers for agriculture and for some low-skilled jobs in the steel, auto, and other urban industries. Robert Blauner has captured the contrast between the non-European and the European immigrant workers of this period and later: "America has used African, Asian, Mexican, and, to a lesser degree, Indian workers for the cheapest labor, concentrating people of color in the most unskilled jobs, the least advanced sectors of the economy, and the most industrially backward regions of the nation."[13]

Large Corporations and the U.S. Business Cycle

Since the 1920s, large corporations, many with an international orientation, have come to dominate the U.S. economy and politics. By the 1920s, a large number of Americans, including recent immigrant workers, were working in the auto industry or in related industries such as steel. Aggressive competition among auto firms in the 1920s resulted in the production of more cars than were needed in the economy. This overproduction, a chronic problem in a capitalist economy, soon resulted in major cutbacks in employment in the auto and related industries, thus helping to trigger the 1930s' Great Depression, which hit especially hard among recent black and Latino migrants to cities. Unemployed whites, including recent immigrants, took over many of the lower-paying jobs previously held by workers of color. Thus, the latter had very high unemployment rates. The federal government grew as political and business leaders tried to develop economic and social programs to save the foundering capitalist system. Still, racial discrimination was perpetuated in the New Deal relief programs of the 1930s; typically, black workers received lower wages than whites, were employed mainly as unskilled laborers, and were often employed after whites.[14]

The Postwar Era: The United States and the World

For three decades after World War II, the U.S. government, the U.S. military, and U.S. multinational corporations substantially dominated the world economy, in large part because industrial societies elsewhere, such as Germany and Japan, had been destroyed by the war. Since World War II, it has become easier for corporations to move capital investments from the central city to the suburbs, from northern to southern cities, and from U.S. cities to cities overseas. Much of this "capital flight" has resulted in economically abandoned central cities, such as Detroit and Newark. The federal government has facilitated this outward expansion of investment and jobs by funding home mortgage programs and highway systems built in accord with the needs of companies developing plants and of middle-class (usually white) workers living outside central cities. As a result, after World War II many white Americans—often the children and grandchildren of European immigrants—fol-

lowed the new industrial plants and allied workplaces to the suburbs.

Into the central cities came other workers and their families—African Americans, Puerto Ricans, Mexicans and Mexican Americans, Native Americans, and Asian Americans. After World War II these immigrants to northern and western cities inhabited residential areas increasingly abandoned by industry and by the children of European immigrants. Among these more recent immigrants were Puerto Ricans, many of whom were recruited for low-wage city jobs in the 1950s and 1960s. U.S. industrial and agribusiness development in Puerto Rico helped to stimulate a large out-migration. Many older cities have seen an increase in black and Latino political and governmental influence in recent years. Today, these city governments often face recurring economic troubles.

Government Involvement Overseas and Asian Immigration

Until the mid-1960s U.S. immigration legislation was so restrictive that most Asians desiring to emigrate could not enter. By the mid-1960s, the discriminatory quotas for Asians had been lifted, and since then there has been an increase in Asian immigrants, especially Chinese, Korean, Filipino, Asian Indian, and Vietnamese immigrants. U.S. support for South Korea during and after its war with North Korea built strong ties between the two countries. A succession of dictators in South Korea drove out some dissenters, who migrated to the United States; other Koreans came for economic or educational reasons. The immigration of the Chinese, the Filipinos, and the Vietnamese is generally related to the involvement of the U.S. government and corporations overseas. The U.S. arming and political support of the Philippine government and of the Chinese government on Taiwan and U.S. participation in the wars in Korea and South Vietnam have played an important role in creating large groups of Filipinos, Koreans, Chinese, and Vietnamese dependent on or oriented to the United States. More recently, increasing corporate and political ties between the United States and mainland China have facilitated the immigration of mainland Chinese. As with earlier immigrants, these Asians generally migrate to the United States seeking better opportunities.

Latin American Immigration and the Sunbelt Boom

Caribbean immigrants to the United States since the 1960s have included Cubans and Haitians moving to Florida. The U.S. government long supported a dictatorship in Cuba, which was overthrown by a guerrilla movement led by Fidel Castro. Many Cuban businesspeople and professionals fled in the first waves of emigration after Castro took power. Often having economic and educational resources, these Cubans established a major economic niche and great political influence in south Florida. After 1980, a significant number of poorer Cubans migrated to the United States, some of them expelled as alleged "undesirables" by the Castro government. Most Cuban immigrants have been welcomed by the U.S. government as political refugees from a Communist government, and hundreds of millions of dollars in federal subsidies have been provided to facilitate their adjustment to a new country. In contrast, Haitians fleeing politically repressive governments on their Caribbean island in recent decades have for the most part not been welcomed by the U.S. government. Many have been forced to return, and most of those allowed to stay have not been provided with the same level of government support as the Cuban immigrants. A major reason for this differential treatment seems to be that the Communist government in Cuba is seen as a political opponent of the United States, whereas the repressive governments in Haiti were long viewed as political allies.

In recent decades much investment capital and federal aid have shifted from northern to Sunbelt cities. The growing economy of the Sunbelt has created a demand for low-wage workers in sectors such as construction and agriculture. Many people have immigrated from Mexico and Central America for economic reasons. Others, like earlier European groups, have come fleeing political oppression. Mexican immigrants make up a significant portion of the undocumented immigrants. They are attracted by the possibility of jobs, and many are pushed by economic problems in their home country. U.S. corporations operating in Mexico have sometimes played a role in generating Mexican out-migration. For example, some U.S. agribusiness firms have stimulated the development of export-oriented agriculture in Mexico, taking over large amounts of land for that purpose and driving off many Mexican peasants who farmed the land to feed their families.

Immigration Restrictions

European immigrants made up more than half of all those coming to the United States during the decade of the 1950s. Their proportion had dropped to one-third by the 1960s and to less than one-fifth by the late 1990s. The change is substantially the result of the abolition of the discriminatory national–origin quotas in the 1965 Immigration Act. Since the 1960s many Asian and Latino immigrants have been viewed as a "problem" by native-born Americans. Congress has passed immigration legislation with provisions limiting this mostly non-European immigration to the United States. Many native-born workers and leading politicians are concerned that the United States cannot absorb so many new immigrants, even though the ratio of immigrants to the native-born population was much higher earlier in the twentieth century than it is today. The percentage of foreign-born in the U.S. population today is smaller than that of many other nations, including several in Europe. Implicit in many white discussions of the new immigrants is a concern that most are from Asia and Latin America—that is, they are not white and not European.[15]

Significantly, the new Asian and Latino immigrants are part of a growing population of Americans of color. In many areas of the United States, such as numerous large cities and the states of Hawaii, New Mexico, Texas, and California, Americans of color are now, or soon will be, the majority of the population. As their numbers increase, they will likely press even harder for egalitarian treatment in social, economic, and political institutions across U.S. society.

SUMMARY

In this introduction we have briefly reviewed the economic and governmental contexts within which particular groups have immigrated and adjusted. We have suggested that the time of entry for particular groups and the resources they bring affect their economic and political success. A complete understanding of the streams of migration to the United States requires an analysis of immigration in light of the economic and political contexts of entry and upward mobility. Capitalist development and expansion, as well as related U.S. political involvement overseas and domestic governmental expansion and legislative action, have not only shaped the context and character of U.S. immigration and the patterns of race and ethnic relations in North America for several centuries, but have also provided crucibles within which the family patterns, distinctive cultures, and political resistance of specific groups have developed.

CHAPTER 3

English Americans and the Anglo-Protestant Culture

Cleveland Amory tells a story about prominent English American families in Massachusetts. A Chicago banking firm wrote a Boston investment company for a letter of recommendation for a young Bostonian. Eloquently praising the young man's virtues, the company's letter pointed out that his mother was a member of the Lowell family, his father a member of the Cabot family, and his other relatives members of other prominent New England families. The bank wrote back, thanking the company but noting that this was not the type of letter of recommendation they had in mind: "We were not contemplating using Mr. _____ for breeding purposes."[1] Apocryphal or not, this story illustrates the elite status of the "proper Bostonians" and suggests their wealth and prominence in the history of New England.

The story underscores the importance of inbreeding, descent, and interlocking family ties over generations. Ethnicity involves cultural or nationality characteristics that are distinguished by the group itself or by important outgroups, but lines of descent are major channels for passing along the distinctive ethnic characteristics to later generations.

Who are these English Americans? They are the third largest ethnic group in the United States, after the Germans and the Irish. If all Americans claiming some English ancestry in the 1990 census are counted, the number is about 33 million.[2] The phrase *English Americans* itself may sound a bit strange. We hear discussions of Mexican Americans, Asian Americans, even Irish Catholics, but few speak of English Americans. One reason for this is that other labels are used to designate the group. Perhaps the most common are the inaccurate terms *Anglo-Saxon* and *white Anglo-Saxon Protestant*. Although in-depth analyses of this ethnic group are rare, numerous authors have commented on its central importance. A prominent historian of immigration makes a typical comment on its impact: "Our American culture, our speech, our laws are basically Anglo-Saxon in origin."[3] Sociologist Milton Gordon's view of the shaping impact of this first large group of European immigrants on the dominant culture of the United States has already been noted: "If there is anything in American life which can be described as an overall American culture which serves as a reference point for immigrants and their children, it can best be described . . . as the middle-class cultural patterns of, largely, white Protestant, Anglo-Saxon origins."[4] This comment suggests the importance of the dominant culture in the adaptation process faced by later immigrant groups. To take another example, Will Herberg has argued for the influence of this group on the self-image of Americans in this way: "It is the *Mayflower,* John Smith, Davy Crockett, George Washington, and Abraham Lincoln that define the American's self-image, and this is true whether the American in question is a descendant of the Pilgrims or the grandson of an immigrant from southeastern Europe."[5] This comment is focused on European Americans, not on Americans whose ancestors came from places other than Europe, but it does underscore how later immigrants had to adapt to the culture implanted by English Americans.

No social science analyst has undertaken a comprehensive analysis of these English Americans, an immigrant group of paramount importance in U.S. history. Why has this group been so neglected? The answer seems to be that many scholars have taken them for granted as the ancient core of U.S. society and culture. A second question concerns the term *Anglo-Saxon.* Numerous sources use the term loosely for persons or institutions of English extraction. Yet Anglo-Saxon is an inadequate designation for the immigrants from England and their descendants. The term derives from the names for the Germanic tribes, the Angles and the Saxons, that came to the area now called England in the fifth and sixth centuries A.D. But other people were there already—the Celts—and the Germanic tribes were followed by the Normans from France. The English settlers of the American colonies already embodied several centuries of the blending and fusion of several nationality types.[6] So, at best, the term Anglo-Saxon is a misleading shorthand for a complex heritage.

Some authors use *Anglo-Saxon* and related terms such as the ethnocentric "old-stock Americans" in even broader senses. The terms are sometimes used in a loose way to also include British groups other than the English—the Scots and the Welsh. Certain other north European groups that have substantially assimilated to the Anglo culture—particularly Scandinavian and German Protestants—are sometimes included in the terms *Anglo-Saxon* and *Anglo-Protestant.* In any event, when the terms *Anglo-Saxon, Anglo-Protestant,* and *British* are used by authors, English Americans and the dominant culture they generated are at the heart of the discussion.

At an early point in history, Americans of English and British descent publicly expressed a sense of superiority and of prominence in the nation. In the late 1780s, John Jay, the first chief justice of the U.S. Supreme Court, wrote in *The Federalist,* "Providence has been pleased to give this one connected country to one united people—a people descended from the same ancestors, speaking the same language, professing the same religion, attached to the same principles of government, very similar in their manners and customs."[7] This very inaccurate and greatly ethnocentric perspective has been a central problem for non-English groups ever since.

THE ENGLISH MIGRATIONS

Some Basic Data

What was the origin of those English Americans whose company now numbers in the tens of millions? As every schoolchild should know, it was migration. Although the English were not the first to come to North America, they were the first to colonize it in large numbers. By the early eighteenth century, there were approximately 350,000 English and Welsh colonists in North America. At the time of the Revolution, this number had increased to between 1 and 2 million.[8]

Migration to the American colonies was very heavily English until 1700. Then the English migration receded to modest levels until well into the nineteenth century.[9] Nearly 3 million English migrated to the United States between 1820 and 1950, with the years between 1880 and 1900 seeing the heaviest flow. The English migration to the colonies, and later to the United States, was one of the largest population flows in this period. The English were not only the first sizable European group in what was to become the United States; they continued to be an important part of the European migration flow until World War I.[10]

The First Colonial Settlements

The migration of the English settlers in the seventeenth century, together with the establishment of settlements, was different from later European migration streams. This movement can be viewed as *colonization migration,* a concept explored in Chapter 2. Colonization, unlike other types of migration, involves the subordination of indigenous people. As we will show in detail in Chapter 7, the first victims of English and other European colonialism on this continent were the many Native American societies. English settlers participated actively in killing off Native Americans and in driving them off their lands. Few of the English colonists were concerned about the brutality and genocide directed at Native Americans. Unlike the French and Spanish who also explored North America, the English had come to establish permanent colonies. The colonies developed under the auspices of the English king and his merchants and were viewed as an extension of the mother country.[11]

Why did the English Crown become interested in North American colonies? Various explanations for colonial development were put forth by English advocates in the colonial period. Commercial objectives were often mentioned; much attention was given to the need for trading posts and for new sources of raw materials, as well as for new markets for English goods.[12] Other colonial advocates emphasized Protestant missionary objectives, the search for a passage to Asia, the need to stop Spanish and French expansion, and the need for a place for England's surplus population. Nonetheless, the central objective of colonization was economic gain: "What England primarily looked for in colonies was neither expansion of territory *per se* nor overseas aggregations of Englishmen, but goods and markets."[13]

The English colonization was a case of Lieberson's migrant superordination (see Chapter 2). It had dire consequences for the preexisting Native American societies. Geographical expansion proceeded rapidly. The French were interested in the fur trade, but the English wanted land for economic colonization and farming.[14] At first, some Native American groups were treated in a friendly fashion, if mainly because the settlers depended on Native American food and advice for survival. The settlers soon gained numerical superiority over the native population, usually forcing Native Americans back into frontier areas or slaughtering them.[15] Few European settlers seemed concerned over the genocidal consequences of their colonialism. In Massachusetts a plague wiped out many Native Americans before the *Mayflower*'s landing. The famous New England minister Cotton Mather commented, "The woods were almost cleared of those pernicious creatures, to make room for a better growth."[16] For most of the European invaders, the Native Americans were viewed as "savages" who should be driven off the valuable land.

The English established large settlements in North America. The first joint-stock companies were formed by merchants under the auspices of James I of England in the early 1600s. Employees of the Southern Company settled Jamestown, a colony where the primary goal was economic. Initially planning to

Pilgrims aboard the *Mayflower* sign the Mayflower Compact.

develop the colony with poor white labor, the leaders at Jamestown soon perceived a labor shortage and bought Africans from a Dutch ship in 1619, laying the foundation for the brutal institution of human slavery in North America. The northern colony of Plymouth was settled in 1620 under the auspices of another royal company. Many of the Plymouth settlers—later called the "Pilgrims"—were Puritans who had broken with the Anglican church.[17] Both settlements nearly expired in their early years because of disease and starvation. The Plymouth colony managed to survive only with the aid of friendly Native Americans. By 1640 there were thousands of English colonists in the New England area; it was these colonists who first regarded themselves as English *Americans*.[18]

David Fischer has identified four distinct waves of English-speaking immigrants between 1629 and 1775. The first group of these were the Puritans from England's eastern counties, who came to Massachusetts primarily between 1629 and 1640. They brought to New England "nucleated settlements, congregational churches, town meetings, and a tradition of ordered liberty."[19] A second wave, which came to Virginia between 1642 and 1675, was different. It consisted of a small number of elite Royalists from the south of England and a large number of indentured servants. The culture of this group was characterized by "extreme hierarchies of rank, strong oligarchies, Anglican churches, a highly developed sense of honor, and an idea of hegemonic liberty."[20] A third wave—Quakers from the North Midlands of England and Wales who came to the Delaware Valley between 1675 and 1725—established a "pluralistic system of reciprocal liberty" based on spiritual and social equality, austerity, and an unusually intense work ethic.[21] A fourth wave came to the Appalachian backcountry from the borderlands of northern Great Britain and northern Ireland between 1718 and 1775. This group represented a variety of ethnic ancestries (English, Scottish, and "Scotch-Irish") and had extreme socioeconomic inequalities, but its members shared the ideal of natural liberty.[22] Each of these four groups had a distinctive type of culture—distinctive speech patterns, architecture, family ways and child-rearing customs, dress and food ways, religious orientation, and organization of public life. Many of these cultural patterns interacted and fused together over time to create the dominant Anglo-Protestant culture of the colonies.

What was the racial and ethnic mix of the colonial population in 1790? The American Historical Association has developed rough estimates of the "national stocks" of the white population in 1790 based on a surname analysis:[23]

Surnames	Percentage of White Population
English	60.1%
Scottish, "Scotch-Irish"	14.0
German	8.6
Irish (Free State)	3.6
Dutch	3.1
French, Swedish	3.0
Other	7.6
Total	100.0%

These estimates give the English the primary position among whites, with other British groups accounting for significant proportions. In addition, it is important to note that African Americans, then mostly enslaved, made up one-fifth of the total population in revolutionary America.[24]

Later Migration

There was a modest flow of immigrants from the British Isles and the rest of Europe between the American Revolution and 1820, but the century following 1820 saw the greatest Atlantic migration in history. The English and other British contributions to this nineteenth-century migration have been neglected.[25] This neglect underscores the ease with which the later English immigrants blended in. As we have noted, nearly 3 million came between 1820 and 1950. However, in the 1910s English migration declined significantly.[26]

Economic motives were paramount for the nineteenth-century immigrants. In Great Britain depressions were numerous, causing widespread unemployment in the textile industry, the largest employer there at that time. Emigration came to be seen as one solution to unemployment.[27] The skills of textile workers facilitated their mobility. As with their predecessors, this immigrant group attained a relatively advantaged position in a country just beginning to industrialize. English immigrants moved in large numbers from manufacturing and mining industries at home to comparable positions in U.S. industry, with their skills helping to spur the dramatic industrialization of nineteenth-century America.[28] When English American workers were eventually displaced by machines or later immigrant groups, they often moved up into managerial, professional, and technical positions. With their help, U.S. industry soon surpassed in productivity the industry of the mother industrial society.[29]

Was adaptation to the dominant culture difficult for these later English immigrants? The ease with which many moved into industry indicates the swiftness of their assimilation at the level of secondary organizations. Their skills kept most from the poverty that the other immigrants usually faced. Larger numbers moved into clerical and professional jobs than was the case with most other white immigrant groups in this period. Acculturation was easy for the English immigrants. They would be more readily hired where the ability to speak English was important. These immigrants also avoided most of the anti-immigrant agitation others faced. Indeed, new English immigrants often shared the ethnocentric or racist views held by previous English settlers, including the stereotyping of Jews, hostility towards African Americans, and hatred of southern Europeans. Structural assimilation in the primary-relations sphere, to use the concept developed by the theorist Milton Gordon, was rapid for them. Marriage with English American citizens was common. Enforced residential segregation did not develop for these English immigrants.[30]

Still, ties to the homeland were not immediately severed. The monarch was widely revered. British taverns flourished in American cities. Organizations such as the St. George's Society were created to aid destitute English settlers, and there were also numerous social clubs. However, the organizations for preserving English culture were fewer and less exclusive than similar organizations among non-English immigrant groups. Many children of English immigrants soon left these organizations. Rowland Berthoff quotes a son of an English immigrant, who was reviewing the Revolutionary War for his father: "You had the King's army, and we were only a lot of farmers, but we thrashed you!"[31] Here, the pinnacle of identificational assimilation has been reached as early as the second generation; the son's identity is clearly English *American.*

Smaller numbers of English immigrants have come to the United States since 1910, generally less than a few thousand each year. In the 1930s, indeed, more people returned to England than came in as immigrants. One distinctive aspect of English emigration since the 1950s is that it has been a "brain drain": a significant proportion of the immigrants in this period have been managerial, professional, and technical workers, including physicians and college professors. Although relatively few compared with the numbers in earlier decades, the departure of these immigrants has generated controversy in Great Britain over the costly loss of highly educated workers.[32]

The modest migration since 1910, coupled with dramatic increases in immigration from outside of England, has had a dramatic demographic effect. Of the major white ethnic groups in the United States in 1790, only the British groups have declined sharply as a proportion of the total U.S. population.[33]

Other Protestant Immigrants

The terms *Anglo-Saxon* and *Anglo-Protestant* have sometimes been used by researchers to include not only the English but also the Scots, the Welsh, and even Scandinavians and Germans. The Welsh entered the colonies in relatively small numbers, beginning in the early 1600s. The total number who came has been estimated at just over 100,000, with many going into industrial jobs or farming. The first generations retained their customs, language, and distinctive communities, but they were soon substantially assimilated to the white Anglo-Protestant mainstream.[34]

In terms of power, the Scots were perhaps the closest to the dominant English group from the 1700s onward, although they would feel Anglo-conformity pressures. Coming from what have been called the borderlands of Great Britain, Scottish Highlanders and Lowlanders, as well as Scottish emigrants to Ireland, came to the new nation in the 1600s and 1700s. By the late eighteenth century, there were perhaps 250,000 Scots, a number to be supplemented over the next century by three-fourths of a million migrants. In the colonial period, some were prosperous merchants, clerks, soldiers, and middle-income farmers, although the majority probably were servants, laborers, and poor farmers. Many settled in rural and frontier areas. They experienced hostility from some English Americans in the early period. Assimilation to the English core culture gradually accompanied inclusion in the economic system, so that by the early 1800s many of the Scots had moved up to parity with the English. They too were becoming an important segment of the white Anglo-Protestant mainstream.

German immigrants made up the largest non-British group during the eighteenth century. Germans constituted nearly one-tenth of the colonists, and in the century after 1820 several million more would come to the United States. Some were Catholics and Jews, but the largest proportion was Protestant. Many became farmers, merchants, and, later, industrial workers. Over several generations much, but by no means all, of the German culture was reshaped by the well-established Anglo-American patterns. Cultural assimilation, together with substantial mobility in the economic and political spheres, came in a few generations for the German Protestants. Yet for years some distinctiveness did persist in the form of certain German customs, festivals, and residential concentrations. The Jewish Germans (see Chapter 6), who had immigrated in the middle decades of the nineteenth century, remained somewhat distinctive, in part because of the vicious anti-Semitism directed against them (and later Jewish immigrants) by many Gentile Americans.

Scandinavian immigrants, such as Swedes and Norwegians, did not enter in large numbers until the 1870s and 1880s. In all, perhaps 2 million came. Many immigrants entered as farmers and laborers, but the second and third generations moved into skilled blue-collar and white-collar positions. Here, too, substantial assimilation to the British American core culture came in just a few generations. Still, some distinctiveness in family customs and residential concentration, especially in midwestern areas, persists even today.

These white Protestant groups from northern Europe assimilated relatively rapidly in the cultural, economic, and political spheres. This assimilation, however, was not always peaceful. In the period of early contact, even some of these white northern European groups suffered physical attacks and extreme cultural conformity pressures from the English American group. This, however, did not last long. Within a generation or so English Americans were marrying with other British Americans, and sometimes with Scandinavians and Germans. By the early twentieth century the designations *white Anglo-Saxon Protestant* and *white Anglo-Protestant* increasingly came to blur the distinction between the English and the later northern European immigrant groups that had gradually but substantially assimilated to the dominant English culture and its related institutions.

The Invention of the "White Race"

The eighteenth and nineteenth centuries saw the emergence of the "white race" as a deliberately constructed social group for the first time in North American or, for that matter, world history. From the beginning, the English settlers and their descendants saw themselves as quite different from Native Americans and African Americans, whom they often stereotyped as "uncivilized," "idolaters," "absolute brutes," and "savages." The English Americans saw themselves as "republicans" of great virtue; they were concerned with protecting the new nation and reserving it, as some explicitly said in the 1790s, for the "worthy part of mankind."[35] By the early 1800s, moreover, the growing importance of the southern cotton plantations for the U.S. economy as a whole (northern entrepreneurs and bankers were often linked to the southern cotton economy) brought a growing demand for Native American land and for African and African American slaves. At the same time, slavery was being abolished, sometimes slowly, in the northern states. The number of free African Americans was growing in the North.

As a result of these developments, the white Anglo-Protestant elite developed the idea of an advantaged "white race" as a way to provide racial privileges for propertyless European American immigrants and prevent the latter from bonding with Americans of color. In his analysis of the idea of whiteness and the white self, William E. B. Du Bois demonstrated how white workers came to accept a lesser economic position and lower wages in return for the "public and psychological wage" that went with whiteness. In return for their acceptance of their economic position, white workers, including new immigrant workers, were allowed and encouraged by the white Anglo-Protestant elite to be part of a racial hierarchy where all whites enforced deference from African Americans.[36]

In his research David Roediger shows how many nineteenth-century European immigrants, who did not define themselves initially as "white" but rather as Irish, German, or Italian, came to construct themselves as "white" as they moved up in U.S. society. This development of a racial ideology and of white nationalism was accelerated during the presidency of Andrew Jackson (1829–1837), and by the late nineteenth century not only the later English immigrants but also immigrants from Scotland, Scandinavia, Ireland, Italy, and Germany had come to accept a place in the "white race," whose racial privileges included the right to personal liberty, the right to travel and immigrate, and the right to vote. Similarly, Theodore W. Allen provides unequivocal evidence on how the U.S. elite's response to labor and union organization and protests among white immigrants in the eighteenth and nineteenth centuries included an increased emphasis on racial solidarity for a socially invented "white race."[37]

NATIVIST REACTIONS TO LATER EUROPEAN IMMIGRANTS

In the 1700s and 1800s some Americans, themselves descendants of earlier immigrants, were hostile to new European immigrant groups. Anti-immigration agitation, or *nativism*, goes far back in American history, but the term was apparently first used in the 1840s and 1850s. Nativists were nationalists who saw themselves as the *only* true Americans. Higham notes three main themes in reactions to immigrants: anti-Catholicism, xenophobia, and Anglo-Saxonism.[38]

Before the American revolution, nativist concern with new immigrants was centered in religious and moral desirability. Certain religious groups (such as Catholics), "paupers," and convicts were discouraged by English Americans from entering the colonies. Antiforeign sentiment was directed primarily at non-English immigrant groups, of which the French Huguenot refugees were one example. Virginia tried to prohibit their immigration, and other colonies placed restrictions on them. At least one Huguenot community was violently attacked by nativists.[39] The Huguenots were joined as targets by other immigrants. As Jordan notes, "in the early years Englishmen treated the increasingly numerous settlers from other European countries, especially Scottish and Irish servants, with much condescension and frequently with exploitative brutality."[40] In Virginia and Maryland discriminatory duties were placed on non-English servants coming into the colonies. Catholics among the Irish were "doubly damned as foreign and Papist."[41]

Established colonists felt some ambivalence about the new immigrants. On the one hand, immigrants provided needed labor for employers, ship captains profited from immigration, and new immigrants were encouraged to settle in frontier areas to increase colonial security. On the other hand, immigrants were sometimes seen as a threat, and English American mobs occasionally tried to prevent their landing.[42]

More Fear of Immigrants

Antiforeign sentiment took legal form in the late 1700s after the Federalist party became concerned about political radicalism among certain new immigrants and about the growing support among non-British immigrants for the Jeffersonian Republicans. The 1798 Alien Act empowered the English American president to deport immigrants considered a threat to the new nation. The period of residence required for citizenship was raised from two to five years in 1795 and to fourteen years in 1798. Attempts were also made to set an exorbitant fee for naturalization. These strategies were designed to limit the political power of the new non-English immigrants.[43]

Numerous attempts were made to reduce the influence of new immigrants by pressuring them to assimilate to the English-dominated institutions. When Benjamin Franklin set up a Pennsylvania school in the 1740s, he was concerned about the many non-English immigrants who did not know the language and customs.[44] Franklin exhibited strong ethnic prejudices and stereotypes about the German immigrants in his region, fearing that they would "shortly be so numerous as to Germanize us instead of us Anglifying them."[45]

Ethnic homogeneity was the goal of the English founding fathers and prominent educators of the eighteenth century. George Washington believed in a homogeneous citizenry. Thomas Jefferson and Benjamin Rush expected those who were educated to fit into a culturally homogeneous mass of Anglo-assimilated citizens. But such unity could be had only by the subordination of other ethnic identities to the Anglo-Protestant identity.[46]

Anti-Catholic sentiment was at the core of much nativist agitation, especially in the nineteenth century. Irish and German immigrants entering during the 1840s and 1850s were periodically targeted by bursts of nativist agitation; a variety of secret societies, sometimes termed the Know-Nothing movement, sought to fight both immigration and Catholicism. (When questioned, members of these societies would supposedly say, "I don't know nothing.") During the 1850s the ethnocentric Know-Nothings were elected to state legislatures, Congress, and state executive offices. They also precipitated numerous violent attacks against new immigrants and Roman Catholics.[47]

Nativism was often coupled with racist ideologies in the nineteenth century, with other northern Europeans joining English Americans in this perspective. U.S. development was seen as the perfect example of what could be accomplished by the "Anglo-Saxon race." This Anglo-Saxonism was picked up by expansionists who lusted after Mexican land in California and Texas. The vigorous thrust into those areas was seen as directed and legitimated by a mandate to colonize "inferior races." One European American expansionist commented that "the Mexican race now see in the fate of the aborigines of the north, their own inevitable destiny. They must amalgamate or be lost in the superior vigor of the Anglo-Saxon race, or they must utterly perish."[48] Anglo-Saxonism was to play an important role in racist thought after the Civil War, for it provided the rationalization for U.S. imperialist military and business expansion overseas, in places such as the Philippines.

The upper classes became a stronghold of Anglo-Saxonism after the Civil War. They were influenced in part by historians in England, who argued for the superiority of the supposed Anglo-Saxon background of England's greatness. There was an Anglo-Saxon school among U.S. social scientists; its guiding idea was that democratic institutions in this country had come from England.[49] These social scientists ignored the Norman (French) impact on English culture. Convinced that English institutions were the most civilized in the world, some U.S. intellectuals came under the influence of social Darwinism, which extended Charles Darwin's evolutionary thinking into the social realm. This perspective contained notions of white Anglo-Saxon racial superiority that were based on a theory of the social "survival of the fittest." One prominent advocate of biological evolution, John Fiske, celebrated the superiority of English civilization and claimed it was the destiny of the English people to populate *all* the world's empty spaces.[50] Even more influential were popular writers such as Josiah Strong, a Congregationalist minister whose book *Our Country* (1885) sold thousands of copies in the United States. Strong was a vigorous advocate of Anglo-Saxon superiority myths, in combination with attacks on Catholics and other non-British immigrants as undesirable aliens in the United States. The English peoples were rapidly multiplying, he argued, and the United States was destined to be the seat of an "Anglo-Saxon race" whose numbers would approach (by the 1980s, he predicted) a billion strong. Survival of the fittest, he argued, dictated the ultimate superiority of the "Anglo-Saxon race" throughout the world.[51]

Racism and Nativism Since 1890

The increase in immigration from southern and eastern Europe and from Asia around the turn of the twentieth century focused anti-immigration sentiment on these groups. For example, Henry Cabot Lodge, an English American aristocrat from New England and a powerful political figure, was fiercely determined to defend the United States against immigrant threats in the 1890s and early 1900s. English Americans in Boston formed the Immigration League to fight the increasing southern and eastern European immigration (see Chapter 5). The league worked diligently for a literacy test, which passed Congress, and associated itself with the eugenics movement started by Sir Francis Galton, a prominent English Darwinist. The early U.S. eugenicists were racist in their thinking on matters of "racial mixing" and argued that heredity strongly shaped moral as well as biological characteristics. They feared that allowing "unfit" southern and eastern European immigrants to enter and procreate would destroy the "superior race" of north Europeans. The unfit should be sterilized, excluded, or even eliminated.[52]

Perhaps the most prominent American to contribute to the development of racial nativism was Madison Grant, an American of English extraction who fused various racist ideas in his influential book *The Passing of the Great Race* (1916). Particularly worried about the influence of newer groups from southern and eastern Europe, Grant claimed that interbreeding with the inferior European "races" would lead to mongrelization. The northern Europeans—the "Nordic race"— were the superior "race."[53] By the 1920s this "scientific" racism helped to fuel pressures for immigration legislation that discriminated against non-British white groups. Various "national origin" quotas were set to restrict immigration from southern and eastern Europe.

The 1920s and 1930s saw an outpouring of this racial nativism on many fronts. Journalists such as Kenneth L. Roberts continued to write wildly about the racial "mongrelization" caused by the new white immigrants.[54] Nativist organizations such as the revived Ku Klux Klan provided a social outlet for those who wished to subordinate African, Catholic, and Jewish Americans and preserve the so-called Anglo-Saxon race. Opposition to foreign immigration resurfaced after World War II, when various members of Congress and (northern) European American organizations opposed legislation permitting displaced persons, such as European Jews and Catholics, to migrate to the United States.

In recent decades a certain type of nativism has persisted, often in a subtle form. Sometimes it has taken the form of stereotyping and harassing those not of northern European ancestry. In recent presidential campaigns, for example, Democratic party candidates have sometimes been targeted because of their southern European ancestry. In the 1984 election, for example, the Italian ancestry of the Democratic vice-presidential candidate, Geraldine Ferraro, was attacked. Among other things, Republicans (many of northern European ancestry) alleged that she and her Italian American husband had connections to organized crime. In the 1990s a number of Italian Americans in politics, such as Governor Mario Cuomo of New York, have suffered similar "mafia" stereotypes.[55] Some Americans of southern European ancestry are still viewed by northern Europeans, if often jokingly, as not fully "American."

Another form of nativism can be seen in the various anti-immigration organizations that have flourished in the last decade or two. Like their predecessors in the early twentieth century, these organizations have opposed and stereotyped recent immigrants, particularly those coming from Asia and Latin America since the late 1960s. Some nativists have focused on the languages of the immigrants, an issue we consider in the next section. In addition, some white supremacy groups, including the Ku Klux Klan, have held rallies across the United States and pub-

A group of "skinheads" poses before a Nazi flag and posters.

lished literature attacking non-European immigrant groups as a threat to "American" jobs and to the Anglo-Protestant culture. These new nativist groups, it should be noted, include not only significant representations of northern European Americans, but also some whites with southern and eastern European ancestries.

THE DOMINANT CULTURE AND MAJOR U.S. INSTITUTIONS

Most analysts of the U.S. racial and ethnic scene have assumed that the dominant culture and major institutions are substantially English or Anglo-Protestant. During the first century of colonial settlement along the east coast, an English heritage integrated most of the colonies. Political, legal, and economic institutions were generally based on English models. Major U.S. institutions were not identical to those in England, however. The dominance of the Anglican church in some colonies soon gave way to religious liberty, and there was also no hereditary ruling class. The availability of land—the basis of much U.S. wealth—guaranteed greater democracy. Traditional English ways were modified under the new colonial conditions.[56]

Language

The United States has no official language, but English is the dominant language in most areas of the society. The lasting dominance of the English language makes conspicuous the impact of early English settlers and their descendants. When Europeans first came, perhaps a thousand Native American languages were spoken, and several hundred of these are still spoken. Today, the number of Americans speaking these original languages is far smaller than those speaking the languages of the European conquerors—English, Spanish, and French.

The principal U.S. language over the last two centuries has not been a simple blend of Native American and early immigrant languages, but an English language that has incorporated words from both European and U.S. sources. W. Lloyd Warner and Leo Srole have argued that "our customary way of life is most like the English, and our language is but one of the several English dialects."[57] Historically, assimilation pressures on non-English-speaking immigrants have first taken the form of language pressure.

As early as the 1740s, native-born Americans of British background attacked later immigrants for their alleged threats to the dominant American culture. From then to the present the dominance of the English language has been a major concern of nativists. As we noted earlier, Benjamin Franklin, an English American, viewed German-speakers as ignorant and a threat to the English language and culture.[58]

Today, about 25 million Americans live in homes in which a language other than English is spoken. Since the 1980s this relatively small group of non-English-speakers has been attacked as un-American by organized nativists, who worry that many newcomers, especially Latino and Asian immigrants, have not accepted English as their primary language. They are especially concerned that Spanish, spoken by 7–8 percent of Americans at home, is challenging the dominance of English. One result of lobbying by nativist organizations has been the introduction of legislation to make English the official language of the United States. In 1986 California passed a ballot proposition that declared English to be the official language of this most populous state in the Union. By the late 1990s, such legislation had been passed in numerous other states. In addition, in 1981 an English Language Amendment to the U.S. Constitution was introduced in Congress; it was reintroduced in subsequent sessions of Congress but died in the 97th Congress.[59]

In 1997 the chair of a group called National English Campaign asserted the group's goals of (1) replacing ethnic group identification and "hyphenated ethnicity" with an "American identity" based on individual citizenship and (2) establishing English as the official language of government, schools, and elections.[60] Such goals suggest fear of a pluralism of racial and ethnic groups and cultures and an emphasis on an English-oriented American identity. Groups like this consider an official English language necessary to maintain a unified United States.

Contemporary organizations with nativist undertones, such as the California English Campaign (said to have 200,000 supporters) and the National English Campaign, have fought bilingual programs on the west coast and across the nation. In 1997 they pressed for a California ballot initiative to limit instruction of immigrant children to one year in their native language before they moved into classes taught in English.[61] Such groups often argue that they are not trying to discriminate against immigrants but wish immigrants to quickly become part of the mainstream by adopting English as their primary language. However, one such group, called U.S. English, was a project of a nonprofit organization that supports immigration restrictions. A member of the U.S. Commission on Civil Rights resigned as president of U.S. English when she learned that its founder held anti-Latino views; among other things the founder had apparently forecast a political takeover of the United States by Latinos.[62] Several anti-immigration and English-only groups appear to share origins as well as ideas.

Latino civil rights leaders have pointed out the discriminatory nature of several actions advocated by pro-English groups, in particular the prohibition of Spanish usage in government agencies, the elimination of bilingual programs in public schools, and the elimination of bilingual ballots in states with numerous Latino voters. A number of research studies have shown that children who are "denied the right to view the world through their language and culture are made to feel inferior" and may react in such negative ways as dropping out of school or engaging in drugs or crime—outcomes that cost not only themselves but the greater society dearly.[63] The implementation of English-only laws can have other negative effects, including the banning of testimony by non-English-speakers in court and the removal of language interpreters in government agencies, including police departments.

Nativist campaigns to promote the English language underscore the traditional dominance of that language—and the uneasiness that descendants of earlier immigrants to the United States still feel in the presence of languages and cultures brought by relative newcomers to this "nation of immigrants."[64] As legal scholar Juan Perea notes, their "first myth is that our national unity somehow depends solely on the English language, ergo we must protect the language through constitutional amendment or legislation. A corollary is that the only language of true American identity is the English language."[65]

What is ironic about these English-only movements is that most immigrants not only recognize that English is the language of social and economic discourse in the United States, but also strive hard to learn the language. English, as we have noted, is in fact the dominant language. In a recent year, for example, about 40,000 immigrants were turned away or were on waiting lists for adult English classes in the city of Los Angeles alone. Significantly, a study by Veltman has shown that three-fourths of Latino immigrants speak English *every day*. In addition, one consequence of this new English-only nativism is to further segregate English Americans from the rest of the world. The lack of knowledge of languages other than English cripples many Americans who go abroad to conduct business or to deal politically with people in other nations.[66]

Religion and Basic Values

The English religious influence on the United States has been of great importance. Although all were Protestant, the various English denominations represented a variety of beliefs and practices. Anglicans in Virginia were characterized by a hierarchy of priests and a liturgical form of worship. This group favored a state church supported by compulsory church taxes. Presbyterian churches in the Appalachian backcountry favored a national church governed by strong ministers and elders. Congregationalists and Separatists in New England favored moderate separation of church and state and more democratic church governance. Baptists (Rhode Island) and Quakers (New Jersey and Pennsylvania) both advocated strict separation between church and state. The communally organized Baptists favored a fellowship-centered form of worship. The spirit-centered worship of Quakers followed from a belief in an Inner Light that dwells in all people.[67] It was these latter groups who set the principle of separation of church and state at the heart of the U.S. political system.

For the first two hundred years, English churches, or derivatives thereof, dominated the American scene. The Anglican church received some early government support, but this privileged position was lost in the Revolution. The disproportionate number of Anglican and Congregational churches was obvious at the time of the Revolution, although Baptist and Presbyterian churches and Quaker groups were by then becoming more numerous. In the century after 1776, English dominance of U.S. religious institutions decreased as Catholic, Jewish, and other religious groups grew with the new immigration.[68]

Will Herberg has argued that the Catholic and Jewish faiths, as well as non-British Protestantism, have been greatly shaped by the "American way of life," his phrase for the dominant Anglo-Protestant culture.[69] One important study of Judaism has shown the substantial impact of Protestant institutions on eastern European Judaism. Immigrant synagogues made major changes over time in response to the dominant culture. For example, Jewish religious schools adapted to Protestant American scheduling and formats. Among Reform Jews, English came to be the language of worship, and the worship itself was modified with the introduction of Friday-night services.[70] The impact of the Anglo-Protestant culture on the non-Protestant religions of later immigrants has been mixed. The new immigrant has been expected to adapt in many areas, but some religious heritage has been preserved. Cultural pluralism is an accurate term for U.S. religious patterns.

Also important is the impact of certain Anglo-Protestant values on later immigrants. The importance of the ascetic (austere and self-denying) Protestantism that many of the early English settlers brought to the colonies cannot be underestimated. "American condemnation of British sexual and political impurities focused on the King. Idleness, wealth, and power had corrupted him."[71] Puritanism was important in establishing the so-called "Protestant work ethic" at the center of the value system—the idea of hard work as a duty of every individual seeking to please God. Richard Baxter, an important English Puritan minister, exemplified this important perspective, advocating not only unnecessary hard work but also avoiding luxury and personal pleasures.[72] "Continuous work was seen as a major defense against the sinful temptations of the flesh; the primary objective of work was to glorify God. Idleness was regarded as sin."[73]

In North America this austere work ethic became distinctive and emphasized and was linked to the pursuit of profit. The emerging capitalistic system in the late 1700s and the 1800s was pervaded by "pursuit of profit, and forever *renewed* profit, by means of continuous, rational, capitalistic enterprise."[74] Benjamin Franklin personified this spirit of capitalism with his famous maxims about time being money, about punctuality, and about the virtues of hard work.

The English influence on early American culture in general was extensive. To cite a few other examples: Major musical and artistic developments in the earliest period were linked to the English (and later British) religious traditions. The first book published in the New England colonies was the *Bay Psalm Book* (1640), which drew on the English tradition. "Yankee Doodle" was probably an English tune, the original lyrics satirizing ragtag colonial soldiers. Only when the Revolution began did American soldiers take it over from the British. Before, during, and after the Revolution, English melodies were the basis of most popular and political songs.[75] The national anthem, "The Star-Spangled Banner," draws on an English drinking song for its melody.

Interestingly, however, over the next two centuries the English influence on U.S. popular music receded dramatically before the pervasive influence of African American music (for example, ragtime, jazz, and rock and roll), Irish American ("Scotch-Irish") country music, and the Mexican American music of the Southwest. Today, popular music is one major area of U.S. culture from which the English influence has almost disappeared.

Education

English and other British Americans took advantage of what few educational opportunities were available in the colonial period; better-off parents sent their children to the few private schools established before 1800. With the public school movement, which began in earnest in the first decades of the nineteenth century, British dominance of public schools became a fact of life. British Americans saw urban schools as a means of socializing non-British immigrants into Anglo-Protestant values and the values of the U.S. industrial system. Most public school systems were established by English or other British American industrialists and educators who shaped curricula and teaching and supervised schools. Although some—for example, John Dewey—believed education gave greater opportunity to poor immigrants, many educators emphasized the social-control aspects of schools. Americanization pressures on immigrant children were often intense. Whether children were Irish, Jewish, or Italian, Anglicization was designed to ferret out non-Anglo-Protestant ways and to assimilate the children to Anglo-Protestant manners, work habits, and values.[76]

As we will see in later chapters, the social-control function of public schools and the British American influence on their structure and operation are still evident today. Later immigrants, such as Asians and Latinos, have faced Anglo-conformity pressures similar to those experienced by earlier Irish and Italian immigrants. Indeed, the schools are often a major battleground for those concerned with making English the government-sanctioned official language.

Political and Legal Institutions

The political and legal institutions affecting all Americans have been shaped, and are still being shaped, by the English political heritage in at least two basic ways: laws and traditions inherited from the English and their concrete application by English immigrants and their descendants. Given the early majority of English settlers in colonial society on the eastern seaboard, English legal institutions soon became dominant. Concern for the rule of law and for the "rights of Englishmen" was central. The famous Mayflower Compact (1620), a political framework theoretically providing for equality under the law, was part of this English political tradition. New England, with its Puritan institutions, often provided the model for later U.S. political and legal developments.[77]

The North American colonies took on a distinctive set of political institutions—often those characteristic of sixteenth-century England. (Although some of these constitutional features were being abandoned in England in the seventeenth century, they still became part of the original political structure on this side of the Atlantic.) The basic ideas include unity of government and society, subordination of government to law, a balance of power between the legislature (Parliament in England) and the executive (the king in England), and heavy reliance on local governments.[78] American political and legal institutions, including the U.S. Constitution, have reflected these ideas ever since. Authority and power were being centralized in England, but here they were separated into three branches—the executive, judicial, and legislative. The position of the U.S. president is unusual: The United States, unlike almost every other modern political system, does not distinguish between the head of government and the chief of state. The Watergate scandal of the Richard Nixon presidential administration in the 1970s and the "Contragate" scandal of the Ronald Reagan White House in the 1980s showed how powerful the U.S. executive branch is relative to Congress. The United States is a new society, but it is an "old" political state.

Another important English influence can be seen in the representative assemblies in the colonies and, later, the United States. The British Crown established these assemblies in the colonies almost from their start, based on the parliamentary model.[79] Gradually these assemblies grew in power vis-à-vis the London government. Indeed, Crown infringements on them helped generate the Revolution.

The U.S. legal framework reflects much English influence. Prior to the Revolution, English common law was asserted to be "the measure of rights of Americans."[80] The colonies had similar legal frameworks, but some negative feeling arose over English common law because of the tension between the new nation and mother England. Some Americans wanted a new U.S. legal code, but for the most part U.S. lawyers only "sought to reshape or add to the existing stock of authoritative legal materials."[81] Although there was variation in how English statutes were brought into the U.S. legal system, their implementation was thoroughgoing: "the use of English statutes was provided for at an early stage in twenty-six of the twenty-eight jurisdictions organized between 1776 and 1836."[82]

Although the U.S. legal system has been patched many times, the basic cloth today is still English common law.[83]

Officeholding

In addition to their fundamental impact on U.S. political institutions, English Americans have had a major impact on the operation of those institutions. The first president of the United States, George Washington, was of English ancestry, as was the forty-second president, Bill Clinton, two centuries later. (Clinton also had Irish ancestors.) English Americans have filled a disproportionate number of major offices in various political contexts throughout U.S. history.

There are few studies of English or British dominance among U.S. officeholders. Maurice Davie notes that "the colonial assemblies were almost exclusively English in makeup."[84] The Declaration of Independence was signed by fifty-six European American men, thirty-eight of whom were English by background or birth; nine were Scottish or "Scotch-Irish," three Irish, five Welsh, and one Swedish.[85] A majority of the members of the Constitutional Convention were also English, and the Constitution was framed around their concerns not only for democratic institutions reminiscent of English institutions but also for the protection of their own property and wealth. As a result, most people of wealth in the new nation—merchants, financiers, shippers, wealthy farmers, and their allies—supported the new Constitution out of economic self-interest. Slaves, indentured servants, poor farmers, laborers, and women had no say in the framing of the U.S. Constitution. The framers of the Constitution perpetuated social class lines similar to those in England.[86]

Studies of U.S. presidents, Supreme Court justices, and members of Congress have revealed a distinctive pattern persisting to the present. Presidents and presidential candidates have been informally "required" to possess ancestry qualifications, preferably British American or northern European ancestry. Of the forty-one presidents from Washington to Clinton, about two-thirds had English ancestry and all the rest had northern European (mostly British) backgrounds.[87] No southern Europeans, Jewish Americans, Latino Americans, Asian Americans, or African Americans have been president. A study of the origins of Supreme Court justices from 1789 to 1957 found that over half were of English or Welsh extraction. In all periods, including the present, British Americans and other northern Europeans have dominated the nation's highest court.[88] An analysis of 162 prominent political leaders (including presidents, representatives, senators, and Supreme Court justices) of the period between 1901 and 1910 found that over half were of English or Welsh origin.[89]

E. Digby Baltzell has traced the rise of English American leaders such as Robert Todd Lincoln, the son of Abraham Lincoln, at the turn of the twentieth century. Lincoln was educated at Phillips Academy and Harvard and became a millionaire lawyer at the heart of the U.S. ruling elite. In 1901, the year of Queen Victoria's death, Lincoln was part of the British and British American establishments that dominated, politically or militarily, much of the world. A northwestern

European Protestant, Theodore Roosevelt, occupied the White House, and J. P. Morgan, a leader in the (Protestant) Episcopal church, had just put together the first billion-dollar corporation. The Senate of the United States was a northern European Protestant millionaires' club.[90]

Even when new immigrant groups managed to break into U.S. politics, as in the case of Irish and Italian Americans, they were usually subservient to Anglo-Protestant leaders who continued to hold the highest political offices. The newer immigrants and their children did gain significant electoral and political power in the first decades of the twentieth century in some U.S. cities, but not at the national level as elected officials. There still has been only one Catholic president, Irish American John F. Kennedy (1961–1963). His presidency marked only a brief shift from a homogeneous political establishment at the very top, for Kennedy was followed by more men of northern European Protestant stock.[91] While the domination of northern European Americans at the very top of national politics persists today, some challenges to this dominance can be seen at political levels below the top. For example, in the mid-1990s the cabinet of President Bill Clinton included a number of Americans whose background was not Protestant or northern European. Clinton's cabinet included people of southern European, Latino, and African American backgrounds, a change marking the growing racial and ethnic diversity in national politics.

What of the English American impact on local governments? A study of New Haven up to 1960 illustrates English political dominance in New England. For many decades a patrician elite there "completely dominated the political system. They were of one common stock and one religion, cohesive in their uniformly conservative outlook on all matters, substantially unchallenged in their authority, successful in pushing through their own policies, and in full control of such critical institutions as the established religion, the educational system (including not only all the schools but Yale as well), and even business enterprise."[92] A study of the mayors of Cleveland in the period between 1836 and 1901 found that most were part of an Anglo-Protestant elite with strong ties to New England. Their political framework was guided by what was termed the "New England creed," one proposition of which was "The good society is white and Protestant."[93]

In recent decades Americans of British ancestry have had to compete with non-British immigrants and their descendants for power in local and state politics, and today the racial and ethnic mix in local and state political institutions varies considerably across the nation. The large cities of the Midwest, East, South, and Southwest have seen the rise to political power of Irish, Italian, and, most recently, African, Asian, and Latino Americans. Still, English and other British Americans continue to exercise great influence in some local politics, especially in suburban politics, although they still receive little mass media attention.

Economic Institutions

The English heritage is reflected in U.S. economic institutions—in the values that shape those institutions and in the actual dominance of English American individuals. Just as the U.S. legal system incorporated portions of the English legal system, the economic system developed under the mercantile and early commercial capitalism that dominated much of northern Europe during colonial times. Then, as we have seen, the British Crown wished to increase the raw materials and the markets available to the home country. To this end, the first English colonies were set up by state-chartered trading companies or were proprietary colonies established by men of wealth.

Mercantile capitalism, which still existed in the colonies at the time of the Revolution, was a state-directed capitalism linked to English nationalism. The American Revolution was in part a clash between English and British American commercial interests, a clash that unified the colonies and brought a political break between two similar economic systems.[94]

Industrial capitalism developed in the United States after 1830, again with intimate connections to the English system. The basic ideas for U.S. industrial development came from England; English capitalists and skilled workers provided much of the know-how for U.S. economic development. After the Revolution, as before, Britain and the United States formed a single Atlantic economy, so close and important were their economic connections.[95]

Direct Participation in the Economy

English and British Americans have often influenced the operation of the U.S. economy through direct control of critical positions. In the beginning they established most of the colonies and controlled much of the land and wealth. In the early period control of the colonies lay primarily in the hands of English and other British American landowners and merchants.[96] However, those who eventually came to dominate many colonies in the late prerevolutionary period were yeoman farmers with their own land.[97] The founders of the colonies had included English aristocrats, but they had died or returned to England by the 1650s. Whatever their background, English Americans with land and wealth needed labor. Because there was no surplus population in the colonies, labor from Europe and Africa was imported. By the 1730s a substantial Irish migration had begun, and a large proportion of these immigrants were indentured servants. The brutal African slave trade eventually supplanted the trade in white servants.[98]

As we move toward the Civil War period and then into the twentieth century, we find few studies on the dominance of the economy by English or British Americans. A study of the wealth of men living in 1860 concluded only that the wealth of "native-born males," doubtless mostly British Americans, was about twice that of "foreign-born males."[99] U.S. industrialization in the nineteenth century was partially fueled by English and Dutch capital. U.S. business elites have long been dominated by Americans of British or other northern European descent. In the nineteenth century, the most famous of these were the industrialists and financiers, many of whom have been regarded as "robber barons." They included John D. Rockefeller, Leland Stanford, J. P. Morgan, Jay Gould, and Jim Fisk, all men of great wealth and power. Their ethnic heritages were typically English, with a few other northern European heritages mixed in. Many of their associates or family members became senators, representatives, and governors.[100]

A study of top executives and entrepreneurs in the late-nineteenth-century iron and steel industry found that few came from recent immigrant families; most were native-born and had fathers with capitalist or professional backgrounds. Most did not fit the image of a poor immigrant "making good," as did the steel magnate Andrew Carnegie, who came to America as a poor boy. Over half were of English or Welsh ancestry; most of the rest were either Scottish or Irish.[101] A survey of two hundred major executives serving the largest companies from 1901 to 1910 found that 53 percent were of English or Welsh origin, 7 percent were Scottish, 14 percent were Irish, and 8 percent were Canadian or British (unspecified).[102]

A few studies have made clear the extent of British American dominance in local economies. For instance, Burlington, Vermont, was dominated in the 1930s by "Old Americans"—those who had been in the United States for four generations, probably heavily English and English Canadian. They controlled banking and manufacturing, and they constituted a disproportionate number of professionals and political officials. Anderson underscores the racial dimension of this dominance: "Traditions of family and name, of power and influence, in the financial and civil life of the community, of race-consciousness, plus a very deep conviction that the Protestant traditions of their forefathers are basically important to the development of free institutions in America, set the Old Americans apart as a group distinct from other people."[103]

A few studies of the economically influential have been done since the 1930s. The "proper Philadelphians" about whom the sociologist E. Digby Baltzell has written typically had English or British backgrounds. This is suggested by the dominance of Episcopalians and Presbyterians in the Philadelphia *Social Register* for the year 1940.[104] These Philadelphians were persons of great power and influence in the 1940s, particularly in banking, law, engineering, and business.[105] In an analysis of the 1950s and 1960s, Baltzell underscored the continuing dominance of British Americans at the national level. Although non-British groups had significantly penetrated the economic and political systems by that point in U.S. history, they had not been as successful in the executive suites of large corporations, where the leadership was "still mainly composed of managers of Anglo-Protestant background."[106]

Contemporary Elites

A 1970s study by Thomas Dye of the top decision makers in the United States identified four thousand people in the top positions in corporations, government, and the public sector. Dye concluded that "great power in America is concentrated in a tiny handful of men. A few thousand individuals out of 200 million Americans decide about war and peace, wages and prices, consumption and investment, employment and production, law and justice, taxes and benefits, education and learning, health and welfare, advertising and communication, life and leisure."[107] Decisions of importance are reached at the middle and lower levels of the society, but it is the few thousand people in these top positions who make the most critical decisions—those affecting the lives of many millions of Americans in all racial and ethnic groups. Dye's research revealed that the social origins of the four thousand were not representative of the U.S. population as a whole. Indeed, most were affluent, white, Anglo-Protestant men. There were only a few African Americans and virtually no Mexican Americans, Native Americans, or Asian Americans. Dye has estimated that these elites were "at least 90 percent Anglo-Protestant" and noted that "there were very few recognizable Irish, Italian, or Jewish names" in the group.[108]

Since the late 1980s, magazines such as *U.S. News & World Report* have proclaimed that there is a different makeup to those in the media, politics, and the universities who most influence American life. Elites "today represent a real break with their predecessors. Almost none of them are WASP's; fewer still are in the *Social Register*."[109] This view of an integrated elite increased with the more conservative political thinking of the 1980s and 1990s. But much of it was and is inaccurate. One must be careful to distinguish social and economic realities from rags-to-riches myths. By the late 1990s the upper reaches of U.S. economic (and other) institutions had broadened to include not only British Americans but also those with other northern European ancestry, particularly German, "Scotch-Irish," and Scandinavian Americans. And by the late 1990s a handful of Catholic and Jewish Americans were beginning to penetrate elite bastions of economic power. Yet, as we begin the twenty-first century, Catholic and Jewish Americans are still not proportionately represented at the top of the economic pyramid. And almost no non-Europeans can be found at the very top of U.S. corporations.

Research studies by Thomas Dye and others in the 1980s and 1990s have found a continuing pattern of disproportionately white and north European Protestant dominance at the top levels of U.S. industrial, public interest, and governmental organizations. One study found that 57 percent of business leaders were Anglo-Protestants, much higher than their proportion in the population. When other white Protestants were added in, the percentage rose to 79 percent.[110]

Catholic critics such as Michael Novak have been outspoken about the persisting influence of Anglo-Protestants:

> In the country clubs, as city executives, established families, industrialists, owners, lawyers, masters of etiquette, college presidents, dominators of the military, fundraisers, members of blue ribbon committees, realtors, brokers, deans, sheriffs—it is the cumulative power and distinctive styles of WASPs that the rest of us have had to learn in order to survive. WASPs never had to celebrate Columbus Day or march down Fifth Avenue wearing green. Every day has been their day in America.[111]

It is important to note the caustic character of this assessment of the economic and other power of the so-called Anglo-Saxon Protestants. In recent decades the acronym *WASP*, originally shorthand for *white Anglo-Saxon Protestant*, has been widely used, often in a derogatory way, particularly by writers of southern and eastern European heritage. One significance of this greater derogatory use of *WASP*, and of the stereotyping associated with the term, is that English and other British Americans have increasingly been challenged for political and economic dominance by Americans from southern and eastern Europe.

English Americans as a Group: Economic and Educational Data

Some English Americans have done well in the higher echelons of U.S. society. What about English Americans as a group? In the 1990 census, about 23 million Americans listed English as their first ancestry, just over 9 percent of the total population; 97 percent of these were native-born. Counting both the first and second ancestries listed on the census forms, nearly 33 million Americans identified themselves as English Americans. The median age for English Americans was forty years—seven years older than the median age of the population as a whole.[112]

In 1990 the educational attainment of English Americans as a group was higher than that of either the total population or the total (non-Latino) white population. (In census tabulations, many Latinos are counted as white, but some are counted as black.) A slightly larger percentage of English American youth was enrolled in school than in either of the larger groups, as the following tabulation illustrates:[113]

	English Ancestry	Non-Latino White	Total Population
Percent of 15–19-year-olds in school	85%	82%	81%
Those 25 years and over with less than fifth grade	.7	1.3	2.7
Those 25 years and over with high school or more	84	79	75
Those 25 years and over with college degree or more	28	22	20

Taken as a group, English Americans were also economically better off than the total population or the total (non-Latino) white population:[114]

	English Ancestry	Non-Latino White	Total Population
Median family income	$40,875	$37,628	$35,225
Per capita income	$18,594	$16,074	$14,420
Family poverty rate	4.5%	7.0%	10.0%

The median income for American families of English ancestry was about 16 percent greater than that of all American families and almost 9 percent greater than that of all (non-Latino) white families. Significantly, the poverty rate for families of English ancestry was less than half that of all American families.

Occupational distribution data show broad similarities between English Americans and the general population, although a somewhat larger proportion of Americans of English ancestry hold white-collar jobs and a somewhat smaller proportion hold blue-collar jobs than in the general population, as can be seen in the following occupational distributions:[115]

	English Ancestry	Non-Latino White	Total Population
Managerial and professional	34%	29%	27%
Technical, sales, administrative	33	33	32
Service	10	12	13
Farming, forestry, fishing	2	2	2
Precision production, craft, repair	10	12	11
Operators, fabricators, laborers	11	13	15
	100%	101%	100%

In addition, English Americans are more likely to be self-employed and less likely to be unemployed than either the general population or the total (non-Latino) white population, as can be seen in the following data:[116]

	English Ancestry	Non-Latino White	Total Population
Unemployment rate	4.3%	5.0%	6.3%
Percent self-employed	8.7	8	6.97

Still, it is also important to note that not all those with English ancestry are well-off in terms of education, income, and occupational position.

ENGLISH AMERICA TODAY

Although they constitute the group whose culture and institutions have usually been the standard for whether or not other immigrants have assimilated, English Americans are rarely written about or researched in the United States. One analysis by the senior author of a large data bank of thousands of articles and stories in hundreds of U.S. magazines, newspapers, newsletters, journals, and other publications that appeared between 1978 and 1997 found not one serious article focusing on Americans of English ancestry. In this sixteen-year period, it was very rare for journalists or editors even to mention English Americans in any context. This neglect of such a powerful ethnic group suggests just how much the English have blended into, or *become*, the sociocultural background of this society.[117]

A few recent studies of white ethnic Americans have found that there is still a large English American group made up of some 33 million or so Americans, who in censuses have claimed partial or total English ancestry. There is still some tendency for those of English descent to marry others with the same background. In an analysis of the most recent data available, Lieberson and Waters found that 56 percent of women of English ancestry had mates who were partly or wholly of English ancestry.[118]

Residential dispersal has been characteristic of the English Americans and other north European Americans. A study by Richard Alba in the state of New York found that those respondents with English ancestry had dispersed throughout the New York region. Their early ancestors had immigrated to the area in the seventeenth and eighteenth centuries, and later descendants had much time to move around. This residential dispersion is probably a major reason that so little attention is paid to this ethnic group. In the New York study, 95 percent of those with English or Dutch ancestry reported mixed ethnic backgrounds; when asked, they might list two or three countries from which their ancestors came. In addition, 40 to 50 percent of those with British backgrounds said that their ethnic identity had no importance to them. Alba cautions that this latter response may mean that many have come to see their English or British American identity as synonymous with a "truly American" identity. Their English or British identity may be so integrated in their minds with what is American that they see no need to identify assertively with their country of origin. In contrast, more recent immigrant groups (for example, southern European Catholics) were much more likely to identify strongly with their national heritage.[119]

While English Americans can be viewed for many purposes as a cohesive ethnic group, regional variations in certain aspects of English American culture are still evident today. As Fischer has pointed out, the concepts of liberty brought by four waves of English immigrants in the 1600s and 1700s evolved in somewhat different ways in the colonies. In New England, the Puritans' concept of ordered freedom, which was codified into written laws, "became an instrument of savage persecution." Ordered freedom involved the liberty to impose individual restraints on the Puritans themselves without interference by outsiders, to grant certain exemptions from these restraints to particular individuals, to practice the "true" religion and persecute dissenters, and to be free of the "tyranny of circumstance," which included want and fear. In Virginia, the idea of hegemonic freedom—the belief that liberty was the birthright of the free-born English and gave those with high status the right to rule people of lower ranks—"permitted and even required the growth of race slavery for its support." In the Delaware Valley, the Quakers' belief in reciprocal freedom, which recognized each individual's right to dissent, caused them to withdraw from the world. In contrast, "the [Appalachian] backcountry belief in natural freedom, which favored minimal government and the supremacy of private interests, sometimes dissolved into cultural anarchy."[120] All those of English descent, however, emphasized the importance of individual freedom as they saw it. All these interpretations can still be found today as different regional variations on the theme of freedom in the still-dominant Anglo culture.

Fischer has also analyzed the relationship between present-day regional diversity in the United States and the distinctive colonial cultures of the four waves of English immigrants. Regional differences in homicide rates provide an interesting example. Homicide rates today are low in the areas of New England in which the early Puritans established a tradition of order and nonviolence, and high in the southern areas that were first settled by immigrants from northern Great Britain's borderlands, whose culture was somewhat violence-prone before emigration. Other social indicators examined by Fischer include education, attitudes toward gender equality, and patterns of local government and public life. Those areas with high rates of high-school and college graduation today are generally the ones whose colonial culture valued education highly. Those states that failed to ratify the Woman's Suffrage Amendment (1918–1921) and the Equal Rights Amendment (1972–1978) were those in whose colonial culture women had a comparatively low status. Moreover, many New England communities today continue the colonial practice of governance by town meetings. Current regional differences in the levels of taxation and public spending are broadly similar to what they were in the colonial period. Significantly, Fischer concludes that "each of the four cultural regions of British America . . . [has] kept its own customs of enculturation for many generations."[121]

One distinctive region is the South, which was settled substantially by English from the borderlands. The largest white ethnic group in the South today is still Americans of English descent.[122] In analyzing the South, sociologist Lewis Killian has referred to English Americans and other white ethnic groups as *white southerners,* and occasionally as *white Anglo-Saxon Protestants.* Killian notes that one part of this southern white population is descended from early Irish immigrants, those often called "Scotch-Irish" (see Chapter 4). There are also large proportions of French, Spanish, or German descent. Killian further argues that English and other British Americans have become mostly submerged in a larger and ethnically diverse white population that has emphasized whiteness above all else: "For a southerner, the salient fact was and is whether he was white or black; all else was secondary."[123]

As we have noted before, the theoretical frameworks of U.S. assimilation analysts generally take the English (or British) Americans and their culture and institutions as the starting point for the analysis of assimilation in the United States. Milton Gordon's important seven-stage framework, discussed in detail in Chapter 2, assumes Anglo-conformity as the general trend of adaptation by subsequent immigrant groups in the American colonies and, later, in the United States. Eventual inclusion of later groups into the dominant culture and society is also assumed by assimilation theorists.

Looking at the history of English Americans, however, power–conflict theorists would accent the ways in which the English colonization process began the establishment of racial–ethnic stratification. The violent subordination of Native Americans by English settlers is a clear example of what Lieberson has called *migrant superordination,* which takes place when a migrating group imposes its will on a native group. The entry of later groups of immigrants and their relegation to a subordinate position in the American stratification system, as was the case for enslaved Africans, can be seen as an example of Lieberson's concept of *indigenous superordination.* Such concepts give attention to the major social hierarchy, with its greatly unequal power and resources, that developed over the course of U.S. racial and ethnic history. The importance of this racialized hierarchy will become clearer in later chapters.

SUMMARY

The purpose of this chapter has been to examine one of the most neglected of all U.S. ethnic groups, English Americans. Their blending into the background makes it difficult to assess the power, location, and achievements of these early immigrants and their millions of descendants. Americans of English ancestry still make up a substantial proportion of the U.S. population, and there is still a significant tendency for them to share certain values and customs and to marry others of English or other northern European ancestry.

It was the English who first colonized on a large scale the area that became the eastern United States. We have detailed what the original English colonization and migrations meant for U.S. institutions, past and present. *Dominance* is the appropriate term for English influence on U.S. religious, economic, and political institutions. The colonization migration of the English created a dominant culture and social structure to which subsequent immigrant groups were required to adapt. The study of assimilation in the United States can begin with the English. For centuries, English migrants and their millions of descendants have been disproportionately represented in key social, economic, and political positions in this society. Between the mid-1800s and the 1990s, they have been joined in their dominant position by certain other European American groups. The result is a more diverse Anglo-Protestant group, but one that still has disproportionately great power.

The tremendous impact of Anglo-Protestant Americans on the culture and institutions does not mean that substantial segments have not stayed working-class or poor. There have long been significant regional and denominational differences within English and British American groups. Episcopalians are a bit different from Congregationalists, and southerners are different from New Englanders.

In recent decades, English and British Protestant dominance has been challenged by Catholic Americans and Jewish Americans, as well as by some non-European groups. Some analysts have argued that Anglo-Protestant influence is on the wane. Schrag, for instance, has argued that Anglo-Saxon Protestants are on the road to cultural decline. In this view, white Anglo-Saxon Protestant domination in areas such as music and the arts came to an end sometime after World War II; the "decline of the WASP" is to be seen in the increasing non-Anglo-Saxon dominance of music, literature, and art. But even Schrag presents a different conclusion for the economic sphere: the Anglo-Protestant "elite still controls its own corporate offices, its board rooms, its banks and foundations."[124] Thus, analyses arguing for the decline of whites of English and British ancestry as a force in this society, as the data in this chapter suggest, are at the least premature.

CHAPTER 4

Irish Americans

Numerous discussions of ethnicity have focused on *white ethnics,* a term some-times used for white Catholic and Jewish Americans. White Anglo-Protestant Americans have, on occasion, blamed these groups for societal problems, such as political machines or antiblack discrimination in U.S. cities. They have sometimes spoken of white ethnic "hardhats" as though they were uneducated buffoons with a corrupt or authoritarian bent. Not surprisingly, white ethnics have counter-attacked, arguing that hypocritical Anglo-Protestants have little awareness of the experiences of Catholic and Jewish Americans. It is the purpose of this chapter on the Irish Americans, and the following chapters on Italian and Jewish Americans, to analyze the neglected experiences of some of the non-English white Americans who helped build the United States.

Irish Americans are one of the major groups, especially those in the cities, that come to mind when white ethnic groups are mentioned. The traditional view of the Irish contains images of parading leprechauns in funny suits, shamrocks, Saint Patrick's Day, and big-city political machines. The Irish, furthermore, are said by some to be among the more conservative and racist of white Americans and to have a greater incidence of alcoholism than other Americans. This superficial imagery is an inaccurate portrayal of the realities of the Irish American experience. Irish Americans have made major contributions to the development of the United States.

How did the Irish come to these shores in the first place? What was their immigration experience? What proportions were Protestant and what Catholic? What conflicts have occurred? How successful have the Irish been? How does the assimilation model fit the Irish experience? Let us turn now to these questions.

IRISH IMMIGRATION: AN OVERVIEW

Placed on the migration continuum from slave importation to voluntary immi-gration, the Irish migration to North America would be toward the voluntary end.

Even so, this movement was less voluntary than the migrations of some other European groups, for economic and political pressures to leave Ireland were great. Those wishing to leave Ireland had a choice of destinations, though many came to the east coast of the United States. The volume of immigration has also varied. Perhaps 200,000 to 400,000 Irish left for the colonies prior to 1787; between 1787 and the 1820s, approximately 100,000 migrated.[1] The heaviest period was between 1841 and 1860, when 1.6 million Irish entered the United States. Migration peaked again in the 1880s and the 1890s, then dropped off sharply in subsequent decades.[2] In the period 1961–1992, almost 107,000 Irish immigrants entered the United States.[3]

In the 1990 census more than 22.7 million Americans listed "Irish" as their primary ancestry, and more than 4.3 million listed "Scotch-Irish." Almost all (99 percent) of both groups were born in the United States.[4] Together, these two groups make up almost 11 percent of the U.S. population. Counting both the primary and secondary ancestries that respondents listed on the census forms, nearly 39 million Americans identified themselves as Irish Americans and 5.6 million identified as "Scotch-Irish" Americans.[5]

The Eighteenth-Century Migration

The Irish first came to the United States in the 1650s, when Captain John Vernon supplied 550 persons from southern Ireland as servants and workers for the English colonists and entrepreneurs in New England; by 1700 a few Irish Catholic families had settled in Maryland.[6] Not until the 1700s did large numbers of Irish arrive on North American shores. A significant proportion of these were from northern Ireland (Ulster) and had some Scottish ancestry, but many were from southern Ireland and could trace their ancestry back into ancient Irish history.

Both push and pull factors influenced Irish immigration. The image of North America as a land of opportunity was a major pull factor, but domestic pressures were also important. In the 1100s the English conquered Ireland. The English rule was often bloody and repressive. By the 1600s, Scots, in increasing numbers, were being encouraged to migrate across the channel to Ireland and to develop lands given to English and Scottish landowners by the king of England. The English conquerors drove many of the native Irish people off the land.[7]

As a result of England's colonization of Ireland, the Ulster (northern) Irish who migrated to North America included a significant number of persons of Scottish ancestry. The latter were the fourth or fifth generation of Scots in Ireland, and they had become Irish.[8] There is some debate among scholars as to how much the Scottish settlers blended with the Irish, but it is clear that some intermixture—cultural and marital—did occur. They identified their primary nationality as Irish, not Scottish.

To what extent were the migrants from northern Ireland in the 1700s joined by those from southern areas? To what extent were these migrants Celtic or Catholic? (*Celtic* refers to those inhabitants of Ireland whose ancestry dates back far before the Roman and English invasions of the island.) These questions are debated by scholars. The traditional view has been that virtually all the immigrants before 1800 were "Scotch-Irish" Protestants from northern Ireland. Henry Jones Ford and James Leyburn claim that the immigrants were generally persons from the North with Presbyterian backgrounds.[9] However, other authors have provided evidence of a large southern (and thus Catholic) component to this migration. Michael O'Brien cites "unquestionable proof that every part of Ireland contributed to the enormous emigration of its people, and while there are no official statistics now available—for none were kept—to indicate the numerical strength of those Irish immigrants, abundant proof of this assertion is found in authentic records."[10]

Tens of thousands of immigrants with old Celtic names appear in various records. Passenger ship data provide evidence of the significant quantity of non-Ulster immigrants. Sixty percent of the 318 passenger ships sailing between 1767 and 1769, and 57 percent of the 576 ships sailing between 1771 and 1774, neither came from nor returned to northern Irish ports. Such evidence is only suggestive, however, since an unknown number of ships from northern Ireland stopping in southern ports for provisions gave the latter as their points of departure.[11]

Andrew Greeley concludes that it is possible that most in the early stream of Irish immigrants were Catholic Irish, at least in their family heritages. Many southern Irish immigrants gave up their traditional Catholicism because of the scarcity of Catholic churches in the North American colonies and because of the extremely hostile Protestant environment in many areas of Ireland and the colonies that made the open practice of Catholicism dangerous.[12] Local laws often required children to be baptized as Protestants, and Protestants were often extremely antagonistic toward "papists." Conversion of the Catholic Irish to Protestantism was common in the early migration. One Episcopalian clergyman wrote to a missionary society that "there were many Irish Papists in Pennsylvania who turn Quakers and get into places as well as Germans."[13] Some scholars have suggested that these early immigrants represented the less devout agricultural proletariat and thus found it relatively easy to sever their weak identification with the Catholic church once they arrived in their new homeland.[14]

Because the northern Irish in the first streams of immigration regarded themselves as Irish rather than Scotch-Irish, the term *Scotch-Irish* was seldom used in the first two centuries of Irish presence in America. The new migrants gave Irish names to their settlements and joined organizations such as the Friendly Sons of Saint Patrick rather than Scottish American societies.[15] The term *Scotch-Irish* came into heavy use only after 1850, when some older Irish Protestant immigrants (and their British friends) sought to distinguish themselves from the more recent Irish Catholic immigrants who were, at that time, the focus of much discrimination.[16] By the late nineteenth century, the issue of the "Scotch-Irish race" and its impact was widely discussed. Prominent politicians engaged in blatant racism when they praised the members of the "Scotch-Irish race" as great pioneers and democrats while damning the "Catholic Irish race."[17]

In his book *The Winning of the West*, Theodore Roosevelt (later U.S. president) dramatized the contributions of the Scotch-Irish frontier people. We had not understood, he argued, the important part "played by that stern and virile people," the brave "Puritans" of the West.[18] In the early 1900s, other U.S. scholars argued, inaccurately, that the Scotch-Irish were not really Irish and that they saw themselves as Scots living in Ireland—a distinct and superior racial type with a different "type of frame and physiognomy."[19]

The view that the Scotch-Irish were part of the Anglo-Saxon or Teutonic "race" was so vigorously argued that it reached the absurd point of denying any Celtic (that is, Catholic) part in the mixture: "Whatever blood may be in the veins of the genuine Scotch-Irishman, one thing is certain, and that is that there is not mingled with it one drop of the blood of the old Irish or Kelt."[20] The data showing large numbers of Celtic Irish in the early migration pose serious questions for this racist glorification of the Protestant Irish.

Early Life

What was life like for the early Irish settlers in an English-dominated society? In North America, perhaps half became indentured servants; others became subsistence farmers or farm workers, often in frontier areas. The English Americans treated Irish servants as lowly subordinates, even to the point of brutality. Discriminatory import duties and longer indenture terms were placed on Irish servants.[21] Irish Catholic servants suffered because of their nationality and their religion. As early as 1704, heavy taxes were placed on Irish Catholic immigrants. Laws were passed discouraging their importation or discriminating against them.[22] With times as hard as this, significant numbers gave up their Catholicism. Not all converted, however. Pressing for religious tolerance, several prominent Irish Catholics wrote President Washington in the late 1700s asking that the full religious rights of Catholics be protected.[23]

Pennsylvania and New England received the first groups of Ulster Irish in the decades before 1740. After 1740, many migrated to the valleys of Virginia and the Carolinas. Many of these also were indentured servants; others became farmers. Immigrants' letters to Ireland reveal that America was considered a land of hope and opportunity.[24] Many eighteenth-century Irish immigrants, encouraged to settle in frontier areas as a barrier against the Native Americans, came into conflict with the latter, as well as with British American landowners on whose land they sometimes squatted.[25]

By 1790, almost 10 percent of the white population of 3.2 million was Irish. The Ulster Irish constituted large proportions of the Georgia, Pennsylvania, and South Carolina populations; those from the southern areas of Ireland were most substantially represented in Maryland, Virginia, Delaware, and North Carolina. The Irish Americans were a large racial-ethnic group at the time of the new nation's birth.[26]

The pull factors motivating millions of Irish Catholics to cross the Atlantic after 1830 were the same as those that attracted European immigrants for centuries to North America, which was portrayed, often in exaggerated terms, as the land of golden opportunity. Push factors loomed even larger. The famine that came to Ireland in the 1840s spurred emigration to the United States. Irish peasants relied heavily on potatoes for food. The potato blight caused a massive failure of that crop, and many people starved to death or died from diseases such as hunger typhus. During these famine years, Ireland actually produced more than twice the food needed to feed the hungry. However, the oppressive English landlords saw to it that most of these foodstuffs were exported to England and elsewhere or consumed by those in Ireland with money. The Irish have said that "God sent the blight, but the English landlord sent the famine." English leaders advocated emigration to the United States and elsewhere as the proper solution for the poor Irish. Many Irish who emigrated to the United States mourned their departure with an all-night farewell ceremony called the "American wake"; they saw their new land as a place of involuntary exile, a condition Kerby Miller sees as the foundation of Irish American homesickness and nationalism. The long history of English interference in and oppression of Ireland lies behind the persisting conflict between the two peoples in places such as Northern Ireland, even as we move into the twenty-first century.[27]

The Atlantic crossing was dangerous. Few ships arrived that had not lost a number of their poorly accommodated passengers to starvation or disease. The survivors usually chose urban destinations. New York became a major center, eventually housing more Irish than Dublin. Like most urban migrants, the new immigrants went where relatives or fellow villagers had settled. Residential segregation for Irish Americans in the nineteenth century had a distinctive form. Huge segregated communities, such as where African and Latino Americans now live, were not the rule. They clustered in smaller, more dispersed settlements than would be the case for later immigrant groups.[28]

These scattered settlements were reinforced by a second large stream of immigrants from Ireland between 1870 and 1900 and by significant but declining numbers of immigrants from 1900 to 1925. These later immigrants were forced out not by famine, but primarily by poverty and the hope for a better life. In New York, Boston, and Philadelphia, poor housing with its attendant disease was frequently their lot. An analysis of New York for 1877 revealed that the death rate for the Irish-born was high, as was the mortality rate for their American-born children. Whole families were consigned to a single room in crowded apartment houses often called *rookeries*. The Irish were overrepresented in the almshouses of some cities. Irish crime rates, high for some categories of minor offenses, were exaggerated by Anglo nativists; the rate of serious offenses was low. The poverty of Irish immigrants had several causes. Many of the immigrants had few skills, but more important reasons for their poverty were low wages and direct institutionalized discrimination against those of Irish descent.[29]

From the beginning, Irish women have been central to the establishment of strong Irish American communities. One distinctive aspect of this immigration was the presence of large numbers of young single women. Because they had no hope of inheritance and little hope of marriage in poverty-stricken Ireland, they saw America as a land of opportunity. Once in the United States, these women did not subscribe to the cult of womanhood that emphasized that the woman's place was only in the home. Most did not live lives of sheltered domesticity but rather became self-sufficient persons with distinctive work histories. They made important social and economic contributions to the upward mobility of Irish Americans into middle-income America.

The famine in Ireland destroyed many Irish families, and for six decades young, unmarried women came to the United States to avoid the terrible life awaiting them in Ireland. In contrast with male Irish immigrants and female immigrants from many other countries, these women were willing to postpone or forego marriage and to work as domestic servants. Many supported families in the old country. Their values, expressed in the decisions they made about work, were fundamental life-choice values that have persisted among Irish Americans today. Among these values was a strong commitment to their Irish heritage and to personal independence. Interestingly, the daughters of these women often became schoolteachers or clerical workers.[30]

STEREOTYPES

The resistance of English Americans to the Irish immigration dates back to the seventeenth and eighteenth centuries. "Papists" were frequently the targets of open hatred. Protestant and Catholic Irish Americans suffered from nativistic concern over their political persuasions, as in the conflicts in the 1790s between the Federalists and the Jeffersonians over restricting immigration. Yet it was the nineteenth-century Irish, poor Catholics from the famine-ridden Emerald Isle, who were attacked the most.

In a study of Civil War public literature on the Irish, Dale Knobel found what he terms the "Paddy stereotype," a view of the Irish that experienced gradual change from the 1820s to the Civil War. From the 1820s to the mid-1840s, this stereotype of the Catholic Irish emphasized what was seen to be their morality, style, and lack of intelligence. Alleged character faults, such as ingratitude, wickedness, and ignorance, were accented in this early stereotype. With the surge in Irish migration in the late 1840s and early 1850s, the image in the literature came to emphasize conflict, hostility, and emotion. Words such as *temperamental, dangerous, quarrelsome, idle,* and *reckless*—characteristics emphasizing conduct as much as character—came into use after 1845. The Anglo-American image of the Irish hardened and became less tolerant as the number of Irish immigrants grew. During the following decades, various phrases that were derogatory to the Irish— such as *Irish buggy* for wheelbarrow, *Irish promotion* for demotion, and *paddy wagon* for a vehicle used by the police to transport criminals—came into use.[31]

Attacks on Irish Catholics took the form of cartoons that stereotyped the Irish by means of outrageous or hostile symbols—an apelike face, a fighting stance, a jug of whisky, a shillelagh. The influential caricaturist Thomas Nast published cartoons of this type in *Harper's Weekly* and other magazines. One of his caricatures shows a stereotyped southern black man and an apelike Irishman, both portrayed as ignorant voters and a threat to orderly politics. "New York's leading cartoonists of the 1870s and 1880s," notes Lewis Curtis, "certainly did not refrain from simianizing Irish-American Paddies who epitomized the tens of thousands of working-class immigrants and their children caught up in urban poverty and slum conditions after their flight from rural poverty and famine in Ireland."[32]

The Ape Image

The apelike image of the Irish was imported from England. With the rise of debates over evolution in England, the poor Irish came to be regarded by many in England and the United States as the "missing link" between the gorilla and the human race. With the constant threat of Irish rebellion on the one hand and the press of evolutionary Darwinism on the other, "it was comforting for some Englishmen to believe—on the basis of the best scientific authority in the Anthropological Society of London—that their own facial angles and orthognathous features were as far removed from those of apes, Irishmen, and Negroes as was humanly possible."[33] In rationalizing the exploitation of the Irish and Africans, racists on both sides of the Atlantic developed dehumanizing animal stereotypes. Notice the comparable position of black and Irish Americans in this mythology. Greeley has underscored the parallels in prejudice and stereotyping:

> Practically every accusation that has been made against the American blacks was also made against the Irish: Their family life was inferior, they had no ambition, they did

Stereotypes of Roman Catholic bishops as crocodiles supposedly threaten Protestant children on American shores.

not keep up their homes, they drank too much, they were not responsible, they had no morals, it was not safe to walk through their neighborhoods at night, they voted the way crooked politicians told them to vote, they were not willing to pull themselves up by their bootstraps, they were not capable of education, they could not think for themselves, and they would always remain social problems for the rest of the country.[34]

Early stage shows made fun of the Irish by using these stereotypes, just as they did with African Americans. In the nineteenth century, the Catholic Irish were often socially defined by those in dominant groups as physically different, and thus as a major "race." Significantly, in the twentieth century, the emphasis on this alleged physical and racial distinctiveness would disappear.

Changing Attitudes

In the early decades of the twentieth century, the harsh attitudes toward Irish Americans gradually gave way to acceptance as nativist hostilities were transferred to newer immigrant groups. In 1921, amid a heated debate regarding the desirability of southern and eastern European immigrants, the *Boston Globe* noted that seventy years earlier Irish immigrants had been deemed undesirable and then concluded: "The undesirable of one generation is the desirable of the next. . . . The standard of desirability is not a fixed standard in the public mind."[35]

Yet not all negative attitudes toward Irish Americans had disappeared. In 1932 white students at Princeton University were given a list of eighty-four positive and negative traits and asked to identify those they associated with ten racial and ethnic groups, including Irish Americans. Five of the top ten traits assigned to Irish Americans—"pugnacious," "quick-tempered," "quarrelsome," "aggressive," and "stubborn"—comprise a stereotype of Irish aggressiveness. Fifty years later, a similar questionnaire given to a predominantly white sample of Arizona State University students found a significant decrease in the negative imagery. Only "quick-tempered" and "stubborn" remained among the top ten traits assigned to the Irish. The Arizona State students added the positive traits of "intelligent" and "loyal to family ties" to their top ten. Significantly, in neither sample did the Irish receive the most negative stereotypes available to the students—the traits of "treacherous" and "sly"—which were attributed to Jewish, Japanese, and African Americans.[36]

In a 1980s nationwide opinion poll that asked respondents whether various immigrant groups had, on balance, been good or bad for this country, Irish Americans received the second-highest percentage of positive answers, only slightly less than English Americans.[37] The reduction in the traditional racial and ethnic stereotyping of Irish Americans that appears to have taken place since the 1930s indicates substantial *attitude-receptional assimilation,* to use Milton Gordon's conceptual term. Yet, even in the 1990s, stereotypes of Irish Americans still exist. In a recent study of white ethnic groups in a large metropolitan area of New York State, about one-fifth of those with Irish ancestry reported encountering stereotypes of Irish Americans as politicians and police officers, heavy drinkers, or poets. They also encountered images of Irish women as "long-suffering." (The drinking stereotype of the Irish in Ireland is strong too, but is also incorrect. Most European countries, as well as the United States as a whole, have higher rates of alcohol consumption than Ireland.)[38]

Irish Catholic Americans have been seen by some analysts as a particularly antiblack group of white Americans. Compared with some other white Americans, though, Irish Catholics have been found to be relatively liberal. For example, a review of 1970s opinion polls came to this conclusion: "Surveys in the 1970s revealed that in the North Irish Catholics were more sympathetic to integrated neighborhoods, integrated schools, and interracial marriages than other white Catholics and white Protestants. Among whites only Jews are more liberal on racial issues than Irish Catholics."[39] In addition, Irish Catholics in the North are more likely than most other white groups to live in racially integrated neighborhoods. Nonetheless, some Irish Catholics in major cities, like other whites, have played a significant role in overt and subtle discrimination against African Americans.

PROTEST AND CONFLICT

From their first decades in North America, Irish Americans suffered not only verbal abuse and stereotyping but also intentional discrimination and violent attacks from Anglo-Protestant Americans. On occasion, Irish Americans have retaliated, even to the point of violence. In other situations they started the racial or ethnic conflict. As we noted in Chapter 2, intergroup conflict often involves a struggle over resources and can be generated by group inequality. This conflict can take both nonviolent and violent forms, and it typically involves racial and ethnic groups with differing power and resources.

Assimilation theorists have usually neglected the conflict that has characterized interethnic and interracial relations. Indeed, some views of U.S. history embody a myth of peaceful progress. In this view the members of each white ethnic group have advanced higher on the socioeconomic ladder by pulling themselves up by their own bootstraps—solely by hard work and diligent effort, not by active protest and collective violence. This image is incorrect. As with other white groups, the Irish Americans have struggled for their "place in the sun" with many other groups, from established Anglo-Protestants to Native Americans. They have been involved in open conflict with groups above and below them in power and status.

Early Conflict

The first major conflict was with the established groups that controlled the major institutions in the North American colonies at the time of the initial Irish immigration. A few eighteenth-century Irish settlements were damaged or destroyed by Anglo-Protestant attacks. For example, British Americans attacked and destroyed an Irish community in Worcester, Massachusetts, in the eighteenth century. There was a great deal of opposition from the already established colonists to both Catholic and Protestant Irish migrants.[40] Conflict sometimes arose between the Irish Protestant farmers in the frontier areas and the British plantation gentry in the coastal areas of the colonies. In the colonial period, the backcountry Irish Americans were seen by English Americans as crude frontier people. Settling in frontier areas, the Irish sometimes defied laws or regulations made by English American officials and engaged in aggressive protest against them, such as in the Whisky Rebellion and the Regulation movement, in order to expand their own political power.[41]

Conflict with Native Americans was part of the Irish American experience. The Irish were often encouraged to settle in the frontier areas of the colonies so that the dominant Anglo-Protestant interests would be protected and shielded from Native Americans to the west. The bloody practice of scalping was institutionalized by English and Irish settlers determined to exterminate Native Americans. Placing bounties on the scalps of Native American men and women became common in New England and the middle colonies. Conflict between Irish Americans who were stealing Native American lands and Native Americans who were protecting their way of life became widespread in Virginia and the Carolinas.[42]

In the 1790s there were violent attacks on Irish Catholics by Anglo-Protestant Americans. In 1798 a disturbance known as the Federal Riot took place at Saint Mary's Church in Philadelphia: Irish opponents of a new anti-alien law who had come to the church with a petition for the congregation to sign were beaten up by a group of Federalist rioters.[43] Although the Irish had a valid reputation for aggressiveness, much of the rioting after 1800 was directed against them because they were immigrants or Roman Catholics.[44] By 1850 most large cities had seen anti-Catholic demonstrations and riots carried out by Protestants. Philadelphia became a center for anti-Irish Catholic violence. There, in 1844, two major riots "resulted in the burning of two Catholic churches . . . ; the destruction of dozens of Catholic homes; and sixteen deaths."[45] In the 1850s Anglo-Protestant nativist groups such as the Know-Nothings played a major role in attacks on Irish Americans.[46]

Conflict over Workplace Conditions

Conflict in mining areas was a major feature of the Irish American experience in the latter half of the nineteenth century. Irish workers and better-paid English workers often did not get along. In the early days of copper mining in Michigan, English and Irish miners competed for jobs.[47] Similar struggles characterized the coal mining areas of Pennsylvania, where the Irish played a major role in developing the anthracite coal mines. Here, they found English and Welsh mining capitalists and English workers in control of skilled work.[48] Working and living conditions were oppressive. Pay rates were low, perhaps $20 to $30 per month. Often, pay was in the form of a "bobtail check": money owed the company for groceries and rent equaled one's wages, a situation of wage slavery.[49] Such oppression and poverty regularly led to violent conflict between the predominantly British Protestant owners and superintendents and the Irish Catholic miners.[50]

A major coal strike in 1875, called the Long Strike, forced many miners to the brink of starvation. The mine owners broke the strike and crushed attempts at unionization.[51] In response, secret Irish organizations linked to the Ancient Order of the Hibernians (AOH) sometimes resorted to assassination and sabotage. The owners reacted with violence against the AOH groups. The Anglo-Protestant establishment engineered numerous shootings of Irish workers, and the miners replied with armed defense and guerrilla warfare.[52] Although called Molly Maguires (after an older organization in Ireland), the protesting miners were not part of that secret organization. Instead, they were members of miners' organizations who went underground when more moderate worker protests failed to improve their oppressive living and working conditions.

Rather than yield to the reasonable requests of the miners for better wages and conditions, the British American and other mine owners hired private detectives to put down the workers' rebellion. One detective gathered information to be used in court cases; twenty miners were hung for engaging in protest. The owners' counterattack in the courts was reinforced by nativist portrayals of the Irish American members of the secret societies as undisciplined and violent. This Anglo-Protestant nativism was evident in the court trials of the miners, whose convictions were apparently influenced by negative Irish stereotypes in the minds of non-Irish judicial authorities.[53]

Conflict with Other Groups

In addition to conflict with British Americans, Irish Americans found themselves competing with groups with fewer economic resources and less power. We previously noted the role of Irish Protestants ("Scotch-Irish") in taking Native American lands on the frontier. As early as the 1840s, Irish competition with African American workers in northern cities engendered substantial distrust and hostility between the two groups. Between the 1840s and the 1860s, Irish workers attacked black workers in several northern cities. During the Civil War, Irish American hostility toward African Americans increased; the two groups competed for many low-paying jobs in northern cities. Irish opposition to black workers was partially economic—the fear of job competition from black Americans moving North. They "valued the security that came from the existence in the country of at least one social class below them."[54] Excluded from discriminatory all-white unions, black workers sometimes were used by white employers as strikebreakers. The use of black strikebreakers on the waterfront, combined with Irish opposition to the Civil War military draft, helped to spur the 1863 Irish riot, usually termed the Draft Riot—the most serious riot in U.S. history. An estimated four hundred white rioters were killed in the streets, together with some free blacks and some white police officers and soldiers. Irish rioters attacked "Yankees," the police, and blacks.[55]

Within a generation or two, Irish Americans had come to see themselves clearly as members of a distinctive "white race." In Chapter 3 we noted how the image of whiteness, and its component view of superiority, came to be fostered by English American elites by the mid-1800s. One Anglo-American ruling class response to farmer and labor unrest among white immigrants in the nineteenth century was to place a greater emphasis on racial solidarity with the immigrants in a "superior white race." By the mid-nineteenth century, many European immigrants who did not initially define themselves as "white" but as Irish, German, Norwegian, or Swedish, had come to see themselves as "white Americans."[56]

Somewhat surprisingly, the nineteenth-century Irish immigrants were important in this drama of celebrating whiteness. Many of the Irish who had themselves been described as "wild," "savage," and "apelike" by the English in England and by English Americans now came to share with their English oppressors a similar negative view of African Americans. Between 1830 and 1890 the majority of Irish Americans came to see themselves as "white" and, as a rule, began to develop the negative prejudices toward African Americans shared by most other whites. Recent historical analysis has shown that, among Irish Americans, the psychological movement from a likely sympathy for the oppression of African Americans to their own version of white-racist thinking was intentionally fostered by the Anglo-American press, by Anglo-Protestant and Roman Catholic religious leaders, and especially by Democratic Party organizations, such as Tammany Hall.[57]

Irish Americans, including Catholic priests and intellectuals, actively challenged the notion of "Anglo-Saxon" superiority, which excluded the Irish as an inferior race, and supported its replacement with the notion that all Europeans should be included within a "superior race" of white Americans. English Americans increasingly, if grudgingly, accepted this change in the racial status of Irish Americans, in part because the Irish had growing political clout in cities across the nation. David Roediger has underscored this politics-makes-strange-bedfellows argument: "The emphasis on a common whiteness smoothed over divisions in the Democratic ranks within mainly northern cities by emphasizing that immigrants from Europe, and particularly from Ireland, were white and thus unequivocally entitled to equal rights." There were dissenters among the Irish in regard to such racist thinking, but they were not able to stem the tide.[58]

Black–Irish conflict has now persisted for more than a century and a half in U.S. cities. Irish American and other white ethnic frustration at black civil rights gains from the 1960s to the 1990s has been a familiar topic in the mass media. Many Irish Americans have felt that African Americans receive a disproportional share of federal government benefits and programs compared with what urban white ethnics receive. Today, serious tensions between black and Irish urbanites exist in major cities such as Boston and Chicago, especially over such issues as school and neighborhood desegregation.

On the West Coast, Irish American workers aggressively fought to maintain their economic position in the mid-nineteenth century. Competition from Chinese immigrant workers led to the development of anti-Chinese racism and to violent attacks on these immigrants in Irish American papers, as well as to meetings and parades demanding prohibition of further Chinese immigration (see Chapter 12). The anti-Chinese protest was often led by Irish immigrants and their descendants.[59] In addition, by 1900 new immigrants from southern and eastern Europe were confronting Irish Americans in the Midwest and on the East Coast. In cities such as Chicago and Boston, Irish control of the Catholic church and of political parties was a major source of friction with these new European immigrant groups; the new immigrants resented Irish American control of the U.S. Catholic church and of city governments and many local jobs.

In the 1930s Father Charles Coughlin (born in Canada of Irish immigrants) and his racist organization, the Christian Front, spread a populist message that included anti-Jewish stereotypes and hostility among many Irish and other Gentile Americans. Coughlin's radio broadcasts reached millions of Americans. In 1938 Coughlin serialized an anti-Semitic document, the "Protocols of the Elders of Zion"—a well-known forgery accusing Jews of political conspiracy—in his magazine. The Christian Front went so far as to circulate a list of non-Jewish merchants who promised not to hire Jewish workers or deal with Jewish businesses.[60]

POLITICS AND POLITICAL INSTITUTIONS

When the Irish began arriving in the seventeenth century, much of the general political framework of the colonies had already been fashioned by the English. Yet those Irish immigrants who came in the eighteenth century did play a modest role in shaping the nation's initial institutions: some were even among the founding fathers. Eight of the fifty-six signers of the Declaration of Independence were Irish immigrants—five from the north and three from the south of Ireland. Four men born in Ireland were members of the Constitutional Convention, together with three other men of Irish descent. At least two Irish Americans were members of the first U.S. Senate, and two were members of the first U.S. House. Before 1800, a few could also be found participating in state and local governments.[61]

Most of the Irish migrating after the Revolutionary War settled in eastern cities, where they often became involved in urban politics. Irish Americans were generally anti-Federalist and supported the democratic faction of Thomas Jefferson. Here, again, there was intergroup political competition. The Federalist-sponsored Alien and Sedition Acts of 1798 were directed in part against Irish immigrants. Irish American opposition to such actions led to the downfall of the Federalists. They turned out as a group to help elect Jefferson as president. A few decades later, the Irish American vote played an important role in electing the first Irish American (Protestant) president, Andrew Jackson.[62]

Political Organization in the Cities

Traditionally, discussion of Irish Americans in politics has focused on Irish Catholics. The common terms used by critics of urban politics are *boss* and *machine.* The theme of corrupt urban machines has been tied to hostile views of

Catholic immigrants. Protestant views have tended to be pious: "In general, the Irish Catholic political machines in the United States have been notoriously and flamboyantly corrupt—a disgrace to Catholicism, to American democracy, and to the Irish people."[63] Commenting on the Irish machine that existed in New York, William Adams argued that "the 'horrible example' of New York politics combined with a rapid increase of pauper immigrants to check the advance of liberal ideas."[64] The tone of such analyses was that the Irish Americans were more unscrupulous and corrupt in their political activities than other white groups. In fact, the Irish immigrants entered a U.S. political system that already had many weaknesses, including no secret ballot and much urban political corruption. Urban machines existed before the Irish Americans came to control them. Anglo-Protestant political organizations—by which those in power secured for their poor constituents jobs, housing, and food—already ruled in numerous cities before there were sizeable Irish American communities.

Why has there been a strong Irish involvement in local politics? Politics was one means to social mobility, a means of achieving power in the face of great Anglo-Protestant opposition. The dominant Anglo-Protestant perspective on government in the nineteenth and early twentieth centuries tended toward a hands-off view, with government staying out of economic affairs as much as possible. It was against this do-nothing background that desperate urban residents, plagued with unemployment, low income, and poor housing, joined large urban political organizations. Taking control of local party organizations, immigrant leaders shaped government programs to benefit the poor. Providing jobs—for example, in real estate projects and construction—was one of the machines' critical functions.[65]

One of the first political machines was New York City's Tammany Society. In 1817, a group of Irish Americans, incensed at discrimination at the hands of this Anglo-Protestant machine, broke into one of its meetings and demanded the nomination of an Irish American for Congress. Although they were driven away this time, a few decades later Irish Americans were able to take over two New York political organizations, including Tammany Hall.

One figure in Tammany Hall, William M. "Boss" Tweed, has long been attacked by critics for his alleged greed and corruption. Numerous articles and textbooks have heralded a totally negative image of Tweed. Yet this image is exaggerated. In reality, Tweed was an urban political leader who represented the underdog, including Irish and Jewish Americans, in nineteenth-century New York. He was tolerant of various religious beliefs, family-oriented, and ambitious. He identified with New York's poor immigrants and worked to build schools and hospitals. He was generally hated by the Anglo-Protestant elite because of his identification with the poor immigrants. Yet Tweed's own ethnic background remains unclear; he was apparently of Scottish or Irish descent. Because of growing Irish political power, Tweed became a powerful leader and rewarded Irish and other immigrant constituents with jobs, schools, and social services. Tweed may well have been less politically corrupt than many Anglo-Protestant politicians who dominated urban politics before and after his era.[66]

With the election of New York City's first Irish American mayor in the 1880s, Irish Americans began to play a major role in New York politics. They held many elective posts and gained heavy representation in appointed positions. They also moved into important positions in the governments of numerous other cities with large Catholic populations. In vigorous competition with English and other British Americans, the Irish gradually won a place in the political sun in Boston, Brooklyn, Philadelphia, New Haven, and Chicago.[67]

By the 1960s these Irish political organizations were gone except in Chicago, where the paramount Irish American boss, Mayor Richard J. Daley, maintained great power into the 1970s. One-fourth of Chicago's fifty aldermen, its mayor, and 42 percent of its ward committee members were Irish. Chicago's political machine was characterized by many complexities. It was responsible for tremendous urban development and renewal. At the same time, construction contracts were awarded in questionable ways to friends of the machine.[68]

Chicago has become a center of Irish American culture and politics. By the 1980s, Daley was dead, and Chicago's Irish-dominated political machine was weakened to the extent that a black mayor, Harold Washington, was elected against the machine's wishes. Soon, however, the Irish were back. In 1989 an Irish American politician, Richard M. Daley, the son of the former mayor, was elected mayor. Today, many major Chicago-area political offices are held by Irish Americans. In fact, Richard M. Daley was re-elected for another term in 1995, and by the end of that term will have served a decade as Chicago's mayor. In contrast, the number of Irish Americans in political office in New York City has declined steadily over the past few decades. By the late 1980s, there were so few Irish Americans in New York City government that the mayor found it difficult to assemble a contingent of top officials of Irish descent to march in the Saint Patrick's Day Parade. However, a recent study of the metropolitan region around New York State's capital city of Albany found that Irish Catholic politicians still exercised significant influence in some of New York's urban areas.[69]

Pragmatism in Politics

For Irish Americans, politics is an honorable profession. Family and friends provide the important networks for entry into political positions. Irish Americans have often developed a political style based on concern for individuals and personal loyalty to leaders. Individual charity is a major feature. One Irish American official put it this way: "When a man is ill in government and without enough time for retirement or health benefits, an efficient man fires him. Yet the Irish administrator says, 'What the hell, he has two kids,' and keeps him on. He knows this is a risky thing, letting him come in at ten and leave at two. So what happens? He gets a little more work out of the others to make it up."[70]

In recent decades Irish American politicians have been influenced by reform movements to clean up corruption. Some have been reformers themselves, playing a major role in bringing down the corrupt leaders of political machines in New York and other cities. Yet the personal, pragmatic, nonideological style of Irish

American politics remains.[71] Pragmatic politics, with its coalition and compromise themes, is a major Irish contribution to U.S. politics. One principle is that a city is a mosaic of racial and ethnic groups and the political machine is a broker, balancing these groups' interests so that a coalition can hang together. Irish American political leaders have often pressed for racially and ethnically balanced tickets.[72] Hence, they have been important in much urban coalition building. Irish American political organizations have also made a major contribution to the bricks-and-mortar development of cities. Without the Irish American contractors linked to the earlier political machines, who would have met the need for public buildings, streets, and subways in many cities?[73]

With suburbanization and intermarriage, this Irish political style has begun to fade, but it has by no means disappeared. One study of fifty-one cities found that those with large Irish American populations were more likely than other cities to have a government (often Irish-dominated) that provided a high level of public services for residents. There was more responsiveness to poor groups, including poor black residents, in these Irish-populated cities than in other cities. Irish American political machines may be fading, but their humane, services-oriented, patronage approach to local government often persists. Some analysts have attempted to link the upward mobility of Irish Americans to a growing "conservatism," noting that in the 1960s and 1970s Irish American electorates in New York and Connecticut preferred the more conservative political candidates in mayoral, gubernatorial, and senatorial races. Elsewhere, however, they have continued to vote for liberal and moderate Democrats in many local and state races.[74] In most cases, Irish Americans have been more liberal than numerous other white Gentile groups. In general, Irish Catholic Americans have had a progressive political tradition. Today, they remain substantially Democratic, with a large proportion of liberal Democrats among them.

National and International Politics

After 1840, the Irish American electorate was increasingly courted by presidential and congressional candidates. Ulysses Grant, the Republican presidential candidate in 1868, wooed Irish American voters; after he was elected he made a few Irish appointments to his administration. In succeeding elections, the Irish American vote has been sought by presidential candidates of both parties.[75]

One study of the period between 1901 and 1910 found that 13 percent of 162 prominent political leaders, including presidents, senators, representatives, and Supreme Court justices, were Irish American (generally Protestants) compared with 56 percent who were of English or Welsh descent.[76] Irish *Catholic* influence at the national level was weak. In a letter to Theodore Roosevelt, Finley Peter Dunne, a prominent Irish American writer, commented on the lack of Irish Catholic influence: "As for the point about Irishmen holding office, I simply wanted to emphasize the fact that Irishmen are the most unsuccessful politicians in the country. Although they are about all there is to politics in the North between elections, there is not, with one exception, a single representative Irish man in any important cabinet, diplomatic, judicial or administrative office that I know about."[77] Penetration at the city level did not necessarily lead to important positions in the federal executive or judicial branches.

Most literature on Irish Americans in politics focuses on Irish Catholics. Millions of Irish Protestants, many of whom live in the South, have received little attention. Andrew Jackson, a Presbyterian from Tennessee who served as president from 1829 to 1837, was the nation's first Irish American president and the only one both of whose parents were immigrants. Woodrow Wilson, a "Scotch-Irish" Protestant from New Jersey, was president from 1913 to 1921. Although this was a crucial time in the history of Ireland, Wilson was not sympathetic to Irish Catholic causes and did not support the Irish fight against England. More recently, at a precedent-setting 1994 Saint Patrick's Day White House dinner, which was attended by prominent Irish American industrialists, academics, politicians, and entertainers, Ireland's prime minister presented President Bill Clinton a genealogy of Clinton's Irish ancestors.[78] (Clinton has both English and Irish ancestry.)

Many Irish Americans, primarily Catholics, have reacted strongly to the English oppression of their brothers and sisters in Ireland. In the late 1800s and early 1900s, numerous Irish nationalist groups came to public attention. Since that time, some Irish Americans have attempted to shift U.S. foreign policy away from its generally pro-English stance.[79] After World War I, the unsupportive stand of Woodrow Wilson and many other Protestants for the concerns of those seeking Ireland's independence was a critical issue for many Irish Catholic Americans.[80]

In subsequent decades the issue of an independent, united Ireland has remained important and has continued to generate financial and political support among Irish Americans. The Irish American senator Edward Kennedy of Massachusetts once introduced a U.S. Senate resolution asking for the removal of British soldiers from Northern Ireland. In the 1980s, IRA fugitive Joe Doherty became a rallying point for Irish American opposition to British rule of Northern Ireland. He was convicted in absentia in Belfast, Ireland, for his part in the killing of a British military officer and held in U.S. prisons from 1983 until he was extradited to Britain in 1992. During the years he was held in prison, Doherty wrote a popular column in the New York newspaper *Irish People* supporting the IRA's cause and received visits from more than one hundred members of Congress, as well as from New York's Cardinal O'Connor, in support of his request for political asylum. In early 1992, following the U.S. Supreme Court's decision to deny Doherty political refugee status and to extradite him, his Irish American supporters protested on a Manhattan street corner named in his honor.[81]

Irish American support for the Catholic Irish cause has created some political tensions in the United States, with some non-Irish politicians criticizing Irish American support of the Catholic struggle in Northern Ireland or U.S. involvement in trying to broker peace between Sinn Fein, the political arm of the IRA, and the British government. In 1994, 1995, and 1997, Gerry Adams, the head of Sinn Fein, was granted a visa to visit the United States—first to participate in a conference on Northern Ireland, then to meet with U.S. government officials following his announcement of an IRA cease-fire in Northern Ireland, and in 1995 to meet with President Bill Clinton. In 1997 Adams came to the United States again to raise funds and to meet with White House officials, although the president did not meet with him—reportedly to put pressure on Sinn Fein for concessions in negotiations over the future of Northern Ireland.[82]

Peace negotiation efforts by some Irish American political leaders and President Clinton's decision to lift a twenty-year ban on official U.S. contacts with Sinn Fein are said by many observers to have played a significant and positive role in encouraging the ongoing peace process in Northern Ireland. In addition, in 1997 Sinn Fein was continuing its efforts in the United States and had success in raising substantial funds from Irish Americans. As of early 1998, the various parties contending over Northern Ireland were still debating conditions for all-party negotiations. The controversy over Northern Ireland's independence from Britain not only illustrates an interethnic struggle (between Catholics and Protestants in Ireland) that continues to the present, but also shows how events in the country of origin of a segment of the U.S. population can long affect ethnic relations within the United States. This theme will reappear in the chapters that follow, as, for example, in the effect of events in Italy on Italian Americans and in Japan on Japanese Americans. The world is still the larger context of the interethnic and interracial relations in the United States.

An Irish Catholic President

Alfred E. Smith, the Democratic candidate for president in 1928, was the first Irish Catholic to carve out an important role in presidential politics. Yet his Catholic religion, his calls for modification of Prohibition, and his lack of knowledge about regions of the United States other than the East counted against him in this first Irish Catholic presidential campaign. Although he lost the election, he managed to equal or exceed the Republican vote in eleven of the nation's twelve largest cities, pulling urban immigrants into a national voting bloc in the Democratic party for the first time in U.S. history. No national candidate could again ignore the importance of the growing non-Protestant vote in the cities.[83]

In 1930, with the exception of one Supreme Court justice, there were still no Irish Catholics holding major positions in the judicial and executive branches of the federal government. Franklin Roosevelt was the first president to appoint Irish Catholics to important positions, which included ambassador to Great Britain, postmaster general, and attorney general. Many Irish Catholics were sent to Congress for the first time as a result of Roosevelt's New Deal electoral landslides. Roosevelt, and subsequently Harry Truman, appointed far more Irish Catholic judges and executive branch officials than had previous presidents.[84]

Not until 1960, more than three hundred years after the first few Irish Catholics had come to the United States and more than a century after sizable Irish American Catholic communities had been established, was the first and only Irish Catholic president elected. Six of the thirty-six presidents, from Washington to Nixon, had Irish American backgrounds, but except for John Kennedy all of these were Protestant Irish, as were more recent presidents, Ronald Reagan and Bill Clinton.

The first Irish Catholic president, John F. Kennedy, is given the oath of office.

President Kennedy was a descendant of Irish Catholic politicians in Boston; he was elected on the "backs of three generations of district leaders and county chairmen."[85] His grandfather had been mayor of Boston; his father was the first Irish American Catholic to serve as ambassador to Great Britain. John Kennedy came from a small, wealthy New England elite, but he was a pragmatic politician: Day-to-day problems of food and shelter for ordinary Americans were critical issues to him. In the 1960 presidential election, Irish Catholic votes in New England, New York, and Pennsylvania helped to create Kennedy's victory. Nationwide, he received an estimated 75 percent of the Irish vote but only 50.1 percent of the total vote. As president, Kennedy acted not only on behalf of Irish Americans but also, to some extent, on behalf of America's other emergent urban groups, appointing the first Italian American and the first Polish American to a presidential cabinet and the first African American to head an independent government agency.[86]

THE IRISH IN THE ECONOMY

As we noted in Chapter 2, one type of structural assimilation involves large-scale movement by members of an immigrant group into the secondary-organization levels of a society, such as into positions in governmental agencies and private economic organizations, including farms and factories. The majority of Irish immigrants started out at the bottom of the economic pyramid, filling the hard, dirty, low-wage jobs in rural areas and in cities. As with other white immigrant groups, most Irish immigrants found jobs through preexisting ethnic networks and thereby avoided free-market competition. "The process was cloaked in favoritism and operated quite independently of qualifications. The result can be called 'ethnic mobility, collective style.'"[87]

The eighteenth-century Irish immigrants contributed significantly to the economic development of the colonies and the new nation. In New England and other northern states, they were important in commerce; they worked as weavers for textile industries and laborers for road systems. In the South they became farm laborers, farmers, and owners of small businesses. Their children moved up the economic ladder over the next few generations, sometimes at the expense of later European immigrants.[88]

Male and Female Work: The Irish after 1830

Irish labor was critical to industrial and commercial development in the United States. Irish immigrants after 1830 typically became urban workers, miners, or transportation workers. Hard, low-paying work was the lot of most. They had migrated looking for work—Irish men found it in unskilled jobs, on the docks and in the factories of large cities; Irish women found it as servants in Anglo-Protestant homes. Many Irish immigrants were single females unattached to family groups. Impoverished in an alien land, these women frequently moved into domestic work where they could live with a family. In the 1855 census of New York City, three-fourths of the domestics were Irish, although the Irish were only one-fourth of the population. Later immigrant women, such as Italian and Jewish immigrants, were not as likely to go into domestic work. This fact had little to do with differences in cultural backgrounds but reflected the different character of later migration: Jewish and Italian women generally came with their families. Irish women who came alone did so not by choice but because of adverse economic conditions in Ireland.[89]

Male immigrants became farm laborers, railroad laborers, miners, and textile workers. Many died helping build transportation systems, as the old saying "There's an Irishman buried under every railroad tie" indicates. As late as 1876, half of Irish-born Americans were still in the worst-paid, dirtiest jobs, compared with 10 to 20 percent of most other white groups.[90] Irish Catholics encountered direct institutionalized discrimination (see Chapter 1) in employment. Stereotyped as dumb, unskilled, or rowdy, Irish American men and women were denied decent-paying jobs by Protestant employers. Few would hire them except for unskilled positions. By the 1840s, Boston newspapers were carrying anti-Irish advertisements with the phrase "None need apply but Americans."[91]

Non-Irish observers have blamed Irish immigrants for the emergence of urban poverty. Against the contributions of such immigrants, argues one scholar, "must be set certain intangible social burdens on the whole community and some definite expenditures, of which poor relief through almshouses, hospitals, and dispensaries was most costly."[92] Many among the Irish became dependent on charity or public aid. But local and state governments in that period actually provided little support for the urban poor—the majority of whom were *not* Irish Americans.

Few among the millions of immigrants and their children moved quickly from rags to riches. Still, many did save some money, and many sent significant sums back to Ireland. This charitable impulse reduced their own chances for mobility in the United States. One study of Newburyport, Massachusetts, revealed that Irish American working-class families were more likely to have accumulated some property (usually housing) than was commonly thought. One price of accumulating such property was a spartan life; another was early employment of children, which reduced their education. Economic advance in one generation did not necessarily bring upward mobility for subsequent generations. In addition, building a separate church and parochial school system meant some drain on family resources.[93]

Irish Catholics began to move up the economic ladder after the Civil War. By the decade after the Civil War, Philadelphia had become a major eastern center for manufacturing and transportation, and the Irish Americans there began to move from unskilled labor to skilled positions. Economic success was reflected in the erection of churches, parochial schools, and charitable institutions. A significant number of Irish Americans in Philadelphia began to move into better housing in middle-income residential areas, although many still found themselves in segregated, inferior housing.[94]

Significant numbers of the Irish Catholics became upwardly mobile near the turn of the twentieth century. They entered the urban economy when expanding industries needed large numbers of low-wage workers. Major cities grew and developed as capitalists centered new types of manufacturing in the industrial heartland, from Pittsburgh to Chicago to Detroit. Powerful urban political machines facilitated mobility by providing jobs and other economic resources for the upward trek. Political machines channeled money into building projects, facilitating the emergence of a business class. Irish Americans were important in a few labor organizations in Massachusetts and New York as early as the 1850s. By the early 1900s unions had emerged among dockworkers, construction workers, and miners. To the present day, Irish Americans have been prominent in labor organizations, including the AFL-CIO.[95]

Irish Americans, especially Irish Protestants, had begun to penetrate business and professional arenas by the middle of the nineteenth century; the 1890 census showed 1.7 percent of foreign-born Irish men in professional positions. A small number of Irish Protestants became wealthy entrepreneurs. Among the handful of native-born U.S. millionaires in the period between 1761 and 1924, 8 percent were Irish, a proportion considerably smaller than the English and Scottish contingent.[96]

Although some progress was obvious for rank-and-file Irish American Catholics by the turn of the century, discrimination and poverty still had an impact. One study of Irish-born immigrants in 1890 Boston revealed an occupational distribution of 0 percent in the professions and 10 percent in other white-collar jobs, with most working in low-skilled jobs. This employment situation contrasted greatly with that of the native-born Boston residents, mostly non-Irish, 47 percent of whom had white-collar jobs.[97]

Mobility in the Twentieth Century

A study of Philadelphia's Irish population in 1900 found evidence of slow movement up the economic ladder. Although a large majority still worked in manufacturing, laboring, and domestic service jobs, some held political office. There was a small but growing middle-income group; a few had become prosperous in business, mining, and construction. This middle-income group soon grew to the point of being stereotyped as "lace curtain" Irish, a description based on the prosperity that enabled this more affluent group to afford lace window curtains. However, fewer than 10 percent of employed men and women held professional or managerial jobs; a majority were still relatively poor.[98]

Information available on mobility among Irish Americans after 1900 suggests increasing economic security for a growing segment. The mostly Protestant descendants of pre-1830 immigrants were still disproportionately concentrated in farming areas, in towns, and in southern and border states. In the late nineteenth and early twentieth centuries, and probably in later decades as well, a significant proportion became relatively prosperous farmers, owners of small businesses, and skilled blue-collar workers, as well as part of the growing clerical-job category. Over time, many blended into the Anglo-Protestant mainstream, though some remained poor and forgotten in rural areas.

By the 1930s Irish Catholics still had not blended into the Anglo-Protestant mainstream. In a study of Newburyport in the 1930s, Warner and Srole found Irish Americans moving closer to native Yankee residents in socioeconomic status. No Irish, however, could be found at the top. The Depression hit Irish Americans hard, postponing for a decade the major economic breakthrough just within their reach. Baltzell's study of Philadelphians in 1940 revealed that few people of wealth and influence were Catholic; white Protestants still dominated the top of the economic pyramid.[99]

Business leadership in the 1940s, 1950s, and 1960s continued to be British American. In those decades Irish American Catholics were less conspicuous in the ranks of leading scientists and industrialists than might have been expected. This may be in part because their ancestors brought little scientific or management experience from the homeland. Some have suggested that modest representation in scientific and managerial fields may have been due in part to the nature of much Catholic education, with its classical emphasis, but it was also because of anti-Catholic discrimination at the higher levels of business and industry.[100]

Recent Successes

Many Irish Catholics have been employed in government—in police, fire, and public works departments; in the courts; and in schools and colleges. In seeking government jobs, like other groups after them (for example, African Americans), they often faced less discrimination than they did in the business sector. In a few cities, the recruitment patterns for government jobs, frequently based on patronage and kinship networks, created a "one-big-family"-style government workforce. Such Irish governmental domination in Boston, to take one example, has been challenged by affirmative action lawsuits beginning in the 1970s and has contributed to tensions there between blacks and Latinos on the one side and Boston's Irish on the other.[101]

In recent decades, Irish Catholics have moved up economically. By the early 1970s, two-thirds of younger-generation Irish Catholic men held white-collar positions, compared with 38 percent of their fathers. Both generations were more likely to be found in better-paid, white-collar jobs than their counterparts in most other ethnic Catholic groups.[102] By the early 1990s, the occupational distribution for Irish Americans closely paralleled that of all (non-Latino) whites in the United States. Scotch-Irish Americans were more heavily represented in managerial and professional job categories and less likely to hold service or blue-collar jobs than all whites as a group. Although Scotch-Irish Americans fared substantially better than other Irish Americans on all economic indicators, both groups had a higher median family income and a lower rate of poverty than (non-Latino) whites as a group. The median income of Irish Americans is now only a little lower than that of English Americans.[103]

Today, Irish Americans hold positions of leadership in all areas of American life. The mass media symbols of Irish American success have typically been athletes, entertainers, politicians, or, less often, entrepreneurs such as Joseph Kennedy. Another group of Irish American heroes has received little notice—the growing group of Ph.D.s and academics. Catholics make up about one-fourth of faculty members in top state colleges and universities, and about half of these are Irish. Irish American Catholics are heavily represented in humanities departments. (Ireland has a very strong literary heritage.) Many graduate-trained Irish Catholics have moved into local, state, and federal government as lawyers, administrators, researchers, and elected officials. Daniel Patrick Moynihan, an Irish American and the U.S. senator from New York, has noted, "So many Irish-Americans have succeeded in various fields that their prominence no longer is noteworthy."[104]

EDUCATION

Organized education on a significant scale for Irish Protestants began after the Civil War. In the South, public schools spread in the Reconstruction period, and by the early twentieth century many of the Protestant Irish had taken advantage of them. The Catholic Irish, in contrast, relied on parochial and public schools in urban areas of the North for organized education. Because of the severe anti-Catholicism of the period, no Catholic schools of any kind existed in 1790. Parochial schools did not become numerous until the period between 1820 and 1840. In cities, some Irish Catholic children were beginning to receive public education, although the intense Anglo-Protestant pressures in the public schools gave strong impetus to the development of separate, church-related schools as a means of retaining ethnic identity. By the late 1800s and early 1900s, the center of the Irish Catholic community in numerous cities was a parish and parochial school system.[105]

By 1960, nearly 13,000 elementary and secondary Catholic schools had an enrollment of 5 million children. Irish Catholic Americans were at the center of this immense network, which was by then a subject of some political controversy in the United States. Financed by Catholic Americans, these private schools had gradually come to receive some public aid as well, bringing opposition from some Protestant and Jewish American groups and not a few court cases on the issue of separation of church and state.[106]

By 1910, Irish Catholics were going to college in large numbers, above the national average for all whites. The educational achievements of Irish Catholic Americans were increasingly impressive, with Catholic colleges being built in significant numbers and college attendance on the increase. The Presbyterian Irish had earlier made important contributions in the area of education, including the establishment of institutions such as Princeton University, to provide an educated ministry for Presbyterian churches.[107]

Today, Irish Americans continue to place great emphasis on education. Indeed, 1990 census data show that the educational attainment of Irish Americans as a group is now equal to that of non-Latino whites as a group. Other data indicate that the educational attainments of both Irish American Catholics and Protestants are increasing relative to the general white population.[108]

In the last decade a number of Irish American leaders have pressed for more coverage of Irish and Irish American history in U.S. schools and colleges. In 1997, Tom Hayden, a California State Senator of Irish heritage, proposed a bill that would reshape the educational curriculum so that children in the racially and ethnically diverse state of California could learn about the potato famines discussed earlier. Hayden was concerned that the children learn about the Irish who emigrated because of the famine and starvation brought on by actions of the English oppressors. Similar efforts to change the educational curriculum to include more Irish history have been made in New Jersey and New York.[109]

RELIGION

In the political and economic spheres, Irish Americans were pressured early to assimilate, nonreciprocally, to the established Anglo-Protestant culture. In the religious sphere, the earliest Irish immigrants, whether Catholic or Ulster Presbyterian, mostly blended into various American Protestant denominations. However, later groups of Irish Catholic immigrants played a major role in firmly establishing what may well be the most influential non-Protestant institution in the United States— the Roman Catholic church. Although the Catholic church has had to adapt to some extent to the preexisting Protestant system, its impact has been to accent the issue of separation of church and state and to reinforce the right of all Americans to choose any faith.

Irish Catholics fought intense anti-Catholic prejudice and sometimes violent discrimination against rooting the Catholic church in Anglo-Protestant soil. New churches sprang up wherever Catholic workers went. Priests had long suffered with the poor in Ireland and in the United States, so they were generally respected. In addition to Catholic church organizations, related benevolent and charitable community organizations were of great consequence for Irish Americans. The omnipresent Ancient Order of Hibernians is but one major example.[110]

The Catholic church's hierarchy in the United States has long been disproportionately composed of Irish Americans. One analysis of Catholic bishops from 1789 to 1935 revealed that 58 percent were of Irish extraction. In the 1970s, one-third of the priests and half of the upper hierarchy were Irish Americans, compared with 17 percent of the total Catholic population. In the 1990s Irish Americans still account for a disproportionate number of Catholic priests but no longer generate a disproportionate number of Catholic bishops in the United States.[111]

In northern cities, many Irish American neighborhoods have been built around a parish church. In certain large cities, local politics has often blended with church and school, as have local stores and taverns.

> Among Irish Americans, that particular part of the urban turf with which you are identified and in which live most of the people on whom you have a special claim . . . is virtually indistinguishable from the parish; when asked where they are from, Irish Catholics in many cities give not the community's name but the name of the parish—Christ the King, St. Barnabas, All Saints . . . and so forth.[112]

In the last few decades, many central city churches have been closed or merged, as Irish Americans have moved to the suburbs. Today, in the suburbs of many cities the Irish Catholic parish survives. Loyalty to the church remains strong; one 1990 survey by the National Opinion Research Center (NORC) found that more than half of Irish Catholics go to services every week, a much higher proportion than among other whites in the survey.[113]

Irish American priests have shaped the U.S. Catholic church in a number of distinctive ways, some conservative and some progressive. Irish American archbishops and cardinals have often been politically and socially conservative, while many local priests have led progressive struggles, such as the struggle for expanded civil rights. For example, the former president of Notre Dame University, Father Theodore M. Hesburgh, symbolizes the liberalism in Irish Catholicism. For many years, including those he spent on the U.S. Commission on Civil Rights, Father Hesburgh has been outspoken in his support for civil rights laws, antisegregation action, and affirmative action benefiting African Americans and other people of color.[114]

ASSIMILATION THEORIES AND THE IRISH

Now we can examine how the theories and concepts discussed in Chapter 2 help illuminate the experiences of Irish Americans. As we have seen, some power–conflict analysts (such as students of internal colonialism) specifically omit immigrant groups such as the "white ethnics" from their analyses, preferring to focus on certain racially subordinated groups because these have endured much greater violence and repression in the North American colonies and the United States.

The assimilation theories of Milton Gordon and Andrew Greeley seem the most relevant for analysis of groups such as Irish, Italian, and Jewish Americans. Yet in looking at these groups from the assimilation perspective, we must keep in mind something many assimilationists tend to forget—the substantial conflict and ethnic stratification that has characterized the experiences of these Americans.

Compared with many other ethnic and racial groups, Irish Americans are several steps higher on the U.S. ladder of economic success and dominance. Each generation of Irish Americans became ever more incorporated into the core institutions than prior generations. The eighteenth-century Irish moved up the social and economic ladders slowly; they were typically Protestants. Substantial assimilation came by the late nineteenth century for many of the descendants of these Irish immigrants. One observer argues that this group blended in rather quickly, for "their social and political activities have mixed freely and spread freely through the general mass of American citizenship."[115] Indeed, by the early 1900s the successful assimilation of the "Scotch Irish" Protestants was being held up as a standard for subsequent immigrant groups to emulate.[116]

Although certain propagandists for the Scotch-Irish, such as Theodore Roosevelt, exaggerated the rapidity of this cultural and structural assimilation, there is much truth to the view that the early Irish immigrants and their descendants assimilated relatively rapidly at the level of the English American culture, slowly but surely at the level of structural integration into the economy and the polity, and gradually at the level of primary social ties. Sometime in the last century, many Scotch-Irish became a difficult-to-distinguish part of the Anglo-Protestant mainstream.

On the whole, assimilation came more slowly for Irish Catholics, who entered in increasing numbers after 1830. Some adaptation to the dominant Anglo-Protestant culture, particularly learning the English language and certain basic symbols and values, is necessary to successful achievements within U.S. institutions. Some cultural assimilation had come early for most Irish Catholic immigrants. U.S. cities offered hope for escape from the oppressive conditions of Ireland, and the expanding industrial environment meant a greater chance for mobility. Significantly, Ireland's customs and U.S. customs often had some similarities. The English language was familiar to many immigrants. While assimilation at all levels took several generations, significant cultural assimilation took place in the first decade.[117]

Religion was an exception. Most of these later Irish Catholic immigrants did not become Protestants. For the Irish American communities, external Anglo-Protestant hostility and a common religious background reinforced a protective separatist reaction. Conflict with the Anglo-Protestant nativists intensified Irish American commitment to the Catholic church. Over time the dominant Protestant culture came to accommodate Catholic and Jewish religious communities. Nevertheless, the Catholic churches made adjustments to the English-dominated milieu in such areas as language and restructured church organizations. Such adaptations made the U.S. Catholic church and school system an important medium within which new Catholic immigrants began their acculturation and even some structural assimilation (for example, priests helped in securing employment).[118]

Has commitment to the Catholic religion declined in later generations of Irish American Catholics? Some analysts have claimed this, arguing that cultural assimilation will thus soon be complete. Some recent studies have not found this to be the case, however. As a group, Irish Americans are among the most likely to attend mass of all Catholic groups. There has been an increase in religious devotion over the last few decades.[119]

In regard to the dimensions Milton Gordon calls *behavior-receptional assimilation* and *attitude-receptional assimilation*—in effect, discrimination and prejudice—there have been substantial changes since the mid-nineteenth century for the Catholic Irish. Stereotyping has declined substantially since the days of the ape-like image, although some negative feelings directed against Irish Catholicism and urban machine politics have persisted among many Protestant Americans. Anti-Catholic discrimination has declined significantly, although it still can be seen at the very highest levels of the U.S. economy and government. As we noted earlier, the United States has had only one Irish Catholic president.

Patterns of Structural Assimilation for the Irish

At the structural-assimilation (secondary-group) level, Irish Americans made slow but significant movement, over several generations, into Anglo-Protestant organizations and institutions. We have seen the steady movement of the Irish from unskilled work into white-collar occupations—and the relatively high occupational levels of Irish American Catholics in recent decades. Residential dispersal, often to suburban areas, has paralleled these developments, although some residential self-segregation persists in some cities in the East and Midwest. After a century of struggle in the political sphere, Irish Catholics are now substantially integrated at the local and state government levels; in the last few decades, they have moved significantly into the judicial, legislative, and executive branches of the federal government, if not yet in representative numbers at the very top. At the local level, Irish Americans have long shaped urban politics in a number of cities.

Some have argued that the higher status accompanying economic assimilation is causing many Irish Americans to move away from the Democratic party.

Looking at the period between the 1940s and the 1960s, for example, Glazer and Moynihan argued that the "mass of the Irish have left the working class, and in considerable measure the Democratic party as well."[120] Yet voting data for roughly that same period suggests continuing Irish American loyalty to the Democratic party. Urban politicians, particularly Democrats, have long given great attention to the Irish American community, and many Democratic party leaders are still Irish. An analysis by Andrew Greeley found that 61 percent of Irish Catholics and 54 percent of Irish Protestants identified themselves as Democrats; 28 percent of Irish Catholics and 22 percent of Irish Protestants labeled themselves as liberal. This suggests that one assimilation theory of ethnic politics—that economic mobility destroys traditional ethnic voting patterns—is not necessarily correct. As of the late-1990s, absorption into a Republican party dominated by white Anglo-Protestants has not happened for the majority of Irish American Catholics—and perhaps even for a majority of Irish American Protestants.[121]

As for structural incorporation at the level of primary-group ties, data on informal groups and voluntary associations point to some interesting trends. Ethnic clubs and organizations, since World War II if not before, have apparently declined in importance for the Irish Catholics. Benevolent societies have declined in numbers; so have the great fund drives to support Irish causes. This probably indicates increasing integration into the voluntary associations of the larger society. Irish American attendance at Catholic parochial schools has also declined, which may mean that children of Irish ancestry are making more friendships across ethnic lines than ever before.[122]

Intermarriage is a major indicator of assimilation at the primary-group level. One national survey in the 1960s reported substantial endogamy (within-group marriage) for Irish Catholics; 65 percent of respondents with Irish fathers also had Irish mothers, and 43 percent of Irish married men had a wife with an Irish father. Yet over half the respondents to the national survey had a non-Irish spouse. One more recent survey of a large metropolitan area in New York found 82 percent of Irish Americans there had mixed ethnic ancestry. And in 1997 one commentator estimated that two-thirds of Irish Americans are now marrying outside the group.[123]

Is There an Irish American Identity Today?

The intermarriage rate poses challenges to continuing Irish American identity. Among the final stages of assimilation is what Milton Gordon and Andrew Greeley have seen as "identificational" adaptation. Ultimately, this type of assimilation would mean a loss of a sense of Irishness and the development of a sense of peoplehood that is solely American or Anglo-Protestant American. One's sense of identity would no longer be Irish. This may have happened for many Irish Protestants, but the majority of Irish Catholics still seem to have a feeling of Irishness, although for some it may be a vague sense.

Some Irish Catholic writers have argued that Irish Americans are losing their ethnic identity because of the decline in immigration from Ireland. Marjorie

Fallows has argued that the American Irish are fully acculturated to the Anglo-Protestant culture; even Irish Catholicism has become generally "Americanized" and fully compatible with the "Protestant ethic." In her view distinctive ethnic traits that are culturally significant are rare among the American Irish today. Fallows and others have argued that even though there are still a few ethnically distinct Irish Catholic communities in northern cities, this does not mean that most Irish Catholics live in such communities. Indeed, they assert that cultural and structural (primary-group) assimilation are all but complete for those Irish Catholics living outside ethnic neighborhoods.[124]

Richard Alba interviewed respondents in eight white ethnic groups in a metropolitan area in upper New York State. He found ethnic identity declining somewhat in significance among Irish Americans, especially in the fourth and later generations. However, those with pure Irish ancestry had a stronger sense of their ethnic identity than most of the other groups examined. Those with mixed Irish ancestry were also loyal to their Irish heritage. They were three times as likely to identify solely as Irish as they were to choose another ethnicity from their mixed background. In addition, the Irish American respondents were less likely than those in other ethnic groups to attach no importance to their ethnic identity.[125]

The Irish Catholic group has changed over generations of contact with the public school system and the mass media, but it has retained enough distinctiveness to persist as an ethnic group into the last decade of the twentieth century. The theory of ethnogenesis discussed in Chapter 2 seems appropriate to Irish Catholic Americans. This ethnic group has been more than a European nationality group. The Irish who came in large numbers after 1830 forged, over several generations, a distinctive U.S. ethnic group. Ethnicity was an important way for the Irish Catholics to attach themselves to the new scene, a way of asserting their own identity in a buzzing confusion of diverse nationality groups. For Irish Catholics, because of nativistic attacks and discrimination, ethnic identity was less voluntary in the first few decades than it was to become later. In the beginning Irish Americans had a cultural heritage that was distinctly different from that of the British American host culture. Over several generations of sometimes conflictual interaction with Anglo-Protestants, the Irish immigrants and their descendants adapted substantially to the host society. This process created a distinctive Irish American ethnic group that still reflects elements both of its nationality background and of the host culture.

The persistence of Irish American ethnicity and its positive and negative functions was evident in the desegregation struggle that took place in South Boston between the 1970s and the 1980s. Boston's predominantly Irish working-class community's vigorous, sometimes violent, opposition to a judge's 1974 school desegregation plan for the area involved more than a legal desegregation struggle. The controversy reflected different views of schooling and of urban communities; the South Boston Irish have seen the central-city schools as a socializing force, reinforcing local and traditional family and community values, whereas many black Bostonians and some suburban whites have viewed desegregated public schools primarily as avenues of upward mobility for all children. Irish

American resistance to desegregation of central-city neighborhoods and schools has been based in part on anti-black prejudices, but it has also been based on the desire of Irish Americans to protect their ethnic institutions against intruders, whoever they may be. Historian Ronald Formisano writes that court-ordered school desegregation "was at one level an attempt by mobile professionals and elites to impose their liberal, cosmopolitan, middle-class values on working- and lower-middle-class people who embraced the values of localism and personalism. The residents of defended neighborhoods certainly saw desegregation in part as an attempt by elite outsiders to change them and their way of life."[126]

In an analysis of opinion poll data, Irish American sociologist Andrew Greeley has examined four survey questions that tap what he views as traditional Irish Catholic sociocultural traits: gregariousness, gathering in a public house, religious intensity, and activity in religious organizations. As of 1987, none of these had been eliminated from Irish American culture; on all four survey questions Irish Catholics ranked higher in social activity than did the national sample as a whole.[127] Greeley concluded that Irish Catholic distinctiveness persists, particularly in certain northern cities.

> On the basis of the evidence available to us, the Irish-American subculture is likely to persist indefinitely. The Irish Catholic Americans will continue to be different in their religion, their family life, their political style, their world view, their drinking behavior, and their personalities. . . . The Irish will continue to be affluent and probably will become even more affluent as they settle down securely amidst the upper crusts of the middle class with a firm foothold in the nation's economic and political, if not intellectual and artistic, elites.[128]

Greeley even found some evidence of a return to higher levels of self-conscious identification among young Irish Americans. Other reports have also indicated a resurgence of interest in things Irish. For example, one 1997 survey reported a growing interest in studying the original Irish language (Gaelic), Irish dance, and Irish music among Irish Americans. And we have noted the pressures being placed on public schools to include more Irish and Irish American history. In addition, there has been some interest in having a Gaelic mass at some Irish American celebrations. Whether this trend will continue remains to be seen. Whatever happens, however, it is clear that the impact of the Irish background on Irish American thought and behavior remains strong.[129]

SUMMARY

The Irish began moving to North America quite early, with indentured servants and farmers entering in the 1700s. This early immigration apparently included more southern, or Celtic, Irish than the often exaggerated accounts of the "Scotch-Irish" have suggested. The majority of the descendants of these early migrants were, or became, Protestants, settling disproportionately in the South and in frontier areas. Many of the descendants of these early settlers became part of the Protestant mainstream over the next several generations. However, a significant proportion remained poor. The Protestant Irish in particular have received little attention from scholars.

After the 1830s, large numbers of Irish Catholic immigrants settled in the cities of the North, where many suffered violence at the hands of Catholic-hating nativists and discrimination by Anglo-American employers. Poverty-stricken Irish Catholics slowly began moving toward economic equality with older groups. Conflict, sometimes violent, marked their climb. Frequently political innovators, the Irish Catholics shaped the political organizations of major cities in order to facilitate their integration into the dominant political and economic institutions. They desegregated U.S. religious institutions by bringing in a strong Catholic church and school complex.

Economic mobility has been so dramatic that by the 1990s Irish Americans ranked at or above the national average for all whites on a number of important socioeconomic indicators, including educational level, occupational distribution, and income. Today, as we move into the twenty-first century, Irish Americans are a major segment of Middle America.

CHAPTER 5

Italian Americans

For many decades Italian Americans have found themselves to be targets of hostility from other racial and ethnic groups, especially Anglo Protestants. This mostly Catholic group has been attacked for being unsophisticated, superpatriotic "hardhats" with connections to the "Mafia." By the 1960s, a counterattack developed. Many white ethnic leaders, including Italian Americans, came to view Anglo-Protestant intellectuals and officials critically: "The ethnic American is sick of being stereotyped as a racist and a dullard by phony white liberals, pseudo black militants and patronizing bureaucrats. . . . He pays the bill for every major governmental program and gets nothing or little in the way of return."[1] Richard Gambino, an Italian American scholar, has noted that "the white elite has shown little understanding of Italian-American history, culture, or problems and less empathy with them."[2]

The militant defense of things Italian and the achievements of Italian Americans had, by the 1980s and 1990s, brought this group greater acceptance among other Americans. Clear signals of the rising prominence of Italian Americans in the United States could be seen in the selection of Geraldine Ferraro, an Italian American member of Congress, as the Democratic party's vice-presidential candidate in 1984 and the substantial national support for New York governor Mario Cuomo as a possible Democratic presidential nominee during the 1990s.

ITALIAN IMMIGRATION

Italian explorers, including Cristoforo Colombo (Christopher Columbus), played a major role in opening the Americas to European colonization and exploitation. An Italian navigator, Amerigo Vespucci, made a number of voyages to the Americas shortly after Colombo's voyages. Because of his early maps, the continents even came to be named after him.[3]

Numbers of Immigrants

Small numbers of Italians migrated to the colonies prior to the 1800s. Schiavo notes that "in Virginia, a small group of Italians settled with Filippo Mazzei in 1774 in order to introduce wine making and Italian agricultural methods."[4] Thomas Jefferson was influenced by Mazzei's intellectual talents and invited other Italian agricultural experts and crafts workers to Virginia. Jefferson was responsible for bringing an Italian architect to design his home at Monticello, Italian artists to create sculptures and frescoes to decorate the U.S. Capitol, and Italian musicians to form the first U.S. Marine Corps band.[5]

Since 1820, more than 5 million Italians have migrated to the United States. Until 1860 the migration was quite small. Between 1861 and 1880, migration picked up a little, totaling 67,500. In the next four decades, Italian immigration became heavy, with more than 4 million recorded immigrants. Prior to 1880, most immigrants were from northern Italy; after 1880 they came in very large numbers from the south. The heavy migration of poor farmers and laborers began just a few decades after the formerly independent regions of Italy were unified into one state.[6]

As we noted in Chapter 2, certain factors are relevant to the study of migration: the point of origin, the destination, the migrating units, and the larger context. As with the Irish, land and agricultural problems triggered much of the Italian out-migration. National unification under a government controlled by northern Italians had brought heavy taxes to southern Italy. Hence, low income, poor soil, a feudal land system, unreasonable taxes, and government corruption were important push factors at the point of origin.[7] The often exaggerated image of the United States as a place of expanding opportunity was a major pull factor. Some came to stay, but for the majority of the early immigrants the United States was seen as a temporary workplace. A considerable portion of the immigration was stimulated by expanding industrial capitalism in the United States; many came as a result of labor recruiting in Italy.[8]

Migration along kinship networks, typical for poor and working-class migrants from European countries, lessened the pain of resettlement. Italians came in large numbers from the same villages. Chains of kin migration across the Atlantic linked areas in Italy and America. Most immigrants headed for urban points; like the Irish, most had had enough of farm life. Industrialized East Coast cities were popular destinations. In larger cities immigrants often went to "Little Italies," where fellow villagers resided.[9] Remigration for Italians was well above that of other groups. In some years in the early 1900s, returnees equalled 60 to 70 percent of new immigrants.[10]

Nativist agitation by Anglo-Protestant groups resulted in legislative attempts to restrict this immigration. Between 1924 and 1965, immigration quotas sharply curtailed Italian immigration. The Immigration Act of 1924 established a small, discriminatory quota for Italians. By 1929, the annual quota for Italians was only 5,802, compared with 65,721 for Great Britain. The quota system was based on Protestant nativists' belief that those countries that had furnished the most "good American citizens"—that is, immigrants prior to 1890—should receive the largest quotas. The British, Germans, Irish, and Scandinavians were given three-quarters of the total, although the demand from those countries had slackened considerably by that time.[11]

Pressure on Italy's small quota produced a backlog of 250,000 applicants by the time the 1965 Immigration Act replaced the discriminatory national–origin quota system. The first stage of the 1965 act allowed the unfilled quotas of some countries to supplement the filled quotas of certain other countries. The number of Italian entrants increased significantly. In 1966, some 26,447 Italian immigrants were admitted; in 1967, 28,487. However, the 1965 act set an annual limit of 20,000 for each country beginning in 1968, and the backlog of Italian applicants again increased. Italian migration continued at a high level in the early 1970s. By the late 1970s, the backlog was exhausted, and since that time the annual number of Italian immigrants has dropped sharply. In the period between 1981 and 1992, a total of about 38,000 Italian immigrants entered the United States.[12] More than 11 million Americans listed Italian as their first ancestry in the 1990 census, most of whom were U.S. born.[13] Counting both the first and second ancestries listed on the 1990 census forms, nearly 15 million Americans identified themselves as Italian Americans, making them the fifth-largest ancestry group in the United States.[14]

Life for the Immigrants

What was life like for the large numbers of Italians who immigrated in the peak period between 1880 and 1920? Most worked as unskilled laborers on transportation systems such as canals and railroads and on water and sewer systems. Pay was low, and individuals as well as families were usually poor. Segregated in "Little Italy" ghettos within cities, Italian immigrants and their children frequently faced economic, political, and social discrimination. There is irony here, since *ghetto* is thought to be a Venetian word first applied to the practice of segregating Jews in Italy in the sixteenth century. In the United States it was the Italian Catholics who found themselves in ghettos. In many cities Italian Americans replaced earlier groups as part of an invasion-succession process. Yet other groups would follow on their heels.[15]

Some analysts have viewed working-class communities in cities as disorganized "slum" areas with little positive social life. This was not true for Italian American communities. As with the Irish before them, Italians developed their own extensive friendship and kinship circles, political clubs, avenues for upward mobility, and community celebrations. Central to Italian American communities were indigenous organizations and festivals, including mutual-benefit societies whose members made monthly payments to ensure a proper funeral upon their demise. In 1927 Chicago had two hundred mutual-aid societies and many other clubs and lodges. Italian newspapers flourished.[16]

Italian American communities, such as the North End of Boston, were laid on the bedrock of kinship networks, with extended-family members living near one another. As a result, and contrary to nativist propaganda, few among first-

An Italian American street festival in Boston.

generation Italian Americans ended up in almshouses. As in Italy, Italian immigrant families in the United States tended to be patriarchal, and kinship solidarity was emphasized. Home ownership was highly valued. The local communities were critical to keeping Italian Americans in certain northern and midwestern cities.[17]

STEREOTYPES

By the end of the nineteenth century, nativist stereotypes of the "apelike" Irish were giving way to negative stereotypes of southern and eastern European immigrants, including Italian Catholics. The stereotypes were harsh and frequently absurd:

> It is urged that the Italian race stock is inferior and degraded; that it will not assimilate naturally or readily with the prevailing "Anglo-Saxon" race stock of this country; that intermixture, if practicable, will be detrimental; that servility, filthy habits of life, and a hopelessly degraded standard of needs and ambitions have been ingrained in Italians by centuries of oppression and abject poverty.[18]

Such indictments appeared in national magazines. In the 1888 *North American Review,* labor activist T. V. Powderly alleged that southern and eastern Europeans were an inferior stock that lived immoral lives revolving around liquor.[19] Italian immigrants were scorned by nativists as "dangerous, contemptible, inferior, and disloyal"—the "off-scourings of the world."[20] Some even interpreted the energy, hard work, and ambition of the immigrants as dangerous. Referring to Italian and other immigrants from southern and eastern Europe, one writer warned in a magazine article in 1913, "Unless Americans are careful, they will take over."[21]

Myths of Biological Inferiority

Popular writers, scholars, and members of Congress warned of the peril of allowing "inferior" stocks from Europe into the United States. Kenneth L. Roberts, a prominent journalist, wrote of the dangers of the newer immigrants making Americans a mongrel race: "Races can notbe cross-bred without mongrelization, any more than breeds of dogs can be cross-bred without mongrelization. The American nation was founded and developed by the Nordic race, but if a few more million members of the Alpine, Mediterranean and Semitic races are poured among us, the result must inevitably be a hybrid race of people as worthless and futile as the good-for-nothing mongrels of Central America and southeastern Europe."[22] The "Alpine, Mediterranean, and Semitic races" generally covered countries of heavy emigration other than those of northern Europe; the Italians and European Jews were thought by such writers to be examples.

Half-truths about disease and illiteracy were circulated about the southern and eastern European immigrants. It was true in some years between 1880 and 1920 that half the adult Italian immigrants could not read and write, but in other years the overwhelming majority were literate. In no year were the charges of total illiteracy leveled at Italian Americans by the press and politicians accurate.[23]

In the first three decades of the twentieth century, Anglo-Protestant stereotypes of the immigrants' intellectual inferiority were based in part on misreadings of the results of new psychological tests inaccurately labeled intelligence (IQ) tests. The term *intelligence test* is inaccurate because the tests measured only selected, learned verbal and quantitative skills, not a broad or basic intelligence. In 1912 Henry Goddard gave Alfred Binet's diagnostic test and related tests to a large number of immigrants from southern and eastern Europe. His data supposedly showed that 83 percent of Jewish and 79 percent of Italian immigrants were "feeble-minded," a category naively defined in terms of low scores on the new English-language tests.[24]

During World War I prominent psychologists developed verbal and performance tests for large-scale testing of many draftees. Although the results were not used for military purposes, detailed analyses were published in the 1920s and gained public and congressional attention because of the racial-inferiority interpretation many Anglo-American psychologists placed on the test scores of the southern and eastern European immigrants among the draftees.[25]

In 1923 Carl Brigham, a Princeton psychologist who would later play a role in developing college entrance tests, argued for the intellectual inferiority of white immigrant groups, including Italian Americans, drawing on data from the army tests. The average scores for foreign-born draftees ranged from highs of 14.87 for

English and 14.34 for Scottish draftees, to an average of 13.77 for all white draftees, to lows of 10.74 for Polish and 11.01 for Italian draftees. The low test scores for groups such as the Italian Americans were boldly explained in *racial* terms; those low-scoring groups were considered not only unintelligent but also "inferior racial stocks." These results were used by psychologists such as Brigham to support the ideology of "Nordic" superiority being espoused by racist theorists such as Madison Grant. Brigham also argued that the sharp increase in southern and eastern European immigration had lowered the general level of American intelligence.[26]

The political implications of Brigham's analysis were proclaimed: Immigration limits were necessary, and political means (for example, government-ordered sterilization) should be developed to prevent the continued propagation of "defective strains" in the U.S. population.[27] Here was pseudoscientific support for such government action as passage of the 1924 Immigration Act, which would soon restrict southern European immigration.

Important in the stereotyping of Italian immigrants is the role of the government, a point underscored by Omi and Winant in their racial formation theory (see Chapter 2). The official definition of these immigrants as undesirable racial or ethnic groups was stimulated by psychologists working with government agencies, in this case the U.S. armed forces, and their research was used by the Congress to support racist arguments to restrict immigration.

The "intelligence" differences measured by the brief psychological tests were assumed to reflect the inferior or superior genetic background of European "racial" stocks. In the early decades of the twentieth century, few seriously considered the possibility that the linguistic (English), cultural (northern European–American), and educational bias in the tests and in the psychologists' interpretive procedures could account for the "racial" differences.[28]

Some immigrant leaders developed strategies for dealing with concern over "blood" lineage. One prominent Italian American leader, Fiorello La Guardia, suffered personal attacks that incorporated stereotypes. For his criticism of officials such as President Herbert Hoover he received letters such as the following: "You should go back where you belong and advise Mussolini how to make good honest citizens in Italy. The Italians are preponderantly our murderers and bootleggers."[29] La Guardia's countertactic was often biting humor. When asked to provide material on his family background for the *New York World*, he saw the ghost of "blood" inferiority behind the request and commented: "I have no family tree. The only member of my family who has one is my dog Yank. He is the son of Doughboy, who was the son of Siegfried, who was the son of Tannhäuser, who was the son of Wotan. A distinguished family tree, to be sure—but after all he's only a son of a bitch."[30] Humor is one useful coping response for hostile stereotyping.

Ethnic slurs and epithets, including *dago, wop,* and *guinea,* that have often been hurled at Italian Americans reveal the intensity of non-Italian hostility. *Dago,* a corruption of the Spanish name Diego, was originally used for Spaniards or Mexicans. After 1880, however, it was applied to Italian immigrants. Similarly, the term *guinea* was an early term for African Americans, whose ancestors had come from the Guinea coast of Africa. After 1880 Anglo-Americans used *guinea* to classify Italians as "no better than blacks."[31] The ease with which epithets are transferred to later racial–ethnic groups reveals not only the fear that established groups have of newcomers but also the way in which the newcomers may come to be classified, as in the case of the Italian immigrants for a time, as somehow *not white*.

The Mafia Myth

Into the late 1990s perhaps the most persistent of Italian American stereotypes has been the image of criminality. By the 1870s Italians were depicted as lawless, knife-wielding thugs looking for a fight. Even a report of the influential U.S. Immigration Commission, issued in the early 1900s, argued that certain types of criminality were "inherent in the Italian race."[32] Yet the validity of the criminality stereotype is disputed by official government data from the early decades of this century. For example, the arrest rate for drunkenness and disorderly conduct for the Italian foreign-born in 1910 was quite low—158 per 100,000 people, compared with 202 for American-born whites. The imprisonment rate in 1910 was much lower than public stereotypes would suggest: 527 prisoners per 100,000 for the Italian-born, compared to 727 for the English and Welsh foreign-born.[33]

Small-scale crime, fostered by poverty and discrimination, was a problem in urban communities, but it usually did not involve a criminal conspiracy. Prohibition catapulted some Italian Americans into organized crime, at the time controlled mostly by Irish and Jewish Americans. By 1940 two dozen Italian American "crime families" were operating in major cities. For many immigrant groups, including Italian Americans, such crime has been one of the only avenues for economic mobility. Unfortunately, the Sicilian term *Mafia* has been used to describe organized crime, though many of these gangsters have been neither Sicilian nor Italian. Significantly, Italian Americans had *low* crime rates in the 1920s and 1930s. What data are available suggest that foreign-born Italian Americans had crime rates close to those for all native-born Americans.[34]

The image of Italian criminality has taken on a widespread mythological character; the stereotype of the Italian American male as a Mafia hoodlum committed to crime and violence persists. Into the 1990s, Italian names for criminals in various TV programs and movies have implied ties to the so-called "Mafia." Without exception, every non-Italian respondent in Waters's study of white ethnics in California and Pennsylvania used the Mafia and gangsters to characterize Italian Americans; most said their ideas were based on media images.[35]

The Mafia myth will not die. In the fall of 1997 the CBS television network aired a miniseries, *Bella Mafia*, about several Italian American wives linked to organized crime. Some Italian Americans, including the National Italian American News Bureau, protested the "gangster" stereotypes of Italian Americans and encouraged viewers to protest by not watching the program.[36] In the late 1990s, other Italian Americans have fought against stereotypes on labels and trademarks.

One lawyer working with the Commission for Social Justice of the Order of the Sons of Italy in America—a group with half a million members—has successfully stopped the federal government from issuing label trademarks that are insulting to Italian Americans, such as product labels with terms like "Mafia Mob" or "Cosa Nostra."[37]

That organized crime continues as a major enterprise cannot be disputed. That a small proportion of Italian Americans have played and continue to play a role in it is not disputed. That these Italian Americans control a nationwide crime syndicate with little help from other racial and ethnic groups can be strongly disputed; that the Italian (Sicilian) term *Mafia* should be used to describe such a hypothetical syndicate can be rejected. Organized crime is an enterprise drawing from most racial and ethnic groups; Italian Americans are a small percentage of such criminals today. FBI statistics show that only 4 percent of the 500,000 Americans estimated to be involved in organized crime belong to Italian American crime networks. In addition, reports in the 1990s indicated that, except in New York City and Chicago's suburbs, the power of Italian American crime families had declined significantly. Federal prosecutions and convictions had broken up most surviving crime families by the 1990s. More recent immigrant groups, including some from Asia and Latin America, had taken over much organized crime in U.S. cities.[38]

Stereotypes and Discrimination

One study of the portrayal of Italian Americans on prime-time television examined a sample of 263 programs for one season in the 1980s. The study found that negative images of Italian Americans outnumbered positive images by two to one. Most of the ninety-six Italian characters in the shows studied were men with low-status jobs. A significant percentage were portrayed as criminals, and many were pictured as "lovable or laughable dimwits who worked in jobs that offered little pay and less prestige." The majority of Italian Americans portrayed on television made grammatical errors, misunderstood English words, or spoke broken English.[39]

One Italian American in California described his experience with ethnic slurs: "When I joined the office in the new location I became a member of the Rotary Club, and of course there were very few Italian members. So the minute I came on board, they started referring to me as the Godfather of the country." He went on to say that he found this humor very degrading, since he had to explain that he had no ties to the so-called Mafia. Numerous other Italian Americans have reported similar experiences, including discrimination in corporate workplaces and much barbed Mafia joking.[40]

The Mafia myth appeared in the 1984 presidential election when a smear campaign aimed at Democratic vice-presidential candidate Geraldine Ferraro, an Italian American, insinuated that *she* had "mob connections" because her husband had inherited a real estate business founded by his father and the brother of a New York crime figure. Recalling the first time her son had been called a "wop," when he was six or seven years old, Ferraro indicated that encounters with anti-Italian attitudes were common. The problem of the Mafia myth has also plagued the presidential aspirations of New York governor Mario Cuomo since the mid-1980s. One of the reasons he gave for not running for president in 1992 was that anti-Italian prejudice would hurt his candidacy: "People who didn't know me said years ago that they would not vote for me because I was apt to have Mafia connections."[41] More recently, a mid-1990s national survey by the Joint Civic Committee found that three-fourths of Americans still viewed Italians as somehow linked to crime.

The Mafia image is not the only negative stereotype to which Italian Americans are subjected. Among all the European ancestry groups included in Alba's 1980s study of white ethnics in a large metropolitan area of upper New York State, the Italian American respondents reported encountering the greatest number of stereotypes. The stereotyped images referred to physical appearance (big noses), mannerisms (talking with hands), family life (being especially family-oriented), as well as alleged Mafia connections. Similarly, Waters's non-Italian white respondents in a California and Pennsylvania study held both negative and positive stereotypes of Italian Americans. Some described Italians as dirty, loud, temperamental, selfish, unambitious, combative, and not very bright; others listed characteristics such as having excellent food, doing well in business, being affectionate, being family-oriented, and being clean housekeepers.[42]

CONFLICT

The myth of peaceful progress is again dispelled by the history of struggles of Italian Americans with Anglo-Protestant nativists, Irish Catholics, and African Americans. Irish and Italian Americans fought on the streets of Boston by the 1860s, and Italian parents accompanied their children to school for protection. In the 1870s Irish American workers on strike in New York attacked Italian American strikebreakers. Four Italians were killed in Pennsylvania in a clash with striking Irish miners.

By the 1880s Anglo-Protestant nativists had initiated attempts to control immigrants from southern Italy, sometimes in the form of vigilante action. In the 1880s in Buffalo, New York, more than three hundred Italians—most of the local Italian population—were detained by police after an incident in which one Italian had killed another; only two of the three hundred were found to be holding weapons. The Italian American community even protested to the Italian government. Replying to the governor of New York, the police chief of Buffalo explained that he thought Italian Americans as a rule carried concealed weapons and were a threat to social order.[43]

In this early period several dozen Italian immigrants were killed by mobs in the South motivated by economic competition and a desire to maintain racial lines. Italian immigrants were viewed as a threat to white solidarity in the South because they were more likely than other whites to support black political rights.

They often worked alongside blacks as laborers or sold to them as small shop-keepers. In one town five Sicilian shopkeepers were lynched for this reason.[44] One well-publicized attack occurred in New Orleans after the 1891 murder of a white police superintendent who was investigating crime among Italian immigrants. A number of immigrants were jailed for the murder, and the police refused to intervene when a large group led by prominent citizens stormed the jail and killed eleven of them. Newspapers and major political figures praised the deed, using the incident to advance the stereotypical theme of criminality. Even President Theodore Roosevelt made negative comments about Italian immigrants, calling the 1891 lynchings in New Orleans "a rather good thing."[45]

More Legalized Killings

Italian immigrants were fired on and forced to leave Marksville, Louisiana, for violating southern racial taboos. Two hundred were driven out of Altoona, Pennsylvania, in 1894. In some areas, Italian immigrants counterattacked. In 1899 an Italian agricultural community in Arkansas suffered vandalism, and its school-house was burned by whites. Groups of Italian Americans armed themselves and patrolled their area, effectively ending the vigilante attacks.[46]

Some killings were legalized. One of the most famous murder trials of all time was that of Nicola Sacco and Bartolomeo Vanzetti, Italian-born workers who were tried for robbery and murder in Massachusetts. Numerous witnesses testified that the defendants were elsewhere at the time of the crime, but the testimony of the Italian-born witnesses was ignored by the judge. Anti-Italian prejudice was very evident at the trial and in the views of the presiding judge. While their guilt or innocence is still being debated, the two men clearly did not receive a fair trial. As suspected "radicals," they were executed in 1927 in the midst of hysteria over left-wing, "un-American" activities.[47]

Conflict with African Americans

Since the 1930s, conflict between Italian Americans and groups lower on the socioeconomic ladder has been part of the urban scene. "Law and order," school desegregation, and busing have been major issues in the northern metropolitan areas. In the 1960s and 1970s Italian American leaders sometimes complained that black Americans were the "darlings" of the white Protestant liberals and received disproportionate press coverage and federal aid. Italian Americans in some areas of such cities as Newark and Philadelphia found themselves surrounded by large numbers of black Americans, who were often poor, migrating from other regions. Realistic fears about urban crime were coupled with exaggerated views of the black role in such crime, much like Anglo-Protestant fears earlier exaggerated the Italian role in urban crime.[48]

In the spring of 1990, a group of Italian American youths attacked and killed a black youth, Yusuf Hawkins, in the predominantly Italian Bensonhurst area of New York City. The attackers believed that the victim was on his way to date an

Italian American girl. Actually, Hawkins had gone to Bensonhurst to inquire about buying a used car. Members of the Federation of Italian American Organizations actively sought to calm racial tensions, calling the attention of Italian residents to their own history of discrimination. Some residents, though, noted that this incident was not unique. One woman told of two of her black Brazilian friends who had been abducted, stabbed, and brutally beaten by a group of Italian American youths in 1988. The victims survived and gave descriptions of their assailants to the police, yet no arrests were made, and the Italian American community there generally ignored that racial incident.[49]

Opinion surveys in the late 1960s and 1970s showed significant antiblack prejudice and strong opposition to neighborhood desegregation among Italian Americans. One found that 70 percent of Italians would object if a black family moved into their area, a figure higher than for whites in general.[50] By the 1990s Italian American attitudes, like those of many other whites, had liberalized on some racial matters. Sixty percent of Italian Americans, compared with 55 percent of all whites, said they would work for improved racial relations, and 85 percent of Italian Americans, compared with 79 percent of all whites, said they would vote for a black presidential candidate. However, on a question asking if they would object to sending their children to a school that was half black, Italian Americans were somewhat more likely to be opposed than whites as a group (19 percent compared with 16 percent).[51] On the whole, Italian Americans seem less negative in their views of African Americans than they were in the past. Yet among Italian Americans, as among other white groups, a sizeable proportion remain openly racist in their attitudes toward black Americans, a situation that has on occasion fueled antiblack violence, such as the Bensonhurst attacks.

POLITICS

The first major Italian influence on U.S. politics was that of Filippo Mazzei, a friend of Thomas Jefferson who came to the colonies to help with agricultural development. Mazzei helped Jefferson bring legal reforms to Virginia. Mazzei's writings speak vigorously of freedom and equality and include phrases similar to those Jefferson later used in the Declaration of Independence—for example, "All men are by nature created free and independent."[52]

City Politics

During and after the great migration of 1880–1920, Irish Americans recruited Italian Americans into the Democratic party. In Chicago, Italian Americans benefited from the political patronage system; many were employed by the city in the 1890s, mostly in menial positions, such as street sweeping. Italian Americans elected an alderman there by 1892, and by the mid-1890s they had a few representatives in the Illinois legislature. Italians had begun to enter elected offices in

New York City by 1900, and by 1920 they were central to city politics—for example, in passing out life-sustaining job favors.[53]

The political participation of Italian immigrants suffered a setback during the "Red Scare" of 1919–1922. The infamous raids conducted by U.S. Attorney General Palmer in this period were aimed largely at immigrant families, often Italian, thought to be radical or subversive. Many aliens were illegally detained or arrested, and some were deported as a result.[54] Such activities had a major dampening effect on Italian American political participation.

By the late 1930s, a few cities, such as New York, San Francisco, and New Orleans, had Italian mayors. Nonetheless, the typical picture was of Italian American communities governed by non-Italian politicians. Substantial gains were made in the next few decades. A number of smaller cities elected Italian mayors, and by the late 1940s Italian Americans had gained great influence in New York City politics. Irish control of New Haven's government kept Italian Americans from moving up for a number of decades, and it was not until the late 1950s that Italian Americans were well represented in government positions there. Over the next two decades, the increasing number of Italian Americans serving as mayors or city-council members became conspicuous in many cities.[55] Prominent Italian American mayors in recent decades have included Anthony Celebrezze (Cleveland), Joseph Alioto (San Francisco), George Moscone (San Francisco), and Frank Rizzo (Philadelphia). Of those who have served as chief executives in major cities, most have been Democrats.

As they did with Irish Americans, Anglo-Protestant urban reform movements have often reduced the benefits going to the Italian American working class. These movements have been aimed at ridding urban politics of machine bosses and corruption. But defeating the machine has meant decreasing the political power of working-class ethnics.[56] Reform in the guise of urban renewal and redevelopment has hurt Italian American communities. For example, the West End of Boston once contained a large, viable, Italian working-class community. In the late 1950s, the area, which had little clout, was designated a "slum" by the politically powerful city fathers and razed for urban renewal. New apartment buildings were built, development that was expected to improve the city's tax base. Several thousand Italian Americans of all ages were forced to relocate, a move that brought them great pain and suffering.[57]

State and National Politics

Very few Italians served in state and national legislatures prior to 1900. One was Francis Spinola, a general in the Union army, a member of the New York legislature, and a member of the U.S. House of Representatives. After 1900, the few successes at state and national levels were based on the concentration of voters in certain cities. Prior to 1950, New York had sent only six Italian American representatives to Congress. The most famous was Fiorello La Guardia. In Congress he was a vigorous supporter of Italian immigration, attacking nativism and the anti-Italian quota system it fostered. He was the first Italian

American to rise through ethnic politics in New York City, where he was elected mayor in 1934. La Guardia showed that Italian Americans could support reform movements aimed at urban machines, in this case Tammany Hall, and promote honest government.[58]

International politics has affected Italian American political activities, just as the Ireland–Britain struggle has long affected Irish Americans. During the Great Depression, the Italian dictator Mussolini became a hero for many Italian (as well as non-Italian) Americans—although antifascist activity was also a significant force in Italian American communities. During World War II, Italian Americans suffered some discrimination. Italian American subversion was widely alleged, but not proven, and the use of the Italian language was prohibited on the radio in New York and Boston. Several hundred Italian Americans, legal residents of the United States, were imprisoned at a Montana concentration camp where Japanese Americans were also interned (see Chapter 11). In addition, more than a half million Americans of Italian American ancestry were officially seen as "enemy aliens" and had their rights curtailed. The property of some Italian Americans was confiscated; some restrictions were placed on travel; nighttime curfews were sometimes imposed; and some Italian Americans living in coastal areas were forced to move away. The justification for ignoring the civil rights of hundreds of thousands of Americans was similar to the rationalizations for the internment of Japanese Americans. They were alleged to represent a security threat. Recently, legislation has been introduced in Congress to require the government to openly acknowledge these violations of the civil rights of Italian Americans.[59] It is significant, however, that the government action taken against Italian Americans was far less substantial than that against Japanese Americans, perhaps because Italian Americans were by that time considered to be "white" by most of the government officials who were involved.[60]

The war contributed to Italian American mobility and assimilation, particularly after 1945. The solidarity with other Americans that was generated by the struggle against fascism in Germany and Japan helped the Italian immigrants and their children assimilate more rapidly to Anglo-Protestant culture and institutions. Italian Americans enlisted in the armed forces and served in ethnically integrated units. (In contrast, African Americans and Japanese Americans served in segregated units.) Novels and films about the armed forces celebrated the ethnic diversity of U.S. soldiers. The war contributed to what Alba terms "a different vision of America, which included ethnic Americans, or more precisely those who were white, in the magic circle of full citizenship."[61]

Following the Great Depression, Italian Americans began to gradually move into the middle levels of state and federal government, including the judicial system. Franklin Roosevelt appointed the first Italian American judge to the federal courts; President Harry Truman appointed the second and third. Only one Italian American (a current Justice, Antonin Scalia) has ever served on the Supreme Court. Progress in congressional representation has been substantial. By the late 1940s, eight Italian Americans held seats in Congress. By the 1950s ever increasing numbers of Italian Americans were serving in state legislatures. John Pastore of

Rhode Island became the first Italian American governor (1946) and the first senator shortly thereafter. In 1962 Anthony Celebrezze became the first Italian American to serve in a presidential cabinet.[62]

Between the 1970s and 1990s, the number of Italian American cabinet members, governors, and state legislators grew. Today, some areas of the country, such as Long Island, have large numbers of Italian American officials, including state legislators. Some local officials have gained national attention. Mario Cuomo, then governor of New York, was a contender for the Democratic party's presidential nomination in 1992. Cuomo was also a keynote speaker at the 1984 Democratic party convention that nominated Geraldine Ferraro as its vice-presidential candidate. It was a source of great pride for many Italian Americans that the first woman nominated for vice-president was Italian American. In 1994 Cuomo, a Democrat, was defeated in a bid for re-election as New York governor by Republican George Pataki, also of Italian ancestry. In the late 1990s, New York City's mayor and one of the state's U.S. senators were of Italian ancestry. New York's mayor, Rudolph Giuliani, a Republican, was heralded as a likely presidential candidate. By the late 1990s thirty-two Italian Americans, representing numerous states, were members of the U.S. House of Representatives.

In the 1960s Republican strategists began a concerted effort to attract the white ethnic vote, including the Italian American vote, away from the Democratic party. Fears about black civil rights actions were fueling white ethnic discontent. Although this strategy produced notable success for a number of white ethnic groups in the 1972 presidential election, survey data for the late 1970s showed Italian Americans still leaning strongly toward the Democratic party. Only 22 percent called themselves Republicans at that time. However, during the 1980s many moved their political allegiance to the Republican party. By 1990, opinion poll data found that 49 percent of Italian Americans called themselves Republicans, compared with 39 percent who called themselves Democrats.[63] More recent analysis of public opinion data on Italian Americans by the National Opinion Research Center indicates that over the last two decades they have moved to the political right on major issues such as capital punishment and the restriction of immigration. Still, the data indicate continuing political liberalism today among Italian Americans on such matters as support for the United Nations and increased government spending to help the poor and the central cities.[64]

As large numbers of Italian Americans have moved to the suburbs, they have become politically and economically more like other white Americans. Nationwide, Italian American organizations have been politically influential. In the mid-1960s, for example, the 130 chapters of the American Committee on Italian Immigration held rallies and lobbied successfully in support of the 1965 Immigration Act, which changed racist immigration regulations. Since its creation in 1976 the National Italian American Foundation, headquartered in Washington DC, has operated as a clearinghouse of information on Italian politicians and political issues of importance to Italian Americans.[65]

Italian Americans have also been concerned with international politics, including the place of Italy on the world scene. Italian Americans, like other U.S.

ethnic groups, have lobbied on behalf of their home country. In the fall of 1997, the United Nations was considering a U.S. proposal to add Germany and Japan, but not Italy, as permanent members of the Security Council. Italian American citizen groups organized protests against what they called a "blatant insult" and argued that Italy should be placed on the Security Council because of its great importance in current UN activities.[66]

THE ECONOMY

Structural adaptation by immigrant groups includes their movement into secondary-organization levels of the host society—into the economic as well as the political and educational organizations. Economic mobility entails the penetration of higher levels of employment and the attendant economic benefits. Italian Americans started near the bottom of the ladder. The small number of immigrants prior to 1880 were mostly artisans, street sellers, and political exiles, primarily from northern Italy. The southern Italian immigrants, who came after 1880, were economically oppressed: They responded to the tremendous U.S. demand for unskilled labor in the late nineteenth century.[67]

Large numbers came to the United States with the aid of *padroni,* labor bosses who linked the new immigrants to employment, food, and housing. Some claim this system was imported from Italy, but others have argued that it was a normal part of U.S. industrialization, which virtually devoured immigrant workers. The padroni acted primarily as agents who secured cheap labor for transportation, construction, and manufacturing enterprises in the United States. Exploitation often resulted from the padrone system. Exorbitant prices were charged by the labor bosses for housing and food; labor abuses were heaped on workers often isolated in camps. By 1909, because of legislation passed in several states, the contractors had begun to change from extralegal padroni to legitimate labor agents.[68]

Early Poverty and Discrimination

Urban poverty coupled with dangerous working conditions was the lot of most immigrants: "The Italian immigrant may be maimed and killed in his industrial occupation without a cry and without indemnity. He may die from the 'bends' working in the caissons under the river, without protest; he can be slowly asphyxiated in crowded tenements, smothered in dangerous trades and occupations (which only the ignorant immigrant pursues, not the native American); he can contract tuberculosis in unsanitary factories and sweatshops."[69] A number of studies documented poor conditions—overcrowding and exorbitant rents in run-down housing, as well as inadequate water and sewage facilities. Death rates from infectious diseases were often high.[70]

Lack of skills affected the first generation of immigrants. Some who came were skilled workers, but overall this group had the highest percentage of unskilled laborers among major immigrant groups in this period. Poor farmers and their families made up the majority. However, a study of Italian-born men in the United States found few of these immigrants employed in agriculture, but a high proportion employed as unskilled workers, such as miners or laborers. Many replaced Irish Americans in building roads and railroads. Few were in clerical fields or the professions. Women were employed primarily in trade.[71]

Background handicaps, such as a poor command of English and lack of vocational skills, were not the only restrictions on occupational opportunity. Discrimination played an important role. Isolate, small-group, and direct and indirect institutionalized discrimination (see Chapter 1) held Italian Americans back. From the first years of heavy migration, the new Italian residents were "abused in public and isolated in private, cuffed in the works and pelted on the streets, fined and imprisoned on the smallest pretext, cheated of their wages, and crowded by the score into converted barns and tumble-down shanties that served as boarding houses."[72] Discrimination in wages was often blatant, as in an ad for laborers to build a New York City reservoir that listed daily wages as $1.30 to $1.50 for "whites" and $1.15 to $1.25 for "Italians."[73] Just as important was discrimination institutionalized in the form of recruitment practices with a built-in bias. At the turn of the twentieth century, informal social networks were then as now the major means of circulating job information. Anglo-Protestant and Irish American sponsors were important in most urban job networks, protecting their own kind and often discriminating against Italian American workers.[74]

Unions

One factor operating against Italian Americans was discrimination by worker organizations, which kept them from moving into many blue-collar jobs in the early 1900s. Some became strikebreakers as a result of that exclusion and also because their poverty-stricken condition led them to be hired as "scabs" by employers seeking to destroy the unions. Not surprisingly, in their first decades in the cities, Italian immigrants were not as active in unions as native-born whites.

However, some later immigrants who brought progressive working-class ideas with them from Italy soon became active in unions. Some were union leaders and took part in major strikes, such as that in Lawrence, Massachusetts, in 1912. Joseph Ettor, an Italian American organizer of the Industrial Workers of the World (IWW), was asked to assist textile factory workers, including Italian American women. The workers had gone on strike over reduced wages after the woolen company in Lawrence refused arbitration. The state militia, made up mostly of native-born white-collar workers, was called in, and one woman striker was killed in clashes between the militia and the 25,000 strikers. The strikers won a small wage increase. The 7,000 Italian Americans were the largest nationality group among the strikers and included prominent union leaders. By the early 1900s Italian Americans were extensively involved in the union rank and file and leadership. Since that time they have been among the strongest supporters of unions.[75]

Textile laborers and armed soldiers face off during the strike by the International Workers of the World at Lawrence, Massachusetts, in 1912.

Upward Mobility

Economic progress came slowly but steadily. The proportion of Italian American workers who were laborers dropped from 50 percent in 1916 to only 31 percent fifteen years later. Small-business and skilled blue-collar positions were more common by 1931.[76] Mobility was evident, but so was the persisting economic differential between Italian Americans and other whites. A study in Newburyport, Massachusetts, in the early 1930s revealed that Italians there were lower than other whites on the "prestige" ladder and somewhat lower on the occupational ladder. The Great Depression slowed advancement, but did not stop it. By 1939 Italian Americans had begun to supplant Jewish Americans as the major group in a number of important unions of skilled workers. They had become numerous in the garment industry and in building trades. Italian Americans paralleled the economic pattern of the Irish, moving up from unskilled to skilled blue-collar positions in a few generations.[77]

Since the 1920s organized crime has provided better-paying jobs for a few Italian Americans in northern cities, although the so-called "good citizens" of the cities, both Italians and non-Italians, were the ones who kept bootlegging, prostitution, and gambling operations going with their patronage.[78] Later, money from organized crime would flow to legitimate enterprises, just as it had earlier for other ethnic groups. Members of families successful in organized crime would eventually move out of illegitimate enterprises altogether. This trend, according to Ianni, supports "the thesis that for Italian Americans, as for other ethnic groups, organized crime has been a way station on the road to ultimately respectable roles in American society."[79] But only a few Italian Americans ever made it up this way. The line between legitimate and illegitimate business, moreover, has often been fuzzy in this society, and not just in the case of white ethnics in organized crime. During the late nineteenth and early twentieth century the Anglo-Protestant "captains of industry" were often involved in a variety of questionable economic and political activities, including illegal ones.[80]

Some Italian Americans became nationally prominent entrepreneurs and scientists. Amadeo Giannini, founder of the Bank of America, made his fortune in California financing generations of small businesses and ranches; he permitted his depositors a voice in bank management. Italian Americans such as Di Giorgio and Gallo began to play major roles in restaurant, agricultural, and contracting businesses. Scientists Enrico Fermi and Salvador Luria won Nobel Prizes. As with groups before and after them, Italian Americans also found upward mobility in sports, as is indicated by the careers of such men as Rocky Marciano and Joe DiMaggio.[81]

Recent Decades

By the 1950s Italian Americans had advanced further, although not to the level of major white Protestant groups. One urban study in the 1950s suggested that second-generation Italian Catholics had yet to equal white Protestants in the proportion holding higher-level white-collar jobs.[82] In the 1970 census, second-generation Italian Americans were less likely to be found in professional and technical jobs and clerical or sales positions than the employed population as a whole. They were, however, more likely than the general population of workers to be employed as managers or officials. They were also more likely than the general population to be found in skilled blue-collar jobs.[83]

The 1990 census showed significant mobility in the occupational distribution for Americans of Italian ancestry. Compared with the total white population, Italian Americans now had a greater proportion in professional, managerial, technical, and other white-collar jobs and a smaller proportion in blue-collar jobs.[84] Although Italian Americans are still underrepresented among top corporate officials, the National Italian American Foundation reported that in 1991 some 150 Italian Americans held top- or second-ranking positions in large American companies. "Our feeling here is that Italian Americans are making a substantial impact—after a very slow century—on American corporate life." Lee Iacocca, former head of Chrysler Corporation, is perhaps the best known among these.[85]

By the end of the 1960s, the income level for Italian American households was higher than that of the typical U.S. household.[86] By the 1990 census, the median family income for Italian Americans ($42,242) was substantially higher than that of all whites ($37,628), and poverty rates for Italian Americans were substantially below those of the larger group. The unemployment rate for Italian Americans was slightly below that of all whites and well below that of the total population.[87]

Some Persisting Problems

Over the last two decades, discrimination against Italian Americans has sometimes been a problem at the highest levels of this society. One study in the mid-1970s in northeastern cities found that Italian Americans were heavily represented among rank-and-file workers in police, fire, and sanitation departments and in public utilities, but generally had weak representation in higher-level administrative positions in city departments.[88] The failure to hire Italian Americans at the City University of New York (CUNY) was documented in a 1970s study of CUNY's higher-level positions that concluded: "In decision-making positions of Dean, Director and Chairman of the system's 18 colleges, there are only 20 Italian Americans out of a total of 504 positions."[89] Only a small percentage of the faculty were Italian Americans, and these tended to be at the lowest ranks.

In 1975 an affirmative action program for Italian American faculty was put into place, but fifteen years later the percentage of Italian American faculty had not increased. Between the 1970s and the 1990s, there was little change. At the beginning of the 1990s, Italian Americans still constituted less than 6 percent of CUNY's faculty, in contrast with the larger percentages on the faculties at private universities in New York City. At that time CUNY's student body was about 17 percent Italian American.[90] In the early 1990s, CUNY professors protested discrimination in the hiring of Italian Americans in a class action complaint against the university.[91] In 1994 CUNY settled a lawsuit brought by the director of the university's Italian-American Institute; CUNY's administration agreed to make the Institute a permanent part of Queens College and to hire a distinguished senior professor in Italian American studies. As of the late 1990s, there was still continuing litigation and dispute over the implementation of the settlement.

Into the 1980s and 1990s, some important private clubs still quietly barred Italian Americans. Italian Americans are underrepresented in the very top positions of major corporations. In addition, in certain areas, especially those with large numbers of new immigrants, poverty has been a problem. In the 1970s, a few Italian American urban communities saw a growing number of poverty-stricken residents. One 1975 report found poverty rates from 15 to 18 percent among families in those New York City census tracts with 50 percent or more foreign-born Italians. Some of these poor were aged immigrants who came in the first two decades of the twentieth century; others were among the thousands who came in the late 1960s and 1970s, after earlier immigration restrictions were removed. Another example involves older Italian Americans in Boston's North End. By the 1980s, this once-vigorous Italian American community of 10,000 had become home to growing numbers of young non-Italian professionals who found the North End a chic place to live. Many of the older Italian residents had been pressured to leave because of gentrification, and economic pressures undercut the quality of life of those who remained. Many longtime community residents fell into poverty.[92]

Yet we must put these problems of poverty and discrimination in perspective. The overall picture of recent occupational and income mobility for Italian Americans, a white ethnic group oppressed on a large scale just a few decades ago, is impressive. At least two among them, Mario Cuomo and Lee Iacocca, have been touted as presidential candidates for the Democratic party. Italian American men are prominent among movie directors. Women of Italian American ancestry have quietly moved into important positions in the mass media, including the writer Anna Quindlen and the co-creator of television's *Murphy Brown* show, Diane English. The majority of Italian Americans have made strides up the socioeconomic ladder, so much so that on many socioeconomic indexes they have surpassed Anglo-Protestants.

EDUCATION

Organized education for Italian Americans began toward the end of the nineteenth century. Many immigrants came from areas in Italy where the poor were provided with little schooling. Half could not read or write. Like many immigrants to the United States, they adopted a pragmatic approach to education, valuing it but asking, "What is the practical value of this for jobs, for later life?" Many poor families made sacrifices to get their first child through elementary school, then expected this child to help, with a job, to get later children through school.

From the start, the Anglo-Protestant establishment imposed a serious obstacle for the educational advancement of Italian immigrants. As they had been with the Irish, Protestant educators were very concerned with the alleged corruption and cultural inferiority of Italian Americans. Many schools became pressure cookers of Americanization in which these educators sought to teach Italian immigrants Anglo-Protestant ways as quickly as possible. Anglo-Protestant norms about health, dress, work, and language were pressed hard on the immigrants and their children. Ethnic discrimination was a fact of school life. These pressures were especially strong for second-generation children, most of whom went to public schools. (Conflict with the Irish, as well as economic problems, kept many Italian parents from sending their children to parochial schools.) Public schools were Procrustean beds shaped in Anglo-centric form. Rather than give in to hostile pressures, some Italian American children even left school.[93]

In spite of such obstacles, Italian Americans made dramatic progress in educational attainment. For example, between 1950 and 1970 the median years of education completed for the native-born children of Italian immigrants rose by 1.5 years. In both 1950 and 1970 these children of immigrants had median levels of educational attainment higher than for the total population of the United States, but a bit lower than for the white population as a whole.[94] More recently, data from the 1990 census show that the educational level of Italian Americans was only slightly below that of all non-Latino white Americans. And native-born Italian Americans had achieved educational parity with the larger white group.[95]

RELIGION

The Roman Catholic church has been important in the lives of Italian Americans. In southern Italy the church was associated with an oppressive landlord system. Male peasants attended mass infrequently, primarily on ceremonial occasions; older women were the most active church members. In the United States, Protestant opposition to Catholicism presented an obstacle to the free practice of religion. In the large cities, Anglo-Protestant social workers in settlement houses often attempted to Americanize the new Catholic population, which consisted mostly of immigrants from southern and eastern Europe. One Protestant minister argued that "public schools, mission schools and churches will do the work to evangelize the immigrants. And it must be done, business pleads for it, patriotism demands it, social considerations require it."[96]

Many Irish Catholic churches were overwhelmed by the number of Italian immigrants. Moreover, for many Italians, the Irish were too orthodox in their Catholicism. Religion was not an intimate part of political identity for the Italian immigrant, as it was for the Irish immigrant, whose religious expression was tied to a nationalist heritage of anti-English agitation. Saints were important to Italian immigrants and their children, as were the religious festivals that played an important role in cementing the Italian community.[97]

Irish American priests often saw the new Italian parishioners in a negative light. They were not considered to be as serious as the Irish American worshippers. Sometimes this tension escalated. Once ethnic parishes for Italian Americans had developed, they were warned away, on occasion forcefully, from Irish American parishes. Italian Americans reciprocated. Many first-generation Italian Americans preferred to send their children to public schools rather than to the Irish-dominated parochial schools.[98] Gradually, Italian Catholicism, with its festivals and ceremonies, took its place alongside Irish Catholicism. By 1900 there were fourteen Italian parishes in New York; and by 1961, seventy-four.[99]

A 1960s study of Italian and Irish Catholics in New York City suggested the controversial conclusion that third-generation Italians were becoming more "Irishized" in their religious practices; the data showed that there was less emphasis placed on the Virgin Mary, that fewer masses were said for deceased relatives, and that more emphasis was placed on generous contributions to the church than in earlier Italian American generations. Significantly, Susanna Tardi's late-1980s study of Italian American Catholics in New Jersey found that only about 40 percent were practicing Catholics, although the percentage was higher for the second generation than for the first or third generation. The incompatibility of the Catholic church's doctrines with real-life issues was cited as a major reason for withdrawing from the church. Among all respondents, the influence of religion in their lives was ranked as significantly weaker than the influence of the family.[100] In addition, in national survey data for the period between 1988 and 1991, only 70 percent of Italian Americans classified themselves as Catholics, and many of those were nonpracticing Catholics. Catholicism today seems less central for Italian Americans than for Irish Americans. Still, in the late 1990s, some Italian American communities, such as that on New York's Long Island, still have parades, feasts, and church bazaars honoring traditional saints or the Virgin Mary.[101]

ASSIMILATION OR ETHNOGENESIS?

Acculturation pressures came early for southern and eastern European immigrants. Unlike the British immigrants before them, they spoke no English nor were they familiar with the customs of Anglo-Protestant society. Often concentrated in so-called "Little Italies," Italian immigrants learned Italian dialects other than their own, and most picked up some English. Cultural adaptation was slowed by factors other than language and community: poverty, the intention of some to return home, and anti-immigrant hostility and discrimination in the new environment.[102]

The first-generation family was in transition, cross-pressured between the old Italian and the new American ways. Families became less patriarchal and kin solidarity often weakened somewhat, as did ties to religion. Children were more on their own. Speaking Italian at home was sometimes a point of intergenerational conflict, since the younger members felt school pressures to speak only English.[103]

A second point of intergenerational conflict was marriage. First-generation parents saw it as a family matter, while many children tended to see it as an individual matter. Given this tension, it is not surprising that second-generation families adapted in different ways. One type substantially abandoned the old ways, changing the Italian name and moving out of an Italian residential area. This was rare. A second type rejected the old ways in part, perhaps by moving out of concentrated Italian American communities but remaining near enough to maintain close ties to the first generation. This was the largest group. A third type stayed in the old community and retained many of the old ways.[104] By the 1980s, the third and fourth generations were coming into their own, and many were moving into the white multiethnic suburbs. At the beginning of the 1990s, Italian Americans were still concentrated in the Northeast; they constituted about one-sixth of the population in several northeastern states such as New York. No longer a predominantly central-city group, they were about as likely to reside in suburbs as the average white American.

Structural Assimilation

Structural assimilation involves the movement of a group into the secondary organizations—the businesses and bureaucracies—of the larger society, as well as into its primary social networks: social clubs, neighborhoods, and friendship circles. Structural movement by Italian Americans over the first several decades came with considerable violence and resistance from earlier groups. Positioning at the lower economic levels was a fact of life for a time.

In recent decades Italian Americans have made impressive gains in employment, income, and education and advances in politics. This upward educational and occupational mobility has contributed to assimilation in other areas, since Italian Americans have had increasing equal-status contact with members of other white groups in the workplace, the suburbs, and colleges—contacts that have in turn created cross-ethnic friendship networks.[105]

The success of Italian Americans and other white ethnic groups is sometimes compared with the relative lack of success of other groups, such as African Americans. Why were the Italian Americans so successful in assimilating over time to Anglo-Protestant institutions and organizations? The answer to this question lies not just in the hard work and sacrifice of several generations of Italian Americans, for those factors are also characteristic of African Americans. It lies also in the timing of Italian immigrants' entry into the United States. Jobs and housing near jobs were available to the masses of Italians who arrived in the last decades of the nineteenth century and the first decades of the twentieth century. The second and third generations emerged with enough economic support from their parents to get the education they needed for the better-paying jobs opening up during and after World War II.[106] Expansion of jobs on the middle rungs of the occupational ladder then made possible the upward mobility of many white ethnic Americans. The poverty and ethnic discrimination faced by these immigrants, although very serious, was never as thoroughgoing as the extreme poverty and severe and institutionalized racial discrimination faced by such groups as African Americans.

By the World War II period, the earlier view of Italian Americans as an "inferior race" held by Anglo-Protestant officials and commentators had been replaced by a conception of Italian Americans as part of the "white race," thereby reducing anti-Italian discrimination in many settings. Wartime solidarity had hastened the assimilation of white ethnics, including Italian Americans, into Anglo-Protestant institutions, including the main units of the armed forces. In contrast, African Americans and Japanese Americans were kept in segregated units. After the war many Italian Americans took advantage of the G.I. grant programs to get a college education at colleges and universities across the United States. At that time, black Americans were still excluded from many of these colleges and universities.

Many Italian American families in the suburbs and central cities have remained enmeshed in kinship and friendship networks composed at least partially of other Italian Americans. Research studies have revealed the persisting importance of these networks, particularly in working-class communities. In his classic 1962 study, Herbert Gans wrote about an "urban village" in Boston, a blue-collar Italian American community with intimate ties between relatives and friends. A 1975 study of Italian Americans in the Bridgeport, Connecticut, metropolitan area found a continuation of close kinship ties, particularly among the first and second generations; later generations were more likely to have non-Italian friends. Even for the younger generations, about 80 percent of friends were Catholic.[107]

Research over the last two decades shows the persistence of informal networks, particularly in urban neighborhoods. One study of Italian Americans in a northeastern city found strong family systems persisting among the several hundred people interviewed. Older Italian Americans were more likely than non-Italians to have younger relatives nearby; parents and their children usually had maintained strong bonds. Although most Italian Americans in this study had non-Italian friends and co-workers, they spent much of their time with their close relatives. Ninety-two percent of the in-married respondents (those with Italian spouses) reported seeing parents daily or weekly, compared with 81 percent of the out-married Italians (those with non-Italian spouses) and 71 percent of the non-Italian Protestants also interviewed. Sixty-three percent of the in-married saw siblings daily, compared with 32 percent of the out-married respondents and 12 percent of the non-Italians. Ties to Italian relatives, including parents, were weaker among the out-marrieds than among the in-marrieds, but most still lived near relatives. The researcher predicted that increasing intermarriage would result in a diminishing family orientation among Italian Americans. In addition, Alba's mid-1980s study in a large New York metropolitan area found that Italian Americans there were one of the most residentially concentrated of white ethnic groups. They were more likely to name a relative as a close friend and had one of the highest rates of intraethnic friendships. Among three generations of Italian Americans in Tardi's late-1980s New Jersey study, sharing problems and needs with family members was the daily norm. Her respondents defined their Italian American ethnicity in terms of a warm and cohesive family structure that they perceived as distinctive among white ethnic groups.[108]

While kinship and primary-group ties often remain strong among Italian Americans, suburbanization has shrunk formerly large ethnic enclaves.[109] A study of the Greater New York area by Alba and his associates found that in both 1980 and 1990, *most* of the nearly 3 million Italian Americans in that area lived outside of Italian American neighborhoods (defined as census tracts with at least 35 percent of the population of Italian ancestry). In the 1990s, New York's Italian Americans are much less concentrated in mostly Italian neighborhoods than in previous decades. Alba reports that "there are important Italian neighborhoods in this region, but they are mostly in cities, where only a minority of Italian Americans are found."[110] The majority now live in the suburbs.

Studies of marriages in New Haven in 1870 and Chicago in 1920 found high rates of in-marriage for Italians: 94 to 98 percent of all marriages were endogamous. In subsequent decades, in-marriage decreased: the New Haven figure was 77 percent by 1950. Twenty-five years later, in a Bridgeport study, 84 percent of the respondents reported both of their parents were of Italian ancestry. However, only 44 percent were themselves married to Italian Americans. Still, the rate of religious endogamy (in-marriage) was high: Most marriages outside the Italian group were with persons raised as Catholics. Exogamous marriages were more likely for those with higher-status educational and occupational achievements. By 1980, according to U.S. census data, fewer than half of all Italian Americans had endogamous marriages; those under thirty with unmixed Italian ancestry had an out-marriage rate of 67 to 80 percent. More recently, one 1997 analysis estimated that 73 percent of Italian Americans in their 30s were marrying outside their ethnic group.[111]

Alba argues that while ethnicity is still important for the first and second generations, a transition is underway for later generations. He sees ethnicity receding for the third and fourth generations, as Italian Americans become more structurally integrated into the mainstream of white America: 54 percent of all Italian American respondents in his mid-1980s upper New York State study reported ethnically unmixed ancestry. Yet, for those born after 1940, the proportion dropped to only one-third. (National survey data also suggest high levels of mixed ancestry for Italian Americans.) Alba predicts that a much more assimilated Italian American group will emerge as the younger generations replace the earlier ones.[112]

Across-the-board assimilation of Italian Americans is progressing, although this group still encounters significant stereotyping and some discrimination. Italian Americans remain underrepresented at the very highest economic and political levels of U.S. society. Even Alba, who has written about the "twilight of ethnicity" among Italian Americans, has noted, "Because networks of sponsorship tend to perpetuate the ethnic patterns of the past, elite levels register only slowly the ethnic changes at lower levels, and the Italian-American gap in representation is unlikely to close anytime soon."[113]

An Italian Identity?

Identificational assimilation involves giving up one's ethnic identity for that of the dominant Anglo-Protestant culture. For many Italian Americans, this is happening only slowly. Ethnic ties and accents are greater in older generations and among all generations in certain ethnic enclaves. In a number of substantially Italian American neighborhoods in northern cities, older Italian Americans and new Italian immigrants of the last few decades are helping to keep alive some visible cultural characteristics. One study of Belmont, a community in the Bronx with a substantial Italian American flavor, found some persisting ethnic neighborhoods and traditions. Once a 100-square-block community of 28,000 Italian Americans, Belmont is now a multiethnic community whose population is only one-third Italian American. Yet Belmont's vitality makes it a symbol of ethnicity beyond the community's boundaries and a magnet for some Italian Americans, including former residents of the area, who come there to socialize, hear mass in Italian, and celebrate festivals.[114]

A sense of ethnic identity has also been found outside the ethnic enclaves. Phyllis Cancilla Martinelli's study of Italian Americans in Scottsdale, Arizona, in the 1980s found that rather than losing their cultural identity, these respondents, almost half of whom had lived in Arizona six or fewer years, had preserved an Italian American subculture. Almost one-fourth reported a strong ethnic identity, and over half had a moderate ethnic identity. Sixty percent maintained daily or weekly contact with relatives locally, and a large percentage of friendships were with other Italian Americans. In the New York State study cited earlier, Italian Americans, even those of mixed ancestry, were the most likely of the various white ethnic groups to feel a sense of ethnic identity and to consider their ethnic identity as very important. Among those of mixed ancestry who identified ethnically, almost three-fourths described themselves solely as Italian American.[115]

A prominent historian, Marcus Lee Hansen, once argued there is generally an increase in ethnic awareness in the third generation of an immigrant group; this substantially assimilated generation vigorously searches out its ethnic roots. Some studies of Italian Americans in the 1970s did find greater pride in ethnicity expressed among third-generation respondents compared with earlier generations. Younger Italian Americans have faced less discrimination and stereotyping than the older generations did. The assimilation of older Italian Americans has made it possible for younger generations to express their ethnicity openly. However, in her New Jersey study, Tardi found a strong pride in ethnic identity among Italian Americans of the first, second, *and* third generations. The structural factors associated with greater freedom to express ethnic pride, such as diminishing overt discrimination and increasing numbers of highly visible Italian Americans in public life, have apparently affected all generations.[116]

Micaela di Leonardo sees ethnicity as a variable, stronger in some areas than in others. Her study of Italian Americans in California found a relationship between the strength of ethnic networks and identity and the work an individual does. Most working-class Italian Americans in California no longer worked with large numbers of other Italian Americans and therefore expressed their ethnic identity differently from shopkeepers and independent professionals, who were free to stress their ethnicity in their work, often in serving an ethnic clientele. The latter groups were more likely than the former to participate in Italian American voluntary organizations and to accent the continuing cohesiveness of the Italian American community. Participation in the economy may or may not destroy ethnic identity, depending on the character of one's participation and on where one works.[117]

The ethnogenesis model of Andrew Greeley (see Chapter 2) seems to fit the Italian experience well. Italians came to the United States with significant differences from the dominant British American group, but they shared some historical background and a Christian tradition with that group. Through interaction in public schools and the influence of mass media, the gap narrowed substantially, but by no means completely. Italian Americans assimilated in major ways to the Anglo-Protestant host culture, but in other ways they retained their distinctiveness. Because of their strong national heritage, residential segregation, and strong community and kinship networks, a distinctive U.S. ethnic group developed over time. Today, Italian Americans are no longer an Italy-centered group dominated by that national heritage. But they also have not become British Protestant American or even simply "American." For the most part, they remain *Italian* and *American*. Very substantial adaptation without complete assimilation currently characterizes Italian Americans as a group.

How long this strong sense of ethnic identity will persist is a matter of debate. Scholars like Richard Alba see structural forces such as increasing intermarriage, increasing levels of education, loss of (Italian) language, and residential mixing in the suburbs as significantly diminishing, if not eradicating, the sense of traditional ethnic identity among Italian Americans over the next several decades. From the perspective of such data, one can raise the question of what Italian American identity means or will mean in the near future. Membership in Italian American organizations is also declining. As we have seen, a sense of Italian American identity has not retarded the increasing rates of intermarriage.[118] Still, there are some modest counter forces. The presence of several hundred thousand foreign-born Italian Americans keeps Italian as a live language and helps maintain some Italian American neighborhoods in U.S. cities. What the future holds for Italian American identity remains unclear.

SUMMARY

Today, many descendants of the Italian immigrants who entered around the turn of the century are clustered in certain northern states. Most remain Catholic, but many are not active in the church. These Americans have played and continue to play an important role in the culture, politics, and economy of the United States. We have focused primarily on the descendants of the streams of migration that spanned the years 1880 to 1920 and earlier, examining the beginnings of this important migration and tracing its often dramatic impact. Poverty and difficult working conditions greeted these hardworking immigrants. They were not prepared for the intense nativist attacks from Anglo-Protestants, who falsely stereotyped Italian Americans as an inferior, immoral, and criminal people. Much nativist activity was aimed at proving Italian American "racial inferiority." The widespread Mafia myth stigmatized Italian American communities. Violent attacks by other white Americans were endured in many Italian immigrant communities.

Political avenues were closed for a time; the economy often consigned Italian Americans to low-paying jobs; public schools tried to make carbon-copy Anglo-Protestants out of them. Yet, in spite of these problems, the immigrants and their descendants persevered and prospered. Particularly after World War II they began to make their mark in politics, the economy, and education. Their economic and political mobility has made them another U.S. success story, although a considerable price was often exacted for that success.

Today, Italian Americans are one of the major groups in the great American drama of blending and pluralism. As a group they have so far retained a significant degree of ethnic distinctiveness, ethnicity that seems likely to persist for some time to come. Yet some observers and researchers are predicting that in the next few decades social forces such as suburbanization and intermarriage will diminish the Italian American ethnic identity and accelerate the identification of Italian Americans with a general "European American" or "white American" identity.

CHAPTER 6

Jewish Americans

Jews have been scapegoats for the hatreds of the dominant peoples in various nations around the globe for thousands of years. From the Egyptian and Roman persecutions in ancient times to the massacres and expulsions in Spain in the late 1400s to the brutal pogroms of the Russian czar in the 1880s to the German Nazi massacres, Jews might be regarded as the most widely persecuted ethnic group in world history. Residing in many lands, the continually harassed ancestors of Jewish Americans forged strong and distinctive cultural traditions. Indeed, some of the intellectual pillars of modern civilization—Karl Marx, Sigmund Freud, and Albert Einstein—were Jewish.

Jewish Americans have contributed much to the success of this nation—as pioneers in trade and commerce, workers in industry, professionals, government officials, and entertainers. They have benefited from a political structure that separates church and state and prohibits religious qualifications for holding public office. Jewish immigrants have come from countries in which they were clearly outsiders, prohibited from owning land, and subjected to government-sponsored persecutions and mass murder. In the United States, Alan Dershowitz points out in his book, *Chutzpah,* "the Jews did not have to evaluate every single event by reference to their own survival."[1] For the most part U.S. law never became the enemy of Jewish Americans. Still, more than any other white ethnic group, they have often been treated as outsiders in the United States.

By tradition, Jewish ethnicity is based on matrilineal ancestry: A Jew is a person whose mother is Jewish. In the contemporary United States, many Jewish writers define Jews as those who identify themselves as Jews. Some Jewish Americans have focused their identity primarily on their religion; others have defined their Jewishness primarily in terms of group membership. Given the many changes experienced by Jewish Americans over the past quarter-century, a major question among many Jewish writers today is if, and if so on what basis, Jewish identity will survive in the United States.[2]

MIGRATION

From 1500 to World War II

The earliest Jewish settlers came as individuals to the Atlantic Coast colonies in the 1600s seeking economic opportunities denied to them in their European countries of origin. The first Jewish community in North America dates from the arrival in 1654 of twenty-three Jews fleeing the Catholic Inquisition in Portuguese-controlled Brazil. Most of these were *Sephardic Jews,* those whose background was the Jewish subculture of Spain. Having been refused entry at their intended destination, the Spanish-controlled Caribbean islands, these refugees also faced resistance in New Amsterdam on the grounds that they would present unwelcomed economic competition. They were grudgingly allowed to settle and later given the right to own land and engage in trade.[3]

Over the next hundred years, small numbers of descendants of *Marranos*—Jews who had been forced to publicly convert to Christianity during the Spanish Inquisition under threat of death but who privately maintained allegiance to Judaism—came to the North American colonies. These were mostly cosmopolitan merchants and traders. In port cities from New York to Georgia, they established small Jewish American communities organized around Orthodox synagogues, but their lives outside the communities were characterized by substantial cultural assimilation—in language, dress, and manners.[4]

Immigration of the more traditional *Ashkenazi Jews* (those from England, Germany, and Poland) began in the early 1700s, and soon this group outnumbered Sephardic Jews. Many were attracted by reports of economic prosperity in the United States. For the most part the new immigrants integrated into the Sephardic communities and adopted their acculturated practices. Estimates of the Jewish American population at the time of the American Revolution range from 1,000 to 2,500—a very small percentage of the population.[5]

After 1820, central European Jews came in dramatically increased numbers in response to declining economic conditions and increased anti-Semitism in Europe, as well as to economic expansion in the United States. These immigrants have often been called "German Jews," although their countries of origin included Bohemia and Moravia as well as Germany. The typical Jewish immigrant of the 1830s and later was a single man, often a poorly educated younger son who had no prospects in the impoverished regions of central Europe where the number of Jewish households was not allowed to increase. This stream of immigrants included peddlers, merchants, and craft workers from small towns. Many settled in the Midwest, Far West, and South, and by 1860 Jewish American communities and synagogues had been established in many cities. Such geographic mobility facilitated acculturation.[6]

Eastern European Jews, the largest group of Jewish immigrants, began to arrive in the 1870s. The overwhelming majority came from Russian-controlled areas, where anti-Semitism, overpopulation, and lack of economic opportunities were major push factors. In Russia in the 1880s, government-sponsored massacres, called *pogroms,* affected all Jews and contributed to an increase in outmigration. German Jews, largely acculturated by the time the eastern-European immigrants arrived, often felt their societal position was threatened by the newcomers. Still, they provided substantial assistance for the large numbers of new immigrants.[7]

Jewish immigration from 1881 to the mid-1920s totaled approximately 2.5 million, with most coming between 1890 and 1914 and in the five years following World War I. By 1914 there were ten times as many Jewish Americans of eastern European descent as there were of German descent. By the mid-1920s, Jewish Americans composed 3.5 percent of the U.S. population. Eastern European Jews constituted a large proportion of all immigrants during this period. Unlike some non-Jewish European immigrants of this period, almost none of the eastern European Jews returned home. Most settled in East Coast cities. As peddlers, street vendors, and unskilled workers, they became part of the growing urban communities. These new immigrants brought with them a distinctive language and culture (both Yiddish), a strong sense of Jewish identity, some Orthodox religious observances, and a determination to succeed in their new homeland.[8]

After the restrictive 1924 Immigration Act, an act aimed at limiting eastern and southern European immigration, the number of Jewish newcomers declined rapidly. Between 1921 and 1936, fewer than 400,000 Jewish immigrants entered the country. During the Great Depression, the number of immigrants from all parts of the globe was sharply reduced. President Franklin Roosevelt's administration did permit some increase in Jewish refugees from Germany after the Nazi persecution became known; yet Roosevelt, and particularly his State Department, did much less than they could have to allow Jews to flee to the United States. The obstacles to Jewish immigration were a disgrace: The U.S. State Department adopted the callous policy of requiring affidavits of financial solvency and good character and used visa regulations to slow the flow of refugees fleeing the threat of Adolf Hitler's death camps. In June 1940, the State Department put an end to most immigration from Germany and central Europe. Because of these actions, more than 400,000 slots within U.S. immigration quotas for refugees from countries under Nazi control were left unused between 1933 and 1943. To some extent these unfilled quotas may represent lives lost to extermination by the Nazis because of U.S. immigration policy.[9]

The 150,000 refugees who did manage to enter between 1935 and the early 1940s included many highly talented people. One-fifth were professionals. Many set up businesses from New York to San Francisco; contrary to the prevailing stereotype, they were no burden on their new homeland. Among these refugees were some of the world's most able scientists and artists, including Albert Einstein.

World War II to the Present

After the arrival of thousands of postwar refugees, Jewish migration again tapered off significantly to an estimated 8,000 annually in the 1950s and 1960s. New sources of immigrants replaced the old. By the 1970s, a significant number of Israelis—estimated at 100,000 or more—had come to the United States. Large numbers were undocumented immigrants ("illegals"). Moreover, between 1966 and 1982, nearly 250,000 Soviet Jews left their country. Before 1975, most went to Israel, but by the late 1970s most were coming to the United States. By 1980 nearly 100,000 had entered. Many more came in the 1980s and early 1990s, when the numbers reached about 36,000 annually. By the mid-1990s, however, U.S. immigration restrictions caused a decline to about 21,000 annually. In one survey of these immigrants, most said they were proud of their Jewish heritage and had left the Soviet Union because of fear of anti-Semitism.[10] In addition, the last two decades have again seen an increase in Israeli immigrants to the United States. The number has risen each year since 1990. Today there are about 200,000 Israeli immigrants in the United States.[11] The cost of helping these immigrants has been borne largely by the Jewish American community.

Since World War II internal migration has brought about a shift of the Jewish American population from cities to suburbs, and the proportions living in the South and West have about doubled. For example, a late-1980s survey of the Rhode Island Jewish community revealed the impact of migration from the Northeast. The population in the largest urban area, Greater Providence, had dropped about one-fifth since the early 1960s, and the state's Jewish population had also declined. The average age for Rhode Island's Jewish population had risen because of declining birthrates and out-migration of the young.[12]

The 1997 *American Jewish Yearbook* estimated the Jewish American population at about 5.9 million—nearly half the world's Jewish population. A very high percentage of the Jewish American population was born in the United States. About half live in three large metropolitan areas—New York-northern New Jersey, Los Angeles-Riverside-Orange counties, and Miami-Ft. Lauderdale. (About 70 percent identified themselves as either Reform or Conservative in terms of religion.) Since the peak year of 1937, the Jewish American population has declined as a percentage of the total U.S. population—to somewhat more than 2 percent in the late 1990s.[13] Still, Nathan Glazer has suggested that Jewish "institutions are on the whole more extensive and stronger than in the 1930s, and Jewish political strength is substantially greater."[14]

PREJUDICE AND STEREOTYPES

Jewish Americans have been socially defined by outsiders on the basis of both (real and alleged) physical and cultural characteristics. In the early 1900s, in the 1930s and 1940s, and even to the present, they have been considered by some non-Jews to be a biologically inferior "race."[15] No white group in history has suffered under a broader range of stereotypes for a longer period than have the Jews. For centuries, Jews have been targets for intensely held prejudices, hostile attitudes, and discriminatory behavior, collectively known as *anti-Semitism*. For almost two thousand years the writings and liturgies of Christendom have been rife with anti-Semitism. Many Christians have held Jews as a group culpable for the death of their Christ; Jews have been cursed and killed as "Christ killers." (Of course, Jesus was a Jew.) From the earliest colonial period, Christian groups in North America brought the "Christ killers" view with them. Many Christian ministers and priests passed along these views to each new generation.[16]

Anti-Semitism has accented a number of other negative themes. One cliché is that many Jews are examples of economic deviousness. Unlike African Americans and Native Americans who are frequently stereotyped by whites as unintelligent, Jewish Americans have been seen as too hardworking, too intelligent, and too crafty. Carey McWilliams has suggested that this "devious" stereotype developed to rationalize the American Jews' relative success as "middleman" merchants and brokers.[17]

Although some early political leaders, such as John Adams, wrote tributes to the achievements of Jewish Americans, positive comments did not predominate in the first few Anglo-Protestant generations. Even Adams's grandson, the intellectual Henry Adams, upset with the rapidly industrializing United States, was anti-Semitic. For him the Jewish American was a symbol of the materialistic world he disliked. By the late 1800s, Jewish Americans had become the scapegoats for angry members of the old-money Protestant elite whose social position, based on ancestry, had been taken over by the newly wealthy (and non-Jewish) captains of industry.[18]

The crude stereotype of Jewish Americans as social climbers became the subject of frequent parodies in the media, including vaudeville, after the Civil War. Clumsy Jewish figures speaking inflected English were depicted in high-society positions. By the 1880s, newspaper and magazine cartoons were caricaturing Jewish Americans as long-nosed, garishly dressed merchants speaking broken English. It was also during this period that Jews began to be excluded from many areas of life. In 1877, a prominent Jewish American banker was denied accommodation in a major hotel. The following year a Jewish American was excluded from the New York City Bar Association, and New York's City College banned Jewish Americans from Greek-letter fraternities. In a growing number of contexts, Jewish Americans were officially classified as outsiders.[19]

One of the most vicious attacks on Jews was the book called *The Protocols of the Elders of Zion*. This highly stereotypical tract was created by the Russian secret police and attempted to show that Jews, as anti-Christian agents of the devil, were seeking to take covert control of the world and to destroy Western civilization. U.S. Gentiles like automobile pioneer Henry Ford worked to spread the vicious stereotypes. In May 1920, a summary of *The Protocols* appeared on the front page of Ford's newspaper in Dearborn, Michigan, boosting the paper's circulation to hundreds of thousands of copies. Gentile leaders in Europe praised the paper for its articles, and by the 1920s this book was being widely circulated in the United States. Ford's paper and *The Protocols* played an important role in a new burst of malicious anti-Semitic stereotypes and agitation across the nation.[20]

In subsequent decades, numerous mass media political cartoons stereotyped Jewish Americans as radicals or "Communist" sympathizers and alleged that "Jews were taking over the government." By 1941, hatred of Jewish Americans had risen to a fever pitch. They were falsely accused by members of Congress, the press, and prominent citizens of bringing the United States into war with Germany. A World War II social science study, reported in the book *The Authoritarian Personality*, found substantial support among samples of non-Jewish Californians for crude stereotypes of Jews as revolutionary, clannish, and parasitic. Ironically, after World War II, a *Fortune* magazine poll found that three-fourths of non-Jewish Americans who felt some groups had more power than was good for the country's economy cited the Jews.[21]

Much evidence confirms the persistence of anti-Semitism even today among many non-Jewish Americans. The president of a major Baptist organization publicly stated that God does not hear the prayers of Jews, and a leader of the conservative Moral Majority group repeated the age-old stereotype that Jews had a "supernatural" ability to make money. Gary Tobin has reported that interviews with Jewish Americans in a number of metropolitan areas at various times in the 1980s revealed a significant incidence of anti-Semitism, typically encounters with negative references or remarks. Between 17 and 28 percent of the respondents reported such experiences during the year prior to their interview. The rate was much higher for young adults: over half of those in Kansas City and Atlantic City, 40 percent in St. Louis, and 46 percent in Washington, DC.[22]

Some older Jewish Americans who experienced hostility, discrimination, and exclusion during the early decades of this century feel that the relatively better current situation is proof that anti-Semitism is no longer a significant problem. Charles Silberman points to the many successes of Jewish Americans and the access they have to most areas of this society. Others, particularly members of the younger generation, are more skeptical. Dershowitz discusses a number of social phenomena that constitute a new variety of anti-Semitism. The "new strains of the old virus" include anti-Zionism and the application of higher standards of moral and political conduct for Israel and Jews in general than for other nations or ethnic groups.[23] In a 1997 survey of Jewish Americans, 40 percent said that anti-Semitism is still a "very serious" problem, with another 55 percent saying it was "somewhat" of a problem. Clearly, anti-Semitism remains a U.S. problem. This survey also found that the top group ranked as anti-Semitic by the respondents was the "religious right." Surveys have also shown that Jewish respondents identifying as religious feel the anti-Semitism the most keenly.[24]

Some recent surveys have found that non-Jewish Americans greatly overestimate the Jewish American presence in the United States—at about 25 percent of the nation, instead of the actual 2 percent. This population estimate may indicate the negative view that Jewish Americans are too dominant in the country.[25]

OPPRESSION AND CONFLICT

In the 1880s, Jewish American merchants in the South suffered violent attacks from non-Jewish farmers who blamed them for economic crises. In the 1890s, the farms and homes of Jewish American landlords and merchants were burned in Mississippi.

In the early 1900s, riots erupted against Jewish American workers brought into factories in New Jersey. Just before World War I in Georgia, Leo Frank, the Jewish part-owner of a pencil factory, was convicted of killing a young female employee, though evidence pointed elsewhere. After being beaten up in prison, he was taken from the prison hospital and lynched by an angry white Gentile mob.[26]

Southern demagogues such as Tom Watson used the Frank case to fuel the flames of anti-Semitism for political purposes. About this time the Ku Klux Klan was revived; it proceeded to wage violence against black, Jewish, and Catholic Americans. In the 1920s and 1930s, crosses were burned on Jewish property; synagogues were desecrated and vandalized. On occasion, the victims fought back. In the 1920s, Jewish and Catholic immigrants attacked parades and gatherings of the Ku Klux Klan in Ohio and New Jersey.[27]

Organized Anti-Semitism and Hate Crimes

Between 1932 and 1941, the number of openly anti-Semitic regional and nationwide organizations grew from only one to well over a hundred. Two dozen were large-scale operations holding numerous anti-Semitic rallies, some drawing thousands. Millions of anti-Semitic leaflets, pamphlets, and newspapers were distributed. Among the more prominent groups were the German-American Bund and the Silver Shirts. As we noted in Chapter 4, Father Charles Coughlin's organizations—the National Union for Social Justice and the Christian Front—became active in anti-Jewish agitation in the 1930s.[28] Early in 1940, the FBI arrested more than a dozen members of a Christian Front group reportedly intending to kill "Jews and Communists, 'to knock off about a dozen Congressmen,' and to seize post offices, the Customs House, and armories in New York. In the homes of the group were found 18 cans of cordite, 18 rifles, and 5,000 rounds of ammunition."[29] Coughlin himself did not openly advocate anti-Semitic violence, but he often defended those who did.

Increased anti-Semitism in Nazi Germany was an important factor in the rising number of neo-Nazi attacks against Jewish Americans in the United States. German Gentiles had long portrayed their Jewish neighbors in terms of negative stereotypes. The Nazi Holocaust began with restrictions on Jewish communities in the Nazi sphere, soon to be followed by deportation to forced-labor camps and extermination by starvation and mass killings. An estimated 6 million European Jews were killed. Extermination and forced migration reduced the Jewish population in countries such as Poland and Germany to just 10 percent of their former numbers. In the United States, the sense of oppression among Jewish Americans was reinforced not only by newspaper reports of European refugees but also by the growing knowledge that the U.S. government was aiding these actions in Germany, at first by continuing normal economic and diplomatic relations and later by turning its back on thousands of refugees.[30]

Violent attacks on Jewish Americans, their property, and their synagogues were common after World War II. More than forty major incidents were reported in 1945 and 1946 in the United States, and there have been numerous attacks each

A common hate crime is the defacing of headstones in Jewish American cemeteries.

year since. The Anti-Defamation League (ADL), established in 1913 as a branch of the fraternal organization B'nai B'rith, now publishes an annual report on anti-Semitic incidents. Generally, only blatant instances of anti-Semitism are reported to the ADL; most personal experiences of subtle discrimination are not reported. The ADL's first survey (1979) included 129 reported cases of vandalism, such as attempted arson and the painting of swastikas on tombstones or synagogues. Between 1979 and 1984, a total of 3,694 incidents was reported. The numbers increased in the late 1980s and 1990s. A record 2,066 incidents were reported for 1994. The numbers have remained in this range; 1,722 incidents were reported in the most recent ADL (1996) report. These acts have included threatening phone calls, attacks on individuals, and acts of vandalism against Jewish-owned property (arson, bombings, and cemetery desecrations). In 1996, a bomb was exploded at the front of a New York City Jewish Center and two men in Wisconsin shot people praying inside a synagogue with a BB-gun. Significantly, in recent years several state legislatures have passed laws making religious desecrations special crimes.[31]

The ADL has reported an increase in the number of anti-Semitic groups participating in the development of a global network of anti-Semites by spreading racist propaganda on the Internet.[32] Moreover, attacks on African and Jewish Americans by the Ku Klux Klan and other white supremacy organizations have reappeared in recent years. One neo-Nazi group, The Order, was formed in Idaho in 1983 to conduct a war against the "Zionist Occupation Government." Members of the group machine-gunned a Jewish American talk-show host in Denver, committed armed robberies, counterfeited money, set fire to a synagogue, and killed police officers trying to capture them. The number of hate crimes by groups of skinheads (young, white neo-Nazis who shave their heads) has also grown in recent years.[33]

Religious Discrimination and Conflict

A number of federal court cases have involved religious discrimination against Jewish Americans. In the 1950s and 1960s, Orthodox Jewish business owners fought local Sunday "blue laws" requiring businesses to close on Sunday, the Christian holy day; they argued that such laws violated their First Amendment right not to be penalized for their religious practices. The Supreme Court rejected their case and upheld the blue laws. In addition, Christian religious observances, such as reciting the Lord's Prayer, were once standard in public schools. The imposition of these practices on Jewish American children was opposed in courts from New York to California. In the 1960s, the Supreme Court ruled against these officially sanctioned religious practices in the public schools.[34] Although in the mid-1980s a more conservative Supreme Court upheld the practice of daily prayers in state legislatures and the local government practice of constructing Christian nativity scenes on public property as part of an official Christmas celebration, the Court reaffirmed the principle of the separation of church and state in a 1992 decision, *Lee v. Weisman*, which involved prayer at a junior high school graduation.[35]

In other cases in which individual claims to religious liberty (especially by non-Christians) are made against the government, the same conservative Court has ruled in favor of government bans on religious expression. In a five-to-four decision, the Court ruled in 1986 that the U.S. Air Force could require an Orthodox rabbi employed as a chaplain to remove his small religious cap, the yarmulke, when working indoors. Since childhood Rabbi S. Simcha Goldman, an Orthodox Jew, had observed the Orthodox tradition of keeping his head covered, a tradition designed to remind individuals of God's omnipresence. The Pentagon decided to spend a large amount of money in court defending its position of preventing Orthodox Jews from wearing the yarmulke while in uniform. Several dissenting justices asked why military authorities had the right to limit religious freedom when civil authorities did not. The impact of these recent cases is to give court sanction to government decisions on which religious expressions are permissible within the government sphere and which are not.[36]

Jewish Americans Fight Back

Fear of street crime and anti-Semitism led to the formation of a few militant self-protective associations beginning in the late 1960s. In 1968, Rabbi Meir Kahane organized the Jewish Defense League (JDL) in New York City, in part to deal with threats against Jewish American communities in cities. The JDL's goals included not only the reinvigoration of ethnic pride but also the physical defense of citizens wherever threatened. The JDL organized armed citizen patrols in New York and other cities to protect communities from street crime. During the 1980s, JDL members protesting the treatment of Jews in the Soviet Union disrupted Soviet diplomatic activities and even tried to assassinate high-level Soviet diplomats. Strober has argued that the JDL touched a "middle-class nerve" and that for many Jewish Americans the traditional organizations had appeared unwilling to vigorously defend Jewish interests.[37] Although most Jewish Americans have strongly disapproved of the JDL's violent tactics, many supported some of its defensive aims, at least in the beginning. In 1990, Rabbi Kahane was assassinated; an Egyptian-born Muslim was charged with his murder but was acquitted by a New York City jury. The assassination did not end the JDL's activities, and the organization has continued to pursue the goal of aggressive defense of Jewish American issues and communities. Indeed, the group has been associated with terrorism in the United States and overseas. The FBI has reported that the JDL and related groups, for example, Kahane Chai, which was founded after Kahane's death, were responsible for a dozen terrorist acts across the United States in the decade before 1995. Because of this terrorist activity, the Anti-Defamation League issued a 1995 report that condemned the "Kahanists' reckless violence against Jews [who do not agree with the group] and non-Jews" and described these extremists as a "cult of violence and racism who speak only for themselves."[38] Clearly, the overwhelming majority of Jewish Americans today do not support such groups.

Black–Jewish Relations

African Americans and Jewish Americans share a long history, much of it filled with examples of mutual support and assistance. Three Jewish immigrants participated in John Brown's armed struggle against slavery in the 1850s, and in 1917 a Jewish newspaper condemned antiblack violence in the East St. Louis riot, comparing it with an anti-Semitic pogrom in Russia. The chairperson of the NAACP during most of the period between 1914 and 1939, Joel E. Springarn, was Jewish. Moreover, the 761st Tank Battalion, an all-black unit in World War II's segregated armed forces, led General George Patton's Third Army and was the first of the groups that liberated the Jews in the Nazi concentration camps at Dachau and Buchenwald. Even though they were denied equality at home, these black troops risked their lives to free the Jewish victims of Nazism. During the civil rights movement of the 1960s, Jewish Americans made up more than half of both the white students who went south to register black voters and the white lawyers who went south to defend civil rights protesters. Some Jewish Americans were murdered by white southerners because they were fighting for black civil rights. Much of the financial support for civil rights organizations also came from Jewish Americans.[39]

However, there has been conflict between Jewish Americans and African Americans since the 1960s. In the 1960s riots and rebellions—and again in similar 1980s and 1990s rebellions—black rioters have sometimes attacked local Jewish

American businesses that they saw as exploitative. This and other developments generated a backlash among many Jewish Americans. In some areas, black street criminals have been seen as responsible for destroying the peace of Jewish neighborhoods. For example, much controversy between black and Jewish Americans has centered in certain areas of New York City. In the early 1990s, there was great tension between Hasidic Jews and blacks in Brooklyn. The Hasidic community in the Williamsburg area of Brooklyn even set up its own crime patrols to police the area against non-Jewish criminals thought to be living nearby. The patrols harassed and beat some black and Latino residents from nearby areas who ventured into the Hasidic community. In the nearby area of Crown Heights, a Hasidic driver accidently ran over a black child, setting off anti-Jewish rioting by angry groups of black residents in which a rabbinical student was murdered. The traffic death, rioting, and murder greatly increased the tensions between the black and Jewish residents of New York City.[40]

Since the 1960s, black anti-Semitism and criticism of Zionism have alienated a significant number of Jewish Americans from active participation in black–Jewish coalitions. And antiblack sentiments are not unknown among Jewish Americans.[41] That economic advancement has been more available to Jewish than to black Americans is one source of black antagonism. In the 1970s some black leaders broadcast anti-Semitic statements aimed at the Jewish merchants and landlords they believed were exploiting their poorer brothers and sisters. A few black leaders seized upon the "abstract idea of the conspiratorial Jew,"[42] as when they falsely blamed Jewish American leaders for President Jimmy Carter's firing of Andrew Young from his post as U.N. ambassador in 1979. Also troubling has been the appearance of political anti-Semitism, illustrated during Jesse Jackson's 1984 campaign for the Democratic presidential nomination. Jackson referred to New York City as "Hymietown" and to Zionism as the "poison weed" of Judaism. Jackson subsequently apologized. In addition, Jackson and a large number of the black delegates to the Democratic convention refused to disavow the comments of another black leader, Louis Farrakhan, whose anti-Semitic utterances included a reference to Judaism as a "gutter religion."[43] Into the late 1990s Farrakhan's statements about Judaism have continued to be a source of tension between the black and Jewish communities.

In her book *Deborah, Golda, and Me: Being Female and Jewish in America*, Letty Pogrebin discusses some reasons for the current tensions between black and Jewish Americans: "The differences between blacks and Jews are rarely more obvious than when each group speaks about its own 'survival,' a word that both use frequently but with quite dissimilar meanings. . . . Blacks worry about their actual conditions and fear for the present; Jews worry about their history and fear for the future." Each group fears the other for different reasons: Jewish Americans fear the greater numbers of blacks in the cities and a few black leaders such as Farrakhan who have periodically made anti-Semitic remarks. African Americans, in contrast, fear Jewish Americans because they are part of the dominant white group.[44]

Still, the tensions between black and Jewish Americans that can be seen in some urban communities have not substantially affected Jewish American commitments to civil rights and antidiscrimination legislation. Among the major white groups in the United States, Jewish Americans are still the most liberal on racial issues. National Opinion Research Center polls from 1980 to 1990 found that Jewish American views on racial matters were closer to those of the black respondents than to those of white Protestants and white Catholics.[45] A 1992 nationwide survey conducted for the Anti-Defamation League of B'nai B'rith found that Jewish Americans were among the least likely of all white Americans to hold negative views about African Americans. Compared with all white Americans, Jewish Americans were more likely to believe that black Americans do not receive equal treatment in the economic, educational, or judicial arenas. Their beliefs on racial matters were generally much closer to those of black Americans than to those of other whites.[46]

Many Jewish American individuals and organizations continue to support black civil rights causes and black communities. For example, even though some Jewish businesses were burned during the 1992 Los Angeles riot, thirty synagogues and Hillel centers (campus organizations for Jewish students), as well as the antihunger organization Mazon, provided large amounts of clothing and food to black churches offering relief to black families in the riot areas. The Los Angeles uprising provoked a number of Jewish American leaders to call for an expansion of Jewish action on behalf of African Americans in the "noble tradition of compassion for the stranger."[47]

The pattern of mutual support can be seen in the highest political arenas in the mid-1990s. For example, a 1994 study by the American Jewish Congress of the votes of the thirty-nine black and thirty-two Jewish members of the U.S. Congress found that the two groups voted alike much of the time on matters of interest to their respective communities, including issues of separation of church and state and social welfare programs.[48]

In the late 1990s, black and Jewish citizens in numerous dialogue groups seek ways to ease tensions between these two traditional allies in the civil rights struggle. For example, in January 1997 some seventy black and Jewish teenagers joined in celebrating Martin Luther King, Jr.'s birthday by working in eight local soup kitchens. Operation Understanding, a cooperative group created in 1985 by an African American Congressperson and a Jewish investment executive, is jointly sponsored by the Urban League and the American Jewish Committee. Each year since its founding, the group has brought together groups of Jewish and black students to travel together. They visit sites of importance to each group, such as Ellis Island, where large numbers of eastern European immigrants entered the United States, or the Mississippi location of the murder of black and Jewish civil rights workers. These groups also work together on projects such as rebuilding the recently burned black churches in the South.[49]

POLITICS

From their first arrival in the colonies, Jewish Americans were treated as outsiders to the political system. Members of the first Jewish community in New Amsterdam were specifically barred from holding public office, and in general voting and officeholding in the colonies were limited to Christians. Still, Jewish Americans made substantial contributions to the American Revolution, and the new government to which the Revolution gave birth brought important benefits to Jewish citizens by establishing the separation of church and state. The Constitution's prohibition of religious qualifications for public office and the Bill of Rights' protection of speech and religious choice granted political freedom at the federal level. However, political enfranchisement was slower to come at the state level. Only five states had removed voting and officeholding restrictions by 1790; six others carried Christians-only provisions for political participation as late as 1876. Until the Civil War, rabbis were prohibited from serving as army chaplains. Still, "anti-Semitism never became rooted in the political tradition of American society," notes Chaim Waxman, as it had in the European political systems from which the immigrants had come. Will Herberg has written: "In America, religious pluralism is . . . not merely a historical and political fact, it is . . . the primordial condition of things, an essential aspect of the American Way of Life."[50]

In the first years of the new republic, the anti-Jewish practices of some Federalist officials, combined with Federalist support for the Alien and Sedition Laws, guaranteed that Jewish Americans would support the liberal Jeffersonian political party, later to become the Democratic party. A few Jewish Americans, mostly Democrats, were elected to local, state, and national offices prior to the Civil War. Although Jews supported Democrats for decades, some voters gravitated to the antislavery Republican party in the 1850s, especially Abraham Lincoln's admirers in the Midwest.[51]

The voting power of Jewish Americans increased as they became more concentrated in northern cities at the beginning of the twentieth century. While some Socialist party candidates received strong support, many Jewish Americans remained Republicans or supported the Irish-dominated Democratic machines, which provided jobs and shelter to needy immigrants.[52] Eastern European Jews became famous for exercising the franchise and undertaking volunteer political activity. Whereas in the early twentieth century Irish Americans used ethnic politics to advance their immediate economic and family interests—to create jobs and patronage—Jewish Americans, although concerned with the same bread-and-butter matters, were more political-issue-oriented, particularly in the matter of expanding civil rights.[53]

Jewish Americans and the Democratic Party

In spite of their conscientious political activity, by 1910 few Jewish Americans had been able to win electoral office, and few had been appointed to high-level positions. An occasional city-council member, one or two state legislators, a judge—this was the extent of their success. At the national level, the impact was modest as well. Many Jewish Americans still voted for Republicans. The appearance of an internationalist Democratic candidate, Woodrow Wilson, brought a majority of Jewish voters to the Democrats for the first time in decades. Wilson appointed a few Jewish Americans to important positions, including the legal genius Louis Brandeis to the Supreme Court.[54]

After Wilson, Jewish American voters generally supported Republican presidential candidates until the late 1920s, although they were shifting to Democratic candidates at the local, state, and congressional levels. In 1920, there were eleven Jewish members of Congress, ten of them Republicans, but by 1922 most were Democratic. New York Governor Al Smith, of poor Irish background, attracted many Jewish Americans to the Democratic party and received substantial support in his 1928 bid for the presidency.[55]

Although Jewish Americans have become increasingly more suburban and middle-income since the 1920s, their vote has not shifted heavily back to the Republican party. Franklin Roosevelt brought Jewish Americans firmly into the Democratic fold in 1932. Roosevelt's anti-Nazi rhetoric and his support of government programs such as Social Security and of union organization won over many Jewish voters. Until Roosevelt, only a few Jewish Americans had served in the executive or judicial branches of the federal government. Benjamin Cohen, Felix Frankfurter, and Louis Brandeis served as advisers to Roosevelt, and Roosevelt appointed Henry Morgenthau, Jr., secretary of the Treasury.[56] Yet Roosevelt's strong regard among Jewish Americans did not lead him to take dynamic political action on behalf of the refugees from Nazi-dominated Europe. One reason for this was his fear of the intense anti-Semitism prevailing in the United States during the 1930s and 1940s, especially among white Gentile members of the U.S. Congress. Anti-Jewish discrimination was then quite common in politics, social affairs, education, employment, jury selection in certain states, and residential restrictions.[57]

Since Roosevelt, the proportion of the Jewish American vote going to Democratic presidential candidates has remained substantial. In 1948, three-fourths of Jewish voters supported Harry Truman. Three-fourths voted for Adlai Stevenson during the Eisenhower landslides, and more than three-fourths supported John Kennedy in 1960. Considerably more than three-fourths voted for Lyndon Johnson in 1964 and for Hubert Humphrey in 1968. In 1976, Democrat Jimmy Carter received 70 percent of the Jewish vote. In 1980, however, Carter received only 45 percent of the Jewish vote in his second bid for the presidency, according to one poll, with the rest split between Ronald Reagan and an independent candidate. This, the lowest percentage given to a Democratic presidential candidate since Franklin Roosevelt, was said to have reflected Jewish concern over Carter's attempts to build bridges to the Arab world. Jewish Americans feared that Israel's security might be jeopardized by Carter's peace initiatives in the Middle East.

But in 1984, according to a *Times*/CBS report, Jewish Americans were the only major white group to give a majority of their votes to the Democratic candidate, Walter Mondale. One reason for this large anti-Reagan vote among Jewish Americans was Reagan's close tie to the religious right. Some of the fundamentalist Christian preachers made anti-Semitic remarks and asserted the dominance of Protestant Christian values over those of other religious traditions. A 1984 poll found that 57 percent of Jewish respondents identified themselves as Democrats, 31 percent as independents, and only 12 percent as Republicans.[58] In addition, liberals outnumbered conservatives among Jewish respondents to the 1990 National Jewish Population Survey, although a significant portion identified themselves as middle-of-the-road politically. The survey also found that most Jewish Americans were registered to vote.[59]

Historically, Jewish Americans have been underrepresented among elected and appointed officials. Just over a hundred Jewish Americans have ever been a U.S. senator, House member, or governor. Recent years have seen some improvement. In 1995 Jewish Americans were represented by thirty-four members in Congress, a number that was down significantly from 1993. The only American of Jewish ancestry to be considered for president was Barry Goldwater (a convert to the Episcopal religion), who was defeated in his bid for the presidency in 1964. So far, only a half-dozen Jewish Americans have ever served on the U.S. Supreme Court, although perhaps one-fifth of the nation's lawyers in recent decades have been Jewish. In 1993 President Bill Clinton appointed the first Jewish American woman to the Supreme Court, Ruth Bader Ginsburg, a strong advocate of women's rights. She was the first Jewish judge to serve on the court since 1969. The first Jewish American in a presidential cabinet was Oscar Straus, appointed by Theodore Roosevelt in 1906. About two dozen have served in cabinets since that time. Jewish Americans have served in significant (although less than representative) numbers in local and state executive and legislative offices. It was not until 1974 that a Jewish American (Abraham Beame) became mayor of New York City. Also in the 1970s, Dianne Feinstein became the first Jewish woman to be elected mayor of a major city, San Francisco.[60]

While these numbers are impressive compared with the limited political power of certain other racial and ethnic groups, discrimination still plays a role in limiting the number of Jewish Americans who occupy the political front lines. The proportion of Jewish Americans in elected office is low given their high proportion among political activists. Although there are more Jews than Presbyterians or Episcopalians in the United States, in recent years Jewish Americans have not held nearly as many congressional offices as have these powerful Protestant groups.[61]

Unions and Community Organizations

Eastern European Jewish immigrants actively protested oppressive working conditions in the 1890s, organizing to fight long hours, low pay, and unsafe working conditions. Tens of thousands of workers struck the New York garment industry in 1910 and inspired union militants elsewhere.[62] New York City data for the 1930s show large numbers of Jewish Americans in food, entertainment, clothing, and jewelry unions. Jewish union leaders went beyond the problems of wages and working conditions to grapple with broader issues, developing health, pension, and educational programs that would be imitated by all unions. Jewish Americans also played an important role in the growth of the American Socialist party between 1905 and 1912 and other subsequent labor–liberal parties.[63]

The organized Jewish American community has long been impressive. One important aspect of this "civic Judaism," to use Jonathan Woocher's term, is the North American Jewish federation movement, now made up of just under two hundred social service and educational agencies representing and serving Jewish Americans. The federation movement originally emphasized philanthropy and Jewish immigrant adjustment, but more recently has stressed social activism and political survival. In the mid-1990s, the federation movement was raising hundreds of millions of dollars for Jewish causes, but was facing some decline in support.[64]

By the 1930s, several civic and civil rights organizations had been established whose importance would persist: the Anti-Defamation League, the American Jewish Congress, the American Jewish Committee, and the United Jewish Appeal. Since 1906 the American Jewish Committee has vigorously fought anti-Semitic prejudice and discrimination in the United States. The American Jewish Congress, established early in this century by eastern European Jews, has also fought for the civil rights of Jewish Americans. Both are large organizations. The Anti-Defamation League has carried out a vigorous civil rights campaign in its mission to root out anti-Semitism. The United Jewish Appeal, established in 1939, has been a successful fund-raising organization that has aided a variety of causes, including war refugees and the state of Israel.[65]

The founding and survival of Israel have been concerns of major Jewish American organizations in the post–World War II period. During the Eisenhower administration Jewish American political pressure to support Israel often went unheeded, but by the 1960s U.S. support for Israel had sharply increased. Since the 1960s, Jewish American political pressure has been mobilized for numerous other causes, such as support for Jews in the (former) Soviet Union and opposition to political candidates taking a tolerant or supportive position toward Arab nations hostile to Israel.[66]

In addition to combating anti-Semitism, some organizations have broadened their focus and worked to eliminate all racial prejudice and discrimination and to ensure the continued separation of church and state. Jewish American commitment to expanded civil rights for African Americans has been strong since the 1800s. Numerous Jewish congregations and their rabbis were active in the black civil rights protests of the 1950s and 1960s. Jewish Americans were also active in the antiwar movement of the 1960s and 1970s.[67] These decades were the period one author describes as the Jews' "golden age," during which many Jewish Americans committed their efforts to the rights of the "underdogs."[68]

In recent years, some Jewish Americans have accused the well-off board members of the American Jewish Committee, the American Jewish Congress, the United Jewish Appeal, and the Anti-Defamation League of being more sympathetic to the needs of employers than to traditional concerns for workers, the poor, and discrimination against black Americans and other people of color. This criticism may be somewhat unfair, but it does highlight a dilemma faced by Jewish Americans today. As the most affluent of the "white ethnic" groups, Jewish Americans might be expected to develop the generally conservative orientation of other high-income white groups.[69] Yet, given their Jewish past and the periodic recurrence of anti-Semitism in the United States, most Jewish Americans remain more liberal, politically and economically, than non-Jewish whites.

THE ECONOMY

From their earliest presence in colonial communities, Jewish immigrants contributed to the prosperity of America. One Jewish immigrant from Poland, Haym Salomon, played a critical role in financing the American Revolution with a loan to the struggling revolutionary government.[70] The opening of commerce in the Americas presented a golden opportunity for European Jews, who had centuries of experience as a "middleman" trading minority in Europe, where they were excluded from land ownership and skilled-worker guilds. Their success in commercial pursuits made them an accessible scapegoat for the non-Jewish poor, who saw them as exploiters, and for the non-Jewish rich, who viewed them as an economic or political threat. The often marginal nature of their businesses, as well as outside white hostility, fostered the growth of an ethnic economy in which Jewish Americans provided economic aid to one another in order to maintain their enterprises and communities.[71]

Establishing an Economic Niche: A "Middleman Minority"?

The rate of penetration of a new immigrant group into the core society depends on its own economic background as well as the economic and political conditions at the point of destination. Most central European Jews were poor when they came. They arrived when frontier development and industrial growth were exploding, and they found that their experience in selling was in demand. As street vendors, they roamed city streets and the countryside. Many eventually became prosperous shopkeepers, and a few even became bankers and industrialists.[72]

By the late nineteenth century, 58 percent of employed Jewish Americans were in trading or financial occupations, 20 percent were office workers, and 6 percent were professionals. The remaining 16 percent were blue-collar workers or farmers. Jewish American entrepreneurs were concentrated in clothing, jewelry, meat, and leather businesses. By the 1890s, a majority of the German and other central European Jews seemed to be moving up the economic ladder. Although they had prospered by the second generation, they were still unable to enter the top positions in an economy whose central industrial enterprises were firmly controlled by British Americans.[73]

Coming in next, the Jewish immigrants from eastern Europe entered the expanding U.S. industrial economy at an opportune time. Most were poor and poorly educated; nearly half the women were illiterate. But their considerable experience in coping with oppression provided them a cultural heritage replete with strategies for finding economic niches in which they could survive. Most settled in the industrial cities, and large numbers found employment in the expanding garment industry. As some moved out of the manual occupations, new Jewish immigrants filled their places at the bottom rungs of the mobility ladder—until discriminatory quotas curtailed immigration in the 1920s. Men, women, and children—whole families—engaged in low-wage manufacturing work. The long hours and poor conditions of the sweatshops of industrial capitalism led to many reform and union movements among these immigrants and their children.[74]

In the early 1900s, more than one-third of the eastern European immigrants were employed in the garment industry, one-fourth were in building trades, and one-fifth were in retail trade. Many wage earners set their sights on a business career. Some moved up the economic ladder from peddler to owner of a scrap-metal yard, or from needleworker to clothing entrepreneur. But those in the second generation were encouraged to seek clerical and sales work. A few eventually worked their way to the head of clothing firms; by 1905 a significant proportion of the clothing industry in New York City was under eastern European Jewish management. A number went into the professions; by 1905 eastern European Jews had a toehold in law, medicine, and dentistry in New York.[75]

Jewish women contributed significantly to family incomes. A Philadelphia study in this early period found that one in three Jewish American households had a woman working outside the home. Most unmarried women worked. Because of the low wages of both male and female workers, families needed the wages women earned outside the home or from taking in sewing or laundry in the home. Wives joined their husbands in the small retail shops that supplied many Jewish neighborhoods. Many women were left to raise their children alone when their husbands died or deserted the family. At least one-fourth of immigrant fathers left their families because of economic (for example, job search) and other reasons. A National Desertion Bureau was established in 1911, which contributed to the support of a hundred thousand deserted wives and their families in this early period.[76]

From the Depression to 1950

About one-fourth of Jewish Americans in Detroit and Pittsburgh in the mid-1930s were owners or managers, compared with about 9 percent of the total population. A study in Newburyport, Massachusetts, estimated that just under half of the Jewish Americans there had moved into the middle-income range. As in the case of Japanese Americans (see Chapter 11), the solidarity of the Jewish American community and its heavy involvement in small and medium-sized businesses were sources of community survival during the Great Depression. Whenever possible, Jewish American businesses dealt with one another and hired unemployed relatives. Crime, including organized crime, was a way out of poverty for a small proportion of first- and second-generation Jewish Americans in the early decades, but it declined significantly as a force with the movement of large numbers out of the working class and the central-city neighborhoods following World War II.[77]

The ethnic economy provided a fallback position for those who faced anti-Jewish discrimination in the 1930s. One of the goals of anti-Semitic organizations was to reduce the number of Jewish Americans in private and public employment. Non-Jewish whites in the teaching, banking, medical, legal, and engineering professions sought to prohibit Jewish Americans from employment in their sectors. In many cities securing skilled blue-collar jobs and clerical jobs was difficult. The Great Depression accentuated the problem. "No Jews need apply" signs were common, particularly in larger businesses and professional institutions. Placement agencies throughout the Midwest, to take just one area, reported that from two-thirds to 95 percent of job listings excluded Jewish Americans from consideration. Jews also faced discrimination in the teaching profession, particularly in smaller cities and at colleges. From 1900 to the 1950s, discrimination was rife in housing; real estate agents from Philadelphia to Boston to Chicago discriminated against Jewish Americans, while neighbors made life miserable for those who managed to pioneer in desegregating an area. Later, even those who managed to move into the suburbs in significant numbers often found Protestant-oriented organizations and recreational facilities off limits.[78]

One of the fears of anti-Semites has been the alleged Jewish dominance of banking. Yet a *Fortune* magazine survey in 1936 found very few Jewish Americans in banking and finance, and a later survey found that only 600 of the 93,000 banking officials in the United States were Jewish Americans. Nor were they very numerous in heavy industries such as steel or automobiles or in public utilities. Their representation was small in the press and in radio. The *Fortune* survey found that the only sectors in which Jewish Americans dominated were clothing, textiles, and the movies. Even in law and medicine, Jews had little representation in powerful positions. The author of the 1936 *Fortune* article seemed puzzled at the clustering in certain industrial and business areas and explained the situation in the stereotypical terms of Jewish American clannishness.[79]

Such patterns were by no means mysterious; they reflected the extent to which Jewish Americans had to work outside mainstream industries and businesses because of blatant institutionalized discrimination. As McWilliams noted in *A Mask for Privilege,* discrimination forced Jewish Americans to become "the ragpickers of American industry." They were channeled by anti-Semitic discrimination into higher-risk economic spheres marginal to the mainstream economy.[80]

After World War II, extensive employment discrimination continued to be directed at Jewish Americans. Job advertising included restrictions, and many employment agencies required applicants to list their religion or ethnicity, which in turn was used to discriminate against them. In spite of this, many Jewish Americans were able to share in postwar prosperity, particularly in new and riskier industries, such as television and plastics. For Jewish Americans the postwar economic pyramid had a modest working-class base and no significant wealthy elite at the top. Jewish Americans remained concentrated primarily in trade, clothing, and jewelry manufacturing; commerce; merchandising; certain light industries; mass communications; and certain professions.[81] The 1957 Current Population Survey found that three-fourths of Jewish American men were employed in white-collar jobs, compared with 38 percent of white Protestants. Over half were by then in professional and managerial jobs, twice the percentage for white Protestants. Less than one-fourth were in blue-collar positions.[82] Research on business executives, presidents, and board chairmen indicates that in 1900 just under 2 percent were Jews; in 1925 and 1950 the figure was between 2 and 3 percent for each year. Given the preponderance of Jewish Americans in commercial and business employment, these proportions are much lower than they would be if there had been no anti-Jewish discrimination. A very large proportion of the Jewish American executives—just under half—made it to the top only in Jewish businesses within the ethnic economy.[83]

From the 1950s to the 1990s

Data from the 1950s show a sizable proportion (30 percent) of Jewish household heads with incomes above $7,500, compared with 13 percent of the total population. This advantaged economic position has continued in each succeeding decade, although a significant minority, mostly elderly, live in poverty. In a 1987 survey in Rhode Island, over half the Jewish American households responding to a question about family income earned more than $40,000 per year. However, more than half of those aged sixty-five and older had annual household incomes below $25,000; one-third of these received less than $15,000.[84]

The 1990 National Jewish Population Survey (NJPS) estimated the 1989 median annual income for all Jewish American households (families and individuals) to be $39,000. In the same year, the median income for all U.S. households was $28,906 and for all white households $30,406. However, 14 percent of Jewish multiperson households were still classified as low-income (that is, with incomes under $20,000 per year). No direct comparison is available for the general population, but 18 percent of all U.S. households had incomes below $25,000 in that year.[85]

Occupational Mobility

Continuing occupational mobility has characterized Jewish Americans since the 1960s. In that decade an estimated one-fourth of male Jewish workers in New York City were in blue-collar occupations. The blue-collar proportions in studies of other cities were lower. Occupational data for New York, Providence, Milwaukee, Detroit, and Boston showed that 20 to 32 percent of Jewish American males were in professional positions and 28 to 54 percent were in managerial–official positions. Over half of all Jewish American workers in each city were in these two categories, while most of the rest were in either clerical or sales positions. In comparison, the majority of the total employed population in each of those cities was in blue-collar positions. More recent research has confirmed this trend toward white-collar employment. More than one-third of the Jewish respondents in the 1987 Rhode Island survey were in professional occupations; most of the rest were in white-collar occupations. The 1990 NJPS also revealed that most Jewish Americans held salaried white-collar positions; 16 percent were self-employed.[86]

Contrary to the stereotype, in recent decades Jewish American executives have not controlled banking in any area of the United States. Excluding one New York bank (31 percent of whose top managers were Jewish), in 1976 only 2.5 percent of the executives in commercial banks nationwide were Jewish. Among the primary areas of Jewish American population concentration, New York (25 percent Jewish) had the lowest proportion of Jewish executives (2.7 percent) and San Francisco (10 percent Jewish population) had the highest proportion (5 percent). A decade later, Abraham Korman found that only 3.4 percent of the executives in ten of the nation's largest corporate banks were Jewish American.[87]

Discrimination against Jewish Americans was common in corporations until the 1970s. Relatively few were employed in managerial positions in major firms such as the leading automakers. A 1980s study of Jewish Americans in the corporate elite found that most were in Jewish-founded corporations or occupied lower managerial positions in other corporations. Those who have cracked the top of the corporate establishment, such as Irving Shapiro, formerly chief executive officer of DuPont, have usually been brought in from the outside (Shapiro was brought in from government). They have rarely been given the chance to start at the bottom of the corporate hierarchy and work up in the usual way. "They are not even remotely close to being the dominant force they are tragically and mistakenly thought to be by anti-Semites."[88]

In the mid-1980s, an estimated 6 to 8 percent of senior executives in U.S. corporations were Jewish Americans. Studying the distribution of Jewish American executives in corporate America, Korman found that the major (Fortune 500) industries he analyzed fell into three significant groups. Group A, those industries in which Jewish Americans constituted less than 5 percent of senior executives (below the overall corporate percentage of Jewish executives), included many of the largest and most powerful corporations in terms of annual sales and number of employees. Of the thirteen diverse industries in this group, the petroleum industry had the lowest percentage of senior executives who were Jewish Americans. Group B included seven industries with proportions of Jewish senior executives (5 to 8 percent) at or near the overall corporate percentage. In only three industries was the level of Jewish senior executives above the nationwide figure: publishing and printing (9.5 percent), textiles and vinyl flooring (9.9 percent), and apparel (26.7 percent). Among service industries in the Fortune Service 500, Jewish Americans constituted approximately 2 percent of senior executives in utilities and transportation and just under 5 percent in life insurance.[89]

In interviews with management consultants and corporate managers, Korman found that the "outsider" status of Jewish managers, was taken for granted; all found the absence of significant numbers of Jewish Americans in high-level executive positions to be predictable. All agreed that in order to succeed in the corporate hierarchy, Jewish Americans must divest themselves of all visible Jewish identity. Some of the Jewish respondents cited specific anti-Jewish actions that had blocked their career advancement; some were denied titles appropriate to their actual duties. Like Asian Americans (see Chapters 11 and 12), many found they could hold professional or staff positions but would never be seriously considered for the higher executive positions.[90]

Until the last decade or two, higher-level government positions have rarely been open to Jewish Americans. One Jewish American recently noted that when he began his career in the early 1960s, "the State Department (and the CIA and FBI) was virtually closed to Jews."[91] Interestingly, in 1997 the mass media made much of the fact that a dozen or so top people in the U.S. State Department were of Jewish background, including Secretary of State Madeleine Albright. This signalled some change in Jewish representation. However, some Jewish Americans find such media attention offensive, since similar attention is not given to the prevalence of Presbyterian or Catholic officeholders in government.

Perhaps because of greater freedom to excel in the academic sphere, many of the nation's writers, scholars, and professors are Jewish American. Jewish Americans are well represented among distinguished scholars at major universities and among top literary figures. They include Nobel laureate Saul Bellow and prominent intellectuals such as Stephen Jay Gould, Irving Howe, and Seymour Martin Lipset.

The effects of anti-Semitism keep many Jewish Americans in the "gilded ghetto," where they find themselves economically successful but frequently denied the full social recognition and political power that success should have brought. Ghettoization has often been subtle, and progress toward inclusion steady but slow. In 1983, for example, New York City finally introduced a law banning discrimination, including anti-Jewish discrimination, in private clubs; the law did not pass until 1985, and then only after the minimum club membership covered was increased from one hundred to four hundred. In May 1992, a bill banning racial and gender discrimination in large private country clubs made its way to the floor of the New York State senate after being blocked for ten years by its white Protestant opponents. In March of the same year, a similar bill banning discrimination in private clubs finally passed the Florida legislature. The American Jewish Congress headed up a coalition of civil rights groups that worked together to get the bill passed. Still, in the 1990s, Florida is one of only a few states with strong laws prohibiting discrimination in private clubs. Experts estimate that three-fourths of the nation's private golf and country clubs have no black members, and many take either no female or Jewish members or only token numbers. Much discrimination has been hidden by secrecy at the higher socioeconomic levels of this society. Exclusion from certain private social clubs and private schools, where much important information is exchanged, creates economic and political disabilities in other spheres—a clear example of the indirect discrimination discussed in Chapter 1.[92]

Discussions of anti-Jewish discrimination still appear periodically in the mass media. In 1997, an employee at a major rental car company reported that he was told by supervisors that Hasidic Jews were "the worst people to rent to." Two employees also reported that supervisors rejected business accounts from Jewish applicants. While the company denied the allegations, the complaints raised the question of whether this type of economic discrimination against Jewish Americans has really disappeared in the United States.[93]

EDUCATION

Education, secular or religious, was not as high a priority for the earliest groups of Jewish immigrants as it was for later groups; the earlier arrivals focused on success in business rather than on entering a profession or preserving the European tradition of religious scholarship. Significant participation in public schools came in the nineteenth century with the surge of eastern European immigrants, for whom secular education was a means of becoming American. Parents often pushed their children to succeed in school so that they could prosper economically and socially. College was especially valued as a door to a career for the young. Adults, too, were eager to learn the customs of their new country; thousands studied English at evening schools established by philanthropic organizations, many of which were operated by the already acculturated Jewish Americans from Germany. Because eastern European immigrants felt it important for their U.S.–born children to retain their Jewish identity, they established numerous Jewish schools that taught Hebrew and religious practices.[94]

Educational mobility for second- and third-generation Jewish Americans came swiftly. Large numbers of students graduated from high schools in northern cities, and a significant number pursued college educations. By 1920 the proportion of Jewish students in New York City colleges and universities was estimated to be greater than the Jewish proportion of the general population. By the late 1930s, almost half of Jewish students in New York City managed to complete high school, compared with only one-fourth of other students. Nine percent of the nation's 1.1 million college students were Jewish Americans, although they constituted only 3.7 percent of the total population.[95]

Discriminatory Quotas for Jewish Students

Jewish progress was countered by discrimination on the part of Anglo-Protestant Americans. Restrictive quotas for Jewish American students were imposed at numerous colleges and universities from the 1920s to the 1950s. In 1918 Dean Frederick Jones of Yale called for a ban on Jewish students because they were winning most of Yale's scholarships and Gentile students were said to be discouraged by their success. In 1922, Harvard University president A. L. Lowell also called for discriminatory quotas on Jewish students. Covert methods of limiting Jewish admissions, such as "character" tests and requirements for "geographic balance" in an entering class, were employed at many schools. With the use of these quotas, Columbia's Jewish enrollment dropped from 40 percent to 15 percent and Harvard's from 21 percent to 10 percent. In the 1920s, three-fourths of Gentile students applying to a major medical school in New York were admitted; the percentage of Jewish students admitted peaked at half but eventually dropped to one-fifth. In the same decade, restrictions were placed on Jewish admissions to law schools and to the bar in various states. Fraternities and sororities, institutions that groomed students from the "right" racial and ethnic backgrounds for success, excluded Jewish Americans.[96]

Jewish Americans were excluded from teaching positions in higher education. Between the 1920s and the 1940s, Jewish Ph.D.s, even the most distinguished, found it difficult to get appointments at Anglo-Protestant-dominated universities. In 1940, fewer than two in every one hundred of the nation's college and university faculty members were Jewish. The sudden increase in college enrollments following World War II created a demand for teachers; by the end of the 1960s the proportion of Jewish faculty members in U.S. institutions of higher education had risen to 9 percent; in elite colleges the figure was 20 percent.[97]

Affirmative Action Programs

Affirmative action programs, which seek to improve educational opportunities and job chances for black and other non-European groups, have become a political issue for many Jewish Americans since the late 1960s. Some have objected to the use of affirmative action goals to benefit these groups. Jewish Americans have long been among the most vigorous supporters of the principle of merit because of the quota restrictions that denied them access to higher education and jobs from the 1920s to the 1950s. Some have opposed recent affirmative action programs, such as those in college admissions, because of Jewish Americans' heavy commitment to higher education, a commitment that reflects the past exclusion of Jewish Americans from many sectors of the academic and business worlds. The college admissions preferences for non-Jewish groups can disproportionately affect Jewish Americans' access to college degrees and perpetuate the effects of anti-Jewish discrimination in the past.[98]

However, voicing support for affirmative action, Harvard law professor Alan Dershowitz, a Jewish American scholar, notes the "real difference between the institutional impact and intensity of the hurt suffered as part of an invidious pattern of racial *subordination* and as part of a benevolent pattern of racial *equalization*." He points out the bias of admission programs, such as those in Ivy League colleges, that hold fairly constant the number of students admitted from certain white Anglo-Protestant pools (descendants and relatives of alumni and those admitted to achieve "geographic balance"), yet at the same time make room for certain affirmative action applicants (Latinos and blacks) by reducing the number of other groups (Jewish and Asian Americans) who are admitted. He argues that it would be much more equitable for those white Anglo-Protestant groups that have long benefited from the exclusion of all subordinate racial–ethnic groups to bear a *heavier share* of the burden of this equalization through affirmative action.[99]

Continuing Achievements in Education

Severe discrimination declined after World War II, and large numbers of Jewish American veterans took advantage of free college and graduate school tuition under the GI bill. Since that time the educational attainment of Jewish

Americans has reached ever higher levels. The 1990 NJPS estimated that only about 6 percent of Jewish adults twenty-five and older had less than a high-school education, compared with almost one-fourth of all white adults in the United States. Approximately half of the women and almost 60 percent of the men were college graduates, compared with 17 percent of all white women and 24 percent of all white men. Many held advanced degrees. Jewish American families place very heavy emphasis on high levels of educational attainment. Today, many U.S. universities have very large numbers of Jewish American students. An estimated 85 percent of Jewish Americans attend college at some time during their lives.[100]

Schooling in Jewish religion and culture also persists. The proportion of second-generation eastern European Jews who received instruction in religious schools was small considering the heavy emphasis traditionally placed on Jewish education in Europe. In New York City the proportion did not exceed one-fourth during the early decades of the twentieth century. Yet surveys of Jewish Americans in recent decades have found strong support among parents for some type of Jewish education for children, and large percentages of both adults and children have reported receiving such education. More than 86 percent of the adult respondents in the 1987 Rhode Island study, and 80 percent of the children in their households, had received at least some Jewish education. The 1990 NJPS estimated that approximately half of all Jewish adults nationwide had received some Jewish education. The renewed emphasis on formal learning of one's heritage and religion in the lower grades has carried over to colleges and universities. In the 1960s, there were more than five dozen faculty positions in Jewish studies; by the 1990s, there were more than three hundred.[101]

RELIGION AND ZIONISM

Religious services for members of the first Jewish community in New Amsterdam were restricted to their homes. In the British colonies, religious freedom was variable, but most restricted Jewish American participation in colonial life. The anti-Jewish bias of other settlers sustained a vigorous oppositional culture, the base for much Jewish protest against religious and political oppression from then to the present. Support for maximizing religious freedom increased after 1790, particularly among Thomas Jefferson and his followers. While the new nation remained fundamentally Christian, religious freedom gradually became law in each of the new states, most by 1850.

Until the 1790s, the Sephardic tradition prevailed in the synagogues. As the numbers of German and other central European Jews increased, some broke away from Sephardic congregations and developed the practice of founding multiple synagogues in a community, each following the traditions of its members. The two hundred synagogues founded by the new immigrants served as an antidote to loneliness as well as a center for religious observances. All but one of these were Orthodox. During the 1850s and 1860s most congregations Americanized their religious practices, in part to achieve greater respectability in the eyes of non-Jews. This Reform movement became organized in the Union of American Hebrew Congregations in the 1870s. The new Reform temples had shorter services, organ music, and English prayers. The changes taking place in U.S. Judaism were articulated by Isaac Mayer Wise, the spiritual leader of German Jewish immigrants in the mid-1800s, who advocated a more optimistic faith that could celebrate democracy in its "temples without tears."[102]

In the 1820s a number of independent Jewish organizations emerged as some philanthropic societies broke away from the synagogues that had founded them. Some service organizations founded over the next few decades had greater memberships than synagogues. Although festivals and rites of passage continued to be celebrated in the synagogue, these independent societies and organizations often came to replace the synagogue as the center of life in the Jewish community.[103]

The role of *Judaism* (the Jewish religion) in Jewish identity was a point of conflict between the German Jews and the new eastern European immigrants. The German Jews saw themselves as Americans whose religion happened to be Judaism. They generally endeavored to be inconspicuous in order to be accepted as true Americans. In contrast, the new immigrants from eastern Europe had a strong desire to maintain their old ethnic identity. Most were Orthodox, observing the Sabbath and kosher dietary laws insofar as the conditions of poverty that defined immigrant life would permit. Theirs was a grass-roots adaptation of Orthodoxy that focused on family and group feeling and stressed charitable acts, support of Jews abroad, and selective observance of rituals.[104]

Conservative Judaism, which began in the late 1880s as a modified traditionalism in reaction to Reform groups, was especially appealing to the U.S.–born generation of eastern European Jews. The Conservative synagogues observed many Orthodox rituals and traditions, although they discontinued the separation of men and women at worship services as well as certain traditional religious practices, such as strict dress codes.[105]

By 1935 Orthodox synagogues had about 1 million members, Conservative synagogues 300,000, and Reform temples 200,000. The authority of the rabbi, as well as the traditional ritual and theology, became less important as one moved from Orthodox to Conservative to Reform congregations. Many synagogues built in the new middle-class neighborhoods in the 1920s were designed as community centers as well as religious centers. However, membership and attendance were low; by the 1930s, only one-fourth of Jewish American families were formally affiliated with a synagogue. The thoroughly Jewish atmosphere of highly concentrated neighborhoods provided a strong sense of ethnic identity; most apparently felt little need to ensure the survival of Jewishness through formal affiliations or extensive religious education for their children. During this period some second-generation eastern European Jews turned away from all branches of Judaism; secularism, socialism, labor radicalism, and Zionism became the new "religions" of many younger Jewish Americans during the crises of the Depression and World War II.[106]

A Jewish elder shows youngsters how to blow a shofar, the ram's horn used in religious observances.

Trends in Religious Practice and Identity

Expanding suburbanization after World War II brought an increase in the number of congregations in the rings around central cities. As a small minority in suburbia, Jewish American families sought a public symbol to affirm their Jewishness and a means to ensure the Jewishness of their children. Synagogue membership and ritual observances saw marked increases. Silberman suggests that "the new suburbanites desperately wanted to be full members of American society, but it was not until that desire began to be realized that they discovered how much they wanted to remain Jews as well."[107]

Jewish American religion currently reflects a substantial interest in the traditional heritage, maintenance of the synagogue as a community center, and home religious practices. Although lighting Hanukkah candles was the only religious ritual always practiced by a majority of the respondents in the 1987 Rhode Island survey, more than half lit Sabbath candles and had a Passover Seder at least sometimes, and two-thirds fasted on Yom Kippur. Most parents felt it was important for their children to know about Jewish customs and beliefs, to become Bar/Bat Mitzvah, to give to charity, to have Jewish friends and marry a Jew, and to read prayers in synagogue services. The two most important issues defining Jewishness for these respondents were having close family ties and remembering well the European Holocaust.[108]

According to the 1990 NJPS, 62 percent of Americans of Jewish ancestry identified as religious. However, less than 5 percent felt that their Jewish identity was based solely on religious group membership. Even among the religious Jews, "cultural group" and "ethnic group" were named the most frequently as a basis of Jewish identity. The survey also noted a general movement away from traditional Judaism. According to the national survey, only 41 percent of entirely Jewish households and 13 percent of mixed households were affiliated with a synagogue or temple in 1990. Among the affiliated, Conservative congregations had the largest proportion of households. The relatively larger household size of those who are affiliated suggests that families with children are the most likely to be active. Moreover, rituals remain important. Well over half of religious Jews and approximately one-tenth of secular Jews reported fasting on Yom Kippur and attending synagogue on high holidays. More than three-fourths of entirely Jewish households and approximately 60 percent of mixed Jewish-Gentile households reported that they attended Passover Seder at least sometimes and lit Hanukkah candles.[109]

Judaism has become one of the major U.S. religious traditions. Modern Judaism is a "voluntary" faith: Jewish Americans can reject it or accept it to varying degrees. Some call this Judaism a "cardiac" religion, emphasizing the heart or one's morals rather than traditional ritual and doctrine. The tolerance that has developed for different denominations within Judaism is similar to that of Protestantism.[110] However, Orthodox Judaism, which bases Jewish identity on descent from a Jewish mother, still involves ritual observance with fewer adaptations to the secular world. In contrast, Reform Judaism accepts Jewish heredity through either a Jewish father or mother and emphasizes humanitarian Jewish principles rather than ritual. It defines Jewishness as a religious preference rather than an all-encompassing identity. Conservative Judaism represents a middle path between Orthodoxy's tradition and Reform's assimilationism. Conservatives are willing to adapt to the dominant culture yet wish to retain much of the form and content of the Jewish tradition.[111]

Zionism

At the heart of modern Jewish consciousness is a concern for the survival and prosperity of the Middle-Eastern nation of Israel. For many Jewish Americans "Israel represents Jewry's positive response to centuries of anti-Semitism in general and to Hitler's attempted genocide in particular."[112] Whether active in religious Judaism or not, many Jewish Americans share the commitment to *Zionism*—the right of Jews everywhere to have a secure national homeland. This commitment to Israel has affected not only Jewish voting patterns and black–Jewish relations (because of pro-Arab sentiments among some black leaders) but also Jewish American philanthropy. Jewish American financial support has been critical to Israel's survival in the face of hostility from nearby Arab governments.

In the 1980s and 1990s, debate increased among Jewish Americans over certain actions of the government of Israel. In the 1990 NJPS, 83 percent of religious Jews and almost half of secular Jews felt an attachment to Israel.[113] Yet, from time to time many Jewish Americans have raised questions about the direction of Israel's development and the wisdom of Israeli leaders. One-fourth of the respondents and most Jewish leaders in the American Jewish Committee's 1989 survey agreed that Israel's continued occupation of territories it has captured would "erode Israel's democratic and humanitarian character." Most favored "territorial compromise for credible guarantees of peace" and peace negotiations between Israel and the Palestine Liberation Organization (PLO) if the latter organization recognized the state of Israel and renounced terrorism.[114]

Since 1990 there have been ongoing negotiations between the Israeli government and the PLO over the future of the Palestinian population. An agreement was reached giving the PLO some political authority over the Palestinian population in certain of the occupied areas, and Israeli troops were withdrawn. A new U.S. organization, Builders for Peace, was created jointly by some Jewish and Arab Americans to funnel new investment capital into the Palestinian areas.[115] A majority of Jewish Americans have backed the peace negotiations between the PLO and the Israeli government, although many remain cautious in their assessments of the possibility of a lasting peace. A 1997 survey of American Jews found that 82 percent supported the creation of a Palestinian state if Israel's security and control over east Jerusalem could be guaranteed.[116]

ASSIMILATION OR PLURALISM?

Two different theoretical perspectives have been used to explain the experiences of Jewish Americans—Anglo-conformity perspectives or cultural pluralism approaches. Most scholarly analyses of Jewish Americans have reflected some type of assimilation viewpoint. The dominant perspective among Jewish Americans themselves has been at least partially assimilationist: the view that some adaptation to the surrounding culture is critical to achieving economic success and avoiding anti-Semitic prejudice and discrimination.[117]

An alternative to the traditional theory of Anglo-conformity assimilation, cultural pluralism can be seen in the views of certain Jewish leaders since the early 1800s. It was Horace Kallen, a Jewish American of Polish and Latvian origin, who best formulated this perspective (see Chapter 2). Kallen argued that for most people, ethnic–cultural group membership was not easily abandoned and that ethnic groups had a right to exist on their own terms; that is, democracy applied to ethnic groups. He argued against the ruthless Americanization advocated by many white Anglo-Protestant nativists. By the 1920s Kallen had given the name *cultural pluralism* to the view that each ethnic group has the democratic right to retain its own heritage. However, some scholars have argued that Kallen's cultural pluralism is not a useful perspective for understanding the adaptive history of Jewish Americans, since massive acculturation and much other assimilation have been facts of life for most.[118]

Patterns of Assimilation

Partial cultural assimilation came relatively quickly for each of the three major streams of Jewish immigrants and their children. Most Sephardic and German Jews rapidly adapted to their environment, picking up English and certain American folkways, but they maintained a commitment to Judaism. They first came in small numbers into a rapidly expanding United States with a vast frontier. Then came the large numbers of eastern Europeans. German Jews pressed these new immigrants to Americanize rapidly. In New York City German social workers came "downtown" to help assimilate the new eastern Europeans. Yet for the most part the two groups remained separate. Most new arrivals were committed to retaining their distinctiveness and their sense of Jewish peoplehood. Their eastern European Jewish (Yiddish) culture, which in the United States became in part an oppositional culture, played a crucial role in perpetuating the Jewish heritage and in resisting anti-Semitism. The immigrants had no illusions that they would cease to be outsiders in a predominantly non-Jewish society, yet they eagerly embraced the opportunities for jobs, for citizenship, and for an education for their children.[119]

Second-generation eastern European Jews were more affected by assimilation pressures and rapidly picked up the language and values pressed on them in the media and the public school system. Like the young Italian Americans discussed in the last chapter, they were caught between the culture of their parents and the dominant Anglo-Protestant culture, a situation guaranteed to create family tensions. Their Judaism, particularly the Reform and Conservative variants, was Americanized. Many members of the third eastern European generation moved out of predominantly Jewish neighborhoods. Still, they too were eager to accent their Jewishness in a combination of religious and secular practices.[120]

In the sphere of structural assimilation at the secondary level of the economy and politics, the central and eastern Europeans advanced quickly. A large portion of German Jews and some eastern European Jews achieved substantial economic success in the first generation. And, as a group, the eastern Europeans moved from a blue-collar concentration to a white-collar concentration in three generations. The initial concentration in certain blue-collar and entrepreneurial categories reflected Anglo-Protestant discrimination as well as the skills that the immigrants brought with them. For many, the ethnic niche economy was critical; often concentrated in "middleman" positions, many prospered. Hard work and mastery of the educational system facilitated upward movement over several generations. However, even today the occupational distribution of Jewish Americans underscores the point that many of the prosperous among them are not yet fully integrated into the upper reaches of the U.S. economy and society. The underrepresentation or absence of Jewish Americans at the very top in many spheres of the economy and politics is indicative of continuing discrimination.

Jewish Americans have, over a few generations, moved well up the economic ladder in the United States. Most came in poor; most today are part of middle-income America. Why were they able to move up the ladder so successfully? Some have explained this in terms of certain basic values and religious traditions. Nathan Glazer has argued that "Judaism emphasizes the traits that businessmen and intellectuals require, and has done so at least 1,500 years before Calvinism. . . . The strong emphasis on learning and study can be traced that far back, too. The Jewish habits of foresight, care, moderation probably arose early."[121]

Others have argued that this image of success growing out of traditional religious values is greatly exaggerated. Jewish American success had less to do with religious factors than with historical and structural factors. Although the eastern European immigrants were among the poorest, least-educated European Jews, they were not illiterate peasants lacking urban experience. During the period between 1880 and 1920, most came from urban areas of eastern Europe, where they had worked in a variety of urban occupations, such as manufacturing, craftwork, and small-scale commerce. Compared with the literacy level of most other immigrants at this time, theirs was relatively high. European Jews migrated to the United States at a time of expanding manufacturing and trade. Their urban backgrounds and skills fit in well with the needs of U.S. capitalism, especially in the textile industry. Steinberg concludes that, contrary to what Glazer has argued, Jewish immigrants did not need to rely only on their traditional religious values; they came in with "occupational skills that gave them a decisive advantage over other immigrants." The fit between Jewish American skills and economic circumstances at a critical time was better than it would be for later migrants (such as African Americans and Puerto Ricans) to the big cities.[122]

Arthur Hertzberg takes another tack and attributes the immigrants' success largely to their "'Jewish head' . . . the heritage of siege mentality, of centuries of being an embattled bastion in a hostile 'exile,' and of having only one tool for survival, the use of one's wits." This is a type of oppositional culture that facilitates survival under anti-Semitic oppression. Hertzberg also noted the unique relationship of the eastern Europeans to their countries of origin, European places in which Jewish life had ceased to be viable. They had an overwhelming need to succeed in the United States; returning to Europe was not an option.[123]

Although American Jews have shown greater geographic mobility than many other groups in recent years, the majority have not achieved full structural assimilation at the informal level. Decreasing residential concentration has not eliminated the informal social cohesion of Jewish Americans. Calvin Goldscheider notes that geographic mobility for this group is based on the same factors as geographic mobility for other Americans: housing markets, family life cycle, and economic constraints. "It is no longer the case," he claims, "that the greater the residential dispersal and integration, the weaker the informal ties to the Jewish community. . . . The evidence from Jewish communities . . . shows that there are few long-term effects of migration on ethnic cohesion."[124]

Thus, in the early 1980s, informal social ties were found to be strong in Los Angeles's large Jewish American community, even though the housing pattern there was dispersed; "the picture that emerges . . . is of a vibrant people whose closest personal associations are with other Jews in the family, friendship, and occupational groupings."[125] In 1987, only one-fourth of Rhode Island's Jews lived in neighborhoods that were half-Jewish or more, yet three-fourths reported that two or more of their closest friends were Jewish. Even among the young, two-thirds reported having mostly Jewish friends. About one-fourth of all the respondents, and a larger proportion of the young, expressed the desire to have more Jewish families living in their neighborhoods.[126] Nationally, however, the figures on friendship are not as high. In the 1990 NJPS, 45 percent of religious Jews, but only 12 percent of secular Jews, reported that most or all of their friends were Jewish.[127]

Intentional discrimination played a major role in frustrating the rise of first-generation Sephardic, German, and eastern European Jews. Even the acculturated children and grandchildren of these immigrants faced anti-Semitic barriers that have stalled structural assimilation in some areas. Discrimination channeled the first eastern Europeans into familiar ghetto communities. In the World War II period, many Jewish Americans even changed their names. In Los Angeles following World War II, for example, just under half of all those petitioning for name changes were Jewish, although Jewish residents made up only about 6 percent of the population. This may seem like a final rejection of Jewish identity. For most, however, a name change was simply instrumental in securing a job and in facilitating structural mobility. Despite the affluence of later generations, some economic and social discrimination persists. Milton Gordon has argued that while Jewish Americans have experienced partial assimilation at the behavior-receptional level (that is, discrimination has declined), less assimilation has occurred at the attitude-receptional level because of the persistence of anti-Semitism.[128]

Intermarriage

Opposed by some on the grounds that it threatens the solidarity and survival of the Jewish American community, intermarriage has generally increased with each successive generation, reflecting the decline of negative mutual images, desires to assimilate, and greater acceptance of ethnic diversity in the United States. Out-marriage has been more common for those Jews who are geographically separated from large Jewish communities. Since the 1960s, the proportion of interfaith marriages has risen steadily—from 11 percent for those who married prior to 1965 to 31 percent during the period between 1965 and 1974 to 57 percent for those who married in the late 1980s. Today, the percentage is still over half of all marriages. This trend has led some observers to predict the disappearance of the American Jewish community within a few decades. However, since 1980, Judaism's increasing acceptance of mixed marriages has resulted in a growing percentage of intermarried couples who, along with their children, embrace Judaism and identify themselves as Jewish. One 1997 estimate, however, put this figure at only one-fourth of all intermarried couples.[129]

In Rhode Island the percentage of marriages in which both partners were Jewish-born declined from 98 percent before 1960 to 62 percent for the years between 1980 and 1987. However, in this later period, 12 percent of the Jewish-born partners married a convert. The Jewish partners in these marriages were almost equally divided between husband and wife. Seven in ten of the Rhode Island respondents said they would accept a child's intermarriage; about half said they would encourage the non-Jewish spouse to convert. The major concern about intermarriage was the future of the American Jewish community.[130] In addition, in the 1990 NJPS, fewer than half the respondents stated that they would support marriage between their child and a non-Jewish person, although only 22 percent of religious Jews and between 3 and 6 percent of other Jews would openly oppose such a marriage.[131]

Assessing the implications of the growing number of intermarriages, observers differ in their view of the implications. For example, Goldscheider argues against Gordon's view that they can be regarded as an unambiguous measure of assimilation to the Anglo-Protestant society. "Strong communal bonds and networks link the intermarried to the community. . . . There is evidence as well that an increasing proportion of American Jews are accepting the intermarried within the community."[132] However, Alan Dershowitz has recently argued in his book *The Vanishing American Jew* (1997) that the Jewish American group will soon disappear if the intermarriage rate remains high and the birth rate low. He argues that the decline of anti-Semitism has reduced in-group solidarity. Because of this he has called for a renewed Judaism and for a reinvigorated system of Jewish education. He also advocates an international conference to consider the future of Jews and Jewish identity worldwide.[133]

Does the Jewish American community generally share this concern that intermarriage is now destroying Jewish identity and solidarity? A 1997 survey indicates that this may not be the case. Asked whether anti-Semitism or intermarriage was the greater threat to the continuing Jewish presence in the United States, anti-Semitism was picked by 61 percent compared with only 32 percent who cited intermarriage. There appears to be more concern for external threats than for the internal threats of concern to recent analysts like Dershowitz.[134]

Recent Immigrants: Strong Jewish Identity

The social and economic adjustment of recent Jewish immigrants raises some interesting issues about assimilation and U.S. culture. The close ties between Israel and the United States make this trek westward easy for Israeli immigrants, who generally are more economically successful than other immigrants. Many come with professional or managerial experience. Israeli immigrants often maintain some distance from native-born American Jews in their language and values.[135]

Immigrants from the former Soviet Union report more difficulty assimilating to U.S. culture. Most left their homeland because of anti-Semitism. While most of the respondents in one recent opinion survey of 900 émigrés rated their lives as Jews, as well as their housing, income, and overall standard of living, better than that in the former Soviet Union, most reported having trouble with English and with initially finding a job. Most considered their cultural environment worse in the United States, and large percentages felt their friendships, social status, and workplace atmospheres were worse in the United States. They liked the freedom and creativity of the United States, but disliked the vulgarity and "low" cultural tastes. This mostly well-educated group of immigrants appears to be assimilating satisfactorily to the U.S. economy and to material conditions but is having trouble with certain social and cultural adjustments.[136]

Steven Gold has examined adaptation among a more diverse group of refugees from the former Soviet Union in two recently established immigrant communities in Los Angeles and San Francisco. In both communities the Jewish population was geographically concentrated; residents of the full-faceted Los Angeles community could lead an active life without any knowledge of English. Many had little contact with other Jewish Americans because of differences in language and culture. However, some, particularly the younger ones with a good education, found desirable jobs and moved into the middle class. Many middle-aged émigrés whose job skills were not transferable or who were unwilling to take a lower-prestige job than they had held in their native country had more difficulty adapting and often remained isolated from fellow émigrés out of a sense of shame. Older émigrés were the least likely to adapt. Few voluntary support organizations had been formed in either California city. Most support came from their extended families. The strong sense of Jewish identity of these new immigrants is yet another factor reinforcing Jewish ethnicity in the United States.[137]

Contemporary Jewish Identity and the Future of the Jewish American Community

What does it mean to be Jewish American in the 1990s? Asked to specify the basis of Jewish identity, 90 percent of the respondents to the 1990 NJPS cited cultural or ethnic group membership; this was true for both religious and secular Jews. Fewer than 5 percent of all respondents defined Jewishness only as religious group membership.[138] Significantly, Israel has been a major focus of this Jewish American identity and consciousness, a focus reducing the possibility of identificational assimilation. In the 1990 NJPS, most religious Jews reported an emotional attachment to Israel, and just under half of secular Jews also reported such an attachment.[139]

The size of the Jewish American population has remained fairly stable since 1970. The Jewish American population in 1970 was about 5.4 million; by 1997 it had risen a bit, to 5.9 million. As we have noted, low birthrates and marital assimilation are seen by some as threats to the continuation of Jewish ethnicity. Most Jewish households are small, averaging 2.2 persons. This reflects the older age of the group as well as the small number of children per family. On the average

Jewish American families have fewer children than the population as a whole, and the core population has almost one-third more elderly persons than the total U.S. population. However, the 1990 NJPS found that virtually all children of Jewish parents were being raised Jewish. Significantly, even though only a small percentage of non-Jewish-born spouses in mixed marriages have converted to Judaism, an estimated 28 percent of their children were being raised Jewish.[140] Commitment to passing on Jewish culture and a sense of Jewish identity to succeeding generations remains strong.

Andrew Greeley's *ethnogenesis* perspective, which we discussed in Chapter 2, recognizes the reality of cultural differences among contemporary ethnic groups (in the tradition of Kallen's cultural pluralism) and seems to fit the Jewish experience. Jewish Americans are more than a single European nationality group. They are a composite group of Sephardic, central European, and eastern European origin. In the United States, the Jewish immigrants and their descendants have forged a distinctive ethnic group, shaped partially by their Jewish and European cultural heritage and partially by adaptation to the Anglo-Protestant core culture. Despite substantial adaptive changes, Jewish American ethnic and cultural distinctiveness remains. Persisting anti-Semitism, and especially respect for an ancient heritage and the socialization of children by parents in this heritage, continue to shape the behavior and beliefs of Jewish Americans.

How strong is Jewish identity? Is it, as Herbert Gans argues, only a "symbolic ethnicity," without much deep and lasting significance? In this view ethnicity for many white ethnic Americans is today little more than a desire to maintain some feeling for ethnic background without strong commitments to ethnic behavior or strong social ties.[141] We have already noted the concern for a vanishing Jewish identity in the recent book of Alan Dershowitz. Some Jewish scholars, such as Arthur Hertzberg, have argued that the weakening of religious ties among Jewish Americans signals that Jewish ethnicity is increasingly symbolic, that "it is well on its way to becoming memory."[142] Other Jewish American leaders have expressed concern about changes at the organization level. For example, the 189 agencies that make up the Jewish federation movement have recently faced a decline in private and governmental support. One 1995 report suggests that federation leaders are worried that assimilated Jewish Americans with a weak sense of identity may not support the movement like their ancestors did. They have created a Commission on Jewish Identity and Continuity and are seeking to strengthen Jewish education.[143]

Still, scholars such as Hertzberg who wish for a revival of true Judaism among Jewish Americans recognize that Jewish ethnicity will probably last at least a few more generations. Alba has pointed out that certain distinguishing features of Jewish culture and history—in particular, their extensive social networks, especially those rooted in religious congregations and schools, and their long tradition of survival as a minority in non-Jewish societies—support the survival of their ethnic identity.[144]

Silberman suggests that the greater acceptance of Jewish Americans in a largely non-Jewish society today, compared with fifty years ago, makes Jewish

Americans less likely to abandon their Jewishness, since their identity has ceased to be the focal point of widespread discrimination and instead has become a badge of pride linked to a worldwide Jewish struggle such as that of Israel.[145] From this perspective, a sense of Jewishness is likely to remain strong for the majority of Jewish Americans for the foreseeable future.

SUMMARY

Jewish Americans, most of whom are descendants of central and eastern Europeans, have become substantially assimilated in the cultural arena. An economically prosperous ethnic group that has made dramatic progress up the mobility ladder, Jewish Americans have struggled against great prejudice and discrimination and not a little violence. Theirs is substantially a success story. But as we have seen, a price has been paid for that success. Significant anti-Semitism persists today, often limiting movement to the very top in the economy and especially in politics. Coupled with the substantial vertical progress over the decades has been horizontal mobility in the form of suburbanization. The first-generation eastern European Jews were concentrated in central-city areas; subsequent generations began moving in large numbers into suburban areas.

Central to an adequate understanding of Jewish Americans today is an understanding of their ties to Israel. The creation of Israel and periodic Arab–Israeli conflicts have generated a strong commitment to Israel, philosophically and financially. Israel continues to be seen among Jewish Americans as a critical place of refuge for a people that has survived the Roman persecution, the Spanish Inquisition, Russian pogroms, and the Nazi Holocaust. Related to this commitment has been the flow of thousands of Jewish Americans to the work camps, towns, and cities of Israel. Yet, recent decades have also seen a significant number of Israeli and Russian Jewish immigrants to the United States seeking to escape the threat of war in their home countries or seeking new economic and political opportunities. These immigrants provide a contemporary reminder of the sojourner character of much of the Jewish experience.

In this chapter we have demonstrated how diverse the United States still is—a diversity that makes for great vitality and creativity. Jewish American participation in U.S. institutions means that this nation is *not* by definition a Christian country; it is a nation of many religious groups, including Protestants, Catholics, Jews, and Muslims. One of the contributions of Jewish Americans has been their stand for the Jewish religious and cultural heritage in spite of nativist discrimination and other opposition—and thereby the expansion of liberty for all residents of the United States.

Jewish Americans have contributed substantially to the emphasis on education in the United States, to high achievement in the arts and sciences, and to the values of justice, tolerance, and fairness. Jewish Americans have not been passive victims of anti-Semitic prejudice and discrimination; they and their organizations have occupied the forefront of the fight against the racial prejudice and behavioral racism that continue to plague U.S. society.

CHAPTER 7

Native Americans

In the early 1990s, Native American groups across the nation held protests as the celebration of the 500th anniversary of Columbus's 1492 voyage to the Americas began. In Washington, DC, two protesters spray-painted "500 years of genocide" on a statue of Columbus, and a third read a list of human rights violations while pouring blood onto the statue. In Tuscon students and representatives of the Apache Survival Coalition held a "drum-in" to protest both the Columbus celebration and the construction of the Columbus telescope on top of a sacred Apache mountain. In Minneapolis protesters held a sunrise ceremony to remember the Native American nations that were destroyed by European immigrants and to celebrate those that survived. Hundreds of protesters organized by the American Indian Movement confronted a Columbus Day celebration in Denver, calling it "a commemoration of centuries of racism in the Americas." In these and many other cities, Native Americans were joined by members of African American, Puerto Rican, Mexican American, and other organizations.[1] Native American activist Suzane Shown Harjo explained the Native American position regarding the Columbus Quincentenary: "As Native American peoples . . . we have no reason to celebrate an invasion that caused the demise of so many of our people and is still causing destruction today. The Europeans stole our land and killed our people."[2]

With this chapter we begin to consider several groups that were racially subordinated in the process of European colonization and expansion in North America. The term *white* as a self-designation for Europeans developed in the context of contact with the darker-skinned peoples of both Africa and the Americas, whom Europeans called *black* and *red*, respectively.[3] As well-armed colonizers, white Europeans achieved dominance and became a numerical majority. People of color were subordinated economically, politically, and culturally. In this and subsequent chapters, we will see critical differences in the past and present experiences of these European and non-European Americans. We will also discover the relevance of power–conflict theories for interpreting the past and present of the subordinated racial groups.

The first victims of European colonization of this continent were the Native Americans—members of the hundreds of nations and smaller groups who were present at the time of the Europeans' entry. Called collectively, and erroneously, "Indians" by their European conquerors, Native Americans have suffered from a variety of stereotypes, from the wooden cigar-store figure to the bloodthirsty savage of the movies to the noble primitive of novels. Distorted images of bloody tomahawks, scalping, feathered headdresses, and warriors on wild ponies have been impressed on the Euro-American mind by sensationalism in magazines, newspapers, movies, and on television.

Coupled with these stereotypes and distortions has been a tendency to ignore the past and present reality of Native American life. Reflect for a moment on the notion of Europeans "discovering" America. In fact, the fifteenth-century European explorers were latecomers, for the continent they happened upon was already peopled by several million inhabitants. The ancestors of these peoples had discovered the continent at least twenty thousand years earlier—when, most scholars believe, they had migrated across the land bridge from Asia to Alaska. Reflect too on the name that Native Americans have had to bear ever since, the "Indians" (*los Indios*), a name bestowed by their conquerors that reflects a colossal geographical error, the assumption that the early expeditions had found the Asian Indies they were seeking.

CONQUEST BY EUROPEANS AND EURO-AMERICANS

Human migration varies from voluntary movement to forced slave importation. This migration often involves a dominant racial or ethnic group that is already established within certain boundaries and is incorporating the new immigrant group into its sociocultural framework. In the case of Native Americans, however, it is the dominant group itself that migrated; that is, the Europeans moved into the territories of Native American groups. This process can be termed *colonization migration*. Unlike other types of migration, colonization migration involves the conquest and domination of a preexisting geographical group by outsiders. Such migration also illustrates *classical colonialism*.

How many Native Americans were there at the time Europeans came into North American history? Early on, some analysts estimated the native population of North America in the year 1500 at between 900,000 and 1,150,000 persons. In recent decades, however, the estimate has been sharply revised upward. A considered estimate by Kirkpatrick Sale puts the number in North America at 15 million at the time of conquest, with tens of millions in Central and South America as well. Thorough assessments by Henry Dobyns and Russell Thornton also support a figure larger than earlier estimates, whose low figures have often been used for the purpose of legitimating the European conquest of an allegedly unoccupied land.[4]

By 1890, European diseases and firepower had sharply reduced the number of Native Americans in North America to approximately 250,000. The population remained below 400,000 until the 1950s, when it began to grow. The 1990 census counted more than 1.9 million people who listed their background as "American Indian." By 1997, there were an estimated 2.1 million Native Americans. Today, most of the 557 Native American groups have fewer than 10,000 members each; only four have populations of more than 100,000. The two largest groups—the Cherokee (308,000) and the Navajo (219,000)—account for 28 percent of all Native Americans. Most Native Americans do not live on reservations; just over one-fifth live on 314 reservations and trust lands. Nearly half live west of the Mississippi. Oklahoma has the largest concentration of Native Americans, followed closely by California and Arizona.[5]

Between 1970 and 1990, the number of Americans claiming Native American ancestry more than doubled. Drawing on archival and interview data, Joane Nagel argues that the large increase in the Native American population reported in the 1990 census is mostly the result of identity "switching"—the change in self-identification by hundreds of thousands of Americans from non-Indian to Indian in response to Native American activism that has promoted Native American pride and enhanced the symbolic worth of being Native American.[6]

The term *Indian* and most names of major Native American groups are terms of convenience applied by European American settlers. In most history books, not one of the major tribes is recorded under its own name. For example, the "Navaho" call themselves *Dine*, meaning "The People."[7] The renaming of Native American nations by outsiders is a result of their subordination and suggests one major difference between colonized groups and European immigrants: Colonized peoples have had little control over the naming process.

Native American Societies: Are They "Tribes"?

Although many people today think of them as a single category, Native Americans have for centuries been a diverse collection of nations and societies, with major differences in population, language, economy, polity, and customs. Some define the common term *tribe* as a group of relatives with their own language and customs who occupy a definite territory. Yet such a definition obscures the great variety in size and complexity of Native American groups, which have ranged from very small nomadic hunting and gathering bands to complex, hierarchically organized nations with large territories.

Early Cultural Borrowing

The cultures of the Native American societies encountered by European colonizers in the Western Hemisphere were often more highly developed than European cultures. These peoples built great cities and roads, developed advanced agricultural systems, and created calendars and numerical systems superior to those of Europeans. Significantly, the European invaders borrowed heavily from Native American agriculture and pharmacology. An estimated 60 percent of the foods (for example, potatoes, corn, peanuts, and many grains) eaten by people around the globe today were first developed by Native Americans in the Western Hemisphere. Many medicinal plants and their derivatives (for example, quinine) were taken from Native Americans. In addition, European Americans such as Benjamin Franklin and Thomas Jefferson both admired and learned from the democratic political institutions of major North American nations.[8]

Geographical Location and Relocation

There were perhaps two hundred distinct groups at the time of the European invasion. Traditionally, Native American societies have been grouped by Euro-American scholars into geographical categories as follows: (1) the societies of the East, who hunted, farmed, and fished, and whose first encounters with whites were with English settlers; (2) the Great Plains hunters and agriculturalists, whose first encounters were with the Spaniards; (3) the fishing societies in the Northwest; (4) the seed gatherers of California and neighboring areas; (5) the Navaho shepherds and Pueblo farmers in the Arizona–New Mexico area; (6) the desert societies of southern Arizona and New Mexico; and (7) the Alaskan groups, including the Eskimo.[9] In this chapter, we will sometimes be speaking of these many societies as though they were one group; at other times we will be speaking of one specific group within this larger category.

Forced migration at gunpoint was the lot of some native groups after they had been defeated. Groups in the West, such as the Navaho, were rounded up after military engagements and forced to migrate to barren reservations. Perhaps the most famous forced march was the "Trail of Tears," in which thousands of Cherokees, Creeks, Chickasaws, Choctaws, and Seminoles were relocated from their eastern lands to "Indian Territory," the eastern half of present-day Oklahoma. Internal migration in the twentieth century has involved relocation from rural areas to the cities. During the 1950s and 1960s, an urban relocation program was expanded by the federal government to cover many Native American groups and numerous cities; a Bureau of Indian Affairs (BIA) branch was set up to oversee relocation services.[10] (We should note that Native Americans are the only U.S. racial–ethnic group with a federal bureaucracy, currently with 12,000 employees, that has had much economic and educational control over reservations.) The scale of this internal migration can be seen in the fact that more than 200,000 Native Americans moved to the cities between the late 1950s and early 1980s, settling for the most part in low-income neighborhoods. By 1990 more than half of Native Americans resided in cities.[11]

Why have Native Americans moved to the cities? The reasons vary. Many GIs and nurses returning after World War II felt estranged from their former lifestyle on reservations. Perhaps most importantly, poverty and high unemployment on reservations pressured many Native Americans, especially younger workers, to seek economic opportunities in cities.[12]

The Colonial Period

Various strategies were developed by the Europeans for dealing with those Native Americans whose land they coveted. These ranged from honest treaty making with equals, to deceptive treaty making, to attempts at extermination, to enslavement like that of Africans, to confinement in barren prison-like camps called reservations.[13]

In the 1600s, the Dutch established several communities on the East Coast that displaced or destroyed Native American societies. A Dutch governor was one of the first to offer a government bounty for Native American scalps, to be used as proof of death; Europeans played a major role in spreading this bloody practice conventionally attributed only to Native Americans.[14] English settlers usually gained dominance over Native Americans, forcing them into the frontier areas or killing them off.[15] Few whites seemed concerned about the genocidal consequences of this brutal expansion. It is often noted that some English settlers relied on friendly Native Americans to survive the first devastating years, but the new settlers soon turned on their neighbors. In New England, for example, a war with the Pequots in 1637 ended when whites massacred several hundred inhabitants of a Pequot village and sent the survivors into slavery. The 1675–1676 King Philip's War with the Wampanoag tribe and its allies, precipitated by the oppressive tactics of the New England settlers, resulted in substantial losses on both sides. The Native American leader, Metacom (known by the English as King Philip), was "captured, drawn, and quartered: his skull remained on view on a pole in Plymouth as late as 1700."[16] Native American survivors were sold as slaves.

Few people today are aware that some Native Americans were enslaved by the European settlers. A 1708 report mentioned 1,400 Native American slaves in the Carolina area. By the mid-eighteenth century, between 5 and 10 percent of slaves were Native Americans. As late as the 1790 census, 200 of the 6,000 slaves in Massachusetts were Native Americans. Native Americans were replaced by Africans as slaves in part because escape was a constant problem with the former.[17]

The English defeat of the French after a ten-year war resulted in the French withdrawal from the continent in the mid-1700s. This move brought many Native American societies into contact with the often less sophisticated and generally more brutal policy of the English.[18]

Treaties, Reservations, and Genocide

With the founding of the United States, Native Americans found themselves in a strange political position. The U.S. Constitution only briefly mentions Native Americans in giving Congress the power to regulate commerce with the tribes. And the 1787 Northwest Ordinance made the following solemn promises:

> The utmost good faith shall always be observed towards the Indians; their land and property shall never be taken from them without their consent; and in their proper-

ty, rights, and liberty, they shall never be invaded or disturbed, unless in justified and lawful wars authorized by Congress; but laws founded in justice and humanity shall from time to time be made, for preventing wrongs being done to them, and for preserving peace and friendship with them.[19]

Washington's secretary of war, whose department had been assigned responsibility for those called "Indians," adopted a policy of peaceful adjustment. By the late 1700s the executive and legislative branches had become actively involved in dealing with the indigenous Americans. In 1790, an act licensing "Indian traders" was passed. A treaty was signed with the Senecas in 1794, and in 1796 government stores were established to provide Native Americans with supplies on credit. Some Supreme Court decisions in the early 1800s laid out the principles that Native American societies had a right to their lands and a right to self-government. At the same time, the Court saw Native Americans as "domestic, dependent nations," thereby helping to provide a legal rationalization for domination of the formerly independent nations.[20]

Federal officials, by action or inaction, supported the recurrent theft of Native American lands. In practice, they approved of ignoring boundary rights wherever necessary.[21] A French observer of the 1830s noted the hypocrisy of high-sounding U.S. treaties: "this virtuous and high-minded policy [of treaty making] has not been followed. The rapacity of the settlers is usually backed by the tyranny of the government."[22] The procedure was often not one of immediate expropriation of land, but rather of constant encroachment by European settlers, a land-taking process sanctioned after the fact by the government (and its army units) and legitimated by treaties.

The subordination of Native Americans was encouraged by Andrew Jackson, a slaveholding president critical of treaty making, who even encouraged the states to defy Supreme Court rulings concerning Native Americans. Gradual displacement gave way to brutally oppressive marches over hundreds of miles at gunpoint, a near-genocidal policy explicitly designed to rid entire regions of those falsely stereotyped by Euro-Americans as "savages." Congress passed the Indian Removal Act in 1830, and within a decade many of the tribes of the East had migrated voluntarily or at gunpoint to lands west of the Mississippi under the auspices of "negotiated" treaties. Atlantic and Gulf Coast tribes, such as the Cherokees, as well as midwestern tribes, such as the Shawnees, were forcibly removed to the Indian Territory in the migration known as the "Trail of Tears." Large numbers died in the forced march, and the relocated peoples faced serious survival problems in the new lands, where unfamiliar agricultural techniques were required and where there was different game that they had to learn to hunt.[23]

Westward-moving white settlers precipitated struggles with the preexisting Plains societies, many of which had by that time given up agriculture for a nomadic hunting and raiding lifestyle. Most Native American groups in this region had participated in intergroup raiding, but the genocidal actions of federal troops and white settlers were a new experience. It was the nomadic, horse-oriented Plains peoples who forever came to symbolize "the Indian" in the white imagination. Mass media presentations have severely distorted the reality of the

An etching of a meeting between U.S. army generals and Sioux and other Native American leaders at North Platte, Nebraska.

Plains wars, which usually did *not* involve chiefs in warbonnets on stallions facing a brave collection of U.S. Army officers backed by heroic men on a sun-swept plain.[24]

Myths about Conflict

Movies and television have portrayed the years between 1840 and 1860 as an era that featured constant conflict between white overlanders and Native Americans. The movies and television have created many unforgettable, often racist images of the West—wagon trains moving across the West, wagons in a circle, whooping Indians on ponies, thousands of dead settlers and Indians, and treacherous "red men." However, research studies by John D. Unruh and others have made clear that these images are largely mythological. Between 1840 and 1860, approximately 250,000 white settlers made the long journey across the plains to the West Coast; far less than 1 percent of those migrants died at the hands of the native inhabitants. Indeed, between 1840 and 1860 a total of *only 362 white settlers and 426 Native Americans* died in *all* the recorded battles between the two groups along wagon train routes. There is only *one* documented attack by Native Americans on a wagon train in which there were as many as two dozen casualties for the white settler-invaders. Most of the accounts of massacres of whites by "wild Indians" are either fictions or great exaggerations of minor encounters.[25]

Unruh's research also highlights the cooperation between Native Americans and the new settlers. Native Americans often provided food and horses for weary white travelers. Some served as guides. Unruh and other historians make clear the crucial role of the federal government and of federal troops in attacking and oppressing the native tribes. By the 1850s, an army of federal agents, from the famous "Indian agents" to surveyors, road builders, and treaty agents, was facilitating the westward migration of white colonizers.

A recurring pattern emerged in the growing conflict between whites and natives. White settlers would move onto native lands to farm. The federal government, by means of a treaty involving threat or coercion, would provide land for the resettlement of the Native American group affected. More white settlers, prospectors, and hunters moving along migratory paths from the East would gradually intrude on these new Native American lands. This land theft would then be legitimated by yet another treaty, and the process might begin again. Or perhaps a federal government treaty promise of supplies or money to those Native Americans living in a restricted area would be broken, and some Native American men would leave the area seeking food or revenge. The U.S. Army would then take repressive action, sometimes intentionally punishing an innocent group and thus precipitating violent uprisings.

Many treaties, part of U.S. law, were masterpieces of fraud; consent was gained by deception or threat. More than three hundred treaties with Native American tribes were made between 1790 and the Civil War. Most were *not* honored in full by the U.S. government. As time passed, treaties established regulations governing Native American behavior and provided for restricted areas called reservations. Many Native Americans thereby became dependent on the federal Bureau of Indian Affairs and on Congress, which by the Civil War could change treaties without the consent of Native Americans. This treaty process was abandoned by the U.S. government by 1871, although hundreds of ratified treaties between the United States and many Native American groups still remain in effect.[26]

White Massacres of Native Americans

Serious treaty violations by whites often led to open conflict. For example, in an 1862 uprising in Minnesota, the eastern Sioux killed some settlers after losing much of their land to the invading settlers and suffering at the hands of white Indian agents. Delays in payment of promised supplies resulted in warriors burning and killing throughout the Minnesota Valley; massive white retaliation followed. About the same time, conflict occurred in Colorado between Native American groups and a state militia left in charge when the U.S. Army was withdrawn to fight the Civil War. Guerrilla warfare by Native Americans was met by savage retaliation. In 1864, Colonel John Chivington, a minister, and his Colorado volunteers massacred nearly two hundred Cheyennes in a peace-seeking band at Sand Creek.[27] The massacre was one of the most savage in western history: "Children carrying white flags were slaughtered and pregnant women were cut open. The slaughter and mutilation continued into the late afternoon over many miles of the bleak prairie."[28]

After the Civil War, large railroad corporations gobbled up millions of acres in the West. Buffalo were slaughtered by the millions, and the hunting economy of the Plains was destroyed. In the late 1860s, a federal peace commission met with numerous Native American groups at Medicine Lodge Creek in Kansas. Reservations were worked out for all the Plains societies, but it was only after two more decades of battles that all groups agreed to settle in the areas designated by the U.S. government.[29]

Settlers, miners, and the army repeatedly violated treaties with the Sioux and moved aggressively into the Dakota Territory. Conflict over the illegal white invasion escalated; troops were sent in to force Sioux bands onto a smaller reservation, even though the Sioux were already on what the government regarded as "unceded Indian territory." In this force was the infamous Colonel George A. Custer. The most widely known battle of the Plains struggle occurred at the Little Big Horn in 1876 when Custer and his soldiers were wiped out by a group of Sioux and allied tribes that had refused to settle on the reservation.

One of the last engagements was the massacre of Native Americans at Wounded Knee Creek fourteen years later. Attempting to round up the last few Sioux bands, the U.S. Army intercepted one group near the Dakota Badlands and forced them to camp. The white colonel in command ordered a disarming of the camp, which was carried out in ruthless fashion. One young Sioux shot into a line of soldiers; the troops replied by shooting at close range with rifles and machine guns. Approximately three hundred unarmed Native Americans, many of them old men, women, and children, were killed on the spot or while running from the camp.[30]

In the Southwest, Native American resistance was, on occasion, substantial. Even after the United States took over the region by military conquest in the 1840s, slave raids on the Navaho by New Mexican settlers continued for a decade or two. Military expeditions were conducted in the Southwest against the scattered Navaho and Apache communities in an attempt to destroy them or hem them in. Colonel Kit Carson succeeded in getting the Mescalero Apaches to agree to reside on a reservation. Establishing headquarters in Navaho territory, Carson began a scorched-earth program, destroying Navaho fields and herds. He then herded his captives three hundred miles to a reservation—the famous "Long Walk" that is central to the Navaho collective memory of oppression. By 1890, most of the remnants of the Native American groups had been forced onto reservations.[31] Still, even on the reservations, most Native American groups maintained their historic cultures, including language and religion, and often drew on their cultures to resist pressures of acculturation to the dominant white culture.

RACIST IMAGES AND STEREOTYPES

Soon after the arrival of European colonizers in the Americas, the stereotypes of Native Americans as lazy and wild and of Europeans as provident and steady, along with classification by physical characteristics, served to distinguish the colonizers from the colonized. Thus, self-identified "hardworking whites" legitimated the dispossession and attempted enslavement of "lazy red savages." Another early European myth, that of the "child of nature" or "noble savage," was a mixture of appreciation and prejudice. French philosophers such as Jean Jacques Rousseau, who had read of European contacts with Native Americans, utilized scanty data to argue for a golden age of human existence when there was only the unsophisticated "primitive" unspoiled by European civilization.[32]

European settlers were shocked at the strength of Native American societies and cultures and at the unwillingness of the native residents to submit to the "civilizing" pressures of the missionaries and landseeking farmers. Violent resistance by Native Americans reinforced the stereotypes of the "bloodthirsty savage." This racialized image became common after the first battles with Native Americans resisting the seizure of their lands. By the mid-1600s, Europeans in New England and Virginia were writing that the Native Americans were "wild beasts" who should be hunted down like other animals. Puritan leaders such as Cotton Mather even saw them as agents of the Devil.[33]

It was the era of westward expansion that imprinted on the Euro-American mind, in dime novels and later in movies and TV programs, the image of "cruel" Native American warriors attacking "helpless" settlers. Yet the much more significant savagery of the white settlers has seldom been accented in the mass media. Carlson and Coburn have commented on the staggering number of Native Americans killed in the mass media: "The Indian, who had been all but eliminated with real bullets, now had to be resurrected to be killed off again with printer's ink."[34] The distorted image of Native Americans as savages can still be found in many textbooks in U.S. schools.

Another erroneous but persisting image is that of the "primitive hunter" who made little use of the land. Most tribes that were forced off lands or killed off were composed *not* of nomadic hunters but of part-time or full-time farmers. Groups such as the Cherokee had, by the removal period of the 1830s, developed their own mills and other agricultural enterprises.[35] They *used* the land stolen from them.

Two paradoxical stereotypes were applied to Native American women by European Americans, both based on the women's relationship with white men: a Princess who saves the white man from her own people and a Squaw who becomes the white man's sexual partner. Rayna Green documents how the image of the esteemed Princess, portrayed as only slightly darker-skinned than Europeans and with distinctly European features, became a symbol of the New World in Europe, a many-faceted "Mother figure—exotic, powerful, dangerous, and beautiful."[36] In contrast, the Squaw, portrayed negatively by white racists as darker, fatter, and cruder than the Princess, shared the negative traits of drunkenness, stupidity, and thievery attributed by whites to Native American men, and her destruction by whites was thereby justified as necessary to the progress of "white civilization."

Studies of elementary, high-school, and college social science textbooks have found a number of negative stereotypes about Native Americans. Most school texts deal briefly with Native Americans, almost always in the past tense, with a few references to pioneer days and occasional use of derogatory terms such as *squaw* and *buck*. Numerous children's books on the market today, including story books, picture books, and coloring books, portray Native Americans as princesses, squaws, warriors, or savages. In an analysis of Houghton Mifflin's history and social science series for kindergarten through eighth grade, Communities United, a group seeking to locate and remove "stereotypes, omissions, distortions, exaggerations, and outright lies about peoples of color" from school texts, found the series to contain "the justifications and trivializations of some of the most vicious social practices in our history."[37] Studies of the mass media have turned up grossly exaggerated stereotypes, including widespread use of the "Indian warrior" image.[38]

Some scholars have criticized the tendency of many white observers to define Native Americans and their ancient traditions in terms of eighteenth- and nineteenth-century Euro-American observations. This limited basis for definition has influenced North American and European art, literature, the mass media, and the mainstream view in general and has contributed to the invisibility of contemporary Native Americans.[39] The Academy Award-winning film *Dances with Wolves* is an example of the media's focus on the past. Although this film presents a more sensitive treatment of intergroup history than most of its predecessors, it sees the historical Native American experience, while regrettable, as proceeding to an inevitable conclusion. The film diverts attention from the present reality of Native Americans, perpetuating the notion that Native Americans are a relic of the past, to be studied only in historical context. As Ward Churchill has stated, "native people are forced to live, right now, today, in abject squalor under the heel of what may be history's most seamlessly perfected system of internal colonization, out of sight, out of mind, their rights and resources relentlessly consumed by the dominant society."[40]

Studies of white attitudes toward Native Americans have been rare. One study in the 1970s updated 1920s research conducted by E. S. Bogardus on social-distance attitudes directed at Native Americans. In Bogardus's 1920s research study, white college students were asked how close, on a scale from 1 ("would marry") to 7 ("would not allow them in nation"), they would allow a given racial or ethnic group to themselves. Bogardus found that white students rejected all close contact (such as friendships) with Native Americans. Using the same social distance scale, the 1970s study found Native Americans still being rejected by white respondents in primary-group relations, such as marriage and club membership. This study also found that white views of Native Americans mixed romantic stereotypes with traditional negative stereotypes.[41]

More than two decades later, stereotypes of Native Americans are still omnipresent in U.S. society. Suzane Shown Harjo, a founding trustee of the National Museum of the American Indian, has noted that whether a stereotypical image is hostile or benevolent, "There is no such thing as a good stereotype. . . . It reduces people or a person to a consumable, easily digestible, prejudged image or word. It sets up a system or prejudice either for or against a person or a people and, in that way, denies the humanity of that person or people . . . or it wrongly characterizes people."[42] In the fall of 1994, the Cable News Network (CNN) aired a rare series, "Native Americans: The Invisible People," which presented the historical circumstances surrounding several contemporary Native American issues, including land-use treaty violations, federal recognition of Native American nations as legal entities, and the protection of Native American sacred sites.[43] It is interesting that CNN should be the first major television network to present in some detail such historical and contemporary realities; CNN's founder, Ted Turner, also owns the Atlanta Braves baseball team and has helped perpetuate negative Native American stereotypes through the team's name and fans' use of the famous "tomahawk chop."

POLITICS

At first, European colonizers and settlers dealt with Native Americans as independent nations. However, as European communities gained strength they began to treat these nations as groups to be exterminated or as dependent wards. Many eastern groups were destroyed. Those remaining in the East were militarily weak enough by the 1830s for the government to force them westward. About the same time, the Bureau of Indian Affairs (BIA) was established to coordinate federal relations with Native Americans; its work ranged from supervision of reservations and land dealings to provision of supplies. Until the end of major battles in the 1880s, the BIA's role of attempting to protect Native Americans put it in direct conflict with a military policy that often sought genocidal extermination.

Under BIA domination, indigenous Native American leaders were often set aside and replaced by white-controlled leaders. Native religions were suppressed, and large numbers of Christian missionaries were imported. BIA rations were usually provided to those who remained on reservations, while U.S. troops chased those who did not. With the termination of treaty making in 1871 and the reduction of all major groups to life on reservations by the 1890s, Native Americans entered into a unique relationship with white America: They were (and are) the only subordinate racial or ethnic group whose life was to be (and is) routinely administered directly by a bureaucratic arm of the federal government. The action of the BIA is a clear example of the role of government in defining and controlling U.S. racial and ethnic groups, a point underscored by Omi and Winant in their theory of racial formation (see Chapter 2).[44]

From the Dawes Act to the New Deal

A major policy shift regarding land took place in the late nineteenth century. Native Americans, liberal white reformers argued, should be taught new rules of land use. They wished to assimilate Native Americans to Euro-American land values. The Dawes Act of 1887 provided that reservation lands be divided among individual families—even though the European tradition of private ownership and individual development of land was an alien value system for most Native

American groups. White advocates of the new policy hoped that small individual allotments (40 to 160 acres) would convert Native Americans into individual farm entrepreneurs. Unallotted lands left over could then be sold to white outsiders. This new federal policy resulted in a large-scale land sale to white Americans; through means fair and foul the remaining 140 million acres of Native American lands were further reduced to 50 million acres by the mid-1930s.[45]

In 1884, a Native American named John Elk moved to the city (Omaha, Nebraska), adapted to white ways, and attempted to vote. Denied this citizenship right, Elk took his case to a federal court, where he argued that the Fourteenth Amendment made him a citizen and that the Fifteenth Amendment guaranteed his right to vote.[46] The court ruled that he was not an American citizen—that he was in effect a citizen of a *foreign* nation and thus not entitled to vote. However, under the 1887 Dawes Act, the "wards" of the government could become citizens if they showed themselves competent in managing their land allotments. Some Native Americans were issued "certificates of competency" by special "competency commissions," which decided if they could function well in the white world. Belatedly, in 1924 Congress passed the Indian Citizenship Act, granting citizenship, including voting rights, to all Native Americans.

Still, the U.S. Supreme Court continued to hold that Native Americans were wards of the federal government, a status not changed by the Citizenship Act. Because of this ward status, many state governments refused to provide services or allow Native Americans to vote in local elections. To make matters more confusing, the federal government on occasion tried to discontinue its services on the ground that Native Americans were officially citizens.[47]

It was not until the 1934 Indian Reorganization Act (IRA) under the New Deal that a new federal policy was developed. Designed by the liberal commissioner of Indian affairs John Collier, the law was explicitly intended to establish Native American civil and cultural rights, allow for semiautonomous tribal governments similar in legal status to counties and municipalities, and foster economic development of reservations. The changes seemed progressive. The IRA would end land allotment, require careful BIA supervision of the sale of lands, and provide for federal credit and preferential hiring of Native Americans in the BIA. Native American groups were supposed to vote on whether they wanted to come under the act.[48]

Yet as progressive as the law appeared, it had serious defects. It ignored fundamental economic problems and maintained the subordinate ward relationship of Native Americans to the federal government. Oklahoma tribes were excluded; the Papago tribe lost control of its mineral resources; and great power was put in the hands of the secretary of the interior, whom some called the "dictator of the Indians." The secretary made rules for elections, could veto constitutions, supervised expenditures, and made regulations for land management on the reservations.[49] One analyst has noted that "the expressed purpose of this law was finally and completely to usurp the traditional mechanisms of American Indian governance (e.g., the traditional chiefs, council of elders, etc.), replacing them with a system of federally approved and regulated 'tribal councils' . . . structured more along the lines of corporate boards than of governmental entities."[50]

Drawing on their own cultures for support, many Native Americans resisted. Many Native Americans saw the IRA as a violation of the sovereignty guaranteed them by treaties with the U.S. government. The law was ratified only by manipulation of the voting process. Although in several cases the IRA lost at the ballot box, those Native Americans who did not vote, including many who refused even to recognize the BIA's authority to hold an election for ratification, were often counted as "yes" votes. On some reservations, dead people's votes were used to ensure passage of the act. Tribes that did not hold an election were automatically reorganized under the IRA's terms. After four years, 189 Native American nations were reorganized. Many of these groups incorporated themselves. Many also developed central councils with constitutions reflecting the values of the surrounding white culture. The seventy-seven groups that succeeded in voting down the act still operated under their traditional cultures and customs. Numerous groups began some self-government, managing their own property and governing their own affairs under federal supervision.[51]

Fluctuations in Federal Policies

In the 1950s, House Concurrent Resolution 108, which called for the termination of federal supervision of Native American groups, brought yet another major shift in federal policy toward Native Americans. The intent of the resolution was to reject the Indian Reorganization Act and return to the policy of forced conformity to individualistic values of land use. Supporters of termination included land-hungry whites outside reservations and conservative white members of Congress seeking to cut government costs, as well as some acculturated Native Americans living off reservations. Between 1954 and 1960, federal guardianship of several dozen Native American groups was "terminated." Because of its negative effects, including the problems of dealing with unfriendly local officials and white land entrepreneurs, this termination policy soon came to be viewed as a failure. For example, in the case of the Menominee, who became a new political unit under Wisconsin state law, distribution payments to individual members soon exhausted the group's funds and thus development capital, the local hospital had to be closed because it did not meet state standards, and local power plants were sold to an outside company. Termination was costly for many Native American groups unprepared to deal with the treachery of the outside white world.[52]

From the 1960s to the 1980s, federal policy shifted yet again, moving away from termination. President Richard Nixon called on Congress to maintain Native Americans' tie to the federal government and to prohibit termination without consent. Congress passed legislation that restored the sacred Blue Lake to the Taos Pueblo, made credit available for business purposes, and established a self-determination procedure whereby Native American nations would assume some administration of certain federal programs on reservations. In the late

1970s, some Native American groups began to run their own schools and social-service programs.[53]

The powers of the Bureau of Indian Affairs have been far-reaching. The BIA defines who is a Native American by determining which "tribes" are officially acknowledged by the federal government. The bureau keeps records of "blood" lines in order to identify who is an "Indian" eligible for benefits. Official status brings a number of benefits to a group, including economic development aid and health, education, and housing benefits for its members. To obtain federal recognition, a group must document a continuous history and prove that its members are Native Americans, a process that many find demeaning and expensive. Several groups have even been denied official recognition by the BIA, an action that amounts to "administrative death" unless the group can successfully appeal its case to the courts or Congress. For example, in 1992 the six-hundred-member Shinnecock group in New York State debated the merits of applying for recognition; it estimated the cost of doing so would be $250,000.[54] In this government-controlled process of defining who is an "Indian" (by "blood") and what is a "tribe," we see again evidence of the racial formation theory suggested by Omi and Winant. Governments often intrude into the process by which racial and ethnic groups are defined.

Today, the BIA continues to supervise tribal government, banking, utilities, and highways, as well as millions of dollars in tribal trust funds. In the early 1990s, the federal government recognized about three hundred of the five hundred surviving groups and held in trust for them 52 million acres of land. The BIA supervises leasing and selling of Native American lands, and, until recently, all control of social services, including education, was in the hands of the bureau or allied federal agencies. Some Native Americans regard the BIA as the lesser of two evils, noting that in recent decades it has to some extent protected them against predatory exploitation from whites and has periodically expanded self-determination and community control. To terminate the BIA would be to end what protection it can provide, giving outside white interests one less barrier to contend with. Indeed, under pressure from private ranching, lumbering, farming, and mineral interests, other major branches of the Interior Department have sometimes opposed the interests of Native Americans.[55]

Since the mid-1980s, growing numbers of Native Americans have called for an end to the colonialism of BIA control and have worked for recognition of their groups as sovereign nations. The Indian Self-Determination Act was amended to enable ten Native American nations to plan for autonomous governance. Government support for Native American self-government was furthered when the U.S. Senate Select Committee on Indian Affairs revealed corruption and mismanagement in the BIA. The committee recommended an end to the federal government's paternalistic control over Native American affairs and the negotiation of formal agreements with Native American nations. One Native American leader pointed out that these federal government actions "still retain the legally groundless presumption that Indian nations are somehow inherently subordinate to the United States," and that the call for negotiated agreements instead of treaties "denies Indian peoples the formal recognition of their national sovereignty implied by treaties."[56]

Even the limited amount of autonomy granted to Native Americans is resented by some other Americans. For example, in 1997 U.S. Senator Slade Gorton (Rep.-Washington) tried to pass legislation that would get rid of the sovereign immunity of Native American governments, which he alleged made it impossible for non-Indians to sue these governments. Native American leaders disagreed and pointed out that Native American governments have given up their immunity when necessary and that individual Native Americans can be sued. Under Gorton's proposal, unless Native American governments give up their immunity from lawsuits, they could not receive $767 million in federal funds.[57] Some analysts suggested that Gorton was still upset about his loss of a major court case when he was attorney general for Washington in the 1970s. At the Supreme Court level, he had lost a case that upheld Native American fishing rights in the Northwest.[58]

Growing Pressures for Political Participation

Native American political participation has often been limited to reservation elections and service in tribal governments. With some exceptions, the reservations have been exempt from state control and taxation; subject to BIA approval, Native American groups have made their own laws and regulations. Native American governments have often combined legislative and executive functions in one elected council, and voter turnout for elections has often been substantial. Political conflict has frequently occurred on reservations between those leaders who prefer to work closely with the BIA and those who support the sovereignty of Native American nations.[59]

Native Americans did not have the right to vote in all states in elections outside reservations before the 1924 Indian Citizenship Act. States such as Utah, Arizona, and New Mexico even barred reservation Indians from voting until the 1940s; as late as the 1960s and 1970s, some states made voting and jury participation difficult. State literacy tests and gerrymandered voting district lines have also reduced Native Americans' voting power in some western states. The number of potential Native American voters has risen to substantial proportions in some nonreservation areas since the 1960s. In some urban areas, Native American voting strength is great enough to function as a *swing vote* (a bloc that can throw close elections one way or another).

The number of Native Americans running for political office increased in the 1990s, although few have been elected. Only a handful of Native Americans have served in state and federal legislatures, most since the 1950s. About two dozen have served in state legislatures since 1900. The New Mexico legislature had its first Native American representatives in 1964. In 1992, thirty-five Native Americans were in fourteen state legislatures, and Larry Echo Hawk was the elected attorney general in Idaho. Very few have ever served in Congress—perhaps a half-dozen representatives and two senators have had some, often modest, Native

American ancestry. The most famous, Charles Curtis, was born on the Kaw reservation in 1860. Said to be one-fourth Native American, Curtis was a representative for fourteen years, a senator for twenty, and vice-president under Herbert Hoover.[60] Since 1935, only three Native Americans have served in Congress; there has not been more than one Native American representative at any one time. Ben Reifel, a Sioux, was a representative from South Dakota from 1961 to 1971. In 1992, Congress's only Native American member, Representative Ben Nighthorse Campbell from Colorado, was elected senator from that state, and in the late 1990s remained the only Native American in either house of Congress.

The slight representation in state legislatures and Congress is paralleled in town and city governments. Even in metropolitan areas with substantial Native American populations, few Native Americans have been elected to city councils, school boards, and county governments. Police harassment of Native American men in towns near reservations is sometimes a problem, in part revealing discrimination by local white authorities. Complaints by Native American leaders in several cities have focused on the lack of efforts to recruit Native Americans as police and parole officers and government attorneys, as well as unnecessarily high arrest rates.[61]

The recent economic improvements that come from gambling operations, which we will note later, have enabled a few Native American groups to contribute significant amounts of money to local and national political campaigns and to fund lobbying in Washington, DC, thereby expanding their political power and influence. Their political influence has already stopped the passage of legislation seen as detrimental to Native American interests. Nonetheless, the large majority of Native American groups have not been able to prosper economically or politically in this manner.[62]

PROTEST AND CONFLICT

Organized Native American protest against subordination has been the most sustained of any group in the history of North America. Violent resistance to Euro-American oppression between 1500 and 1900 produced some of the greatest protest leaders the continent has seen.

The end of the period of armed conflict did not end protest. The character of the protest changed. By the late nineteenth century, a number of new protest organizations had sprung up. One was the Indian Rights Association, founded by white Quakers concerned with protecting and "civilizing" Native Americans. By exposing the corruption and oppression on reservations, such progressive groups did lay the basis for reforms in federal policy. One of the first organizations formed by Native Americans was the Society of American Indians, created in the early 1900s. The goals of this self-help-oriented national organization included developing pride and a national leadership and improving educational and job opportunities.[63]

In the 1920s, a prominent white advocate for Native Americans, John Collier, organized the American Indian Defense Association to fight attempts by

Republican officials to establish "executive order reservations" not covered by treaty and accessible to exploitation by whites who wished to extract minerals. The National Congress of American Indians (NCAI) was formed in the 1940s and pressed for education, legal aid, and legislation. An influential organization, the NCAI vigorously opposed the termination policy of the 1950s and 1960s and campaigned for the "war on poverty" of the 1960s and for the self-determination policy of the 1970s and 1980s. NCAI, with some three hundred member groups, is the oldest and largest Native American advocacy group. In the 1990s, the group has campaigned against Native American stereotypes, including sports teams' use of Native American names and symbols. The National Indian Youth Council, created in 1961, has fought vigorously for the civil rights of Native Americans, sometimes organizing civil disobedience and developing a "Red Power" ideology. The Youth Council has been active in education and has taken up causes critical to the protection of Native American lands.[64]

Protest actions and civil disobedience movements increased in the 1960s, with at least 194 protest activities occurring between 1961 and 1970. These actions continued a long tradition of coaxing white-controlled institutions into concessions—the great strength of organizations such as the NCAI. Civil disobedience involved such activities as delaying dam construction, occupying offices or other government facilities, picketing, and staging sit-ins.[65] Some of the protest actions since the 1970s have brought changes benefiting Native Americans.

In one widely publicized action, students began the nineteen-month occupation of California's Alcatraz Island in November 1969; they were replaced by one hundred Native Americans claiming unused federal lands under provisions of an old treaty. The intent of the protestors was both symbolic and concrete—to dramatize the plight of Native Americans and to establish a facility where Native Americans could celebrate their ancient cultures. In the same period protesters made several attempts to seize other unused federal property, including Ellis Island in New York harbor, and occupied BIA offices in protest against BIA policies.[66]

In 1968, the American Indian Movement (AIM) was organized by Native Americans to address problems ranging from police brutality to housing and employment discrimination. An Indian Patrol, established by the organization to supervise contacts between Native Americans and the police, pressed for improvements in police behavior. AIM grew to more than a dozen groups in cities and on reservations. In the spring of 1973, AIM organized a large-scale occupation of Wounded Knee, South Dakota, a hamlet on the Pine Ridge reservation. Several hundred AIM members participated in the seventy-one-day armed protest of the Justice Department's sending federal agents to Pine Ridge to support a Sioux leader, who was favored by the federal government, when he was challenged by AIM activists wishing to replace him with a traditional Council of Elders.[67]

In its attempts to convict AIM protestors, the federal government, with President Nixon's encouragement, behaved like a police state and used illegal wiretaps, altered evidence, and paid witnesses—which led to dismissal of the case by a federal judge. Afterward, government agents participated in a campaign to destroy the movement and were thought by some observers to be involved in a dozen suspicious murders and accidents involving AIM members. Two hundred AIM members were harassed and arrested, but only a dozen or so were ever convicted. This was an example of an open confrontation between militant Native Americans and a Native American establishment propped up by BIA and other white officials.[68]

AIM now has chapters in cities across the nation. AIM has organized "survival" schools for Native American children, operated a radio station in South Dakota, and participated in an encampment at Big Mountain on the Navaho reservation to prevent the forced removal of Native Americans from their land.[69]

In the 1990s, AIM and other Native American organizations have led initiatives to protest the use of Native American names, sacred symbols, and "tomahawk chop" gestures by sports teams and their fans. Some protest efforts have focused on the World Series and the Super Bowl. For example, before the 1992 Super Bowl, AIM sponsored a two-day conference on racism in sports. These nationally televised sports events brought degrading caricatures into the homes of Native Americans who otherwise have little contact with white fans' and teams' behavior. "We couldn't ignore it anymore," one Native American woman stated. "People started coming up to me at work and going, 'chop-chop' and 'woo-woo.'" Some names like *Redskins* (a racist epithet) are extremely derogatory. Native Americans consider all team names such as *Redskins, Chiefs,* and *Braves,* as well as caricatures used by the teams, to be offensive stereotypes. The parody of sacred chants, face paint, headdresses, and drums for entertainment purposes is viewed as a blasphemous assault on Native American culture, since all of these have spiritual significance.[70] These protests have continued into the late 1990s. In the summer of 1997, the National Coalition on Racism in Sports and the Media joined local protesters in Cleveland in demonstrations against the Cleveland baseball team's use of the "Chief Wahoo" symbol. Called the "Indians," Cleveland's team has come under intensive criticism for several years for the use of this caricatured image, which is seen as extremely negative and racist by Native American and other critics. Some of the team's defenders have tried to argue that the caricatured logo honors the first Native American to play baseball with a nineteenth-century baseball team in Cleveland.[71]

Using interviews with Native American leaders in the movement to eliminate the use of Native American sports mascots, Laurel Davis has examined several of the movement's arguments. First, such mascots and related fan actions are based on myths and stereotypes of Native Americans as wild savages and ferocious, bloodthirsty warriors and ignore the historical reality of the European takeover of Native American lands and the genocidal policies toward native nations. "The holocaust and oppression of Native Americans [are rendered] invisible, justified, or even glorious. . . . Native Americans were only viewed as 'positive' symbols of a proud fighting spirit after they were conquered, and only after large scale resistance to white control was eliminated."[72] The particular symbolism chosen by sports teams also stereotypes Native Americans as an historical rather than present-day people. Native Americans are portrayed as a generic "Indian" group rather than as diverse and distinctive nations and are thus robbed of control over their public image. The use of these symbols in sports events often trivializes and mocks the religious significance of Native American sacred symbols and can adversely affect the self-image and self-esteem of some Native Americans, including Native American youth. The vigorous and emotional opposition among some white men to the elimination of Native American sports symbolism may even suggest that the protest movement threatens a particular version of white American (or white masculine) identity that is rooted in the mythology of the American West. One Native American leader has noted the following statement made by a prominent pro-football player: "The reason there's so much violence in football is we can't kill Indians anymore."[73] Another Native American leader stated, "If people thought [the use of Native American mascots] was trivial, they wouldn't need to debate it."[74]

AIM protests in 1996–1997 included efforts to free Leonard Peltier, a Lakota/Ojibwa. Seen by many, including Amnesty International, as a political prisoner, Peltier has been in a federal institution for two decades. He is accused of shooting two special government agents in a confrontation between Native Americans and government agents at the Pine Ridge Reservation in South Dakota in 1975. Initially, several other men were also accused, but only Peltier was tried and sentenced to life in prison. Even federal government officials now admit that it is unclear who shot the federal agents, and numerous members of the U.S. Congress have supported a new trial. Millions of people around the globe have signed petitions or joined groups protesting Peltier's confinement as a *political* prisoner.[75]

The Native American civil rights movement and other activism have achieved some gains in raising the consciousness of the general public and the nation's mass media leadership. Films portraying Native Americans as savages and white people as heroes became less common in the 1990s. Films such as *Powwow Highway* and *Dances with Wolves* have portrayed Native Americans in a more sympathetic, if still paternalistic, light. In the 1970s, some colleges and universities, including Dartmouth and Stanford, dropped the name *Indians* for their sports teams. In 1992, in direct response to AIM protests, the *Oregonian* became the first newspaper to discontinue using names that stereotype Native Americans. In an editorial the managing editor of this Portland daily stated, "We will not be a passive participant in perpetuating racial or cultural stereotypes."[76] A member of the Missouri House of Representatives introduced a bill to prohibit state financial support for the Kansas City Chiefs' stadium if the team discriminated against Native Americans or mocked their sacred symbols.[77] In the 1990s, a coalition of petitioners has sued to force the Washington Redskins football team to change its name. A number of high schools across the nation have changed their team names from such terms as Indians and Redskins and removed offensive mascots and images. In September 1997, the Los Angeles Board of Education voted unanimously to eliminate all Native American mascots in all local schools. Money was provided to the schools to paint over the images and purchase new uniforms. The alumni of several of the schools protested the ban as hurting school spirit and costing too much money.[78]

Protests against the Columbus Quincentenary in the early 1990s had a noticeable impact on commemorative events planned nationwide. Native

American groups called for a more accurate accounting of history that presented the encounter of two old cultures rather than the discovery of a virtually uninhabited wilderness by Europeans. In addition to demonstrations at the Quincentenary events, Native American leaders talked with white Quincentenary planners and convinced many to include the native perspective in major events, exhibitions, and documentaries. The National Council of Churches adopted a resolution urging their member denominations to refrain from celebrating an event that had resulted in the genocide of indigenous peoples.[79]

Fishing Rights and Land Claims

Fishing rights and land claims have been at the heart of the conflict between Native Americans and whites. In the Pacific Northwest and the Great Lakes region, Native American nations have struggled with whites for a century over fishing rights. Shootings and court battles have occurred in the state of Washington over Native American rights to catch fish, particularly salmon and trout—rights guaranteed by treaties between the nations and the federal government more than a century ago. White anglers and commercial fishing companies object because their fishing opportunities are reduced when Native Americans exercise their treaty rights. A major court decision, *U.S.* v. *State of Washington* (1974), ruled that the treaties did reserve fishing rights for Native Americans that are different from those allowed whites. The court ordered the state of Washington to protect Native American fishers.[80]

White fishers defied the court's decision, protesting that it discriminated against them, and the state of Washington appealed the decision. Native American fishers were harassed and physically assaulted, and protests were directed at the judge who ruled in their favor. The federal government spent millions of dollars to increase the fish available in the area and to compensate whites who suffered economic hardship. In 1979, the U.S. Supreme Court upheld the lower-court ruling, and government enforcement gradually reduced illegal fishing by whites. This decision helped to revitalize reservation economies in the state of Washington. In the words of a Native American leader, "the opportunities created directly or indirectly from the legally secured right to fish are the difference between staying and leaving" for many young families in more than two dozen communities.[81]

In the mid-1980s, following an agreement between Wisconsin treaty nations and state officials to honor Native American fishing rights, some Native American fishers became the targets of physical and psychological harassment by vigilante whites. Anti–Native American violence by whites in Wisconsin escalated to include gunfire, arson, and beatings. Nonetheless, by the 1990s Native American groups in both Wisconsin and the Pacific Northwest had realized significant gains in the struggle to regain their treaty fishing rights.[82]

Historically, Native American lands were taken without adequate compensation. The cause of land-claims conflict on the East Coast was stated in a report by the U.S. Commission on Civil Rights:

> The basic Eastern Indian land claim is that Indian land in the East was invalidly transferred from Indians to non-Indians in the 18th and 19th centuries because the Federal Government, although required to do so, did not supervise or approve the transactions.[83]

In recent decades many indigenous groups, such as the Oneida in New York and the Passamaquoddy in Maine, have pressed land claims in federal court. A number of tribes have won their cases, and some of the illegally taken lands have been restored. Prior to 1960, the U.S. Indian Claims Commission had denied most claims for compensation for land taken. However, Native American and other pressures on the federal government since then have resulted in increases in the compensation paid by the commission.[84]

In recent years, the Sioux have pursued the return of the land in U.S. courts and in the United Nations. In 1980, after a lengthy court battle, the U.S. Supreme Court awarded the Lakota Sioux $122.5 million for more than 7 million acres taken illegally in the 1870s. Although the land (including the Black Hills) had been guaranteed to the Sioux nation by an 1868 treaty, it was stolen by whites a few years later. When gold was discovered in the area, whites came into the center of the reservation. After a war between the Sioux and the U.S. army, the Lakota and others were dispersed and lost control of much of their land. Significantly, this cash award was refused by the Lakota, who reiterated their position that their land was not for sale and that the land itself should be returned to them. In 1987 U.S. Senator Bill Bradley from New Jersey introduced a bill to return substantial land to the Lakota and to offer the money as damages instead of as payment for stolen land. The bill gained considerable support from the Lakotas before it was withdrawn by its sponsor in 1990.[85]

Recently, Sioux leaders have taken their case to the United Nations, where some have been part of the U.N. committee writing a Declaration on the Rights of Indigenous Peoples. Provisions included in the declaration are the "restitution of the lands, territories and resources" and the "enforcement of treaties." Needless to say, the U.S. government has tried to get changes in the draft declaration.[86]

Many land claims by indigenous nations in Minnesota, Arizona, Massachusetts, Alaska, Hawaii, Nevada, New York, and South Dakota remain unsettled. In the mid-1990s one Minnesota group, the Mille Lacs, won their case when the court declared that the 157-year-old treaty that granted them hunting and fishing rights was still valid and must be respected.[87]

White backlash against Native American land claims, fishing claims, and other militant protest led to the creation of a national organization called the Interstate Congress for Equal Rights and Responsibilities and a variety of other antitreaty organizations. Senator Mark Hatfield of Oregon publicly noted that this "very significant backlash . . . by any other name comes out as racism in all its ugly manifestations." Some white members of Congress, supporting the backlash, introduced bills to break treaties, overturn court decisions, and extinguish native land claims, arguing that the demands by Native Americans had soured longtime "friendly relations." Native Americans responded that they were seeking what was *legally* theirs. Whites had become hostile because of the expense of living up to U.S. law and, as one tribal leader noted, "because of the lack of educational systems to teach anything about Indians, about treaties."[88] White stereotypes about Native Americans and ignorance of important treaties have played a critical role in the opposition to Native American struggles for social justice.

The Native American Rights Fund (NARF), a nonprofit national legal defense firm, has represented various tribes in lawsuits and negotiations for treaty-guaranteed land, water, and natural resource rights and for restoration of the status of tribes as separate, sovereign nations. NARF's hundreds of victories include land returned to the Passamaquoddy and Penobscot nations in Maine. NARF has secured Native American control over taxation, local courts, and educational programs and economic enterprises on reservations.[89]

Reports from human rights groups have documented an increase in harassment and violence perpetrated by right-wing extremists against Native Americans over the last decade. Native Americans have been the victims of property crimes as well as beatings and murder. In 1995, some 4,800 racial hate crimes were reported. More than 60 percent targeted African Americans, and about a sixth of the crimes targeted Native Americans or Asian Americans. Many of hate crimes against Native Americans have occurred in rural western white communities that border reservations, although Native Americans in urban areas have also been targeted. Many Native Americans feared reporting hate crimes to white law enforcement officials because of the lack of seriousness with which such crimes have been treated in the past. Those incidents that are reported seldom receive any media coverage. Rodney Barker, author of *The Broken Circle* (1993), the story of a series of hate crimes against Native Americans in New Mexico, reported that numerous Native Americans had personally told him about hate incidents they or their families had experienced, "but the newspaper was refusing to carry those reports. . . . Everyone tries to dissociate themselves from the historical pattern and say, 'Well, this is an aberration, it's not representative of what's going on here.' And yet, how many of those (crimes) does it take before you see the pattern is still in evidence?"[90]

THE ECONOMY

For white immigrant groups, structural assimilation at the secondary level has usually involved upward movement into ever higher levels of the economy. Economic mobility has been modest and uneven for Native Americans. The colonialism model best fits the way in which Native Americans have been incorporated into the U.S. economy without getting on the escalator to economic equality. Before being forced onto reservations, most native groups, which ranged from the Pueblo agriculturalists of the Southwest to hunting societies on the Plains to mixed agricultural-hunting societies elsewhere across the continent, had self-sufficient, land-based economies.

The loss of land to whites destroyed traditional economies. Speaking at a meeting of the Connecticut Humanities Council, Melissa Fawcett Sayet, a

Mohegan elder, has explained how she cried in anguish when her high-school teacher taught the concept of *Manifest Destiny*, which stated that the United States had a right to expand from the Atlantic Ocean to the Pacific and would inevitably do so. Her white audience then became defensive. By the 1880s, Native American nations had lost millions of acres as white "civilization" proceeded westward; millions more acres were lost with the breakup of the remaining lands under the 1887 Dawes Act. Native American lands were usually reduced to areas considered the least valuable to white settlers and entrepreneurs, although in recent years some of that land has been found to be rich in natural gas and other valuable natural resources. In the 1990s, Native Americans control only 3 percent of the land in the continental United States, although indigenous peoples "still retain unassailable legal title to about ten times the area now left them."[91]

Economic exploitation accompanied the growth of industrial capitalism and urbanization in the late nineteenth century. The encroachment on Native American lands by white lumbering, ranching, and railroad interests redirected resources from rural Native American lands to fuel growth in urban centers. Bison and other game were killed for skins to be sold in Eastern cities, and white ranchers and farmers took lands for cattle raising and agriculture, hastening the impoverishment of Native Americans in the West. Rural poverty increased as corporations reached out from metropolitan centers to develop more and more land; this in turn pressured many Native Americans to migrate to the cities. Joseph Jorgensen has argued that the poverty of rural Native Americans is "not due to rural isolation [or] a tenacious hold on aboriginal ways, but results from the way in which United States' urban centers of finance, political influence, and power have grown at the expense of rural areas."[92]

Poverty and Land Theft

The poverty of many reservations is rooted in the destruction of local economies and often in mismanagement by BIA officials. Testifying before a congressional committee on the food situation in the winter of 1883, a member of the Assiniboine nation pointed out that its members were healthy until the buffalo were destroyed, and that the substitute BIA rations were not adequate:

> They gave us rations once a week, just enough to last one day, and the Indians they started to eat their pet dogs. After they ate all their dogs up they started to eat their ponies. All this time the Indian Bureau had a warehouse full of grub. . . . Early [the next] spring, in 1884, I saw the dead bodies of the Indians wrapped in blankets and piled up like cordwood in the village of Wolf Point, and the other Indians were so weak they could not bury their dead; what were left were nothing but skeletons.[93]

Government agents were officially responsible for supplies, instruction in farming, and supervision of lands. Yet many agents were notorious for their corruption or incompetence. Many desired to make their fortunes at the expense of those for whom they were responsible. The "agency towns" growing up on reservations developed a stratified system in which there was little equitable contact between Native Americans and paternalistic white officials. After the 1890s, the BIA attempted to expand farming on some reservations. Yet white officials still built paternalistic systems in which Native Americans had little part other than that of unskilled laborers or small farmers.[94]

The reorganization policy of the 1930s, which provided for Native American self-government, put a partial brake on corruption and blatant land theft, but serious economic problems persisted. Federal policy fluctuated between tribal self-determination and forced individualism. Termination experiments threw some Native American groups to the "outside white wolves." Some lands were sold to pay taxes, and many Native Americans fell deeper into poverty as land resources were depleted.

Native American lands have been taken for dams, national parks, and rights-of-way for roads. The sale of lands to white lumbering and mineral interests continues. Attempts by Native American nations to control the use of their lands have led ranchers and other white interests to argue that self-government by Native Americans is an unreasonable threat to "rational" development. Much of the substantial money made in agriculture or ranching on reservations has flowed to whites, who lease large proportions of the usable land. Facing discrimination and often having limited technical schooling, technical assistance, and capital to buy seeds, livestock, or machinery, the Native American farmer has frequently been faced with suffering a low yield or else leasing to outsiders.[95]

Land, Minerals, and Industrial Development

In recent decades, the federal government has taken some action on the economic problems of reservations. Federal antipoverty programs have brought some job and training benefits, mostly temporary. The BIA strategy of urban relocation and employment assistance has encouraged or facilitated the movement of thousands of Native Americans to cities. Urbanites earn more than those on reservations but are often dissatisfied with urban life. Many return to reservation areas after a few years; lack of economic success is cited as the major reason. Studies have also shown a relationship between the negative economic experiences of urban migrants, such as low wages and unemployment, and their relatively high arrest rates. Many Native Americans in cities still face discrimination, poverty, and low-wage, dead-end jobs.[96]

The federal government has attempted to attract industrial plants to reservations. Yet many jobs in plants built on or near reservations have gone to white workers. Government funds have all too often expanded corporate profits, with modest gains for rural Native Americans. The BIA has encouraged cottage industries, such as the revival of traditional arts and crafts, which has helped improve the economic situation on some reservations.[97]

Federal development projects on reservations, including dozens of resorts and industrial parks, have generally failed. Occupancy rates at the industrial parks have been 5 percent, largely because they are located in rural areas lacking the amenities many corporations desire. A *Forbes* magazine article noted that

Native American "reservations do not seem fertile ground for the seeds of capitalism. Reservation resources are generally the province of the tribe rather than individuals and shared equally among the membership." Native American values accent the group rather than the individual and are thus alien to individualistic capitalism. This group emphasis helps explain the limited success of attempts to foster the "entrepreneurial spirit" on reservations and to increase the number of Native Americans operating small businesses.[98]

Native American reservations in the United States encompass about one-third of all low-sulphur coal, 6 percent of oil and gas reserves, and half of all known uranium reserves. Corporate executives have eagerly eyed these mineral resources, and a few have called for the abolition of the reservations and the Bureau of Indian Affairs so that these mineral resources can be exploited.[99] Historically, when mineral resources have been found on Native American land, the land has frequently been taken over by white entrepreneurs and corporations. An example is the 1952 mineral extraction agreement between the Navaho Tribal Council and Kerr-McGee Nuclear Corporation. Over a period of eighteen years, Kerr-McGee employed 150 Navaho men to mine uranium on Navaho land, paying them only about two-thirds of the prevailing off-reservation wage. Once the easy-to-reach deposits were mined, the company closed the facility, leaving acres of radioactive debris that threatened the water supplies of downstream communities. By 1980, thirty-eight of the miners had died of cancers related to their mining of uranium, and ninety-five more had similar cancers.[100]

Three dozen tribes made national headlines in the 1970s when they announced the creation of the Council of Energy Resources Tribes (CERT) and hired a former Iranian oil minister to help them get better contracts with white-owned companies. Many whites worried that tribes were going to behave like OPEC and seek to be completely independent in making contracts with energy corporations.[101] By the mid-1990s, CERT's membership had expanded to fifty-seven Native American groups. By providing technical and financial assistance to help member groups control their own energy resources, the organization has brought some jobs and increased income to some reservations.[102]

Persisting Economic Problems

Before 1940, most Native American men were poor farmers or unskilled workers. With increasing rural-to-urban migration, the proportion in farm occupations has dropped dramatically—from 68 percent in 1940 to 24 percent in 1960 and only 5 percent in 1990.[103] Native American workers in cities have usually been concentrated in the secondary labor market—that sector of urban economies, characterized by job instability, low wages, and little job mobility, that is typically composed disproportionately of Native American, African American, and Latino workers. The primary labor market—that sector characterized by skilled jobs, high wages, and significant mobility—is predominantly composed of white workers. The following census figures (the most recent data) compare the occupational distributions of Native Americans in 1990 with those of whites.[104]

	Men		Women	
	Native American	*White*	*Native American*	*White*
Managerial and professional	15%	27%	22%	30%
Technical, sales, and clerical	16	22	40	45
Service	14	8	23	15
Farming, forestry, and fishing	5	4	1	1
Precision production	23	20	3	2
Operators, fabricators, laborers	27	19	11	7
	100%	100%	100%	100%

Today, Native Americans are far less likely than white Americans to hold managerial or professional positions. Native American men are concentrated in blue-collar and service-sector jobs. The majority of Native American women hold clerical, sales, or service-sector jobs.

Through the years, unemployment rates for Native Americans, both on and off reservations, have been far higher than for most other groups. In 1940, one-third of all Native American men were unemployed, compared with fewer than one-tenth of white men. By 1960, the rate had risen to 38 percent, compared with just 5 percent for all men. This increase reflected in part the move from agriculture to the less certain work opportunities in urban areas. By 1970 the rate had dropped to 12 percent for men, still three times the national figure.[105] The 1990 unemployment rate for all Native American men (15 percent) was also three times that of white men, and the rate for all Native American women (13.1 percent) was almost three times that of white women.[106] In that year the unemployment rate for Native Americans living on reservations was 25.6 percent; on some reservations the rate even exceeded 50 percent.[107] (These rates do not include the large proportion of Native American workers who have given up looking for work.) Native Americans have endured the longest Depression-like economic situation of any U.S. racial or ethnic group.

For decades Native Americans have also had the lowest median family income, and the lowest per capita income, of any racial or ethnic group. The income of Native Americans on reservations has been lower than that of those living in non-reservation areas. In 1939, the median income of men on reservations was less than one-fourth of the median income for all U.S. men. In 1990, the median income for Native American families living on reservations was still only 38 percent that of all U.S. families, and the median income for all Native American families was 62 percent of the general population. More than 26 percent of all Native American families and 47 percent of those on reservations fell below the official poverty line.[108] Part of Native Americans' economic improvement since the 1930s may be an effect of the large increase of people who now identify themselves as Native American. That is, people of mixed ancestry now reclaiming their heritage are frequently more affluent than those of unmixed ancestry.[109] Still, at the beginning of the 21st century, Native Americans as a group remain the poorest of all Americans.

Poverty and unemployment mean inferior living conditions. Generally speaking, Native Americans face the worst housing conditions of any group in the United States. Today, Native Americans are much more likely than European Americans to have inadequate nutrition, to die of tuberculosis or diabetes, to live in small apartments or houses, and to have inadequate water and sanitation facilities. The mortality rates for Native Americans of all ages, including infants, are higher than for the nation as a whole. Death rates from alcoholism and tuberculosis are more than five times those of the total population. Although life expectancy for Native Americans has increased significantly in recent years, it is still below the national average. Inadequate medical facilities, coupled with poor nutrition resulting from low incomes, constitute a major part of the problem. Cutbacks in federal health programs in the 1980s and 1990s have reduced access to medical care for many Native Americans.[110]

Today, Native Americans are more urban than rural. The Los Angeles metropolitan area, with almost 58,000 Native Americans in 1990, has the largest urban concentration. One study reported 117 distinct groups represented there. Oklahoma City has the highest percentage of Native Americans—more than 4 percent of the city's population. Many Native Americans in those two urban areas have experienced some economic mobility in recent decades. In 1990, the median Native American family income in these urban areas was somewhat above that of local black and Latino families but substantially below that of local white families. The poverty rate of Native American families in the Los Angeles area (11.4 percent) was only slightly higher than that of the area's general population (10.2 percent), although in Oklahoma City, Native American families' poverty rate (17.6 percent) was far above that for the city's total population (10 percent).[111]

Recent Economic Developments

The substantial court-awarded judgments received by some Native American groups have seldom brought them much collective benefit, in part because of the BIA's practice of dividing a large portion of these awards among individuals. One exception is the Saginaw Chippewa of Michigan, who with the help of the advocacy organization First Nations secured legislation to permit a $10 million judgment to be paid directly to the group. They used the funds for scholarships, health insurance, and security for home mortgages, strategies designed to increase self-sufficiency.[112]

In recent decades, several dozen Native American groups have developed gambling enterprises in an attempt to improve local economies. In the late 1990s, there were 237 gambling places run by Native American groups in twenty-nine states. However, some mass media reports have greatly exaggerated the economic return from these operations. Most Native Americans have not benefited economically from gaming. For example, one critical *Washington Post* report notes that the majority of the nation's 557 Native American groups have no casinos, and only forty-eight tribes receive annual returns of more than $10 million from casinos. The Oglala Sioux reservation's casino is typical. Housed in a few trailers, the operation earns only $1 million a year for the reservation's mostly poor residents.[113]

Where gambling revenues are significant, they have paid for educational and health-care facilities, water and sewage treatment plants, job training, roads, and housing, and have reduced unemployment. For some groups, profits from gambling enterprises are their first regular, independent income. Still, white investors, lenders, and management firms have claimed a large share of the revenues from many of the gambling operations. One federal government investigation found that many tribes had been victims of economic exploitation, theft, and embezzlement by white management firms.[114]

In recent years, many reservation leaders have been approached to provide landfill space for out-of-state garbage; some have been urged to store nuclear waste. Reservations are attractive to waste management companies because of their low population density and because they are not subject to state environmental regulations or state taxes. Enforcement of federal pollution regulations has been lax on reservations. Waste management firms expect that the prospect of substantial income will convince impoverished tribes to accept landfills. Yet most tribes have rejected the offers. One leader on the Rosebud Sioux reservation stated, "Here it is, almost the twenty-first century, and we're still fighting the invaders, only now they're trying to make us take their trash."[115] There is a growing body of research on the widespread problem of government and private

In recent years several Native American groups have developed gambling enterprises to boost their local economies.

dumping in communities populated by Native Americans, African Americans, and Latinos. Dumping is described by some as "environmental racism."

EDUCATION

The formal educational experience of subordinated Native Americans began early in the reservation period. Influential whites supported education as the channel of forced acculturation to white culture. In the white-controlled schools, the "wild Indians"—as whites stereotyped them—could be civilized. By 1887, 14,300 children were enrolled in 227 schools, most operated by the BIA or by religious groups with government aid.[116]

Yet, by 1900, only a small percentage of Native American children were receiving formal schooling. In the Southwest, perhaps one-fourth of the school-age children in the four decades after 1890 had experience with BIA and other boarding schools; a small percentage of the rest attended public schools. From the beginning the BIA and mission schools were run according to a strict Anglo-conformity assimilationist approach. Intensive efforts were made to destroy Native American ways; students were punished for speaking their native languages. The facilities and staff of most boarding schools were often inadequate either in quantity or in quality.[117]

By the mid-1930s, some boarding schools were being replaced by day schools closer to home, and a bilingual educational policy was being discussed. Increasingly, public schools became the context for Native American education. The Johnson-O'Malley Act provided federal aid for states that developed public schools for Native Americans. Yet, by 1945, large proportions of Native American groups were still not enrolled in formal schools.[118]

Enforced acculturation has been an issue in public schools, where white administrators and teachers have viewed Native American cultures as a major problem. Whites have blamed educational problems on cultural differences and emphasized the contrast between the collective values of Native Americans and the individualism of white Americans. Many teachers have attempted to make their pupils "less Indian." To this day, school textbooks have provided little to help the children identify with their own culture.[119] The one-way assimilation perspective of BIA-supported education programs is evident in the fact that bilingual programs provided for Native American students with limited English proficiency were designed not to enhance the students' understanding of their own language but solely to "improve their ability to read, write, speak, and understand English."[120]

Since the 1960s, Native Americans have increasingly pressed for social change. In part because of this pressure, government aid to primary, adult, and vocational education has expanded substantially since the 1960s. Government attention has been refocused on local public and BIA schools, and many federal schools have developed advisory boards composed of Native Americans, have added Native Americans to their staffs, and have included classes in native art, dance, and language. However, in the words of an AIM member, "the curriculum taught in Indian schools [has] remained exactly the same, reaching exactly the same conclusions, indoctrinating children with exactly the same values as when the schools were staffed entirely by white people."[121]

The movement of many Native Americans to the cities has resulted in a decline in the proportion of Native American children in BIA schools in recent decades. In 1970, only 25 percent of Native American children enrolled in school attended BIA schools; in the mid-1990s, the proportion had dropped to less than 10 percent. Most of the other children now attend local public schools. In 1991, a Department of Education task force, most of whose members were Native Americans, issued a report concluding that both local and federal educational systems have failed to meet the needs of Native American students. The report cited the absence of a Native American historical perspective in the curricula, the loss of Native American language ability, the shift away from Native American spiritual values, and the overt and subtle racism of white teachers and administrators as major barriers to Native American students' educational success in school. The report called for the implementation of multicultural curricula embodying respect for Native American history and culture and for programs that would guarantee that Native American students learn English well.[122]

In recent years a desire to increase the relevance and effectiveness of their children's education led Rosebud Sioux leaders to draw up an education code of their own to increase the group's authority over the public schools on their reservation. This was the first action of its kind in the nation. The leaders worked to gain support from education officials at the state and federal levels and thus to implement their plan without the need for a court battle.[123]

More than 127,000 Native Americans are enrolled in colleges nationwide.[124] Approximately 18,000 of these attend twenty-three Native American–controlled community colleges, where efforts are made to integrate Native American history and culture into courses and where more attention is given to Native American students' values and needs. The first reservation community college was established in 1969 on the Navaho reservation in Arizona with federal government funds. However, these reservation colleges are typically small and poorly financed. Some are not fully accredited, and most are two-year institutions that emphasize vocational education.[125]

The educational attainment levels of Native Americans have remained consistently below those of the general population. Some educational gains were made during the 1960s. Although the number of Native Americans with fewer than nine years of schooling decreased, at the end of that decade high-school graduation rates remained far below the national average. By 1990, fewer than two-thirds of Native Americans over the age of twenty-five were high-school graduates, compared with three-fourths of all persons in that age range.[126] Today, school enrollments vary greatly among reservations, with 95 percent of the children on the Pima and Papago reservations in Arizona enrolled, but only 35 percent of the Alaskan Eskimos.[127] The Department of Education task force report mentioned earlier put the proportion of Native American students who drop out after tenth grade at 36 percent, the highest of any racial or ethnic group and more than twice that of whites.[128]

RELIGION

In the summer of 1977, some Navaho leaders came to Sante Fe, New Mexico, to take back religious and other ceremonial "artifacts" that a museum had collected. For many white museum visitors, these prayer sticks, medicine bundles, and other items were curiosities provided to entertain and perhaps inform. But for the Navaho they were sacred objects stolen from their rightful Native American owners. After holding a religious ceremony, the Navaho leaders reclaimed the sacred objects. One said, "We will take them home and teach the younger generation what these things mean."[129]

Many sacred objects belonging to Native American groups still remain in white hands. Since the 1960s, Native Americans have periodically requested that museums return thousands of religious and art objects, particularly those illegally acquired. Many Native Americans have protested the display of Native American skeletal remains in museums and have called for the return of the remains for proper burial ceremonies. Following enactment of the Indian Arts and Crafts Act (1988) and the Indian Graves Repatriation Act (1990), the federal government now requires museums to catalog their holdings of Native American remains and sacred objects and consult with relevant Native American groups about returning these holdings.

Pressures for acculturation to Euro-American culture have been clear in the case of religion. The Spanish conquerors brought Roman Catholic priests to reduce southwestern tribes to a mission-centered life. Later, white settlers sometimes attempted to convert what they stereotyped as the "heathen Indians" to Christianity. Some Native Americans have joked that "when [the Christian missionaries] arrived they had only the Book and we had the land; now we have the Book and they have the land."[130] With the reservation period came a jockeying among Christian denominations for control; reservations were often divided up so that Episcopalians got one, Methodists another, and Catholics yet another. For a number of reasons, including fear of whites, many Native Americans became affiliated with a Christian denomination.[131]

Revitalization Movements as Protest

From the Pacific Islands to Africa to the United States, colonized peoples have lashed out at European oppressors by joining millenarian movements, often led by visionaries and oriented to a "golden age" in which supernatural events will change oppressive conditions. Among the most famous Native American millenarian movements were the Ghost Dance groups that emerged on the Great Plains. In the 1870s, the prophet Wodziwob told of a vision in which the ancestors of Native America came on a train to Earth with explosive force, after which the

Earth swallowed up the whites. A number of Native American groups joined in the movement in the hope of salvation from white oppression. The movement declined when no cataclysm came but experienced a resurgence in the late 1880s when the new prophet Wovoka experienced a vision ordering him to found another Ghost Dance religion. Religious fervor spread through the Plains tribes. The cooperation among all Native Americans preached by this movement did increase solidarity. Disturbed at the resurgence of millenarianism, white officials tried to suppress it. The Sioux who were massacred at Wounded Knee in 1890 were fleeing the reservations in order to hold Ghost Dance ceremonies.[132]

Peyotism, reflecting another way of protesting white cultural pressures, surfaced as the Ghost Dance movement was being destroyed. Long used by individual practitioners to treat sickness, peyote rituals became a group religion in 1880. Between 1880 and 1900, it spread throughout the Plains. The new religion reflected an ambivalence toward Christianity. Peyote rituals involved singing and praying but were distinctive in the visionary experiences induced by eating peyote (a hallucinogenic cactus plant).[133]

Attacks by Christian missionaries and government officials welded believers together, and in 1918 the Native American church was formally incorporated as an association of Christian groups protecting the Sacrament of Peyote. By the 1920s, white legislators in seven states had passed antipeyote laws, and the BIA had issued proclamations banning its use. Nonetheless, the opposition stimulated church growth. In the 1930s, the progressive commissioner of Indian affairs, John Collier, came to the defense of indigenous religions and allowed the resurgence of the old ways, although this brought charges that the government was fostering "paganism."[134] By the 1960s, 40 percent of Native Americans on some reservations were Native American church members.[135] In the early 1990s, the Native American church had about 250,000 members in twenty-seven affiliated chapters composed of hundreds of tribes across the country.[136] Protection of the sacred peyote sacrament was not assured to Native Americans in all states until the Religious Freedom Restoration Act was passed in 1993.

In contrast to Christianity, most of the traditional religious beliefs and practices of Native Americans are not exclusive; as is also the case with many Asian religions, a person can be both a Christian and a traditional believer. Because of this, a great variety of traditional and Christian religious practices now coexist among Native American groups.

Questioning Christianity: Oppositional Cultures

Using the standard of their own cultures, a number of Native American leaders have criticized Christianity as a crude religion stressing blood, crucifixion, and bureaucratized charity rather than true sharing and compassion for people. Closely related to this criticism is renewed opposition to the dominant European American culture. Native leaders stress that white Europeans are newcomers who sharply accelerated war on the continent, destroying many animal species and betraying the Native Americans who aided them in becoming established here.

Europeans destroyed the ecosystem and polluted the environment. Respect for land and nature is a common theme in many Native American cultures. In 1970, a Hopi wrote to President Richard Nixon protesting strip mining and other forms of destruction of the western aboriginal lands: "The white man, through his insensitivity to the way of Nature, has desecrated the face of Mother Earth. The white man's advanced technological capacity has occurred as a result of his lack of regard for the spiritual path and for the way of all living things."[137]

Today, many Native Americans argue that the solution to problems of environmental damage lies in recognizing the superiority of Native American religious values, including a respect for the environment and a strong sense of community. This is an example of the role of oppositional cultures in U.S. society. Native American respect for land and ecology is strongly rooted in ancient cultures and has long been a basis for opposition to the dominant Euro-American culture's land-use values. In recent years many whites, interestingly, have come to recognize the importance of the Native American approach to the land.

ASSIMILATION AND COLONIALISM

Theoretical analysis in the field of racial and ethnic relations has long neglected the condition and experiences of Native Americans. Native Americans are distinct among U.S. racial and ethnic groups, in that the classical external colonialism model is relevant to analyzing their encounters with Europeans. In the earliest period, Native American societies on the Atlantic Coast saw their lands seized and their members driven off or killed by outsiders. It was clear that the European strategy was usually to destroy or remove indigenous peoples who stood in the way of settlement. This process would recur as European Americans moved westward from the Atlantic over the next several centuries. The policy of genocide coexisted with a reservation policy.

Assimilation Perspectives

Some white observers have argued that the opportunity to assimilate is more open for Native Americans than for other people of color.[138] In the 1920s and 1930s, even a few Native American professionals argued that Native Americans should voluntarily follow the lead of the white immigrant groups and blend quietly into the Euro-American culture.

How might assimilation theorists view the past and present adaptations of Native Americans? Applying an assimilation model to Native Americans, one might accent the extent to which traditional cultures have undergone Europeanization. Schools and missions in the nineteenth century brought changes in religion, language, and dress styles to many Native American groups. Other changes, such as in land-ownership orientations, have also been substantial. Assimilationists have argued that Native American cultural traditions are the major barriers to further acculturation. These analysts seize on the cultural adaptations that many Native Americans have already made and cite them as evidence of movement toward gradual inclusion in the Euro-American culture.[139]

Living patterns and the sense of Native American identity today vary widely. For example, the Sioux and Navaho have a strong group identity, whereas certain other groups have for the most part lost their old ways and identities. Some reservation groups, such as the western Pueblos, the Navaho, and the Sioux, confine their social contacts substantially to people of their group; others, such as a significant segment of the Blackfeet in Montana, have intermarried with whites and substantially acculturated to European American ways. Some of the small California tribes, such as the Nomlaki and the Yuki, have "forgotten ancient customs, abandoned the native language, and look upon themselves more as extended families than as members of any particular tribe."[140]

The persistence of Native American languages has been significant. Several dozen Native American languages are still spoken in the United States today. Intensive, often forced, acculturation has not necessarily resulted in the demise of Native American cultures. Many cultures have survived extremely unfavorable conditions.

Structural assimilation at other than low-paid job levels in the economy has come slowly for Native Americans. Not until the urban migration of the last few decades could many Native Americans be viewed as moving into the economic mainstream. Urban integration has often involved less well paid blue-collar positions and poor housing conditions. Some political integration has taken place in towns and cities.

Limited structural assimilation at the primary-group level has come slowly, although it is greater in urban areas than on the reservation. One study in Spokane, Washington, found little social integration of Native Americans into white voluntary associations in that area. Some shift can be seen in urban family patterns, which today often involve less emphasis on extended families than in the past. Increases in marriage with whites have occurred in some cities. One Los Angeles study found that one-third of the married Native American respondents had white spouses. Census data have shown a similar pattern among urban Native Americans nationwide, although the rural rate of intermarriage is about half that in urban areas. Intermarriages between members of different Native American groups have been common in cities.[141]

An assimilationist theorist might argue that some adaptation has occurred on other dimensions of assimilation suggested by Milton Gordon (attitude-receptional, behavior-receptional, and identificational assimilation). Some movement can be glimpsed in the area of white attitudes; the traditional stereotyping of Native Americans by whites appears to have declined somewhat. Blatant discrimination appears to have decreased in certain sectors of the society. Still, as we have seen in the sections on economy, education, and politics, many types of direct and indirect discrimination still restrict Native Americans today.

Attachment to ancestral identity seems particularly strong among most of those who have predominantly Native American ancestry. Some West Coast tribes have exemplified perhaps the weakest sense of identification. A study of the

Spokane tribe in the late 1960s found over half identifying themselves in interviews as definitely Native American, while one-third identified themselves as definitely more white. Today, many Native American groups persist as cultural islands. A number of organizations, including the National Congress of American Indians and the National Indian Education Association, have tried to build a "pan-Indian identity" and promote unity across many tribes. In the 1980s and 1990s, regular pan-Indian conferences and Pow Wows have been held in all regions of the United States. But this effort has been only partially successful. There have been conflicts within these organizations among members of various Native American groups—as well as in the BIA schools among students. Local group membership remains very important for many Native Americans, and most on reservation lands identify themselves in local terms, such as Navaho or Sioux, rather than as pan-Indian.[142]

The greatest pan-Indian identity has developed in urban areas, where intergroup contacts and intermarriage are common. In addition, one study found that Native Americans in Los Angeles have experienced a degree of spatial assimilation as evidenced by some residential dispersion within predominantly white neighborhoods; however, many urban Native Americans are scattered among low-income neighborhoods populated by poor whites and other people of color.[143]

Power–Conflict Perspectives

Because of the colonial history of Native Americans, some theorists have persuasively argued that power–conflict models have greater relevance to the Native American experience. Analysts such as Robert Blauner cite Native Americans as a clear case of an externally colonized minority.[144]

Power–conflict analysis accents the deception, genocide, and land theft involved in the subordination process. Much assimilation rhetoric—"civilizing the Indians"—was a cover for exploitation by land-hungry white settlers. There was great pressure, even force, involved in treaties and laws providing for individual Native Americans to become "citizens" only after meeting such criteria as accepting individual land allotments. Unlike assimilation analysts, power–conflict analysts look at the broad sweep of the acculturation process and see the *force* behind much of it. This theme is evident, for example, in the statement by the commissioner of Indian affairs in 1879:

> Indians are essentially conservative, and cling tenaciously to old customs and hate all changes: therefore the government should *force* them to scatter out on farms, break up their tribal organizations, dances, ceremonies, and tomfoolery; take from them their hundreds of useless ponies, which afford the means of indulging in their wandering, nomadic habits, and give them cattle in exchange, and compel them to labor or to *accept the alternative of starvation*.[145]

On the reservations, forced acculturation was often the rule in missions and boarding schools, where children were isolated from their families.

Since the 1970s, some Native American children have even been removed from their homes to white foster homes or institutions. White social workers have sometimes argued that the homes of poor Native Americans are not "fit" places for these children. Anthropologist Shirley Hill Witt has written of one Mormon child-placement program that aggressively sought the placement of Native American children. A former president of the Mormon church reportedly stated:

> When you go down on the reservations and see these hundreds of thousands of Indians living in the dirt and without culture or refinement of any kind, you can hardly believe it. Then you see these boys and girls [placed in Mormon homes] playing the flute, the piano. All these things bring about a normal culture.[146]

It is ironic that white culture should be held up as the "normal culture" against which poor Native Americans are judged, because the poverty in the lives of Native Americans is substantially the result of whites' destruction of Native American resources, theft of land, and discrimination. The Indian Child Welfare Act, passed in 1978, has gradually achieved a significant reduction in the number of Native American children removed from their parents and placed in non–Native American homes.

Power–conflict analysts accent the one-way character of assimilation pressures. A study of Native American college students at the University of Oklahoma found that success in college was linked with two different sets of factors. Those who had done well in high school and on college entrance tests tended to do well at the university. Significantly, those with a strong Native American identity were more likely than assimilated Native Americans to fail and drop out, regardless of their academic ability. One major problem is the white-oriented university context. The expected changes are unidirectional: The Native American student (like other students of color) is expected to conform to the Eurocentric college environment. White institutions do not change significantly to reflect the cultures and needs of Native American students.[147]

At all educational levels, Native American children face great acculturation pressures; many capitulate, sometimes adopting white stereotypes of themselves and often dressing and behaving in Anglo-preferred ways. This behavior damages the inner self and creates great stress for many. Caught between their native culture and Anglo pressures, some even commit suicide. An Oklahoma study found that suicide rates among young Native American males have been increasing; those with the highest rate were those who were the most assimilated to white culture. Historically, suicide has been rare among young Native Americans. In recent years, it has been at epidemic levels. One study reported that the suicide rate for Native American high-school students on reservations was four times that of their white counterparts; 17 percent of these teenagers had attempted suicide.[148]

A colonialism analyst would stress that many Native Americans remain isolated politically and geographically—on the reservations, in rural areas, or in segregated urban areas. They are often colonized on their own lands. Whites are often ignorant of Native American conditions. In Oklahoma there has been a prevalent white misconception that the reservation Cherokee tribe is dying out. Yet the group is one of the largest in the nation, clinging tenaciously to its language and values. Albert Wahrhaftig and Robert Thomas have suggested that this white "fiction serves to keep the Cherokees in place as a docile and exploitable minority population."[149] By denying the existence of viable and enduring Native American communities, whites can ignore their Native American neighbors and their persisting problems that are rooted in colonialism.

Perhaps the strongest argument for the relevance of a colonialism model can be found in the data we examined on Native American income, employment, housing, education, and political participation. Although there have been some important gains, Native Americans as a group remain on the lower rungs of the socioeconomic ladder. Poverty characterizes life for many in rural areas and cities. Since the 1970s, many reservations have had extremely high unemployment rates. On the Rosebud Sioux reservation in the early 1990s, 90 percent of adults were jobless. In urban areas, Native Americans have had to face to a disproportionate degree low-wage jobs, absentee landlords, and racial discrimination. Native Americans are relative latecomers to the cities, and many have found their "place" to be defined by whites as the secondary labor market and segregated urban neighborhoods. In the 1980s, President Ronald Reagan's supply-side economic policy brought significant cutbacks in social programs for Native Americans on the reservations. As a result, many Native American groups began gambling operations or negotiated with corporations to develop mineral resources for outside whites to utilize. The image of an *internal colony* remains appropriate for analyzing the situation of many Native Americans on reservations.

Many Native Americans are fighting back aggressively against the vestiges of colonialism, such as the racist symbols used by many sports teams and the dumping that constitutes environmental racism. A renaissance of Native American cultures can be seen in the many protest movements and Pow Wows in recent decades. Power–conflict analysts are the most likely to emphasize the importance of this struggle against white pressures and oppression. This resistance is rooted in the historical cultures of Native American tribes, the oppositional cultures that have placed great emphasis on harmony with the world and nature and on the foolishness of selfish individualism and materialism. The oppositional cultures of Native American groups provide a valuable source of the fundamentally humanitarian, earth-centered values that seem to be declining in the larger society.

SUMMARY

Native Americans today remain highly diverse. There are many different rural and urban groups, but most are still subordinated to whites who have greater economic, political, and bureaucratic (BIA) power. Native Americans are the descendants of the only groups that did *not* immigrate to North America in the last five hundred years. They were brought into the European American sphere over a long period, during which many Native Americans fought fierce battles with the invaders. Genocide, the destruction of all Native Americans, was often the goal of the white invaders. The many battles were followed by the present reservation era with its long line of white bureaucrats and officials seeking to dominate or exploit Native Americans. Even white social scientists have exploited Native Americans for research purposes, as is illustrated by the Native American quip: "What is a Navaho family?" Answer: "Three matrilineal generations and one white anthropologist living together in an extended family."

Often stereotyped by whites as culturally inferior, Native Americans have suffered and still face exploitation and discrimination in the economic, political, religious, and educational spheres. In the economic sphere, they have seen their lands taken, their young forced by job circumstances to relocate to often inhospitable cities, and their upward mobility limited by continuing racial discrimination. While recent decades have seen some economic gains, progress has been slow and has yet to be matched by substantial political progress, particularly off the reservations. The BIA, although it has become more progressive and now employs many more Native American officials than in earlier years, remains an outside governmental bureaucracy. Indeed, in the last decade the BIA has been the target of numerous attacks and congressional investigations for inefficiency and mismanagement, as well as periodic budget cuts.

For many decades, protest organizations, secular and religious, have underscored the strengths and the discontent of Native Americans. In recent years, Native American activists have emphasized the cultural uniqueness of the Native American respect for the greater human community and for all aspects of the natural environment. Groups have organized to regain fishing rights and lands that were stolen. Calls for maintaining cultural distinctiveness and recognizing the superiority of Native American oppositional cultures have been heard. Vigorously opposing celebrations of Columbus's "discovery of America," Native Americans accented the uniqueness and brutality of their continuing colonization. Native Americans have a unique position in regard to citizenship, since they existed in America prior to any European settlement or government. Indeed, some members of groups such as the Iroquois have argued that they are *not* citizens of the United States nor do they want to be. They predate the European invasions, so they are citizens of their own nations.

The desire for full recognition of their sovereignty is strong among numerous Native American nations. While the federal government has made some progress in recent years in returning land and control of various aspects of life to many Native American groups, most still have a colonial relationship to the federal government. This can be seen, for example, in the reservation-based colleges. Although these colleges do much to meet the needs of Native American students, Native Americans lack full control of them since their accreditation and a large part of their funding remain in the hands of federal agencies. Thus, in recent years many Native American nations have pressed for a government-to-government relationship that would replace the current internal-colonial relationship with the federal government of the United States.[150]

CHAPTER 8

African Americans

A few years ago one of the nation's most talented young journalists, Leanita McClain, committed suicide. Just thirty-two years old, she had won several major journalism awards and was the first African American to serve on the *Chicago Tribune's* editorial board. Why did such a talented black woman commit suicide? The answer is doubtless complex, but one factor looms large: the problem of coping with a culturally different, often racist and discriminatory white world. Reviewing McClain's life, one writer has analyzed the conformity to white ways that is faced by middle-class black employees in historically white workplaces: "Black women consciously choose their speech, their laughter, their walk, their mode of dress and car. They trim and straighten their hair. . . . They learn to wear a mask."[1] Black Americans in the corporate world not only face blatant discrimination but also suffer greatly from the pressures to adapt to the values and ways of that overwhelmingly white world.

Many African Americans have family trees in the United States extending back to the 1600s and 1700s, before the American Revolution. They are among the oldest settlers in North America, far older as a group than many prominent white immigrant groups. There is a tragic irony here. That a people who have been here almost as long as the first European settlers should still find themselves so discriminated against, so unwelcome in many traditionally white institutions and places, is a problematical dilemma not only for assimilation theory (see Chapter 2) but also for the future of this nation.

FORCED MIGRATION AND SLAVERY

White immigrants, for the most part, came to North America voluntarily. Most Africans had no choice; they came in chains. African Americans exemplify the slave-importation end of the migration continuum discussed in Chapter 2. Their destinations were determined by slave traders and buyers. The enslavement of

Africans was seen by many whites as a solution to their desire for cheap agricultural labor in the South and elsewhere in the Americas.

The European Trade in Human Beings

Dutch and French companies early dominated the forcible importation of Africans; England entered the trade in the 1600s. Fed by European desires for wealth, the African slave trade soon saw the institutionalization of trading alliances between certain African rulers, who wanted European goods, and white slavers, who wanted human beings to sell. Some African coastal rulers, motivated perhaps by greed or fear of European firepower, succumbed to the slave-trade pressure and established themselves as go-betweens serving European slave traders.[2]

Once captured, those enslaved were often chained in corrals called barracoons, where they were branded and held for transportation. The voyage was a living hell. Enslaved Africans were chained together in close quarters, with little room for movement. The horror was summed up by a young African:

> I was soon put down under the decks, and there I received such a salutation in my nostrils as I had never experienced in my life: so that with the loathsomeness of the stench, and crying together, I became so sick and low that I was not able to eat, nor had I the least desire to taste any thing. . . . On my refusing to eat, one of them held me fast by the hands, and laid me across, I think the windlass, and tied my feet, while the other flogged me severely. . . . One day, when we had a smooth sea and moderate wind, two of my wearied countrymen who were chained together (I was near them at the time), preferring death to such a life of misery, somehow made through the nettings and jumped into the sea.[3]

Suicides were common among the kidnapped Africans, and uprisings brought death to Africans and sailors alike. The widely believed white myth that Africans passively endured their fate is contradicted by the 155 recorded shipboard uprisings by Africans between 1699 and 1845; many other violent attacks on the white slavers went unrecorded.[4]

In 1619, twenty Africans were brought to Jamestown by a Dutch ship, and by the mid-1600s the slave status of Africans had been fully institutionalized in colonial laws. From the mid-1600s to the 1860s virtually all African immigrants were imported for involuntary servitude. Estimates of the number of Africans brought alive into the Western Hemisphere are in the range of 10 to 15 million. Most were brought to the West Indies and South America, only 5 percent to North America. Before 1790, an estimated 275,000 Africans were brought into the colonies; between 1790 and the end of the legal slave trade in 1808, another 70,000 were imported. The total for the entire slavery period was approximately one-half million.[5] In addition to those arriving alive, millions more died in the process of enslavement and transportation.

A number of prominent European Americans in the early period of this nation were slaveholders, including George Washington, James Madison, and

Thomas Jefferson. In an early draft of the Declaration of Independence, the young Jefferson went so far as to attack slavery, but was careful to blame it on England's King George. As a result of southern slave owners' opposition, Jefferson's anti-slavery language was not included in the final version of that founding document. One of the greatest democratic manifestos in world history was severely compromised by the unwillingness of white Americans to include African Americans within its framework.[6]

Slaveholding interests forced the recognition of slavery in three major sections of the U.S. Constitution: a provision that each slave be counted as three-fifths of a person for the calculation of congressional representation (of whites); a fugitive-slave provision; and the postponement of prohibition of slave importation to 1808. Although the slave trade was officially abolished as of 1808, the ban was not enforced. Thousands of Africans were still forcibly and illegally imported.[7]

In 1860, only one-fourth of the 1.6 million white families in the South owned 3.8 million African Americans. A majority of the enslaved African Americans were chained to the larger farms or plantations, where they performed most of the labor and produced agricultural products to be marketed for the profit of slaveholders and their many descendants (the latter still benefiting today). Most plantation owners were agrarian capitalists attuned to trade for a money profit. The wealth and power of the slaveholding gentry rose dramatically as a result of slave-based agriculture. This white plantation gentry dominated the U.S. economy and the federal government from 1800 to the Civil War.[8] We noted in Chapter 2 the emphasis that some power–conflict theorists put on government's role in creating racial arrangements. For centuries the U.S. and southern state governments passed laws benefiting the powerful slaveholding gentry and reinforcing the racial definition and oppression of African Americans.

The Lives of Africans under Slavery

There has long been a magnolias-and-mint-julep mystique about the slave system, which lingers on, particularly in the South and in Hollywood movies such as *Gone with the Wind*. According to this white imagery, residing in a big, white plantation house with multiple columns surrounded by magnolia trees, a paternalistic white master "cared kindly" for "contented, happy slaves."

Slave autobiographies describe the true oppressiveness of the living conditions. Most rose before dawn, then worked in the house or the fields until dark. Food, clothing, and housing were crude and often inadequate. The whip and chains were mechanisms of control. Some masters were extremely cruel, such as the owner of one African American, who told about moving from Georgia to Texas: "Then he chains all the slaves round the necks and fastens the chains to the hosses and makes them walk all the way to Texas. My mother and my sister had to walk. Emma was my sister. Somewhere on the road it went to snowing, and Massa wouldn't let us wrap anything round our feet. We had to sleep on the ground, too, in all that snow."[9] African Americans could not legally protest such brutality, for slaveholders controlled the state militias and the courts.[10]

Many accounts of slavery do not specifically discuss the special plight of African American women. Yet they were at the center of the U.S. slave system. Most black women, as one put it, "worked in the fields every day from 'fore daylight to almost plumb dark."[11] The brutality of the slaveholders was not tempered when it came to the women: "Beat women! Why sure he [master] beat women. Beat women just like men. Beat women naked and wash them down in brine."[12]

Eugene Genovese has argued that slavery was in part a "paternalistic" system. For the white masters, paternalism rationalized the subordination of other human beings considered to be in need of the care of whites. For those enslaved, paternalism meant some recognition of material needs. Yet a paternalistic system is dangerous for the oppressed, for it tends to foster divisions in terms of master-granted privilege (for example, "house slaves" versus "field slaves") and thus can make organization for resistance difficult. Genovese has been criticized for exaggerating the paternalistic aspects of slavery, but many researchers consider his view important. Both accommodation and violent resistance were among the reactions to an alternately brutal and paternalistic system.[13]

African American families have long been a preoccupation of whites, including white social scientists; even the contemporary problems of poverty and "broken" families have been traced back to the assumed constant breakup of black families in slave days. Until recently, supportive family life was viewed as nonexistent for the majority of enslaved African Americans. Yet there is now considerable evidence of paternalistic slave owners fostering families and, most significantly, of enslaved African Americans working hard to preserve and protect their families to the extent possible under extreme conditions. Research has shown that typical slave families were protective, supportive environments that helped African Americans to survive. Those enslaved frequently deserted brutal masters in family units, and a common cause of desertion was the desire to find lost loved ones. In an extensive analysis of families on large plantations, Herbert Gutman found that enslaved African American women were expected to have their children by one man; that the names of fathers were given to sons; that adoption was used to ease the disruption caused by death within and breakup of families; and that many African American families persisted over several generations. The threat to the family was great. Marriages were likely to be broken up at some point, most often by death but frequently by the white slaveholders. An accurate picture of the slave family must include both aspects: the strong African American attempts at family stability and the frequent disruption of families by brutal slaveholders.[14]

In the face of physical torture and white attempts to eradicate their cultures, the many peoples of Africa among those enslaved—the Yorubas, Akans, Ibos, Angolans, and dozens of other groups—became a single African American people and forged their own oppositional culture, an African American culture.[15] Drawing on deep African spiritual roots, these new Americans shaped their own religion, their own art and music, their distinctive versions of Afro-English, and their own philosophical and political thinking about racial oppression, liberation, and social justice. In the colonies and later in the United States, the pressures on

African Americans to conform to the dominant Eurocentric culture forced them to become *bicultural,* to know both the dominant culture and their own culture as well. Since the days of slavery African Americans have struggled to maintain this oppositional culture, a culture part African and part an African American adaptation to the concrete history of white oppression. This culture has provided the foundation for active black resistance to white oppression since the seventeenth century.

Active Slave Resistance

Enslaved African Americans had many reactions to their oppression. They often had to be submissive, but this was only one response to white domination and brutality. An assertive reaction grounded in African and African American culture was common. Both types of response were important components of many a slave's repertoire for coping with the savagery of slavery. Depending on circumstances, one or the other might come to the forefront. Many African Americans used their wits to escape as much forced work and punishment as possible; they observed the servile etiquette when necessary, but many also rebelled in dozens of small and large ways, even attacking whites violently when possible.[16]

Antislavery action took several forms, including violent resistance, flight to the North, suicide, and psychological withdrawal. Those fleeing slavery became a serious problem for white slave owners, serious enough to prompt inclusion of a fugitive-slave provision in the U.S. Constitution. The most famous route was the Underground Railroad, the network of former slaves and other antislavery citizens, black and white, who secreted and passed along tens of thousands of those fleeing to the North between the 1830s and the Civil War. One of the famous "conductors" on this railroad was an African American woman and former slave, Harriet Tubman, one of the greatest of U.S. heroes. She reportedly went back south nineteen times, risking her life to deliver more than three hundred African Americans to freedom. Southerners committed to the "happy Sambo" view of their black workers sometimes went to absurd lengths to explain the fugitive-slave problem. The white physician Samuel Cartwright, incredibly, attributed the problem to a strange disease, "drapetomania," by which he meant the unhealthy tendency to flee one's owner![17]

Nonviolent slave resistance took the form of a slow working pace, feigned illness, and strikes. Violent resistance was directed at the property and persons of slave owners or overseers. Tools, livestock, fields, and farmhouses were destroyed; white masters and overseers were killed. Collective resistance included revolts and conspiracies to revolt. There is evidence of 250 slave revolts or conspiracies to revolt, a count that does not include numerous mutinies aboard slave ships. Newspapers of the day provide considerable evidence of an extensive white fear of such uprisings.[18]

In 1800, a group of enslaved African Americans led by Gabriel Prosser in Henrico County, Virginia, gathered weapons and planned to march on Richmond.

The Virginia governor took immediate action to protect the state capital from the rebels. A thousand armed men rendezvoused, but a heavy rain cut them off from the city, and they disbanded. Betrayed, the leaders were quickly arrested; at least thirty-five, including Prosser, were put to death. In 1811, several hundred armed slaves attacked whites on plantations near New Orleans. White troops violently suppressed the rebellion, killing several dozen African Americans. Others were executed by a firing squad, and their heads were publicly displayed.[19]

Nat Turner, a self-taught man with religious leanings, led a famous rebellion that took place in Southampton County, Virginia, in 1831. Turner recruited seventy slaves in a single day. His revolutionaries attacked, and dozens of whites were killed. The black revolutionaries were eventually defeated by hundreds of white soldiers. Turner escaped but was later captured and executed.[20] These leaders of slave revolts could be included among the great revolutionary heroes, for they took seriously the principle of "liberty and justice for all." In his analysis of slave revolts, Sterling Stuckey has shown that African culture and religion were a major source of the black revolutionaries' philosophy and inclination to rebellion.[21]

Slave revolts intensified the fears of whites, many of whom were near panic following a revolt. Revolts contradicted the apologists' notion of "happy slaves"; given the opportunity, those enslaved sometimes did resist violently. Slavery wasted the lives, talents, and energies of millions of African Americans and stole the possibility of creating wealth for their descendants. But the enslavement of African Americans also brought major costs for whites and their descendants. Southern whites lost much of their own humanity and morality, as well as much of their own freedom of speech and press, because of the legal controls and requirements of the totalitarian slave system.

Many African Americans played an important role in liberating their brothers and sisters from oppression by creating or joining organizations to abolish slavery. Frederick Douglass, a former slave, was one of the most important leaders among the abolitionists. In a July 4, 1852, speech in Rochester, New York, Douglass spoke eloquently: "What, to the American slave, is your Fourth of July? I answer: A day that reveals to him, more than all other days of the year, the gross injustices and cruelty to which he is the constant victim. To him your celebration is a sham."[22] Another influential African American abolitionist was the former slave Isabella Van Wagener, better known as Sojourner Truth, who was born a slave in New York in the 1790s; in the mid-1800s she became an influential lecturer against slavery and also an early advocate of women's rights across the United States.

Outside the Rural South

Between the 1600s and the early 1800s, many northern whites either owned African Americans or considered the U.S. slave system legitimate. Significant numbers of enslaved African Americans could be found in northern states. The North was built in part on forced black labor and in part on the labor of European immigrants. As Benjamin Ringer puts it, "despite the early emancipation of slaves in the North, [racialized colonialism] remained there, not merely as fossilized remains but as a deeply ingrained coding for the future."[23] Consider Massachusetts, where slavery was legalized in 1641, three years after Africans were brought in. Massachusetts merchants played a central role in the North American slave trade. Not until the 1780s did public opinion and some court cases come together to abolish slavery in New England. Even then, it was not a recognition of the rights of African Americans that ended slavery, but rather pressure from the growing number of white working people who objected to having to compete with slave labor. In New York, slaves made up 7 percent of the population by 1786. Not until 1799 was a statute of emancipation passed there—and one providing for only partial emancipation at that. Understanding that slavery was long entrenched in the North's economic and legal system is important for understanding the type of internal colonialism (see Chapter 2) that African Americans still face today in the urban North.[24]

Even before the Civil War, "Jim Crow" laws in the North enforced the segregation of free African Americans in public transportation, hospitals, jails, schools, churches, and cemeteries. Racially segregated railroad cars were established early in Massachusetts. In all northern cities, many whites enforced severe antiblack housing discrimination and segregated housing areas at a time when most southern cities had no comparable segregation because southern slaves often lived in or near the residential areas of the slavemasters.

RACIST IDEOLOGIES AND STEREOTYPES

Dominant racial groups, such as white Americans, develop beliefs to rationalize their economic, social, and political domination. In pamphlets, books, and articles, many white theologians, intellectuals, and political leaders devised racist theories of the biological, mental, and moral inferiority of African Americans to rationalize their exploitation as slaves. Negative views of African peoples existed in Europe before the founding of North American colonies, but these did not develop into a systematic ideological racism until the 1700s. We have previously described the eighteenth-century notions of racial hierarchy put forward by European scholars like Johann Blumenbach, which included a social construction of an "African race" viewed by Europeans as biologically and intellectually inferior to "Caucasians." On this side of the Atlantic, Thomas Jefferson took up these European notions and developed his own ideological racism that personified the moral dilemmas of whites in the eighteenth century: He wrote an indictment of slavery in the original draft of the Declaration of Independence, yet he was the owner of two hundred African Americans. He wrote vigorously of his opposition to interracial sex and miscegenation, yet he is reported to have had a black mistress who bore him children. He periodically wrote of the racial inferiority of African Americans, but he also argued that they should be free.[25]

Seeing African Americans As Inferior: White Stereotypes

At an early date, the dark color of enslaved Africans and African Americans was singled out by many white Americans as unusual and ugly. By the mid-1800s, racist defenders of slavery were portraying African Americans as an inferior human group and as "apelike," a stereotyped image applied earlier by Anglo-Protestants to Irish Americans.[26] Since the days of slavery, whites have often depicted black Americans in negative terms. Black men and women have been alleged to have an offensive odor. Black women have been stereotyped as immoral; black men, as oversexed and potential rapists. Extreme white images of black sexuality probably reflect deep white psychological problems with the idea and reality of racial mixing. White guilt and anger may ultimately be linked to the historical fact that much interracial intercourse before 1865 involved the forcible rape of black women by white men, particularly by overseers and slave owners. Patricia Williams, a law professor, has illustrated this point by relating the story of Austin Miller, her great-great-grandfather, who as a thirty-five-year-old white lawyer, bought Williams's eleven-year-old black great-great-grandmother Sophie and her parents. Miller soon forced the child Sophie to become the mother of Williams's great-grandmother Mary. Like many African Americans, Williams must deal with the reality that her white ancestor was not only a prominent lawyer but also a *rapist* and *child molester.*[27]

A burst of renewed interest in "scientific racism" occurred in the decades right before and after 1900, when a number of U.S. scientists agressively argued for the inferiority of certain racial groups, including Americans of southern European as well as African descent. As we noted in Chapter 5, many observers, relying heavily on the so-called "intelligence tests," attempted to prove that southern and eastern Europeans were mentally and racially inferior; other prominent scholars used the tests to make the same arguments in regard to African Americans. Since the last decades of the nineteenth century, both intellectuals and white political leaders, including U.S. presidents, have sometimes adopted crude racial theories to explain the poverty-stricken conditions of white immigrants and of African Americans.[28]

The Pseudoscience of "Intelligence" Testing

The theme of intellectual inferiority along racial lines has received much public attention since World War II.[29] Earlier in the twentieth century this perspective was applied to white immigrant groups considered inferior to Anglo-Protestants; in the last few decades the focus has been on Americans of color. For example, a few white social scientists, such as Arthur Jensen and Richard Herrnstein, have alleged that differences in "intelligence test" (IQ) scores are not determined just by environmental factors such as learning, socialization, and socioeconomic circumstances, but reflect real genetic differences between black and white groups. A key argument here is that differences in intelligence can be reliably measured by the relatively brief paper-and-pencil and object (or symbol) manipulation tests called

"IQ tests." In their view, groups with low social status or income are, on the average, intellectually and genetically inferior to those groups with greater status and income levels because the former average lower scores on these so-called IQ tests. These writers sometimes argue that poor and rich Americans, or black and white Americans, have different types of intelligence, perhaps requiring different educational techniques. They also express concern about high black birthrates, which they believe will result in a lowering of the national IQ. Jensen's research on intelligence focused on the speed of the brain's nerve signals and on myopia as measures of intelligence allegedly favoring groups such as Jewish and Asian Americans over African Americans.[30] Most recently, in a best-selling book *The Bell Curve*, Richard Herrnstein and Charles Murray have argued yet again for the discredited theory that there are significant genetically determined differences in IQ between black Americans and white Americans. Significantly, in this recent work Herrnstein and Murray make a special point of admitting that environment has "something to do with racial differences."[31]

Although the reactionary views of Jensen, Herrnstein, and Murray have been successfully critiqued by many social scientists, especially for playing down the environmental effects and pervasive cultural impact on test results, their notions about black intelligence have spread to some U.S. academics and journalists and to politicians around the globe. For example, Michael Levin, a philosophy professor at a New York college, has cited Jensen's research on white and black IQs to support his own arguments against affirmative action programs, arguing that "on average, black Americans are significantly less intelligent than whites."[32]

The Jensen and Herrnstein arguments have occasionally been reiterated by influential politicians in the United States and elsewhere. In 1971, Patrick Buchanan, then an adviser to President Richard Nixon who was himself to become a Republican presidential candidate in 1992 and 1996, picked up on Herrnstein's arguments. In a memo to Nixon, Buchanan alleged that "every study" showed black groups had lower IQs than white groups and that Herrnstein's views about race and IQ provided "an intellectual basis" for perhaps cutting back certain government social programs. This "scientific" racism has spread to other countries. In Japan, former prime minister Yasuhiro Nakasone commented that "the United States is lower [in intelligence scores] because of a considerable number of blacks, Puerto Ricans, and Mexicans."[33]

In the 1930s, a number of social psychologists began questioning whether IQ test results could be used as evidence of genetically determined racial differentials. Citing data on the extremely oppressive conditions suffered by black people, they argued that black–white differences in IQ test scores reflected differences in education, income, and other living conditions. A number of studies showed that IQ test scores of black children improved with better economic and learning environments, as when black children from segregated southern schools attended integrated northern schools. Most strikingly, results from large-scale IQ testing in earlier decades showed black children and adults in some northern states scoring *higher* than whites in some southern states.[34] Using the logic of analysts such as Jensen, one would be forced to conclude that white southerners were mentally and "racial-

ly" inferior to black northerners. White analysts would doubtless avoid this interpretation; obviously they, as defenders of a theory of black inferiority, do not wish
to argue that data on IQ might actually show black intellectual superiority. Rather,
they would accept an environmental explanation for uncomplimentary regional
IQ-score differentials for whites. Differentials favoring whites are also most reasonably interpreted as reflecting environmental conditions, not genetic factors.

Some analysts have focused on the cultural bias—specifically, the white
middle-class bias—inherent in traditional U.S. achievement and other psychome-
tric tests (including IQ, SAT, and GRE tests), which measure only certain types of
learned skills and certain acquired knowledge, skills and knowledge not equally
available to all racial and ethnic groups because of discrimination and inadequate
educational facilities. Researchers have found that achievement-test taking itself is
a skill white middle-class children are more likely to possess, because they and
their parents are most familiar with such testing. White middle-class children take
many such tests, and in doing so they enjoy a built-in advantage over most other
children.[35]

The most fundamental problem for those who insist on racial differences is
the equation of "intelligence" test results with general intelligence. From the
beginning, the so-called intelligence (IQ) tests have been intentionally misnamed.
These tests are at best measures of selected verbal, mathematical, or manipulative
skills. They do not measure many aspects of human abilities, such as creativity and
imagination. They do not measure farming, fishing, musical, artistic, and many
other skills that reflect human intelligence. Intelligence is something much broader than what a few short paper-and-pencil or symbol-manipulation tests can measure. More broadly, intelligence can be viewed as a complex ability to deal cre-
atively with one's environment, whatever that environment may be. Only a small
portion of human intellectual ability can be revealed, at best, on any short test.
Given this problem of what social scientists call the "validity" of a measure, the
modest and brief IQ tests clearly do not reveal what the defenders of racial
inequality claim they do.[36]

Contemporary Antiblack Prejudices and Stereotypes

To what extent does the white public still accept negative stereotypes of African
Americans? In one 1990s nationwide opinion survey 38 percent of the white
respondents felt blacks were "more prone to violence than people of other races,"
and 35 percent felt that blacks preferred welfare over work. Thirteen percent felt
that blacks were less intelligent "than people of other races." Three-fourths of the
sample accepted at least one of eight stereotyped images of African Americans.
The survey also found that the most prejudiced whites (those who accepted four
or more antiblack stereotypes) tended to be older and less well educated than the
population as a whole. However, two-thirds of white college graduates did in fact
express some antiblack prejudice.[37]

These negative, often hostile stereotypes can be harmful for African Americans
across a spectrum of life experiences. For example, in a survey of practicing psychi-

atrists, Doris Wilkinson found that "cultural conditioning to racial beliefs and attitudes . . . pervades therapeutic contexts in which minority women are clients."[38]

Most white Americans admit to pollsters that they hold some antiblack attitudes. For example, in a mid-1990s National Opinion Research Center survey, 59 percent of white respondents took an antiblack position on at least one of the following items: (1) Do you think there should be laws against marriages between blacks and whites?; (2) White people have a right to keep blacks out of their neighborhoods if they want to, and blacks should respect that right; (3) Blacks shouldn't push themselves where they are not wanted; (4) A law says that a homeowner can decide for himself whom to sell his house to, even if he prefers not to sell to blacks; (5) Do you think blacks get more attention from government than they deserve?[39] Education has some effect on antiblack attitudes, but not as much as one might expect. While three-fourths of those whites with less than a high-school education took an antiblack position on one or more of the statements, about 58 percent of high-school and junior-college graduates, and 50 percent of college graduates, showed a similar pattern of antiblack responses. Only the group of whites with some graduate education had a majority rejecting the antiblack position on all of these items.

Examining white views on social change, John McConahay has described what he calls "modern racism": the white view that black Americans have illegitimately challenged cherished white values and are making illegitimate demands for changes in racial relations. This white hostility is reflected in negative views of certain black actions and achievements. McConahay and his associates have argued that the most extreme antiblack stereotypes and white opposition to all desegregation have to some extent been replaced by new prejudices and stereotypes.[40]

Many whites today publicly state their support for equality of opportunity, unlike the racists of the 1950s who espoused segregation. Most whites believe that serious racism is no longer widespread and that African Americans today have fully equal opportunities. In one 1994 NORC survey, only one-third of whites agreed that "blacks have worse jobs, income, and housing than white people . . . mainly due to discrimination." Sixty percent disagreed with this statement. A recent survey for the National Conference of Christians and Jews found that a large majority of whites felt that blacks have an equal opportunity for a quality education and equal opportunities for skilled jobs. A majority also felt blacks have an equal chance to get decent housing.[41] Clearly, black and white Americans differ dramatically in how they see the continuing reality of discrimination in the United States. In a 1996 survey in central Pennsylvania researchers found that "Eight of 10 blacks said they felt the differences in jobs, housing and income were primarily due to discrimination. Most white people, on the other hand, said they thought the differences were due to a lack of will power or motivation."[42] Three-fourths of the black respondents thought the justice system was racially biased, compared with only one-fourth of the whites. Indeed, the majority of whites thought that discrimination against whites was now a serious problem.

A majority of whites also feel that black Americans are too demanding, paranoid, and pushy. A recent *Times-Mirror* national survey found that 51 percent of whites agreed that equal rights have been pushed too far in the United States, a proportion up from 42 percent in 1992.[43] In national surveys a majority of white

Americans indicate vigorous opposition to government programs that would aggressively attack racial discrimination in employment, housing, or other areas of society. Desegregation defined as a few black employees at work, a few black students in the schoolroom, or a few black families in a large residential community is acceptable to a majority of whites. But more substantial desegregation and thoroughgoing integration brought about by vigorous government action are not acceptable.[44]

Survey data show that between 1973 and 1994 the proportion of whites who supported a law that prohibited racial discrimination by a homeowner increased from 34 percent to 59 percent. In a 1994 national survey a majority supported this open-housing law, but fully 35 percent of whites nationwide, and half of whites in some parts of the South, did *not,* preferring instead a law that would give a white homeowner the right to refuse to sell to a black person.[45] It is clear from these recent survey data that some whites still favor segregation. The ideal of equality and fair play remains, at best, an abstraction when it comes to the racial attitudes of many white Americans.

Negative portraits of African Americans in the mass media remain a serious problem. One analysis of the racial groups represented by characters in television programs found that the percentage of black characters increased from .05 percent in the late 1950s to 17 percent during the 1992–1993 season. However, black television figures continue to be disproportionately represented as criminals: During the season analyzed, half the black characters in reality-based shows, such as COPS and AMERICA'S MOST WANTED, committed crimes, compared with only 10 percent of the white characters.[46] In addition, the majority of television programs featuring black Americans are situation comedies, often with stereotypical black characters, that fail to present a well-rounded portrait of African Americans.

Do racial prejudices and stereotypes generate or support racial discrimination? One recent review of twenty-three research studies found a significant but moderate relationship between negative racial attitudes and discriminatory actions in the expected direction. Whites who express prejudice are more likely to discriminate than those who do not. These researchers also note that experimental studies show that white respondents "systematically alter their expressed racial attitudes and behaviors to appear in a more socially desirable-unprejudiced and egalitarian-light." For example, experimental research (generally using less obtrusive measures) suggests that the increase in positive white racial attitudes during the 1960s–1970s represented a conforming to a more liberal climate rather than a basic change in racial attitudes.[47]

INTERRACIAL CONFLICT

Antiblack Violence

Behind the U.S. slave system's veneer of civility were the bloody instruments of social control—the whip and the guns. Free blacks also suffered at the hands of whites. Before the Civil War, white-dominated race riots directed at free blacks occurred a dozen times in northern cities. The most serious race riot in U.S. history in terms of casualties was the 1863 antidraft riot in New York City, during the Civil War. The rioters were mostly working-class whites, including many Irish Americans, who were angry at being drafted to fight a war to which they were not committed.

The end of the Civil War brought an increased threat of violence, including lynching, against the former slaves. *Lynching* is one of the most brutal forms of collective violence that human beings engage in. It is a group killing carried out by vigilantes seeking revenge for an actual or imagined crime by the victim. Before the Civil War, most lynchings in the United States were carried out by white mobs against whites. After the Civil War, lynching became a means of keeping African Americans subordinated, or "in their place," as white southerners often said. Recorded lynchings show the following racial pattern:[48]

	White Victims	Black Victims
1882–1891	751	732
1892–1901	381	1,124
1902–1911	76	707
1912–1921	53	533
1922–1931	23	201
1932–1941	10	95
1942–1951	2	25
1952–1956	0	3

There have been occasional lynchings since the 1950s, including the hanging of a black man by Klan members in 1981 in Mobile, Alabama. At least half of all lynchings went unrecorded. The actual number has been estimated to be at least 6,000. In many periods there was an "inclination to abandon such relatively mild and decent ways of dispatching the [lynch] mob's victim as hanging and shooting in favor of burning, often roasting over slow fires, after preliminary mutilations and tortures . . . a disposition to revel in the infliction of the most devilish and prolonged agonies."[49]

Lynchings were a show of force by whites fearful of black assertiveness. Brutal lynchings, whites expected, would make black residents afraid to challenge segregation and repressive laws. White lynchers were seldom punished for their crimes, and many lynchings took place with the acquiescence of police officials. The decrease since World War II is somewhat misleading, since by then public lynchings had largely been replaced by "legal" and secret lynchings. Legal lynchings include numerous killings of innocent blacks by white police officers. Secret attacks by whites also resulted in hundreds of deaths of black citizens and some white civil rights workers in the South between the 1940s and the 1960s.[50]

Black southerners moved to northern cities to escape oppressive conditions, but in the North they met more violence. Clashes with whites became frequent as black workers and their families moved into northern cities. In a white riot in 1900 in New York City, for instance, a substantially Irish American police force encouraged working-class whites to attack black men, women, and children wherever they could be found. One of the most serious white-dominated race riots occurred in 1917 in East St. Louis. White workers, who saw black workers as a job threat, attacked a black community. Thirty-nine black residents and nine of the white attackers were killed. This riot was followed in 1919 by a string of white riots from Chicago to Charleston.[51]

Opposition to black workers searching for better jobs has long been a cause of white violence. Black workers often become scapegoats whenever a serious economic downturn threatens white livelihoods. African Americans, as well as Asian, Latino, and Jewish Americans, have regularly been singled out as targets of anger, even though they have little or nothing to do with the troubles facing whites. Many white workers have little understanding of how a capitalistic system works. Many do not recognize, for example, that their job cutbacks and job displacement are often the result of white employers and investors seeking better profits in low-wage areas outside the United States.

White supremacy groups have long been in the forefront of those blaming black, Latino, and Jewish Americans for problems rooted elsewhere. The Ku Klux Klan, the leading white supremacy group for most of the twentieth century, gained strength in the 1920s and again in the 1970s and 1980s.

Other racist groups, such as the White Aryan Resistance (WAR), have emerged in recent decades. One recent count found more than 300 Klan, neo-Nazi, skinhead, and other white supremacist hate groups involving an estimated 25,000 white Americans active in the mid-1990s. In addition to the activists, another 200,000 whites are thought to be passive supporters, including those who buy white supremacist publications.[52] White supremacy groups have been involved in numerous attacks on and murders of blacks and other minorities, although until 1987 no supremacist group had been found guilty of such violence. In that year a court awarded $7 million to the family of Michael Donald, the 1981 victim of a Klan lynching.[53] In 1993, an appeals court upheld a $12.5 million judgment against WAR for its role in laying the foundation for a skinhead gang murder of a black man.[54]

Newspaper reports have documented the existence of paramilitary training camps where supremacists are reportedly preparing for a "race war." In just one year in the mid-1990s, thirty-five white supremacists in thirteen states were arrested on explosives and weapons charges after law enforcement agencies discovered six weapons arsenals, thirteen explosives stockpiles, and a variety of bombing plots.[55]

In recent years, there have been numerous hate-motivated murders and hate-inspired assaults, including many against African Americans. The Southern Poverty Law Center's Klanwatch, which conducts a comprehensive hate crime survey, estimates that fewer than half of all hate crimes are reported to police and that many hate crimes that are reported are not classified as such.[56] In one Iowa incident, a black doctor was awakened in the night when a firebomb was thrown through his bedroom window. He later found the word "nigger" scraped on his car door. In a mid-1990s Texas incident, the home of a black family was pelted with eggs and their car was set ablaze in the street outside their home.[57] In recent years many have called for increased penalties for those carrying out hate crimes.[58]

Black Protest against Oppression

As with other groups we have examined, it is important to distinguish violence used to oppress black Americans from violence used by black victims to *resist* oppression. Since the 1930s, black urbanites have, on occasion, violently rebelled against oppressive conditions. Historically, white violence to enforce discrimination and oppression has preceded black violence against white oppression.

A few riots involving pitched battles between black residents and white police officers, often sparked by a police incident, occurred in the 1930s and 1940s, particularly in New York City. Underlying causes of these riots involved antiblack discrimination by whites. Job discrimination and restrictions on political participation have periodically prompted black Americans to lash out in violent riots. In the 1960s and 1970s, dozens of U.S. cities experienced black uprisings against local symbols of white oppression: especially white police officers, businesses, and landlords. Large-scale black rebellions occurred in Los Angeles in 1965, in Detroit and Newark in 1967, and in Washington, DC, in 1968. An angry generation of African Americans showed their willingness to engage in violent protest against racism and economic problems, and the impact was felt across the nation.[59]

Rebellions against oppressive conditions have continued in the 1980s and 1990s. In the spring of 1980, black anger over local economic and political conditions exploded in a major riot in Miami. Black residents lashed out at white and Cuban American police officers and the larger white society, burning and looting stores. The three days of rioting cost sixteen lives, caused 400 injuries, and resulted in $100 million in property damage. A poll after the riot asked a nationwide sample of African Americans if they thought the rioting was justified. Twenty-seven percent said "yes" and another 25 percent were unsure.[60] Black anger at the reality and effects of racism broke out in other cities as well in the early 1980s, from Chattanooga, Tennessee, to Washington, DC.

Three more uprisings occurred in Miami between 1982 and 1991, all triggered by incidents involving white or Latino police officers shooting to death an African American or being acquitted for such a killing. In Los Angeles in the spring of 1992 the acquittal of police officers videotaped in the process of beating an unarmed black man triggered the most costly uprising so far in the twentieth century. During days of rioting in South Central Los Angeles, more than 10,000 blacks and Latinos (actually, more Latinos than blacks) were arrested, and more than 50 people were killed. Property damage exceeded $1 billion. At one point 20,000 police officers and soldiers patrolled the area.[61] Rioting also broke out in other cities. As in the 1960s riots, the underlying conditions fuelling the uprising included racial discrimination, poverty, unemployment, and poor housing.

The role of white officials and police officers in generating or accelerating rioting, while overlooked by most white Americans, has been very significant; police malpractice, especially the commonplace brutality directed against black men and women, has often precipitated or accelerated rioting.

Police malpractice and brutality targeting people of color remain major problems in cities across the United States. In a search of articles appearing in major newspapers between January 1990 and May 1992, one researcher found reports of 130 incidents of serious police brutality against citizens. White police officers were involved in more than nine in every ten of these cases; black or Latino citizens were the victims in almost all (97 percent) of the police incidents. Significantly, an officer was punished in *only 13 percent* of the incidents, and the usual punishment was slight.[62]

Occasionally, hidden police violence becomes public. In 1991 a white photographer in Los Angeles captured on videotape the beating of Rodney King by white police officers, while more than a dozen other officers watched. Initially, the white Los Angeles police chief did not condemn the officers, saying only that the beating was an "aberration." In a recent nationwide poll, three-fourths of black respondents said that the police in most cities treat black citizens less fairly than white citizens of the same income and educational level; two-thirds felt that blacks were treated less fairly than whites by judges and the courts.[63]

THE ECONOMY

An optimistic assimilation theory can include the idea of gradual secondary-structural assimilation in the U.S. economy, one aspect of which is the mobility over several generations of most in a particular racial or ethnic group into higher levels of employment (see Chapter 2). Whether this assimilationist interpretation can be applied to the long history of African Americans is questioned by power–conflict theorists. One test of such optimistic theories is the extent of African American economic progress since slavery.

Over the course of nearly 400 years of U.S. history African Americans have been critical to the building of this society's wealth and prosperity. From the 1600s to the late 1990s they have provided much hard labor for economic development. Their labor was stolen as they toiled in fields and houses or in the craft shops of the cities, building up the great wealth of the white slaveholding class. Put into southern and northern banks, that slave-generated wealth was reinvested or loaned out, and thereby helped to fuel the nation's industrial and commercial development, both in the South and in the North.

In the decades just before the Civil War, free black Americans in the northern states found themselves competing with white immigrants, such as the Irish, for jobs. Sometimes they were displaced from unskilled and skilled jobs by these new white immigrants. As we noted in Chapter 4, the job opportunities of these white groups were often determined by their racial or ethnic heritages or by social networks rather than by experience or qualifications. In addition, in their attempt to move up the economic ladder, Irish and other European Americans increasingly came to see themselves as privileged and superior "white Americans."[64]

In the South the economic separation of blacks from whites that was established during slavery "generated vastly disparate rankings in the class system. Thus, it was inevitable that the descendants of slaves would inherit this structural pattern."[65] Discriminatory employment patterns continued after the Civil War when newly freed African Americans began to compete directly with whites in the South. Black workers were usually segregated in unskilled "Negro jobs" and blocked on racist grounds from taking skilled employment in the newly expanding industrial sectors in the South.

With no major land reform accompanying their emancipation, most former slaves were forced to sell their labor to those controlling the agricultural system—often their old slave masters. Exploitative, semislave farm labor became the lot of many. Black sharecroppers and tenant farmers were tied to one farm or one rural area by mounting debts owed to a white-controlled lending system. Having less money and much less legal protection than whites and facing racial discrimination in land and consumer-product transactions, most freed blacks were unable to become independent farmers of means in the South. Those in the cities fared little better. Most men were confined to service sector jobs. Unemployment was common. Few manufacturing jobs, including those offering employment to white women, were open to black women.[66] Reflecting on the high rate of stillbirths among black mothers, a black physician commented: "Why should we be surprised at the great number of still-births among our women? . . . They do heavy washing, make beds, turn heavy mattresses, and climb the stairs several times during the day, while their more favored white sister is seated in her big armchair, and not allowed to move, even if she wanted to."[67]

The Migration North

In 1900, nine black Americans in ten still lived in the South. Soon, however, the bustling economy in northern and border cities, the declining significance of "King Cotton" in the South, and the cruelty of southern segregation stimulated increasing numbers to move North. After the 1920s' anti-immigrant legislation and the subsequent decline in foreign immigration, the demand for black laborers in northern industries increased. Thousands of poor black farmers, unable to finance the technological innovations necessary to circumvent the pestilence of the boll weevil, were driven from their farms to the cities. The major push factors were racial segregation and the declining viability of cotton farming; the major pull factor was industrial employment.[68]

The migration North accelerated during World War II. By the mid-twentieth century, millions of African Americans had migrated to what many saw as an economic "promised land." What were their common destinations? Large cities in the Northeast, Midwest, and West. These migrants generally were forced to settle in low-income areas already occupied by black families, swelling their size. Some assimilation theorists argue that this northern migration brought great opportunities for economic mobility to African Americans, whom they see as just another in a line of urban immigrant groups (such as the Irish and the Italians) successfully seeking their fortunes in the city. However, if we accept this view, we would expect that black economic gains between 1900 and the late 1990s would have dramatically closed the black–white gap. The reality, however, has been quite different.[69]

The racial division of labor in the cities was enforced by discriminatory law, violence, or informal discrimination. The urban economy can be divided into at least two major employment sectors. The primary labor market, composed mostly of privileged white workers, is characterized by skilled jobs, high wages, and job ladders offering significant upward mobility. The secondary labor market, composed disproportionately of African Americans and other workers of color, is characterized by instability, low wages, and little upward mobility. The dramatic rise of corporate capitalism after 1900 that created employment for large numbers of workers also resulted in union organizing to expand workers' wages and rights. To counter the white workers' demands, white employers offered certain concessions, including separating the white workers from less-privileged black workers in the workplace. In this way, white workers got what Du Bois has called a "psychological wage" (that is, the sense of white superiority and privilege) in return for taking less in monetary wages than they would have gotten by organizing more aggressively with black workers. Positions in the secondary labor market were often assigned to black Americans and other workers of color. Thus was born the split labor market described in Chapter 2.[70]

The increasing numbers of black men and women moving out of farm occupations found themselves channeled into relatively unskilled jobs in urban industrial and service sectors. The principal occupations of black men became porter, truck driver, janitor, and cook. Black women served as maids, restaurant workers, and dressmakers as white women began to move into clerical and professional jobs.[71] Census figures for 1930 revealed the continuing dominance of agricultural and domestic service jobs. Of every 1,000 black workers, 648 were in agricultural or domestic service jobs, compared with 280 of every 1,000 whites. Most of the remainder were in other unskilled blue-collar positions.[72] Highly educated black men and women were frequently forced to do menial jobs. Most of the few black professionals were teachers, ministers, and physicians serving the black community; likewise, black business people usually served a black clientele. As a result of discrimination and segregation, black incomes were sharply lower than those of whites.[73]

Most labor unions had traditionally been segregated. By the late 1930s, black pressure and federal legislation had forced many American Federation of Labor (AFL) unions to begin to reduce discrimination in recruiting black workers. The new Congress of Industrial Organizations (CIO) began with an official nondiscriminatory policy in order to attract black workers in the automobile, steel, and packing industries. In 1930, at least twenty-six major unions officially barred black workers from membership; by 1943, the number had dropped to fourteen. Nonetheless, official discrimination was usually replaced by widespread informal exclusion or restriction of black workers.[74]

Economic Changes Since the 1940s

The 1940 census revealed a continuing and heavy concentration of black workers in agriculture and the secondary labor market of cities. During World War II, industries with severe labor needs were forced to make significant concessions to black demands for better job opportunities. The proportion of black employees in war-related industries increased from 3 to 8 percent over the war years. Under pressure from black civil rights and union leaders, President Franklin Roosevelt issued executive orders that reduced racial discrimination in war-related industries. However, at the end of the war this progress came to an abrupt end: Layoffs hit black workers much harder than whites.[75]

During the economic expansion between 1955 and 1972, the proportion of African Americans in professional, managerial, sales, clerical, crafts, and operatives jobs increased and the proportion in unskilled and service jobs decreased. The largest increase was in the clerical category. By the 1980s, the growth in the proportion of black employees in better-paid job categories had slowed, and by the late-1990s black workers were still less likely than white workers to be in the better-paid managerial, professional, technical, sales, and crafts categories. In the mid-1990s, only 19 percent of black workers were employed in managerial and professional jobs, compared with 29 percent of white workers. In contrast, black workers were much more likely than white workers to be in blue-collar jobs in the service, operative, transportation, and handler-laborer categories (44 percent compared with 26 percent).[76]

Even within the white-collar categories black workers tend to be in subcategories with lower pay and less job status. For example, within the professional–technical category, black employees today are most commonly found in such fields as social work, kindergarten teaching, vocational counseling, personnel, dietetics, and health care. They are less often found among lawyers and judges, dentists, artists, engineers, and professors at historically white universities. In addition, whites are more than two-and-one-half times as likely to be self-employed as are blacks.[77]

Persisting Discrimination in the Workplace

Sixty percent of white respondents in a recent Associated Press poll thought blacks and other minorities had the same opportunities as whites. Yet 70 percent of blacks in the survey reported that blacks did not have the same opportunities.[78] Surveys such as this indicate that most whites refuse to accept the experienced testimony of African Americans that they still face serious discrimination in the workplace and other arenas of U.S. society.

A number of research studies have confirmed that discrimination today continues to confront black employees working for wages and also those trying to succeed in business on their own. In two recent studies, Joe Feagin supervised interviews with several hundred middle-class African Americans in more than a dozen cities. Many told stories of discrimination in employment or business settings that document the types of discrimination discussed in Chapter 1. You will recall that isolate discrimination involves the actions of an individual acting alone, such as a white manager expressing antiblack views by discriminating against black employees without the support of fellow workers or a discriminatory company policy. Following is a description of the actual experiences of the successful owner of one small consulting firm:

> I have a contract right now with a southwestern city government; and I practically gave my services away. I had to become very creative, you know. I wanted the contract because I know I could do the work, and I have the background and the track record to do it. However, in negotiating the contract, they wanted to give it to all these other people who never had any experience . . . simply because they're a big eight accounting firm, or they're some big-time institution. So, I had to compete against those people. But it was good because it proved that I could be competitive, I could give a competitive price, and I could finally win a contract. But it was a struggle.

She then explained that a professional panel evaluating the bids gave her the highest rating because of her track record. But a barrier was thrown up, because

> the director of their department made a very racial statement, that "they were very sick and tired of these niggers and these other minorities because what they think is that they can come in here and run a business. None of them are qualified to run a business, especially the niggers." (Now, a white person, female, heard this statement, and because they had some confrontational problems—I think the only reason she really told me was because of that.) He was going to use that, not overtly, but in his mind that was going to be his reason for rejection. . . . Even though they [the panel] all recommended me (I got all five consensus votes), he was going to throw it out. . . . I had to really, really do some internalizing to keep myself from being very bitter. Because bitterness can make you lose your perspective about what you want to accomplish. Because you know there are so many roadblocks out there—it's just stressful trying to do these kinds of things—but I really had to do that just to keep from going off the deep end.[79]

This instance of discrimination involved a white man's blatant attempt to restrict a talented black person's advancement, apparently without the overt support of other whites in the organization. Such examples of isolate discrimination motivated by racial prejudices are still common. This victim was unusual in having proof of the attempt at racial exclusion.

Small-group discrimination is also common, North and South. Small-group conspiracies, arranged by prejudiced white supervisors or union officials wishing to subvert company or union regulations that require the hiring or promotion of qualified black employees, continue to be omnipresent, although they are often hard to document.[80]

Direct institutional discrimination consists of organizationally prescribed actions carried out routinely by whites in companies and businesses. Today, this typically takes an informal, sometimes even covert, form. Examples include outright exclusion, the relegation of black employees to special jobs, or retarding the mobility of black employees beyond the entry level. One Urban Institute study sent comparable white and black applicants to the same employers to apply for jobs. A significant proportion—more than one-fifth—of the black applicants suffered job discrimination at the entry stage.[81]

Discrimination in Corporations

Once a black person is hired, discrimination does not end. Having reluctantly torn down traditional exclusion barriers in the 1960s and 1970s, many white managers have retreated to a second line of defense: hiring black workers for nontraditional jobs and putting them in conspicuous or powerless positions. Analysis of the corporate world by management consultant Kenneth Clark and research studies by sociologist Sharon Collins have documented that African Americans moving into professional and management jobs in corporations frequently find themselves tracked into special "job ghettos," such as members or heads of departments of affirmative action, "community affairs," or "special markets."[82] Black professionals and managers "are rarely found in line positions concerned with developing or controlling production, supervising the work of large numbers of whites or competing with their white 'peers' for significant positions."[83] One 1990s study of ninety-four large corporations found that only 6 percent of management positions and 2 percent of upper management positions were held by white women or by African Americans, Latinos, or Asian Americans.[84]

An example of racial problems in major corporations came to public attention in late 1996 when *The New York Times* quoted from the taped transcript of a 1994 meeting of several top executives at the international oil company Texaco, the nation's fourteenth largest corporation, to discuss a lawsuit filed by black employees. According to the transcript, these top corporate officials did not take the black complaints of discrimination seriously and discussed destroying documents requested by the black plaintiffs. Black employees were called "black jelly beans" who all agree with diversity efforts and who "seem to be glued to the bottom of the bag." One top executive said that he was "still having trouble with Hanukkah. Now we have Kwanzaa." (Kwanzaa is an African American winter festival.) Significantly, the federal Equal Employment Opportunity Commission found that Texaco had discriminated against black employees in regard to promotions.[85] Moreover, in an affidavit filed with the court suit, a white manager in a midwestern office reported to his boss, a senior executive in Texas, about a discrimination complaint made by a black employee. His boss reportedly told him that he would "fire her black ass." When the manager pointed out that Texaco's official policy protected those who complained of discrimination from dismissal, the senior executive reportedly said: "I guess we treat niggers differently down here."[86] Court documents obtained by *The New York Times* also showed that only six (0.7 percent) of Texaco's 873 highest-paid executives were black, and that no black person had ever held one of the top 49 jobs in the firm.[87]

The clearest evidence of the corporate world's glass ceiling is the fact that in the mid-1990s not a single one of the Fortune 500 companies had an African American executive at its head. Nor could an African American be found as chief executive officer of the next 500 largest firms. According to a recent report of the federal Glass Ceiling Commission, about 95 percent of the holders of top corporate positions (vice presidents and above) are white (non-Latino) men, yet they make up only 39 percent of the adult population. Government affirmative action policies have done little to alter this white male dominance at the very top of U.S. economic (and other major) institutions.[88]

African Americans face discrimination as consumers as well. A study of automobile buying experiences that used black and white, male and female testers with similar dress, economic stories, and bargaining scripts revealed both racial and gender discrimination. An examination of more than 180 negotiations at ninety Chicago dealerships found that white men were quoted much better prices than were black men, black women, or white women.[89]

In every facet of this society, examples can be found of white privilege and black harm that have been passed along from one generation to the next. Sometimes, whites argue that they "have not discriminated against blacks and have not profited from racism" and thus that they, as innocents, "should not have to pay any price through programs such as affirmative action." Yet these whites overlook the many ways in which they benefit from the access their parents, grandparents, or great-grandparents had to land, jobs, and wealth in periods when access was completely denied or severely restricted for African Americans. Indeed, *legal* subordination and segregation of African Americans were not ended in the United States until relatively recently, that is, until the civil rights acts of the 1960s. Today, the wealth of many white parents is at least in part inherited from earlier ancestors and benefits their children in terms of an ability to pay for higher education, to help start businesses, to buy houses, and even to provide "cultural capital" enabling children to do better in school and on tests such as the Scholastic Aptitude Test (SAT). Once created in situations where others are excluded from gaining it, wealth can bring many unearned benefits to subsequent generations.

Government Action and Inaction on Discrimination

Government action on discrimination has been a hotly debated issue. As we noted earlier, some opponents argue it has gone too far, even to the point of large-scale "reverse discrimination" that favors people of color. Other analysts, with much more evidence, argue that federal government policies have always been modest and since the early 1980s have had a lessening impact on racial discrimination in such spheres as employment and housing because of the weakening of federal civil rights enforcement by the conservative Reagan and Bush administrations in the 1980s and early 1990s.

The pathbreaking 1964 Civil Rights Act and its later amendments prohibit discrimination in employment. The federal Equal Employment Opportunity Commission (EEOC) was created to enforce the 1964 act, primarily by investigating complaints, seeking conciliation, and—since 1972—filing suit to end employment discrimination by labor unions, private employers, state and local governments, and educational institutions. A major Supreme Court decision, *Griggs* v. *Duke Power Co.* (1971), defined remediable discrimination to include white practices that were "neutral in terms of intent" but that disadvantaged black employees. Until the 1980s, the federal courts and the EEOC played a major role in reducing racial barriers in traditionally white employment arenas.

Under the Reagan and Bush administrations in the 1980s and 1990s, however, the EEOC became much less active in attacking racial discrimination in workplaces. During the Reagan era, the EEOC reduced the number of field investigations of the critical class-action complaints of discrimination as well as other broad, institutionally focused investigations of employment discrimination. The Reagan administration destroyed or weakened other civil rights enforcement agencies, and, for the most part, President George Bush continued this negative approach to civil rights. In addition, Presidents Reagan and Bush appointed several conservative justices to the U.S. Supreme Court, which subsequently handed down a number of backtracking decisions on employment and other civil rights issues.

In the late 1980s, a new civil rights bill was proposed to overcome the limitations of recent and conservative Supreme Court decisions. President Bush initially opposed the bill, but after a congressional struggle (and some weakening of provisions) he signed the 1991 Civil Rights Act. In 1993 the Clinton administration began to enforce civil rights laws more vigorously. As of the late 1990s, government enforcement of civil rights has increased but still has not recovered from the Reagan-Bush era.

Strong civil rights laws do not guarantee real equality of opportunity in everyday settings. Few of the millions of cases of racial discrimination perpetrated by white Americans each year against African Americans and other Americans of color are countered by effective private or government remedies. U.S. government agencies have neither the resources nor the staff to vigorously enforce antidiscrimination laws. Over the last decade or two, many African American victims of discrimination have given up on the federal government in dealing with their problems. Indeed, in a 1989 decision one of the few liberal justices then on the Supreme Court, Harry Blackmun, asked whether the conservative white majority on the court, and by implication in the country, "still believes that race discrimination—or, more accurately, race discrimination against nonwhites—is a problem in our society, or even remembers that it ever was."[90]

Unemployment, Income, and Poverty

For decades the black unemployment rate has been about twice the white unemployment rate:[91]

	Black (or Nonwhite)	White	Ratio
1949	8.9%	5.6%	1.6
1959	10.7	4.8	2.2
1969	6.4	3.1	2.1
1975	13.8	7.8	1.8
1980	14.3	6.3	2.3
1985	15.1	6.2	2.4
1990	11.3	4.7	2.4
1995	10.4	4.9	2.1
1998 (Apr.)	8.9	3.6	2.5

In 1985, the black-white unemployment ratio reached a record high of 2.4 and remained above 2.1 in 1995. Related to the high unemployment rate is the fact that in economic recessions black workers tend to lose their jobs at twice the rate of white workers and tend to be recalled at a slower rate. In some cities the unemployment rate for blacks has risen to more than four times the white rate. One major reason for this inequality is the movement of capital and jobs to suburbs. The majority of new jobs in the last two decades in metropolitan areas have been created outside the central city areas where most African Americans live.

Even higher than the unemployment rate for African Americans is the *under-employment rate,* which includes those with no jobs, those working part-time, and those making poverty wages. Nationwide surveys have found that large numbers of black workers have part-time work even though they want full-time work, receive very low wages, or are discouraged workers (those who have given up looking for work). It has been estimated that one-third of black workers fall into these subemployment categories, while the proportion for whites is much lower. U.S. Labor Department data for the mid-1990s showed that the proportion of blacks working part-time because they could not find full-time work was twice that of white workers.[92]

Since the 1950s, black family income has remained at 52 to 61 percent of white family income.[93]

Black (or Nonwhite) Income As a Percentage of White Income

1950	54%
1954	56
1959	52
1964	54
1969	61
1974	58
1980	58
1985	58
1990	58
1995	60

Census data also show that in 1995 black per capita income was only 60 percent of white per capita income.[94]

Families headed by single, separated, or divorced mothers tend to be poorer than those with both parents present. The proportion of black families headed by women increased from 18 percent in 1950 to almost 48 percent in 1994.[95] In the 1990s, well over half of black female headed families with children under 18 years old live in poverty.[96] "Families headed by black women are primarily poor, not because they do not have husbands, but because they do not have jobs."[97] Like black men, black women face major employment problems in part because of intentional discrimination in the present and in part because of the effects of past discrimination.

Whatever the type of family, African Americans average significantly fewer dollars than whites. In the late 1990s, black families were more than four times as likely as non-Hispanic white families to live in poverty. One-third of all black Americans, and 46 percent of black children, fell below the government poverty line. Between 1974 and 1993 the number of black Americans living in poverty increased from 7.2 million to more than 10.9 million. In the mid-1990s, a much smaller proportion of black families than white families owned their own home (42 percent compared with 70 percent), and more than two-thirds of black families nationwide could not afford to buy a modestly priced house in their community.[98]

We have previously noted the fact that many whites have inherited significant economic and cultural (for example, educational) wealth from their parents and earlier ancestors. Because of slavery, legal segregation, and continuing informal discrimination, African Americans have had little opportunity to build up multigenerational wealth. Today, black households as a group have a much lower net worth than white households.[99] The median net worth of white households is almost ten times that of black households. In addition, the types of assets held by white households are different from the types held by black households.[100] Almost three-fourths of black households' assets, compared with less than half of white households' assets, are held in durable goods such as housing and vehicles. White households hold more than three times as much of their wealth in interest-bearing bank accounts or stock shares than do black households.

Poor African Americans: An "Underclass"?

Since the 1970s, a number of scholars and media commentators have described segments among poor black Americans as an "underclass." In *The Declining Significance of Race* (1978), William J. Wilson argued that this underclass is the most serious problem for black Americans and that the rise of the black middle class since the 1960s has resulted from shifting economic conditions and new government policies. Since the late 1970s, many commentators have argued that equal employment legislation all but eliminated the split labor market in which black labor suffered direct segregation. In their view, the central problem for African Americans today is not antiblack discrimination but rather the economic conditions of the poor. In *The Truly Disadvantaged* (1987), Wilson argued that the major problem of poor African Americans is unemployment, a structural condition that in his view should be eradicated by government job programs. Playing up the behavioral characteristics of poor black Americans, Ken Auletta argued that racism has played little part in the formation of the black "underclass," which is mostly the result of an inferior class culture. Since the 1980s, arguments like Auletta's have been echoed in the writings of dozens of white analysts and some black neoconservative analysts, who contend that the black community has been polarized into an affluent middle class and the very poor. They allege that racial discrimination has mostly been eradicated for middle-class black Americans, thus lessening the need for affirmative action programs, which primarily benefit the middle class.[101]

In some scholarly work and much mass media analysis, the plight of the black poor is discussed as though their economic conditions were not the main problem; their values and behavior are said to be the main source of their problems. Moreover, racial discrimination is seen as having little to do with this group's high unemployment and underemployment rates, low incomes, and poor housing conditions. From this perspective, poor black Americans have become locked into a lower-class "culture of poverty," with its allegedly deviant values, immorality, broken families, juvenile delinquency, and lack of emphasis on the work ethic. These stereotype-based arguments about poor Americans are recent versions of largely discredited culture-of-poverty arguments that have been made at least since the 1960s.[102]

Perhaps the greatest weakness of arguments focused on the alleged cultural inferiority of poor African Americans is the neglect of major structural factors. They face many problems created by top business excecutives who are moving U.S. jobs overseas, as Wilson emphasizes. This lack of jobs has nothing to do with the culture of these workers and their families. In addition, racial discrimination is still commonplace in employment and housing. If the notion of the irrelevance of racial discrimination for the poor were true, poor African Americans should face roughly the same social, economic, political, and housing conditions as comparably poor white Americans. But this is not the case. For example, because of past and present discrimination poor black families do *not* live in integrated neighborhoods with poor white families. African Americans, including low-income workers, are *more* likely to be laid off in recessions than white Americans. Poor African Americans are *less* likely than comparably poor whites to get unemployment compensation when they are laid off. They tend to hold lower-paying and less secure jobs than even poor whites. And they face far more discrimination at the hands of white police officers and other whites than do poor whites.

The role of past and present racial discrimination in the problems of poor African Americans must be recognized. Past discrimination (much of it relatively recent), coupled with blatant, subtle, and covert racial discrimination today, is the likely reason for most black poverty, unemployment, and underemployment.[103]

Housing Discrimination

The 1968 Civil Rights Act officially banned most housing discrimination in the United States. However, this and subsequent housing laws have largely been unenforced, and discriminatory practices in housing persist widely across the nation. Using white and black testers, housing audit studies for the 1995 to 1997 period in New Orleans, Montgomery, Fresno, and San Antonio have found very high (61 percent to 77 percent) discrimination rates for black testers seeking rental housing. (Discrimination against Latinos was also found.) This widespread discrimination is often covert, such as a white landlord falsely telling a black renter that an apartment has just been rented. In addition, the movement of capital and jobs out to suburbs or other countries contributes to persisting racial segregation and housing inequality in cities. For some time most new jobs in metropolitan areas have been created outside the urban cores where many Americans of color reside. According to Douglas Massey and Nancy Denton, this commonplace "residential segregation is the institutional apparatus that supports other racially discriminatory processes and binds them together into a coherent and uniquely effective system of racial subordination."[104]

Racial apartheid is still the reality in U.S. cities. Metropolitan areas grew by 15 percent between 1980 and 1992, but during this period the proportion of Americans living in suburban areas rose to about half the nation's population. The white population of central cities has decreased, and most suburbs are now predominantly white. Today about three-fourths of whites live in suburbs or nonmetropolitan areas, while the majority of people of color live in cities. White fears about the new sociospatial reality of our cities seem to be increasing. Ironically, whites now fear the residential segregation that they have created by more than a century of exclusionary racial practices. As William J. Wilson has written, "In the eyes of many in the dominant white population, the minorities symbolize the ugly urban scene left behind. Today, the divide between the suburbs and the city is, in many respects, a racial divide."[105]

This divide has serious consequences. One 1990s study by *The New York Times* journalists examined two adjacent but largely segregated working-class residential areas of Chicago, one white and one black. According to the field interviews, the whites live in an insulated world where they "live out entire lives without ever getting to know a black person." The study found racial fear and suspicion of the other group in both residential areas. However, the black residents were "fearful because much of their contact with white people was negative," while "whites were fearful because they had little or no contact."[106]

POLITICS AND PROTEST

Before 1865, African Americans, whether slaves in the South or "free" men and women in the North, were not allowed to participate as equals with whites in the political system. Most were disenfranchised. Between the 1600s and 1860s, some petitioned white legislatures and executive officials for redress of their grievances; most petitions were ignored. The Civil War brought an end to slavery and increased black participation in electoral politics. The 1866 Civil Rights Act made black men full citizens, at least in principle. The Thirteenth Amendment to the U.S. Constitution abolished slavery, the Fourteenth Amendment asserted that the civil rights of black Americans could not be denied by the states, and the Fifteenth Amendment guaranteed black men (but not women) the right to vote.

From Reconstruction to the 1920s

The Reconstruction period after the Civil War came to the South as a breath of fresh air. Federally enforced Reconstruction policies were precipitated by southern unwillingness to make major changes in the treatment of freed slaves or to prevent the unrepentant leaders of the Confederacy from resuming power. A brief period of limited federal military occupation resulted. During Reconstruction, black southerners made political gains. Black men gained the right to vote; new state constitutional conventions included black delegates, although in most states *white* southerners were the *majority* of all delegates.[107] Between 1870 and 1901, twenty black men served in the U.S. House and two in the Senate. Hiram R. Revels and Blanche K. Bruce were U.S. senators from Mississippi, the first African Americans to serve in the Senate.[108]

Black southerners were generally in the minority in state legislatures. During Reconstruction southern state governments were mostly controlled by whites who had not been active supporters of the Confederacy, including white farmers of modest means. But the conservative forces in the South soon brought an end to Reconstruction. The so-called Redemption period began with the Hayes Compromise of 1877, which removed the few remaining federal troops and thereby eliminated much federal protection of freed slaves. Reconstruction was the first period in U.S. history in which African Americans gained a significant measure of freedom and justice. Although considerable racial segregation existed in this period, the racialized system was not nearly as all-encompassing as it would become in the segregationist years after the 1890s. Freedom here, racial segregation there, mixing here, racial exclusion there—such was the fluidity of the Reconstruction era.

By the early 1900s, enforced racial segregation became the rule in the South, and a Supreme Court decision nailed the lid on the coffin of southern racial progress. The decision in *Plessy* v. *Ferguson* (1896), a case upholding racial segregation in Louisiana railroad cars, delivered a major blow by asserting the legality of so-called "separate but equal" facilities for blacks. The all-white Court reasoned that racism was natural, that "legislation is powerless to eradicate racial instincts or to abolish distinctions based upon physical differences, and the attempt to do so can only result in accentuating the difficulties of the present situation."[109]

In 1915, the Supreme Court began a slow swing back to the protection of some black civil rights by declaring the grandfather clauses for voting unconstitutional. Voter registration increased very slowly. By the 1920s, the black movement to the cities had brought a few black leaders to the political forefront, particularly in the North. Independent political organizations were established in a few cities, but the only major success was that of Adam Clayton Powell, Jr., in New York City. In 1945, Powell became a black member of Congress, the fourth in history and the first from outside the city of Chicago in the twentieth century. In the North, the black vote was at first strongly tied to the Republican party, but by the 1930s it had begun to shift to the Democratic party.[110]

The Limits of Black Progress: Political Discrimination

Black voter registration increased sharply in the South between the 1940s and the 1970s, from 250,000 to 4 million voters. A big jump in registration came after passage of the Voting Rights Act in 1965. Some whites argued that inadequate civic training and less education would render newly enfranchised blacks unable to organize effectively. Yet since their enfranchisement in 1965 black southerners have developed effective political organizations and campaigns. In 1965, there were approximately seventy black elected officials in the South. Three years later, the figure had climbed to 248; by the 1990s it was several thousand. Recent research has clearly demonstrated that this increase was the result of voting rights legislation, which one analysis called "perhaps the single most successful civil rights bill ever passed."[111] Even so, black officials have as yet attained proportional equality in only a few areas of the South.

Into the 1980s and 1990s, black voters have continued to face attempts to reduce the efficacy of their political participation. Research by Chandler Davidson and by Frank Parker has demonstrated that electoral discrimination persists in such forms as vote dilution, gerrymandering, the changing of elective offices into appointive offices, and unnecessary revisions in qualifications for office.[112] A major example of vote dilution is the at-large electoral system, whereby candidates are elected citywide rather than from smaller districts. In cities across the nation, this system has been demonstrated to sharply reduce the participation of black candidates and voters in local campaigns. As long as black voters constitute well under half of the voters in a city, black candidates are unlikely to win elected office in an at-large system because many whites will rarely or never vote for a black candidate. The Supreme Court, in *City of Mobile* v. *Bolden* (1980), required black plaintiffs to prove that at-large electoral systems were intentionally set up to discriminate. The Court ruled that evidence of the severe negative racial impact of such systems was not enough. In the early 1980s, the Reagan administration, responding to conservative white supporters, tried to weaken the Voting Rights Act, which was up for extension. However, in 1982, after a long battle, civil rights forces were able to get Congress to pass a twenty-five-year extension of key provisions of the act and to add an amendment allowing the U.S. Justice Department to prosecute local government officials for discrimination in electoral procedures without having to show racial prejudices on the part of these officials.[113]

African American voters also face discrimination in the form of purges of voter-registration rolls, unannounced changes in polling places, intentionally difficult registration procedures, and threats of retaliation. These practices have been documented from Alabama to Texas.[114] The persistence of these practices has led to new debates over remedies. Since the early 1980s, voting rights issues have been at the center of debates about democracy in the United States. Just after becoming president in 1993, Bill Clinton nominated Lani Guinier, a distinguished black law professor, for an assistant attorney general post. Because she supported vigorous enforcement of the voting rights law, Guinier was labeled a "quota queen" by some conservatives in the media, a reference to the hostile label of "welfare queen" often applied by whites to black women. Many white politicians and journalists took up the theme articulated in the *Wall Street Journal* by conservative activist Clinton Bolick, who inaccurately charged Guinier with supporting "racial quotas" in elections.[115] Guinier's actual views on voting rights were not outside the mainstream. Moreover, Guinier and other scholars have pointed out that the enforcement of the Voting Rights Act has increased the number of black-majority voting districts, yet it has not reshaped local and state legislative bodies to give black officials a proportionate influence on daily operations.

Guinier has suggested additional remedies that might increase black influence on government bodies, one of which is cumulative voting, a procedure in which each voter is given a number of votes equal to the number of positions to be filled in a legislative body. If ten members of a commission are being elected, each voter gets ten votes and may use them to vote for one candidate for each of the positions or cast all ten votes for one candidate. This strategy is thought to increase the probability that a black candidate will be elected in an area in which the majority of voters are white. Cumulative voting is a departure from most existing voting rules, but it is not unprecedented. Some cities, such as Alamogordo and Peoria, have already experimented with this procedure, and it is used in selecting corporate boards of directors. In law journal articles, Guinier has suggested that other mechanisms, such as the requirement of legislative "supermajorities" to pass most laws, should be considered if cumulative voting and traditional strategies do not improve real black political power. In the 1980s, the Reagan administration agreed to just such a supermajority mechanism to redress voting rights complaints in Mobile, Alabama. This remedial procedure stipulated a five-vote majority on Mobile's seven-member city commission to pass legislation. The intention was to ensure that at least one of Mobile's three black commission members would have to vote in favor of any new law.[116]

Have black elected officials in the South been able to accomplish anything? Some argue that black votes and elected officials can accomplish much for black voters, while others see black citizens as unable to gain much through an electoral process controlled by whites. In most jurisdictions black officials have not been able to dramatically reorder local priorities in employment, housing, and education. Yet they have often been able to force an expansion of capital-based services for black residential areas. In his study in Florida, political scientist James Button found that black officials were often more effective in changing employment opportunities for their constituents than in improving capital-based services. Black officials also have had a positive influence on voter turnout by their black constituents. They have become a "direct and effective conduit for political input from black citizens" and the legitimacy of being elected officials has given them "influence and power in the public realm that other black leaders and organizations [have] rarely had."[117]

The number of black elected officials in the nation increased sharply between 1964 and the mid-1990s, from about 100 to more than 7,400. The proportion of women among these officials has grown dramatically, from less than one in twelve in 1970 to more than 25 percent in the 1990s.[118] Since the 1960s, African

Americans have won mayoral elections in a number of major cities with large black populations: Washington, DC, Philadelphia, Detroit, Chicago, Cleveland, New York City, Los Angeles, Atlanta, and Birmingham. In addition, a few predominantly white cities, such as Seattle and Kansas City, have also elected black mayors. In 1990, the state of Virginia, once the capital of the Confederacy, elected L. Douglas Wilder, the grandson of a slave, the first African American governor of any state.

The Federal Government

The New Deal era (1933–1940) was the first period since Reconstruction in which the federal government gave attention to the needs of black citizens. Breaking with previous exclusionary practices, Franklin Roosevelt appointed more than one hundred African Americans to important positions. New Deal programs helped black Americans survive the Great Depression, but the important economic recovery agencies generally discriminated in favor of white citizens.[119]

Between 1901 and 1929, Congress had no black members, and from 1929 until 1945, only one. In 1945 Adam Clayton Powell, Jr., (New York) joined William Dawson (Illinois) in the House, and ten years later, Charles Diggs was elected from Michigan. For the first time in the twentieth century, Congress had three African American representatives. However, black gains increased with the registration of new black voters after the civil rights revolution of the 1960s. By 1992, there were twenty-six black members, including four women, in the U.S. House. The redrawing of election districts following the 1990 census to bring states into compliance with the 1982 amendments to the Voting Rights Act, which confirm the right of African Americans to an equal opportunity to elect candidates of their choice, increased the number of black-majority congressional voting districts. This in turn contributed to a major increase in black congressional representation. In 1997, there were thirty-nine black representatives, including eleven women, in the U.S. House and one black woman (the first ever), Carol Moseley Braun from Illinois, in the Senate.[120]

The first black person ever to serve in a presidential cabinet was Robert Weaver, appointed Secretary of Housing and Urban Development by President Lyndon Johnson in 1967. Johnson also appointed Andrew Brimmer the first black member of the Federal Reserve, Thurgood Marshall the first black Supreme Court justice, and Patricia Harris the first black ambassador.[121] From the 1970s to the 1990s, this pattern has persisted under both Republican and Democratic presidents—a few token black appointments in (usually lesser) positions in the presidential cabinet and one appointment on the Supreme Court. However, no black person has ever served as head of the major executive branch departments, such as state, defense, and the treasury. The overall pattern in federal legislative, executive, and judicial positions is still one of continuing and significant underrepresentation for African Americans.

In federal elections, the black vote has sometimes been very important. For example, in 1944 black voters played a role in Roosevelt's fourth election; in 1948 they were important to Truman's election.[122] The black vote in a few key states reportedly decided the 1960 presidential election in favor of the Irish Catholic John Kennedy. Black voters also played a role in electing Lyndon Johnson in 1964 and Jimmy Carter in 1976. During recent elections, African American voters have continued to help elect white and black (usually Democratic) members of Congress sympathetic to liberal and civil rights issues, to some extent offsetting the conservative impact of many white voters. African American voters have been important in pressing the nation in the direction of its basic political ideal of "liberty and justice for all."

The Republican Party's Appeal to White Voters

There is a good reason why most black voters have sometimes found themselves voting for losing presidential candidates since the late 1960s—the barely disguised prowhite strategy of the Republican party. Developed by Republican conservatives in the early 1960s, this political strategy was used by Richard Nixon in winning the 1968 presidential election. The prowhite approach was celebrated in Kevin Phillips's *The Emerging Republican Majority*, for a while the "Bible" of many Republicans. Phillips explicitly suggested that Republicans did not need "urban Negroes" and other "vested interests" to win.[123] Republican targeting of white southern and suburban voters was effective in the 1980 and 1984 Reagan campaigns and took an even more aggressive form in the 1988 George Bush campaign. In 1988, decisions made by Bush and his campaign manager, Lee Atwater, led to a dramatic television advertisement centered on the photo of a black man ("Willie" Horton) who was convicted of raping a white woman. The man's actual name was William Horton, but he was renamed "Willie" by political strategists, presumably to summon up a more sinister image than "William" would have. (Diminutive names such as "Willie" have often been applied by whites to African Americans, without the latter's input.) In addition, Horton was an atypical rapist, for about nine in ten rapes of white women are by *white* men. Yet the campaign ads showed no white male rapists. The Horton ad was successfully employed to recruit white voters. Candidate Bush stood behind the ad, and Atwater admitted the prowhite strategy: "The Horton case is one of those gut issues that are value issues, particularly in the South."[124]

In recent decades, the Republican party has moved from the party of Abraham Lincoln that advocated expanded civil rights to one opposed in practice to aggressive action (including affirmative action) to redress racism. Once the recipient of a majority of the black vote, the Republican party now receives little of that vote. Indeed, the Republican national conventions of the 1980s and 1990s have had very few black delegates.[125]

During the 1990s, speeches and ads by some Republican candidates for election or reelection (for example, Senator Jesse Helms in North Carolina) have included "code words" that are politically charged, such as "racial quotas" and "unqualified minorities," in attempts to convince whites to vote for Republican candidates. In part as a result of these direct racial appeals to whites, the overwhelming majority of black voters have continued to support Democratic candidates at the local, state, and national levels.

Still, this black allegiance has not been enthusiastic because in some cases white Democratic candidates have also used barely disguised antiblack tactics to court white voters, as in Bill Clinton's attack on the black rap singer Sister Souljah in the 1992 presidential campaign. Clinton reprimanded Souljah for her attempts to explain how the violence black youth have so far turned on themselves and their communities might yet be turned on whites. Clinton incorrectly characterized Souljah as personally advocating violence by black young people. Clinton voiced his harsh criticism of Souljah at a meeting of the Rainbow Coalition (headed by the black civil rights leader Jesse Jackson), where she was being honored for working to get out the black vote. The Clinton strategy showed he could, as Democratic officials put it, "stand up to black leaders" and apparently increased Clinton's support among white voters.[126]

African American Organization and Protest

The fundamental values of the oppositional culture of African Americans have provided a source of resistance to discrimination and have also sometimes become part of the evolving cultural mix that may eventually replace the dominant Eurocentric culture. A major aspect of black oppositional culture is a respect for civil rights and liberty. This value commitment is one of the greatest sources of support for civil rights and civil liberties in the United States today. Over the centuries black resistance to racism has ranged from legal strategies, to the ballot, to nonviolent civil disobedience, to violent attacks on the system.[127]

The goals of African American protest movements in the twentieth century have included the desegregation of public accommodations and schools and the opening of housing and employment once reserved for whites. In 1905, criticizing what was seen as a prowhite accommodationist position of such black leaders as Booker T. Washington, W. E. B. Du Bois and other black and white liberals formed the Niagara movement to focus on legal and voting rights as well as economic issues. Not long thereafter, some of these leaders helped create the still-influential National Association for the Advancement of Colored People (NAACP).

We have previously pointed out the importance of black nationalist thought and action. From the 1900s to the 1950s, Du Bois played a role in the development of pan-African nationalism as a partial solution for the conditions of oppression faced by people of African descent. In 1919, working with other black leaders, Du Bois put together the first Pan-African Congress, to which nearly sixty delegates from fifteen countries came. Speaking for the "Negroes of the world," the Congress called for the abolition of all forms of slavery and for curtailment of colonial exploitation. Cultural nationalism was also apparent in the 1920s Harlem Renaissance, an explosion of writing and arts focused on black values and traditions.

Black organizations directed at self-help and philanthropic activity, such as the Urban League, were created in the early twentieth century. The efforts of these new organizations resulted in increased aid for the urban poor and also some erosion of legal segregation. Legal action became a major strategy for fighting racist barriers. One of the first NAACP victories was a 1917 Supreme Court decision, *Buchanan* v. *Warley,* which knocked down a Louisville, Kentucky, law requiring residential segregation—one of the first steps in reversing the segregationist position the Court had taken in the late 1800s. However, most Supreme Court decisions before the 1930s hurt the cause of black rights by reinforcing segregation in schools, transportation, and the jury system.[128]

Against fierce resistance the NAACP began a large-scale attack on segregation in schools, voting, transportation, and jury selection. Beginning in the 1930s NAACP and other lawyers won a series of cases that over the next several decades expanded the legal rights of defendants, eliminated the all-white political primary, protected the voting rights of black citizens, reduced job discrimination by unions, voided restrictive housing covenants, and desegregated schools and public accommodations. The separate-but-equal doctrine of *Plessy* v. *Ferguson* increasingly came under attack. Dramatically reversing its position in that 1896 case, the Supreme Court in *Brown* v. *Board of Education* (1954) ruled that "in the field of public education the doctrine of 'separate but equal' has no place."[129]

By the 1940s and 1950s, African American communities were generating more militant anti-discrimination strategies. During World War II, a threatened large-scale march on Washington, DC, to be led by A. Philip Randolph and other black leaders, helped pressure President Roosevelt to issue an order desegregating employment. After World War II, Randolph and other leaders organized against the peacetime draft on the basis that black citizens should not serve in a segregated army. After unsuccessful attempts to persuade black leaders to back down, President Harry Truman set up an agency to rid federal employment of racial discrimination and a committee to oversee desegregation of the armed forces. As a result, the U.S. military became, and still is, the most desegregated of major U.S. institutions.[130]

The 1950s and 1960s brought an increase in black protest against antiblack discrimination. One protest strategy was the boycott, such as that of segregated buses in Montgomery, Alabama, in the mid-1950s, where black seamstress and NAACP member, Rosa Parks, refused to give up her seat on a segregated bus to a white person. Her arrest triggered a successful boycott by the black community that brought the boycott leader, Dr. Martin Luther King, Jr., into national prominence. Growing black resistance to segregation spurred the creation of the Southern Christian Leadership Conference (SCLC), led by Dr. King.

In 1960, black students began the sit-in movement at a white-only lunch counter in Greensboro, North Carolina, touching off a long series of sit-ins throughout the South by thousands of black southerners and their white allies. The Freedom Rides on interstate buses came in 1961; blacks and whites tested federal court orders desegregating public transportation and demonstrated a lack of compliance throughout the South. Near Anniston, Alabama, the first bus of Freedom Riders was burned; in Birmingham, the riders were attacked by an angry mob of white segregationists.

In the spring of 1963, King and his associates launched a series of demonstrations against discrimination in Birmingham, Alabama. Fire hoses and police dogs were used against demonstrators, many of whom were children, gaining the movement important national publicity. An agreement desegregating businesses and employment ended these protests, but another round of demonstrations was touched off when a black home and motel were bombed. Then came the massive 1963 March on Washington, in which King dramatized rising black aspirations for freedom in his famous "I have a dream" speech before thousands of white and black demonstrators.[131]

Direct action against segregation in the North began in earnest in the 1960s with boycotts in Harlem, sit-ins in Chicago, school sit-ins in New Jersey, and mass demonstrations in Cairo, Illinois. The Congress of Racial Equality (CORE) accelerated protest campaigns against discrimination in housing and employment. School boycotts, picketing at construction sites, and rent strikes became commonplace. In 1964, protestors in New York threatened a stall-in to disrupt the opening of the World's Fair. Led by Stokely Carmichael, the Student Nonviolent Coordinating Committee (SNCC) germinated a "Black Power" movement. The

Dr. Martin Luther King, Jr., gives his "I have a dream" speech at a large civil rights demonstration in Washington D.C. in 1963.

growing number of organizations oriented toward black nationalism and self-help included the Black Panthers, a group of young black men and women who started breakfast programs for children and engaged in surveillance of local white police officers to reduce police brutality in cities. The Nation of Islam ("Black Muslims") pressed for black pride and established black-controlled social programs and businesses. Pride and consciousness grew in all segments of the black community in the North, particularly among the young.[132]

White commentators on the nonviolent civil rights era have suggested that the image of Dr. Martin Luther King was mostly a media creation and that the civil rights movement was mostly a middle-class movement. Neither is true. Many local demonstrations included large-scale participation by African Americans from all economic backgrounds. Research on the development of these resistance movements has demonstrated they were grounded in organized activism that was in turn rooted in what Aldon Morris has called "a well-developed indigenous base."[133] This broad base included community churches, clubs, and other voluntary organizations whose role in providing money and mobilizing people enabled activists in organizations such as the SCLC and SNCC to be successful in fighting racism and legal segregation.

Progress and Retreat

During the Johnson administration in the 1960s, the civil rights movement played an important role in pressuring Congress to pass three major pieces of legislation prohibiting discrimination in employment, voting, and housing—the Voting Rights Act of 1965 and the Civil Rights Acts of 1964 and 1968. In the 1970s these important acts were amended and expanded, and some effort was put into implementing and enforcing them.

However, many of these advances were threatened and undercut during the 1980s and early 1990s under conservative political administrations. From 1981 to 1989, President Ronald Reagan greatly expanded military spending but cut back many social programs, such as job training and funding for civil rights enforcement agencies. As a result, civil rights agencies reduced enforcement activities, such as class-action suits aimed at discriminatory employers and compliance reviews of government contractors. The Reagan administration tried to cut back the Voting Rights Act and federal programs for increasing employment among African Americans and other groups. Reagan played down the significance of racism and argued that black leaders such as Coretta Scott King were intentionally exaggerating the magnitude of racism and were "doing very well leading organizations based on keeping alive the feeling that they're victims of prejudice."[134]

As we have noted, the Bush administration (1989–1993) continued the negative approach to African Americans, who responded by pressing their fight to improve civil rights enforcement. Bush appointed conservative Supreme Court justices, whose decisions limited discrimination victims' right to sue. These events, and the Willie Horton ad campaign, convinced most black citizens that the federal government had turned its back on them. Bush did finally sign the 1991

Civil Rights Act, which was designed to overcome the restrictions of these Court decisions, but only after a long political struggle.

Civil rights groups have continued to protest on behalf of expanded opportunities for people of color. Washington, DC, and other cities have seen demonstrations against discrimination and the weakening of civil rights enforcement. From time to time, the NAACP Legal Defense Fund, the Leadership Conference on Civil Rights, and other civil rights organizations have mounted enough pressure to stop government officials from achieving certain conservative goals. For example, they have helped block right-wing appointments to federal judgeships, including Supreme Court positions.

The arrival of Bill Clinton in the White House in 1993 brought renewed hope among African Americans for aggressive enforcement of civil rights laws and new programs expanding job opportunities. By 1995, some of these expectations had been met. Clinton's civil rights record was better than those of Reagan and Bush: He appointed more African Americans and women to important government positions, including judgeships, than they did, and his administration put greater emphasis on the enforcement of civil rights laws by the U.S. Department of Justice.

In 1994, class-action suits brought on behalf of black individuals (including a group of secret service agents) who had reportedly suffered racial discrimination at Denny's restaurants were resolved by a consent decree in which the company agreed to pay $46 million in damages. Assistant Attorney General Deval Patrick, an African American appointed by Clinton, noted the decree was one solution for discrimination in public accommodations: "There will be a high price to pay for unlawful indignities, and the Justice Department will exact that price whenever the law is violated."[135] This aggressive Department of Justice involvement in discrimination lawsuits was a clear break from the policies of the two previous Republican administrations.[136]

Nonetheless, the 1994 and 1996 elections signalled the likelihood of backtracking on civil rights enforcement by the new U.S. Congress. The Republican party now had control of both houses of Congress for the first time in several decades, and the conservative congressional leaders made clear their desire to cut back or eliminate federal affirmative action efforts to increase the representation of people of color (and white women) in the better-paying jobs in the U.S. workplace. The conservative white leadership showed hostility toward federal efforts to increase the representation of people of color in business contracting with local and federal governments. As of the late 1990s, this resurgence of conservative white political power at the national level has generated new organizational activity in support of civil rights enforcement and the expansion of equal opportunity among African Americans and other Americans of color in communities across the nation.

New Political Organizations

Because of the persistence of widespread racial discrimination, African Americans have repeatedly organized movements for expanded civil and economic rights. For example, in 1983 Jesse Jackson announced his candidacy for president of the

United States. Jackson and many of his supporters had learned their political skills in civil rights efforts. Jackson and other leaders put together a strong grassroots campaign grounded in a diverse organization called the Rainbow Coalition, which included black, white, Latino, and Native American activists who supported a progressive agenda. By 1984, the group had registered 2 million new voters. Jackson won nearly 4 million votes in Democratic party primaries—one-fifth of all the votes cast—and went to the Democratic national convention with many delegates. Although Jackson's ancestors had come to the United States centuries before the ancestors of some white Democratic and Republican candidates, Jackson was the first African American to reach this level in politics. He lost the nomination but succeeded in creating multiracial political organizations in many states. The new voters registered by his supporters helped elect numerous liberal whites to the U.S. Congress.[137]

In 1988, Jackson again campaigned for the Democratic presidential nomination with the Rainbow Coalition as his base; again he took many delegates to the Democratic national convention. Two million Americans voted for him in the primaries. He was strongly supported by black voters, many of whom became hopeful that an African American might actually be elected president. However, a problem for any black candidate is that a significant proportion of white voters tell pollsters that they will not vote for a black person under any circumstances.[138]

Jesse Jackson stirred many Americans to participate in U.S. politics for the first time, especially people of color and those committed to a progressive political platform. He was the first presidential candidate in U.S. history to develop a strong public position on issues of great concern to black and other women of color. He and the Rainbow Coalition took public positions in favor of the Equal Rights Amendment, choice on the abortion issue, the principle of equal pay for equal worth, and a woman as a vice-presidential candidate.

Sociologist Patricia Hill Collins has demonstrated that black women were an integral part of the civil rights movement of the 1960s, even though leadership roles were generally reserved for men. Collins has criticized black male leaders for not addressing issues relevant to black women, as distinct from the general issue of racial discrimination, until the 1980s. Today, black women have gained more leadership positions in groups like the Rainbow Coalition and are pressing for increased attention to the joint effect of sexism and racism on African American women.[139]

EDUCATION

During the post–Civil War Reconstruction period, black southerners gained their first access to schools, sponsored by either the federal government or private organizations. However, by 1900 all public schools in the southern states were legally segregated under an official "separate but equal" rule. The educational facilities for black students were grossly inferior, and little government money was spent on black children. In 1900, some southern counties spent ten times as much per capita for the education of white children as for that of black children.[140]

In spite of this relentless discrimination, African Americans pressed on toward their dream of a good education. By the early 1900s, a million and a half black children were enrolled in schools. The South had thirty-four black colleges. In the late nineteenth century the nationally known black leader Booker T. Washington advocated vocational education for southern black youth. College curricula focused on skills suitable for an agricultural economy, which, unfortunately, was declining. Other African American leaders, especially W. E. B. Du Bois, felt that Washington was too conservative on racial matters.[141] Although Washington was restricted by the limits of a racist system, he played a significant role in expanding schooling opportunities for southern black youth.

African Americans have continued to take advantage of educational opportunities. Median educational attainment for those twenty-five years old and over went from 5.7 years in 1940 to 9.8 years in 1970 to 12.4 in 1990.[142] The black–white differential narrowed significantly over this period. In 1940, whites on average had nearly three years more education than blacks. By the early 1990s the black–white differential was less than one year.[143] The educational attainment gap, however, has narrowed much more than the economic gap between blacks and whites.

Still, educational opportunities and attainments for blacks are not equal to those for whites. In the mid-1990s, only 73 percent of blacks over the age of twenty-four had completed high school, compared with 82 percent of whites; 13 percent of blacks had completed four years of college, compared with 23 percent of whites.[144]

The Desegregation Struggle

The movement toward school desegregation began in earnest in the 1930s with an NAACP legal attack. Lawsuits attacking discrimination in graduate schools were the first to spotlight the "separate-but-equal" doctrine for the racist sham it was. In the 1930s and 1940s, a series of federal court decisions forced the desegregation of the University of Missouri, University of Oklahoma, University of Maryland, and University of Texas law schools. Then in 1954, black parents won the most famous school decision of all, *Brown v. Board of Education of Topeka*. This decision forced the desegregation of Topeka schools and several other school systems and set in motion, albeit slow motion, government action to desegregate all school systems. In the South, this government action met massive resistance. White judges, fearing violent reactions by white southerners, allowed school desegregation to proceed at a snail's pace during the first decade after the *Brown* decision. Most white-dominated school systems ignored or circumvented the *Brown* precedent as long as they could, and most black children remained in segregated schools. Some whites set up private white schools or resorted to violence. In 1956, President Dwight Eisenhower was forced to federalize the Arkansas National Guard to protect the black children braving violent white mobs to desegregate a Little Rock high school.[145]

The 1960s and early 1970s brought widespread desegregation throughout the South and court orders to desegregate some northern school systems. Some such orders, for example, in Boston, resulted in violent white resistance. In *Swann v. Charlotte-Mecklenburg Board of Education* (1971), one of a series of court cases following *Brown* that expanded the attack on segregated schooling, the Supreme Court upheld the use of busing as a legal means of disestablishing a dual school system. In *Keyes* v. *Denver School District No. 1* (1973), the Court ruled that evidence of government-imposed segregation in part of a school district, such as selective attendance zones, is sufficient to prove segregation and to require desegregation. Segregated schools now included those created by the deliberate location of new schools to reinforce existing segregation patterns. The following year, however, the Supreme Court began to back off from the implications of school desegregation in a ruling that rejected the inclusion of suburban districts in central-city desegregation plans. In *Milliken* v. *Bradley* (1974), the Court overturned a lower-court order requiring the integration of the substantially black Detroit city school system with the surrounding white suburban school systems. Since then, few metropolitan-wide desegregation plans have cleared this Court hurdle. The *Milliken* decision slowed the pace of school desegregation significantly.[146]

White opposition to desegregation has long centered on the issue of busing, although school busing in fact dates back to the early 1900s.[147] School desegregation cannot be accomplished in many large cities without involving large-scale busing and the suburbs. In contrast, desegregation in smaller cities, those with populations of less than 200,000, usually involves much less extensive organizational change or busing. As an alternative to busing, many school boards could redraw gerrymandered districts or locate all new schools on the boundaries of segregated residential areas so as to maximize natural desegregation. In addition, the desegregation of a school's staff, extracurricular activities, or curriculum requires no busing.[148] African American leaders have long suggested that the lack of serious efforts toward desegregation in many school systems indicates much of the white debate over busing is calculated to obscure the real issue—white opposition to white and black children attending the same schools.

In its early years, school desegregation reduced the number of African American principals and teachers and thus had a negative impact on many black communities. Over several decades most desegregation occurred at white schools, where white teachers and principals predominate, rather than at black schools, where black teachers and principals were common. In such cases desegregation significantly reduced the number of black teachers with whom many black children come in contact.[149] Fewer black teachers has meant fewer role models for black children. A number of studies have also shown that black teachers tend to expect greater educational achievement from black pupils than white teachers do.[150]

The Current Public School Situation

Today, decades after the U.S. Supreme Court declared racially segregated public schools inherently unequal, there is ample evidence that *Brown* has not provided equal educational opportunity for most children of color. Federal judge Robert Carter, one of the NAACP's lawyers in the *Brown* case, has condemned the nation's "dismal progress" toward educational equality: "Thus far, for most black children the constitutional guarantee of equal education opportunity which *Brown* held was secured to them has been an arid abstraction, having no effect whatsoever on the bleak offerings black children are given in the deteriorating schools they attend."[151] Although a 1994 national poll found almost 90 percent of Americans supporting the ideal of opening schools to all racial groups, recent analyses of school desegregation have indicated that since the 1980s resegregation has occurred in many public schools.[152] This is in part the result of Reagan and Bush administration policies that opposed mandatory desegregation and supported voluntary desegregation and neighborhood schools. These administrations also cut back programs designed to aid black and other subordinate-group schoolchildren and supported tax deductions for parents who paid private-school tuition. Today, two-thirds of black students still go to schools where the majority of students are not white; one-third go to schools with enrollments that are less than 10 percent white.[153] The states with the highest proportion of intensely segregated schools are in the Northeast, where about half of black students attend schools that are 90 percent or more children of color. The most intensely segregated schools tend to be in central cities with fragmented school districts and no significant cross-district desegregation plans.[154]

Research studies have found that schools with the highest proportion of African American students also have the highest rates of poverty.[155] Because of the heavy reliance of public schools on local tax revenues, schools in poverty areas tend to be poorly funded and to have larger classes, outdated books and equipment, and generally inferior facilities.[156]

Social science research has revealed some important lessons about current patterns of school desegregation. In some cases school desegregation has encouraged housing desegregation. Diana Pearce has reported that cities with metropolitan-area school desegregation plans experienced much more rapid housing desegregation than cities without such plans. The extent of housing desegregation in cities of similar size and racial mix was directly related to the scope of their school desegregation programs. Cities with school desegregation plans covering only the central cities had less housing desegregation than cities that desegregated both central cities and suburban areas.[157]

Racial tracking and other forms of racial discrimination still persist within our school systems. A 1996 report by the community organization ACORN on New York City schools entitled *Secret Apartheid* found widespread racial steering.[158] Trained testers, posing as parents, were sent to twenty-eight elementary schools in half of New York City's thirty-two community school districts. Of the ninety-nine visits made by testers, fifty were made by whites and forty-nine by people of color. All but one of the visits were unannounced. The white parent-testers were able to speak with an educator, such as the principal or assistant principal, much more often than the black and Latino parent-testers. Whites were two-and-one-half times more likely to get a school tour than testers of color, and on the average whites were given much more information. School staff members were more likely to mention programs for gifted children to white testers than to the black and Latino testers. The report describes these actions as "institutional racism" that is likely rooted in conscious racial prejudices, malign neglect by public officials, and the "dysfunction that results when a vital public responsibility is managed by people whose racial, class, and cultural reality is totally different from that of the people whom they are supposed to serve."[159]

Desegregation today has many dimensions and consequences. For example, St. Louis is one of a handful of U.S. cities with a court-ordered desegregation plan bringing together poor inner-city children with those in the mostly white suburbs. By the desegregation plan's eleventh year (1994–1995), African American students made up at least 15 percent of the student population in all but two of sixteen suburban school districts. Drawing on interviews with 300 educators, parents, students, and lawyers, a recent evaluation study of the impact of St. Louis desegregation reported that many black students had achieved academic, and sometimes social, success in integrated suburban schools. Those who have succeeded in the suburban schools tend to have strong parental support or are especially gifted academically, athletically, or artistically. Although a small percentage were so intent on assimilation that they developed a "raceless persona," most "struggle[d] endlessly to maintain their self-esteem and to carry their cultural heritage with them to the other side of the color line so that whites might partake of it and eventually learn to value it."[160] However, each year about one in ten of the black students who transferred to the white schools found the social demands of white suburbia too great or the hostile attitudes of white teachers too intolerable and returned to their central-city neighborhood schools.[161]

According to the St. Louis researchers, a large proportion of the African American students among those who did not transfer to the suburban schools appeared to be "beaten down" by years of degradation, economic deprivation, and political powerlessness; they distrusted the white world and thus chose to remain in their neighborhood schools. However, some of them have also rejected the goal of integration, focusing like the returned students on their oppositional culture and solidarity within the black community.[162]

White hostility in desegregated schools has many negative effects on African American children. Indeed, since 1980 many local black leaders have shifted their emphasis away from comprehensive school desegregation plans to other educational objectives. For example, black groups in Atlanta, where the school population is predominantly black, settled a desegregation lawsuit without a racial-balance plan in exchange for complete desegregation of the school faculty and administration.[163] In addition, many black educators have become more concerned with the survival of black children, especially black males, than with desegregation. Educators in some cities with substantially black school enrollments, such as Atlanta and Washington, have developed a curriculum with more emphasis on the cultural heritage of African American children.

In a growing number of cities, including Milwaukee and Detroit, African American educators are creating special schools, or programs within public schools, for poor African American males. Spencer Holland, director of Morgan State University's Center for Educating African American Males, has articulated the philosophy behind African American–centered programs: "The problem I have with the old guard is that we can't use their tactics in the '90s. . . . Integration tactics don't matter to the lives of the children I deal with. We black people have to take care of these black children now."[164] This new thrust is a survival strategy for supporting black children and black community institutions in the face of continuing antiblack discrimination, which takes the form not only of individual discrimination but also of direct and indirect discrimination in educational institutions.

College Attendance and College Experiences

Since the 1950s African American students have gone to college in large numbers. Today, black young people have strong aspirations for college. In a 1994 poll, 96 percent of black youths aged 11 to 17 stated that their biggest hope or dream for their future was to go to college.[165] Yet in the early 1990s, the proportion of black students entering college immediately after high-school graduation was less than three-fourths that of white students.[166] In the mid-1990s, the proportion of African Americans between the ages of 25 and 34 who were college graduates (12.8 percent) was just over half that of whites in this age group (24.5 percent).[167]

For many decades, most black college students in the South were restricted to all-black colleges. Desegregation in the 1960s opened up many historically white colleges and universities for black students, and outreach programs encouraged their enrollment. By the 1970s, three-fourths of black college students nationwide were in predominantly white schools. The dream of a college education in a desegregated environment seemed to have come true. Still, many black students today attend historically black colleges, where the campus culture is usually more hospitable to black students than that of traditionally white schools. Significantly, the majority of black faculty members teach at historically black colleges.[168]

At predominantly white colleges, African American students face serious racial problems. Murty and Roebuck have noted that "Frequently black students find white universities to be hostile places where they are seen as 'special admits' and beneficiaries of affirmative action. Moreover, adjustment requires adherence to white cultural norms, thereby necessitating the abandonment of black cultural roots."[169] Black students establish their own social networks, in part because of their exclusion from white networks. Half the black students questioned in a University of Michigan study said they did not feel they were part of campus life. Many reported they were disenchanted with their college environments. Most black students come to white campuses having been victims of discrimination, and this does not disappear on the white campus. In the Michigan survey 85 percent of the students reported that they had experienced discrimination on campus, including comments by professors that "black students aren't very bright" and blatant acts such as "KKK" and "nigger" being painted on a house owned by a black organization.[170]

Research conducted by Joe Feagin in the 1990s at a major historically white university found a similar pattern of isolation and discrimination experienced by African American students. A questionnaire given to a random sample of three dozen juniors and seniors asked them to assess this statement: "Today the [State University] is a college campus where black students are generally welcomed and nurtured." Only two (6 percent) of the thirty-six agreed, while 89 percent strongly disagreed or tended to disagree and 6 percent answered, "not sure." One young black woman stated:

> Sometimes I'm like, "God, if I was white, I'd have the best time." . . . They get to have parties at frat houses; they don't have to pay for it. You know, they just have the best time. Everything is geared toward them. Their [campus] paper is geared toward them. Everybody agrees. . . . This university does cater to white students. The commercial strip near the university is for white people. You know, bars everywhere—all white boys in it, no black people. The frat row's white. No black Greeks, nothing. So they're coming from where they're coming from.[171]

A tragic aspect of the racial barriers at predominantly white colleges is that African American students identify these colleges not primarily with educational experiences to be savored but rather with an "agonizing struggle" with campus racism just to get a college degree.

RELIGION AND CULTURE

The first major stereotyping of Africans was in terms of what Europeans saw as their "savagery." The irony of militaristic, slave-trading, warring Europeans seeing Africans as "savage" was lost on white Europeans at the time and has been lost on most of their descendants. Significantly, the Africans imported into the colonies brought African religions with them. At first, slave owners feared that "Christianizing" the Africans would put notions of freedom into their heads—as though they did not already have the idea of freedom. Protestant missionaries were instructed, and laws were passed to make it clear, that conversion to Christianity did not bring freedom along with it. Actually, many slave owners encouraged white missionaries, particularly Baptists and Methodists, to convert African Americans so they could be better controlled.[172]

Conversion to Christian symbolism did not eradicate African religions and culture. African American religion mixed African and European elements, and the African values often prevailed over the European.[173] As some slaveholders had feared, the Afro-Christianity of the slaves sometimes became linked to protest. The view of God that many slaves held—for example, the emphasis on God's having led the Israelites out of slavery—was different from what slaveholders had hoped for. Hidden by Christian symbolism, slave spirituals often embodied a deeper yearning to be free. Regular religious meetings were part of Afro-Christianity, and some gatherings hatched conspiracies to revolt. Black slaves were often permitted to preach to gatherings, and some of these preachers became resistance leaders, including leaders of slave revolts. The freedom discourse African Americans developed in private was often different from the religious discourse they used in the presence of their white masters and oppressors.[174]

Because slaves and free blacks were generally excluded from white churches in the cities, they developed their own formal church organizations. In Philadelphia, Absalom Jones and Richard Allen, after being mistreated at a white Methodist church, established their own Free African Society in 1787. Later, Jones established the first Negro Episcopal church, and Allen played a role in the emergence of the African Methodist Episcopal church.[175]

The role of these churches in African American communities became especially important after the Civil War. Churches were mutual-aid societies, ministering to those facing sickness and death, and they functioned as centers for the pooling of economic and other resources. Education often came as religious education. New schools were established after the war, many under religious auspices. Black churches continued to function as community and schooling centers. With the migration to the cities during and after World War I, some African Americans shifted to a less otherworldly religious style. Urban social welfare and civil rights activity increasingly became part of black religious life. In addition, new urban religious groups became religious and political forces. One is the Nation of Islam mentioned earlier, a group that broke with the Christian background of African Americans. For decades, Nation of Islam leaders have pressed hard for a black-oriented theology suffused with black pride and a self-help philosophy. Militant Afrocentric leaders have arisen from this movement, including Malcolm X and, more recently, Louis Farrakhan.[176]

Today, Protestant churches still predominate among African Americans. They include a great diversity of groups, from the older Methodist and Baptist denominations to newer evangelical groups. Whatever its form, however, the black church is often, as a minister recently explained, "the hub of existence in the black community," a "holistic ministry," and a "social center."[177]

Religion and Protest Movements

Organizations protesting oppressive conditions have been rooted in African American religion from the beginning; religious gatherings and leaders have played a role in spreading protests against racism since the days of slavery. In the twentieth century, ministers have often been political leaders. The nonviolent civil disobedience movement that was important from the mid-1950s to the 1970s had significant religious underpinnings.[178] The prominent minister-leader Dr. Martin Luther King, Jr., who was raised in an intensely religious family with a record of fighting for civil rights, came naturally to his essentially religious view of the legitimacy of nonviolent protest as a way of winning concessions while at the same time healing the wounds of oppressed and oppressor. He led black citizens in effective protests, for which he earned a Nobel Peace Prize, and he died a hero whose example today inspires both black and white Americans.[179]

The effectiveness of churches in providing political leadership, as in mobilizing millions of formerly disenfranchised voters, is deeply rooted in African American culture. The call-and-response format of many black religious services, which allows the congregation to give the minister direct feedback on the sermon,

African American author and teacher Toni Morrison is a Nobel Prize winner.

has provided a context for response to calls to register to vote or to participate in other political activities in the civil rights speeches of leaders such as Dr. King or the Reverend Jesse Jackson. Black political leaders have harnessed the religious sentiments of an oppressed people to mobilize support for political action. Moreover, from the days of the slave spirituals to more recent blues, jazz, and gospel traditions, African American music and singing have reflected a strong element of protest against discrimination.[180]

RECENT BLACK IMMIGRANTS

In 1994, Colin Powell, a retired U.S. Army general and the son of Jamaican immigrants, was mentioned as a possible presidential candidate for the 1996 elections. For a time, General Powell, who had served as head of the Joint Chiefs of Staff in the early 1990s, was called by some "the most respected figure in American political life."[181] Powell is a representative of one of several different ethnic groups that today make up the broad group called African Americans.

Approximately 5 percent of the African American population in the 1990s—about 1.6 million people—is made up of immigrants from Africa and the Caribbean who have come since 1970.[182] The 1990 census reported more than 200,000 African-born individuals living in the United States, most arriving since 1980, with the largest concentrations in New York, California, Massachusetts, and Texas.[183] This is a highly educated population; 43 percent of those over twenty-four years old are college graduates. A higher percentage hold professional positions than one finds among whites. This group has a higher median family income and lower unemployment rate than other African Americans. In spite of their educational achievements, however, they are still less well-off economically than whites.[184]

The 1990 census also reported almost 1.1 million black Americans of Caribbean ancestry. (This does not include Latino groups such as Puerto Ricans). One-third have immigrated to the United States since 1980, and more than 60 percent live in New York or Florida.[185] Caribbean Americans include a number of different national-origin groups, including Martinicans, Guadeloupeans, Haitians, Trinidadians, and Jamaicans. Each group has its own history, language, and culture. Among these Caribbean Americans, Jamaicans are the largest group (39 percent) followed by Haitians (27 percent).[186]

Significantly, the members of each group usually do not identify themselves as "Caribbean Americans" but rather expect their particular culture and identity to be acknowledged and respected by other Americans. These immigrants sometimes view themselves as African Americans and sometimes as an ethnic group distinctive from native-born blacks within the general black group. Nonetheless, the Afro-Caribbean Americans have no choice in how they are viewed, as black Americans, by the dominant white group.[187]

In recent years, Haitian immigrants have received more public attention than other Caribbean newcomers. After winning independence from the French in 1804, Haiti became the first independent black republic in the Western Hemisphere. In order to support U.S. business interests on the island, the U.S. military occupied Haiti from 1915 to 1934, withdrawing only after a military dictator, Francois "Papa Doc" Duvalier, who was friendly to U.S. interests, had been installed. Under Duvalier's rule political repression in Haiti became severe.[188]

Since the 1970s, thousands of Haitians have sought political refuge in the United States. Sometimes, the immigrants have been victims of con artists who lured them to exchange their life savings for a boat ticket. Haitian immigrants, most of whom were fleeing a brutal dictatorship in desperation, were permitted to enter the United States until 1981. However, in marked contrast to the Cuban refugees fleeing political persecution between 1960 and 1994, who automatically qualified for permanent residence under U.S. anticommunist cold-war legislation and were provided with financial support from the U.S. government (see Chapter 10), Haitians received no financial support from the U.S. government but were left to cope on their own or with the assistance of private charities. Between 1981 and mid-1994, most Haitians were refused entry to the United States; the U.S. Coast Guard intercepted Haitian immigrants at sea and returned them to Haiti, where they have often faced persecution or death. This U.S. immigration policy drew harsh criticism from U.S. and international human rights organizations. One such group, Amnesty International, described Haitian prisons as torture and death traps. Beginning in 1981, those reaching the United States were held at several detention centers around the country; later, some Haitian detainees were moved to an army base in upper New York State, an area whose severe winters differ radically from the Haitian climate.[189]

The ouster in the fall of 1991 of Haiti's democratically elected president, Jean-Bertrand Aristide, by military leaders created another flight of Haitians to the United States. However, as an example to stop attempts to immigrate, the U.S. government repatriated 500 immigrants in late 1991. After a U.S. court ordered a halt to such repatriations, Haitian refugees were then taken to a tent city at the U.S. naval base in Cuba. A small percentage of these were granted permission to apply for political asylum but were given no guarantee their applications would be approved.[190] In May 1994, President Bill Clinton announced that the United States would no longer send any Haitian refugees home without a hearing.[191]

Following the U.N.- and U.S.-supported overthrow of Haiti's military government in late 1994, large numbers of the Haitian refugees opted to return to their native island. Aristide was restored to his presidency.[192]

The Economic and Educational Situations

As a group, Caribbean Americans are better off economically than African Americans as a group, although their situation is closer to that of other African Americans than to that of white Americans. The occupational distribution, income, and poverty status of Caribbean Americans vary significantly according to their immigrant status and length of residence in the United States. Consider their occupational status as displayed in the following table based on 1990 census data:[193]

	White Americans	All African Americans	Caribbean Americans
Managerial and professional	29%	18%	20%
Technical, sales, and clerical	33	29	30
Service	12	22	26
Farming, forestry, and fishing	2	1	1
Precision production	12	8	9
Operators, fabricators, laborers	13	21	13

Compared with African Americans taken as a group, Caribbean Americans are a bit more likely to hold white-collar jobs, somewhat more likely to hold service-sector jobs, and much less likely to hold other blue-collar jobs. However, within the Caribbean group, the second generation and those in the United States the longest hold a larger proportion of white-collar jobs than the others; for example, one-third of the recent arrivals hold service-sector jobs, and only 13 percent hold professional or managerial jobs.[194]

It is often the case that immigrants are willing to take lower-wage jobs and do less desirable work than native-born Americans of any group. In a study of native-born and immigrant black workers at a New York City worksite, Mary

Waters found that white managers preferred to hire black immigrants rather than native-born blacks for low-wage food-service jobs because the former were thought to be "more flexible" and "loyal." The black immigrants' tendency to separate the hierarchy of the U.S. workplace from U.S. society's more general racial hierarchy caused white managers to see them as "nicer to be around most of the time." Yet, the white managers at the worksite also reported that, compared with native-born African Americans, the Caribbean immigrants were "more likely to challenge racial ceilings on the job and institutional racism."[195]

In 1990, the median family income for Caribbean Americans was substantially higher than that of African Americans as a group but still well below that of whites. In addition, Caribbean American families were almost twice as likely to be in poverty as white families but only half as likely as other black families. The larger number of workers per family among Caribbean Americans accounted in part for their higher median family incomes compared with other black families.[196]

	White Americans	All African Americans	Caribbean Americans
Median family income	$37,628	$22,429	$31,493
Family poverty rate	7%	26.3%	13.7%

Within the Caribbean group, more recent arrivals have much lower family incomes and a much higher poverty rate. In 1990, Caribbean Americans who entered the United States before 1980 were much nearer the white group in both median family income ($35,901) and poverty rate (10.6 percent).[197] Elaine Sorensen and María Enchautegui report that between 1979 and 1989, a period of overall decline in real earnings, black immigrant men, who made up approximately 6 percent of the total black male labor force in 1989, experienced an 11 percent increase in real hourly wages, while native-born black men experienced an 8 percent drop.[198] The likely explanation for this is the larger proportion of skilled and college-educated workers among Caribbean immigrants, particularly those who arrived before 1980, compared with all African Americans. As the following data on persons over twenty-four years old show, Caribbean Americans have somewhat higher levels of education than African Americans as a group, but they are well below the educational attainment levels of white Americans as a group.[199]

	White Americans	All African Americans	Caribbean Americans
High school graduate or higher	79%	63%	67%
College graduate or higher	22%	11%	15%

In addition, within the Caribbean group members of the second generation have a higher educational attainment than do the immigrants, particularly the recent immigrants.[200]

Racial Experiences and Discrimination

The relatively recent Caribbean and African immigrants have had a different racial history than African Americans whose ancestors came as slaves. Most significantly, they usually have not endured legal segregation. They have come primarily from countries where black people are the majority and have a significant role in major social institutions, including politics, education, and the economy. In the Caribbean nations, many if not most of the police officers, top government officials, professionals, managers, and white-collar workers are of African ancestry. Most Caribbean immigrants have not grown up under white domination but only experience it when they immigrate to the United States.

Because they have lived in a black-run society, Caribbean Americans tend to question the matter of racial categorization. A Haitian perspective on racial matters is illustrated by a humorous story about "Papa Doc" Duvalier's reply to a journalist who asked him what percentage of the Haitian population was white:

> "Ninety-eight percent." The startled American journalist was sure he had either misheard or been misunderstood, and put his question again. Duvalier assured him that he had heard and understood the question perfectly well, and had given the correct answer. Struggling to make sense of this incredible piece of information, the American finally asked Duvalier: "How do you define white?" Duvalier answered the question with a question: "How do you define black in your country?" Receiving the explanation that in the United States anyone with any black blood was considered black, Duvalier nodded and said, "Well, that's the way we define white in my country."[201]

African Americans who have grown up in the United States are constantly dealing with discrimination and are routinely reminded of the social significance of their African origin. Yet in their home countries most Caribbean immigrants were not so constantly reminded of their racial identity. "In societies where the majority of people are black . . . there are many times and arenas in which it is possible to forget about one's race and to not be racially aware."[202] In addition, having no (or low) racial consciousness allows individuals to focus more on goal achievement rather than racial discrimination.

Haitian American sociologist Yanick St. Jean has noted that many Caribbean immigrants continue to see themselves as culturally different, as "foreigners" in the United States regardless of their length of residence. For that reason they feel, usually erroneously, that white Americans are more likely to accept them than they are to accept other African Americans and that racial discrimination is mainly directed at the black "others" and only indirectly at them.[203] Indeed, in interviews with Caribbean American workers, Waters found that many shared a few white stereotypes of native-born African Americans.[204]

Although they have a strong black or African identity, Caribbean and African immigrants sometimes distance their identity from that of native-born African Americans. One reason for this is that there has been some friction between the immigrants and the native-born African Americans, many of whom expect the immigrants to reject their island identities, languages, and heroes and to speak without a detectable foreign accent. Immigrants' distancing may be a form of protection against this cultural devaluation and questioning. St. Jean has noted that for Caribbean and African immigrants "the level of resistance to assimilation into African American groups is extremely high. As one social scientist correctly said: 'They want to be black; they are proud of being black; they just don't want to be black in the United States.'. . . The notion of blackness in this country is so different from their own. In the Caribbean, blackness is strength. In the U.S. it is not. Assimilating means moving from a positive image to a less than positive one. Somehow it is the end of a cherished life, and people fight for their lives."[205]

Initially, many Caribbean immigrants think that native-born African Americans exaggerate the level of racial discrimination they face in the United States. After some time in this country, however, they often change their view, because they too experience the racial exclusion and other forms of discrimination faced by other African Americans. When asked in a recent interview by the authors, "How do you personally feel being black in a mostly white society?" one Caribbean American professional, Marc R. (a pseudonym), stated:

> I usually interact with American whites from a distance. Most are acquaintances, not friends. Coworkers do not know who I am, what I really want. I am not invited to their informal gatherings. Occasional exchanges in hallways are only superficial. I feel I am expected to live in an intellectual ghetto, a very special and preset place which I call "colonization of thinking." From all appearances, I am expected to fail. I am denied even the basic respect due to me as a human being. In sum, the more dues I pay to this society the less respected I feel. Some things I would never admit to. They are just too demeaning.

> I feel my differences are neither acknowledged nor respected. I am a Haitian American. I cannot and will not discard my Haitian origins. But in this society everyone must move in the same direction. It simplifies. It unifies. And to the extent that it also inferiorizes, the denial is a perfect tool to keep "others," and blacks in particular, within the boundaries of American cultural definitions. If and when my differences are acknowledged, AIDS, poverty, and religion are quick to surface as if these were synonymous with Haitian.

Why is there an association in the minds of many white Americans between AIDS, "voodoo" religion, and Haitian American immigrants? Many Americans have believed, quite erroneously, that AIDS originated in Haiti or that Haitians have extremely high rates of AIDS. Indeed, officials in the U.S. Food and Drug Administration accepted this stereotyping to the point of banning (in 1990) all blood donations by Haitians, an action that provoked major civil rights protests. The evidence contradicts the notion that Haitians have a uniquely high AIDS rate. One report found that the new AIDS case rate in San Francisco was *ten times* that of Haiti and that the rates in New York and in Boston were also significantly higher than the rate in Haiti. Yet people in these cities were not generally banned from donating blood. Medical anthropologist Paul Farmer has examined this matter in detail and concluded that white stereotyping and discrimination that targets Haitian Americans is deeply rooted in racist images of "savage and exotic" African peoples.[206]

Haitians are not the only ones who face such stereotyping. Other Caribbean Americans face a devaluing of their culture. Indeed, many white Americans hold prejudices not only in regard to African Americans but also in regard to their African and Caribbean cultures and backgrounds. For many white Americans Caribbean Americans are just another African American group to be targeted with racist images and stereotypes.

ASSIMILATION FOR AFRICAN AMERICANS?

Assimilation Theories

Social theorist Milton Gordon has argued that the theory of assimilation is applicable to both ethnic and racial groups. He applies his scheme to black Americans, whom he sees as assimilated at the cultural level in terms of language and Protestant religion, with some black–white cultural differences remaining because of "lower-class subculture." Beyond acculturation Gordon sees little integration to the "core" (white Anglo-Protestant) society at the structural level, little intermarriage, little erosion of prejudice or discrimination, and no demise of group identity.[207]

As we noted in Chapter 2, Gordon writes optimistically about the eventual assimilation of African Americans, a trend he sees in the growing black middle class. For that reason, Gordon and other assimilationist scholars sometimes call for an end to remedial programs such as affirmative action. Optimistic assimilation-oriented analysts have often evaluated black progress in terms of cultural, economic, and social integration. Sociologist Talcott Parsons argued that racial and ethnic inclusion is basic to U.S. society and that this process encompasses black Americans.[208]

Some social scientists and other analysts have argued that there has been a major collapse in traditional racial discrimination in recent decades, that assimilation of black Americans into the core economy and society is well underway. What these assimilationist scholars view as dramatic economic progress for the black middle class is cited as proof of ongoing black assimilation. In their view the major problem is the troubled black "underclass," whose difficulties are not primarily questions of current discrimination. While recognizing discrimination as a barrier for black Americans, some assimilationists have in effect blamed black Americans for their slower economic and social mobility, particularly in the last few decades. In a famous report in the 1960s, Daniel P. Moynihan viewed black families headed by women as a serious retardant to progress. These arguments have been resurrected in the 1980s and 1990s, and some scholars have again pointed to a subculture of poverty among low-income black families as a major barrier to

progress. The theme of certain white scholars and mass media analysts sometimes boils down to "Why can't black people be like us?" suggesting that black
individuals, like the white immigrant groups before them, should be able to
assimilate, to move up gradually through the various levels of the economy, society, and polity—if they will only work hard and address their own subcultural
and value problems.[209]

Power–Conflict Perspectives: The Continuing Significance of Racism

Power–conflict analysts reject the optimistic assimilationist view of African
American mobility and assimilation, which from their perspective amounts to a
denial of the pervasiveness and persistence of racial barriers. The current condition
of black Americans is much more rigidly hemmed in and resistant to change than
that of white ethnic groups because of the extreme character of most Africans' incorporation into and oppression within this country. Once the system of racial subordination was established, those whites in the superior position, and their descendants, have continued to monopolize the lion's share of inherited economic and
political resources. Since the 1960s, legal segregation in employment, education, and
housing has been replaced by informal, but still extensive, racial discrimination.

In his theory of internal colonialism Robert Blauner argues that major differences exist between African Americans and white ethnic groups in regard to
social and economic oppression.[210] Africans were enslaved and brought across the
Atlantic Ocean in chains. Incorporated into the economy against their will, they
and their descendants provided hard labor at the lowest occupational levels, first
as slaves, later as tenant farmers, then as urban laborers. Even with the northward
migration their lesser economic and social position and status relative to whites
were unaltered. African Americans became a subordinate part of the growing economic system. This point reveals a major problem in traditional assimilation theory: Historically, incorporation into the society and economy has occurred most
often at the lower economic levels, those offering only modest chances of upward
mobility. African slaves suffered attempts to destroy their cultures and were often
forced to give up many of their traditional ways as part of their incorporation into
slavery. The Protestant religion and the English language were forced upon them.
Africans were forced to give up control of their own bodies, which became the
property of whites; miscegenation was frequently forced on them by white
slaveholders who raped female slaves. In contrast with the assimilation view,
power–conflict theorists emphasize the *forced* acculturation and secondary-
structural assimilation of African Americans.

Power–conflict perspectives take a different view of the lack of full assimilation of black Americans into the economy and society in recent decades. They
assign little importance to a subculture of poverty, but instead emphasize persisting discrimination. As we noted previously, when white ethnic groups such as the
Irish began arriving in U.S. cities, they did not gain socioeconomic mobility solely on the basis of fair competition. In the process of coming to see themselves as
"white," they sometimes displaced and discriminated against free blacks, who

were usually relegated to the lowest-paying jobs. By the mid-nineteenth century, white immigrant workers were crowding black workers out of numerous occupations. Black workers were forbidden by law to enter such crafts as blacksmithing and mechanics, and Irish and German immigrants began to fill jobs once held by black workers.[211]

After the Civil War, most African American families in the South remained where they were and became poor tenant farmers and sharecroppers, for the new industrial machine mostly drew workers from southern and eastern Europe, not from the South. Discrimination prevented African Americans' structural assimilation into the economy on an equal-status basis. After 1910, with the trek northward, black southerners moved into low-level jobs in urban industries; not until World War II, did a large proportion of black workers find better-paying jobs in industry. By the end of that war a decline in demand for black labor had begun, and with it a growing urban unemployment problem that persists to this day. Black migrants found that the opportunity awaiting them in northern cities was much paler than the promised-land image that had drawn them. Discrimination severely limited opportunities in jobs and housing. Since World War II, the demand for black labor in cities has been reduced not only by racial discrimination but also by corporate automation and capital flight to the suburbs and low-wage areas overseas.[212]

Irish, Italian, and other nineteenth- and twentieth-century European immigrants benefited from urban political organizations, which played an important role in providing them jobs and thus in facilitating their upward mobility in the first decades of the twentieth century. When African American workers came into northern cities during World War II, the period of great public construction there had ended. In most cities, black communities were never able to benefit as much as white ethnic groups from the local political patronage system.[213]

In Chapter 2 we noted the development of a renewed Afrocentric perspective that builds on the pan-African theory of Du Bois. This Afrocentric approach emphasizes the role of European imperialism in dispersing Africans around the globe and in damaging and reshaping African cultures. In assessing U.S. society, this approach has examined closely the continuing Eurocentric bias in the dominant culture. The Euro-American worldview includes the myth of white cultural superiority and a celebration of individualism and materialism over cooperative and spiritual values. Afrocentrists believe that because of the negative impact the Euro-American view has on African Americans, the latter must direct their efforts to recreate cultural alternatives informed by their African heritage; they must develop a reinvigorated oppositional culture.[214]

Perhaps the most important emphasis of power–conflict analysts is the fact that discrimination is not dead or dying. White racism handicaps African Americans today in all major institutional arenas, from public accommodations to employment and business, to schooling, and to housing. Power–conflict theorists are usually pessimistic about further incorporation of African Americans into these critical institutional arenas absent a major change in the racist attitudes and discriminatory actions of the white majority.

SUMMARY

The social, economic, and political progress of African Americans was severely restricted by slavery and subsequent legal segregation. Even at the time of the first great waves of white European immigrants in the early 1900s, African Americans, many of whom were "old" (tenth-generation) Americans, were still sharply segregated and oppressed. Jim Crow frustrated the lives of freed slaves and several generations of their descendants. Later on, a northward trek reflected protests against southern oppression, protests "by the feet." Other types of black protest against subordination, nonviolent and violent, have punctuated the long course of black–white relations. The segregation period was followed by a long epoch, still in process, of widespread and informal racial discrimination.

As we move into the twenty-first century, most African Americans live in cities, North and South. The migration of African Americans has changed; more are now moving to the South than are leaving the region. Yet wherever they live, they face continuing racial discrimination and economic inequality. The Civil Rights Acts of 1964, 1965, 1968, and 1991 have made many formal acts of discrimination illegal, but they have not ended the millions of cases of blatant, subtle, and covert discrimination in business, jobs, housing, education, and public accommodations that African Americans face each year in the United States. Government antidiscrimination programs are much too modest and understaffed to remedy this widespread discrimination. The specter of "slavery unwilling to die" can be seen today: Informal barriers to voting continue in the South; most black children still attend de facto segregated schools; most black families live in segregated residential areas; most black workers in all income classes face informal discrimination by banks, real estate agents, landlords, and homeowners; many black defendants are tried by juries in which black citizens are underrepresented if not absent; and most black workers face subtle or blatant discrimination in the workplace.

The impact of racial discrimination remains painful, stifling, and cumulative. Reflecting on the costs of racism, a successful black entrepreneur has commented on what it is like to be black today in a predominantly white society:

> *One step from suicide!* What I'm saying is—the psychological warfare games that we have to play everyday just to survive. We have to be one way in our communities and one way in the [white] workplace or in the business sector. We can never be ourselves all around. I think that may be a given for all people, but [for] us particularly, it's really a mental health problem. It's a wonder we haven't all gone out and killed somebody or killed ourselves.[215]

CHAPTER 9

Mexican Americans

In recent years, the term *Hispanic* has been widely used to designate persons of Mexican, Puerto Rican, Dominican, Cuban, and Central and South American heritage. *Hispanic* is an English-language word derived from *Hispania*, the Roman name for Spain. This term emphasizes the Spanish heritage of these groups while ignoring the other (for example, Native American and African) components. *Latino*, an alternative collective designation, which recognizes the Latin American origins of these groups, is a Spanish-language word and therefore more acceptable to many Spanish-speaking Americans. As Edward Múrguía has pointed out, these collective terms suggest different attitudes toward incorporation into or separation from the dominant Anglo culture. In this view, *Hispanic* suggests assimilation, or aspirations toward assimilation. *Latino* suggests cultural pluralism and cultural maintenance, including the continued use of the Spanish language.[1]

On a national level and in large cities such as Chicago and San Francisco, whose Latino populations contain more than one national–origin group, a collective Latino identity may contribute to a broader sense of community. It may help the subgroups to achieve the collective strength to address common problems of education, bilingualism, jobs, and discrimination. Smaller national-origin groups, especially new entrants from Central and South America, may also derive advantages from a collective Latino identity. Still, combining these diverse national–origin groups into one category masks their diversity behind an implied homogeneity. As we will see in this and the following chapter, Latino groups differ on many economic and political indicators; combining data on individual groups to describe all Latinos does not accurately describe any one group. The various groups differ in their histories and in certain cultural forms—for example, in food, religious shrines, and music. Geographic distinctiveness also remains: Mexican Americans are concentrated in the Southwest, mainland Puerto Ricans in the Northeast, Cuban Americans in the Southeast. In many areas, those in one Latino group have little contact with members of other groups. Some observers forecast the development of a "dual ethnicity" based primarily on national origin and secondarily on a collective identity in the context of broader Latino issues.[2]

Latinos are currently the fastest-growing segment of the U.S. population, numbering about 29 million in the late 1990s, nearly 11 percent of the U.S. population. Recent census reports indicate that about the year 2005 the number of Latino Americans will exceed the number of African Americans. Demographers estimate that in about 2050 Latinos will comprise one-fourth of the U.S. population.[3] The pride Latinos feel in their heritages can be seen in their desire to maintain the Spanish language as well as other cultural patterns. The growing numbers of Latinos provide support for both goals. Spanish-language media; Latino religious, charitable, and social organizations; and the commercial availability of Latino products and services have all increased in recent years.

Latinos generally maintain strong communities. In a nationwide survey conducted by Strategy Research Corporation, nine out of ten Latino adults identified themselves as "very Latino," and more than eight in ten projected that they would be "very Latino" ten years in the future. Eight in ten reported that their close friends were "very Latino," and seven in ten identified their neighborhoods as "very Latino." Most were more comfortable speaking Spanish than English and spent more time watching and listening to the Spanish mass media than the English mass media. Based on language use and behavioral, attitudinal, and aspirational measures, the survey ranked the assimilation level of these respondents relative to the dominant European American culture. (We use the terms *whites* and *European Americans* interchangeably in this chapter and elsewhere in this book. Both terms refer to "non-Hispanic whites," as the U.S. census terms them.) Half of all Latino adults were classified as relatively unassimilated; only one in ten was ranked highly assimilated and four in ten partially assimilated. Although Latino youth were more than three times as likely to be highly assimilated to the dominant culture as their adult counterparts, fully two-thirds of them identified themselves as "very Latino" and projected that they would remain so ten years in the future.[4]

In this and the following chapter we examine the three largest Latino groups in the United States: Mexican Americans, mainland Puerto Ricans, and Cuban Americans—groups with diverse histories and heritages as well as different experiences in U.S. society. In the mid-1990s, Mexican Americans made up nearly two-thirds of the U.S. Latino population, mainland Puerto Ricans almost 11 percent, and Cuban Americans almost 5 percent.[5] Other Latino groups, such as Central Americans, many of whom are refugees from political turmoil and persecution, made up the rest. This chapter focuses on Mexican Americans.

Among white Americans, one stereotypical view of Mexicans is of sleepy farmers under big sombreros, "wetbacks," mustachioed banditos, a diet of tortillas, and folk Catholicism. Such popular images are often supplemented by negative treatments of Mexicans and Mexican Americans in schoolbooks that distort the history of the Southwest, as in the myths that glorify freedom-loving, heroic white Texans confronting a backward Mexican people. In addition, both popular and scholarly accounts of life in the Southwest frequently omit significant references to Mexican American contributions to the development of the United States. (*Southwest* refers here to California, Arizona, New Mexico, Colorado, and Texas.)

THE CONQUEST PERIOD, 1500–1853

Early European expansion touched not only the Atlantic coast of North America but also the West. Beginning in the early 1500s, Spaniards conquered, colonized, and sought to Catholicize the native population in what is now Mexico and the southwestern United States and to concentrate it in agricultural and mining communities for economic exploitation. Since few women migrated to the Americas, sexual liaisons, often forced, between Spanish men and indigenous women were common. Teresa Amott and Julie Matthaei classify forced sexual relations as a key aspect of Spanish domination along with colonization and coerced conversion to Christianity. Offspring of these unions, sometimes called *mestizos* ("mixed peoples"), came to outnumber the Spanish colonizers and to occupy a middle social position below them but above Native Americans, persons of mixed Native American and African heritage, and African slaves. Mexican legend considers the Native American mistress of the Spanish conqueror Cortés to be the mother of *La Raza*, the Mexican people.[6] After centuries of economic exploitation, Mexico finally won its independence from Spain in 1821.

Before the 1830s, Mexicans had established numerous communities in what is now the southwestern United States. Several thousand people with a Mexican way of life and a self-sufficient economy lived on Mexican land grants along the Rio Grande in what would become southern Texas. An estimated four thousand Mexican settlers lived in the Texas area in 1821. Soon thousands of European American settlers (some with African slaves) from the United States flooded the area, and in a few years the new settlers outnumbered the indigenous Mexican population.[7]

The Texas Revolt: Myth and Reality

Both the new U.S. immigrants and the Mexican population in the Texas province strongly supported a decentralized system of Mexican government. By 1830, some Mexican residents there had joined the new white settlers to protest actions by the central government. Mexican government actions, including freeing slaves and placing restrictions on U.S. immigration, angered many white settlers. The causes of the Texas revolt are complex, including not only government policies in Mexico City but also the racist attitudes of the white immigrants toward Mexicans, the resentment of white slaveholders toward Mexican antislavery laws, and the growing number of U.S. immigrants coming in illegally from the North. Until recently, few analysts have been inclined to see the 1836 Texas revolt as blatant territorial aggression by U.S. citizens against another sovereign nation, which in the end it was, but rather have excused the behavior of the Texans and blamed an oppressive Mexican government for the conflict.[8]

Myths about the revolt that praise the Texans' heroism persist. Perhaps the most widely known is the legend of the Alamo, which portrays some 180 principled native-born Texans courageously fighting thousands of Mexican troops. Actually, most of the men at the Alamo mission, in the center of what is now the city of San Antonio, were newcomers, not native Texans. Many, such as James Bowie and Davy Crockett, were adventurers, not men of principle defending their homes. In addition, the Alamo was one of the best-fortified sites in the West; its defenders had twice as many cannons, much better rifles, and much better training in riflery than the poorly equipped Mexican recruits. According to one myth, all the defenders died fighting heroically. In fact, several surrendered. After a series of further skirmishes General Sam Houston managed a surprise attack that destroyed much of the Mexican army in the area.[9]

The Texas rebellion was a case of U.S. settlers going beyond an existing boundary and intentionally trying to incorporate new territory into the United States. The annexation of Texas in 1845 precipitated a war with Mexico. Provocative U.S. troop actions in a disputed boundary area generated a Mexican attack, which was followed by a declaration of war by the United States. The poorly equipped Mexican army lost. Some historians have questioned the view of this war as honorable, citing evidence that Mexico fell victim to a U.S. conspiracy to seize territory by force. U.S. soldiers and Texas Rangers murdered civilians and committed other atrocities in Mexico. In 1848, the Mexican government was forced to cede the Southwest area for $15 million. Mexican residents had the choice of remaining there or moving south; most stayed, assured on paper of protection of their legal rights and their language and cultural heritage by Article IX of the Treaty of Guadalupe Hidalgo.[10]

By the 1850s, the population of Texas had grown to 200,000, most of whom were white immigrants. Gradually these new settlers, particularly ranchers and farmers, used legal and illegal means to take much of the land still owned by the existing occupants. Eventually most of the original Mexican landowners lost their lands.

California and New Mexico

In the early 1800s the 7,500 non–Native American residents of California lived on Mexican-run ranches and missions. After gold was discovered in 1849, however, huge numbers of whites poured into California, taking over lands and political control from the Mexicans. The means of takeover ranged from lynching to armed theft to legal action.[11]

The fifty thousand Mexicans in New Mexico had long maintained their own traditions. Their well-established villages—Sante Fe dates from 1598—provided the organization to withstand some of the European American onslaught. Most of the land was owned by the richest 2 percent of the population; the rest was held by the poor. Many landholders did fairly well under U.S. rule, continuing to play an important role in the region's commerce and politics. Nonetheless, most eventually suffered great losses of private and communal lands.[12]

By the mid-nineteenth century, the U.S. system of private land ownership was replacing the Mexican system of communal lands. In spite of treaty promises, old land grants were ignored, and the land was treated as U.S. government land. Everywhere Mexican landholders lost most of their land. The invasion of the Southwest was not a heroic period in which U.S. settlers liberated unused land. It was in fact a period of imperialistic expansion and the colonization of a communal people who had long resided in the area.[13]

THE IMMIGRATION PERIOD

Estimates of the number of Mexicans within the new territorial limits of the expanding United States range up to 118,000 for the 1850s. In the decades to follow, millions of Mexican migrants entered the United States, pushed by political upheavals and economic conditions in Mexico and pulled by expanding opportunities and the demand for unskilled labor in fields and factories north of the border. Many had family ties to what was once old Mexico.

Peak immigration periods have been 1910–1930, 1942–1954, and 1965 to the present. Immigrants can be divided into five major categories: (1) those with official visas ("legals"); (2) undocumented immigrants ("illegals"); (3) braceros (seasonal farm workers on contract); (4) commuters (those with official visas who live in Mexico but work in the United States); and (5) "border crossers" (those with short-term permits, many of whom become domestics).[14] The exclusion of Asian immigrants by federal action (see Chapter 11) and the pull of World War I era industrialization sharply decreased the number of U.S. laborers available for agricultural work. Consequently, Mexican workers were drawn into the Southwest by the demand for labor. Under pressure from U.S. employers federal authorities waived immigration restrictions, allowing more than seventy thousand Mexican workers to enter the United States legally during World War I.[15]

Mexican migration increased in the 1920s, with 500,000 workers and their families entering the United States. Improved canning and shipping technologies opened new markets for agricultural produce. U.S. business interests usually opposed restrictions on Mexican immigration. Agencies in cities such as San Antonio specialized in recruiting Mexican workers for agriculture as well as for jobs in urban industries–in the North as well as the Southwest. Programs that issued temporary work-permits were periodically expanded. The Immigration Act of 1924, which barred most southern and eastern Europeans, did not exclude Mexicans. Mexico had become a main source of cheap labor for the Southwest and the Midwest. Yet many white nativists, including prominent academics at leading universities, strongly objected to the growing Mexican population in the United States, which they feared would create a "race problem" that was greater than "the negro [sic] problem of the South" and threaten white racial and cultural "purity" in the Southwest.[16]

The Border Patrol of the Immigration and Naturalization Service, created in the 1920s, has played a major role in the lives of Mexicans and Mexican

Americans. In 1929, legislation made illegal entry into the United States a felony. Although given the formal authority to keep out all undocumented workers, the Border Patrol has tried to regulate the flow of undocumented Mexican workers, allowing enough to come in to meet the work demand of agricultural and other business interests. In times of economic depression and recession, however, the Border Patrol has conducted exclusion and deportation campaigns; in better times, exclusion has been less rigorous.[17]

During the Great Depression of the 1930s, federal enforcement of literacy tests and local government hostility greatly reduced the flow of immigrants. In addition, considerable pressure was put on Mexicans already here, whether citizens or not, to leave the country. Some left voluntarily. Many workers, however, were forcibly deported in massive border campaigns; thousands, including U.S. citizens, were expelled in organized caravans by social service agencies eager to reduce their expenditures.[18]

Braceros and Undocumented Workers

World War II changed the U.S. attitude toward Mexican workers. A 1942 Emergency Farm Labor (*Bracero*) agreement between the United States and Mexico once again provided Mexican workers for U.S. agriculture. Seasonal workers were given temporary permits to work in the fields. In two decades, nearly 5 million braceros were brought in. Not surprisingly, this government program stimulated the migration of undocumented workers, and many employers became eager for these low-wage workers. Approximately 3.3 million documented migrants entered the United States between 1821 and 1991; since the 1920s, somewhere between 6 and 9 million undocumented migrants have also entered. Many of these were temporary immigrants who returned to Mexico.[19]

The entry into the United States of low-wage and undocumented Mexican labor has periodically met considerable public opposition, particularly since World War II. Union officials have called for restrictions that will protect jobs of citizens. Growing concern among nativist whites led to the inclusion of restrictions on legal Mexican immigration in the 1965 Immigration Act, which set an annual limit of 120,000 persons from the Western Hemisphere. This limit was later lowered to only 20,000 per year for Mexican immigrants.[20] Attempts to deal with undocumented immigrants have often focused on intensified Border Patrol policing and legislation concerning immigration screening.

The U.S. economy depends heavily on undocumented immigrants. Luis Alberto Urrea, who grew up on the Texas-Mexico border, has explained well how hard working and essential the undocumented workers really are: "They come here to make their best efforts, to work—to work *hard*—to better themselves, to enjoy a better world, to get educated, and to prosper. It's the American dream writ large. They're just writing it in Spanish." He continues that these immigrant workers are the "financial backbone of Dole, Green Giant, McDonald's, Stouffers, Burger King, the Octopus car wash chain, Del Monte, Chicken of the Sea, Heinz, Hunt's, Rosarito, Campbell's *m-m-m good*, Wendy's, Taco Bell, Lean Cuisine, Dinty

Migrant Mexican *braceros* harvest a tomato crop in a Texas field in 1959.

Moore, Hormel, midnight shifts, front lawn raking, pool scrubbing, gas station back rooms, blue-jean stitching, TV assembly, athletic-shoe sole gluing" and many other such jobs.[21] Indeed, Mexican workers and U.S. employers in the southern areas of the southwestern states all are linked together in one international labor market.[22]

The Mexican government has made little effort to stop undocumented migration, which relieves severe poverty and population pressures on that side of the border. High rates of inflation, several devaluations of the Mexican peso, and widespread unemployment in Mexico have produced a substantial flow of workers into the United States in recent years, although the number of workers entering illegally is far less than press accounts suggest. For example, a 1994 Urban Institute study reported that virtually all of the 1 million Mexican border-crossers apprehended by the U.S. Immigration and Naturalization Service (INS) annually "are temporary labor migrants who are caught more than once by the INS and who do not intend to live in the United States in any case. . . . A large reverse flow into Mexico goes virtually unnoticed and unreported."[23]

The best estimate for the total number of undocumented immigrants living in the United States in 1994 was about 3.5 million, just under one-third of whom were from Mexico. The *majority* were from Europe, Asia, and other Latin American countries. In the early 1990s, an estimated 200,000 to 300,000 undocumented immigrants entered the United States each year. Leo Chávez's study of undocumented Mexican men and women in southern California, which spanned most of the 1980s, found that most were between 19 and 29 years of age, had little education and few work skills, and were single or had temporarily left their family in Mexico. Most had friends or relatives in the United States through whom they found employment; those without contacts were particularly susceptible to work-related abuses. The low-paid, often impermanent jobs available to undocumented immigrants offer very limited economic opportunities. The principal reason for their migration is economic, and many have faced life-threatening circumstances to get to the United States. They work hard and expect to rely on their own resources.[24] Contrary to some stereotypes, undocumented workers actually have low rates of use of welfare, food stamps, and unemployment compensation programs. Typically, they pay out more in income and other taxes than they receive in government benefits. Most recent studies report that undocumented immigrant workers have either no impact on, or in some cases actually increase, the employment rate of native-born workers.[25] The major exception to this general finding is in large urban areas where there are many unemployed workers of color. For the lowest wage job categories in these areas, native-born workers are sometimes displaced, at least in part, by the undocumented workers.

The 1986 Immigration Act and Undocumented Immigrants

Growing concern over the presence of undocumented immigrants in the United States led to passage of the 1986 Immigration Reform and Control Act (IRCA). Its provisions authorized: (1) legalization of undocumented immigrants resident continuously since 1982; (2) sanctions for employers who hire undocumented aliens; (3) reimbursement of governments for the added costs of legalization; (4) screening of welfare applicants for migration status; and (5) special programs to bring in agricultural laborers.[26] Just over 3 million undocumented immigrants applied for legalization by the January 30, 1989, deadline; 1.7 million applications were ultimately accepted for adjustment to legal residence, representing approximately two-thirds of the estimated eligible population. Mexican immigrants made up three-fourths of those granted IRCA legalization.[27]

Latino analysts feared that IRCA would encourage employers to discriminate against anyone who looked like an immigrant. Indeed, a 1989 federal government study found that numerous firms were discriminating against U.S. citizens in the hiring process in order to insure that they were not hiring undocumented workers. More recent research has found a similar response by many employers and "an IRCA-induced decline in job opportunities" and a lowering of total earnings for "unauthorized-looking natives."[28] A 1990 Immigration Act was passed to correct some of these problems in the 1986 law. Nonetheless, employer discrimination against "immigrant-looking" native-born workers, particularly Latino Americans continues to occur.

Congressional and public debates over this regulatory legislation revived anti-immigration arguments of the past. Many native-born residents worried about the character and values of the new immigrants. Native-born whites were concerned that the United States could not absorb so many immigrants, even though the ratio of immigrants to the native-born population was much higher in earlier decades than in the late twentieth century. For instance, in 1910 the foreign-born constituted 14.6 percent of the U.S. population; in the mid-1990s, the figure was only 8 percent, giving the United States a smaller percentage of foreign-born than many other nations, including England, Germany, Switzerland, Australia, and Canada.[29] Given its long history of successful absorption of immigrants, it is unlikely that the United States will be overwhelmed by these new immigrants. Implicit in many discussions of the new immigrants seems to be a concern that most of them are from Latin America and Asia—that is, that they are not white.

Anti-immigrant stereotypes and political action saw a resurgence in the 1990s. Mostly white citizen groups forced Proposition 187 onto the California ballot, and it passed with a substantial majority in 1994, although three-fourths of Latino voters opposed it. Proposition 187 severely restricts access of undocumented immigrants to public services, including schools and hospitals, and requires public employees to report undocumented immigrants. Immigrant-bashing has been common among white political candidates during some recent election campaigns in California, and a number of anti-immigrant groups aggressively supported the proposition.

In 1996, the U.S. Congress passed yet another immigration act, the Illegal Immigration Reform and Immigrant Responsibility Act (IIRIRA), which focused on cutting down the flow of undocumented immigrants. This law along with certain welfare-reduction legislation established regulations that restrict legal immigration as well. IIRIRA increased the number of INS border control agents as well as other law enforcement operations and imposed an income requirement for families wishing to sponsor immigrant relatives. Sponsoring families must have an income well above the poverty line and must be financially responsible for immigrant relatives they sponsor. These new requirements discriminate against prospective sponsoring families among Latinos because Latino family incomes are, on the average, lower than those of white families. About two-thirds of new legal immigrants now come into the United States under the sponsorship of families.[30] The 1996 legislation was motivated in part by a concern that immigrants are likely to become dependent on public welfare programs. Yet recent research on Latino immigrants contradicts these often stereotyped notions. Generally, Latino immigrants are employed at higher levels and use welfare programs less often than other major racial-ethnic groups in the United States. In addition, most immigrant children are in two-parent families at about the same proportion as for white families.[31]

Population and Location

Official census estimates of the Mexican-origin population in the United States show an increase from 1.3 million in 1930 to 14.6 million in 1993.[32] In the late 1990s, most Mexican Americans are native-born.[33] More than 90 percent now live in urban areas, especially in the southwestern states. Today, however, many are moving from the Southwest to other regions of the country in a search for better economic opportunities.[34]

STEREOTYPES

Early Images

European Americans confronted social class, cultural, and lifestyle differences when they interacted with the Mexican residents of the Southwest. As a result whites came to hold stereotypes about the alleged laziness, backwardness, and poverty they attributed to the Mexican "race." The white slaveholders who came to the Southwest already had a well-developed racial ideology rationalizing the subordination of African Americans; for them it was easy to stigmatize the generally dark-skinned Mexican Americans as intellectually and culturally inferior.

"Greaser" is one contemptuous term applied to Mexican Americans since the Mexican War, perhaps deriving from the activities of Mexicans who greased wagon axles. Alleged Mexican cowardice became a stereotype after the defeats suffered by the Mexican army in the 1830s and 1840s. When cultural and value differences emerged, whites were quick to define the Mexican approaches as "backward." In the 1850s, John Monroe reported to Washington that the people of New Mexico "are thoroughly debased and totally incapable of self-government, and there is no latent quality about them that can ever make them respectable."[35] Ironically, the knowledge of ranching, agriculture, and mining of these Mexicans had laid the foundation for successful economic development of the Southwest.

The heavy Mexican immigration after 1900 triggered more verbal and physical attacks on Mexicans by European Americans. Mexican labor camps were raided by the Ku Klux Klan and other white supremacist groups and the workers beaten. The 1911 federal Dillingham Commission on immigration argued that Mexicans were undesirable. A "Brown Scare" hysteria developed in California between 1913 and 1918 amid fears that the Mexican Revolution would spread to the United States. Mexican immigrants were characterized by whites as a menace to local communities' health and morals, and public pressure for their deportation mounted.[36] In the 1920s, a prominent white member of Congress stereotyped Mexicans as a mixture of Spanish and "low-grade Indians" plus some slave "blood"; in his view they were a mongrelized people. In 1928 an "expert" witness appearing before the House Immigration Committee testified to the racial inferiority of Mexicans, branding the "Mexican race" a threat to the "white race."[37] Nativist scholars and popular writers alike expressed fear of "race mongrelization" as a result of contact with Mexicans. In 1925, a Princeton economics professor spoke fearfully of the future elimination of Anglo-Saxons through interbreeding in "favor of the progeny of Mexican peons who will continue to afflict us with an embarrassing race problem."[38]

Much white commentary since the 1920s has stereotyped the Mexican American male as a crime-oriented villain with a knife in his pocket. For example, a report by a white lieutenant in the Los Angeles Sheriff's Department after the 1943 Zoot Suit Riots (discussed in the following section) alleged that the Mexicans' desire to spill blood was an "inborn characteristic," a view endorsed by his police chief. Much racist stereotyping linked alleged social or cultural traits to genetic inferiority: "The Mexican was 'lawless' and 'violent' because he had Indian blood; he was 'shiftless' and 'improvident' because that was his nature."[39]

Since the 1920s, the results of so-called IQ testing (see Chapter 8) have been used to argue for the intellectual and racial inferiority of Mexican Americans. As in the cases of Jewish, Italian, and African Americans, from time to time a few white commentators have argued on the basis of paper-and-pencil tests that Mexican American children are of lower intelligence.[40] However, some scholars have made a strong case for the total inappropriateness of this argument based on the simple fact that most IQ tests have been administered in English to children whose primary language is Spanish.[41] Nativists have often based their opposition to Mexican immigration on the allegedly low intelligence of Mexicans.

Modern Stereotypes

George Murphy, former senator from California, once argued that Mexicans were "ideal for 'stoop' labor—after all, they are built close to the ground."[42] A California judge, ruling against a Mexican American youngster in an incest case, invoked a racist criminality image with genocidal overtones when he asserted in court:

> Mexican people, after 13 years of age, think it is perfectly all right to go out and act like an animal. We ought to send you out of the country—send you back to Mexico. . . . You are lower than animals and haven't the right to live in organized society—just miserable, lousy, rotten people. Maybe Hitler was right. The animals in our society probably ought to be destroyed because they have no right to live among human beings.[43]

Numerous whites, including government officials, have stereotyped Mexican Americans as passive and fatalistic. Such a stereotype has been reinforced in some social science studies that have viewed Mexican American culture as one of passivity, lack of protest, fatalism, *machismo*, and extreme family orientation. Anthropologists such as Oscar Lewis and William Madsen have portrayed what they thought was a folk culture of fatalism and familism in the villages of Mexico, a view that has been extended to Mexican American life.[44] Other social scientists have criticized these traditional views of Mexicans and Mexican Americans as distortions and pointed out the errors in assuming that life in villages studied decades ago was the same as life in Mexican American communities today. Moreover, the diversity of Mexican American culture from southern Texas to New Mexico to California has been overlooked. Researcher Lea Ybarra has noted that male domination in Mexican American families varies with class and educational background, just as it does among other racial and ethnic groups.[45]

Latino Americans provide a challenge to social science definitions of racial group and ethnic group, as their history and realities provide evidence to view them as both racial and ethnic groups. Certainly, outsiders have seen Mexican Americans in both racial and cultural (ethnic) terms. Some have accented their cultural characteristics as the major indicators of their distinctiveness. Others have seen them as an "inferior race," accenting dark skins and Indian or other physical features thought to be typical of the group. Research in Texas has suggested one likely result of this racial stereotyping over time: Darker-skinned Mexican Americans do not do as well in occupational and income attainments as lighter-skinned Mexican Americans, whose physical characteristics are generally more acceptable to white Americans.[46]

Over the last few decades some of the harshest stereotypes have begun to fade from public view, although negative attitudes are still expressed by whites in social surveys. In a 1982 nationwide poll, 34 percent of the respondents felt that Mexican immigrants had been bad for the United States; only 25 percent felt Mexican immigrants had been good for the country.[47] A recent survey by the National Conference of Christians and Jews regarding interethnic attitudes found that a majority of whites believed that Latinos "tend to have bigger families than they are able to support." One-fifth of whites felt Latinos lacked "ambition and the drive to succeed."[48] In addition, white attitudes tend to be optimistic in regard to the integration of Latinos into the larger society. A majority of whites in the aforementioned survey thought Latinos had equal access to a quality education, decent housing, and skilled labor jobs.

For several decades, the mass media, both through advertising and entertainment programming, have been major perpetuators of stereotypes. "Frito Bandito" ads, once used by the Frito Lay Corporation, portrayed Mexicans as criminals. One deodorant company's ads pictured a grubby-looking Mexican bandit with the caption: "If it works for him, it will work for you." Some tequila advertisements in college and other newspapers have recently used representations of a supposedly lazy peon in a large sombrero sleeping on a burro, a border-town prostitute, and a thieving bandito.[49] Mexicans have also been cast as banditos by the U.S. entertainment media. Movies of Pancho Villa's raids in Texas, to take one example, have emphasized this criminal image and ignored the relationship of the guerrilla raids to prior exploitation by U.S. settlers. In prior decades, TV programs often presented Latino women as flirting senoritas or prostitutes and Latino men as "lazy, fat, happy, thieving, immoral creatures who make excellent sidekicks for white heroes."[50]

As a result of protests from Mexican American communities and leaders, the most extreme stereotypical depictions of Mexican Americans in advertising and the media have decreased over the past several years. For example, in 1991 protests forced a taco restaurant chain in Houston to discontinue a TV ad that featured a stereotypical Mexican American figure. But problems remain. A recent study of the portrayal of Latinos in television programming, commissioned by the National Council of La Raza, reported that today's shows either ignore Latinos or present them disproportionately as criminals. Media scholar Charles Ramirez Burke commented: "The way we are treated in movies represents a way that we are marginalized in the larger society. In that way it is a very accurate portrayal."[51] The study found that Latinos made up only 1 percent of TV characters during the 1992–1993 season, down from 3 percent in the late 1950s. Sixteen percent of Latino characters in network series programs, such as *Baywatch* and *Acapulco H.E.A.T.*, committed crimes, compared with only 4 percent of white characters; 45 percent of Latino characters in reality-based shows, such as *COPS* and *America's Most Wanted*, were criminals, compared with 10 percent of white characters on these shows.[52] Robert Lichter, coauthor of the La Raza study, noted: "Basically these shows consist of whites arresting minorities."[53] The report also praised a few TV shows, such as *NYPD Blue*, for a more positive portrayal of Latinos.

Mock Spanish

In recent research anthropologist Jane Hill has examined the widespread use of a mocking type of Spanish by otherwise monolingual (in English) whites in the Southwest and across the nation. This Mock Spanish includes made-up terms such as "no problemo," "el cheapo," "watcho your backo," and "hasty banana," as well as the seemingly humorous use of phrases such as "numero uno," "the big enchilada," and "no way, José." On the surface these terms may seem light-hearted, but they have deeper meanings, including "a highly negative image of the Spanish language, its speakers, and the culture and institutions associated with them."[54] Mock Spanish, which is common in gift shops, in board rooms, and at country-club gatherings, is created and perpetuated primarily by middle- and upper-income, college-educated whites who create greeting-card texts, coffee-cup slogans, Saturday morning children's cartoons, video games, and political cartoons. Hill cites the example of a Mock Spanish greeting card with the term "Fleas Navidad," which is a pun on the Spanish Christmas greeting *Feliz Navidad*. Scenes in movies like *Terminator 2* use Spanish terms such as "adios" and "hasta la vista, baby" in an insulting way not common among native Spanish speakers. Anglo Americans may first learn this mocking Spanish in school yards and from the mass media. In a society in which openly racist talk is frowned upon, Hill suggests, this Mock Spanish is used to perpetuate negative stereotypes and images of Mexicans and Mexican Americans: "Through this process, such people are endowed with gross sexual appetites, political corruption, laziness, disorders of language, and mental incapacity."[55] This is done even though the use of Mock Spanish appears to show an appreciation for Spanish language and culture.

VIOLENT CONFLICT

The Early Period

Coercion was a fundamental factor in the establishment of white domination in the Southwest. Mexican land and agricultural development were taken over by deception, theft, and force. The competition for land led to a new system of inequality. Both elite and rank-and-file Mexicans became subordinate to the invaders.

The Mexicans resisted, beginning with the taking of Mexican lands in the 1830s and 1840s. Throughout history folk ballads have sung the praises of "bandits" who have been social rebels unwilling to bear quietly the burdens imposed on their people. Typically their acts are regarded as crimes by those in the dominant group, but *not* by people in the subordinated group. Such rebels have been protected and praised by the common people; in some cases they have become legends.[56]

Among the heroes in Mexican legends are Juan Cortina and Pancho Villa. Cortina was typed as an outlaw and cattle thief by white Americans, but he became a Robin Hood figure to many Mexicans. He was certainly more than a thief, for he fought against the oppression of poor Mexicans in the Texas borderlands. In a series of guerrilla raids along the border, his followers clashed with the local militia and the oppressive Texas Rangers. In the 1850s and 1860s, Cortina fought the injustices of the white intruders, issuing formal statements of grievances detailing the biases in the U.S. legal system and land theft by white settlers. Colonel Robert E. Lee was sent to put down Cortina's rebellions but succeeded only in limiting his guerilla activities. Later, between 1910 and 1925, numerous clashes occurred along the Texas border from El Paso to Brownsville in which hundreds of Mexicans and whites were killed.[57]

Lynching and public whipping became ways of controlling Mexicans and Mexican Americans; numerous lynchings of Mexicans were recorded in the nineteenth century. Much of the lawlessness by whites against Mexicans in the Southwest had an official or semiofficial status. Law enforcement officers such as the Texas Rangers terrorized Mexican Americans. The image of the Texas Rangers has been sugarcoated in exaggerated stories of heroism. Americo Paredes has demonstrated that the myth of the heroic Rangers covers up the oppressiveness of a police force used by the dominant group to exploit the Mexican American population. White ranchers and farmers exploited their Mexican workers with the aid of the Texas Rangers.[58]

More Attacks by Whites

Later decades in the twentieth century also saw open conflict. The so-called Zoot Suit riots in the summer of 1943 in Los Angeles began with attacks by white sailors on Mexican American youths, particularly those dressed in baggy attire called "zoot suits." Groups of whites roamed Los Angeles beating up the young Mexican American zoot-suiters. Mexican American groups sometimes organized retaliatory attacks on the sailors. Why did these attacks occur? The local media exaggerated Mexican American crime. Police harassment increased, sometimes to the point of brutality. A few biased but well-publicized court trials involving Mexican American youths stirred up local white prejudices. The unusual dress of these youths became a focus of much media attention. One study found that in the three years leading up to the riots there was a sharp decline in *The Los Angeles Times*'s use of the term *Mexican* and a corresponding increase in an unfavorable use of *zoot suit* in connection with Mexican Americans. So intense was the paranoia during the rioting that the white Los Angeles City Council seriously discussed making the wearing of zoot suits a criminal offense.[59]

Protests since the 1960s

During the 1960s and 1970s, three dozen Mexican American protest-oriented rebellions took place in southwestern cities. Young Mexican Americans, including groups such as the Brown Berets, took to the streets to fight back against harassing police actions they saw as oppressive. Among the most important group actions were the East Los Angeles protests. In August 1970, police attacked demonstrators at the end of a National Chicano Moratorium on the Vietnam War march in which twenty thousand Mexican Americans took part. (The term *Chicano* was preferred to *Mexican American* by activists in the 1960s and 1970s. By the late 1970s activists were debating its use, and today it is used alongside the term *Mexican American* by many activists and researchers.) Police claimed that some deputies had been attacked by Mexican American demonstrators during the march. Four hundred were arrested; dozens were injured; two dozen police cars were damaged. Another violent protest along the route of a Mexican Independence Day parade resulted in one hundred injuries and sixty-eight arrests.[60]

Throughout the Southwest police forces, which included few if any Mexican Americans, were used, sometimes illegally, to end legal strikes and protests by Mexican American workers. Some cases have resulted in deaths to innocent civilians. Between 1965 and 1969, the U.S. Justice Department received 256 complaints of police malpractice from persons with Spanish surnames; in the late 1960s, the American Civil Liberties Union received 174 such complaints in California alone. From the 1960s to the 1990s, the common practice of preventive police patrolling in Mexican American communities, with its "stop and frisk" and "arrest on suspicion" tactics, has periodically led to unfavorable police contacts for Mexican American men. Harassment of this type intensifies negative attitudes toward the police. A recent poll found that two-thirds of Latinos in Los Angeles reported that incidents of police brutality were common in their city; 35 percent of this group said that racist attitudes were very common among law enforcement officers. At public hearings in 1991, an independent citizens' commission investigating the Los Angeles Police Department heard testimony from Mexican Americans that the department "acted like an army of occupation" treating them like the "enemy." Later that year, following the fatal shooting of a Mexican American youth, leaders from a large number of Mexican American organizations called for an independent citizens' commission to investigate the Los Angeles County Sheriff's Department as well. Witnesses said the nineteen-year-old victim had yelled at officers who had struck his friend at a neighborhood birthday celebration. This was one of several controversial shootings involving white police officers in the 1990s.[61]

These police brutality incidents were part of the buildup to the spring 1992 riot—many called it a rebellion—in south central Los Angeles in which many Latinos joined African American residents in protest against racism, police brutality (see Chapter 8), and oppressive living conditions in the city. The majority of those arrested for protesting and looting were Latino residents of Los Angeles. Police brutality incidents have continued to make news in California. In 1996, Riverside County (California) sheriff's deputies were video-taped clubbing a Mexican woman and man, both undocumented immigrants, with batons in the process of arresting them. In this case, one of the deputies was fired, and the immigrants were eventually awarded a monetary settlement for the beating.[62]

In the mid-1990s, widespread anti-immigrant sentiment and the introduction of Proposition 187 in California did more to organize Latinos than anything since the Latino movements of the 1960s. Mexican Americans responded to the new nativism with school walkouts and protests.[63] A large 1994 demonstration in Los Angeles against Proposition 187 illustrated the broad-based community support for Mexican American political concerns. In October 1996, some thirty thousand Latinos, including many Mexican Americans, demonstrated in Washington, DC to protest restrictions on immigrants. These demonstrators also called for an increased minimum wage, better educational programs, an end to discrimination against Latinos, and an increase in Latino voter turnout.[64] While the march was relatively small by Washington standards, it did mark what is likely to be the first of many demonstrations across the nation as the Latino population continues to grow and flex its political muscle against anti-Latino legislation and discrimination.

THE ECONOMY

We have previously discussed the incorporation of Mexicans into the U.S. economy, first by violent conquest and later by the takeover of their lands. An estimated 2 million acres of private lands and 1.7 million acres of communal lands were lost between 1854 and 1930 in New Mexico alone.[65] Across the Southwest, those Mexican Americans who lost their lands often became landless laborers, as did later immigrants. In the 1850s, one-third of Mexican Americans in the rural labor force in south Texas were ranch and farm owners, one-third were skilled laborers or professionals, and one-third were manual laborers. By 1900, the proportion of ranch and farm owners had dropped to 16 percent, while the proportion of manual laborers—many working for large white ranches and farms—climbed to two-thirds. A similar shift took place in the cities: A predominantly skilled labor force had become a predominantly unskilled labor force.[66]

Increasingly, Mexican workers found their opportunities limited by overt, sometimes violent, discrimination. For example, in the 1850s two thousand white miners attacked Mexicans in Sonora, killing dozens and destroying a community. A Foreign Miners Act in California placed a license tax on "foreigners" to force

Mexican miners out. By the 1880s, many Mexican Americans were laborers working in the expansion of railroads. Mexican Americans were the original *vaqueros* (cowboys) on ranches across the Southwest, and large numbers became agricultural workers in this region. Working conditions in agricultural "stoop" labor were so severe and pay so low that few competed with Mexicans and Mexican Americans for these jobs before the Great Depression. Mexican American women were concentrated in agriculture, domestic service, and manufacturing, particularly in the garment industry and in canneries. Regardless of the job, Mexican American men and women generally earned less than whites and were usually assigned the more physically demanding tasks.[67]

Persisting Job Discrimination

Institutionalized discrimination has been a major problem. For decades agricultural firms, oil companies, mining companies, and other industries paid different rates for "whites" and "nonwhites," the latter including Mexicans and Mexican Americans. Wages could be kept low by Anglo employers because of the constant availability of undocumented workers. Many unions also have a record of discrimination against Mexican Americans. In the 1920s and 1930s, the California Federation of Labor worked for their exclusion from labor organizations. Numerous industrial unions excluded Mexican Americans from membership. Attempts to create farm labor unions date back several decades, but they were not successful until the 1960s.[68]

In 1930, Mexican Americans were still heavily employed in low-wage manual labor. The 1930 census revealed that out of nearly 3 million Mexican American residents, only 5,400 were in clerical positions. During the Great Depression, the fact that many poor Mexican Americans were on government relief led to increasing white hostility. A number of local government welfare agencies began a program of forced repatriation to Mexico. Between one-third and one-half million persons of Mexican origin, both U.S. citizens and noncitizens, had been sent back to Mexico by the mid-1930s.[69]

The 1940s saw some improvement in the employment situation, but discriminatory and other barriers kept most Mexican Americans in low-wage positions. In 1943, President Roosevelt's belated antidiscrimination order and the increasingly tight labor supply temporarily opened up some jobs at decent wages to Mexican Americans, but virtually none, however qualified, moved up into skilled or supervisory positions.[70] Poorly paid jobs and housing discrimination restricted most Mexican Americans to living in segregated urban *barrios*, which were often concentrations of inferior or deteriorating housing. Restrictive covenants in property deeds often excluded Mexican Americans from better housing areas.[71]

In the 1950s and 1960s, many Mexican Americans occupied secondary-labor-market positions as farm workers, including migrant workers, urban laborers, or service workers, earned wages that were far below those of whites and had high rates of disabling work injuries.[72] Some lived in labor camps with very inadequate housing and sanitation facilities. Here is one description of the life of a farm worker's family:

> I was never a happy child; in fact I never felt that I was a child since I had to work from an early age. . . . In 1950 my father, Gustavo, bought a little one-room shack behind his mother-in-law's house, and here my parents and eight children lived. Dad's economic situation at the time was very bad and since he worked as a farm laborer he was only paid 60 to 70 cents an hour, hardly enough to feed eight kids much less clothe them and provide for medical attention.[73]

Other Mexican Americans worked in food-processing plants and other industries in the southwest, many of which were brought to this low-wage area by European American capitalists to increase business profits. For example, a large garment industry developed in this region to take advantage of unemployment in the female labor force. Beginning in 1965 the United States and other countries began building labor-intensive transborder manufacturing plants, called *maquiladoras,* in the northern border region of Mexico to take advantage of low-wage labor and weak environmental and worker-safety standards there. In the early 1990s, almost 1,800 U.S.–owned maquiladoras employed nearly 500,000 people in furniture, electronics, textile, food-processing, metal-refining, and other industries. Wages in the maquiladoras are far lower than in the United States; employers save an average of $16,000 per worker per year compared with U.S. wages. Worker turnover is as high as 400 percent in some border plants. Large numbers of Mexican workers live in cardboard shacks without water, heat, electricity, or sanitation facilities. Some workers report that they work in the maquiladoras just long enough to earn money to migrate to the United States.[74]

Many employers in the Sunbelt and the Midwest have sought undocumented workers because they will work for very low wages and can be exploited more easily than U.S. workers. If they protest oppressive working conditions, an employer can turn them in to immigration authorities. Employers in some service industries rely on undocumented workers and have found ways to circumvent the 1986 immigration law that prohibits hiring them.[75]

In the late 1990s, several investigative reporters have found Mexican immigrants working under slavery-like conditions. One New York report found deaf immigrants being forced to sell trinkets for very low wages and to live in extremely crowded and dirty conditions. The relatively few exploited immigrant workers who come to public attention are only part of a very large group of immigrant workers forced to work under extreme employment conditions. For example, in the United States many restaurant workers toil for very long (for example, fourteen-hour) shifts at wages below the legal minimum. Similarly, many farm workers and domestic workers work very long hours for less than the minimum wage. Laws prohibiting such working arrangements are poorly enforced.[76]

Employment testing has documented continuing discrimination in U.S. cities. When matching pairs of whites and equally or better qualified Latinos applied for the same job, one-third of the Latino job hunters in Chicago and 29 percent of those in San Diego encountered discrimination.[77] In a similar study conducted in Washington, DC, in 1992, one in five of the Latino applicants encountered discrimination. Although discrimination was found in all job categories, it was more likely for white-collar, customer-contact jobs than for blue-collar jobs and more likely for jobs requiring less education than for those requiring a college degree. Discrimination occurred twice as often against Latino men as against Latino women, but it was as common among companies claiming to be "Equal Employment Opportunity" employers as among those who made no such claim.[78]

Language discrimination in the workplace is a chronic problem. In the 1990s, the Equal Employment Opportunity Commission (EEOC) has reported an increase in the number of complaints received against U.S. employers who bar Spanish-speaking employees from speaking their native language in both job-related and private conversations while at work. An attorney for San Francisco's Employment Law Center has noted that English-only rules are common. Many legal scholars feel that such practices constitute national–origin discrimination and thus violate Title VII of the 1964 Civil Rights Act. The EEOC's regulations state that an English-only rule is presumed to be discriminatory unless the employer can show a strong business necessity for the rule.[79]

A major U.S. Supreme Court decision on this issue is *Garcia v. Gloor* (1981),[80] which upheld an employer's right to fire employees for speaking Spanish. Hector Garcia, a Mexican American employee of a lumber company, was fired for answering a fellow Mexican American employee's question in Spanish. The Court reasoned that Title VII of the 1964 Civil Rights Act did not equate national origin with primary language and thus that language discrimination was permissible. In a more recent case (1988), the U.S. Court of Appeals for the Ninth Circuit came to the opposite conclusion after evaluating a similar English-only rule: "The cultural identity of certain minority groups is tied to the use of their primary tongue."[81] Referring to EEOC regulations, the court stated that "English-only rules . . . can 'create an atmosphere of inferiority, isolation, and intimidation' [and] can readily mask an intent to discriminate on the basis of national origin."[82] This case was appealed to the U.S. Supreme Court, but the parties reached a settlement before the Court considered the case.[83] In 1991, a federal district judge in California ruled that an English-only requirement for employees in a meat-packing plant was discriminatory. Fluency in English had not been a requirement when the employees were hired.[84]

Unemployment, Poverty, and Income

Unemployment rates for Mexican Americans have been high for decades. In 1993, the unemployment rate for Mexican Americans was 11.7 percent, almost twice the rate for whites (6.1 percent). In addition, Mexican American workers were more highly concentrated in low-wage job categories than were European American workers:[85] (Census data treat some Latinos as white and present both a "white" category and a "non-Latino white" category. Data labeled "white American" here represent the latter census category and do not include Latinos.)

	Men		Women	
	White American	Mexican American	White American	Mexican American
Managerial and professional specialty	29.2%	8.7%	30.9%	13.6%
Technical, sales, and administrative support	21.7	13.8	43.9	40.7
Precision production, craft, and repair	18.7	20.5	1.7	2.8
Operators, fabricators, and laborers	17.8	29.9	6.6	15.2
Service occupations	8.8	15.2	16.0	24.9
Farming, forestry, and fishing	3.7	11.9	0.9	2.8
	99.9%	100.0%	100.0%	100.0%

Notice that Mexican American men are concentrated in the operative, laborer, production, and service worker categories. Mexican American women are located primarily in sales, clerical (typists), service (maids), and operative categories.

Although there is a growing Mexican American middle class, many working families remain below the poverty line. Mexican American incomes have been consistently low compared with those of white Americans. Researchers Edward Telles and Edward Múrguía examined income differences among Mexican American men based on physical appearance. Although intragroup differences in income were not as great as the income gap between Mexican Americans and white Americans, dark and "Native American–looking" Mexican Americans were found to earn substantially less than their lighter, more "European-looking" counterparts. Most of this earning differential could not be accounted for by variations in employee qualifications but was found to be attributable to discrimination by employers in U.S. labor markets.[86]

The following table compares 1992 family income levels and poverty rates for mainland U.S. Latinos of Mexican, Puerto Rican, and Cuban origin with those of the European-origin population:[87]

	Puerto Rican Origin	Mexican Origin	Cuban Origin	European Origin
Median family income	$20,301	$23,714	$31,015	$40,420
Families with incomes of $50,000 or more	14.6%	14.9%	27.0%	37.5%
Percentage of families below poverty level	32.5%	26.4%	15.4%	7.3%
Percentage of children less than 18 years old below poverty line	52.1%	39.5%	22.3%	13.2%

Notice that on family income and poverty measures, mainland Puerto Ricans ranked lowest among the three Latino groups, followed by Mexican Americans. Cuban Americans were closer to the European American population on poverty measures than they were to Mexican Americans or mainland Puerto Ricans.

In 1992, the median income for Mexican-origin families was only 59 percent of that of European-origin families. The median income for Mexican American men ($13,622) was less than 55 percent of that of European American men ($24,994); the median income for Mexican American women ($10,098) was 71 percent of that of European American women ($14,241) but only 40 percent of that of European American men.[88] One must also keep in mind that Mexican American families have more workers than European American families.

In 1993, Mexican American families were almost four times as likely to be in poverty as white families, and almost 40 percent of all Mexican American children below eighteen years of age were living below the poverty line.[89] In 1996, the U.S. Bureau of the Census issued data indicating that U.S. median household income had finally increased for the first time since 1989. During the same period, however, median household income for Latinos decreased by 5 percent. The poverty rate dropped for the nation in 1995 but did not decrease for Latinos.[90]

A recent study in southern California found that, contrary to what one might expect given affirmative action programs, economic conditions have become worse for Mexican American workers over the last three decades. Between 1959 and 1989, the median income of Mexican American men declined from 81 percent of that of white men to only 61 percent. (The declining pattern was true for African American workers as well.) Discrimination and lower educational attainments were cited as major reasons for the widening income gap.[91]

Is There a Latino Underclass?

As we saw in Chapter 8, the concept of a troubled *underclass*—characterized by long-term unemployment, multigenerational poverty, high violent-crime rates, a severe school dropout problem, teenage pregnancy, and long-term drug use—is pervasive in some analyses of African Americans. Many prominent social scientists, media analysts, and politicians have accepted the underclass conception as an accurate explanation for major racial and ethnic problems in U.S. cities. However, the scholarly and journalistic consensus on the underclass is profoundly conservative and often amounts to a modern version of the old notion of an "undeserving poor." Much discussion of communities populated by so-called underclass Americans emphasizes little that is positive, constructing a portrait full of errors, misconceptions, and omissions.

The recent book *In the Barrios* was the first to take an in-depth look at poverty issues for urban Mexican and other Latino Americans. Most previous discussion of the central city poor had focused on African Americans. The case studies reported in this volume demonstrate that underclass theory is of little use in analyzing the diverse Latino communities. Assessing Latino populations in Los Angeles, Tucson, Albuquerque, Laredo, Houston, Chicago, Miami, and New York, these scholars examine the communities' oppositional cultures, institutional strengths, viability, and humanity—as well as their urban problems.[92] Even in the face of substantial poverty and political and economic discrimination, the communities reveal very strong family and community support structures, Latino organizations, and enclave economies. Avelardo Valdez points out that the social and economic conditions in Laredo, along with its border location, facilitate illegal drug trafficking and use and associated illicit activities, yet the area's strong Latino extended families and residential stability have created "a strong sense of community structure and identification."[93] Carlos Velez-Ibanez describes strong extended households, a commitment to homeownership, and strong political action to preserve community viability among South Tucson's impoverished Mexican Americans.[94] Several case studies in this book demonstrate how small local businesses and off-the-books enterprises such as street vending promote the economic vitality of Latino communities. Indeed, recent reports from the census bureau indicate that the number of Latino-owned businesses increased significantly between 1987 and 1992, from about 490,000 to nearly 863,000.[95]

The flow of immigrants into a number of these Latino communities has also promoted economic viability by buttressing the local enclave economy and maintaining a demand for businesses providing Latino goods and services. Writing about Houston, Nestor Rodríguez demonstrates how the "concentration of the poor" that underclass theorists emphasize as negative can be positive for poor Mexican American communities. The residential concentration of Mexican immigrants in Houston has stimulated the development of an enclave economy, reinforced job and housing networks, and provided a supportive cultural setting.[96] Joan Moore and James Diego Vigil discuss Mexican American communities in Los Angeles and find a complex portrait: widespread poverty, continuing immigration, and strained social institutions together with a strong enclave economy, many extended families, growing political power, and vital religious organizations.[97]

Contrary to the conventional underclass theory, these researchers find no one pattern in the responses of Latino families and individuals to poverty conditions. The character and shape of poverty varies somewhat from community to community, but each has used its own oppositional culture and its own social, economic, and religious resources to work out survival strategies. While many of the characteristics associated with the conventional underclass portrait can be found in Latino communities, such conditions do not fundamentally *define* the sociocultural character and core realities of these communities. Important formal and informal organizations buttress Mexican American and other Latino neighborhoods. The core of these communities remains extended family and other social networks, as well as strong Latino cultural frameworks; these are reinforced by religious organizations and, often but not always, other important community organizations.

These Latino communities have provided a basis for enclave economies (see Chapter 2). In southwestern cities many Mexican immigrants have shown their entrepreneurial spirit in a range of merchant and small business activities. For example, the number of licensed Latino enterprises in Los Angeles grew sevenfold in the decade prior to 1993, while the population only doubled. In addition, three of the most common names among home buyers in California in recent years have been Latino.[98] Such evidence strongly suggests that large numbers of Mexican Americans are putting down roots in U.S. soil and are developing strong and lasting communities.

POLITICS

Mexican American involvement in politics has historically been limited by discrimination. Before 1910, some Mexican Americans did hold office in territorial and state legislatures; usually handpicked by whites, they served in the governments of California, Colorado, and New Mexico. There were no strong political organizations for Mexicans immigrating in the decades just after 1900, as there were in northern cities for other groups of immigrants.[99]

White ranchers and those who controlled railroads, mining interests, land companies, and other large enterprises usually dominated local and state politics in the Southwest. Until recently, these interests made sure that Mexican American voting strength was kept low. Methods of discrimination varied from state to state, but common devices used to reduce voting included the poll tax, the all-white primary, and threats of violence. Between 1910 and the 1940s, few Mexican Americans voted, often because of discrimination or fear of Anglo retaliation. Over subsequent decades voting strength was expanded by legal victories in the form of the Twenty-fourth Amendment, which banned the poll tax, and a California court case knocking down an English-only literacy requirement for voting.

Still, in some areas gerrymandering of voting districts has continued to dilute Mexican American voting strength and thus to prevent the election of Mexican American political candidates. Some lawsuits, for example *Garza* v. *County of Los Angeles* (1990)[100] and *Williams* v. *City of Dallas* (1990),[101] have challenged the intentional fragmentation of the Latino voting population and the discriminatory effects of at-large city council seats. The lawsuits have forced some white-controlled governments to create single member districts with Latino voting majorities, and these new districts have elected Latino political officials.

Voter registration and voter turnout among Mexican Americans have risen substantially over the last several years. For example, Latino (mostly Mexican American) voter participation in California in 1994 increased 45 percent over that of 1990. Compared with the size of the Mexican American population, however, the number of Mexican Americans who vote appears small. For Mexican Americans the issue of voting is complicated by the low median age (23.5 years compared with 33 years for the general population and 38.9 years for Cuban Americans)[102] of the population as well as by the large proportion who are legal permanent residents who must become naturalized citizens to qualify to vote. In the mid-1990s, more than two-thirds of Latinos in California were either too young to vote or were not U.S. citizens. Many of the state's 3.2 million legal permanent residents who are eligible to become naturalized have not made this choice because of strong ties to their homeland.[103]

Growing Political Representation

World War II brought hundreds of thousands of Mexican American workers into wartime industries and the armed forces. With this movement came an uphill fight to expand political participation. Numerous examples of slowly expanding, sometimes regressing, participation can be seen in the counties and cities of the Southwest from the late 1940s to the present. For example, Los Angeles, which has the largest Mexican American population of any city in the United States, elected its first Mexican American city council member in 1949 but had no Mexican Americans on its council between the early 1960s and the early 1970s. In the late 1980s, fewer than 2 percent of all elected officials in the Los Angeles area were Mexican American.[104] In 1991, Gloria Molina, the daughter of a Mexican immigrant laborer and a former Los Angeles city councilmember, became the first Latino, and the first woman, ever elected to the Los Angeles County Board of Supervisors, filling a position created by court-ordered redistricting designed to remedy Latinos' lack of representation. Three years later she became the board's chair.[105]

The 1960s and 1970s saw some changes in several types of political representation. By the 1960s, Mexican Americans had moved from no representation on school boards to 470 officials among the 4,600 board members in the Southwest. Since the 1980s, the number of Mexican Americans serving at all political levels has increased significantly. Two major cities (San Antonio and Denver) and several smaller ones have had Mexican American mayors. The *National Roster of Hispanic Elected Officials* reported a 1994 total of 4,276 Latino elected officials in the five southwestern states where most Mexican Americans live, and of 5,466 officials nationwide, almost one-third of whom were women. Three-fourths of all Latino elected officials today serve on school boards or in city governments, although increasing numbers are moving up to state and even national offices. Between 1984 and 1995, the number of Latinos in state legislatures nationwide increased from 113 to 158. Most of these are Mexican American. In 1995, New Mexico had the largest number (42) of Mexican American state lawmakers; they constituted 38 percent of the New Mexico state legislature.[106] In Texas, where approximately one-fourth of the state's voting age population is Latino,[107] Mexican Americans made up 18 percent of the state house and 23 percent of the state senate in 1995. And the number is still growing in the late 1990s. At regular meetings of Mexican Americans affiliated with the Texas Democratic party, one sees not only more Mexican American elected officials from all governmental levels but also white Democrats seeking to win statewide office.[108]

In California, a state in which 14 percent of eligible voters are Latino,[109] the number of Latinos in the state legislature doubled between 1990 and 1995—from 7 to 14; in 1995 they represented 12 percent of the state's lawmakers. Most of the fourteen are Mexican American; six are women, including California's first Latina state senator. At least three represent districts in which the majority of registered voters are not Latino. These numbers have continued to increase in the late 1990s.[110]

Still, the number of Mexican American elected and appointed officials at the state and national levels remains low. Only a tiny handful of Mexican Americans have served as state governors, including two in New Mexico and one in Arizona. In 1992, President Bill Clinton appointed two Mexican Americans to Cabinet posts: Henry Cisneros as Secretary of Housing and Urban Development, and Federico Peña as Secretary of Transportation. In 1995, only six Mexican Americans held statewide offices, including Texas's attorney general and New Mexico's secretary of state. There were only eleven Mexican Americans in the U.S. House, and not one Mexican American served in the U.S. Senate. This level of representation was too low to give this group major political clout in either legislative body.

Support for the Major Parties

At the presidential level, Mexican American voting has traditionally been Democratic. In 1960, John Kennedy won an estimated 85 percent of Mexican American votes, which was more than enough to make the difference for him in winning the states of New Mexico and Texas. In 1964, Lyndon Johnson won an estimated 90 percent, and in 1968, Hubert Humphrey won 87 percent. Mexican Americans stayed with the Democratic party through the 1970s and 1980s, and they voted overwhelmingly for Jimmy Carter in 1980. Three-fourths of the Latino voters in Texas supported Walter Mondale over Ronald Reagan in 1984. In the 1990, 1992, and 1994 national elections, 70 percent of Latino voters nationwide again supported Democratic candidates.[111]

The majority of Mexican American voters have generally cast their votes for the more liberal or progressive political candidates at all government levels. In the 1996 presidential election Latino voters, who are in the majority Mexican American, for the first time voted at a rate greater than the national rate. In 1996 alone there were a million new Latino voters. The Latino turnout had an important impact not only on the presidential election but also on a variety of local and state elections from New York to Florida, Texas, and California. Democratic candidates did especially well, on the average garnering 65–70 percent of the Latino vote.[112]

The Courts

Underrepresentation in the judicial system—both as jurors and as judges—has been common. In *Hernandez* v. *Texas* (1954), the U.S. Supreme Court upheld an appeal of an all-white jury's conviction of a Mexican American defendant on the grounds that Mexican Americans were excluded from jury service. The court noted that the lack of Mexican American representation on any jury over a period of twenty-five years in a county that was 14 percent Mexican American was evidence of discrimination.[113]

Not until the 1960s was the first Mexican American federal judge appointed. By the end of that decade, only two of the fifty-nine federal district judges in the five southwestern states, 3 percent of the nearly one thousand state judges, and 3 percent of district attorneys and public prosecutors in twenty-two Southwest cities had Spanish surnames. In the 1970s and 1980s, these numbers slowly improved. Many Mexican American applicants have been denied police positions by the indirect discrimination of height and weight requirements and by explicit English-language requirements, as well as by too-low scores on conventional English-language qualifying examinations. Also, very few Mexican or other Latino Americans have served at the higher levels of the U.S. Department of Justice or other federal law enforcement agencies.[114]

Given this underrepresentation, it is not surprising that discrimination in the criminal justice system has been documented. Arizona, California, and Colorado have required jurors to be able to speak English, screening out many Spanish-speaking citizens; the pool of jurors in numerous states has until recently been selected by whatever method has suited (usually white) jury commissioners. Mexican Americans charged with crimes have usually been judged by juries containing few if any of their peers. Courtrooms in which no one, including judges, understands Spanish present a language problem for some Mexican American defendants. Besides the absence of Spanish interpreters in courtrooms, other harmful practices have included excessive bail, poor legal counsel, and negative views by white judges of Mexican American defendants.[115]

The exclusion of jurors on the basis of racial group or national origin was declared unconstitutional by the U.S. Supreme Court in *Batson* v. *Kentucky* (1986). In subsequent cases, however, prosecutors have successfully excluded Latinos from juries on the basis of language. In 1989, an all-white jury convicted Jose Razo, Jr., a Mexican American youth, of armed robberies largely on the basis of a confession he had voluntarily made to the police. His defense attorneys argued that the confession was made in order to protect others and while the defendant was under the influence of drugs. One of his attorneys objected when the prosecution dismissed two potential Latino jurors but withdrew the objection after the judge stated that California law would compel her to declare a mistrial and begin anew if the dismissal of jurors were found to be based on discrimination.[116]

An early-1990s U.S. Supreme Court decision upheld a prosecutor's exclusion of bilingual Latino jurors who had hesitated before agreeing to accept the official English translation of the Spanish-language testimony that they would hear in the trial. Legal scholar Juan Perea has noted that it is common for bilingual people to hesitate when answering a question in their second language (English). They might want to carefully consider whether they would accept without question another's English translation of testimony they had heard in their native language of Spanish. In contrast, in 1991 a judge in San Diego County, California, dismissed fifteen indictments handed down by the county's grand jury, because the pool from which the grand jurors were selected did not represent a fair racial cross-section of the county. The population of San Diego County was more than 20 percent Latino, but the grand jury pool was only 3.4 percent Latino.[117]

The Chicano Political Movement

Disenchantment with the accommodationist perspective of some middle-class Mexican American leaders led to the emergence of the Chicano movement in the 1960s and 1970s, a militant political movement that sought greater political power and that emphasized a nationalist identity.[118] Lacking influence in mainstream politics, many Mexican Americans joined the new La Raza Unida party (LRUP) during this period. LRUP's goals included representation of all people by a local government that served the needs of individual communities as well as an end to poverty and injustice.

LRUP's major successes occurred in Crystal City, a south Texas city mostly populated by poor Mexican Americans. A cannery had come to that area in the 1940s, followed in the mid-1950s by the Teamsters' Union. The union gave workers job security and some political resources for electoral campaigns. During the 1960s, LRUP became a leading political force in the area, and by 1970, Mexican Americans had won control of the school board and city council. These new leaders hired more Mexican American teachers, teacher aides, and administrators, started bilingual programs, and added Mexican American history to the school curriculum. Mexican Americans were hired or promoted at all levels of the city bureaucracy. Millions of dollars in federal aid poured in to support programs in health, housing, and urban renewal.[119]

Out of power for the first time, local whites counter-attacked, withdrawing their children from school, boycotting school taxes, and firing some Mexican American employees. White teachers resigned, complaining of a redirection of school activities toward Mexican American goals. Refusing to tolerate self-government by the Mexican American majorities, white state officials succeeded in cutting off state and federal funding, almost bankrupting the city government, and then blamed the Mexican American leadership for failed programs.[120] Although internal conflicts played a part in LRUP's demise, harassment and repression, including efforts to keep LRUP off the ballot and to coopt its leaders, were major factors. By the 1980s, Mexican Americans were identified no longer with LRUP but rather with the state Democratic party. Yet LRUP had brought about the democratization of some southwestern communities, raised the political consciousness of many Mexican Americans, and prompted Mexican American political participation on an unprecedented scale.[121]

Mexican American women held a range of important leadership roles within LRUP. Women composed the vast majority of Mexican Americans elected to office in the Crystal City area. In the words of Mexican American writer Marta Cotera, "Feminism has come easily for Chicanas because of the woman's traditional role and strength as center or heart of the family. . . . The tradition of activism inherited from women's participation in armed rebellions in Mexico and in the political life of Mexico has also strengthened the Chicanas' position."[122] Mexican American feminists have faced major barriers. From the beginning to the present, many issues of greatest concern to them, including poverty and discrimination, have not been central to the mainstream women's movement. They have also encountered sexism from some Mexican American men who resisted women moving beyond their traditional roles. Women who sought their own liberation were accused of betraying the Chicano movement and of identifying with individualism, a concept seen as antithetical to Mexican American culture. As a result, much of the work of these feminists has had to be accomplished in their own organizations outside the Chicano movements.[123]

Another political victory came in San Antonio, whose politics had long been controlled by the white business elite. In 1981, Henry Cisneros, who later served as Secretary of Housing and Urban Development in the Clinton administration, was elected mayor of San Antonio, the first Mexican American mayor of a large metropolitan area. His victory was the culmination of ten years of organization. In 1977, neighborhood organizers working through Communities Organized for Public Service (COPS), an activist neighborhood organization, and other Mexican American organizations got out the vote for a referendum on single-member districts. With this support the referendum passed. A few months later the citizenry elected a city council with a majority of Mexican American and black representatives.[124]

Other Organizations and Protest

Union organization has a long history among Mexican Americans. The first permanent organization was the Confederacion de Uniones Obreras Mexicanas (CUOM), organized in California in 1927 with 3,000 members. A 1928 strike by the CUOM was stopped by deportation and arrests. Coal miners, farm workers, and factory workers struck in New Mexico, Arizona, and Texas in the 1930s, as Mexican Americans were beginning to make their way into mainstream unions. Mexican American women participated in strikes as members of the International Ladies Garment Workers Union. During this period armed police were often used to break up union meetings and strikes.[125]

Mutual-benefit associations developed early among Mexican Americans. These included worker alliances that pooled resources and provided social support as well as religious brotherhoods. By the 1920s, a number of Mexican American newspapers were being published. The League of United Latin American Citizens (LULAC) was organized in southern Texas in the 1920s. Oriented toward civic activities, LULAC pressed for a better deal for Mexican Americans; since the 1960s LULAC has worked to break down discrimination on many fronts.[126]

A number of post–World War II organizations reflected growing militancy. After a Texas cemetery refused to allow the burial of a Mexican American soldier, the American G.I. Forum was established to organize Mexican American veterans and to work for expanded civil rights. In Los Angeles the Community Service Organization worked to organize voting strength. Two groups that formed about 1960—the Mexican American Political Association, a California organization, and the Political Association of Spanish-Speaking Organizations, a Texas organization—focused more explicitly on political goals. Mexican American protest intensified in the 1960s, reflecting growing political consciousness. "Corky" Gonzales and his associates worked in Denver in support of school reform and against police brutality. New youth organizations were formed throughout the Southwest, including the Mexican American Youth Organization and the Brown Berets, a militant organization that set forth a program of better education, employment, and housing. A new ideology of *Chicanismo* was developed, espousing a philosophy of antiracism and decolonization.[127]

Among the protests were those led by Reies Lopez Tijerina. The Alianza Federal de Mercedes was founded in 1963 by Tijerina after he had spent a number of years researching the old Mexican land grants in the Southwest. In July 1966, a group of Alianza members marched to Santa Fe and presented a statement of their grievances about Anglo theft of Mexican land grants. Another group camped out without a permit on Kit Carson National Forest land, once part of a Mexican communal land grant. Forest rangers who tried to stop them were seized and tried for violating the old land-grant boundaries.[128]

Since the 1980s, voter registration has been a major focus. The Southwest Voter Registration Education Project, located in San Antonio and Los Angeles, has participated in hundreds of voter-registration campaigns and has joined the Texas Rural Legal Aid organization to file lawsuits seeking to dismantle discriminatory election systems and thereby expand the impact of Mexican American voters. The Mexican American Legal Defense and Education Fund (MALDEF), founded in 1968 to address problems of jury discrimination, police brutality, and school segregation, is also an active force for change. In the redistricting that followed the 1990 census, MALDEF has worked to assure voting strength and more equitable representation of Latino citizens in several states, including Texas, California, and Illinois.[129]

Today, Mexican American women remain active in grass-roots organizing. Mothers of East Los Angeles (MELA) is an effective grass-roots organization that works to defend its community's quality of life. For example, at an early 1990s neighborhood meeting MELA members confronted the representative of an oil company wishing to build a pipeline through the center of a Latino community in Los Angeles:

> "Is it going through Cielito Lindo [former president Ronald Reagan's ranch]?" The oil representative answered, "No." Another woman stood up and asked, "Why not place it along the coastline?" Without thinking of the implications, the representative responded, "Oh, no! If it burst, it would endanger the marine life." The woman retorted, "You value the marine life more than human beings?" His face reddened with anger and the hearing disintegrated into angry chanting.[130]

Unions for Low-Wage Workers

Important developments in unionization took place in the 1960s—the creation by Jessie Lopez, Dolores Huerta, and César Chávez of the Agricultural Workers Organizing Committee (AWOC) and the National Farm Workers Association (NFWA). By 1964 the NFWA had a thousand members. In 1965, the first big strike

Cesar Chavez marches at the head of
United Farm Workers during a 1979 protest.

was organized. Workers in AWOC struck the Delano, California, growers: The
NFWA met in Delano and voted to join the strike, demanding hourly wages of
$1.40. Growers refused to talk; picket lines went up; guns were fired at farm work-
ers. The NFWA remained nonviolent in the face of much provocation by white
growers and police officers. A grape boycott was started in 1965 and spread across
the country. Picket lines went up wherever grapes were sold. A massive march on
Sacramento was organized. In 1966, the AWOC and the NFWA merged into the
United Farm Workers Organizing Committee.[131]

Unionization was more difficult in Texas. The attempt by the United Farm
Workers to organize in the Rio Grande Valley in the 1960s and 1970s moved slowly because of imprisonment of strikers and leaders and the intervention of the
hated Texas Rangers.[132] In 1973, the largest winery in the United States, Gallo
Brothers, chose not to renew its contract with the United Farm Workers and
signed with the more conservative Teamsters. As other wineries followed suit,
many observers argued that Chávez and his union were dying. Yet the struggle
continued. Governor Jerry Brown of California worked for legislation to protect
farm workers, and in 1975 signed the Agricultural Labor Relations Act, which provided for protection for union activities and established a labor board to run
secret-ballot elections.[133]

The United Farm Workers, the most successful farm workers' union in U.S.
history, altered the structure of power in rural California by using the power of
organized numbers to pressure for economic and political change. In the late
1980s, the UFW and the charismatic Chávez addressed the issue of pesticide

spraying of farm products in a nationwide campaign to force large farmers to "stop poisoning workers and consumers." The UFW won a partial victory in 1991 when the Environmental Protection Agency agreed to ban one deadly pesticide, parathion, from use on all but nine crops. Parathion has been implicated in more than seventy deaths and thousands of illnesses among farm workers.[134] In 1994, the Clinton administration signed an agreement to settle a lawsuit brought by farm workers and environmentalists five years earlier. If approved by the court, the agreement would require the Environmental Protection Agency, over a two-year period, to ban thirty-six of the most widely used agricultural chemicals that have possible links to cancer and to review an additional forty-nine chemicals.[135]

In the spring of 1994, one year after the death of César Chávez, more than eighty farm workers and former farm workers, some of whom had made the first such pilgrimage twenty-eight years earlier, walked the 340 miles from Delano to Sacramento, California, signing up thousands of new UFW members along the way. Addressing a rally of more than 10,000 farm workers, their descendants, and supporters at the state capitol, UFW president Arturo Rodríguez stated, "Conditions for farm workers are as bad as they were twenty years ago. Wages are worse now than they've ever been."[136] Today, many farm workers still earn less than minimum wage, and because of lack of enforcement of the 1975 Labor Act many farm workers who favor unions are fired by their employers.[137]

In the late 1990s, an increasing number of Mexican Americans are to be found in mainstream unions representing auto workers, miners, railroad, cannery, garment, steel, and construction workers, teamsters, and dockworkers.[138] Unionizing efforts have been successful among undocumented workers, challenging the commonly held assumption that undocumented workers are willing to tolerate poor working conditions based on their fear of deportation.[139]

EDUCATION

In the first three decades of the twentieth century, little attention was given to the education of Mexican Americans. The whites who controlled the agricultural economy of the Southwest pressed for low-wage labor without the expense of education. Schooling for laborers was usually minimal.[140] Before World War II, Mexican American schoolchildren from Texas to California were often segregated, although school segregation for this group was different from that for African Americans. As a rule, Mexican Americans were segregated not by state law but either by local laws or by informal gerrymandering of school district lines. Discrimination in housing reinforced school segregation.[141]

In some areas, such as Lemon Grove, California, children of middle-class Mexican American families were allowed to attend white schools. Such arrangements had little impact outside the immediate area, although the practice probably served to reduce middle-class Mexican American resentment.[142] The economic hardships and forced repatriation movements during the 1930s diverted the attention of most Mexican Americans from the pursuit of equal educational opportunities.

Persisting Educational Problems

After World War II, Mexican American communities began to press hard for changes in the educational system. A major conference in Texas in 1946 called for an end to segregation, the adoption of a Mexican-oriented curriculum, better teacher training, and better school facilities. A federal court's decision in *Mendez* v. *Westminster* (1946) ruled that the segregation of Mexican American children in "Mexican" schools in California violated the Fourteenth Amendment because these children were not separated on valid educational grounds but on the basis of their surnames. Significantly, much of the social and educational theory expressed by the judge in the *Mendez* case anticipated the Supreme Court's ruling in *Brown* v. *Board of Education* almost a decade later. After the *Mendez* decision, California laws allowing school segregation were repealed.[143]

Yet de facto segregation has persisted to the present. In the mid-1990s, most Mexican American students still attend schools made up mostly of children of color. The proportion of Mexican American children in many public schools in the Southwest has increased significantly, in part because of segregated housing patterns. In addition, many of the more than 1,000 predominantly Mexican American schools continue to have inferior educational resources. Although the Mexican American Legal Defense and Education Fund (MALDEF) has challenged inequalities in public school funding in several court cases, unequal funding persists across the country. Mexican Americans also remain underrepresented among teachers and administrators in most school systems in spite of modest increases in their numbers. Guadalupe San Miguel, Jr., argues that greater success might have been achieved in eliminating educational discrimination had efforts concentrated on replacing educational policymakers rather than simply challenging educational policies. The major obstacle for Mexican American communities has been their lack of political power.[144]

In the recent past, some schools with high percentages of Mexican American students rigidly prohibited manifestations of Mexican American subculture, some going so far as to enforce dress and hair codes for students. Teachers anglicized the names of children (for instance, Roberto became Bobby), downgrading the heritage of the children. White teachers' treatment of Mexican American children in the classroom is another persisting problem. Teacher practices have been shown to have a strong relationship to student achievement. One study of teacher behavior in classrooms found that the average teacher praised white children 35 percent more often than Mexican American children, questioned them 20 percent more often, and used their ideas 40 percent more often.[145]

For many years, Mexican American children in Texas and California were overrepresented in classes for the mentally retarded. Most Mexican Americans in these classes were "six-hour retarded" children—capable of functioning in the outside world yet mislabeled largely as a result of the cultural discrimination in school testing methods. Tests were usually conducted in English. As early as the 1930s, the educator George I. Sanchez fought against the inequity of interpreting test scores apart from an understanding of the ways in which test results reflected the past experiences of the children tested and the "educational negligence on the part of local and state authorities" with regard to Mexican American children.[146]

A 1970s study in Riverside, California, found that all of the white children in classes for the mentally retarded showed behavior abnormality, compared with less than half of the Mexican American children. Although certain discriminatory practices, such as placement in classes for the "mentally retarded," had been eliminated from most schools by the 1980s, vestiges of bias and discrimination remained. In the mid-1990s, schools still place too many Mexican American children in learning-disabled classes, and school textbooks usually neglect Mexican American history.[147]

Current Educational Issues: Bilingualism and Achievement

Writing about the historical treatment of language in the interaction between the dominant culture and other U.S. cultures, Juan Perea points out that "America has always been a land of many different languages and cultures."[148] The Articles of Confederation were officially published in three languages—English, German, and French. California's first state constitution (1849), published in both Spanish and English, provided that "all laws, decrees, regulations, and provisions" be printed in both languages. From the first, the laws of the territory of New Mexico were published in both Spanish and English; this practice continued during the first forty years of New Mexico's statehood. Education in most schools in that territory was provided in Spanish. Later, nativists succeeded in having languages other than English labeled "foreign" and in getting laws passed restricting their use (see Chapter 3). Such actions are "attempts to exclude certain unpopular Americans from the definition of what is American."[149] We will examine the nativist attack on Spanish speakers and ethnocentric proposals for English as the "official language" in Chapter 10.

When placed in classrooms in which instruction is given only in English, children with a limited proficiency in English frequently become discouraged, develop low self-confidence, and fail to keep pace with their English-speaking peers. This condition affects many Latino students. (Bilingual education for Puerto Rican and Cuban American students will be discussed in Chapter 10.) In 1968, Congress passed the Elementary and Secondary Education Act, which set up a mechanism for the federal government to fund bilingual programs in public schools to meet the needs of language-minority children. By 1973, however, no southwestern state had taken more than token steps; only 5 percent of the Mexican American children in the Southwest were being affected by federally funded bilingual programs in the 1972–1973 school year.

A 1974 Supreme Court decision (*Lau* v. *Nichols*) established a child's ability to understand classroom instruction as a civil right, making it illegal for school systems to ignore the English-language problems of language-minority groups. Since 1968, federal programs have provided over $1 billion for local school district programs to increase the English proficiency of children whose primary language was not English. Yet apart from a few stellar programs in schools with sensitive principals in scattered public school systems, the overall picture of bilingual education is one of snail-like progress—and often of white opposition.[150] One federal study found that most school systems had few qualified bilingual teachers and were unable to accurately assess the English-language needs of their language-minority students.[151]

Although the median education level for Mexican Americans has increased since 1950, it remains significantly behind national figures. Between 1950 and 1980, the median schooling for Mexican American adults increased from 5.4 to 9.6 years, decreasing the gap but still much lower than the national median of 12.5 years. The 1980 census reported that less than 38 percent of Mexican Americans over twenty-four years old were high-school graduates, and by the mid-1990s, the proportion was still less than half. The corresponding figures for the total population in those two years were 67 percent and 80 percent, respectively.[152]

A wide gap exists between the rate of college graduation for Mexican Americans and that for the population as a whole. Access to higher education was provided for veterans during the 1940s and 1950s by the GI bill. This access was increased for nonveterans during the 1960s and 1970s by federal education programs in the wake of a national civil rights movement. Yet today the proportion of Mexican Americans completing college is still low. The following table compares the educational attainment in 1993 of persons over twenty-four years old who are Mexican American, mainland Puerto Rican, and Cuban American with the European origin population.[153]

	Mexican Origin	Puerto Rican Origin	Cuban Origin	European Origin
Less than five years of school completed	15.4%	8.2%	5.3%	0.8%
High-school graduate or more	46.2%	59.8%	62.1%	84.1%
Bachelor's degree or more	5.9%	8.0%	16.5%	23.8%

The high-school and college graduation rates for Mexican Americans are the lowest of the three Latino groups and are far lower than the graduation rates of European Americans. The educational attainment of the Mexican-origin population today provides evidence of decades of limited economic and educational opportunities. Research shows clearly that more education, particularly beyond high school, would enable Mexican Americans to decrease the wage differential with white Americans. However, as Martha Jimenez of the Mexican American

Legal Defense and Educational Fund has recently noted, "It's a vicious circle. This wage differential makes it so everyone in the family has to work, which is one of the biggest reasons for the dropout rate."[154]

This dropout rate—some would call it the "pushout rate"—for Mexican American students in public schools remains high. Variations in reporting methods for dropout rates (annual, longitudinal, or overall) and the fact that students drop in and out of school, and sometimes re-enroll somewhere else, make it impossible to arrive at an exact figure, but estimates of the dropout rate for all Latino groups combined range from two to three times that of non-Latinos, and Mexican Americans rank at the low end among the various Latino groups. Poverty and the need to earn money to help support their families are major obstacles for these students. School counselors often advise those who have fallen far behind to drop out. Nonetheless, a few schools have increased graduation rates for Mexican American students significantly—in at least one case to 95 percent—by providing programs to address such student concerns as jobs, substance abuse, and teen parenthood.[155]

In the late 1980s, researchers Harriet Romo and Toni Falbo began tracking a group of 100 Mexican American high-school sophomores who were at high risk of dropping out of school.[156] Within two years, 40 percent had dropped out. Only nineteen of the original 100 graduated at the end of their senior year, and only one student remained in school the following year. Many of those who graduated did so with the help of special programs, and their skills were scarcely better than those of the students who dropped out. Interviews with the students revealed that their school experience had often been demeaning and demoralizing. Some expressed the feeling that someone was "always on my back." Many of the students felt they were better off after they left school. One girl remarked about her job: "At least they care whether I come or not."

Nonetheless, education was highly valued by both the students and their families; the anguish of school failure was keenly felt. "School failure involves threats to the self-esteem of the students as well as the status of the family and results in complex intra-family tensions and conflicts. . . . After a student dropped out, parents felt devastated and angry."[157] In most of these families, the mothers were primarily responsible for their children's education. The mothers derived much of their own sense of self from the successes of their children and tended to blame themselves, or felt that school personnel blamed them, for their children's failures. These mothers' strategies for helping their children stay in school involved giving encouragement and pointing to individual models of success. Most had limited schooling themselves and were unable to help their children with schoolwork. They often did not understand the school system. Few mothers had the confidence to approach the school for help, and those who did felt themselves at a disadvantage. They reported experiencing frustration over the school's unwillingness or inability to provide help and sometimes encountering hostility from teachers, counselors, or administrators. Yet those parents with strong parenting skills were able to defy the odds and keep their adolescents in school.

Ethnographic research by Concha Delgado-Gaitan and Henry Trueba has shown that Mexican immigrant families are very interested in the education of their children, although they have little knowledge about how to become involved in U.S. schools. This research also shows that public schools in the United States typically make little effort to involve immigrant parents with their children's education in a meaningful way.[158]

In a critique of the major explanations offered for the poor school performance by many students of color, including Mexican American students, Catherine Walsh argues that attributing school problems to alleged individual or cultural inadequacies is only blaming the victim. Simply blaming incompatibilities arising from the cultural differences between Latino students and the white-dominated educational system on the victims is to overlook the historical and ongoing sociological and ideological significance of these differences. That all culturally different students do not perform equally poorly in school points to the relevance of additional factors. The problem is one of unequal power relationships. To locate the root of school problems one must look to the character of the school system, not to the student. For example, the mainstream school curriculum is built on the dominant culture and the centrality of the English language and usually equates individual and group success with adopting that dominant culture and language. Mexican American history, culture, language, and life experiences are typically ignored. Latino cultures are seen by the dominant group as negative environments from which students need to escape. Walsh suggests that poor school performance is often a response to alienating and oppressive conditions that have robbed them of identity, dignity, and voice. Learning or not learning can be a political statement. Walsh quotes Frederick Erickson, who states that to overcome resistance to learning one must establish

> trust in the legitimacy of the authority and in the good intentions of those exercising it, trust that one's own identity will be maintained positively in relation to the authority, and trust that one's own interests will be advanced by compliance with the exercise of authority.[159]

Including the Spanish language and Mexican American culture in the classroom, involving students' parents in the learning process, and increasing interaction between students and teachers are important steps toward improving education for Mexican American children. But these steps are inadequate by themselves. From Walsh's perspective, the severe imbalance of power and authority needs to be corrected. Mexican American students would then be accorded respect and the possibility of establishing a positive identity in public schools.

Since the 1970s, a debate has raged over the obligation of public school systems to educate the children of undocumented Mexican aliens. State officials, especially in southwestern states, have complained that educating these children is a burden on their citizens. In Texas, one court case arose out of officials' attempts to charge the children of undocumented aliens a special fee to attend school. After an extended struggle in the lower courts, the Supreme Court ruled in 1982 that all children had to be provided with schooling and that children could not be discriminated against on the basis of parental condition, such as immigrant status.[160] More recently, the ballot initiative Proposition 187 explicitly barred the children of undocumented parents from California public schools. However, viewed in terms of the 1982 Supreme Court decision, this aspect of Proposition 187 appears to be unconstitutional.

RELIGION

Mexican immigrants to the Southwest have not been accompanied by Catholic priests. The Catholic church and its doctrines are seldom major factors in the lives of migrants. However, what has been termed *folk Catholicism*, a blend of Catholicism and certain non-Catholic beliefs and rituals, has played an important role.[161] Many immigrants have been hostile to the established church in Mexico, and most have not been prepared for a U.S. Catholic church dominated by Irish American and other white priests. In the first decades of immigration, little provision was made for the religious schooling of Mexican Catholics. Before 1940, the church provided little sustenance or aid to a Latino population troubled by poverty and discrimination.[162]

In the 1950s and 1960s, some priests began to take an active role in union activities. In the 1960s, War on Poverty programs were sometimes operated in connection with church projects, and a number of "lay protest" and "priest protest" groups were formed to deal with urban poverty and related problems. Yet in some areas the Catholic hierarchy prohibited priests from participating in protest organizations. The Los Angeles cardinal, for example, refused to provide priests for the Delano farm workers on strike in the 1960s. Moreover, the hierarchy of the U.S. Catholic church has sometimes discriminated against Mexican Americans. Very few Mexican Americans had achieved positions of responsibility before the 1960s; the first Mexican American bishop was designated, in San Antonio, in 1970. By the mid-1980s, only eighteen of the nearly 300 bishops in the United States were Mexican American; by mid-1990s the number was still low— only twenty-two.[163]

The Catholicism of most Mexican Americans has been described as somewhat similar to that of Italian Americans, with a general allegiance to the church but less active participation than for Irish Catholics. In the 1940s, Tuck found that most Mexican Americans in San Bernardino, California, were baptized, married, and buried with a priest in attendance, but participated infrequently in church activities. The power of the church was found to be great in affecting attitudes on such issues as venereal disease campaigns and unionization. In recent years, however, this influence of the church on secular issues appears to be on the wane; rejection of the church position on abortion and birth control has been widespread.[164]

Nonetheless, in many areas the Catholic church still creates a central place for Sunday mass and Latino holiday celebrations and community gatherings. Celebrating the feast day of Our Lady of Guadalupe is increasingly popular in

Latino communities. In cities such as Chicago, some older parishes have seen large increases in their Spanish-speaking parishioners and have re-oriented their services to the needs of Latino members. The U.S. Catholic church has also created a number of new churches in West Coast areas where immigration from Mexico has been substantial.

A 1994 study reported that the proportion of Latinos who identified as Catholic had dropped from 90 percent to about 70 percent over the last several decades.[165] Many of those not identifying as Catholic are today identifying with U.S. Protestant denominations, particularly with evangelical groups. Some Latinos have converted to Jehovah's Witnesses and other evangelical groups that welcome new immigrants and make them feel, as one person put it, like "part of a family."[166] Dozens of evangelical and Pentecostal churches have been created in urban Latino communities, often in empty storefronts and abandoned churches.[167]

ASSIMILATION OR COLONIALISM?

An assimilation perspective is implicit or explicit in many prominent research studies of Mexican Americans. In addition, recent political commentators such as the conservative Linda Chávez have argued that, apart from recent immigrants, Mexican Americans are gradually becoming assimilated like white ethnic Americans. Assimilationists argue that Mexican Americans are moving up the mobility ladder just as the European ethnic groups did, and thus are proceeding slowly but surely into the American mainstream at all the assimilation levels described by Milton Gordon.[168]

An assimilationist looking at Mexican American history might emphasize that only 100,000 Mexicans were brought into the United States as a result of military conquest. Most immigrants came later. Most have been able to improve their economic circumstances relative to their condition in Mexico. Moreover, aspects of traditional Mexican culture began disappearing as acculturation proceeded.[169] For the first generation of Mexican Americans, cultural assimilation made itself felt mainly in terms of adjustments in language and certain workplace values. Religious and other basic values were less affected; respect for Mexico remained strong. For later generations, there has been increased structural assimilation into the economy and even more cultural (for example, language) adaptation. The Mexican American family is traditionally depicted as a large, extended, patriarchal unit; however, this is most descriptive of family patterns in agricultural towns in earlier decades. Urbanization and increased incomes have opened up the possibility of separate residences for nuclear families, and the number of large, extended families in urban areas has declined. Fertility trends and family values have increasingly become similar to those of other Americans.[170]

However, from the traditional life of rural villages to the faster-paced life of the urban barrios there has been substantial cultural persistence. Most notable has been the Spanish language, which has persisted as the primary language or as part of a bilingual pattern for a majority of families. Closeness to Mexico has been given as an important reason for the persistence of the Spanish language. Surveys in Los Angeles and San Antonio have found that most Mexican Americans wished their children to retain ties to their Mexican culture, particularly to language, customs, and religion. An early 1990s survey found that most Mexican Americans were bilingual to some extent, but a significant minority had little fluency in English.[171] Significantly, the 1990 census found that half of Los Angeles' Latino (mostly Mexican American) population did not speak English "very well."[172] Although almost all Latino adults in the survey mentioned above felt that it was very important for their children to become fluent in both Spanish and English, most immigrant parents and their children recognize the clear social and economic advantages of learning English. Studies in San Diego and south Florida have found that 66 to 80 percent of immigrant school children prefer English to Spanish.[173]

Structural assimilation at the economic level has come slowly even for the second and third generations; discrimination and the concentration of a majority of workers at the lower wage levels persist. Problematical too has been the limited participation of Mexican Americans in political institutions, although recent progress can be seen in some areas. Efforts of the Southwest Voter Registration Project and the success of court cases suing for single-member districts have increased Mexican American voter strength. Developments on Milton Gordon's dimensions of behavior-receptional assimilation and attitude-receptional assimilation have varied considerably within the Mexican American group and over time. Widespread prejudice and severe discrimination faced the Mexicans who were conquered in the expansion of the United States, as well as the immigrants since 1900. Over time, however, many lighter-skinned Mexican Americans in larger cities were treated with less prejudice and discrimination. Darker-skinned persons have often been treated the same as African Americans. Today, considerable prejudice and discrimination are still directed against darker-skinned Mexican Americans in many parts of the United States.

The Limits of Assimilation

Structural absorption at the primary-group level and marital assimilation have not yet reached the point where one can speak of moderate-to-high assimilation for Mexican Americans as a group. Some increases in intergroup friendship contacts were found in studies in the 1970s, particularly for Mexican American children in desegregated environments, although most still had predominantly Mexican American friends. In one study, fewer than 5 percent of Mexican American respondents in San Antonio had predominantly white friends; the proportion in Los Angeles was about 15 percent. In a 1991 survey, the vast majority of Latinos (mostly Mexican Americans) in the Southwest, West, and Central regions of the United States reported that their close friends (as well as their neighborhoods) were Latino.[174]

Data on intermarriage indicate that a majority of all Mexican American marriages are still within the Mexican American group. In San Antonio the proportion of Spanish-surname individuals marrying outside the group slowly increased from 10 percent in the period between 1940 and 1955 to 16 percent in 1973. In Los Angeles, the proportion of individuals marrying outside the group increased from 9 percent in the period between 1924 and 1933 to 25 percent in the years 1960 and 1961. In Texas and New Mexico, in the 1980s, the proportion of Mexican Americans marrying outside the group stabilized in the 5-to-24-percent range. One exception to these relatively low out-marriage rates appears in a study for all California counties, which found out-marriage rates to be between 34 and 36 percent for the 1970s.[175] Early 1990s data indicate that, for all generations taken together, about 26 percent of marriages are outside the Latino group.[176] However, the 1990s rate of out-marriage appears to be higher for younger generations of Mexican Americans. A recent estimate for native-born Mexican Americans in southern California puts the out-marriage figure at approximately 50 percent.[177]

Some conservative assimilation analysts, such as Nathan Glazer, have questioned the extent of Mexican Americans' identification with things Mexican. Glazer has characterized the militant Chicano movement of the 1960s and 1970s as "one of extreme views espoused by a minority for a short period." This view overlooks the fact that the majority of younger Mexican Americans supported the Chicano movement, even if they did not actively participate in its activities, and that many in the older generation—that is, the families of the activists—were quietly supportive. In addition, the perspectives and actions of the Mexican American activists in the 1960s as well as in the 1990s reflect themes of militancy and change rooted in their cultural heritage.[178]

Connor has argued that the diversity of self-identification labels used by persons with ties to Mexico—designations such as *Hispano, Chicano, Mexican, Mexican American, Latino, Spanish,* and *Hispanic*—indicate a significant diversity of opinion about identity within this growing community.[179] Some whose ancestry dates back before the U.S. conquest of northern Mexico prefer terms such as *Spanish.* Some scholars have emphasized that outside oppression forced many, particularly in earlier decades, to hide their Mexican origin under the euphemism *Spanish American*; thus, this term is not necessarily a sign of identificational assimilation. Middle-income Mexican Americans in the 1920s began to use such terms to hide from prejudice. In recent decades there has been a shift back to *Mexican* and *Mexican American.* In one survey the preference of respondents in Los Angeles was for *Mexican* or *Mexican American,* whereas in San Antonio the majority preferred *Latin American.* Few in either city wanted to be called just "American." In a survey of households in the Southwest and Midwest, most respondents preferred to be called Mexican American, Mexican, or Chicano.[180] Pride in Mexican identity thus remains strong.

Identification as Mexican American or Chicano can vary with social class, age, and experience. A recent research project at the University of California found that many middle-class Mexican American undergraduates had been sheltered by their parents and parochial school teachers who had encouraged them to think of themselves as "white" and to assimilate fully to Anglo-American ways. These students often experienced shock in coming to the UC campus, where they were con-

Mexican Americans in a Mexican Day parade in Chicago.

sidered to be "Chicano" and part of a racial group that was a victim of discrimi-nation.[181] The campus experience brought these students out of their sheltered families and into a highly racialized society. In addition, David Montejano has documented considerable class differences in ease of assimilation for Mexican Americans, with upper-middle-class professionals facing fewer barriers than members of the working class and immigrants.[182] Similarly, Múrguía has argued that the Anglo-Protestant group allows certain Mexican Americans, particularly those who are lighter-skinned or middle-class, to assimilate on a more or less equal-status basis. Yet in his view group assimilation cannot go as far as it has for other Catholics, such as the Irish. The differences are narrowing, but assimilation to the dominant culture and institutions will stop short of complete absorption.[183]

A study by Strategy Research Corporation (SRC) indicates a slow rate of assimilation with some regional and generational variations. The SRC study groups together various "Hispanic" groups into one general Hispanic category and then presents the data broken down by region. Since most of the Hispanic Americans in the West, Central, and Southwest regions are Mexican Americans, we will focus on SRC data from these regions. Almost 90 percent of the Hispanic adult respondents in the West and Central regions and more than two-thirds of those in the Southwest described themselves as "very Hispanic." When asked how Hispanic-oriented they would like to be in ten years, the percentage replying "very Hispanic" remained virtually unchanged in the Southwest and dropped only a few percentage points in the other two regions. Very small percentages in each region saw themselves as minimally Hispanic (from less than 1 percent in the West to just over 4 percent in the Southwest). The percentage who would like to be minimally Hispanic in ten years more than doubled in the Southwest but rose only slightly in the West and Central regions. Significantly, young people below the age of eighteen in all three regions consistently rated themselves as less Hispanic and projected a lower level of Hispanic identification for themselves in the future than did their adult counterparts. But the proportions identifying themselves as minimally Hispanic were still extremely low (ranging from 2.5 percent to 10.6 percent).[184]

In addition to these self-descriptions, the SRC study ranked respondents' level of assimilation on the basis of identification, language used, and behavioral, attitudinal, and aspirational measures. Only some 13 percent were judged to be fully assimilated; that is, they were thought to have given up most of their Latino culture. Approximately half (49 percent) were ranked partially assimilated; although reasonably comfortable in both Spanish and English, their Spanish-language skills predominated and they retained strong ties to Latino culture. The remaining 38 percent, classified as relatively unassimilated, spoke very little English. Largely recent immigrants, they are the fastest-growing segment of the Mexican American population in the United States.[185]

Regional and generational differences were apparent in language-use patterns. A large majority of the Hispanic adults in the West and Central regions felt most comfortable speaking Spanish and spoke it more frequently than English at home and on social occasions. Interestingly, the use of Spanish was less dominant among adults in the Southwest, where the majority of Mexican Americans reside. While a majority felt most comfortable speaking Spanish, fewer than half spoke it more frequently than English at home or on social occasions. More than half of the youth in the West and Central regions felt most comfortable speaking Spanish, whereas a large majority of their counterparts in the Southwest felt most comfortable with English. In all three regions, Spanish was spoken far less frequently at home and on social occasions by the youth than by adults. An overwhelming majority of the adults in all regions considered it very important for their children to learn to read and write both Spanish and English well. These data suggest that if the immigration streams from Mexico and other parts of Latin America ever abate, the linguistic (and probably other cultural) assimilation of the population will increase dramatically, especially as the population ages.[186]

Today, however, persisting immigration streams create problems for an assimilation analysis. The influx of significant numbers of Mexican immigrants into established Mexican American communities in recent years has helped reproduce and perpetuate the traditional culture of Mexican American communities, has supported in-group marriages and has encouraged the maintenance of Spanish as a primary language. In addition, Mexican American businesses have been supplied with new customers as well as a source of low-wage labor, thereby stimulating the growth of an enclave economy. These immigrants, as well as those from Central and South America, have furnished both the means and the reason for the growth of various enterprises, such as restaurants offering authentic cuisine, spiritualist shops offering nonmedical healing, and Spanish-language media. This indicates a clear pattern of segmented assimilation (see Chapter 2).

Mexican Americans have also had an impact on the larger society, although most assimilationists have given this aspect of group incorporation little attention. Some of the larger society's adaptations to the growth of the Latino population is relatively superficial, such as the growth of Mexican fast food outlets. But other societal adaptations, such as Spanish language ballots, Internal Revenue Service forms, and bilingual education, represent a recognition of the reality of a distinctive and different culture. Advertising directed toward and mass media serving Latino populations have also increased, particularly in areas such as Los Angeles, Houston, and Miami. In addition, recognition of the changing character of the U.S. consumer market has prompted several corporations, such as large retail chains and phone companies, to aggressively recruit bilingual employees. Some observers have even spoken of the "Hispanicizing of America."[187]

Mexican immigrants and their children have had a significant influence in the political arena. They increase the population base for electoral representation and the concerned constituency of Mexican American officeholders. The international political concerns of many immigrants have helped to expand the political involvement of Mexican American leaders and activists into a broader political arena, including a deep concern for relations between the United States and Mexico.[188]

Applying a Power–Conflict Perspective

Power–conflict analysts would emphasize the extent to which Mexican Americans have *not* moved toward speedy incorporation into the dominant culture and its institutions. The best that assimilation analysts can argue is that the trend is toward assimilation, for substantial economic and political assimilation is not a reality for the majority of Mexican Americans.

Internal colonialism analysts accent Mexican American history, particularly its origin in the ruthless conquest of northern Mexico in the period between 1836 and 1853. The situation for the early Mexican, whose land and person were brought into the United States by force, is one of classical colonialism. Some parallels can be seen between the Mexican American experience and that of externally colonized populations: Land is taken by military force, the native population is subjugated economically and politically, the indigenous culture is suppressed, and the colonizing power favors a small elite to help maintain the outside domination.[189]

One problem in applying the colonialism perspective to Mexican Americans is that most entered as immigrants *after* the conquest. Internal colonialism analysts underscore the differences between Mexican and European immigrants. Unlike Europeans, Mexican migrants have not come into a new environment. People of their background were already in the southwestern United States. Socially and culturally, they have moved within one geographical area, all of which was originally controlled by Mexicans. Moreover, little time is required to move back and forth across the border—in sharp contrast with the time of travel required of most European immigrants.[190]

Perhaps the most significant difference was that the heritage of the colonial situation, with its practices of discrimination and cultural subordination, shaped the receiving conditions of the later Mexican immigrants. "The colonial pattern of Euro-American domination over the Mexican people was set by 1848 and carried over to those Mexicans who came later to the Southwest, a land contiguous to Mexico and once a part of it."[191] Later subordination of Mexican immigrants by force has included rigorous Border Patrol searches and deportation of those immigrants (and sometimes citizens) deemed unworthy by Anglo-American authorities.

Later Mexican immigrants were channeled into an environment in which low wages, absentee landlords, inferior schools, and discrimination have limited their progress and mobility. John Ogbu has suggested that the rejection of public education by many Mexican American youth is a direct reaction to their colonized status.[192] For many decades, residential segregation has also reflected racial discrimination. Mexican Americans are not like European immigrant groups, whose level of segregation has declined sharply with length of residence in the United States. Discrimination in employment and housing persists.

In Chapter 2 we discussed the book *Race and Class in the Southwest* by Mario Barrera, who analyzes Mexican Americans using a modified internal colonialism model that emphasizes institutionalized racism and capitalism as factors in racial inequality. Barrera argues that each of the major classes of capitalism, such as the capitalist class and the working class, contains important segments that are defined by characteristics such as racial group. Each of the major classes contains a racial–ethnic line that separates those suffering institutionalized discrimination, such as Mexican Americans, from those whites who do not. Consider the example of the working class. While Mexican American workers share a similar class position with white workers in that both are struggling against employers for better wages and working conditions, the former are in a subordinate economic position because of structural discrimination along racial lines. The dimensions of this discrimination include lower wages for the same or similar work and concentration in certain lower-wage occupations.[193]

Internal colonialism analysts argue that white employers have created a split labor market from which the latter have profited greatly; they have focused the attention of white workers on Latinos (and African Americans) as a job threat for white workers. Given the dual-market segmentation of the labor force by employers, it is not surprising that white workers often try to solidify their positions and keep other workers out of the privileged jobs reserved for themselves. This is a type of internal colonialism in employment.

Mexican Americans have been subordinated much more than European immigrant groups ever were. Great psychological as well as economic benefits have accrued to the white oppressors. The acculturation of Mexican American children and adults has involved much pressure and some coercion, as we have seen in the public schools. Racial stereotyping, especially of darker-skinned Mexican Americans, has played a major role in establishing and preserving the racial hierarchy of the Southwest. Theories of biological inferiority have been used to justify taking land and exploiting Mexican American labor. This discrimination and subordination benefit most whites directly or indirectly:

[It] is a complex cultural system of racial and cultural domination which produces privileges above and beyond the surplus value generated solely by capitalism—privileges from which all members of the dominant social groups (despite their class) derive benefit directly or indirectly.[194]

Power–conflict analysts see the real hope for decreased oppression and an improved economic, political, and cultural situation in the Mexican American protest movements of the past and present.

As we noted previously, a distinctive aspect of Mexican American communities today is the constant infusion of undocumented workers. Particularly in the Southwest, this undocumented immigration provides renewal of ties to Mexico and reinforcement of Mexican culture, thereby undergirding Mexican communities and identity. These immigrants provide much low-wage labor for the Southwest's corporations, farms, and ranches. Their presence has become the center of continuing controversy over U.S. immigration laws and policies. This influx of immigrants creates serious problems for those applying the assimilation perspective to Mexican Americans, because the close ties to the traditional Mexican culture—the closest for any immigrant group in U.S. history—significantly slow cultural and social assimilation by providing an external supportive foundation.

SUMMARY

Mexican Americans have an ancient and proud ancestry, predominantly Native American ("Indian") but with significant Spanish and African infusions. Their vital cultural background is partly Native American but heavily Spanish in language and religion. After the European American conquest in what is now the U.S. Southwest, Mexican Americans became part of the complex mosaic of racial and ethnic groups in the United States. They have suffered much stereotyping similar to that of other groups of non-European ancestry, and discrimination in economics, education, and politics has been part of their lot from the beginning.

The literature on racial and ethnic relations has often compared the situations of Mexican Americans and African Americans, the largest subordinated groups in the United States. Both groups face substantial, and often similar, prejudice and discrimination at the hands of white Americans late in the twentieth century, especially in jobs, business, and housing, although many lighter-skinned, middle-class Mexican Americans probably face less discrimination from Anglo whites than most middle-class African Americans.

At the attitudinal level, Mexican Americans and African Americans are often sympathetic to each other's problems. One study of Mexican American attitudes in Texas found more positive feelings toward African Americans than were found among whites, more sensitivity to discriminatory barriers, and more support for civil rights protest. Differences between the two groups appeared in the area of protest strategies. The researchers found that African Americans were significantly more militant than Mexican Americans on selected issues, more dissatisfied with civil rights progress, and more approving of civil rights demonstrations.[195] This difference has sometimes made it difficult for the two groups to work together politically against the dominant group. In some situations the two groups even find themselves competing for limited benefits granted by the dominant group. Nonetheless, there have been several attempts to build black–brown coalitions, including the building of the Rainbow Coalition in the 1980s and 1990s (see Chapter 13). The future may well bring more political coalitions.

CHAPTER 10

Puerto Rican and Cuban Americans

Puerto Rico and Cuba, both Spanish-speaking islands in the Antilles, are the points of origin for two of this nations's largest Latino groups. Since its independence from Spanish rule, Cuba has, in the words of Cuban American editor Enrique Fernandez, "oscillated between a corrupt democracy and dictatorships of both right and left, accompanied by a humiliating dependence on a superpower."[1] This political oscillation has generated important out-migrations that have contributed greatly to the development of vital Latino communities in the southeastern United States. Cuba has a heroic history of its own, replete with heroes such as Jose Martí, the nineteenth-century poet and leader in the struggle for independence whose maxim for Cuba was "a nation . . . but no master." The struggle for independence continues to be an important theme in the present history of Cuban Americans.

Puerto Rico was once part of the Spanish empire, but for nearly a century has been a commonwealth within the U.S. empire. Although all Puerto Ricans are American citizens, Puerto Rico is not a state. Puerto Ricans send nonvoting delegates to the U.S. Congress but cannot vote in U.S. federal elections. Today, there is much debate over the future of the island; different political factions press for independence, for statehood, or for a continuation of the current commonwealth status. Unlike the Cuban case, these political debates have been relatively unimportant to Puerto Rican out-migration; the migration to the U.S. mainland has been most significantly influenced by the economic pull of the mainland economy, coupled with the ease of migration for these U.S. citizens. Many Puerto Ricans return regularly to an island that maintains a complex relationship with the United States. Generally more prosperous than most of their Caribbean neighbors, island Puerto Ricans are still only "quasi-citizens of the United States. They can give their lives fighting for the country in U.S. forces, but they cannot vote in national elections. They have only observer status in the U.S. Congress, but they can migrate to the mainland freely."[2] Puerto Ricans are unique among Americans, since they are U.S. citizens whether they reside on the island or are migrants to mainland cities along the eastern seaboard. Today, the number of expatriates and their descendants living on the mainland is just over 2.4 million.[3] Today the population on the island is nearly 4 million. If both groups are included, Puerto Ricans make up about 2.5 percent of the U.S. population.[4]

Both Cuban Americans and mainland Puerto Ricans today play a critical role in expanding and maintaining Latino culture in a multicultural United States. (In this chapter the term *mainland* refers to the U.S. mainland, as distinct from the U.S. territory of Puerto Rico.) Both groups express a strong identification with their cultural traditions, and, in spite of much internal discussion about return to the home islands, both groups are committed to carving out a permanent place on the U.S. mainland.

Puerto Ricans

FROM SPANISH TO U.S. RULE

Borinquén, the original native name for Puerto Rico, had a population of about 50,000 in 1493 when violent Spanish imperialism reached the island. Spain used the native people there (the Taino) as forced labor in mines and fields. Forced labor, disease, and violent suppression of rebellions caused a decline in the native population, so slaves were imported by the Spanish from Africa to fill the gap. The absence of women among the Spanish colonizers led to marriages between Spanish men and Native American or African women, producing a blended population of significant size. Over time, the population included a growing number of free blacks, since Spanish law allowed slaves to purchase their freedom. By 1530, only 369 of Puerto Rico's 3,049 inhabitants were European-born Spaniards. During the nineteenth century, immigrants and refugees from numerous countries, both European and Latin American, made their way to Puerto Rico. The census of 1827 found that the proportions of whites and people of color in Puerto Rico were almost equal. By the end of the century the island's population comprised thirty-four nationalities. Puerto Ricans today are the product of many racial and ethnic streams.[5]

In 1897, Puerto Ricans pressured the Spanish government into granting them internal autonomy. The following year, during the Spanish-American War, U.S. troops occupied the island. In the peace treaty that ended this brief war (1899) Spain gave Puerto Rico to the United States, whose leaders saw it as a useful station for warships and a profitable agricultural enclave. After four centuries of Spanish colonial rule, Puerto Rico came under U.S. control with no input from its local inhabitants, thereby losing the autonomy so recently won from Spain.[6]

As a U.S. possession, Puerto Rico was headed by a governor from the mainland appointed by the U.S. president. Puerto Rican scholar Maldonado-

Denis wrote the following description of Puerto Rico's governors during this early period:

> The criterion used by the President of the United States to choose the colonial governor and his cabinet was, with very few exceptions, one of compensation for political favors received. Many of these men came to Puerto Rico without knowing the language or, at times, even the location of the island. . . . The same can be said of many of the bureaucrats sent to Puerto Rico in the colonial free-for-all: they were ignorant and prejudiced, with the feelings of superiority common to all colonizers.[7]

Acts of the locally elected legislature were subject to veto by the U.S. Congress, the president, or the governor, and English became the mandatory language in schools. In 1917, the Jones Act awarded U.S. citizenship to all Puerto Ricans. Islanders have long been divided over the character of their political ties to the United States.[8]

In 1948, Puerto Ricans were permitted to elect their own governor. In 1952 the Commonwealth of Puerto Rico, the idea of Governor Luis Muñoz Marín, was created with its own constitution (approved by the U.S. Congress). Considerable home rule was granted Puerto Ricans, including the right to elect their own officials, make their own civil and criminal codes, and run their own schools. In 1948, Spanish became the official language in schools, and the Puerto Rican flag was allowed to fly. However, these changes came about only with the permission of the U.S. government, the colonial power that still oversees Puerto Rico. Puerto Ricans living in Puerto Rico still have no vote in national elections and no senators or House members. Their only representation in the U.S. Congress is by a nonvoting commissioner. In addition, the Commonwealth status has an important economic dimension, since it includes strong economic ties to the United States.

When the United States took over Puerto Rico, much of the land was owned by small farmers who raised coffee, sugar, and other foodstuffs. In 1899, Puerto Ricans owned 93 percent of the farms. Under U.S. control, heavy taxes and restrictions on credit forced many farmers to sell their land to U.S. companies. Independent farmers growing coffee were driven out by the U.S.-forced devaluation of the Puerto Rican peso and the closing of European markets that came with U.S. occupation. By 1930, large absentee-owned companies controlled 60 percent of sugar production and monopolized tobacco production and the shipping lines; by 1952, sugar production dominated the island's economy. The island moved from a locally controlled, diversified economy to one dominated by sugar interests and under external control. Many peasant farmers and their families were forced to seek jobs with the absentee-owned sugar companies. Puerto Ricans have thus become low-wage labor for international corporations, and in the slack employment seasons thousands have endured terrible poverty.[9]

Until the 1930s, Puerto Rico was ruled as an agricultural colony under various U.S. decrees that determined life on the island, from currency exchange to the amount of land a person could own. When 1930s (New Deal) reforms came to Puerto Rico, U.S. governor Rexford Tugwell envisioned a program for the island that would include agricultural and industrial development.

After World War II, agricultural development was forgotten, and, in the late 1940s, a program called Operation Bootstrap, designed by Puerto Rican governor

Marín to bring about economic development by attracting U.S. industrial corporations to the island, was implemented. Lured by a ten-year exemption from local taxation as well as by lower wages than on the mainland, some 1,700 factories came to the island by 1975, creating manufacturing jobs and bringing a boom in construction. Real annual per capita income increased almost sevenfold during this twenty-five-year period, and Puerto Rico's gross domestic product tripled between 1950 and 1970. However, the tax exemptions for most of these new industries left the burden of financing the infrastructure (sewers, water, electricity) on the local population, resulting in a high personal income tax. Operation Bootstrap's emphasis on urban industry and neglect of agriculture tilted the island farther away from its heritage of locally owned farms. Loss of agricultural land to industrial development even forced the island to import food. Today, little of the island's economy is agricultural, and sugar is no longer of any importance. Industry mainly takes the form of manufacturing plants.

By the 1970s, massive unemployment had led approximately one-third of the island's population to migrate to the mainland; since then the island's official unemployment rate has remained at least as high as 10 percent. The return of many Puerto Ricans to the island from the mainland during the mid-1970s caused even greater unemployment. In recent years, recessions have brought cutbacks in Puerto Rico's petrochemical plants, increasing unemployment rates. Numerous companies have left the island, some looking for cheaper labor and tax exemptions elsewhere.[10] One Puerto Rican immigrant testified at a U.S. Commission on Civil Rights hearing that he came to the mainland because the company he worked for had used up its exemption from taxes, and its executives had decided to move from the island rather than pay taxes.[11] The official unemployment rate peaked at 23 percent in 1983 and stood at 16.8 percent (19 percent for men and 13.3 percent for women) in 1993.[12] Some analysts have estimated the real unemployment rate (including part-time workers) to be 40 percent or higher.

In 1996, the U.S. Congress passed legislation ending the tax incentive that encouraged U.S. manufacturing firms to locate in Puerto Rico, where they have had little or no federal income tax obligation. The tax exemption will be phased out over the years between now and 2006. As a result, the 300 U.S. canning, textile, pharmaceutical, electronics, and other factories on the island may eventually move to cheaper labor and taxation areas around the globe, thereby creating another serious job crisis for the island and, possibly, a new large-scale search for jobs on the mainland.[13]

MIGRATION TO THE MAINLAND

Migration Streams

The number of Puerto Ricans in the United States before the island became a U.S. possession was small and consisted largely of prosperous merchants, political activists, and tobacco workers. Some 2,000 Puerto Ricans lived on the mainland in 1900; most of these were in New York City. Significant immigration to the mainland in response to unemployment and poverty on the island began in the late 1920s, and a somewhat smaller group came in the late 1930s. By 1940, mainland Puerto Ricans numbered almost 70,000; most continued to reside in various sections of New York City. Over the next two decades the number increased more than tenfold, to 887,000, the period called the "great migration." A major reason for this was the previously mentioned Operation Bootstrap, which resulted in a net loss of jobs and included active encouragement (such as in radio ads) to emigrate. Between 1945 and 1970, about one in three Puerto Ricans left the island. Thousands were farm workers forced out of work by the aforementioned changes in agriculture. Puerto Rican communities were established in New Jersey, Connecticut, and Chicago, although the majority of new immigrants continued to settle in New York.[14]

Many a tourist who has seen Puerto Rico has probably asked, "Why would anyone want to leave such a beautiful island?" Piri Thomas answers succinctly: "Bread, money, gold, a peso to make a living. . . . Wasn't that the greatest reason all the other different ethnic groups came to America for, freedom from want?"[15] Another Puerto Rican writer, Jack Agueros, describes the impact of the surge of new immigration on established Puerto Rican communities on the mainland:

> [World War II] ended and the heavy Puerto Rican migration began. . . . Into an ancient neighborhood came pouring four to five times more people than it had been designed to hold. Men who came running at the promise of jobs were jobless as the war ended. They were confused. They could not see the economic forces that ruled their lives as they drank beer on the corners, reassuring themselves of good times to come while they were hell-bent toward alcoholism. The sudden surge in numbers caused new resentments, and prejudice was intensified. Some were forced to live in cellars, and were then characterized as cave dwellers. Kids came who were confused by the new surroundings; their Puerto Ricanness forced us against a mirror asking, "If they are Puerto Ricans, what are we?" and thus they confused us. In our confusion we were sometimes pathetically reaching out, sometimes pathologically striking out. . . . Education collapsed. Every classroom had ten kids who spoke no English.[16]

The island's political and economic ties to the United States made possible a variety of favorable investment and trade arrangements for U.S. firms, ultimately displacing large numbers of workers on the island and creating the need for mass emigration.[17] The Puerto Rican government encouraged migration as a safety valve to reduce the pressures of unemployment. Pull factors were also important. Many came to the mainland as contract laborers. Puerto Rican workers brought to southern New Jersey farms in the mid-1940s were

> flown up here to a strange land, in the dark of the night, and by morning some are in the farmers' fields ready to work. There is no time for any sort of adjustment. The Puerto Rican is plunged into a strange environment with not even the advantage of a common language among these strangers.[18]

Beginning in the mid-1940s, corporations sent recruiters to Puerto Rico seeking cheap labor for the booming postwar economy. Workers came to textile sweatshops in New York; steel mills in Pennsylvania, Ohio, and Indiana; foundries in

Wisconsin and Illinois; and electronics industries in Illinois. Many of these immigrants hoped to earn money on the mainland and then return to the island. But for the large majority marginal employment or chronic unemployment gave them little choice but to become permanent residents of mainland urban areas. For example, Puerto Ricans who came to work in coal mines in Dover, New Jersey, in the mid-1940s stayed to work in factories in that area.[19]

The decades since 1970 are sometimes called a period of "revolving-door" migration. Many Puerto Ricans fleeing declining industrialization on the island have arrived in U.S. cities that are periodically plagued with unemployment. A series of recessions along with deteriorating neighborhoods and living conditions on the mainland have combined with love for the island, family ties, and a desire to nurture children in island culture to prompt many Puerto Ricans to return to the island. Often these same people come back to the mainland after a time because of lower wages and poor working conditions on the island. In the 1990s, manufacturing wages on the island have been about half of those on the mainland, and Puerto Rico's per capita income has been half that of the poorest U.S. state. For many who come to the mainland to work, intending to accumulate enough money to start a business and begin a new life on the island, the cycle of migration and return becomes a familiar pattern. Some analysts have argued that this circular migration is one reason for the lower educational and economic status of Puerto Ricans living on the mainland. Each return to the island is accompanied by the hope of success, although few have achieved that success. Moreover, in recent years the number of professional and other well-educated Puerto Rican workers coming to the mainland has increased, in part because of an absence of appropriate jobs on the island.[20]

In 1993, approximately 40 percent of all Puerto Ricans—more than 2.4 million people—resided in mainland communities in virtually every state. Puerto Ricans now make up almost 11 percent of all Latinos on the mainland.[21] Increasingly, many Puerto Ricans have settled in areas other than New York. Both Connecticut and Florida have large and growing Puerto Rican populations.

PREJUDICE AND STEREOTYPES

Puerto Ricans have been stereotyped in ways similar to Mexican Americans and African Americans. The first white stereotypes were probably developed by U.S. military officials and colonial administrators. (In this chapter, as in Chapter 9, the term *white* refers to those identified by the U.S. census as non-Hispanic whites.) In the 1890s, for example, a white U.S. officer noted that "the people seem willing to work, even at starvation wages, and they seem to be docile and grateful for anything done for them. They are emotional."[22] Other officials saw Puerto Ricans as "lazy natives."

Images of lazy, submissive Puerto Ricans persist, particularly among white officials who deal with Puerto Rican clients. White teachers have held images of Puerto Ricans as lazy and immoral. Alfredo Lopez reports being at a college meeting in New York where an experienced teacher from a poor school spoke on instill-ing the "middle-class values" of thrift, morality, and motivation in the children. Lopez asked the white teacher about her image of Puerto Rican children:

> It was when I asked what morality was and where it was practiced among middle-class people or what motivation was lacking in our people and how she discovered this, or finally, how the hell a person could be thrifty on eighty-four dollars a week, that she began to do some thinking.[23]

Often referred to by the derogatory term *spic*, Puerto Ricans have been viewed, as were the Italians and Mexican Americans before them, as a criminal lot. An Aspen Institute conference report noted that the English-language news media exaggerate certain aspects of Puerto Rican and Mexican American life—poverty, gang violence, and illegal immigrants. Crimes by Puerto Ricans have been sensa-tionalized in the New York City newspapers and other mass media; this has helped foster the image of Puerto Ricans as criminals. J. Edgar Hoover, a former director of the FBI, promulgated this perverse stereotype:

> We cooperate with the Secret Service on presidential trips abroad. You *never* have to bother about a President being shot by Puerto Ricans or Mexicans. They don't shoot very straight. But if they come at you with a knife, beware.[24]

Hoover's crude stereotype of Latino Americans as dumb-but-sinister knife carri-ers is still common in the United States.

In the 1950s, when large numbers of migrants began coming to the main-land, the Puerto Rican government circulated pamphlets trying to prepare migrants for prejudice they were likely to face. One read as follows:

> If one Puerto Rican steals, Americans who are prejudiced say that all Puerto Ricans are thieves. If one Puerto Rican doesn't work, prejudiced Americans say all of us are lazy. . . . We pay, because a bad opinion of us is formed, and the result may be that they discredit us, they won't give us work, or they deny us our rights.[25]

This pamphlet recognized the ways in which whites unfairly generalize, and it clearly implied that negative stereotypes are translated into discrimination against Puerto Ricans who are looking for jobs. A majority of Puerto Ricans inter-viewed in a recent New York City survey felt that Puerto Ricans were discrimi-nated against by non–Puerto Ricans on the mainland.[26]

Stereotypes of Puerto Rico and Puerto Ricans have been circulated by social scientists as well. For example, Nathan Glazer and Daniel Moynihan argued in their famous 1963 book *Beyond the Melting Pot* that Puerto Rican society was "sadly defective" in its culture and family system. They characterized Puerto Rican families as weak and disorganized. Glazer and Moynihan suggested that this allegedly weak family structure was the reason Puerto Ricans on the main-land did not move into better-paying jobs.[27]

Similarly, in a famous book titled *La Vida*, anthropologist Oscar Lewis honed his influential but stereotyped "culture of poverty" concept, which emphasizes the allegedly defective subculture of those in poverty. Lewis initially developed this perspective based on research on low-income Puerto Ricans on the island. Then, in the 1960s, he applied the concept to the poor in the United States, arguing that the culture of the poor is "a way of life which is passed down from generation to generation along family lines."[28] The poor, he contends, adapt in distinctive ways to their living conditions, and these adaptations are transmitted through the socialization process. Lewis's negative culture-of-poverty generalizations have greatly influenced the contemporary popular emphasis on the supposedly pathological traits of poor communities. What is missing from such "culture of poverty" analyses is a clear discussion of the role of unemployment and underemployment in generating extremely oppressive conditions for poor Americans.

Stereotypes of Puerto Ricans as drug users and criminals influence police actions in Puerto Rican communities in U.S. cities, which are often more closely patrolled than other areas. In the words of one Puerto Rican rights activist, "There is this idea that young Hispanics are all drug abusers who come here to terrorize people." Significantly, however, a survey in New York State found that Latino teenagers actually use drugs *less often* than white teenagers do.[29] Unfortunately, such data have not yet corrected the racial bias in drug-use stereotypes circulated in many police departments or in the mass media.

A recent report on the local economy in New Britain, Connecticut, revealed a new form of stereotyped images of Puerto Ricans. The report, issued by some white members of the city's business elite, alleged that the "poor language skills," "poor family values," and work ethic of Puerto Ricans contributed to the city's economic problems and suggested that Puerto Ricans should be encouraged to leave the city. In response, in the spring of 1997 a large group of Puerto Rican residents organized the Puerto Rican Organization for Unity and Dignity to counter overt anti-Latino stereotyping and discrimination and to press for expanded political clout.[30]

Color Coding and White Prejudices

As with other non-European groups, racial prejudices and stereotyping are reflected in discrimination against Puerto Ricans and have a negative impact on their self-images. To understand the Puerto Rican experience on the mainland we must first look at the situation in Puerto Rico, for, although prejudice and discrimination exist on the island, there is a considerable difference between the two areas. The phenomenon of "passing" on the mainland, in which a light-skinned individual hides his or her African ancestry in order to pass for white and bypass discrimination, is not necessary in Puerto Rican society. Puerto Rican society, like other Latin American countries, recognizes a spectrum of several racial categories based on multiple physical characteristics and not just skin color. Puerto Rican society is also much more racially integrated than mainland U.S. society. A Puerto Rican family's members may represent a variety of skin colors. Moreover, an individual's treatment in terms of housing, political rights, government policy, and other social institutions is often not racially differentiated. Finally, Puerto Rican culture represents a complex synthesis of multiple and diverse cultural elements, whereas acculturation on the mainland is (with a few exceptions such as music) one-way, with Latino groups typically adopting dominant-group cultural values rather than the reverse.[31]

Americans of European descent tend to see Puerto Ricans as a "nonwhite" group, lumping them with African Americans or Mexican Americans. Until they come to the mainland, most Puerto Ricans have seldom had to deal with blatant color-based discrimination. Overt racial discrimination on the mainland comes as a shock to most immigrants. Recalling an experience in high school when a girl whom he had asked to dance turned him down, Piri Thomas, a Puerto Rican who grew up in Spanish Harlem (*El Barrio*) and eventually became well known as the author of the autobiographical *Down These Mean Streets,* wrote about his confusion and anger at whites' denial of his identity as a Puerto Rican:

> "Who?" someone asked.
>
> "That new colored boy." . . .
>
> I couldn't see them, but I had that for-sure feeling that it was me they had in their mouths. . . .
>
> "Listen, Angelo. Jus' listen," I said stonily. . . .
>
> "Do you mean just like that?" . . .
>
> "Ahuh," Marcia said. "Just as if I was a black girl. Well! He started to talk to me and what could I do except be polite and at the same time not encourage him?"
>
> "Christ, first that Jerry bastard and now him. We're getting invaded by niggers."[32]

The imposition of discrete and rigid mainland categories of black and white on Puerto Ricans, whose home culture sees racial-ethnic diversity on a continuum, creates confusion and anger, whether the individual is called "black" or "white." The denial of personal identity inherent in such a racial identification is the issue. Statements such as "You don't look Puerto Rican," or "Are you 100 percent Puerto

Puerto Rican American author Piri Thomas.

Rican?" commonly confront Puerto Ricans on the mainland. Faced with the task of categorizing Puerto Rican school children as either "Negro" or "Caucasian" in 1954, New York State officials were aware of the invidious divisions that would arise if Puerto Rican families were asked to divide their children. The officials proposed abandoning the racial terms and listing these children simply as Puerto Rican even though this would imply that Puerto Ricans were a distinct racial category.[33]

Research by Angel Martínez has revealed a substantial difference in the self-perception of Puerto Ricans and how they thought North Americans perceived them. When asked to classify themselves, most chose neither white nor black but a mixed category of brown. However, most felt that other North Americans saw them as either white (58 percent) or black (42 percent).[34]

The 1980 census was the first to ask every individual whether he or she was Hispanic; it included subcategories for Mexicans, Puerto Ricans, Cubans, and other Hispanic persons. A separate item asked for the "race" of each individual. Fewer than 4 percent of the Puerto Ricans from the New York City area stated their "race" as black; 44 percent classified themselves as white. Almost 48 percent wrote in "Spanish" in the space labeled "Other–Specify." This indicates, among other things, the conflict between the polarized U.S. racial structure and the cultural–racial continuum with which Puerto Ricans identify.[35]

ECONOMIC AND RELATED CONDITIONS: THE MAINLAND

Writing about his experiences as an early immigrant, Jesús Colon has explained that Puerto Ricans did the dirty work of the society and that poverty was usually their lot. Jesús and his brother worked different hours, and to save money they even shared their working clothes: "we only had one pair of working pants between the two of us."[36]

Discrimination in employment was common for Puerto Rican immigrants; those with darker skin usually suffered the most. In *Down These Mean Streets*, Piri Thomas recounted a 1945 interview for a job as a door-to-door salesperson. He was not hired; a lighter-skinned friend was. Dark-skinned Puerto Ricans, he discovered by asking other applicants, were discriminated against by the white employer:

> "Let's walk," I said. I didn't feel so much angry as I did sick, like throwing-up sick. Later, when I told this story to my buddy, a colored cat, he said, "Hell, Piri, Ah know stuff like that can sure burn a cat up, but a Negro faces that all the time."
>
> "I know that," I said, "but I wasn't a Negro then. I was still only a Puerto Rican."[37]

Occupation and Unemployment

Puerto Rican immigrants have brought with them a wide spectrum of skills. Some are artists and musicians; others are skilled in wood or other crafts. Some operated their own business on the island; others held positions of responsibility in the educational, medical, legal, or political systems. On the mainland, however, the skills of many immigrants have gone largely unnoticed and unused. Regardless of their background, Puerto Ricans have been offered few choices for employment. Mainland Puerto Ricans have often done the "dirty work" for whites. Many have been forced to take low-level jobs in factories or restaurants in New York City. They have cleaned up as busboys and janitors; they have worked in garment industry sweatshops that paid low wages; they have driven taxis. Many have faced recurring unemployment.[38]

The following table shows the occupational distribution for employed Puerto Ricans on the mainland in 1993:[39]

	Men		Women	
	European Americans	Puerto Rican	European Americans	Puerto Rican
Managerial and professional	29.2%	15.5%	30.9%	18.5%
Technical, sales, and administrative support	21.7	18.0	43.9	48.4
Service occupations	8.8	22.4	16.0	19.9
Farming, forestry, and fishing	3.7	1.8	0.9	—
Precision production, craft, and repair	18.7	15.1	1.7	2.4
Operators, fabricators, and laborers	17.8	27.3	6.6	10.8
Totals	99.9%	100.1%	100%	100%

Puerto Rican men are still concentrated in lower-paid blue-collar and service jobs. Once mostly domestics and less-skilled blue-collar workers, Puerto Rican women are now concentrated in sales and clerical jobs. Both Puerto Rican men and women are substantially underrepresented in managerial and professional occupations. Today, Puerto Rican men are only about half as likely to hold managerial or professional positions as European Americans and are more than two and one-half times as likely to be employed in service jobs. In addition, Puerto Ricans in white-collar jobs tend to occupy the lower-paid positions, such as teacher or librarian. In many East Coast areas, Puerto Rican laborers have done much of the low-paid field work that has put vegetables on U.S. tables, often working seven days a week and living in substandard housing conditions.[40]

Unemployment at all points has been much higher for mainland Puerto Ricans than for white workers. Unemployment and subemployment rates for Puerto Rican men and women have consistently been among the highest of any racial or ethnic group in northeastern U.S. cities. In March 1993, 14.4 percent of mainland Puerto Ricans were officially unemployed, compared with 6.1 percent of whites.[41] Moreover, these official rates show only the tip of the iceberg, for they reflect no more than half the actual number of Puerto Ricans who are unemployed or subemployed. To ascertain the total number of unemployed and subemployed Puerto Ricans we must add the large numbers who are discouraged from looking for work because of long-term unemployment, who are working part-time but who want full-time work, and who make very low wages.

Employment Discrimination and Other Social Barriers

Institutionalized discrimination rooted in color coding and linguistic prejudice has restricted Puerto Rican access to many job categories, contributing both to the concentration of Puerto Ricans in low-level employment and to their high unemployment rates relative to other groups. In New York City, for example, Puerto Ricans have been severely underrepresented (relative to their percentage of the population) in local and state government jobs. This is at least in part because they are less integrated into the job information networks traditionally dominated by whites. In many cases, Puerto Ricans are screened out of jobs by tests that are, unnecessarily, given only in English. Such a procedure is discriminatory when Puerto Rican applicants are capable of doing the jobs and the screening tests are not job-related. Even trash collection jobs, for example, have sometimes required screening tests, on which those who speak English and have a high-school diploma score better. As with Mexican Americans, many Puerto Ricans find themselves unfairly stigmatized as being of "low intelligence" because of their limited command of English.[42]

Institutionalized discrimination can also be seen in height and weight requirements that use white men as the standard. Such requirements have sometimes disqualified Puerto Rican applicants for police and fire department jobs. Even Puerto Ricans' status as U.S. citizens has been a source of discriminatory treatment. Some have been asked by local government officials, apparently unaware that Puerto Rico is part of the United States, to prove that they, as Puerto Ricans, are U.S. citizens. For other jobs, citizenship status has proved to be a handicap. In a Civil Rights Commission interview a Puerto Rican woman in California said,

> I've had about six or seven jobs since I came here. What happens is that they hire you temporarily and get rid of you as soon as possible because you don't belong to the right race. I'd even say that bosses here prefer Mexicans (particularly illegals) because they know that unions don't represent them, so they can be exploited easier. At least Puerto Ricans have citizenship and can get into unions.[43]

Racial discrimination is a major factor in the employment possibilities of Puerto Ricans. White Americans tend to classify Puerto Ricans as "black" or "nonwhite" and may discriminate against them for the same reasons they discriminate against African Americans. Historically, many U.S. unions, especially those representing skilled and craft workers, have excluded or restricted Puerto Ricans. Union, private, and governmental authorities have sometimes winked at these practices. "Unions did not facilitate the economic integration of Puerto Ricans as they had for other groups," writes Rodríguez. As a result, "Puerto

Rican pay rates and benefits were (and are) inferior to those of other workers doing the same jobs."[44]

Industrial Restructuring

A variety of changing structural factors in the U.S. economy have contributed to high unemployment rates for Puerto Ricans. Early Puerto Rican immigrants came to the mainland, especially to New York City, to fill manufacturing jobs, primarily in the garment industry. By the time of the migration of 1946–1964, however, the central cities of the United States, and especially New York City, had generally entered a period of industrial decline. As New York City moved from an industrial economy to a service-oriented economy, production jobs once open to Puerto Ricans began to disappear. Between 1960 and 1980, New York City lost many manufacturing jobs, and this decline continued into the 1980s and 1990s. The availability of low-level service jobs did not keep pace with the decline in production jobs.

Technological innovations—automation, computerization, and the use of robots—further eroded the number of less-skill blue-collar production jobs. In addition, many plants moved to the suburbs, the South, or overseas, taking jobs out of the geographical reach of inner-city Puerto Ricans who did not qualify for most of the new white-collar jobs created in the city. Lack of retraining and education for white-collar jobs leaves Puerto Rican workers in New York increasingly part of a large surplus labor force.[45]

Marta Tienda and William Diaz have argued that the primary reasons for the sharp deterioration in the economic position of Puerto Ricans were the decline of inner-city manufacturing in the northeastern cities and the continuing circular migration to Puerto Rico. The most important reason for the rising poverty and unemployment faced by Puerto Ricans between the late 1970s and the late 1980s was the "drastically reduced job opportunities in industrial Northeastern cities like New York, Newark, and Pittsburgh, as well as in Puerto Rico."[46] In addition, circular migration, the constant movement of Puerto Rican workers back and forth between Puerto Rico and the mainland in search of jobs, causes significant disruption to families and educational attainment. It exacerbates the fundamental economic problems created by economic dislocation, capital flight, and discrimination in northeastern cities.

The presence of employed workers is crucial for any community's survival. For example, Mercer Sullivan describes an area of Brooklyn where unemployed and displaced Puerto Ricans live in dire straights, yet reside next to employed blue-collar workers who help maintain viable institutions in that local community. Some unemployment can be more or less handled by a community as long as it does not become dominant.[47]

Income and Poverty

Puerto Ricans are one of the poorest groups in the United States. Between 1959 and 1974 Puerto Rican family incomes declined from 71 percent of the national average to only 59 percent. Poverty or near poverty was the lot of most families.

Accounts of oppressive conditions are not unusual. Felipe Luciano described life during this period as a Puerto Rican:

> You resign yourself to poverty—my mother did this. Your face is rubbed in shit so much that you begin to accept that shit as reality . . . my stomach rumbling. My mother beating me when I knew it was because of my father . . . the welfare investigator cursing out my mother because what she wants is spring clothing for her children.[48]

Puerto Ricans were the only group in the United States to see a decline in family incomes in the 1970s and 1980s. Between 1979 and 1984, median family income for mainland Puerto Ricans fell in real terms (adjusting for inflation) 18 percent—more than the huge 14 percent drop for African Americans and the 9 percent decrease for Mexican Americans.[49] Puerto Ricans continue to have one of the lowest median family incomes of any U.S. group. Data from the 1990 census show that only Dominicans and Hondurans ranked lower than Puerto Ricans on this economic indicator.[50] In the mid-1990s, median family income for mainland Puerto Ricans was still only half that of whites.[51] The 1994 Census Bureau population survey reported a median family income for Puerto Ricans of $20,929, which is just over two-thirds that of Cuban Americans ($30,581), the most affluent Latino group. Almost 37 percent of mainland Puerto Ricans fell below the federal poverty line, compared with less than one-tenth of whites.[52]

The desperate nature of some Puerto Ricans' situations is evident in their use of public assistance for both couple-headed and single-parent families; this is especially significant in light of the hostility that most have for such public aid. "I'd rather starve than go on welfare" is an often stated sentiment among Puerto Ricans regardless of their poverty status.[53]

Housing Problems

Discrimination against Puerto Ricans is significant in the area of housing. A Rutgers University professor of law contended at one Civil Rights Commission hearing that Puerto Ricans have suffered more than African Americans from housing discrimination. Puerto Ricans have been excluded from most decent housing markets and get the "housing scraps" no one else wants.[54]

Compared with other groups, Puerto Ricans use a larger percentage of their income for housing and are more likely to live in dilapidated or deficient housing. In 1993, fewer than one-fourth of Puerto Rican households owned or were buying their own home, compared with more than 70 percent of white households.[55] As low-income renters, many Puerto Ricans are vulnerable to the devastating impact of urban decay. Overcrowding and deteriorating housing are characteristic of numerous neighborhoods. The South Bronx, home to the largest and densest mainland Puerto Rican community, is a grim example. Once composed of stable communities, this area has been gutted by highway construction, redlined by bankers, and abandoned by employers and government agencies. Since 1970, the South Bronx has lost much of its housing stock and population. In addition to psychic stress and severed friendship and community ties, neighborhood decay has had a negative impact on education and has increased the distances residents must travel to shopping and workplaces. Clara Rodríguez describes the effects on residents of depopulation and commercial and industrial flight:

> Certain neighborhoods were swept with devastation, leaving local landscapes where one or two buildings were the lone survivors of an unabated process of destruction. . . .
>
> It is difficult to convey the psychic despair that is felt by people who experience the daily loss of people and places that make up their world. One day there was a super-market to shop at, the next day it is closed. Last week you had friends or relatives up the street, today they too are leaving. Your own home edges closer to the brink of decay as the buildings on the block empty. The continual reminders of surrounding decay multiply with each day.[56]

Discrimination is an omnipresent problem not only in housing but in most other areas as well. In one survey in New York City, 80 percent of Latinos (mostly Puerto Ricans) reported having been mistreated by the police. More than 70 percent reported mistreatment by landlords, employers, shopkeepers, elected officials, the courts, and the schools. When asked a general question about the frequency and extent of discrimination against Latinos, a majority of the respondents felt there was substantial discrimination in all areas of life.[57]

EDUCATION

In 1993 more than 8 percent of mainland Puerto Ricans over twenty-four years old had completed less than five years of school. This was more than ten times the percent for whites at this low educational level. Approximately 60 percent of Puerto Ricans over twenty-four years old had completed high school, compared with more than 84 percent of whites. Eight percent had completed college, about one-third the figure for whites.[58]

High dropout rates, or more accurately *pushout* rates, for Puerto Rican students remain a nationwide problem, although variations can be found from one area to another. These rates tend to be highest in central-city school districts. In spite of its high position among the states in per-pupil expenditures and teacher salaries, New York ranks near the bottom in student retention. New York City has a particularly dismal record in educating Puerto Rican students, whose retention rates there are lower than for any other group. Tracking the school population's racial–ethnic composition by grade level shows a precipitous decline in Latino enrollment in New York City schools at the ninth grade. Some have characterized the poor education opportunities of Puerto Rican youth as "premarket discrimination"—that is, discrimination that inhibits future success in the labor market.[59]

The low college graduation rate for mainland Puerto Ricans restricts upward mobility. As for African and Mexican Americans, the historically white college or university setting is often an alien environment for Puerto Rican students. Mila Morales-Nadal has noted the determination and struggles of Puerto Rican women, among the poorest of all people of color, to get an education in order to secure a decent job. "It is not uncommon for some mothers to take their children with them to class in some public colleges." She concluded that within the context of higher education intercultural exchanges that respect and value the language, culture, and identity of Puerto Ricans are vital to the empowerment of Puerto Rican youth.[60]

At least since the great migration, Puerto Ricans have struggled against an educational system that has failed many of their children. Pressing for in-depth studies to examine their educational problems, some Puerto Rican communities have also developed local organizations to work for change. When the findings and recommendations of these numerous critical studies are ignored by school boards, Puerto Ricans have sometimes turned to the courts. Nonetheless, the educational system has proved highly resistant even to court-mandated change, for white school administrators' attention to the rights and needs of culturally different students has often been halfhearted.[61]

Barriers to Social and Economic Mobility

Few Puerto Ricans have moved into influential positions in the field of education, and Puerto Ricans have little control over the educational policies and curriculum decisions affecting their children. School authorities frequently are insensitive to Puerto Rican history and culture; the standard curriculum is often based on the implicit assumption that Puerto Ricans are culturally and linguistically deficient. Neglect of Puerto Rican history and culture by the schools contributes to a lack of self-esteem among students. The schools attended by most students have a high concentration of Puerto Rican and other students of color, yet both the actual number of Puerto Rican teachers and administrators and the ratio of Puerto Rican teachers and administrators to Puerto Rican students are extremely low.[62] Segregated schooling has serious negative implications: low retention rates, a large majority of students who read below grade level, high student–teacher ratios, less-qualified teachers, and low teacher expectations. As we have noted previously, a strong correlation has been established between teachers' expectations and students' actual academic achievement. Those students, in any group, whose teachers expect them to achieve are much more likely to succeed.

Language

As we noted in the chapter on Mexican Americans, most U.S. schools today are not structured to deal with students who do not speak English. Prior to the American Revolution, however, bilingual education (in such languages as German, for example) was common and continued to be available to many immigrants and their children in private, and sometimes publicly funded, schools in the eighteenth, nineteenth, and early twentieth centuries. It is only in the last half of the twentieth century that bilingual education has become "un-American" and highly politicized by anti-immigrant organizations.

Limited English proficiency creates multiple handicaps for Puerto Rican students, as it does for other Latino groups. Children who are unable to understand

English instruction fall behind native-English-speaking classmates. Puerto Rican students are sometimes assigned to low-ability groups, to "language-disabled" classes, or to lower grades. On the average, Puerto Rican students do not do as well as non-Latino white students on achievement tests, most of which are given in English. A psychologist in Philadelphia commented on the inaccuracy of English-language test scores:

> In my clinic, the average underestimation of IQ for a Puerto Rican kid is 20 points. We go through this again and again. When we test in Spanish, there is a 20 point leap immediately—20 higher than when he's tested in English.[63]

Many of the new Spanish-language achievement and "IQ" tests are only translations of English-language tests, a practice that passes along the other cultural biases that exist in the tests. The predictive validity of the standardized tests used for college and graduate school entrance (the SAT and GRE) is considerably lower for Latinos than for whites. Use of such tests has been considered discriminatory by many critical observers.[64]

Schools can be places of oppression or of support. Educator Henry Giroux has written that learning is "not merely . . . the acquisition of knowledge but . . . the production of cultural practices that offer students a sense of identity, place, and hope."[65] Puerto Rican educator Herman La Fontaine has noted that "our definition of cultural pluralism must include the concept that our language and our culture will be given equal status to that of the majority population."[66] Puerto Rican educators argue that children should be taught to read and write well in Spanish first, taught subjects in that language, and then taught English as a second language. Some civil rights groups have pressed for expanded and effective bilingual education programs for Latino children. Indeed, a goal of Puerto Rican organizations in their struggle against the New York City school system has been a comprehensive educational program in which the strengths and values of Puerto Rican culture and the Spanish language are recognized. The outcome of their struggle so far has been a bilingual program that is designed to teach English as a replacement language and that devalues biculturalism.[67]

Some researchers report that high-school students in bilingual programs have higher attendance and completion rates and that such programs contribute to more positive self-concepts for students. Nonetheless, in most instances bilingual programs have not become part of the mainstream school curriculum. Viewed by conservative officials as luxuries, bilingual programs were heavily cut in the 1980s. A leader of Philadelphia's Puerto Rican Alliance argued that this showed a "blatant disregard of a right the courts have already recognized."[68]

Official English Policies and Spanish Speakers

As we have noted in Chapter 3, support for English as the official U.S. language has grown over the last decade or two. Much of this nativist movement has targeted Spanish and Spanish speakers such as Puerto Rican and Mexican Americans, especially in Florida and the southwestern states. An amendment to the Arizona Constitution went so far as to make English the language "of all government functions and actions," but a federal judge ruled in 1990 that this law violated free speech as protected by the U.S. Constitution.[69] Nativism directed at Spanish speakers can be seen in this passage from a Council on Interamerican Security paper:

> Hispanics in America today represent a very dangerous and subversive force that is bent on taking over our nation's political institutions for the purposes of imposing Spanish as the official language of the U.S. and indeed of the entire Western Hemisphere. . . . They represent a serious threat to our cherished freedoms and our American traditions. . . . If we desire to preserve our unique culture and the primacy of the English language, then we must so declare rather than sitting idly by as a de facto nation evolves.[70]

Xenophobic nativists praise official-language and English-only government policies as a means to unify diverse groups within U.S. society and to promote Anglo-Protestant cultural values. Educator Catherine Walsh reports that instead "such efforts toward linguistic cohesion resonate with a kind of colonial domination, a hegemony that threatens to silence the less powerful [and attempts] to render invisible the complex, abstract, socio-ideological nature of language."[71] Language is one of the ways in which people define themselves. Far from simply a set of neutral symbols, language shapes thought and thus is inseparable from personal identity and everyday life. In her years as a teacher and researcher, Walsh documented the daily struggle faced by language-minority students over *whose* language and therefore whose knowledge, perspectives, and experiences are recognized and accepted and whose are omitted or belittled. She quotes one young bilingual student:

> "Sometimes I two-times think," she said. "I think like in my family and in my house. And then I think like in school and other places. Then I talk. They aren't the same, you know."

Realizing that the language context of her home was not only different but less acceptable than that of the school, this child often told her teacher, "It makes me feel funny, all alone . . . different."[72] The negative effects of the limited bilingual education provided in public schools on Mexican American students, which we discussed in Chapter 9, are equally negative for Puerto Rican students in northeastern cities.

POLITICS

In Puerto Rico, voting by registered voters runs to 60 percent or more. Yet among mainland Puerto Ricans voting rates have been as low as 20 percent in some urban areas. The low level of political participation by and representation of Puerto Ricans on the mainland can be explained along the lines of other exploited racial and ethnic communities: a lack of education, weak electoral support of Puerto

Rican candidates by whites, a lack of campaign funds, a lack of representation in Democratic party leadership, and a feeling of hopelessness regarding possibilities for political change. In a survey of Puerto Ricans in New York City who were not registered to vote, the most frequently cited reasons for not voting were "not interested in politics" (29 percent) and "voting makes no difference" (24 percent). More than one in four stated that language barriers were important in keeping them from registering to vote.[73] Voter registration and turnout has generally increased for Puerto Ricans since 1990, especially in areas where governments are responsive to the needs of Puerto Rican communities. In the 1994 general election, for example, Puerto Rican voters in Pennsylvania played a decisive role in the reelection of one U.S. Representative.[74]

Election to political office has been slow to come for Puerto Ricans on the mainland. Since the 1930s, Puerto Ricans have participated in Democratic party politics in such states as New York and New Jersey, but until recent years that participation has usually been token. The first Puerto Rican American was elected to the New York State assembly in 1937; it would be fifteen years before another was elected. In 1965, Herman Badillo became the first Puerto Rican to be elected president of a New York City borough; six years later he became the first voting member of Puerto Rican background in the U.S. House. Since that time the South Bronx has continuously had a Puerto Rican representative in Congress. Robert Garcia, who followed Badillo, played an important role in building political bridges between African Americans and Puerto Ricans in New York, noting that "blacks and Puerto Ricans are natural allies as defined by our common position on the bottom rung of the socioeconomic ladder."[75] In 1965, he and several other state legislators formed a black–Puerto Rican caucus in the New York legislature. More recently, a Congressional Hispanic Caucus was created to focus on issues of importance to the Hispanic community. In 1990 Jose Serrano was elected to fill Garcia's seat. Puerto Rican representation in the House tripled in 1992 with the election of Nydia Velazquez (D.–New York) and Luis Gutierrez (D.–Illinois) to fill seats created by redistricting following the 1990 census. All three were reelected in mid-1990s elections. Moreover, in 1997 the newly re-elected President Bill Clinton appointed Aida Alvarez as head of the Small Business Administration, the first Puerto Rican to hold a cabinet-level position.[76]

Puerto Ricans have served on a number of city councils and as mayors of small towns and a few cities. Miami, Florida, had a Puerto Rican mayor from 1973 until 1985. Electoral successes at the local level have created a foundation for representation in several state governments. In 1995, New York had four state senators (two male and two female) and seven state assembly members who were Puerto Rican. By the late 1990s, Puerto Ricans had won twenty-one elected positions in New York City. Moreover, in the mid-1990s Illinois had one Puerto Rican state senator and two Puerto Rican state assembly members; Connecticut had four Puerto Rican state assembly members; Kansas had one Puerto Rican state senator; and Pennsylvania and California each had one Puerto Rican state assembly member. The majority of these officials have been elected since 1990.[77]

The long-term effects of institutional discrimination can be seen in state and city government employment, in which Puerto Ricans are significantly underrepresented. As a result many Puerto Ricans feel they are not part of the political system, and they often report being treated as nonpersons by government and private agencies. Government officials serving them are usually not Puerto Rican and seldom speak much Spanish. Government services have historically been less accessible to Puerto Ricans, and job training and employment services have been slow in coming to numerous Puerto Rican communities.[78] One exception to this pattern is the city of Paterson, New Jersey, where many Puerto Ricans are now employed in government jobs. With four Puerto Ricans, including three women, on the city's nine-member council in 1995, Paterson had the highest percentage of Puerto Rican representation in the nation.[79]

Starting in the 1980s, the Midwest–Northeast Voter Registration Education Project, which operates in eighteen states with significant Latino populations, has conducted thousands of voter-registration campaigns and registered more than a million new voters, many of whom were Puerto Rican. In the late 1980s, the governor of Puerto Rico announced a campaign to register mainland Puerto Ricans to vote. At that time an estimated 400,000 eligible Latinos, mostly Puerto Ricans, in the New York City area alone were unregistered. Local leaders welcomed this unique intervention by a non–mainland Puerto Rican leader, which demonstrated the close political alliances between the mainland and island communities. The project, which was funded by the Puerto Rican government, was implemented in 1988 by the Department of Puerto Rican Community Affairs in the United States, an agency that also provides information and referral for educational, employment, legal, and other social services. By the time the project closed in the early 1990s, it had registered more than 84,000 new voters in New York City, and Puerto Rican voter turnout in city council elections was increasing significantly. This resulted in an increase in the number of Puerto Rican members on the New York City council.[80]

PROTEST

In Puerto Rico

In Puerto Rico, the period of U.S. rule has periodically been punctuated with protest against the subordinate status that colonial domination entailed. Contrary to the stereotype of Latino docility, Puerto Ricans have fought hard to retain their language and culture and for self-determination. In the 1930s large numbers of Puerto Ricans attacked the colonial government buildings in periodic protests, and in 1934 there were strikes in the sugarcane fields. The Nationalist party, led by a Puerto Rican hero, Harvard-educated Pedro Albizu Campos, began pushing for expanded freedom and for independence. In March 1937, Nationalist party marchers who had joined a legal march in Ponce were massacred. By bringing in two hundred heavily armed police, the U.S. colonial governor set the stage for violence. A shot was fired, probably by the police, and a pitched battle ensued, with twenty dead and 100 injured, mostly marchers and bystanders.[81]

In the fall of 1950, police raided Nationalist party meetings and houses. This precipitated an armed revolt that spread to five cities. Hundreds of people were killed. Two thousand people were arrested for actively advocating independence. On the mainland Puerto Rican nationalists seeking independence attacked the residence of President Harry Truman and members of the U.S. House while they were in session.

The future of Puerto Rico is a major political issue on both the island and the mainland. The platforms of both the Republican and the Democratic parties have supported statehood for Puerto Rico. Although on the island pro-statehood sentiment has increased over the last few decades, in a nonbinding plebiscite in 1993 voters in Puerto Rico narrowly favored continuing the island's commonwealth status (48 percent to 46 percent for statehood). A small percentage (4.4 percent) voted for independence.[82] Significantly, in recent years several hundred Puerto Ricans have renounced their U.S. citizenship, viewing it as a colonial imposition.

In 1996 the pro-commonwealth party lost ground as the pro-statehood party received just over half the vote for its candidate for governor. The following year nine U.S. senators introduced a bipartisan bill to set up a plebiscite in 1998 (and every four years, if necessary) on Puerto Rican statehood. A similar bill was approved overwhelmingly by the House Committee on Resources in the summer of 1997. Supporters of statehood argue that commonwealth status is a second-class status. In contrast, opponents fear the economic changes and loss of Puerto Rican culture that statehood might bring. Writing in the elite journal *Foreign Affairs* in 1997, Ruben Berrios Martinez, President of the Puerto Rican Independence Party, stated:

> As a state, Puerto Rico is bound to pay the heaviest of prices: cultural assimilation. In the American system the only way out of an ethnic ghetto is through cultural assimilation into the Anglo-American mainstream, which would subordinate the island's Spanish language and distinct culture. . . . In any case, assimilation is unacceptable to Puerto Ricans, including statehooders.[83]

One sign of the threat of cultural assimilation is the view of some mainland whites, including politicians, that Puerto Rico should not become a state unless it adopts English as its official language.[84]

On the Mainland

Arriving for the most part desperately poor and already stigmatized by whites as inferior, Puerto Ricans on the mainland have developed community organizations to deal with discrimination and other problems. Some of the major organizations are the Puerto Rican Legal Project, the Puerto Rican Legal Defense Fund, the League of Puerto Rican Women, the Puerto Rican Teachers Association, the Puerto Rican Forum, and the Puerto Rican Family Institute. The Puerto Rican Teachers Association has worked to increase representation of Puerto Ricans among teachers and principals and to expand bilingual programs. Puerto Ricans have been active in labor and union organizations on the mainland since the late 1800s.[85]

Protest activity increased in the 1960s and 1970s. In the spring of 1969 the Young Lords, a militant protest group patterned after the Black Panthers, occupied the administration building of McCormick Theological Seminary to publicize poverty in Chicago. They took over a church, opening a day-care center and school for the community. They protested the use of urban-renewal land for a tennis club, and they set up a "people's park" on other urban-renewal land.[86]

A New York group formed a Young Lords political party. In December 1969, these Young Lords occupied the First Spanish Methodist Church in New York City for eleven days and organized a day-care center, a breakfast program, and a clothing distribution program. They created a newspaper, *Palante* (Forward), and led a demonstration of two hundred Puerto Ricans protesting squalid conditions at a local hospital.[87] The Young Lords, which had begun as a Chicago street gang, developed their own protest style. Children of poor immigrants, they articulated a thirteen-point program for a democratic-socialist society. They called for "liberation and power in the hands of the people, not Puerto Rican exploiters." At the peak of their influence, the Young Lords had chapters in twenty cities. Militant Puerto Rican groups such as the Young Lords were subject to police repression, including infiltration of their groups and prosecution of some leaders, sometimes in rigged trials. Other leaders were co-opted into government antipoverty programs. The Young Lords gradually disbanded in the early 1970s. In 1989, many former members celebrated the militancy of the group and the twentieth anniversary of its founding. Many former members are today influential Puerto Rican professionals and leaders in community organizations.[88]

In the 1990s, many organizations in Puerto Rican communities have been working for a better quality of life and increased decision making in the political process. The Puerto Rican Legal Defense and Education Fund has engaged in litigation in support of civil rights; an organization named Aspira has worked on improving education; the National Puerto Rican Forum has focused on employment and job training. The National Puerto Rican Coalition, representing more than 115 local organizations, has served as a liaison between Puerto Rican communities and federal government officials and lobbied for educational, health, economic, and civil rights programs.

Community Protest

Puerto Rican communities have protested discrimination. For example, in Cleveland, Orlando Morales, a young man serving two life sentences, was viewed by community groups as innocent. Much evidence indicated that Morales did not commit the murder for which he was convicted. Many in the Puerto Rican community felt the twenty-two-year-old Puerto Rican had been railroaded and actively protested what they saw as discrimination in the criminal justice system. Three hundred angry Puerto Ricans engaged in a protest meeting at Cleveland's Spanish American Committee Hall. In addition, community organizations in Chicago have protested housing discrimination and police brutality. Police injustices targeting Latinos, including derogatory language and unwarranted arrests and searches, as well as the use of excessive physical force, have reportedly been common in Chicago. A major riot involving hundreds of Puerto Ricans occurred in Miami in 1990 after six police officers were acquitted in the fatal beating of a Puerto Rican drug dealer. Residents of the extremely poor Puerto Rican neighborhood said the violent uprisings had a lot to do with the sense of alienation and powerlessness in the Miami community. They pointed to factors as diverse as the scarcity of Puerto Ricans in powerful government and business positions and the absence of Puerto Rican music on Spanish-language radio stations. "Cubans get everything; we get nothing," one resident stated.[89]

Some protest movements have brought important changes. For example, pressures from Puerto Rican activists led to the founding of a community college in the South Bronx and helped create an open admissions program at the City University of New York. City and state governments have provided more funds for community projects and hired more Puerto Ricans. Some public schools have added more Puerto Rican studies and bilingual programs and hired more Puerto Rican teachers.[90]

Coalitions of grass-roots organizations and older established groups were created in the 1980s, among them the National Congress for Puerto Rican Rights. Through such mechanisms traditional and militant leaders have tried to bridge the long-standing gap between them and to improve the socioeconomic conditions of Puerto Ricans. In the 1990s, the leaders and members of several state branches of this National Congress pressed state and local governments for equal justice in the courts and for better schools for Latino children; they participated in protest demonstrations, sometimes together with black organizations, against government indifference and police brutality. They have also been active in pressing the mass media for better reporting on Latino communities.

Annual parades honoring Puerto Ricans are now held in cities in New York and New Jersey. In the summer of 1997, a strong sense of Puerto Rican identity and a concern with discrimination could be seen during and following a large-scale parade by 200,000 people, which included elected officials and celebrities. A few days before this Puerto Rican parade, a local white business leader urged area businesses to close their doors and protect their premises during the parade. In addition, a former New York columnist writing in a prominent British magazine called Puerto Ricans "fat," "dusky," and "semi-savages." These actions, which triggered protests among Puerto Rican leaders, reveal continuing negative stereotypes of Puerto Ricans among white business and media elites.[91]

RELIGION

Traditionally, most Puerto Ricans have been Catholic, but on the mainland they have generally been led by non–Puerto Rican clergy. The supportive framework that parishes gave to many previous Catholic immigrant groups has largely been missing. One exception to this dependence on non–Puerto Rican clergy has been the Bishop of Puerto Rico, who visits Puerto Rican parishes on the mainland.

Scholar Joseph Fitzpatrick has argued that Puerto Rican religion is more a religion of the community than of the parish. Community celebrations and processions are important, as is reverence for the Virgin Mary and the saints. Formal church worship is less important than communal celebrations and home ceremonies. But many remain devoutly religious whether or not they attend mass regularly. On the mainland, Puerto Ricans have shared parishes with black and other Latino parishioners. Latino caucuses have developed within the Catholic church to press for Spanish-language services and more priests of Latino background. In Fitzpatrick's words, "the principal demand of the Puerto Ricans and other Latinos is for a policy of cultural pluralism in the church that will provide for the continuation of their language and culture in their spiritual life and the appointment of Puerto Ricans and other Latinos to positions of responsibility."[92] For several decades, the Catholic hierarchy was not welcoming to the new immigrants from the island, but gradually the Catholic church has moved to integrate Puerto Ricans and other Latinos more centrally into parishes and leadership positions.

In the 1990s, the Archdiocese of New York has been estimated to be about 40 percent Latino. Yet only about 4 percent of the priests are Latino, and this lack of leadership from Puerto Rican and other Latino groups is creating a serious problem for the Archdiocese. While the church has made significant attempts to reach out to the Latino poor, it has not yet developed a sensitivity to Latino language and culture.[93]

Many Puerto Ricans have left the Catholic church for pentecostal and other evangelical churches, which they feel offer a warmer reception and a community feeling. Protestant fundamentalism has made significant inroads into Puerto Rican communities, as it has in other Latino communities. Many of these communities now have numerous storefront evangelical churches. New York City alone is said to have 1,400 Latino pentecostal and other Protestant churches.

ASSIMILATION OR COLONIALISM?

Assimilation Issues

In an influential book on Puerto Ricans, Fitzpatrick uses an assimilation model to interpret Puerto Rican experiences. While in his 1964 book the assimilation theorist Gordon found little assimilation of Puerto Ricans into the dominant culture and society, a few years later Fitzpatrick reported a significant degree of assimilation. Fitzpatrick noted substantial cultural assimilation, particularly for many mainland-born Puerto Ricans who have identified with U.S. society and adopted English as a second language. Yet other scholars, such as Walsh, have argued that this cultural adaptation is limited and gives a "false hope of inclusion in [the dominant] environment." Walsh found that Puerto Rican schoolchildren often deny knowing Spanish when speaking with non-Latinos, even if they use Spanish at home and in their community. Similarly, in *Up from Puerto Rico*, Padilla has argued that second-generation Puerto Ricans often have a different reference group, the mainland society rather than island society, and as a result many hide their Spanish-language facility in an attempt to assimilate culturally.[94]

The pressure to assimilate culturally has been intense, as Maldonado-Denis notes: "Regardless of what Glazer and Moynihan argue in *Beyond the Melting Pot*, the American ethic is a messianic one, and all ethnic groups are required to assimilate culturally as a condition for achieving a share in the material and spiritual goods of American society."[95] For Puerto Ricans, these cultural assimilation pressures begin in Puerto Rico, where for decades the colonial government pressured Puerto Ricans on the island to assimilate to U.S. culture, such as by requiring the use of English in schools. Today, there is evidence of significant cultural assimilation. In an early 1990s survey, Strategy Research Corporation ranked the cultural assimilation level of Latinos on the basis of language use and behavioral, attitudinal, and aspirational measures. The majority (59 percent) of mainland Puerto Rican heads of household were classified as partially assimilated. However, fewer than 10 percent were ranked as highly assimilated, and 32 percent were considered relatively unassimilated.[96]

There is significant Puerto Rican resistance to complete cultural assimilation. The Puerto Rican quest for identity "is taking the form of a strong assertion of the significance of Puerto Rican culture, including language, and also the definition of Puerto Rican interests around militant types of political and community action."[97]

Puerto Ricans waving the flag of Puerto Rico in a New York City parade.

Among Puerto Ricans themselves, some argue that Puerto Ricans in the United States must assimilate more thoroughly to the dominant culture in order to find better jobs and achieve a higher position in this society. Some even argue that this can be done with a minimum of soul selling—that is, with a strong persistence of Puerto Rican culture. Others worry about the heavy cost of thoroughgoing cultural assimilation in terms of the identities of Puerto Ricans; they are concerned that assimilation pressures, as with other subordinated racial and ethnic groups, will lead to rootlessness.

As we have noted in previous chapters, white school teachers are frequently engaged in an ongoing struggle with Latino students. The outcome of this struggle varies; students may become culturally assimilated, fully or to a lesser degree, or they may drop out. Researchers have found that favorable, or fair, treatment of Latino students in school increases as their "difference," as perceived by the non-Latino teacher, decreases. For earlier white European immigrants, acculturation frequently resulted in some denial of ethnicity; differences became the source of fear, even shame, as noted by the Italian immigrant Leonard Covello:

> We soon got the idea that Italian meant something inferior and a barrier was erected between [children] of Italian origin and their parents. This was the accepted process of Americanization; we were becoming Americans by learning to be ashamed of our parents.[98]

For people of color, however, full cultural assimilation and loss of racial-ethnic identity are impossible; the differences usually are too visible and too important in the racial judgments made by powerful whites. Rather than becoming de-racialized or de-ethnicized "Americans," Puerto Ricans and other people of color remain distinctive and subordinated.

Today, there seems to be some decline in blatant discrimination against Puerto Ricans in jobs, but the level of discrimination remains substantial. In addition, blatant and subtle forms of mistreatment continue in other areas such as the renting and purchasing of housing. For the most part, the level of assimilation in this regard is relatively low. Moreover, secondary-structural assimilation at the level of higher-paying white-collar jobs has been slow; there remains a disproportionate concentration of Puerto Ricans in blue-collar, service, and lower-wage, white-collar jobs, as well as among the unemployed. Problematical, too, has been the relatively low level of participation of Puerto Ricans in mainland political institutions. Here, too, there has not been substantial assimilation.

Structural assimilation of Puerto Ricans at the primary-group level and marital assimilation have not reached levels comparable to those of white immigrants. A New York study of 400 Puerto Ricans found "almost incessant interaction between the parents and their married children." In spite of, or perhaps because of, their wrenching experiences of migration to the mainland and three decades there, the first generation of immigrants has maintained a high level of social integration with their children and grandchildren. The better jobs and educations of many in the second generation have not broken up this family integration. However, out-marriage seems to be more significant for the second generation. Over half of the U.S.–born Puerto Ricans who are married have a Puerto Rican spouse, compared with more than 80 percent of the island-born migrants. Out-marriages, however, are typically to other Latinos and to African Americans rather than to non-Latino whites.[99]

Generational conflict has been a problem for Puerto Rican families. Children grow up in the mainland culture and pick up values that often conflict with traditional values. For instance, the traditional chaperoning of girls has given way to the less restrictive mainland dating patterns. The street life of boys in large barrios is more difficult to supervise. Moreover, identificational assimilation has come slowly for Puerto Ricans. Most, whether island-born or mainland-born, still see themselves as Puerto Rican. One study of two generations of Puerto Rican families in New York City found that both generations had acculturated to some extent to the mainland culture, "but internally, in the symbolisms linking them to the island, they experienced less change." Even those born on the mainland retained strong symbolic ties to the island of Puerto Rico. More than half of the first generation of migrants to the mainland and 45 percent of their children saw themselves as *solely* Puerto Rican in terms of values. The rest saw themselves as partly Puerto Rican and partly "North American." Not one of the four hundred persons in the sample identified himself or herself as purely "North American" in terms of values. The second generation apparently had as strong an allegiance and sense of identity with Puerto Rico as the first generation.[100]

Power–Conflict Views

Power–conflict analysts would agree that there has been heavy Anglo-conformity pressure on Puerto Ricans, but they would stress how colonized Puerto Rican Americans remain. Assimilation into the economic and political mainstream has been rather slow, which suggests that non-European migrants such as Puerto Ricans are not, contrary to the views of some assimilation analysts, just like the European immigrants in earlier periods of the twentieth century.

Issues of Puerto Rican identity and history surfaced in a late 1997 debate among some Puerto Ricans about a new Puerto Rican Barbie doll issued by Mattel corporation in its Dolls of the World series. Critics argued that its appearance (skin and hair) was "too white" and did not reflect Puerto Ricans' strong Native American and African ancestries. Some also argued that the description of the island on the doll's box neglected this history as well as the colonial oppression of the island by the United States.[101]

Puerto Ricans have had the distinctive experience of *external* colonialism. Unemployment in the U.S. "possession" of Puerto Rico has often been cited as a major reason for out-migration; the prosperity of the mainland economy has been cited as an important pull factor. But unemployment and mainland prosperity would not have created the long streams of migration from this Caribbean island without the long colonial relationship. The economic history of Puerto Ricans is grounded in the history of the colonial relationship between the United States and the island of Puerto Rico. After the war with Spain, the United States took the island by force as an external colony. Since that time the inhabitants have been subject to U.S. economic and political intervention. Indeed, it was the creation of a one-crop agricultural society dominated by absentee sugar companies that orig-inally created a large group of agricultural workers seeking other work.

With the later industrialization of Puerto Rico under the auspices of large U.S. firms, many Puerto Rican workers became part of a growing surplus labor population, one that often made its way to the industrialized northeastern cities on the mainland. These immigrants from an external colony became part of the internal colonialism of U.S. central cities. Puerto Ricans live, for the most part, in segregated communities. Colonialism theorists would argue that there is also today a co-opted Puerto Rican elite that has a social control function in keeping the Puerto Rican population from rebelling against oppressive conditions.[102]

Internal colonialism could be seen in the Reagan and Bush administrations' "urban enterprise zone" proposals of the late 1980s and early 1990s, which signifi-cantly reduced taxes and regulations on corporations that opened plants in urban poverty areas, thus recognizing these Latino and black communities as areas for eco-nomic exploitation. Frank Bonilla and Ricardo Campos have compared this "puer-toricanization" of central-city communities to the economic colonialism of Operation Bootstrap in Puerto Rico. Under Operation Bootstrap, Puerto Rico's poverty and low wages became its main assets in attracting U.S. multinational corporations.

In the case of Puerto Rico, corporations were encouraged by various incen-tives to come in and profit from exploiting cheap labor. The "puertoricanization" of certain central-city areas makes them corporate havens of profitability similar to the island of Puerto Rico. Various government urban-renewal schemes, new and old, for exploiting Puerto Rican and African American workers show the logic of modern capitalistic expansion, which leads "not only to the introduction of the peoples and problems of colonialism into the metropolis, but also to the transfer there of colonial 'solutions' [such as urban enterprise zones] and practices."[103]

Cuban Americans

We will now turn to the situation of Cuban Americans, the third-largest Latino group in the United States. Like Puerto Ricans, this group has its roots in an important Caribbean island.

PATTERNS OF IMMIGRATION

Early Immigration: 1868–1959

Virtually all migrations from Cuba to the United States have stemmed from polit-ical upheaval and economic distress on the island of Cuba. Nineteenth-century wars of Cuban independence brought the first Cuban immigrants to the United

States. Most were from Cuba's middle and working classes; many were professionals and business people. Although some of these immigrants went to New York, Philadelphia, and Boston, most chose to settle in south Florida because of its proximity to Cuba and the similarity of its climate to that of the island. By 1873, Cubans were the majority of the population in Key West, Florida. Ybor City and Tampa became home to a large number of Cubans after 1885 when cigar factories located there. Considering themselves exiles and expecting to return home soon, members of these communities were highly committed to the independence of their homeland from Spain. They contributed both soldiers and financial assistance to the war in Cuba. When Cuba won its independence in 1898, many exiles returned home. However, for tens of thousands of Cubans who had lived in the United States for more than twenty years, return was not an option; the United States was the location of their homes and jobs and the birthplace of their children. Among the major contributions of these early Cuban Americans to their adopted homeland were the organization of Florida's first labor union and the establishment of Key West's first fire department and bilingual school.[104]

These early Cuban exiles were politically active at the local level and lobbied for a U.S. policy that would support Cuba's liberation from Spain. However, for some time the U.S. government did not share the exiles' enthusiasm for the independence of their homeland. The United States even supported Spanish colonialism over Cuban independence. Later, during the thirty-year war between Spain and Cuban rebels, the United States made several attempts to purchase the island from Spain. Finally U.S. troops were sent to Cuba, and after Spain was driven out in 1898, the U.S. occupied the island. In 1902, Cuba became a U.S. protectorate. The Platt Amendment to the 1900–1901 U.S. military appropriations bill gave the United States the right to military intervention in Cuba to preserve the island's "independence" and to protect life, property, and individual liberty. During the first two decades of the twentieth century, U.S. involvement in Cuban politics took the form of military intervention to settle political disputes. After the 1920s, military actions were replaced with diplomatic interference. So great was U.S. power in Cuban affairs that no elected president of the island who was opposed by the United States could remain in office long. Cuba was in effect a colony of the United States from 1898 until 1959.[105]

During this period U.S. financial domination of Cuba was no less extensive than political domination. Within fifteen years after Cuba gained independence from Spain, U.S. investments grew from an estimated $50 million to an estimated $220 million. By the late 1920s, the United States controlled three-fourths of Cuba's sugar industry. By 1960, U.S. businesses controlled 90 percent of Cuba's mines, 80 percent of its public utilities, half of its railways, 40 percent of its sugar production, and one-fourth of its bank deposits. Cuba was indeed an economic colony.[106]

The political turbulence that accompanied a succession of corrupt and repressive dictators in Cuba during the first half of the twentieth century brought some political exiles to the United States. For many, their stay in the United States was brief; returning to Cuba, they were often replaced in the United States by

those Cubans from whose power they had earlier fled. During the corrupt dictatorship of former army chief Fulgencio Batista in the 1950s, the refugees numbered between 10,000 and 15,000 per year.[107]

Recent Immigration: 1959 to the Present

The migration of large numbers of Cubans to the United States occurred after
Cuba's 1959 revolution. Fidel Castro, the young rebel leader of the grass-roots insurrection that overthrew Batista, came to power in that year. To the majority of
Cubans, Castro's victory brought hope for social, economic, and political reforms.
Land grants to tenant farmers, guaranteed compensation for small sugar growers,
and the nationalization of public utility companies were among Castro's stated
goals. However, such reforms were mostly not in the interest of Cuba's business,
industrial, and political elites or of the island's U.S. investors. Exaggerated views of
the Cuban revolution's threat to U.S. business and political interests, suspicions that
Castro was a Communist, and Castro's declarations that he would not tolerate
manipulation of Cuba by the U.S. government led to open U.S. hostility toward
Cuba, a break in diplomatic relations between the two countries, and a U.S. policy
of welcoming refugees from Cuba's "Communist oppression" to the "free world."[108]

The first major stream of immigration began with Cuba's elite—former government officials, bankers, and industrialists who had done well under the Batista
dictatorship and feared Castro's revolutionary political orientation. These were
Cubans whose economic position in Cuba was directly related to Cuba's political
and economic relationship with the United States. The second wave started in
1961, when large numbers of middle- and upper-income Cubans began to flee the
revolution, preferring exile from their native island to life under Fidel Castro's
increasingly authoritarian Communist government. This group was composed of
middle-level professionals, managers, merchants, and landlords and included
more than half of Cuba's doctors and teachers. Many cited loss of job, possessions,
or sources of income as reasons for their departure. Others reported harassment,
persecution, or temporary imprisonment or fear that they would be imprisoned.
More than 14,000 children were sent alone to the United States by parents who
feared having their children educated by a Communist state. Both of these waves
of immigrants were mostly composed of light-skinned Cubans. (The island's population was 27 percent black, according to the 1953 Cuban census.) By 1962,
almost 200,000 Cubans had entered the United States. Smaller numbers continued
to arrive by small boat or by way of other countries after air travel between Cuba
and the United States was suspended in 1962.[109]

As with earlier Cuban immigrants, south Florida, only 90 miles from Cuba,
was the logical destination. Because they were fleeing a Communist government,
they found the U.S. government a willing host. In the first years, from the point of
view of both the immigrants and the U.S. government, the Cubans were refugees
forced into temporary exile with the firm intention of returning home as soon as
the Castro regime was overthrown. This is a major reason why most of the
refugees chose to stay in the cities of south Florida.

To provide for the immediate needs of these refugees, the Eisenhower administration created the Cuban Refugee Emergency Center in Miami and allocated $1 million in federal funds. This aid was expanded by the Kennedy administration in 1961 in the form of a Cuban Refugee Program that assisted refugees with resettlement, helped them locate employment, and provided for maintenance, health services, education and training programs, aid for unaccompanied children, and surplus food distribution. The nation's first federally funded bilingual programs were started for Cubans in Dade County, Florida, in the late 1960s. The Cuban Refugee Program lasted from 1961 until 1974 and provided a total of nearly a billion dollars during its lifetime. This federal government aid was a major asset in helping Cuban refugees build and sustain their own communal and economic infrastructure. Cubans are the only large group of Latin Americans who have been granted political refugee status and on that basis have been able to qualify for federal financial aid.[110]

A third stream of Cuban immigrants, totaling more than 250,000, arrived between 1965 and the late 1970s. Almost five thousand relatives of those refugees already in the United States were allowed to leave from the Cuban port of Camarioca in late 1965 aboard hundreds of boats arriving from Miami. This flotilla exodus was followed by an airlift negotiated by the U.S. and Cuban governments. Push factors for this largely light-skinned, working-class and small-business group included concern with economic scarcities and hope for a higher standard of living in the United States, in addition to disagreement with Cuba's political regime. As with earlier groups, these refugees settled mainly in south Florida, although by the 1970s some were spread among many Cuban communities throughout the other forty-nine states. A nationwide study of 300 immigrant families in 1968 found that relocation patterns reflected family associations: More than three-fourths of the families in this study had relatives already in the United States. The study also found that occupational orientation was an important criterion in selecting a relocation city. For example, some with a background in government chose Washington, while some whose background was in business or finance chose New York City.[111]

By the late 1960s, increasing numbers of Cuban immigrants had begun to think of themselves as permanent residents of the United States, more interested in improving their lives and less involved in efforts to bring about the demise of Castro's government. Many owned businesses and homes and had become integrated into the social, economic, and political institutions of their community. Many became naturalized citizens.

The Mariel Immigrants

A fourth stream of immigrants, the sudden influx of 125,000 Cubans in 1980 often called the "Mariel boatlift" (after the port from which they sailed), gave rise to myths and distortions among non-Cuban Americans. Popular images characterized the Mariel refugees as undesirables—poorer and less educated than earlier waves of Cuban immigrants and containing a large percentage of criminals and the mentally ill. This group included some who left voluntarily and some, considered undesirable by the Cuban government, who were forced to leave. However, of the entire group, only a few hundred were mentally ill and required institutionalization, and fewer than one in five had been in prison in Cuba. Among this latter group, almost one-fourth were political prisoners, and the offenses of an additional 70 percent consisted of some form of dissent or other acts that were not crimes in the United States. Fewer than 2 percent were subsequently imprisoned in a U.S. federal penitentiary. The education level of this Mariel group was similar to that of the Cuban immigrants of the 1970s, and most represented the mainstream of the Cuban economy and society. More than 11 percent were professionals, including many teachers; some 71 percent were blue-collar workers. However, unlike the earlier waves of Cuban immigrants, who were mostly light-skinned, approximately 40 percent of the Mariel group were darker-skinned Cubans with substantial African ancestry. More than half came to waiting families or sponsors, and two-thirds of the rest were easily placed in communities across the nation. By the mid-1980s, most Mariel refugees had been absorbed by Cuban American communities. However, a small number did remain in detention camps several years after arrival because U.S. government officials feared they were criminals.[112]

Because their reasons for immigration were substantially economic, the Mariel immigrants were ineligible for the federal financial support available to political refugees. They were allowed to stay in the United States by the Carter administration's creation of a special immigration category, "Cuban-Haitian entrant," which included eligibility for emergency assistance, medical services, and supplemental income, most of which was paid for by the federal government. Upon arrival the Mariel immigrants were housed in tent cities in the Miami area and flown to military bases in Arkansas, Florida, Pennsylvania, and Wisconsin. Some were held in these makeshift processing centers for an extended time while the government attempted to identify refugees who might be "dangerous." Yet as noted above, the vast majority of Mariel immigrants were neither marginal nor criminal. Many were angry at the contrast between their actual conditions and the exaggerated reports from exiles visiting Cuba concerning the wealth and ease of life in the United States. Disillusionment and crowded conditions in the detention centers led to several inmate riots and violent confrontations between the refugees and the National Guard troops in charge of the centers. In addition, from August 1980 into 1983 a few Mariel immigrants participated in airplane hijackings in an effort to return to Cuba.[113]

In 1994, the Cuban government lifted its ban on emigration, and soon 35,000 Cubans left for Florida, mostly on rafts and small boats. Reversing earlier policy, the U.S. government stopped admitting Cuban migrants, sending them to camps at the Guantanamo Bay Naval Station. In negotiated agreements in 1994–1996, the U.S. government agreed to increase to at least 20,000 the annual visas granted to Cubans, while the Cuban government agreed to halt the mass exodus of refugees. The U.S. government agreed to send back those who had not departed legally. Both governments agreed to make the migration more orderly and safer for the immigrants. As a result of these agreements, a large number of Cuban immigrants

Some of the Cuban refugees not allowed into the United States were held at the Guantanomo naval base in Cuba.

have been legally admitted to the United States, including immediate relatives of U.S. citizens. Still, in the summer of 1997, Phyllis E. Oakley, a U.S. Assistant Secretary of State, pointed out in testimony to Congress that the number of immigrants was not reaching the allowed quota because of high exit fees imposed by the Cuban government. Discussions over immigration issues continued between the two governments in the late 1990s.[114]

In the late 1990s, about 1.5 million Cuban Americans live in the United States, a significant increase over the last two decades. Most live in urban areas. In the mid-1990s the median age for Cuban Americans was almost forty-four years, older than the population as a whole and other Latino groups.[115] Lisandro Perez notes that "the overrepresentation of the elderly among Cubans has clear origins. Dissatisfaction with socialist revolutionary change was likely to be highest among the elderly. In issuing permits, the Cuban government has given preference to the dependent elderly while restricting the emigration, for example, of males of military age."[116]

INTERGROUP CONFLICT

One major result of the Cuban migrations over the last few decades has been a change in the population mix of south Florida. By the late 1980s, Latinos had become a majority of the population in the city of Miami. The 1980 Cuban migration swelled Miami welfare rolls, increased overcrowding in the schools, and created $30 million in expenses for local governments already hurting from cutbacks in federal programs. The millions of dollars paid out to care for the new influx of Cubans angered many non-Latinos; many of the latter unfairly blamed all Cubans for many local social problems.

Tensions accelerated with Miami's African American residents, many of whom argued that Cuban Americans were taking jobs away from them. The larger and generally more affluent Cuban American community today controls many of its own businesses, small and large, and Cubans are usually preferred in hiring there. In one 1980s mayoral election, 95 percent of African American voters voted against the Cuban American candidate. Since 1980, more major racial riots have occurred in Miami than in any other U.S. city. Miami's 1980 Liberty City riot and 1982 Overtown riot by poor African Americans were precipitated in part by police involvement in the killing of black men. The Overtown uprising involved a Cuban American police officer shooting a black man who was playing a video game. More rioting took place in 1984 when the officer was acquitted of charges in connection with the killing. After the riots some Anglo landlords and businesses that had been damaged were replaced by Latino landlords and businesses. One former black school official complained that "after a generation of being Southern slaves, blacks now face a future as Latin slaves." The shooting of an unarmed black motorist by a Latino officer in 1989 precipitated another major uprising in predominantly black areas of Miami. More than 280 people were arrested in three days of rioting. After the shooting the U.S. attorney for Miami began an inquiry into complaints of police brutality by Anglo and Latino officers toward African Americans. Latino officers themselves asked not to be assigned to black areas of the city where antipolice hostility remained high after the riot. The tensions have continued into the late 1990s.[117]

Cuban American leaders angered the local black community when they ignored visiting black officials, including South African president Nelson Mandela, who maintained friendly relations with the Cuban government. In addition, black groups have sued the Cuban American–controlled local governments for what they see as the obstruction of fair political representation for black voters. The head of a new local civil rights group, People United to Lead the Struggle for Equality, recently commented: "We are very much on edge here, and it's getting worse because of the constant elimination of African Americans from jobs and political offices. They [Cuban Americans] are becoming the oppressor."[118] Intergroup rivalry and competition can be seen clearly in south Florida today, with a very old immigrant group (African Americans) often losing in a power struggle with a new immigrant group (Cuban Americans).

Inconsistent U.S. government treatment of the often light-skinned Cuban refugees and the dark-skinned Haitian refugees, discussed in Chapter 8, has been another source of intergroup tension in south Florida. Thousands of Haitians, as well as hundreds of thousands of Salvadorans and Guatemalans, have been refused refugee status in the United States since the 1970s; many have been deported to face death at the hands of their own dictatorial governments.

In a clearly political maneuver, the Cuban immigrants were for some years defined as "political refugees" eligible for U.S. citizenship by friendly U.S. officials, while most Haitian and Central American immigrants were classified as "economic refugees" ineligible even for entry into the United States. (However, in 1994 the federal government began to place more restrictions on Cuban immigrants.) This differential government treatment of immigrants and potential immigrants has fueled tensions between Miami's Cuban and Haitian communities in the 1990s.[119]

STEREOTYPES AND DISCRIMINATION

Cuban Americans are sometimes stereotyped as a predominantly affluent group. As we will see in the following section, Cuban Americans as a group are generally more prosperous than other Latino groups. However, this relative affluence should not be exaggerated, for a significant proportion of Cuban Americans live in modest circumstances or poverty. The Children's Defense Fund has reported that the poverty rate for Cuban American children rose by 71 percent during the 1980s, a greater increase than for any other Latino group.[120]

Non-Latino whites have sometimes expressed distaste for the Spanish language and other aspects of Cuban American culture. Cuban Americans have faced language discrimination in various places and contexts. For example, in the late 1980s the voters of Florida, by an 83-to-17-percent margin, approved an "official English" initiative hostile to the state's Latino population. The initiative mandated that the state government's business be conducted in English. One Cuban American leader noted that such legislation "opens the way for bigotry and discrimination."[121] In addition, some private clubs in south Florida have excluded Latinos and other minority groups. Federal district judge Kenneth Ryskamp's connection to a Miami country club with such a policy was one of several actions that led the Senate Judiciary Committee to reject his nomination by the Bush administration to a U.S. court of appeals seat in the early 1990s. The country club's white members wanted a place where they did not have to hear Spanish spoken. In most regions of the United States, the Spanish that might be heard by middle- and upper-income whites is spoken primarily by working-class Latinos. In south Florida, however, Spanish speakers make up a majority of the Miami population and are to be found in every social class. Judge Ryskamp echoed the sentiments of many prejudiced European Americans when he complained that his wife was annoyed because many store clerks spoke mostly Spanish and that it was difficult for her to shop because stores mainly stocked merchandise preferred by their Spanish-speaking customers.[122]

Like other Latinos, Cuban Americans have experienced discrimination at the hands of European Americans. In the 1960s, signs outside some apartment buildings in Miami greeted Cuban immigrants with the message, "No Dogs, No Kids, No Cubans." The new immigrants not only faced housing discrimination but also employment barriers. One Cuban American FBI agent, Fernando Mata, helped to bring a successful 1988 lawsuit against the FBI. As a result of the lawsuit the FBI was forced to eradicate patterns of employment discrimination against its Latino employees. After the lawsuit Mata, a decorated counterintelligence specialist, lost his security clearance and was suspended by the FBI because of allegations that he was spying for Cuba. However, many FBI agents and civil rights activists outside the agency saw no proof of spying activity and argued Mata was being harassed because of the discrimination lawsuit.[123]

THE ECONOMIC SITUATION

Many Cuban immigrants experienced a dramatic decline in occupational status when they entered the U.S. economy. For example, a 1966 survey of Cubans in the Miami metropolitan area found that the percentage of immigrants who were employed as professionals, proprietors, technicians, and managers dropped from just over 48 percent to just under 13 percent, while the percentage of those employed as unskilled laborers doubled (32 percent in the United States compared with 16 percent in Cuba). Even though many were willing to take jobs far below their previous occupational level, unemployment was widespread in south Florida. Yet most did not migrate to other regions, but preferred to remain in the Cuban community in south Florida.[124]

The increased Cuban presence in south Florida has made Miami much more important as a center for Latin American and other international trade. The area's economic growth has brought an increase in the number of international corporations establishing headquarters for Latin America in the Miami area, as well as an increase in the volume of international trade. Miami has become, in the eyes of many observers, the "capital of Latin America" because of its centrality in Latin American trade and banking as well as in the underground economy of the drug trade.[125]

A 1968 nationwide survey of Cuban immigrants across the United States found that fewer than half of those who had been employed as professionals in Cuba held professional positions in the United States; the proportion who held unskilled jobs had risen from 5 percent in Cuba to 25 percent in the United States. Interviews with immigrants revealed that as they increased their English proficiency, their educational background and work experience often helped them climb to a position at or near their former level within a few years of resettlement.[126]

Compared with other Latino groups, Cuban Americans have enjoyed a high degree of economic success. There are several interrelated reasons for this. Some researchers have pointed to individual strengths; the high-level educational and occupational characteristics and aspirations of many Cuban immigrants, especially the earlier arrivals, prepared them for success. Other researchers have emphasized that the large numbers of immigrants in one economic community (Miami), an "ethnic enclave," make possible the development of support networks to facilitate economic adjustment. Discussing the development of the Cuban American enclave in Miami, sociologists Alejandro Portes and Robert Bach suggest that Cubans have done relatively well economically because they migrated not as poor individuals in isolated circumstances but rather as a group that had substantial resources, access to important social networks, and support from major federal programs. Silvia Pedraza has suggested that these government programs advanced the structural assimilation of Cuban immigrants by reinforcing their initial social-class-of-origin advantage and thereby creating a cumulative advantage. The wide range of occupations and skills among the Cuban immigrants facilitated the development of a large and interdependent local economy capable of providing jobs and incomes for many members of the Latino immigrant community in south Florida, including some from Central and South America. Once created, the enclave economy gave Cuban American entrepreneurs access to a periodic stream of labor from Cuba. Appeals to group solidarity, to the Cuban identity of the laborers, sometimes helped certain Cuban businesspeople to exploit their own laborers.[127]

While individual and group factors are important in the economic adjustment of Cuban Americans, they do not fully account for the substantial mobility displayed by this group. A third factor must be considered: the economic organization of the Cuban American family. As Perez points out, the Cuban American family is generally "organized around realizing aspirations of economic achievement." Although few Cuban women participated in the paid labor force prior to the revolution, gainful employment became an economic necessity for upward mobility in the United States; after immigration Cuban women viewed work outside the home as an opportunity to help the family advance. Cuban American women, including those who are married with husband present and those with young children, are more likely than other Latino women to be in the paid labor force; Cuban American women are also more likely to work full-time and year-round than other Latino women. On the average, Cuban American families have fewer children than other Latino families, and thus fewer disruptions for the women in the paid labor force. Significantly, three-generation families under one roof are more common among Cuban Americans, providing a source of safe child care and additional wage earners.[128]

Among Latino groups, Cuban Americans have relatively high levels of income and education. A comparison of family income and poverty rates and levels of educational attainment for Mexican Americans, Puerto Ricans, and Cuban Americans was presented in Chapter 9. Cuban Americans are much nearer the non-Latino white population on most measures than they are to Mexican Americans or mainland Puerto Ricans. The rate of college completion for Cuban Americans is more than twice that of mainland Puerto Ricans and almost three times that of Mexican Americans.[129] The 1992 median family income for Cuban Americans was 77 percent that of Anglo whites. In contrast, the median family income for mainland Puerto Ricans was half that of Anglo whites; for Mexican Americans it was 59 percent. We noted previously that in 1994 Cuban Americans' median family income ($30,581) was almost 50 percent higher than that of Puerto Ricans.[130] However, we should not overlook the possibility of discrimination in the case of Cuban Americans. Given the relatively high level of education among Cuban Americans, their median income figure is lower than it would be for comparably educated whites. Employment discrimination at the hands of European Americans has been a problem for Cuban Americans since the 1960s.

As we have already noted, the prosperity of Cuban Americans compared with other Latino groups does not mean that all Cuban Americans are affluent. In 1992, the poverty rate for Cuban American families was almost twice that of whites; almost one-fourth of Cuban Americans under age 18 and over age 64 lived in poverty.[131] Economic success is not a reality for all Cuban American families.

POLITICS

The expectation that the Fidel Castro regime, and the period of exile, would be short-lived led most post–1959 Cuban immigrants to remain politically inactive at the local and state levels for a number of years, although from the time of their arrival they had a strong desire to influence U.S. foreign policy toward Cuba. The mid-1970s saw an increase in the number of naturalized citizens that was followed by an increase in voter registration and participation in local and state politics. In the 1980s, the Cuban American marketing director of the *Miami News* stated, "Cuban-Americans are definitely super-conservative. Communism for us is the enemy. On domestic issues, we will be more toward the center . . . but the Cuban business community is still more in favor of Reaganomics than Mexicans or Puerto Ricans."[132] However, Antonio Jorge and Raul Moncarz point out that although Cubans tend to identify with the Republican party, which they consider more likely than the Democratic party to be anti-Castro, they left a legacy of progressive politics in Cuba. Some social reforms, such as an eight-hour work day, free school lunches, and a minimum wage, instituted in the 1930s, have remained in effect through a succession of Cuban dictators.[133]

Since the 1980s, Cuban Americans have become more politically active than other Latino groups. Cuban Americans now hold many elective and appointive offices in Florida, including powerful positions in the Florida legislature. In 1997, the mayor and city manager of Miami, the head of Dade County government, the superintendent of the Dade County public schools, the county police chief, two presidents of major local colleges, and many of Dade County's state legislators were Cuban American. Similar advances have been made in urban areas in other states, particularly New Jersey. In 1993 Ileana Ros-Lehtinen, a Cuban American from Miami, became the first Latina to serve in the U.S. House of Representatives. In the mid-1990s two more Cuban Americans, Lincoln Diaz-Balart from Florida and Robert Menendez from New Jersey, joined Ros-Lehtinen in the House.[134]

Many Cuban Americans have remained psychologically involved in the politics of Cuba. They are yet one more example of how many U.S. racial–ethnic groups remain actively concerned about or involved in the politics of their home countries. Indeed, some U.S. analysts, particularly conservative critics of multiculturalism, have worried that U.S. foreign policy is no longer unified, but has become a balkanized collection of the overseas interests of numerous racial–ethnic groups in the United States.[135]

The Cuban American National Foundation, established in 1981 with offices in Miami and Washington, has become one of the most active conservative organizations in the United States. It has been very influential in lobbying members of Congress on legislation dealing with Cuba, and a few of its leaders exercised great influence in the Republican administrations of the 1980s and early 1990s. Moreover, some Cuban exiles have engaged in paramilitary training and plans for terrorist acts against the Cuban government. Cuban exiles recruited by the CIA were involved in the unsuccessful Bay of Pigs invasion in 1961. Members of at least one of the militant anti-Castro groups in the United States continued to practice mock invasions well into the 1990s. In 1991, three Miami Cubans entered Cuba by boat with small arms and explosives, but they were captured, tried, and convicted of sabotage.[136] Since 1985 Cuban Americans have been active in the operation of Radio Marti, a federally funded station, and its affiliate, TV Marti, which transmit news and public affairs programming from Washington to Cuba via Florida.[137]

In November 1997, the funeral of Jorge Mas Canosa, one of the major anti-Communist leaders in the Cuban American community and a founder of the Foundation, was attended by thousands. His death was thought by some to open up the possibility of more moderate voices—those who seek some relaxation of tensions with the government of Fidel Castro—eventually coming to the forefront in the Cuban American community.[138]

The collapse of the Soviet Union brought severe economic hardships to Cuba, for the two countries had been closely linked by trade for three decades. Significantly, the Antonio Maceo Brigade, a progressive Cuban American organization, reported that between September 1991 and February 1992 fifteen thousand Cuban Americans in Miami signed a petition calling for the United States to lift its economic blockade of Cuba in order to ease the island's economic plight. During this same period, conservative Cuban Americans sought more U.S. government support for raids designed to topple Castro's government and to introduce multiparty politics in Cuba. In January 1992, five thousand Cuban American counterdemonstrators in New York City, including several hundred from Miami, protested proposals to end sanctions against the Castro government at an international rally against the economic blockade.[139] In addition, Republican victories in the 1994 congressional elections brought a number of prominent anti-Castro politicians to the forefront of U.S. foreign policy. One of these, Senator Jesse Helms (R.–North Carolina), even called for a military overthrow of Castro.

The involvement of Cuban Americans in the politics of Cuba is yet another example of the way in which the development and situations of U.S. racial and ethnic groups interact with and are dependent upon the world context. In this sense, U.S. racial and ethnic relations are intrinsically international.

ASSIMILATION OR COLONIALISM?

Assimilation Issues

Cuban Americans are one of the recent additions to the bubbling cauldron of the United States. Like other Latinos they have faced prejudice and discrimination including language discrimination and exclusion from certain Anglo-dominated organizations.

Efforts to maintain the old Cuban culture and social order, as well as to bypass country club discrimination by whites, led to the creation in the 1960s of the Big Five Club, a Miami social club originally composed exclusively of members of five elite Havana yacht and golf clubs. As of the early 1990s, the Big Five Club's membership included some sixteen hundred families. To attract younger members, the club lowered its initiation fee for families with children below the age of twenty-four. As with other immigrant groups, members of the younger generation seem less interested in maintaining old ways by joining such social clubs. According to one president of the Big Five, "The ones born in this country feel they are more American than Cuban."[140]

Identificational assimilation has come slowly. Many Cubans living in the United States continue to consider themselves exiles rather than immigrants and to speak of their "fractured identity." Others—especially those who left Cuba as children and those of the American-born generation—say they have a "double" rather than a "split" identity. One poll found that only 29 percent of Cuban-born household heads living in the Miami area expressed an intention to return to Cuba permanently if the Castro government were to fall.[141]

The preservation of Cuban culture and identity in an "enclave" (a concentrated community) in south Florida has represented a crucial foundation for Cuban Americans' economic and political integration into U.S. society. Portes and Bach found that the strong enclave community created by the first groups of Cuban immigrants was rooted in old kinship and friendship ties and formed the social and economic context into which later immigrants entered. In 1973 and 1974, these researchers interviewed 590 Cuban male immigrant heads of household at the time of their arrival in Miami. The respondents were interviewed again several years later. In the initial interview 99 percent of these respondents expressed an intention to remain in Miami, and, significantly, at the time of the final interview 97 percent still resided there. The strong Cuban enclave community provided a context in which the average immigrant could partially adapt to U.S. culture and yet carry out many of life's routine activities within a Cuban American setting. Six years after these respondents entered the United States, more than one in five were self-employed in the Cuban American community and almost half worked for a Cuban American business. For most, economic assimilation was not directly to the dominant economic institutions but to the enclave economy in south Florida. Group economic integration with only modest individual assimilation at the cultural level was the pattern for the first generation.[142]

Cuban Americans are not the only immigrant group to achieve a degree of prosperity and economic power during the first generation in the United States. Like Jewish and Japanese immigrants in the first half of the twentieth century, Cuban immigrants did not follow the model of waiting their turn in the urban queue, as had Irish and Italian immigrants in an earlier period. Instead they advanced in an economic niche as small-business owners, laying a foundation for their children's educational and occupational mobility into business and professional jobs. The economic enclaves created by the first generations of Jewish and Japanese Americans did not become part of the pattern of typical urban group succession. Nor is it likely that the enclave economy created by Cuban Americans in south Florida will pass in turn to another immigrant group. The presence of a large and cohesive group of immigrants provides a context of social support and economic concentration for Cuban Americans that does not exist for other current immigrant groups. The economic concentration and success have provided a foundation for some political integration, at least in south Florida.[143]

Cultural-assimilation pressures on Cuban immigrants have created cross-generational problems similar to those of earlier European immigrants. Language assimilation is significant for the younger generation. One 1980s survey of Miami's Cubans revealed that the young preferred to listen to English-language programs on radio and TV, whereas their parents switched back and forth between English and Spanish programs. Like other immigrant grandparents before them, the grandparents preferred to hear and speak the mother tongue. Parents and grandparents worried about the excessive freedom and lack of parental respect of teenagers in U.S. cities. Parents and grandparents tended to emphasize Cuban traditions and food; the grandchildren often preferred things American. Moreover, the older generations were found to be more strongly committed to overthrowing Cuba's Communist government and to returning home. The less politically active youth saw the United States as their permanent home. Nevertheless, family and community ties were strong, and the young were proud of their Cuban identities.[144]

Strategy Research Corporation's Latino study found a similar generation gap. SRC's ranking of the assimilation level of Latinos found Cuban Americans to be the least culturally assimilated of all Spanish-speaking groups based on language use and behavioral, attitudinal, and aspirational measures. Fewer than 4 percent of Cuban American heads of household were classified as highly assimilated; just over 26 percent were rated partially assimilated, and 70 percent were ranked relatively unassimilated. The high density of Cuban Americans in south Florida and the older average age of this population are major factors in the lower level of assimilation. This same survey reported other measures of assimilation by region. Among Latinos in the Southeast, 57 percent of whom are Cuban Americans, the vast majority of adults felt more comfortable speaking Spanish than English and spoke Spanish more often at home and on social occasions. A majority gave Spanish as the language they spoke more frequently at work, although almost one-third answered "both Spanish and English" to this question. Fewer than one-third of these adults reported that they spoke, read, or wrote

English well. A very large majority considered themselves "very Hispanic" and expected to be "very Hispanic" ten years in the future.[145]

However, the SRC survey presented a very different picture of younger Latinos (mostly Cubans) in the Southeast. Fewer than half of those under the age of eighteen classified themselves as "very Hispanic," and only 40 percent felt they would be "very Hispanic" ten years in the future. Compared with those over eighteen, Latinos in this younger group were almost eight times more likely to expect that they would be only minimally Hispanic ten years in the future. Language assimilation was dramatic. Almost three-fourths of this age group spoke English at school and felt more comfortable speaking English than Spanish. A large majority reported that they spoke, read, and wrote English well, and a majority reported that their reading and writing ability in Spanish was only very poor to fair. About half reported that they used both languages on social occasions, although over half said they spoke Spanish more frequently at home. Yet without exception, the adult respondents in this region felt that it was important for their children to be able to read and write Spanish. The young are making greater strides toward cultural assimilation than their parents are eager to accept.

Cuban Americans in Miami have assimilated selectively, with the older generation especially preserving language and social and cultural traditions. In numerous cultural and social areas the younger generation seems to be moving away from the old ways, even from the enclave community, and assimilating to the dominant culture and institutions. This pattern is similar to earlier immigrant groups such as Italian Americans. In other areas of the nation, smaller Cuban American communities are more fully integrated into the larger community. Even in these areas, however, some aspects of traditional Cuban culture are celebrated. For example, Los Angeles now has a Cuban Cultural Festival that features Cuban food and music.[146]

A Power–Conflict Perspective?

To our knowledge, no one has applied a power–conflict perspective to Cuban Americans. Some might argue that the internal colonialism and other power–conflict perspectives are not relevant to interpreting the development of the predominantly light-skinned Cuban American group, which has not been victimized as much by thoroughgoing long-term economic and political discrimination as have other Latino groups. Many who migrated to the United States before 1980 were the beneficiaries of the economic and political colonialism of Cuba at the hands of the United States prior to the 1959 revolution. Instead of becoming low-wage and surplus labor forces for non-Latino industrialists, as was (and is) the case for many Puerto Ricans, most Cuban Americans have become part of a Miami area niche economy that has helped speed their economic and social mobility in the United States.

The opportunities and accomplishments of the U.S.–born generations of Cuban Americans (at least of the lighter-skinned majority), which include growing numbers of professional and managerial workers, seem more similar to those of certain white ethnic groups (for example, Italian Americans) at a comparable point in time than to those of other Latino Americans. Indeed, it may be the case that over time the adaptive development of Cuban Americans may be a variation on the ethnogenesis model, much like the long-term adaptation of white ethnic groups such as Jewish and Italian Americans. However, this can occur only if the second and later generations of Cuban Americans disperse residentially from what is now a highly concentrated and cohesive community in south Florida. Even now, the south Florida enclave community has not been able to resist the pressures for assimilation that now are having an impact on the second and third generations of Cuban Americans. Residential dispersion would likely accelerate this assimilation process.

One major obstacle, however, to full assimilation of Cuban Americans to the dominant Anglo culture and institutions is language. As we have seen in this and previous chapters, powerful English-speaking whites have organized to fight against Spanish and Spanish speakers and to try to impose English as the dominant language. Such nativist movements mark a type of cultural colonialism that rejects cultural pluralism if it threatens the dominance of the core culture. Even though most Cuban Americans appear to be light-skinned to white Anglos, they will not be fully accepted by the dominent group until they reject the Spanish language and other aspects of their Cuban culture. Thus, a significant Cuban sacrifice on the altar of white nativism and ethnocentrism will be required for the majority of white Americans to welcome Cuban Americans into the dominant culture and society. Even then, Cuban Americans whose ancestry is predominantly African will not likely be admitted into white society. Given the persisting problems of discrimination and cultural imperialism, some might argue that a power–conflict perspective is indeed appropriate for the case of Cuban Americans.

SUMMARY

Puerto Ricans, the second largest Latino group in the United States, are an important and distinctive American group with an ancient heritage. Like Mexican Americans, they represent a fusion of Native American, Spanish, and African heritages. Today, Puerto Ricans are a divided nation, with one foot on the mainland and one foot in Puerto Rico, a Caribbean island. The more or less external-colony situation of the island population complicates the picture. There has been a debate among Puerto Ricans as to whether they are one nation with one set of problems with a few variations or two nations with different sets of problems.

The issue of class also enters this debate. The island is a self-contained society with a variety of classes, including both a local capitalist class and a local working class, as well as a small elite of U.S.–based multinational capitalists. Some argue that social-class problems on the island are different from those on the mainland. On the mainland, Puerto Ricans tend to be primarily a working-class people; there are few mainland Puerto Rican capitalists. Other commentators play down the class divisions and stress that there is only one Puerto Rican nation. As one Puerto Rican social scientist puts it, "No matter how we see ourselves internally, the Yanqui always sees us and deals with us as one class and one people with the same problems. Therefore we should band together and not divide ourselves to fight for our nation against the colonizer."[147]

Puerto Ricans have the lowest median family income and the highest incidence of poverty of the three major Latino groups in the United States. By contrast, Cuban Americans, the third largest Latino group in the United States, are relatively better off; compared with the other Latino groups they have higher levels of education and income. Like Puerto Ricans, Cuban Americans came as immigrants from a Caribbean island. Today they are basically an urban population concentrated in the southeastern United States. A major reason Cuban Americans have done relatively well is that most of the early immigrants migrated not as poor individuals but rather as a group that had important resources and access to social networks. Smaller families and a higher level of participation of Cuban American women in the paid labor force have contributed to the impressive economic upward mobility of this group. The achievements of Cuban Americans underscore the advantages of migrating under the auspices of strong family and friendship networks and of receiving significant federal government support.

A distinctive aspect of this important Latino group has been the development of a politically powerful urban community centered in Miami. The size and economic diversity of the Spanish-speaking population in south Florida have allowed this group to develop a strong enclave economy and to maintain many Cuban cultural practices as well as use of its mother tongue, Spanish. Yet as is the case with other immigrant groups, members of the younger generation are beginning to move toward the dominant culture in many areas, including that of language use, much to the chagrin of many in the older generation. In the United States, cultural assimilation pressures are powerful, especially for the native-born offspring of new immigrant groups.

CHAPTER 11

Japanese Americans

THE GROWTH OF THE ASIAN–PACIFIC POPULATION

Changes in U.S. immigration laws since the 1960s, especially the elimination of racist immigration quotas, have allowed a substantial increase in immigration from Asia and the Pacific Islands. Asian-Pacific Americans are one of the fastest-growing racial-ethnic groups in the United States. Contrary to the view of many other Americans, Asian-Pacific Americans are not a homogeneous population. More than a dozen groups of Americans have roots in Asia or the Pacific Islands. Since their earliest days of immigration, Asian-Pacific groups have sought to maintain their own distinctive cultures and identities. The consciousness of "Asian Americans" as a group is a rather recent phenomenon dating from the late 1960s.[1]

In 1940, Asian–Pacific Americans were less than half of one percent of the U.S. population. By 1990, they numbered more than 7 million—almost 3 percent of the total population. The following table shows the number in each of several different groups according to the most recent census:[2]

	1980 Census	1990 Census	Percent Change
Chinese	812,178	1,648,696	103%
Filipino	781,894	1,419,711	82
Japanese	716,331	866,160	21
Korean	357,393	797,304	123
Asian Indian	387,223	786,694	103
Vietnamese	245,025	593,213	142
Hawaiian	172,346	205,501	19
Cambodian	16,044	149,047	829
Laotian	47,683	147,375	209
Hmong	5,204	94,439	1,715
Thai	45,279	91,360	102
Samoan	39,520	57,679	46
Guamanian	30,695	47,754	56

In 1990, the largest of the Asian–Pacific groups, about 1.6 million, was Chinese American. Filipino Americans were not far behind. Japanese, Korean, Asian Indian, and Vietnamese Americans constituted the other large Asian American groups. We will examine Japanese Americans in this chapter and then turn to certain other Asian American groups in Chapter 12.

INTRODUCTION: JAPANESE AMERICANS

Japanese Americans are one of the oldest Asian American groups. At the beginning of the 1990s, Japanese Americans comprised 12 percent of Asian Americans. Although more than half of all Asian Americans live in western states, Japanese Americans are the most heavily concentrated in this region, with 80 percent living in those states. Among Asian American groups, Japanese Americans have the highest percentage who are U.S.–born, an indication of the group's early entry into the United States and of the small number of recent immigrants.[3]

For some non-Asian Americans, Japanese Americans conjure up crude racial stereotypes of "crafty Orientals," images of the militaristic Japanese expansionism of the 1930s and 1940s, or resentment of "unfair" Japanese economic competition today. Even in recent years, political speeches and the graffiti of vandals have included such phrases as "fat Japs" and "little Japs," and we have seen vandalism and violence targeting Japanese and other Asian Americans. A *Boston Globe* writer summed up some common anti-Japanese incidents:

> A Honda Civic is bashed in Pennsylvania; Japanese-American community centers are vandalized; an American car salesman is fired for saying on national TV that he buys what is best for his money; a Japanese offer to purchase the Seattle Mariners baseball team sets off a national outcry; writers on Japan topics feel required to state they have never been employed by the Japanese. Frighteningly, a Japanese businessman in California is killed, apparently after receiving an anti-Japanese threat.[4]

Many of these verbal and physical attacks seem to have been motivated by whites' fear of Japanese imports or corporations in the United States or by resentment of Japanese competition in world trade. Anti-Asian hostility has increased during economic recessions as non-Asians have frequently sought scapegoats for problems usually rooted in the faulty economic decisions of non-Asian executives, investors, or workers.

MIGRATION: AN OVERVIEW

The Serial Migration of Asians

Asian Americans include many immigrant groups: the Chinese, Japanese, Koreans, Filipinos, Vietnamese, and Asian Indians, as well as smaller groups. In his pathbreaking book on Asian immigration to the United States, Ronald Takaki has shown that prominent white historians of immigration have often neglected Asian immigrants in the epic story of U.S. migration. Takaki suggests that such a Eurocentric history serves no good purpose, that we Americans have "come from many different shores—Europe, the Americas, Africa, and also Asia."[5]

To a striking degree, the immigration of major Asian groups has proceeded in serial fashion. This has not been by chance; it is largely the result of the actions of white employers and workers, who were often motivated by racist prejudices to stop the immigration of a particular Asian group. As we will discuss in more detail in the next chapter, the first large group of Asian immigrants to the United States were the Chinese. Early Chinese immigrants came to Hawaii, where U.S. planters were becoming influential by the mid-1800s. Later on, from the 1860s to the early 1880s, the Chinese migrated in large numbers to the West Coast to do low-wage work in construction and other industries. After racist agitation and exclusionary legislation stopped most Chinese immigration to the U.S. mainland in the 1880s, Japanese workers were aggressively recruited to fill the demand for labor on farms and in construction and mining projects.

The cutoff of Japanese immigration in 1908 (to be discussed shortly) in its turn spurred white American employers to recruit Filipinos to fill the continuing labor needs of farms on the mainland and in Hawaii. In addition, the recruitment by white employers of other Asian laborers, including Koreans and Asian Indians, during the first two decades of the twentieth century was designed to reduce the dominance and ability to organize of Japanese American workers in the labor markets of Hawaii and the United States.[6]

Early Immigration

Japan's initial contact with the United States involved gunboat diplomacy. In 1853, U.S. commodore Matthew Perry sailed warships into Tokyo Bay, and with a show of force won a treaty granting the United States trading rights with Japan. In a few decades there would be much trade between the two nations.

The colony of Hawaii was the first destination for Japanese immigrants coming within the U.S. sphere. At least 231,000 migrated there between 1868 and 1929. European planters sought low-wage laborers for their fields. At first, Chinese laborers were brought in under labor contracts. After 1884, thousands of Japanese laborers were brought to the Hawaiian plantations, usually under contract labor agreements. There were relatively few white laborers in the islands, and the Japanese immigrants became part of a racial hierarchy headed by the European American planters. When the labor agreements expired in 1894, most immigrants stayed on, thereby laying the basis for Hawaii's present-day Japanese American communities. Propertied European Americans worked to ensure their control of the islands, with many lobbying for annexation by the United States. In 1898, Hawaii came under the territorial control of the U.S. government.[7]

Japanese workers were numerous on the islands. Dependent on the plantations owned by a few big corporations, they learned they could not "advance themselves through individualism and small business," as they did on the mainland. Rather, as laborers, they adopted a class-based strategy of "unionization, politics, and collective action."[8]

Mainland Migration

Between the 1880s and the so-called Gentlemen's Agreement in 1908 (see below) more than 150,000 Japanese entered; between then and the 1920s another 100,000 came. The immigrants to the mainland moved into a greater diversity of economic positions, from farm labor and mining to shopkeeping and truck farming, than did immigrants to Hawaii. Some came under contract to employers, others under the auspices of relatives, and yet others on their own. The pre-1908 Issei often had a harder time than those who came afterward, since the later immigrants were able to move directly into Japanese American communities.[9] (*Issei, Nisei, Sansei,* and *Yonsei* are Japanese terms for the first four generations of Japanese Americans. The Issei were born in Japan.)

Like the Chinese before them (see Chapter 12), the Japanese immigrants faced discrimination from whites. Many white employers favored immigration; many white workers and unions opposed it. At the turn of the century, one mayor of San Francisco campaigned against the Japanese, arguing they were "unassimilable" and a competitive threat. In 1905, California newspapers began a campaign against the so-called "yellow peril," which they saw as a threat to public schools. Both houses of the California legislature passed a resolution calling for exclusion of the Japanese on the grounds that they would not assimilate, given their racial differences. Because of this racist agitation and other factors, President Theodore Roosevelt arranged for a prohibition of Japanese migrants. In negotiations in 1907 and 1908, Roosevelt persuaded the Japanese government to agree to an infamous Gentlemen's Agreement, whereby no passports would be given by Japan to any Japanese workers except those already in the United States and their close relatives.[10]

Unlike the Chinese, Japanese immigrants were able for a time to bring in wives and families. Between 1908 and 1920, thousands of Japanese "picture brides" entered the United States following wedding ceremonies conducted in Japan to husbands they had never met. The large proportion of women and children among Japanese immigrants in the period between 1910 and 1920 even led some white supremacy groups to allege that this "disloyal alien race" was taking over and would soon overpopulate California.[11]

More Racist Agitation and Restrictions

The same white writers who proclaimed the threat posed by southern and eastern Europeans to "Anglo-Saxon superiority" often expressed fear of Asian migrations as well. Organized white groups, including the American Legion and the California Farm Bureau Association, pressed for exclusion of the Japanese. By the 1920s, the U.S. Congress had succumbed to this racist agitation. It passed the 1924 Immigration Act, which established racist quotas based on a formula giving preference to "Nordic" nations and excluded Japanese immigration with a provision prohibiting all "aliens ineligible for citizenship" from entry into the United States. In an earlier decision, *Ozawa* v. *United States* (1922), the Supreme Court had paved the way by ruling that only those immigrants of white or African origin could become citizens of the United States. One of the most striking features of the new government restrictions on immigration was that Japanese and other Asian immigrants already in the United States, unlike their European counterparts, were prohibited from bringing the wives they had left behind. The intention was clearly to prevent the development of Asian American families. The 1922 Cable Act was even more extreme, requiring any U.S. woman, whether white or Asian American, who married an alien ineligible for citizenship (an Asian) to lose *her own* citizenship. In contrast with northern European immigrants, Asian immigrants were considered very undesirable by whites and were not permitted to assimilate in important ways.[12]

Government action against Asians, spurred by labor unions and hate groups, persisted. Much of the U.S. labor movement supported direct exclusion of Japanese immigrants until after World War II. Not until 1952 did the federal government provide even a small quota for the Japanese and permit first-generation Japanese Americans to become naturalized citizens, and not until 1965 were the anti-Asian restrictions removed from U.S. immigration law.[13]

In 1880, there were only 148 Japanese Americans. By 1920, the number had grown to 111,000. As late as 1965 there were only about 1 million Asian Americans, of whom Japanese Americans were the largest group. The 1965 Immigration Act permitted new immigrants, and since the 1970s non-Japanese Asian and Pacific peoples have predominated in the migration from Asia. There were 3.7 million Asian Americans in 1980, an increase of more than 100 percent from 1970. By 1990 there were 7.3 million Asian Americans, of whom about 866,000 were Japanese.[14]

Since the abolition of the racist 1924 immigration law in 1965, it has been possible for large numbers of Japanese immigrants to enter the United States. But relatively few have taken advantage of the opportunity to immigrate, and their numbers have been lower than those of other Asian groups (see Chapter 12). In recent years the immigration of a relatively small number of Japanese professionals and executives of American branches of Japanese corporations and their families has contributed to the revitalization of some Japanese American communities.

STEREOTYPES

Non–Asian Americans have held a range of stereotypes about Japanese Americans. In recent years Japanese Americans and other Asian Americans have sometimes been seen as "model minorities"—groups who are said to be successful in moving up in U.S. society. In addition, movies about the Vietnam War have portrayed Asians as devious, corrupt, or evil "gooks," and anti-Asian graffiti such as "Look out for the Asian invasion" and "Stop the Yellow Hordes" have been scrawled on college dorm walls and numerous highway overpasses.[15]

Non-Asians often lump all Asian Americans into one group that is smeared with anti-Asian stereotypes. Whites applied stereotypes of early immigrants, especially the Chinese, to later Japanese or Korean immigrants. All Asian groups have suffered from similar stereotypes, such as that of the "dangerous and wily Oriental." In the early years, Chinese immigrants were stereotyped as "docile," "crafty," or "dirty." Initially, some whites evaluated the new Japanese migrants less negatively than the Chinese immigrants, considering them less threatening and more family-oriented than the Chinese. Soon, however, white images of the Japanese came to contain the negative notions that the Japanese were docile and servile. The new immigrants often heard white cries of "Jap go home."[16] Since these early days, the word "Jap" has become a derogatory epithet hurled by some non–Asian Americans against this group of Americans.

Within a short period, many Japanese laborers managed to gain some land to farm, usually by contract, shares, or leasing. Hostile white farmers and workers exaggerated this Japanese American land ownership, which was growing but never involved more than a small percentage of western farmland. Another widespread view was that the Japanese Americans were incapable of being shaped by the dominant culture because of their different culture. V. S. McClatchy, a Sacramento editor, argued that the Japanese were "for various reasons unassimilable, and a dangerous element."[17] The irony in this racist view was clear to anyone who understood that state or federal laws *prohibited* Japanese immigrants from becoming citizens, from directly owning land, and from marrying whites—and thus from even trying to assimilate along these dimensions.

From U.S. presidents and senators to ordinary citizens, many whites belabored the differences between themselves and Japanese immigrants. James Phelan, U.S. senator from California, argued that Japanese Americans were a great threat to the "future of the white race, American institutions, and Western civilization."[18] Again we see how the construction of "whiteness" is based on extremely biased views of the meaning of "civilization" as well as a strong negative view of hated outgroups.

The movie industry has played an important role in circulating stereotypes of Asian Americans—just as it has for other Americans of color. Historically, movie images have been part of a broad stereotyping of Japanese Americans as inscrutable, treacherous, and immoral. In the formative period of the movie industry in the early twentieth century, Chinese and Japanese characters were usually pictured as outsiders and villains. Asians and Asian Americans were crudely stereotyped as "inscrutable," poor at speaking English, and dangerous or treacherous.[19] Between 1900 and the 1920s, the vicious image of the forward, buck-toothed "Jap" exploded in the mass media. In his widely circulated "Letters of a Japanese Schoolboy," the journalist Wallace Irwin stimulated stereotypes about Japanese Americans, including a mode of speech parodied with phrases such as "so sorry, please." White legislators spoke of the alleged immorality of Japanese Americans, even using the apelike image applied earlier to Irish and African Americans.[20]

Public opinion surveys in the 1920s and 1930s indicated that anti-Japanese prejudices were accepted by most white Americans, especially those on the West

Coast. In a survey of white students' attitudes in California in 1927 the stereotypes frequently mentioned were negative. The Japanese were thought to be dishonest, treacherous, and unfairly competitive.[21]

War Propaganda

From the 1890s to the 1930s, anti-Japan sentiment grew among non-Asians. The Japanese people were considered an "inferior race" with the brashness to challenge European and American interests in the Pacific region. Before the attack on Pearl Harbor, white politicians and labor leaders were portraying Japanese Americans as disloyal. This image expanded after Pearl Harbor, and rumors of spying circulated by the thousands, including such wild stories as Japanese American farmers planting flowers in a pattern to guide attacking airplanes.[22]

California's attorney general (later U.S. chief justice), Earl Warren, depicted Japanese Americans as dangerous and threatening. And in 1943, General John L. DeWitt, the West Coast military commander, argued, "A Jap's a Jap. . . . The Japanese race is an enemy race and while many second- and third-generation Japanese born on United States soil, possessed of United States citizenship, have become 'Americanized,' the racial strains are undiluted."[23] With no evidence whatsoever, the national press argued that there were many enemy agents in this "large alien population." Indeed, the main reason for the existence of this alien population was the racist U.S. law that prohibited first-generation Japanese Americans from becoming citizens. Significantly, no Japanese American was ever proven to have collaborated with the enemy during World War II. The alleged disloyalty was a racist notion in the minds of many white Americans.

Surveys by the War Relocation Authority after the war revealed that Japanese stereotypes were commonplace. Slowly the stereotypes began to change. By the 1960s, new stereotypes had developed, some with apparently positive aspects. Magazines and newspapers frequently praised Japanese Americans for being highly acculturated and successful. However, as Ogawa has noted, the "highly Americanized" and "successful citizens" stereotypes are not entirely positive, for they suggest that one must act or think "white" in order to be a good U.S. citizen. The assumption underlying these stereotypes is that since Japanese Americans have become English-speaking, work-ethic models of virtue, they can now be *accepted by whites*. The "superior, successful citizen" image has also been used to defend the U.S. record on racial relations more generally. Whites who hold this view often argue that other non-European Americans can make it too if they work hard and assimilate culturally like the Japanese Americans.[24]

Recent Distortions, Stereotypes, and Omissions

One study of the images of Japanese Americans in history textbooks found not only this "successful minority" stereotype but also numerous distortions of Japanese American history. For example, one prominent textbook used in public schools tiptoes around the oppressive and discriminatory circumstances of early Japanese American history, speaking of Japanese being "added" to the population. There is a serious omission in such textbooks—the fact that U.S. employers in Hawaii and California actively recruited and exploited Japanese laborers. Most textbooks also do not deal adequately with the character and impact of the 1924 Immigration Act. That act was grounded in the racist stereotypes of white legislators in the U.S. Congress and violated the Gentlemen's Agreement with Japan. It stopped the immigration of Japanese entirely, over the objections of the Japanese government.

Frequently, the internment of Japanese Americans in concentration camps during World War II (to be discussed shortly) is not adequately portrayed. Most textbooks see the camp experience as part of the "hysteria of war" and do not discuss the long history of anti-Japanese agitation and discrimination that led to the illegal imprisonment of U.S. citizens of Japanese descent. Moreover, one textbook suggests that Japanese Americans "have forgiven the government for violating their rights during World War II." The fact is that the imprisonment is well remembered by Japanese Americans. None has forgotten the experience, and many have not forgiven the U.S. government.[25]

The stereotyping or misperception of Japanese Americans has taken place at the highest levels of U.S. society. In the mid-1980s, Senator Spark M. Matsunaga of Hawaii, a Japanese American, was assisting the White House in hosting a reception for visiting Japanese officials. The U.S. secretary of state, Alexander Haig, mistook Senator Matsunaga for one of the officials and shook his hand, wishing him a nice visit! In recent years Senator Daniel Inouye, a Japanese American who lost an arm fighting for the United States in World War II, received hate mail telling him that he should "go home to Japan where he belongs." Other Japanese American officials have reported that white Americans frequently congratulate them on how well they speak English, as though they were foreigners. Many white Americans seem unaware that the nation has Japanese American elected officials, that such officials' place of birth is the United States, and that their native language is English.[26]

One issue that has become more central in the 1980s and 1990s is the use of ethnic and racial group symbols and caricatures as mascots for sports teams. During the 1991 World Series, for example, the use of Native American caricatures by the Atlanta "Braves" baseball team created much protest from Native Americans and others, who noted that such symbols were racist in form and content. A number of sports teams have given up these caricatures and stereotyped symbols of various American racial and ethnic groups. For example, in 1991 Shoreline Community College in Seattle abandoned its Samurai Warrior mascot, a Japanese caricature, because of its racist overtones.

A serious caricature of the Japanese is developed in Michael Crichton's 1991 best-selling novel, *Rising Sun*, and in the movie of the same name. The Japanese businesspeople and other Japanese characters in this murder mystery set in Los Angeles are portrayed, to quote one reviewer, as "inscrutable, technologically proficient, predatory aliens who . . . subsist through unpalatable foods, manipulate *everything* and *everyone,* and enjoy kinky, violent sex with white women."[27] This novel's characters encompass several of the negative stereotypes and prejudices with which whites have targeted Asians and Asian Americans since the beginning of this century.

In 1994 a white disc jockey for a San Francisco radio station was suspended indefinitely for anti-Asian comments he made on the air and for allowing callers to make racist anti-Asian remarks. The disc jockey reportedly spoke of the "stinking Japanese" and told a Japanese American caller that he would hate the Japanese until he died. He also predicted another war with Japan. The station received vigorous complaints from several Asian American groups, including the Japanese American Citizens League (JACL).[28]

REPRESSION AND VIOLENT ATTACKS

Japanese Americans have suffered not only from hostile prejudices but also from economic discrimination and physical attacks. The first major acts of violence against the Japanese immigrants came within a decade of their arrival in large numbers. After the 1906 San Francisco earthquake, mob violence directed at Japanese Americans increased. Scientists sent by Japan to help with earthquake relief were attacked by white men and boys, and local newspapers condoned the vicious actions. Japanese American businesses were boycotted, and shopkeepers were attacked.[29]

The anti-Japanese exclusion movement sometimes turned to violence, as in California in 1921, when large numbers of Japanese farm workers were driven out of certain farm areas. Moreover, in the 1930s, white farmers in Arizona petitioned the governor to throw out Japanese American farmers. When this failed, attempts were made to drive them out by force. The threat of such violence spreading to California led the legislature to consider a bill restricting Japanese American agricultural enterprises. At the beginning of World War II the violent attacks escalated. In 1942 alone there were dozens of attacks on Japanese Americans and their property from Seattle to San Diego.[30]

Concentration Camps in the United States

In this century, only one U.S. racial or ethnic group has had a large number of its men, women, and children imprisoned for years behind barbed wire—Japanese Americans. The military victories of the Japanese government in the 1930s and 1940s, including the sudden attack at Pearl Harbor, increased fears of a Japanese invasion of the U.S. mainland. White members of Congress and the mass media parroted the old anti-Japanese stereotypes and escalated fear of Japanese Americans across the United States. By January 1942, the evacuation and imprisonment of Americans of Japanese ancestry was being suggested. Some whites were motivated by economic self-interest; white organizations such as the Western Growers Protective Association seemed committed to destroying Japanese American business competition.[31]

Police raids on Japanese aliens, which had begun after the Pearl Harbor attack, were intensified in a frantic search for spies; more than two thousand aliens were arrested without evidence of disloyalty. Japanese American businesses were forced to close. Citizens were illegally detained by local police, evicted by landlords, and fired by employers.[32]

In the first phase of federal action against Americans whose ancestry was linked to countries at war with the United States, a small number of Japanese, German, and Italian aliens were moved from sensitive areas and their travel was restricted. Then came the second stage. On February 19, 1942, Executive Order 9066 was issued by President Franklin Roosevelt and validated by Congress. It ordered the secretary of war to establish military areas from which any person could be excluded. The West Coast military commander established the western parts of California, Washington, and Oregon, as well as the southern part of Arizona, as areas where no Japanese, Italian, or German aliens could reside. However, the only American citizens who, in large numbers, were detained in assembly centers and later transported under guard to barbed-wire concentration camps were those of Japanese ancestry.[33]

Japanese Americans forced out of their homes in San Francisco await transportation to U.S. concentration camps.

Japanese American businesses usually had to be sold quickly and at a loss. By the fall of 1942, inland areas in the West housed about 120,000 Japanese Americans, more than two-thirds of them native-born U.S. citizens whose only crime was to be perceived by whites as racially different.[34] Racist oppression behind the barbed wire took many forms. At the Tule Lake Camp in California the white administration arranged for camp inmates to be hired out to white personnel as domestics at the low wage of $30 per month. Part of this wage was taken by the camp administration and spent on recreational facilities for white personnel. Low-price barber shops and cafeterias for whites working in the concentration camps were staffed by Japanese Americans paid wages befitting slaves, such as $16 per week for waitresses. Barracks were typically bare-board buildings with few furnishings, and conditions were primitive, with whole families forced to live in small rooms or partitioned-off areas. Many camps were in areas that were very cold in winter and dusty much of the year. Conditions were especially difficult for Japanese American women, who "faced severe racism and traumatic family strain."[35]

Japanese Americans protested their treatment in these concentration camps in numerous demonstrations; six thousand even renounced their U.S. citizenship. Gradually, several thousand college students and workers on special agricultural assignments were released from the camps; others were released to the U.S. Army, where, ironically, many served in Europe with extraordinary valor in segregated units under white officers.[36]

In late 1944, the order to evacuate was rescinded. Most of those imprisoned returned to the West Coast and found farms and businesses in white hands or in ruin, household goods destroyed, and local whites hostile if not violent. The U.S. government spent about $250 million on the evacuation; Japanese American economic losses are estimated to have been at least $400 million. The psychological costs and other human losses were and remain incalculable.[37] Fifty years later some of the barracks from the concentration camps were put on display at the Japanese American National Museum in Los Angeles.

Why the Camps Were Created

Why were Japanese Americans imprisoned? Some commentators have emphasized the military angle. Others have focused on anti-Japanese prejudice among whites and on the role of white business people in their hostile struggle with Japanese American competitors. Yet others have accented the role of West Coast politicians who sought the white public's favor by selecting an issue supported by white prejudices. The U.S. Supreme Court upheld the military decision without investigation—even though two-thirds of those evacuated were U.S. citizens. This evacuation was a clear violation of the civil rights guaranteed all citizens by the U.S. Constitution.[38]

The record shows that President Franklin Roosevelt and other white political officials held racist attitudes toward Japanese and other Asian Americans. Roosevelt believed that the Japanese had less developed skulls and were racially inferior, and he and other political and business leaders saw the emerging struggle in the Pacific as a racial war. Racist attitudes made it easier for top U.S. government officials to order the internment of large numbers of American citizens of Asian descent (but not large numbers of citizens of German or Italian descent) in barbed-wire camps.[39]

Japanese Americans fought valiantly but unsuccessfully in the courts and in demonstrations. At the Santa Anita Assembly Center in California, Japanese American evacuees confronted authorities over the rumored appropriation of personal property. A group of angry Japanese destroyed camp property and attacked a police officer; armed military police suppressed the rioting. In the fall of 1942, internees called a strike at the Poston camp to protest the imprisonment of two Japanese Americans.[40] In December 1942, at the Manzanar camp in California, an assault on a Japanese American who had collaborated with whites and the imprisonment of the attacker led to a mass meeting of 4,000 and demands for an investigation of camp conditions. The camp director, escorted by military police with machine guns, met the crowd. A crowd again formed at night and was fired upon; two Japanese Americans were killed.[41] Ironically, this oppression of Americans occurred at a time when the U.S. government was hypocritically proclaiming the values of "freedom" and "democracy" to a war-torn world.

Recent Violence

After World War II, most Japanese Americans moved back to California where they continued to face racial oppression in the form of economic discrimination as well as violent attacks on themselves or their property. The racial epithet "Jap" became part of commonplace anti-Japanese graffiti. Hate crimes, including murders, assaults, threats, and harassment, targeting Japanese and other Asian Americans—in their homes and businesses, in their places of employment, and in public places—have persisted as we move into the twenty-first century.[42]

THE POLITICAL ARENA

Because of racist U.S. naturalization laws, the Issei and other first-generation Asian Americans were not allowed to become citizens until the 1950s. Most second-generation Japanese Americans, the Nisei, did not become old enough to vote until the 1940s, and the World War II imprisonment was a severe setback in their struggle to participate in U.S. politics.[43]

Some political and civic organization occurred in the 1930s, when older Nisei formed Democratic political clubs in a few West Coast cities. The JACL, under Nisei leaders, advocated the accommodation strategies of self-help and individual enterprise and pressed moderately for civil rights and for citizenship for the Issei. Voter-registration campaigns were inaugurated, but attempts to get candidates to run usually stopped at the planning stage.[44]

Compensation Pressures and Political Progress

Since World War II the JACL, together with other Japanese American organizations, has won some important political and legal victories. By 1946, the JACL and some newer organizations were pressing for compensation for evacuation losses, for citizenship for the first generation, and for changes in discriminatory laws. Meager compensation for business and property losses finally came in the form of the 1948 Japanese American Evacuation Act. Japanese Americans were paid less than 10 percent of their losses.[45]

Japanese American organizations pressed the U.S. government for more adequate repayment for losses suffered. Belatedly, on September 17, 1987, the U.S. House passed a law including a formal apology to Japanese Americans for the internment and providing $1.2 billion in reparations. The bill contained an admission that the "basic civil liberties" of Japanese Americans were violated as a result of "racial prejudice." The Senate passed the bill, and it was signed by President Ronald Reagan. The House passed the bill after years of foot-dragging by congressional leaders and opposition from the Reagan White House.[46]

However, federal funding of the compensation for Japanese Americans took two more years because of more foot-dragging. The first checks were not distributed until the fall of 1990; by 1994, all checks had been mailed. Each of the remaining internees, or his or her heirs, was to receive $20,000. President George Bush wrote each internee a letter of apology. Some, such as Robert Matsui of California, refused the check but accepted the apology letter, saying, "All of us feel like we are home again." The legislation and apology signaled the public admission of discrimination against Japanese Americans by the government. Many hoped it would provide an improved civil rights environment not only for Japanese Americans but for the many new Asian migrants to the United States. Again, we see that civil rights organizations and movements of oppressed minorities have often been the strongest advocates of the "liberty and justice for all" tradition of the United States.[47]

Unfortunately, some whites were unwilling to see these Japanese Americans receive the justice due them. In one Japanese American community in Oxnard, California, for example, anti-Japanese leaflets were circulated that said, among other things, that no apology to Japanese Americans for their unconstitutional imprisonment was necessary because the Japanese government had detained U.S. soldiers in World War II. It appears that some non-Asians are still unable to distinguish between Japanese Americans, who are citizens of the United States, and the Japanese government.[48]

Pressure from Japanese American organizations, including the JACL, helped win two political victories in the 1970s: the repeal of the infamous Title II of the 1950 Internal Security Act, which permitted government imprisonment of citizens deemed potential collaborators with an enemy in time of crisis, and the rescinding of Executive Order 9066, which ordered the wartime imprisonment of Japanese Americans.[49]

Government Officials

Political organization aimed at electoral victories has increased decade by decade. Major gains have usually come first in Hawaii. Some Nisei were registered to vote in Hawaii as early as 1917. In 1930, the first were elected to office, two as members of the territorial legislature; by the late 1930s there were nine Japanese American officials among nearly 100 elected officials. Later, returning World War II veterans, intent on expanding their political participation, became active in Democratic attempts to overthrow the traditional Republican domination of the islands. Several were elected to the Hawaii legislature; in the late 1950s their efforts facilitated Congress's conferral of statehood after years of anti-Asian opposition. War hero Daniel Inouye was elected the first U.S. representative from the new state and the first Japanese American in Congress. Spark Matsunaga became the second to serve in the House, in 1962, when Inouye became a senator. In 1964, a second House seat was won by Patsy Takemoto Mink, the first Japanese American woman to serve in Congress.[50] In 1995, Inouye and Daniel Akaka, a native Hawaiian American, were Hawaii's U.S. senators, and Mink represented that state in the U.S. House.

Political victories on the mainland have been difficult because of the dilution of Japanese American votes in the predominantly non-Asian populations of most western areas. Few were elected to office until recent decades. In the 1960s, a few Japanese Americans were elected to city council offices in Los Angeles County, Oakland, and San Jose. In 1972, Carl Ooka was elected a county commissioner in the state of Washington, the first Japanese American elected to office in that state.[51]

Since the early 1970s only a handful of mainland Japanese Americans have held elected positions at higher levels of local, state, or the federal government. In 1976, Samuel I. Hayakawa, a prominent professor and semanticist, was elected a U.S. senator from California, the first Japanese American senator from the mainland. In the mid-1970s Norman Mineta of California became the first mainland representative of Japanese descent to the U.S. House. Robert Matsui was elected to the California delegation a few years later. He and Mineta led the House effort in the late 1980s to pass the bill providing compensation for the World War II internees.

Political empowerment has come slowly in the West. Historically, Asian Americans, including Japanese Americans, have often been reluctant to participate actively in politics out of fear of intensifying discrimination against them. Even in the 1990s, in states like California, Japanese Americans are less likely to be registered to vote than whites. Some analysts have speculated that Japanese and other Asian Americans tend to view politics and politicians as corrupt or disreputable or that Asian Americans tend to vote for white politicians rather than run their own candidates because they feel that whites have "more political clout."[52] In addition, Japanese and other Asian Americans who venture into the political arena sometimes face overt racist comments or actions. In 1992, a Democratic party leader at a Spokane, Washington, party meeting reportedly referred to the owners of a local hotel as "chinks," provoking strong protests from Asian American Democrats. In February 1993, at a meeting to examine the incident, the Democratic party's white vice-chair bowed and clasped her hands in front of her in response to a Japanese American participant who would not shake her hand. The Asian American participants found the vice-chair's gestures offensive. The JACL sued the state Democratic party for discrimination against Asian Americans.[53]

By 1990, about one of every ten Californians was Asian American, but a far smaller percent of the state's top elected officials were Asian Americans. Only three members of the state's forty-seven-member delegation to Congress were Asian. Not one Asian American served in the state legislature. Only 1 percent of city council and school board seats were held by Asian Americans. There are signs of change, however. In the late-1990s, a number of aides and assistants to California elected officials are Asian American. They may in their turn seek elected office.[54]

Some western cities have seen pan-Asian political cooperation. For example, in the late 1980s, Warren Furutani, a Japanese American, was elected to the Los Angles school board with the help of Filipino and Asian-Pacific Americans, as well as Japanese Americans. He developed an agenda of school issues of concern to all Asian Americans.[55]

Politics, Stereotyping, and Competition with Japan

Acts of violence and vandalism by white Americans against Japanese Americans have often been motivated by fear of economic competition from Japan, a contemporary variation of the classic racist view of "Oriental hordes" threatening white America. For example, an exhibit at a Flint, Michigan, auto show in the 1980s portrayed a car with a Japanese face falling like a bomb on Detroit.[56]

In recent years, Japan's economic development has surpassed that of the United States in a number of manufacturing areas. One U.S. media response has been to print "buy-American" cartoons featuring caricatures of "wily Japs" and "crafty Orientals." Old stereotypes have reappeared in conversations among whites and in newspaper articles. Increasing unemployment in the recessions of the 1980s and 1990s has fueled a tendency among some non-Asians to blame the Japanese for U.S. economic troubles. This scapegoating has been reflected in political action. Anti-Japanese protectionist bills have been introduced in Congress. In the 1990s, Democratic party leaders have proposed bills that would slash Japanese imports. White congressional leaders have frequently ignored Japanese investments in the United States that have created many thousands of new jobs. Japan's investments and competitive economy have not been major causes of U.S. recessions; the real causes lie elsewhere—often in poor U.S. corporate management and overseas investments by U.S. firms (capital flight).[57]

Japanese executives and investors who have come to the United States in recent years have sometimes faced racist agitation. In 1992 a Japanese business-person was killed in the Los Angeles area. Police investigated the possibility that he was murdered by a non-Asian worker who blamed him for U.S. economic troubles. Not long before his death, he had been threatened at his door by a man who blamed him for a 1990s economic recession. Stereotyping remains evident in anti-Japan discussions in the United States.[58]

Protest Organizations and Group Pride

At the turn of the century, white delegates arriving at one anti-immigrant convention were met at the door by Japanese Americans with leaflets arguing against attempts to exclude Japanese immigrants. This was the beginning of a long series of books, speeches, and pamphlets by Japanese and Japanese Americans protesting exclusion attempts. A few voluntary associations, such as the Japanese Association, were formed in the early 1900s to combat exclusion activities and other anti-Japanese discrimination.[59]

Labor protests were part of the early Japanese experience. Japanese workers in Hawaii participated in at least sixty work stoppages protesting poor working conditions in the five decades after 1870. Substantial labor organizing took place on the mainland. There were a few strikes for better wages and working conditions in the 1890s; after 1900 their number increased. In 1903, more than 1,000 Japanese American and Mexican American agricultural workers jointly struck white farmers in California. Japanese American workers were also involved in agricultural and mining strikes in California, Utah, Colorado, and Washington. Up to the 1940s, Japanese American and Mexican American workers cooperated in strikes against exploitative white farmers. Unfortunately, conservative white labor leaders, such as Samuel Gompers, often blocked the admission of Japanese Americans into older unions with the racist argument that Japanese Americans were racially different and unassimilable.[60]

As we have noted, during the 1940s Japanese Americans protested their incarceration in the World War II concentration camps; thousands renounced their citizenship and returned to Japan after the war. During the 1960s, new pan-Asian organizations and publications appeared, often established by the younger generations. Journals such as *Amerasia Journal* urged collective action and attention to problems of Asian Americans. Distorted and sugar-coated images of Asian American success were challenged as a renewed sense of group pride developed.[61]

One sign of group pride can be seen in the development of Asian American studies programs in a number of colleges and universities across the United States in recent decades. Several campuses of the University of California, including Berkeley and Los Angeles, and the California State University, including San Francisco and Long Beach, as well as the University of Washington and the University of Hawaii, have developed important Asian American studies programs. Most of these programs have become institutionalized with a core of faculty. In the 1990s, Asian American scholars have urged a rethinking of these programs, with an eye to encouraging more research on Asian Americans, adding courses to accommodate recent immigrants, and improving relations with Asian American communities.[62]

Hate crimes directed against Japanese and other Asian Americans have increased on some college campuses. In early 1997, some 700 Asian American students at Indiana University (Bloomington) received hate (e-mail) messages in three separate incidents. In the summer of the same year, a white student, apparently concerned about the large number of Asian American students at the University of California (Irvine), awaited trial on charges of e-mailing death threats to sixty of these students.[63] Because of such hostility, which often increases as the number of Asian American students grows at a campus, many Japanese American and other Asian American students have become even more interested than before in the development of strong Asian American organizations and academic programs on their campuses.

THE ECONOMY

Most Japanese immigrants started out at the bottom levels of the economic pyramid, filling the hard jobs on farms, mines, and construction projects. One California study in 1909 found 65 percent of Japanese American workers in agriculture, 15 percent in domestic service work, 15 percent in small businesses, and 5 percent in other lines of work.[64]

In the first decades the new residents worked for as little as $.50 to $1 per day in agriculture. Japanese workers generally received less than whites. For instance, while white sawmill laborers were paid $2.60 to $3.50 per day in the state of Washington, Japanese laborers received only $1.75 to $2.75. This pattern of racially discriminatory wage rates was true for many jobs. In cities Japanese Americans often became service workers, laborers, or the domestic servants of whites.[65]

Finding an Economic Niche

Gradually, many first-generation Issei began to arrange for land to farm on their own. Although the amount of land Japanese Americans owned was not large, their economic role was concentrated and important, particularly in the area of market gardening. They grew almost 100 percent of certain crops. In urban areas, where institutionalized discrimination kept them out of manufacturing and white-collar employment, some went into small businesses. The Issei came to play a "middleman minority" role in several western states. By 1909, there were at least 3,000 Japanese American businesses in these states. By 1929, there were nearly 2,000 in Los Angeles alone. An estimated 30 percent of Japanese Americans were involved with Japanese American businesses as employers or employees. Operated on a small scale, some enterprises catered primarily to a Japanese American clientele, but many eventually served a non-Asian clientele. The Issei's group solidarity helped them create a niche economy, and this small-business economy in turn reinforced their group solidarity. Edna Bonacich and John Modell conclude that "the Japanese minority filled a particular and specialized niche in the western economy and was important to it, providing key products and services."[66]

Most Japanese immigrants came from eleven southern prefectures in Japan, and each was represented by an association in the United States. These prefectural clubs could act as mutual-aid associations for immigrants in a hostile environment. They aided the movement of immigrants into the economy by providing training for workers and directing clients to businesses. Restaurants and cleaning operations succeeded because they could usually draw on prefectural networks for reliable workers and loans. Informal money-pooling organizations and credit-rotating associations called *tanomoshi* provided capital for small entrepreneurs who could not secure funds from banks.[67]

White opposition to the new immigrant workers and businesses built swiftly. In urban areas, the white-controlled labor movement often led the opposition. Boycotts and anti-Japanese advertising were used by white groups, as in the Anti-Jap Laundry League's attempt to drive Japanese Americans out of the laundry business. One problem for racist whites was that the Japanese immigrants were very hardworking competitors who resisted attempts to drive them from their businesses.[68]

A 1913 California Alien Land Law, passed under pressure from white farmers, stipulated that aliens could not buy land or lease it for more than three years; nor could they pass on land to their children. All Issei were forced to remain "aliens" because of the racially discriminatory naturalization laws. This California land law interfered with agricultural activity, but some ways were found to circumvent it, such as registering ownership of lands under the names of children. Such practices brought new laws prohibiting Issei from leasing land and from holding it in the names of children. These discriminatory laws reduced the number of Japanese American farms from over five thousand in 1920 to four thousand in 1930. Those who remained in farming relied on tenant or truck farming. New organizations such as the Japanese Cooperative Farm Industry organized the flow of farm products to Japanese American retailers in cities. Japanese American farmers had again demonstrated their ingenuity and knack for success. But the wartime evacuation destroyed their farming and marketing operations once more.[69]

Forced out of farming by land laws and attracted to the booming cities, many Japanese Americans became gardeners or nursery operators. The 1930 California census showed that half of male Japanese workers were in agriculture or gardening, one-fourth were in trade or business, 2 percent were in the professions, and a large percentage of the rest were in other urban occupations.[70]

By the beginning of World War II, some Japanese Americans in cities were moving into white-collar positions. One study estimated that half the men in highly urbanized Los Angeles County in 1940 were in white-collar positions and about 40 percent were in semiskilled and unskilled blue-collar positions.[71] Then the economy collapsed. Median economic losses per family in Los Angeles from the forced wartime evacuation were estimated at about $10,000 (in 1940 dollars) in goods, property, income, and expenses. The figures were similar elsewhere. Many

of those who could not regain their businesses and farms after 1945 went into contract gardening and private household work.

In her research on the labor of Japanese American women before World War
II, Evelyn Nakano Glenn found that "from the moment they arrived, Japanese
American women labored alongside the men to secure their own and their families' livelihood."[72] Much of the hard work done by the women was unpaid family
labor on farms and in small businesses, but some Issei women and their daughters worked as domestic servants to whites. Before World War II, discrimination
against these women was so strong that most were unable to move into white-
collar work as did European immigrant women and their daughters. The Japanese
American domestics often resisted oppression, usually in covert ways such as eva-
sion of work pressed on them by exploitative white employers. This resistance
gave them a sense of self-reliance that was critical for their development and for
that of their children. They sometimes struggled against husbands as well; their
subordination to white women in their domestic employment was reinforced by
subordination to husbands at home. Yet they struggled to maintain dignity, and
"despite the menial nature of employment, the Issei achieved a sense of their own
strength, and in some cases, superiority to employer and husband within their
own area of competence."[73]

The Postwar Economy

The booming postwar economy was in need of labor, and many white employers
hired Japanese American workers. Yet racial discrimination continued to affect the
second generation; certain occupations were still off limits. For example,
University of California education departments discouraged Japanese American
students from considering the teaching profession because of the difficulty of
placement in the state's schools.[74] Self-employment continued to be important. By
1960, there were 7,000 Japanese-owned businesses in the Los Angeles area, most
of them gardening businesses. Hotels, groceries, and laundries made up the next
largest categories. The "middleman minority" model seems to fit the Issei generation well, but the second and later generations have gradually moved away from
the niche economy of small businesses to professional and other white-collar jobs.
In 1960, about half the Nisei were still involved in niche businesses, but many others used the education provided by parents to move into white-collar jobs.[75]

Occupational Mobility and Persisting Barriers

In recent decades, numerous books and articles have related the Japanese
American experience as a story of achievement. The usual socioeconomic indicators in census data do show that Japanese American progress since the 1950s has
been dramatic. For example, in 1990 both Japanese American women and men
were more likely to hold managerial or professional jobs than were their white
counterparts (33 percent, compared with 30 percent, for women; and 40 percent,
compared with 27 percent, for men). Only 29 percent of Japanese Americans held

blue-collar jobs, compared with 38 percent of whites. The unemployment rate for Japanese Americans was half that of whites and less than half that of all Asian Americans as a group.[76]

Income data also reveal economic success. Nationally, according to the 1990 census, the median income for Japanese American families was more than one and one-third times as much as that for white families. In addition, only a small percentage of Japanese American families (3.4 percent) fell below the federal poverty line, a figure lower than those for whites (7.0 percent) and for all Asian Americans as a group (11.4 percent). Note, however, that Japanese American workers are concentrated in two states, Hawaii and California, which have high wages and a high cost of living. For example, the difference in median incomes between Japanese American families and white families in California ($53,151 compared with $46,291) is not as great as that between Japanese American families and white families nationally ($51,550 versus $37,628). Per capita income for Japanese Americans in California ($20,951) is actually a little lower than that for whites ($20,960). Japanese American families in California are also a bit more likely than white families to have two or more family members in the labor force.[77]

Even though Japanese Americans have achieved significant economic success, they continue to face subtle exclusion from prominent positions in most businesses, in movies and television, in politics, and in certain civil service areas, such as local police and fire departments. Indirect discrimination in the form of height and weight requirements has played a role in some occupational areas. Positions at the highest administrative, managerial, and professional levels have often been closed to Japanese and other Asian Americans, particularly on the West Coast. Whites with poorer credentials or lesser ability have often been promoted at a faster rate.[78]

In 1988, Harry Kitano and Roger Daniels reported that only 159 (0.6 percent) of the 29,000 directors and top executives of the one thousand largest U.S. firms were Japanese or other Asian Americans, yet at that time Asian Americans made up about 2.6 percent of the U.S. population.[79] A *Wall Street Journal* story noted that Asian Americans have a very hard time climbing corporate ladders because "ironically, the same companies that pursue them for technical jobs often shun them when filling managerial and executive positions."[80] Top corporate executives have been quoted as saying that Asian Americans, including Japanese Americans, are best as technical workers and not as corporate executives. Because of this stereotype, they are hired as engineers and technicians but are not usually considered for major management positions. Knowing that discrimination awaits them if they depart from the white stereotype, many younger Asian Americans have pursued scientific and technical educations and rejected the humanities and the social sciences. The promotional ceiling also exists in higher education. A study of the University of California at Berkeley found that only one of the 102 top administrators there was an Asian American, even though the university student body was 25 percent Asian American.[81]

Blatant discrimination still occurs in some employment settings. In 1989, a third-generation Japanese American, Bruce Yamashita, entered the Marine Corps'

Officer Candidate School at Quantico, Virginia. A talented young man with a law degree, Yamashita faced racist discrimination from the first day, when a sergeant told him to "go back to your own country." Other sergeants called him by the names of Japanese-made motor vehicles (Kawasaki and Honda). A fellow officer candidate enquired as to why he had not joined the Japanese army. None of the Marine Corps officers intervened to stop the racial harassment, and Yamashita was terminated for "leadership failure." In 1994, after a five-year legal battle during which Yamashita, with the assistance of the JACL, uncovered a pattern of discrimination against non-European American officer candidates, the U.S. Navy Secretary commissioned Yamashita a captain in the Marine Corps reserves. The Marine Corps also made an apology.[82]

Overall trends in the U.S. economy have affected the employment opportunities of Japanese Americans. Many Japanese American students' career choices have been influenced by the past discrimination that channeled Japanese Americans into certain occupations, such as public school teaching. Moreover business opportunities are still limited by the anti-Japanese sentiment of many white Americans. Asian Americans report a glass ceiling in corporations and exclusion from white business networks. In 1992, several businesspeople, including corporate executives, created the Japanese American Chamber of Commerce to foster business development among Japanese Americans.

That Japanese Americans have achieved remarkable economic success against enormous odds is clearly indicated in statistics from the last four decades. What they could have achieved without persisting discrimination can only be imagined.

EDUCATION

Racism and Segregation

Like other immigrant groups, the Issei had a strong, lasting commitment to education. Most viewed education in pragmatic terms, as a way out of the arduous jobs of the farms and nurseries and as a route to better-paying positions. Issei parents enrolled their children in school more often than parents in most other immigrant groups, and many pursued formal education for themselves.[83]

In 1906, the mayor of San Francisco, in a move supported by local newspapers, secured a resolution from the board of education setting up a segregated public school for Asian children. At the time there were fewer than one hundred Japanese American children in two dozen schools. Reflecting classic white fears of racial mixing, one white member of the California legislature spoke of the danger to the "pure maids of California" posed by older Japanese students in primary grades. The Japanese government protested the segregation, and the federal government took court action to force the San Francisco Board of Education to give Japanese American children the equal rights promised them by a United States–Japan treaty.

Some white Californians were so angered by this rare federal show of support for Japanese Americans that they began to talk about secession. President Theodore Roosevelt and San Francisco officials worked out a compromise, and after three months out of school, most Japanese American children were allowed to return. Overage Japanese pupils were excluded. In return, the infamous Gentlemen's Agreement, aimed at stopping Japanese migration, was executed by Roosevelt.[84]

A common stereotype was that Japanese immigrants' children were displacing other children in California schools. However, even by the late 1930s, Japanese children were present in small proportions in all but two or three schools in California. The agitation over schools brought an increase in racial segregation pressures. California legislators made several attempts to segregate Japanese children, and by 1930 four school districts had segregated schools for Asian Americans.[85]

Language Schools and Japanese Educational Progress

Japanese Americans developed their own language schools that focused on education in the Japanese language and in traditional values such as respect for elders. One reason the Issei established these schools was to strengthen community bonds; by 1928 there were more than 4,000 pupils in 118 schools. White racists vigorously attacked the language schools as centers of emperor worship and Buddhism that were allegedly aimed at making children disloyal to the United States. The California legislature even passed a bill, vetoed by the governor, abolishing the schools. The white exclusionists' stereotyped view of these schools was sharply out of touch with reality.[86]

By the 1930s, Japanese Americans were making great strides in public education, from the primary grades to the college level, in spite of the entrenched discrimination. At several branches of the University of California the ratio of Japanese American students to the Japanese American population was a little larger than the comparable figure for the total California population. A 1930 survey of a large number of Japanese Americans in California showed the average educational level for men over twenty born in the United States to be 12.5 years. The figure for women was also relatively high. The educational attainments of Japanese Americans were already at least equal to those of California whites.[87]

The wartime evacuation and imprisonment interrupted these educational attainments. Second- and third-generation Japanese Americans received part of their schooling in the barbed-wire camps. After the war, educational discrimination against Japanese Americans was relaxed, and major gains resumed. Since the 1970s, the median educational level for adult Japanese Americans has been substantially greater than that for all adult Americans.[88] Census data for 1990 show that among Japanese Americans over twenty-four years old, 88 percent are high-school graduates and 35 percent are college graduates, compared with 79 percent and 22 percent of whites, respectively, in this age group. Only about 3 percent of Japanese Americans aged 16 to 19 are high-school dropouts, compared with 9 percent of their white counterparts. Among those between the ages of 18 and 24, 64 percent of Japanese Americans are enrolled in college, compared with 37 percent of whites.[89]

Nonetheless, the educational sphere still contains more than a few traces of discrimination. We have noted the commonplace underrepresentation of Japanese Americans in higher administrative positions in corporations and in public education. Japanese and other Asian Americans also continue to be underrepresented in certain graduate programs and departments at U.S. universities because of the direct and indirect impact of white stereotypes about the scientific and technical abilities of Asian Americans. Moreover, although the education levels of Japanese Americans are significantly higher than those of the white population, some research studies have suggested that their income levels are lower than one would predict on the basis of their high levels of education. In the United States, the financial payoffs of a college education still vary according to racial group and ethnicity.[90]

RELIGION

Japanese immigrants brought Buddhism and Shintoism with them. These religious traditions have remained significant in the United States. Once the Japanese arrived, Protestant missionaries converted many to Christian beliefs. Some Protestant missions provided support for immigrants who were establishing themselves in a difficult environment. The missions were crucibles of acculturation in which young Japanese Americans began to absorb the language and values of the dominant culture. When the missions grew, they became full-scale Japanese Protestant churches segregated from other churches. By the 1920s, there were thousands of practicing Japanese American Protestants.[91]

Buddhist temples were founded in major coastal cities in the decade after 1900. By 1920 there were two dozen temples in the West. Buddhist groups made significant adaptations to the new environment, with Christian-style Sunday schools and church organizations. As they did with the Japanese language schools, white racists and exclusionists made the outrageous claim that the temples were hotbeds of emperor worship and antipatriotic teaching. The white attackers were ignorant of the fact that Buddhism does not involve emperor worship.[92]

A survey of Japanese Californians in the 1930s found that whereas three-fourths of first-generation immigrants were Buddhist, only 39 percent of the second generation were. A majority among the Nisei were Christian. Japanese Americans were becoming a Christian group. However, adoption of Christian practices did not usually entail a complete break with the past, for many considered themselves Christian *and* Buddhist.[93]

Before and during World War II, there was jingoistic agitation that branded Buddhism and Shintoism as un-American. The wartime evacuation closed churches on the mainland. Buddhist temples were closed in Hawaii, and priests were imprisoned. World War II brought destruction to Buddhist temples; many were vandalized. After the war the number of Buddhist temples increased across the United States as Buddhism regained its important position in Japanese American communities.[94]

By the 1980s, there were several dozen Protestant churches in the Japanese Southern California Ministerial Fellowship, with numerous others scattered up and down the West Coast and across the country. Moreover, in the mid-1990s the Jodo Shinshu Buddhist Churches of America had sixty-five temples across the United States with approximately 20,000 members, and there were a number of smaller Buddhist groups. One study of Japanese Americans in San Francisco found that these churches were second in importance only to the family in cementing the community; two-thirds of those interviewed were at least occasional participants in church activities. Still, the percentage of Buddhists among Japanese Americans is small and declining. Buddhist groups have tended to attract older members; younger Japanese Americans have preferred Protestant churches.[95]

There has been a resurgence of interest in Buddhism in the last decade among Asian and non-Asian Americans. Buddhist festivals have been celebrated in Japanese and other Asian American communities. One of the astronauts who died in the space shuttle explosion in 1986 was Air Force Lieutenant Colonel Ellison Onizuka, the first Asian American in space and a member of the Buddhist

A Buddhist temple in Los Angeles, California.

Churches of America. Onizuka's Buddhist funeral made many non-Asian Americans aware of the presence of several thousand Buddhists in the U.S. armed forces.[96]

ASSIMILATION PERSPECTIVES

An assimilation perspective has predominated in much analysis of the situation of Japanese Americans. Indeed, Japanese Americans have been viewed as the most assimilated of all Asian American groups. Assimilation analysts emphasize that the younger generations have intermarried at high rates and often have little facility in the Japanese language. For a variety of reasons, Japanese Americans are often seen as the most adaptive, in cultural and certain structural terms, of all non-European immigrant groups.

Today, most Japanese Americans are not immigrants. Because few Japanese immigrants have come to the United States in recent decades, the ties to the home country are not as strong for other Asian American groups. One study in Los Angeles County found that 70 percent of Japanese Americans were born in the United States and that only 14 percent had come to the United States since 1970. Among major Asian American groups, Japanese Americans have the smallest proportion of immigrants. Most were born and have grown up under the pressures and influence of the dominant culture and institutions.[97]

From the assimilation perspective one might argue that cultural assimilation came at an early point for most Issei, although some acculturated to the language and other aspects of the dominant culture more rapidly than others. One segment of the Issei sought to survive white discrimination by isolating themselves from the outside world and immersing themselves in things Japanese; many others sought to acculturate rapidly, at least in those areas where acculturation was permitted, while maintaining strong social and cultural ties to their relatives and friends. Assimilation analysts would also suggest that cultural assimilation, especially in regard to language, religion, and orientation to white-collar and corporate employment, has come rapidly for later generations. In one survey, although most Issei reported they could get along in English, many reported some language difficulty. Historically, the influence of the Issei in the Japanese community was wide-ranging, but their ability to cope with the dominant culture was restricted by the massive discrimination they faced. The second-generation Nisei, in contrast, became bicultural; that is, they have operated successfully in both Japanese American communities and in mainstream institutions. Moreover, several studies of the Sansei have underscored the apparent closing of the gap with some aspects of the dominant culture. For example, one study found that Nisei and Sansei respondents showed substantial acculturation in that they spoke mostly English at home and did not often read Japanese literature. Kitano and Daniels reported in 1988 that 49 percent of all Japanese Americans in Los Angeles County spoke only English, the highest proportion for any Asian American group there.[98]

By the late 1990s, certain key community institutions seemed to be in decline. Several important newspapers for Japanese Americans have ceased publication in recent years. In late 1997 *Rafu Shimpo*, a Los Angeles newspaper in publication since 1903, was in financial trouble, with subscriptions down to only 4,000. The readers of these newspapers are mainly the Nisei, who are being replaced by younger generations that appear to be less interested in these traditional community publications.[99]

Structural assimilation at secondary-group levels has been significant for Japanese Americans, particularly in the economic sphere. As we have seen, many analysts have dramatized this aspect of assimilation. Many have argued that Japanese Americans represent a remarkable success story in the economic progress they have made in the face of discrimination. Relatively high levels of occupational attainment, income, and education are characteristic for second- and later-generation families. Explanations for this success have tended to focus on values and community organization. Ivan Light, for example, has opted for a traditional-culture explanation in examining the development of the small-business economy among Japanese Americans, a niche economy that sets them apart, in his view, from certain other non-European Americans such as African and Mexican Americans. Light accents the role of a "culturally preferred style of economic organization," by which he means the rotating-credit associations and similar organizations set up by immigrants from Japan. On a related issue, Kitano and Daniels have shown that most Japanese American families own their own homes and have strongly adhered to homeownership values, more so than white Americans.[100]

What Milton Gordon refers to as behavior-receptional assimilation and attitude-receptional assimilation showed little change until after World War II. Intense discrimination and prejudice marred the lives of the Issei and Nisei for the first sixty years. Since World War II discrimination and prejudice directed at Japanese Americans have decreased. Some researchers have reported that white attitudes toward Japanese Americans improved dramatically between World War II and the early 1980s. For example, Paul Spickard argues that in the early 1900s Japanese Americans were seen by whites as the "lowest of the low" and were grouped with black Americans, but that in recent years whites do "not see them as very different from themselves, and that fact is remarkable."[101] Spickard judges white attitudes from marriage rates; he is influenced by data showing that 30 to 60 percent of third-generation Japanese Americans, depending on the region and city, have married non-Japanese, as opposed to 2 percent or so among the first generation. The third-generation figures are in the same range as those of many white ethnic groups and contrast sharply with the current 2 percent intermarriage rate for black Americans. Spickard argues in effect that whites generally do not feel hostile about Japanese–white marriages, especially those involving white men and Japanese American women.

However, Spickard is too optimistic in reading intermarriages as indicative of positive white views. As we have noted, recent years have seen renewed white hostility and discrimination toward Japanese and other Asian Americans, especially during economic recessions. In one 1980s survey, a significant number of Japanese Americans reported having faced discrimination. One-fifth of those surveyed (31 percent of the Nisei and 13 percent of the Sansei) reported experiencing considerable discrimination as adults, and another 65 percent reported a little discrimination. Only 13 percent reported never having experienced discrimination. In addition, three-fourths of the sample felt that Japanese Americans did experience discrimination; the majority disagreed with the statement that Japanese Americans do not face job discrimination. Given the reluctance of many Japanese Americans to speak ill of their country, these responses likely underestimate the actual amount of discrimination, especially the subtle variety, that Japanese Americans face.[102]

Assimilation analysts tend to focus on assimilation at the level of primary social ties and voluntary associations. Assimilation in these areas did not occur to any significant degree until after World War II. In earlier decades Japanese immigrants migrated under the auspices of family members already in the United States. School employment and small-business relationships were usually their main contacts with non-Japanese; most remained socially within their own group, in part because of discrimination. Even in recent decades the Issei have tended, much more than later generations, to reside in extended families and to localize their ties within Japanese American communities.

A number of researchers have found that primary-group integration with outsiders has been limited for the Nisei but is more extensive for the Sansei. One study of 148 Japanese American men looked at the primary-group level. Two-thirds had mostly Japanese Americans as close friends; the Sansei were a little more integrated with whites than the Nisei. However, majorities in both groups reported living in neighborhoods where 50 percent or more of their neighbors were white. The proportion of Japanese Americans living in heavily Japanese American neighborhoods declined from 1915 to 1967. By the late 1960s, over half lived in predominantly non-Japanese neighborhoods. Residential integration had increased significantly.[103]

One 1960s study found that only a minority of the Nisei and Sansei respondents preferred that their children associate only with other Japanese Americans. Data since the 1960s suggest a trend toward primary-group assimilation, especially for those in the third and fourth generations who have moved away from areas with a critical mass of Japanese Americans. However, in areas where this critical mass exists, such as Los Angeles County and Seattle, primary-group assimilation and marital assimilation have not been as significant as in cities where there are fewer Japanese Americans.[104]

Until the late 1940s, antimiscegenation laws in western states made Asian–European marriages illegal. Aside from the Japanese war brides of returning soldiers, there was almost no marriage with outsiders until the 1950s. Los Angeles data show an out-marriage rate of 2 percent in the years between 1924 and 1933 and a rate of 11 to 20 percent for the 1950s. Surveys in the 1950s and 1960s showed strong but declining preferences among some Nisei and the Sansei for Japanese American marriage partners. In 1967, a national survey of the Sansei discovered that one-third had out-married or were planning to out-marry. Studies of marriage licenses in California counties in the 1970s found the proportions out-marrying to be closer to half.[105]

One analysis of 1980 census data found that 34 percent of Japanese Americans in the United States had married outside their group. The importance of this study is that its sample is national and therefore larger than the western samples used by studies showing higher rates of out-marriage. For example, a study of out-marriage rates by Kitano and Daniels for Los Angeles County for the years between 1975 and 1984 found that the proportion of Japanese Americans marrying non-Japanese increased from 55 percent to 63 percent between 1975 and 1977, then decreased to 51 percent in 1984. The researchers suggested that there may be some decline in out-marriage in Los Angeles County in recent years. Still, several researchers have suggested that in the West out-marriage rates for Japanese Americans in the third and fourth generations may be high enough, especially outside the larger Japanese American communities, to dilute the sense of Japanese American identity in the future. A critical issue will be how the children of these marriages view their identities.[106]

Looking at Japanese Americans in the context of Gordon's concept of identificational assimilation, it seems clear that few have rejected their cultural heritage for a purely "American" identity. The sense of Japanese identity is still strong in all generations. Most Japanese Americans are now bicultural, with a foot in both worlds. In addition, substantial differences in value orientations between Japanese and white Americans have been found. The authors of one study asked Japanese Americans whether they saw differences in Japanese American and white orientations toward social affairs, church life, and family relations. Large percentages saw significant differences, from 42 percent for social life to 65 percent for family life and 75 percent for church life. Interestingly, the Sansei were more likely to see differences than the Nisei. The authors of this study suggest that Japanese Americans do *not* see themselves as assimilating rapidly to the dominant culture in regard to family and church life.[107]

Developing a broad overview of the assimilation process, Kitano and Daniels argue that Japanese and other Asian Americans can be grouped into three major categories based on (1) degree of overall assimilation to the core culture and institutions and (2) strength of "ethnic identity." They argue that many in the third and later generations and those isolated from large communities are in a "high assimilation, low ethnic identity" category; that is, they have made many adaptations to the dominant culture in terms of language and lifestyle and retain only weak ties to the old language and culture. These Japanese Americans have strong social ties to whites or have married whites. The other large group of Japanese Americans belongs to a "high assimilation, high ethnic identity" category. These people move easily in both the Japanese American community culture and the dominant culture. In contrast with the first group, they are more knowledgeable about Japanese American history and culture and have a stronger racial–ethnic identity. A third and much smaller group includes those who have migrated in recent decades and those who spent much of their lives within the Japanese

American communities; they are said to be in a "low assimilation, high ethnic identity" category. Marriages are within the group, and Japanese identity is very important. In addition, Kitano and Daniels are careful to note that the degree of assimilation is a relative matter even in the case of the first two subgroups because many whites in the larger society still regard Japanese Americans as racially distinct, and this visibility forces "the retention of ethnic identity, no matter how slight."[108]

An assimilation theorist might conceivably view Japanese Americans as a clear-cut example of Andrew Greeley's concept of ethnogenesis—partly in but partly outside the dominant white culture and society. To our knowledge, no analyst has developed this perspective on Japanese Americans, although Petersen has argued that this group has become a "subnation" in the United States, achieving integration in the economic sphere and making some cultural adaptation, but often maintaining cohesive, family-centered communities.[109] However, the high intermarriage rate signals a decline of residential concentration for younger generations, which is a problem for a subnation thesis.

The younger generations of Japanese Americans seem to be among the most integrated of all non-European groups into European American culture and communities. Still, how this assimilation and integration will play out in the future is unclear. For example, some Japanese Americans view the children of mixed marriages as Japanese American and are working to integrate them into traditional Japanese American culture or communities. Sometimes called *Hapa*, those of mixed ancestry are seen as the leading edge of changes among Japanese Americans. Greg Mayeda, one Japanese American leader, has explained that eventually the typical Japanese American will be a Hapa:

> "Community leaders must recognize this and encourage Hapas and their multicultural families to participate in Japanese-American organizations and customs. If given the opportunity, Hapas can unify and reinvigorate the Japanese–American community."[110]

A Power–Conflict View

Few analysts have interpreted the Japanese American experience systematically from a power–conflict point of view. One power–conflict analyst, Robert Blauner, has suggested that Japanese Americans might be viewed as a partially colonized racial group. Many early Japanese immigrants worked in a position of debt servitude or migrated to the United States under pressure. This was particularly the case for thousands of contract laborers who went to Hawaii and later moved on to the mainland.

Over the centuries there has usually been an important economic relationship between the labor needs of U.S. capitalism and the streams of immigrant workers. For some time Asian labor filled the needs of a booming frontier capitalism on the West Coast. Chinese and Japanese laborers were seen by whites as "colored" labor with far fewer rights than their white counterparts. Because the United States was an imperial power in the Pacific region, U.S. agents had easy entry into Asian countries and could more or less dictate treaties and agreements benefiting employers. U.S. capitalists actively recruited Asian laborers because they could be made to work for very low wages. Employers thus had the backing of their government in securing low-wage labor from countries such as Japan and China where the United States had the greatest influence. Neither China nor Japan then possessed the power that European nations had to protect immigrant workers. Moreover, Japanese immigrants could not become citizens under U.S. law, so they could easily be excluded if they later became unsuitable to employers.[111]

In the beginning Japanese Americans, much like Mexican Americans, were often forced by discrimination to become low-wage laborers in the fields. The alien-labor laws barring land ownership for the Issei, the complete exclusion of Japanese immigrants in 1924 on the grounds of "race," and the massive imprisonment in World War II underscore the semicolonial treatment that Japanese Americans—unlike European immigrant groups—have endured. Their experiences were not the same as those of the European immigrants in whose experiences the assimilation models are grounded.

Acculturation might also be viewed differently from a systematic power–conflict analysis. The pressures to acculturate were largely coercive. Early commitment to cultural assimilation in Japanese communities can be seen as a reaction to severe white discrimination. By about 1910 numerous Japanese American leaders were exhorting their constituents to be exemplary in their hard work and deference to whites in order to command some acceptance by whites. In the public schools, acculturation pressures took the form of attacks on the Japanese cultural heritage. Japanese Americans have many experiences similar to the racial exploitation of African, Mexican, and Native Americans.

Some Asian American scholars have raised a question about the bias in the assimilation model itself. The assimilation theory of Robert Park and other early social scientists emerged in a period of intense white agitation against Japanese immigration and reflected those scholars' usually racist views of the Japanese. Moreover, applying the assimilationist perspective to Japanese and other Asian Americans prior to the 1950s is very inappropriate in one fundamental respect. Asians were prevented from even trying to assimilate politically and in other ways. Unlike European immigrants, Japanese and other Asian immigrants were denied the right to become naturalized citizens. Government agencies and officials have played a central role in defining racial groups in the United States. In the 1922 *Ozawa* case, the Supreme Court ruled that Asian immigrants were *not white* and thus could not become citizens. In a similar case the next year, *U.S. v. Bhagat Singh Thind*, the same racist reasoning was applied to an Asian Indian seeking to become naturalized. The Court declared that, in contrast to the children of Asian parentage, "the children of English, French, German, Italian, Scandinavian, and other European parentage, quickly merge in to the mass of our population and lose the distinctive hallmarks of their European origin."[112] This explicitly racist reasoning by an arm of the federal government misses the point that at the time—and indeed into the 1950s—Asian immigrants were not even allowed political and civic assimilation in the United States.

Criticizing the "Model Minority" Stereotype

Paramount among the weaknesses in the traditional assimilation perspective has been the "model minority" stereotype. During the 1980s and 1990s virtually every major newsmagazine and television network has periodically carried glowing reports on the achievements of Japanese and other Asian Americans in various occupational categories and in education.[113] The success of Japanese Americans, frequently viewed as rooted in their values and family styles, is cited not only in the media but also by prominent white writers as a reflection of U.S. opportunities and as a model for what other people of color, particularly African Americans and Latinos, could achieve if they would only follow the Japanese American example.[114] Stereotypes of Japanese Americans as paragons of hard work and docility carry a negative undercurrent. Suzuki has suggested that the "model minority" image of Asian groups such as Japanese Americans was created not by these groups but rather by white American outsiders, including non-Asian scholars and media analysts, for ideological reasons.[115] As black Americans protested in the streets during the 1960s, these whites created the model minority image in order to suggest that black Americans could achieve the American dream simply by working harder. The assumption underlying this idea was that Asian Americans were more like whites in their attitude toward work.

As we have noted, recent scholarship has questioned much of this imagery. Pre-World War II educational opportunities greater than those available to legally segregated African Americans helped prepare many Japanese Americans for white-collar jobs opening up after the war. It was not Asian values alone that brought success but access to education and white-collar jobs. Critics of the model minority notion have also noted other factors in the economic success of Japanese Americans: the early role of the Japanese government in supporting immigrants and the availability of an important small-business niche in West Coast areas.

Japanese Americans, at an early point, created many successful businesses through which they served one another and the basic needs of a frontier economy. Japanese American employers and employees saw themselves as a single group confronting the hostile outside world. Out of economic necessity employers and employees, many having kinship or regional ties, worked together against hostile white competitors. Success came at the price of being ghettoized in the small-business economy and, later, in certain professions. As with Jewish Americans, Japanese Americans have, to a substantial degree, succeeded as a group in U.S. society by carving a distinctive niche for themselves—a process of adaptation not completely in line with the idealistic assimilation models. The long-term effects of discrimination are still reflected in the concentration of Japanese Americans in the small-business economy and in certain professional and technical occupations.

Moreover, the movement of Japanese Americans into white-collar jobs does not necessarily signal emancipation from economic discrimination. A study of Japanese American workers in the San Francisco metropolitan area found that those in white-collar jobs were clustered in such occupations as computer programming, clerical work, architecture, engineering, chemicals, dentistry, and pharmacy. The highest level white-collar personnel, such as managers, financial officers, and management analysts, still tended to be white men.[116]

A study of minority-owned businesses found that most of those owned by Asian Americans were in retail trade (such as grocery stores and restaurants) and selected services (such as laundries). Gross annual receipts were modest for the majority of Japanese American firms. In addition, some research has revealed that Japanese Americans do not get as much payoff from their high levels of education as do comparably educated whites. Moreover, Japanese American families have higher incomes but they also have more workers per family than do white families.[117]

Paul Takagi has pointed to another bias in the traditional cultural-background explanation of Japanese American success—the idea that the racial–ethnic groups whose values are closest to those of the dominant white group are the ones who will be, and should be, successful. In other words, success is evaluated only in terms of values prized by the dominant white group. Although Japanese Americans have acculturated in numerous ways, the price they have paid in terms of conformity, lost creativity, and lost contributions to this society has been great.[118] Even in the 1990s, Japanese Americans report that no amount of acculturation protects them from whites who insist on seeing Asian Americans as outsiders. Ronald Takaki, a professor at the University of California, visited an East Coast city where a taxicab driver congratulated him on his good English and inquired how long he had been in the country. Takaki told the driver his family had been here for three generations—since 1886.[119] Despite the fact that many Japanese Americans have grown up in mostly white neighborhoods and gone to mostly white schools and colleges, they often report subtle discrimination and do not feel they are fully accepted by large numbers of white Americans. This is one reason for the growing interest in Asian American studies on college and university campuses.[120]

One must also remember the world context of racial and ethnic relations. From the beginning Japanese immigration and Japanese American integration into the dominant culture and society have been shaped by U.S. intervention in the capitalist world economy. The action of the U.S. government in forcing Japan into the world economy in the nineteenth century was eventually followed by the recruitment of many low-wage laborers for U.S. business enterprises. Today, as the Japanese economy vies successfully with the U.S. economy for Pacific and world dominance, the world economy still forms the backdrop. New economic alliances on the Pacific Rim, such as the Association of Southeast Asian nations, are bypassing the United States. Japan is the most powerful economy in these alliances, and that economic success is one reason there has been relatively little recent migration from Japan to the United States, apart from the temporary migration of business executives and investors.

Unfortunately, there is a negative side to the prosperity of Japan and other Asian nations in the world economy: Some non-Asian Americans, angry over domestic economic troubles, confuse Japanese Americans with the Japanese and blame both unfairly for economic troubles caused by U.S. employers investing overseas or by the federal government. This stereotyping is yet another constant indication to Japanese Americans that somehow they have not been accepted as "true Americans" by many other Americans.

SUMMARY

Japanese Americans are an important group in U.S. racial history. In the beginning they were severely exploited and treated as an "inferior race." Many entered as laborers, facing violence and intense discrimination. They endured complete exclusion as a result of racist immigration legislation. They endured laws against land ownership. During World War II, they suffered the only large-scale imprisonment of U.S. citizens in barbed-wire concentration camps. Against terrible odds they prospered. They are an immigrant group whose economic mobility has been substantial. Yet, for all their acculturation and economic assimilation, Japanese Americans are still not fully included in the dominant Euro-American institutions. Whether they will be the first non-European group to be fully assimilated—politically, socially, and economically—remains to be seen.

It is important for students of racial and ethnic relations to realize that the success story of Japanese and other Asian Americans is partially a myth. Japanese Americans have suffered in the past and still suffer from discrimination in the private sector. Fewer Japanese Americans than whites can fully realize earnings levels that parallel their relatively high educational levels. Few rise to top management in Fortune 1000 corporations, major law firms, or major government agencies.

In general, Japanese Americans have been stereotyped or misunderstood by insensitive whites, including state and federal government officials. For example, in the 1970s Lionel Van Deerlin, California representative and head of the House Subcommittee on Communications, commented that Asian Americans did not need to be considered a disadvantaged minority group because they were "more prosperous than [majority] Americans." Yet in the communications industry, as of that date, not one television or radio station was owned by a Japanese or other Asian American, and a survey of four San Francisco television stations showed that Asian American men were underrepresented, relative to their proportion in the local labor force, at three of them.[121]

More recently, this attitude has been expressed on a more or less regular basis by white officials across the United States. Japanese Americans are still considered a "model minority" with no need of special government protection against discrimination. Yet as we have seen in this chapter, there is still much anti-Japanese sentiment among white Americans, prejudice that results in discrimination and some anti-Japanese violence. White Americans must change their attitudes and practices if Japanese Americans are ever to enjoy equality in the United States. David Mura, the author of *Turning Japanese: Memoirs of a Sansei*, has recently argued that whites must see that the "problem of race is one of giving up power." In his view whites must begin to take part in "dismantling racism and redistributing power."[122]

Perhaps one day the population of the United States as a whole will be more like the members of the crew of the space shuttle Challenger (who, through no fault of their own, died in a tragic 1986 explosion). Working harmoniously together, that seven-person crew included an African American born to sharecroppers (Ronald McNair), a Jewish American of the Orthodox faith (Judith Resnik), and a Japanese American of the Buddhist faith (Ellison Onizuka). Onizuka, the grandson of Japanese laborers who immigrated to Hawaii to work on a coffee plantation in the 1890s, was born on a coffee farm. He worked hard, became an aerospace engineer, and participated in two space missions. As the first Asian American astronaut, Onizuka has come to symbolize for many Asian Americans the heroic character of their struggle for success and equality in the United States.

Hawaii is the first state in which no racial or ethnic group constitutes a majority of the population. Japanese Americans are the single largest group in Hawaii, but they are not a majority. Compared to other areas of the United States, racial-ethnic relations in Hawaii have long been more cooperative and less conflict ridden. While Hawaii has seen some interracial tensions, and the native Hawaiians have suffered much poverty and discrimination, some observers have suggested that Hawaii can provide a few lessons on how diverse racial and ethnic groups can work with each another to build a viable multicultural society.[123]

CHAPTER 12

Chinese, Filipino, Korean, Vietnamese, and Asian-Indian Americans

In the spring of 1992, Elaine H. Kim, a Korean American professor at the University of California, Berkeley, wrote insightfully in a national newsmagazine about the major Los Angeles riot that had taken place a few weeks earlier. She noted how the mass media had played up visual images of violent conflict between African American rioters and Korean American merchants, while ignoring the long histories and social contexts of these two groups. She argued that both Korean Americans and African Americans have been the victims of a long tradition of racial violence and discrimination at the hands of white Americans. Recalling her own experiences, Kim noted that

> my schooling offered nothing about Chicanos or Latinos, and most of what I was taught about African-Americans was distorted to justify their oppression and vindicate the forces of that oppression.[1]

Then she added:

> Likewise, Korean-Americans have been and continue to be used for someone else's agenda and benefit, whether we are hated as foreigners who refuse to become "good Americans," stereotyped as diligent work machines or simply treated as if we do not exist. Throughout my childhood, the people who continually asked, "What are you?" knew nothing of Korea or Koreans.[2]

Proud of her Korean heritage, Professor Kim wishes Korean history and culture were better known across the United States. She tells, for example, the story of Sohn Kee-chung, a courageous Korean marathon runner in the 1936 Olympics in Germany, who won the gold medal in front of Nazi leaders who viewed Asians as an inferior race.

Korean Americans are one of five major Asian American groups—each with a strong identity and a rich history and culture—that are analyzed in this chapter. The others are Chinese, Filipino, Vietnamese, and Asian-Indian Americans. Although these groups have contributed much to the dynamic development of the United

States in the late twentieth century, they still suffer greatly from stereotyping and discrimination at the hands of white and other non-Asian Americans.

MIGRATION: AN OVERVIEW

In the 1980s and 1990s, the fastest-growing immigrant groups were mostly Asian American, including Chinese, Filipino, Korean, Vietnamese, and Asian-Indian Americans. Table 12–1 documents the changing scale of this immigration since the early nineteenth century.[3]

Few Filipinos, Koreans, Vietnamese, or Asian Indians immigrated to the U.S. mainland before the 1960s. Thereafter immigration increased dramatically. The number of Filipino, Korean, and Vietnamese immigrants rose from so few that records were not kept of their arrival to a total of more than 2 million in the most recent period. Chinese immigration has followed a different pattern, with two major periods. The first began about 1850 and lasted until the passage of the 1882 Chinese Exclusion Act, which prohibited direct immigration from China. Although some Chinese immigration occurred in the years following the 1882 act, large-scale immigration did not resume until the immigration reforms in 1965. As can be seen in Table 12–1, a substantial majority of all Chinese immigrants to the United States have come recently.

The 1924 Immigration Act generally excluded people in Asian countries from immigrating to the United States. A 1952 Immigration and Nationality Act superseded previous laws and began to eliminate some of the anti-Asian racism inherent in the 1924 act. The 1952 act established three principles for immigration policy: (1) reunification of families; (2) protection of the domestic labor force; and (3) immigration of persons with needed skills. It permitted small-scale Asian immigration and for the first time made immigrants from Asia eligible for citizenship. Finally, in 1965 Congress took a major step toward providing Asians the opportunity to immigrate on a scale similar to that of earlier European groups. The 1965 Immigration Act abolished the national-origins quota system (see Chapter 11) and established an annual quota of 20,000 for individual Asian countries. Not surprisingly, the percentage of Chinese, Filipinos, Koreans, Vietnamese,

TABLE 12–1 Asian Immigration

	1820–1900	1901–1920	1921–1940	1941–1960	1961–1980	1981–1993
Chinese*	305,455	41,833	43,835	41,910	347,564	647,880
Filipino	**	**	**	19,307	453,363	681,235
Korean	**	**	**	6,231	302,164	402,322
Vietnamese	**	**	**	335	177,160	593,741
Asian Indian	694	6,795	2,830	4,843	207,930	363,010

*Figures include Hong Kong after 1951.
**Data not reported before 1951.

and Asian Indians among the total number of immigrants to this country rose from 0.2 percent for the years between 1901 and 1920 to 32 percent for the years between 1981 and 1993.

Chinese Americans

The Chinese have been the largest single group of Asian immigrants to the United States. Chinese migration began in substantial numbers in the decade before the Civil War, with a quarter million coming during the three decades after 1860. Most Chinese men entered as low-wage workers, brought in to do the "dirty work" for white employers along the West Coast. Many were recruited to remedy labor shortages in railroad work or to fill menial positions in such personal service areas as laundry and restaurant work that whites on the West Coast did not want to do.

Relatively few women were among the immigrants, and those who did immigrate usually came alone, often brought by force to work as prostitutes. Some escaped to missions run by religious denominations. According to the 1870 census, 61 percent of Chinese women in California were prostitutes. In 1875 Congress passed a law prohibiting the importation of Chinese women for prostitution—the first direct regulation of immigration in U.S. history. Significant numbers of Chinese women were not permitted to enter the United States again until the 1940s. In contrast, between 1946 and 1952, almost 90 percent of Chinese immigrants were women, typically wives of Chinese men who had immigrated many years earlier.[4]

As the 1870s began, the U.S. economy entered a depression; at the same time, Chinese Americans were becoming numerous and more successful. White resentment of these Asian immigrants spread throughout the country. White labor leaders, newspapers, politicians, and the general public accused Chinese Americans of driving wages to a substandard level and of taking jobs away from whites. In short, they blamed the Chinese for the country's economic difficulties.[5] The attacks on Chinese Americans finally led to the 1882 Chinese Exclusion Act, which officially prohibited direct immigration from China. Over the next few decades the Exclusion Act effectively reduced the flow of Chinese immigrants, which had reached a high of 123,201 in the years between 1871 and 1880. Because most early Chinese immigrants were male, the exclusion of new immigrants resulted in a 40 percent decline in the Chinese American population between 1880 and 1920.[6] The Chinese Exclusion Act was extended for ten years in 1892 and indefinitely in 1904. In 1905 President Theodore Roosevelt affirmed his support for the racist act, stating that Chinese laborers must be kept out of this country "absolutely."[7] The Exclusion Act was not repealed until 1943, when China became a wartime ally. At that time a very small quota of 105 was set for Chinese immigrants.[8]

The second major period of Chinese immigration took place after the 1960s immigration reform legislation. Between 1961 and 1980, nearly 348,000 Chinese, mainly from Hong Kong and Taiwan, came to the United States. Even larger numbers have entered since 1981. During this period the proportion from Hong Kong and Taiwan fell to less than 40 percent as the proportion from the mainland grew. Between 1980 and 1990 the Chinese American population more than doubled, from 806,000 to more than 1.6 million.[9] In the mid-1990s, Chinese Americans constituted about one-fourth of all Asian Americans. Almost one-third were born in the United States, and more than half lived in western states.[10]

Filipino Americans

When the islands that make up the Philippines were handed over to the United States by Spain at the end of the Spanish-American War, a colonial relationship was imposed. Filipino desires for independence were ignored by an imperialist United States, and U.S. forces killed many Filipino fighters seeking independence. Soon after the U.S. government seized the islands, a commission was sent to determine how to Americanize them. Between 1901 and 1913, a U.S. form of government was established, and a new system of public education was introduced in which U.S. teachers taught Filipino children U.S. cultural values.

William Howard Taft, the first governor of the Philippines and later a U.S. president, inspired a plan to Americanize the colony by sending young men to college in the United States. These students were taken into U.S. homes; after they finished their studies in such fields as education or agriculture, they were to return to the Philippines to teach.

By the 1920s and 1930s, the overwhelming majority of Filipino immigrants to the United States were peasant farmers who sought employment as unskilled laborers. Since the Philippines was a territory of the United States, Filipinos were exempt from the anti-Asian exclusionary provisions of the 1917 and 1924 Immigration Acts. This exemption allowed them to immigrate freely to the United States; they were recruited by white employers to work in the sugar plantations of Hawaii and in fields along the West Coast. Relatively few came to the mainland in these early years; by 1924 only 6,000 lived in the continental United States.[11]

After the passage of the 1924 Immigration Act, employers increased the recruitment of Filipinos as laborers on the West Coast to replace the Asian and other immigrant workers excluded by the act. Between 1924 and 1929, approximately 24,000 Filipinos came to the state of California to do low-wage work. As their numbers increased, so did anti-Filipino sentiment among whites. In 1934, Congress responded to this sentiment by passing an act granting deferred independence to the Philippines and simultaneously imposing an annual immigration quota of only fifty persons per year.[12]

Although Filipinos could enter the United States without restriction until 1934, almost all advantages ended there. Filipino Americans held an ambiguous legal position that was not resolved until 1946, when they were finally declared eligible for U.S. citizenship. Most states did not allow them to practice law, medicine, or other professions. As noncitizens, Filipinos did not qualify for federal relief funds in hard economic times. At the outbreak of World War II, Filipinos' status as noncitizens exempted them from the draft and prohibited them from volunteering for the U.S. armed forces. However, Congress began moving toward citizenship for Filipinos during the war, since it made little sense for the United States to fight for Philippine freedom from Japanese rule while denying Filipino Americans the right to citizenship.

During World War II, some 30,000 Filipinos were recruited to fight with the U.S. armed forces battling the Japanese army in the Philippines. At the end of the war these guerilla fighters were promised by General Douglas MacArthur and President Franklin Roosevelt that they could come to the United States and become U.S. citizens if they wished. However, the U.S. government backed out of the promise nine months before the official deadline, leaving thousands of veterans stranded. Not until the Immigration Act of 1990 were the veterans actually granted the right to U.S. citizenship. By that time many had died.[13]

Between 1950 and 1970, the number of Filipinos residing in the United States almost doubled. Immediately after World War II, most Filipino immigrants still found themselves restricted largely to jobs as laborers, mostly in agriculture. Whereas most earlier immigrants had been male and had not established families in the United States, these newer immigrants were typically men and women between the ages of twenty and fifty who brought their children with them, hoping to find better economic opportunities.[14] An expert on Filipino migration has noted that "most people leave the Philippines to get a job."[15] In addition, many have come to be united with family members who migrated previously.

Since 1970, Filipino immigration has continued. The 1990 census counted 1.4 million Filipino Americans, making this group the second largest group in the Asian–Pacific census category. Today, almost two-thirds of Filipino Americans are foreign-born; 69 percent live in western states.[16] Filipinos are the largest Asian American group in California. In the early 1990s, a quarter million Americans of Filipino ancestry lived in the San Francisco area, which is sometimes called the "capital of Asian America" because of its large Asian American population. Moreover, in some San Francisco Bay area suburbs Filipino Americans are a majority of the population. Filipinos are also numerous in some parts of the Midwest. For example, an estimated 100,000 Filipino Americans resided in the Chicago area in the early 1990s.[17]

Korean Americans

The immigration of Koreans to the United States began in the early 1900s. Approximately 7,000 emigrated to Hawaii between 1903 and 1905. By 1905 approximately 1,000 Korean Americans lived in California. Most immigrants came seeking better living and working conditions, but they too were confronted with discrimination, deplorable working conditions, and low wages. They were segregated along with Mexican and African Americans, refused housing in all but the poorest areas, and denied service in restaurants and other public facilities. After learning of these conditions, Japan, which occupied Korea beginning in 1910, pressured the Korean government to ban emigration. This ban effectively restricted the entry of Koreans into the United States for many years.[18]

Even after these restrictions were imposed a small number of Koreans—mainly "picture brides" and students—were able to emigrate to the United States. Since most who arrived before the 1910 restrictions were single men, and since interracial marriage was not an option because of white prejudice and anti-inter-marriage laws in the United States, the picture bride system was developed. Korean men sent pictures of themselves to prospective brides in their homeland. From 1910 to 1924, more than one thousand brides came to the United States. In addition, several hundred students entered between 1899 and 1940, some as refugees from Japanese colonial oppression.[19]

During World War II, the U.S. government classified Korean immigrants as subjects of Japan. Korean Americans living in Hawaii were classified as "enemy aliens," and those with jobs on defense projects were, to their chagrin, classified as Japanese and required to wear badges of identification. Korean American workers were understandably outraged, since Japan had been Korea's enemy and colonizer for so long. However, their protests only gained them the right to print the words "I am Korean" on their identification badges.[20]

During the heavy U.S. involvement in the Korean War in the 1950s, the people of South Korea saw prosperous Americans up close and came to regard the United States as a place to be admired. Strong U.S. support for the South Korean government, which allowed little domestic political freedom, built strong political and economic ties between the two countries. Most Koreans who immigrated from 1950 to 1965 were wives of U.S. soldiers; as such they escaped the immigration quota system. These wives continued to migrate after 1965, since the United States has maintained troops in Korea to the present.

The changes in the immigration laws in 1965 opened new possibilities for immigration. The lack of economic or educational opportunities in Korea compared with those in the United States has regularly stimulated the emigration of young people. Moreover, some immigrants have been political dissidents opposed to the dictatorial regimes that dominated South Korea for decades. Others have been students who completed their education and stayed. Once established, the first immigrants sometimes used the family reunification clause of the immigration laws to bring in family members. Between 1960 and 1965, only a few thousand Koreans entered each year, but after the 1965 Immigration Act the numbers began to increase; within a decade the annual number exceeded 30,000. Immigration peaked at 35,849 in 1987 and has declined each year since.[21] Improvements in South Korea's economy over the last decade contributed to this decline, as did Korean disenchantment with the United States as a land of opportunity following the 1992 Los Angeles riot during which many Korean American-owned businesses were looted or damaged. Since the late 1980s, a growing number of Korean business people and students have come to the United States on temporary visas.

During the 1980s, the Korean American population more than doubled. The 1990 census counted almost 800,000 Korean Americans, almost 12 percent of the Asian American population. More than one-fourth were born in the United States; 43 percent lived in the western states.[22] By the late 1990s, many Korean Americans

Korean Americans march peacefully in front of businesses destroyed in the 1992 Los Angeles riot.

were moving from the West Coast, and often settling in the cities of the Midwest or East Coast.

Vietnamese Americans

The Vietnamese do not have a long history of immigration to the United States. Most immigrants arrived after 1975, when U.S. involvement in the Vietnam War ended abruptly. The United States first became involved in Vietnam in an attempt to help French military forces maintain colonial control in the area. When the French forces withdrew in 1954, and Vietnam was divided in two, the United States became a military ally of the South Vietnamese government, a non-Communist political dictatorship. U.S. troops and dollars flowed to a war that gradually became unpopular in the United States. In Saigon, the capital of South Vietnam, U.S. military and civilian authorities made plans to evacuate a great number of South Vietnamese in the face of the advancing enemy forces. Included in the evacuation were those Vietnamese and their families employed by the U.S. government or U.S. businesses, those at risk of losing their property or lives when a Communist government took over. As Communist troops approached Saigon in April 1975, the controlled evacuation that had been planned became instead a confused and tragic event. In one week, thousands of Vietnamese left their country. People jammed the airport and the U.S. embassy, climbing fences and clinging to helicopters. Those who could not get on airplanes fled by sea.[23]

In the spring of 1975, large numbers of refugees from Southeast Asia began to enter the United States. The Vietnamese were admitted outside the usual immigration process because they were considered political refugees.[24] As Table 12–1 shows, very few Vietnamese immigrated before 1961, in part because of the anti-Asian immigration laws. Changes in immigration laws, U.S. military involvement in Vietnam, and the fall of Saigon in 1975 contributed to the increase in immigrants. Between 1975 and 1980, more than 166,000 Vietnamese entered the United States.

In the period between 1980 and 1990 the number of Vietnamese Americans grew 142 percent—the largest percentage increase of the major Asian American groups. Approximately 80 percent of Vietnamese Americans are foreign-born; approximately 55 percent live in western states. At the beginning of the 1990s, the nation's largest Vietnamese community was in Orange County, California, where more than 71,000 lived.[25]

Asian-Indian Americans

Of all the major Asian–Pacific groups in the United States, perhaps the least well known is the group the census bureau calls "Asian Indians"—those who have immigrated from India. The first Asian Indian immigrants were Sikhs who worked on the railroads or in agriculture on the West Coast in the mid-1800s, but the number of Asian Indians remained small until the 1960s. They have immigrated in significant numbers since the 1965 Immigration Act abolished racial quotas.[26]

The 1990 census reported almost 787,000 Asian-Indian Americans. More than three-fourths of these were foreign-born, and more than four in ten had come since 1980. Three somewhat different periods are evident in this migration. In the 1960s, many of the immigrants were male professionals and managers, and most easily found jobs. Their wives, however, were generally not well educated. Their children are now coming of age. A second group, which arrived during the 1970s, included a mixture of immigrants, with more well educated professional women among them. A third group, which has come since the early 1980s, includes more relatives sponsored by the earlier immigrants. Compared with earlier immigrants, they tend to be less well educated and more likely to move into service work such as taxi driving or family-owned businesses such as groceries and motels.[27]

Unlike other Asian Americans, the majority of Asian-Indian Americans do not live on the West Coast. More than one-third live in the northeastern states, and just under one-fourth live in each of the midwestern and southern regions. Approximately 190,000 live in the greater New York City area and another 56,000 in the Chicago area.[28] In many metropolitan areas, they have had the economic resources to move directly into suburbs rather than settling first in central-city areas, as have other Asian immigrants. As a result, Asian-Indian Americans are more scattered geographically than other immigrant groups. There are no large urban concentrations as there are for other Asian American groups. Even so, wherever there is a substantial Asian Indian population in a metropolitan area, there is usually an Indian house of worship.

STEREOTYPES

Anti-Asian stereotyping and hostility have a long history in the United States. One common stereotype about Asian Americans is that they are essentially the same physically and culturally. Japanese Americans are often mistaken by non-Asians for Chinese Americans, who in turn may be mistaken for Vietnamese or Korean Americans. Asian Americans are often viewed by non-Asians as "foreigners" rather than as Americans because of their non-European appearance. Films and television programs have sometimes portrayed Asians as faceless, fanatic, maniacal, or willing to die because they do not value life. Stereotyped images, such as the "evil Jap" of World War II and the "Communist gook" in China, Korea, and Vietnam, were created primarily by white Americans and have been recycled as U.S. foreign policy has changed from decade to decade. This uninformed and stereotypical way of thinking, sometimes called *Orientalism*, is common among non-Asian Americans and probably shapes most discrimination directed at Asian Americans.[29]

One prominent Chinese American leader recently commented: "To the larger society, Asian Americans are either invisible, or forever foreigners, or honorary whites, or problems."[30] In 1994, Chinese American journalist Helen Zia told a university audience that Asian Americans were often thought of as either sinister foreigners competing for jobs or college admissions or as emotionless technical nerds.[31] Negative stereotypes have serious implications. Recently a white member of the State Board of Education in South Carolina made this comment at a board meeting: "Screw the Buddhists and kill the Muslims." Even with this type of outburst, he was allowed to keep his position.[32]

Asian American groups have also been stereotyped as "model minorities." According to this stereotyped view Asian Americans have moved ahead rapidly in U.S. society, generally unhindered by prejudice or discrimination, mainly by applying traditional values of hard work and thrift. They are also seen as especially ambitious. Indeed, there are many exemplary individuals in Asian American communities, but the model minority stereotype overstates their economic situation, as we will see later in this chapter.

Specific Images of Asian Americans

The first Chinese laborers on the West Coast became subjects of white workers' derision and suspicion. They were called "coolies" and were maligned by whites as "heathen," "mice-eaters," and "Chinks." Some of these stereotyped images have persisted for more than a century. One source of change, however, came in the 1940s. After the United States declared war on Japan in 1941, China and the United States became allies against Japan. The Chinese were suddenly friends of the United States. Soon after the United States entered World War II, *Time* magazine printed the following racialized explanation of the "differences" between the Chinese and the Japanese:

HOW TO TELL YOUR FRIENDS FROM THE JAPS: Virtually all Japanese are short. Japanese are likely to be stockier and broader-hipped than short Chinese. Japanese are seldom fat; they often dry up and grow lean as they age. Although both have the typical epicanthic fold on the upper eyelid, Japanese eyes are usually set closer together. The Chinese expression is likely to be more placid, kindly, open; the Japanese more positive, dogmatic, arrogant. Japanese are hesitant, nervous in conversation, laugh loudly at the wrong time. Japanese walk stiffly erect, hard heeled. Chinese, more relaxed, have an easy gait, sometimes shuffle.[33]

Ironically, those who put together this wildly stereotyped statement thought they were writing something positive about their new "friends," the Chinese Americans. Yet it is in fact an example of the crude and negative stereotyping of Asian Americans that has long been part of white thinking in the United States.

The stereotypes of Filipino immigrants have sometimes fluctuated according to this group's usefulness to the white employers recruiting them as low-wage labor, especially for the plantations of Hawaii. When these employers were recruiting young male Filipinos, they characterized them as "not too intelligent" and "docile." But when these workers were no longer needed, they were often stereotyped as "lazy, shiftless, and unmanageable."[34]

The Vietnamese arrived in the United States at a time when unemployment was high, and many non-Asian Americans feared that these new refugees would take jobs from them or drain sources of public assistance. During the mid-1970s, this anti-Vietnamese sentiment was reflected in a Gallup poll in which 54 percent of the respondents felt that Vietnamese refugees should not be permitted to stay in the United States.[35] Many white leaders and the white public seemed to wish they could forget Vietnam and its people. Some whites and other non-Asian Americans still see all Vietnamese as "the enemy" because of the U.S. experience in Vietnam and still use the racist term *gooks*. Vietnamese Americans represent a culture different from that of a large segment of U.S. society, and many non-Asians have regarded them as strange, clannish, and hard to approach.[36] Indeed, a survey of the Vietnamese residents of Orange County, California, found that six in ten thought anti-Vietnamese prejudice was a problem there.[37]

In 1990 the musical *Miss Saigon*, produced in London and New York, was sharply criticized by Vietnamese Americans for its racial stereotyping. Critics argued that the central character, a Vietnamese "bar girl" abandoned by a white GI, is a crude stereotype. Because of this Vietnamese and other Asian American leaders called on Asian American theatergoers and actors to boycott the popular play.[38] A 1994 study of images of people of color in news coverage found numerous examples of Asian Americans stereotyped as manipulative, mysterious, and inscrutable. The study also found widespread trivialization of Asian customs, ridicule of Asian American pronunciation, and use of derogatory clichés and inflammatory phrases such as "Asian invasion," which tends to reinforce the view of Asian Americans as hostile foreigners.[39]

Chinese and other Asian Americans became targets of widespread stereotyping in the late 1990s in the investigation of alleged illegal political campaign contributions. Under heavy pressure to raise money for the Democratic party in the 1996 national political campaign, John Huang, a Chinese American, and several other

Asian American fundraisers raised several million dollars in contributions, some of which were alleged to have been illegally contributed by overseas donors. National media discussion included considerable negative stereotyping of Chinese and other Asian Americans as mysterious, underhanded, and corrupt. Investigations of illegal contributions focused heavily on Asian Americans, causing civil rights leaders to charge that this small minority among the political fundraisers had been unfairly singled out. Commenting on Huang's testimony before a U.S. Senate investigating committee regarding his fundraising activities, a white Republican senator from Kansas made fun of what he thought to be Chinese American speech patterns: "No raise money, no get bonus." The senator contended this stereotyped language was not intended as a slight. However, such commentary reveals that elite white Americans still harbor strong negative stereotypes of Asian Americans.[40]

The cover of a spring 1997 issue of the conservative magazine *National Review*, relating to the aforementioned campaign fundraising investigations, showed caricatures of President Bill Clinton and his wife Hilary as slant-eyed, buck-toothed Chinese in Mao suits and Chinese hats. This magazine cover drew protests from Chinese and other Asian Americans. Daphne Kwok, leader of the Organization of Chinese Americans, described these images as racist and offensive because they resurrect stereotypes making fun of the physical characteristics and dress of Asian Americans as they are seen by many non-Asian Americans. Since the nineteenth century, white cartoonists expressing fear of the so-called "Yellow Peril" have portrayed Chinese and other Asian Americans in these stereotyped terms. Appearing on NBC's *Today* show with Daphne Kwok, John O'Sullivan, editor of *National Review*, admitted the caricatures were an attempt to portray Asian characteristics but refused to apologize for them. In April 1997, representatives of several civil rights groups protested outside the magazine's New York offices and called for a boycott of the magazine.[41] In the view of many Asian Americans, the dominant media and elite stereotypes of Asians and Asian Americans had shifted from "model minorities" to dangerous or unassimilated foreigners.

DISCRIMINATION AND CONFLICT

Hate Crimes*

Violence, harassment, and vandalism directed against Americans of Asian descent have occurred across the United States since the earliest days of Asian immigration. Until recently, few local or state governments have collected data on ethnoviolence. Where data have been collected, Asian Americans are often disproportionately represented among victims.[42] In 1993, 236 anti-Asian hate crimes were

---

* The widely used term *hate crimes* is somewhat inaccurate because many such attacks are generated not by hate but by fear or other emotions. And many are not crimes. The National Institute against Prejudice and Violence has suggested the term *ethnoviolence*.

reported to law enforcement officials. By 1996, according to data collected by the National Asian Pacific American Legal Consortium, the number had more than doubled; 534 attacks were reported across the nation. These hate crimes have ranged from the killing of a Vietnamese American student in California to numerous incidents of verbal slurs or hate messages being painted on the homes or businesses of Asian Americans. More recently, in April 1997 several Asian American students were denied service at a Syracuse restaurant. When they left, they were beaten by white male patrons, and the restaurant's security personnel reportedly did not try to intervene. Asian American leaders have attributed the increase in these hate crimes to growing anti-immigrant sentiment and to anti-Asian images in the mass media.[43]

The U.S. Commission on Civil Rights has noted that ethnoviolence is underreported, especially in the case of Asian Americans, many of whom are recent immigrants who distrust the police, have a limited understanding of individual rights under U.S. law, and may have a limited knowledge of English.[44] In some areas, the number of anti-Asian hate crimes reported to the police has declined over the past few years. For example, in Boston, Massachusetts, which was the first U.S. city to have a specialized police unit on hate crimes, forty-one cases were reported in 1986, but only twenty-two cases were reported in each of the years 1993 and 1994, even though the police department's outreach efforts did not decline during that period. One Boston law enforcement officer has observed a disillusionment among some Asian American victims because of the lack of swift and stern punishment given to the perpetrators of hate crimes by the courts. These victims feel that the work days and pay they lose attending court hearings are wasted when a judge gives the perpetrator only a suspended sentence. Such outcomes discourage Asian American victims from reporting their cases to the authorities.[45]

The U.S. Civil Rights Commission has found that adequate police protection is not provided to many Asian American communities. In cities from Boston to Los Angeles, Asian American community organizations are urging local officials to investigate and prosecute hate crimes more rigorously.[46] Many police departments appear insensitive to Asian American individuals and cultures, and some are overtly hostile. When Asian Americans do have contact with white police officers, their rights are sometimes jeopardized by language barriers. Few police departments have adequate interpretive services for non-English-speaking immigrants. The California attorney general's office has estimated that fewer than half the crimes against Asian Americans are reported. When Asian Americans do report a crime, they frequently do not receive justice. The Asian and Pacific Islander Advisory Committee of the California attorney general's office has reported that "one of the most commonly repeated experiences is one in which the perpetrator is allowed to go free and the victim [an Asian American] is arrested."[47] One controversial police strategy is the photographing of youths simply because they fit a "gang profile." Some Asian American communities have begun to organize to challenge this and other forms of police harassment. A spokesperson for one such organization explained, "Culturally, the Asian community does not speak out against such things as police harassment. By nature, our people do not complain or report abuse, so by having some speak out, we hope to encourage others to do the same."[48] Not surprisingly, a growing number of Asian Americans are attending community-sponsored forums and workshops on U.S. government and citizens' rights.

Chinese Americans

During the 1860s and 1870s, anti-Chinese sentiments were common in union policies and political platforms as well as in the press. Chinese immigrants were violently attacked by whites in California and other western states. In recent decades, Chinese Americans have not been immune from such attacks. One Chinese American woman in New York City was pushed in front of a subway train by a man who said he had a "phobia about Asians."[49] In California recently an eighteen-year-old white supremacist was charged with a dozen felony crimes, including the attempted murder of a Chinese American city council member and the firebombing of NAACP and the Japanese American Citizens League (JACL) offices in Sacramento.[50]

The inability of non-Asians to differentiate among individuals of different Asian backgrounds has been a factor in the murder of at least two Chinese Americans. Public monitoring of racially motivated actions against Asian Americans began in 1982 with the death of Vincent Chin, a Chinese American, in Detroit. Two laid-off white auto workers, apparently believing Chin was Japanese and blaming him for the problems of the auto industry, started an argument with him and then used a baseball bat to beat him to death. A Michigan judge sentenced each man to only three years' probation and a fine of $3,780. Asian and other Americans expressed outrage at the extraordinarily lenient punishment, and the U.S. Commission on Civil Rights concluded that the leniency in this case was "suggestive of very little value being placed on an Asian American life."[51] The U.S. Department of Justice later brought federal charges against the white assailants for civil rights violations. A U.S. district court jury found one of the defendants guilty of violating Chin's civil rights, thereby acknowledging the racial motivation of the attack. The other defendant, apparently not directly involved in the beating, was acquitted. The guilty defendant was sentenced to twenty-five years in prison, although his conviction was later overturned by an appellate court for technical reasons. In his retrial, he was acquitted.[52]

A similar incident took place in Raleigh, North Carolina, in 1989. This time the Chinese American victim, Ming Hai Loo, was killed by two white brothers who thought he was Vietnamese and were angry about U.S. battle deaths in Vietnam. In 1990, the brother who struck the fatal blow was sentenced to thirty-seven years in prison for second-degree murder and simple assault, but with the possibility of parole after serving four-and-a-half years. The maximum penalty for such crimes under North Carolina's law is life in prison. The other white assailant, who made hostile racist remarks, received a six-month misdemeanor sentence. The following year he was found guilty in federal court of violating the victim's civil rights and received a four-year sentence, which was shorter than the minimum sentence specified by federal guidelines. Significantly, this case was the *first* successful federal prosecution of a civil rights case in which the victim was Asian American. Yet it received almost no media attention, a neglect that perpetuates non-Asian Americans' lack of awareness of anti-Asian violence and makes such incidents likely to occur again. A report of the U.S. Commission on Civil Rights has stated that "many Americans view racial hatred purely as a black–white problem and are unaware that Asian Americans are also frequent targets of hate crimes."[53]

Anti-Asian attacks are examples not only of racist violence but of the confusion of whites and other non-Asians about Asian Americans. Many non-Asians are not aware that there are more than a dozen major groups among Asian–Pacific Americans and often mistake a person from one group for someone from another such group. This type of thinking may have been reflected in several incidents during the summer of 1997 in which White House Secret Service guards treated Asian Americans (including in one case White House interns on a tour) entering the White House as though they were suspicious or foreigners.[54]

Filipino Americans

Filipino Americans, among the oldest of Asian immigrants, have endured violent attacks. In the early period of immigration there were many clashes in California between Filipino and white farm laborers. In 1929, white farmers in the Imperial Valley, the Sacramento Valley, and the San Joaquin Valley depended heavily on migratory Filipino labor; by 1930 Filipinos represented 42 percent of all non-European labor working on California farms. Because of prevailing patterns of discrimination, Filipino wages were considerably lower than the wages of whites. As a consequence of the heavy use of Filipino farm labor in the 1920s, intense competition developed between native-born white and Filipino immigrant laborers for farm work when the 1930s Great Depression hit California.[55]

On October 24, 1929, an anti-Filipino riot by whites took place in a small farming community in the San Joaquin Valley. The riot resulted from white workers' bitterness over white farmers' use of Filipino workers for harvesting crops. The anti-Asian attacks began at a carnival where whites were shooting some young Filipinos with rubber bands as the Filipinos walked with white women. After a few days of harassment, a young Filipino farm laborer used a knife to defend himself when a white group attempted to corner him. He escaped, but a white mob formed. The whites went to a nearby labor camp, ordered all Filipinos out, then burned the camp to the ground. The local police chief refused to take action against the white mob despite the criminal acts.

The most prolonged anti-Filipino riot in California occurred near Watsonville in early 1930. This riot reflected a decade of increasing tension between white and Filipino American workers. The tension in Watsonville was exacerbated by an interview in the local newspaper with a white official who blamed the Filipino Americans for local tensions. A series of anti-Filipino demonstrations then erupted. At one point, a vigilante mob of 500 white youths marched on a Filipino American dance hall. In this case, police stepped in to curtail the violence. The white-dominated press misreported the incident as Filipino Americans marching and rioting in the streets.

On January 22, 1930, the anti-Filipino attacks reached a peak when 400 white vigilantes attacked the Northern Monterey Filipino Club. One person was killed, and a large number of Filipino Americans were severely beaten. Law enforcement officials who tried to protect them were taunted with cries of "Goo Goo Lovers." The local paper added to the tension by printing stories that condemned the dance halls frequented by Filipino Americans and the practice of Filipino men socializing with white women.

Racial hostility has been a recent problem as well. In 1991, white guests at a party at Chicago mayor Richard Daley's Grand Beach, Michigan, estate reportedly called two Filipino American youths racist names and threw them out. The youths came back with some white friends, and there was a violent brawl. In this case whites both attacked and defended the Filipino American youths.[56]

Korean Americans

Koreans are relatively recent immigrants, yet they too have been hit hard by anti-Asian violence. Like some white ethnic merchants, Korean merchants in some African American communities have faced hostility, and in a few cities their businesses have been primary targets of violence. Local residents have charged that Korean merchants treat black customers rudely and refuse to hire black employees or to extend credit. Another source of black bitterness is the largely unfounded belief that the federal government helps Korean Americans start businesses; in fact, Korean Americans usually pool their personal and family resources to purchase businesses in low-income neighborhoods.[57]

During the last decade black residents in New York and California have boycotted and demonstrated against Korean businesses. Each group has accused members of the other group of racially motivated violence.[58] In 1991, a Korean American storekeeper in Los Angeles shot and killed a fifteen-year-old black customer, Latasha Harlins, whom the storekeeper mistakenly thought was shoplifting. Black rage over this incident, which intensified after a white judge imposed a lenient sentence on the merchant, played a role in the major 1992 Los Angeles riot.[59]

Like Jewish American and other white ethnic merchants in similar situations, Korean Americans have sometimes become "middleman minorities," groups that Bonacich has described as "the footsoldiers of internal colonialism."[60] The poverty area store is often the first step in ethnic entrepreneurship. Thus, Korean American merchants can be viewed as both exploiters and exploited. They generally operate family businesses, must charge high prices to survive, and make a modest to excellent profit in working-class communities whose black residents often do not have the transportation to shop elsewhere. The high prices are resented by the black residents, who also may harbor anti-Asian stereotypes. At the same time, many Korean American merchants have become fearful of all young blacks because they or their friends have been robbed by a few. The Korean immigrants' stereotyping of young blacks is made worse if they viewed U.S. movies in Korea before they emigrated. Because U.S. movies often portray black (and Latino) Americans in a negative light—as mostly criminals, for instance— Korean immigrants may be predisposed to view them negatively even before they arrive in the United States.

Historian Mike Davis has described the looting and burning of 2,000 Korean-owned businesses (about 40 percent of all businesses damaged) during the 1992 Los Angeles riot (see Chapter 8) as the direct product of "the black community's unassuaged grief over Harlins's murder."[61] Walking the streets during the rioting, he was repeatedly told, "This is for our baby sister. This is for Latasha." Many local black and Latino residents saw the "riot" as an urban uprising. Los Angeles's half-million Korean Americans, however, felt betrayed by the U.S. justice system as they saw white police officers protecting large shopping centers owned by wealthy whites while smaller, Korean-owned stores were being destroyed by the rioters. A Korean American university student told Davis, "Maybe this is what we get for uncritically buying into the white middle class's attitude toward blacks and its faith in the police."[62] Social scientist Elaine Kim has commented that "the so-called black–Korean problem masks a deeper racism in this country. . . . When the Los Angeles Police Department and the state government failed to respond to the initial outbreak of violence in South Central, I suspected that Korean–Americans were being used as human shields to protect the real source of rage."[63]

In recent years conflict has also erupted between Korean Americans and Latinos in California. Researchers have found strong antagonism between the two groups. For example, many of the rioters burning and looting Korean American businesses during the L.A. uprising were Latinos. Korean American garment industry contractors are seen by their low-wage Latino immigrant employees as profit-seeking exploiters who are indifferent to workers' well-being. In their turn, these Korean American contractors report frequent verbal disputes in the workplace and acts of sabotage and vandalism. Yet the Korean American contractors are themselves exploited by the white manufacturers who make extensive use of a subcontracting strategy designed for flexible and profitable production of garments.[64]

Vietnamese Americans

Many recent Vietnamese immigrants fished as a livelihood in their homeland, and it has seemed natural for them to do so in their new country. To pursue this dream, some moved to fishing communities on the Texas Gulf Coast. In the late 1970s, they had been encouraged to move to that area because of its labor shortage. They generally took low-paying jobs, such as cleaning fish or working in restaurant kitchens, and in these positions they were tolerated by the white community. But as they began to buy shrimp boats and offer considerable competition to the white fishers, the attitudes toward them changed. Many whites in the area have resented the success of the Vietnamese Americans and have blamed them for the economic recessions that came to the Gulf Coast.

These Vietnamese Americans have experienced open hostility from their Anglo and Latino counterparts since they began fishing. A 1979 conflict between Vietnamese Americans and whites in Seadrift, Texas, culminated in the shooting death of a white fisher. Two Vietnamese refugees were arrested for the shooting, which followed an argument over the placement of crab traps. Within hours of the death, three Vietnamese boats were burned, one house was fire-bombed, and an attempt was made to bomb a packing plant where Vietnamese Americans worked. The attacks caused most of the Vietnamese refugees to flee to another town. The Vietnamese Americans were eventually acquitted of the shooting. In response to this verdict, some whites turned to the local Ku Klux Klan for "protection of their industrial interest."[65]

Since the late 1970s, Vietnamese Americans have faced racial violence in a number of cities across the country. For example, Boston had 339 civil rights crimes reported in 1980, a number of them targeting Vietnamese immigrants. Between 1983 and 1987, the Boston police department reported that nearly one-fourth of the racial violence in the city was directed at Vietnamese and other Asian Americans. In 1989, five Indochinese children were killed in Stockton, California, by a white man partially motivated by racial hostility.[66]

Asian-Indian Americans

Asian-Indian Americans have also faced racial hostility and discrimination. Anti-Indian leaflets have been circulated in several New Jersey cities. According to a 1997 news report on New Jersey schools, Asian Indian children have faced racist behavior from other students. For instance, one young girl reported that she was called derogatory names and physically abused just because of her Indian ancestry.[67] In addition, exaggerated stereotypes of the successfulness of Asian Indians have contributed to interethnic political struggles in several states, including California. For example, attempts to include Indians as Asians in affirmative action programs designed to help Asian American businesses have been vigorously opposed by non-Asians in San Francisco.[68]

ORGANIZING AND ACTIVISM IN THE POLITICAL ARENA

As we mentioned in the chapter on Japanese Americans, a number of Asian Americans have distinguished themselves politically, including U.S. Senators Daniel Inouye and Samuel I. Hayakawa, in spite of anti-Asian prejudices. Yet these senators, elected from states that have a larger proportion of Asian American voters than the nation as a whole, are rare examples of Asian American success at the top of the U.S. political system. In general, Asian Americans have been significantly underrepresented in the political system, especially in western states where large numbers reside. This underrepresentation became conspicuous in the 1990s, when Asian American leaders in California protested a court redistricting plan. Federally mandated redistricting in California, based on the 1990 census, had created seven new congressional districts. However, the new districts, as they appeared in the court plan, did not increase the likelihood of new Asian American lawmakers in a state with a large Asian American population but which at the time had no Asian Americans in its senate or assembly.[69]

As we move into the 21st century, Asian Americans have achieved extremely limited political representation except in Hawaii. Federal appointed offices, including U.S. Congressional staff positions, have largely been inaccessible. In the mid-1990s, less than 1 percent of senior congressional staff positions were held by Asian Americans. In 1995, California had only three Asian American members of Congress (Robert Matsui, Norman Mineta, and Jay C. Kim) and only one Asian American (Treasurer Matt Fong) in an elected position at the state level. A serious lack of representation existed at the local level as well, even in areas with substantial Asian American populations. For example, no Asian American has ever served on New York City's council even though that city's Asian American population now exceeds 800,000. A large proportion of Asian Americans have immigrated too recently to be eligible to vote, and the voting rate of eligible Asian Americans is relatively low. White prejudice and discrimination also play a role in the modest level of Asian American political involvement. Participants in Civil Rights Commission conferences have pointed to several barriers to political participation: (1) apportionment policies that dilute the voting strength of Asian American voting blocs; (2) the unavailability of Asian-language election materials; and (3) anti-Asian sentiments among non-Asian voters and in the mass media.[70]

Pan-Asian Organizations and Coalitions

Nineteenth-century Asian immigrants, divided by language and cultural differences and historical tensions between their countries of origin, held fast to their distinctive cultural identities, resisting the tendency of non-Asian Americans to lump all Asians together. In addition, early Asian communities "were not above denigrating, or at least approving the denigration of, other Asian groups" in order to improve their positions in U.S. society.[71] By the 1960s, native-born Asian Americans outnumbered foreign-born Asian Americans by a ratio of two-to-one in California. Language and cultural barriers were fading, thereby paving the way for the development of a pan-Asian identity and solidarity based on common experiences of racial oppression in the United States. Beginning on college campuses in the late 1960s and spreading to community activists and professional organizations by the mid-1970s, pan-Asian organizations and news media helped forge a group consciousness among Asian American students, artists, and professionals.

Use of the term *Asian American* originated during this period as the term *Oriental*, with its roots in European colonialism and imperialism, was rejected.

Asia is east (oriental) only if the point of reference is Europe. "Oriental" has long been associated with white stereotypes of deviousness, passivity, and acquiescence; for many, "Asian American" means respect and empowerment.[72]

Yet not all Asian Americans were empowered by the pan-Asian movement of the 1960s and 1970s. In general, Asian American women were restricted to subordinate roles, and those who challenged sexism in the movement were ridiculed as traitors to Asian American nationalism.[73] Feeling alienated from the mainstream women's movement, Asian American women have formed their own groups within the context of their Asian identity, sometimes emphasizing their triple oppression based on their gender, their racial group, and their class.[74]

Within the pan-Asian movement, some members of the smaller Asian American groups have resented the dominance of the larger Chinese and Japanese American groups. Reactions of Asian American groups to the early pan-Asian movement ranged from support to apprehension and hostility.[75] It was not until the 1980s that a national pan-Asian political organization specifically addressed Asian American concerns. The first major political effort began in 1986 with the founding of the Asian-American Voters Coalition, which included national and local organizations representing Japanese, Chinese, Asian-Indian, Filipino, Korean, Vietnamese, and Thai Americans.[76] The organization sought to consolidate Asian American citizens into a more effective bloc of voters that could have a significant impact on elections in California, Texas, New York, and Illinois; to protect Asian Americans' civil rights; and to fight anti-Asian legislation, distorted media images, racial violence, and employment discrimination.[77] In the 1990s, the Asian Pacific American Legal Center of Southern California has taken action to protect Asian immigrants' rights to speak their native language in workplaces and has addressed various community issues, such as keeping Asian language books in local public libraries.

In the fall of 1997, twenty Asian American organizations, including the Japanese American Citizens League and the Organization of Chinese Americans, joined to form the National Council of Asian Pacific Americans (NCAPA). A Chinese American was named interim head of the organization, whose members are concerned with such problems as hate crimes, discrimination, immigration restrictions, and the singling out of Asian Americans during the investigation of illegal political campaign contributions.[78]

Coalitions with non-Asian groups have also been created. For example, Latino, African, Vietnamese, Korean, Chinese, and other Asian American leaders in the Los Angeles area created the Multicultural Association for Voter Registration to encourage all people of color to register to vote and to become more active politically. Such coalitions reflect an awareness that cooperation can generate political power. More recently, Korean American community organizations' support for Latino hotel workers unions involved in a dispute with the owner of a Los Angeles hotel was hailed by Latino union leaders as a "wonderful example" of coalition building between Latino and Korean Americans.[79]

Chinese Americans

Perhaps because Chinese Americans have had the longest history of immigration of the five groups studied in this chapter, they have been the most politically active of these groups. Chinese American political activity was modest in the late nineteenth century but increased in the years between 1917 and 1920, shortly after the revolution in China. Increasingly, Chinese Americans became involved in a wide variety of political organizations and spent much time discussing political developments in China. A number of labor-oriented organizations were created and tried to organize laborers in New York's Chinese American communities, where the largest concentration of Chinese Americans then lived. These attempts generally proved unsuccessful, however, because much of the labor there was organized along family networks.[80] Between 1900 and 1930, the important Chinese language newspaper *Chung Sai Yat Po* (CSYP) was an important advocate of civil and political rights for Chinese Americans, including the rights of Chinese American women. The paper's emphasis on political events in China, where the role and status of women were progressing toward equality, contributed to the social and political awakening of Chinese American women.[81]

A second period of major Chinese immigration, after the immigration reforms of 1965, revived political activity among Chinese Americans. Explaining barriers to expanded political activity, Michael Woo, one of the few Chinese Americans in city government, has noted that "cultural traits" are a major challenge to the "Asian community in getting out the vote" because Chinese and other Asian Americans "traditionally view all political activity as suspect." Woo added, however, that more and more Asian Americans are breaking with tradition and becoming active in election campaigns.[82] Earlier, Irving Chin, chair of the Chinatown Advisory Committee to the Borough President of Manhattan, had told a U.S. Senate committee that Chinese American political activity had been limited because of problems with English, fear of and lack of familiarity with government, and a traditional reluctance to engage in political action. In addition, Professor Ling-chi Wang, a San Francisco community activist and later chair of the Asian American studies department of the University of California, Berkeley, spoke to the same committee in support of government social programs. Wang testified that the unemployment rate in San Francisco's Chinatown was double the citywide average, that available housing was substandard and that the incidence of tuberculosis was far above the national average.[83] A movement on behalf of expanded civil and political rights for Chinese Americans and other Asian American groups has paralleled the growth of the Chinese American population.

As the number of Chinese American immigrants in the United States has increased and as many of these immigrants and their children have concentrated in particular geographic areas, they are becoming more influential in U.S. politics. Concerned about a range of local and national issues, including attacks on immigrants and certain social programs, Chinese and other Asian Americans are involving themselves politically to try to influence events in both the nation and their local communities. One example is Monterey Park, California, a Los Angeles suburb of 60,000 people, three-fourths of whom are Asian and Latino Americans. This is one of the largest Chinese immigrant settlements in the United States. Although Chinese Americans are the most numerous group in Monterey Park, a number of other Asian American groups are well represented. When white city council members passed a resolution saying that Monterey Park did not consider itself a sanctuary for "illegal aliens" and that English should be the official language of the United States, many Asian Americans in the community were outraged. No fewer than 4,000 people signed petitions demanding that the city council rescind the resolution, which it did. The controversy over the resolution indicated a serious rift within the community between fearful whites, who often contend that the Asian Americans are not trying "to assimilate" and are "taking over," and Asian Americans, many of whom are socially concerned suburbanites with successful businesses.[84]

By the late 1990s, Chinese Americans were growing in influence in several California cities. They sat on city councils in several Los Angeles–area communities and in San Francisco. In 1996, Gary Locke was elected governor in Washington state, the first Chinese American to serve as governor of a state other than Hawaii. Chinese Americans have also become increasingly active in national politics. Many Chinese Americans have pressed both major political parties to select Chinese American candidates. Few Asian Americans have served in the U.S. Congress. Daniel K. Akaka, currently senator from Hawaii, is the only person of Hawaiian or Chinese American ancestry to ever serve in the U.S. Senate. Chinese Americans contributed large sums to the Democratic party during the 1996 election campaign, and in the late 1990s a majority of Chinese Americans were voting for Democratic party candidates.

Chinese Americans are growing in political influence at state and national levels. Chinese and other Asian American civil rights groups have spoken out strongly and testified before Congress for the continuation of affirmative action programs. Since 1989 many Chinese Americans have also become more involved in pressing for changes in U.S. government policy toward China. The killing of protesting students in Beijing's Tiananmen Square in 1989 prompted the creation of a new organization called the Committee of 100. Headed by leading Chinese Americans, including architect I.M. Pei, the organization has sought to have an impact on government policy toward China. Moreover, many Chinese Americans have pressured the U.S. government to take stronger action to persuade China to improve its human rights policies.[85] The late 1997 visit of Chinese President Jiang Zemin was viewed with mixed emotions by Chinese Americans. Many were proud that China was becoming a superpower and welcomed the visit, while others protested openly against China's repressive human rights policies.

Filipino Americans

The nation's most successful farm workers' union, the United Farm Workers (see Chapter 9), was created by a merger between a Mexican American organizing drive and a Filipino labor organization, the Agricultural Workers' Organizing Committee (AWOC). The two groups conducted a major strike against poor working conditions on the grape farms of California. The head of AWOC, Larry Itliong, was an energetic Filipino American activist who worked to organize farm laborers from Alaska to California to South America.[86] A number of other Filipino American labor and political organizations have been created, including the Filipino Organizing Committee, which was created in the San Francisco area in the 1970s to facilitate greater political participation for Filipino Americans.[87]

New resistance tactics have emerged in the 1980s and 1990s. The National Filipino American Council, a group of 3,000 Filipino social, community, and civil rights groups across the nation, has fought for fair immigration laws. In 1992 and 1997, Filipino Americans held national empowerment conferences to generate political strategies and a movement to secure political positions in cities where they make up a significant percentage of the population. The 1997 conference was organized by the Council and a number of other Filipino organizations. One concern of the 1997 gathering was to get the Filipino Veterans Equity Act passed, legislation that would finally give Filipino veterans of World War II the veterans benefits long promised to them by the U.S. government.[88]

Despite their large numbers, Filipino Americans have rarely been elected or appointed to political offices. In the mid-1990s, the California legislature had no Filipino American members, even though Filipinos have the highest naturalization and citizenship rate of any California immigrant group. Few Filipino Americans have held any elective offices at other government levels. One rare exception was in the Los Angeles area. In 1992, the first Filipino American was elected to the city council in Carson, a community near Los Angeles.

International political events seem to be pulling Filipino Americans ever more into U.S. political debates. A number of Filipino American organizations have responded to the Philippine government's call for investment in the islands to help overcome the recurring economic crises there. This is further evidence of the global influences on racial and ethnic groups in the United States. In addition, the overthrow of the Ferdinand Marcos dictatorship and the coming to power of Corazon Aquino in the Philippines in the late 1980s boosted Filipino American pride. Filipino identity was strengthened by the advent of political democracy in the Philippines. This political trend in the homeland seems to have reinforced the commitment of many Filipino Americans to greater political participation in the United States. Significantly, in 1997 Filipino American leaders in San Francisco protested the installation of a huge granite column celebrating Commodore George Dewey's victory over the Spanish in Manila Bay in 1898. Filipino American leaders also pressed for recognition of the Filipino struggle for independence, which was crushed by the United States in a bloody struggle, after which the Philippines became a major U.S. colony in the Pacific.[89]

Korean Americans

Korean American political activity, like that of Chinese and Filipino Americans, has sometimes been inspired by events in the homeland. For example, during the years between 1905 and 1919 many Korean Americans were active in the fight for

Korean independence from Japan. Japan, however, successfully maintained its colonial dominance over Korea, and after 1919 the Korean independence movement declined. Korean Americans who had devoted energy to the cause of independence did not sustain their political movement, and their organizations reemerged as nonpolitical.[90]

In recent years, Korean Americans have gradually gained more political visibility. Although Korean Americans have been active in the Asian-American Voters Coalition, discussed earlier, until the early 1990s not one had held a major political office in the western states. In 1992 in California, Jay C. Kim became the first Korean American—and the first Asian immigrant—ever elected to the U.S. House. After the 1992 racial riot in Los Angeles, the local Korean-American Coalition also became more active. Jerry Yu, a member of the coalition, has commented that during the riot "Korean Americans really saw with their own eyes the lack of political strength that we as a community have."[91] In the 1996 presidential election, Korean and other Asian Americans became active in registering voters and in supporting Democratic party candidates. During the Democratic party's January 1997 inaugural celebrations, 1,000 Korean and other Asian Americans attended the first ever Asian American inaugural ball, an indication of growing political influence. Still, Asian American leaders were critical of President Clinton for not appointing Asian Americans to his cabinet. They vowed to further increase the number of Asian American voters and candidates in upcoming campaigns, as well as to increase the activity of Pan-Asian organizations.[92]

Many Korean Americans maintain close ties to Korea. After the Los Angeles riot in 1992 (an election year in the United States) several officials from the Republic of Korea promptly visited the riot areas of Los Angeles, arriving even before U.S. presidential candidates. Moreover, when the country of North Korea faced serious food shortages in 1996–1997, Korean Americans sent more than a million dollars for food and other assistance.[93]

Vietnamese Americans

The country of origin has also remained important for Vietnamese Americans. In recent years the icy political and economic relationship between Vietnam and the United States has begun to thaw. In a 1989 survey of Vietnamese Americans in Orange County, California, about half felt that establishing diplomatic ties with Vietnam would be a good idea for the United States and that they might return home for a visit under such conditions.[94] The issue of reestablishing ties to a Communist homeland has been a topic of debate within Vietnamese American communities since the 1980s, just as it has for Cuban American communities (see Chapter 10).

In 1989, a white city council member in Orange County told a group of Vietnamese Americans wishing to parade that "if they want to be South Vietnamese, go back to South Vietnam." The permit was turned down by the city council because the parade to honor the Vietnamese war dead was not seen by local whites as truly "American." Vietnamese stores and signs were defaced by white vandals. After political protest from the Asian American community, however, the white council member apologized for his comments. Although the protest indicated growing political activity, by the early 1990s no Vietnamese Americans were on any city council in Orange County, even though the county had a very large Vietnamese American population. Even so, in the 1990s the county has had an active Vietnamese-American Political Action Committee working for expanded political participation and influence for Vietnamese Americans.[95]

Vietnamese Americans have begun to move up the social, political, and legal ladders like other immigrant groups before them. In the last two decades they have created numerous community organizations and institutions, including Buddhist temples and Vietnamese radio stations. In the early 1990s, a group called the Vietnamese Community of Southern California was created to develop employment, immigrant, and youth programs and to unify some 300 Vietnamese American organizations in that area. Gradually, Vietnamese Americans are moving into important government positions. For example, in 1997 Thang Nguyen Barrett became a Santa Clara County Municipal Court Judge, the first Vietnamese American to serve as a judge in California.[96]

Asian-Indian Americans

Because of their relatively recent arrival in the United States, Asian-Indian Americans have so far had relatively little political visibility. In the history of the U.S. Congress, only one Asian-Indian American has ever served, Californian Dalip Singh Saund, a representative elected in the mid-1950s. However, by the early 1990s, Asian-Indian Americans were starting to form a number of political organizations and networks designed to increase political influence. As a result of such activity in Ohio, the first Asian-Indian American to be appointed to a state governor's cabinet was Pitambar Somani, who became Ohio's director of health in the mid-1990s. Moreover, in the last decade Asian-Indian Americans have organized to fight racial hostility and discrimination in a number of U.S. cities.[97] For example, a group in Hartford, Connecticut, has pressed for changes in discriminatory licensing requirements for foreign-born physicians. The Hartford group has also lobbied for expanded U.S. government aid for India; this provides yet another example of the influence of the home country and the international context on the political orientations of U.S. racial-ethnic groups.[98]

Growing Asian American political influence has been accompanied by an increasing trend toward Pan-Asian coalitions. Pan-Asian political organizations have been created in cities from New York to Los Angeles and San Francisco. Asian American student organizations at West Coast universities such as UCLA are now Pan-Asian organizations and include members whose ancestry stems from numerous Asian countries. These student groups have pressed for expanded Asian American studies programs.[99] In addition, many people of color, particularly civil rights leaders, have called for coalitions between Asian Americans and older groups such as African Americans in order to bring much-needed progressive reforms on racial matters to the United States. In contrast, some observers have speculated about whether white leaders and political organizations, espe-cially in areas where whites are becoming a minority of the population (for exam-ple, in California about the year 2002), will soon seek to build coalitions with Asian Americans in order to maintain substantial white political control.

THE ECONOMY

The U.S. Civil Rights Commission has documented the exploitation of Asian immigrants who are unaware of their rights by white employers who violate laws regarding safe working conditions, wages, and hours. The commission has noted that Supreme Court decisions in the late 1980s have failed to protect Asian American workers from racial harassment and other discrimination. As we have noted previously, the 1991 Civil Rights Act was designed to undo the effects of some of these conservative Court decisions. Well-educated Asian immigrants with professional experience in their homelands have faced employment barri-ers in the United States. Many find that their experience and credentials are dis-counted or ignored by white employers. Generally, well-educated Asian Americans are hired for research, engineering, or other technical positions, but they are underrepresented at all levels of management in most large U.S. com-panies. A Civil Rights Commission study found that U.S.-born Asian American men with good English proficiency were less likely to hold managerial positions than white men with comparable qualifications. Asian Americans are even less likely to hold top executive positions in corporations. Asian American managers and professionals report a "glass ceiling." In 1990, they made up only 0.3 per-cent of the top executives in Fortune 500 companies—about one-tenth of their percentage in the total population. This percentage had changed little by the late 1990s. Moreover, a large majority of Chinese and Filipino American profession-als and managers responding to a recent survey in San Francisco felt that racism had blocked them from advancing in their jobs.[100] A 1994 study found that in the field of urban health care and research and development, where Asian Americans make up more than one-fourth of the work force, fewer than 1 per-cent of senior executives are Asian American. Another study of Asian American managers in California found that they were often seen as docile workers who could be hired and fired at will because they would not complain. White stereo-types of Asian American professionals and managers still result in economic exploitation.[101]

The previously noted Civil Rights Commission study found racially based employment discrimination to be even more severe for Asian American women. These workers are vulnerable not only to racial discrimination but also to sexual harassment and other gender discrimination on the job, and many have little knowledge of their legal rights. They are frequently excluded from the critical informal networks of their co-workers, and hence enjoy fewer sources of support than white women when confronted with sexual harassment. In one instance cited by the commission, an Asian American woman working at a military base in San

Francisco encountered severe retaliation after reporting sexual harassment. After she reported the retaliation her working conditions became so intolerable that she suffered a nervous breakdown. The Civil Rights Commission report noted that "because of the stereotypic expectation of compliance and docility, a formal complaint from an Asian American woman might have been considered as a personal affront or challenge."[102]

Discrimination based on language proficiency or accent is common. In a 1990 judicial decision, the Ninth Circuit Court of Appeals upheld an employer's right to consider an applicant's verbal skills when these were relevant to job performance, although the court cautioned employers not to misuse language proficiency to discriminate on the basis of national origin. Recent Asian (and Latin American) immigrants are adversely affected by English-only rules in the workplace, many of which have been found by the courts to be inappropriate because no business necessity for such language requirements can be demonstrated.[103]

Chinese Americans

In the nineteenth century, Chinese immigrants were recruited to fill the lower rungs of the occupational ladder in the United States. Some became small merchants and crafts workers, but most worked as unskilled laborers. Chinese workers were employed to build railroads in California as early as the 1850s, but the first large-scale use of Chinese labor—more than 12,000 workers—was in the construction of the transcontinental railroad, which was finally completed in 1869. By 1880, Chinese Americans numbered at least 135,000. Most lived in California, and there they became an important factor in the state's economy. They converted swampland in California to rich farmland; their skills in planting, cultivating, and harvesting were used extensively at white-owned vineyards, orchards, and ranches. Some farmed as sharecroppers; others grew vegetables for the general market.

Chinese factory workers were an important part of the California economy after the Civil War. By the early 1870s, Chinese workers made up most of the labor force in woolen mills and most of the cigar makers in San Francisco; by the mid-1870s they were a majority of the shoemakers and garment workers. Chinese American entrepreneurs developed shrimp fisheries, which by the 1880s were exporting a million pounds annually. Chinese American workers were also a mainstay of canneries in the Pacific Northwest. Thousands more operated or worked in laundries and served as domestic servants. Most labored long hours in poor working conditions for very low wages.[104]

The need for large numbers of factory workers in defense plants during World War II opened employment opportunities for thousands who had previously been confined to laundry and restaurant jobs. An estimated 30 percent of young Chinese American men in New York City found jobs in defense plants. Between 1940 and 1950, more than one-third of Chinese American men remained in service occupations, but the percentages in craft, technical, and professional occupations more than doubled. War industries also provided employment opportunities for Chinese American women in clerical and technical jobs in defense plants.[105]

The prospects for many recent Chinese immigrants have not been much better than those for the early immigrants, because many lack money, skills, and the ability to speak English. Most have settled in preexisting Chinese American communities in large cities such as New York and San Francisco, where many of the men have worked in restaurants or other service jobs and thousands of women have labored in nonunion garment factories in or near the Chinese American residential areas. Conditions in these sweatshops are often substandard or dangerous, and pay is often below the minimum wage.[106]

Some postwar immigrants are engineers, doctors, mathematicians, and scientists. Some were trained in China and fled after the Communist victory there in 1949; others received their education on the island of Taiwan, where schools prepared them for emigration to the United States. Still others completed their advanced studies in the United States and found employment in U.S. industries and universities. Members of this well-educated group of immigrants have found better jobs and generally have had an easier time adjusting to their new country than the large number of poorer immigrants.[107]

Table 12–2 presents 1990 census data on the occupational distribution of the five Asian American groups considered in this chapter as well as that of European Americans.[108] Today, Chinese Americans are heavily concentrated in white-collar jobs; 35.8 percent hold professional and managerial positions. The proportion rises to 43 percent for those born in the United States. The proportion of Chinese Americans exceeds that of whites in this category (28.5 percent). However, Chinese Americans are also overrepresented in service-sector jobs compared with whites (16.5 percent versus 11.5 percent). They are only half as likely to hold skilled blue-collar jobs as are whites and somewhat less likely to hold less-skilled blue-collar jobs. In 1990, Chinese Americans' unemployment rate was lower than

TABLE 12–2   Occupational Distribution by Ethnic Group

	Chinese American	Filipino American	Korean American	Vietnamese American	Asian-Indian American	White American
Managerial and professional specialty	35.8%	26.6%	25.5%	17.6%	43.6%	28.5%
Technical, sales, and administrative support	31.2	36.7	37.1	29.5	33.2	32.6
Precision production, craft, and repair	5.6	7.4	8.9	15.7	5.2	11.6
Operators, fabricators, and laborers	10.6	11.0	12.8	20.9	9.4	13.4
Service occupations	16.5	16.8	15.1	15.0	8.1	11.5
Farming, forestry, and fishing	0.4	1.5	0.7	1.4	0.6	2.4
Totals	100.1%	100%	100.1%	100.1%	100.1%	100%

that of the population as a whole and the lowest among all Asian groups except for Japanese Americans.[109]

The Chinese American community is represented at both extremes of the economic spectrum. An Wang, the former head of Wang Laboratories computer firm who died in 1990, became a billionaire. He was fifth on Forbes's 1983 list of the wealthiest Americans and was still on the Forbes Four Hundred list of richest Americans in 1989. One of the nation's leading architects, I. M. Pei, may be the most famous Chinese American, at least to non-Chinese. Several Chinese American women, including Amy Tan and Jade Snow Wong, are prominent novelists.[110] At the other extreme, the 1990 census reported that 11 percent of Chinese American families lived below the poverty line.

Table 12–3 presents 1990 census data on income and poverty for the Asian American groups considered in this chapter and for white Americans.[111]

The median family income for Chinese Americans ($41,316 for all Chinese American families and $56,762 for the U.S.–born group) is higher than that of white families ($37,628), and a larger percentage of Chinese American families reported incomes of $100,000 or more (10 percent versus 6 percent). Yet the proportion of Chinese American families living in poverty in 1990 was also greater than that of white families. The economic range within the Chinese American community is directly related to length of residence. U.S.–born Chinese Americans tend to be better educated, to hold managerial or professional jobs, and to live outside the so-called "Chinatowns" of the larger cities. In 1990 their poverty rate was only 3 percent. However, the more recent immigrants tend to have less education, to be unemployed or hold low-wage jobs, and to live in inner-city communities. The 1990 poverty rate of this group was high—more than 20 percent.[112]

Filipino Americans

Filipinos were first recruited as farm workers for the sugar plantations in Hawaii and farms along the West Coast. The vast majority of these workers were single men who endured a grueling schedule and meager wages. Their typical day began at 4 A.M.; with one fifteen-minute break for breakfast and a half hour for

TABLE 12–3   Income Level by Ethnic Groups

	Chinese American	Filipino American	Korean American	Vietnamese American	Asian-Indian American	White American
Median family income	$41,316	$46,698	$33,909	$30,550	$49,309	$37,628
Percentage of families with incomes of $100,000 or more	10%	8%	7%	4%	14%	6%
Percentage of families below poverty level	11%	5%	15%	24%	7%	7%

lunch, the men worked until 3 or 4 P.M. The wage for this labor remained the same from 1915 to 1933—an incredibly low $18 to $20 per month.[113]

In the early 1930s, thousands of Filipino American workers, a group that constituted 40 percent of the agricultural work force in the Salinas Valley of California, formed the Filipino Labor Union (FLU). An FLU-led strike of lettuce workers in 1934 met with violent opposition from white growers supported by local police officers. The strikers eventually won wages of $.40 an hour and recognition of the union. Subsequent actions by the FLU led to a Mexican-Filipino union chartered by the American Federation of Labor. "The FLU represented . . . the entrance of Filipinos into the labor movement in America. . . . The involvement of the Filipinos in the labor movement reflected a changing consciousness—a sober recognition of shattered dreams and a new sense of ethnic unity."[114]

In the 1950s and 1960s, many Filipinos entered the U.S. workforce when the U.S. armed forces, especially the Navy, began recruiting Philippines residents. This continuing process has created military-related Filipino communities on the West Coast. Filipinos are the only non–U.S. residents recruited into the U.S. armed forces. In addition, hospitals in California have recruited Filipino nurses, who have later become U.S. citizens. Many Filipino scientists, engineers, and other professionals have emigrated because of political turmoil and economic crises at home, sometimes creating a serious shortage of such professionals in the Philippines.[115]

One analysis of 1980 census data for Filipino Americans in California found considerable occupational and economic inequality between Filipino Americans and white Americans. Filipino men, whether U.S.-born or foreign-born, had only about two-thirds the income of white men. Filipino women had only about half the income of white men. The study also revealed inequality in the occupational distribution of Filipino Americans compared with that of the white population. In the managerial and professional ranks, Filipino men were mostly accountants, civil engineers, and electrical engineers, while women were mostly registered nurses, elementary school teachers, and accountants. Few Filipino Americans were found among public administrators, financial managers, marketing managers, physicians, attorneys, architects, aerospace, industrial, and mechanical engineers, and social scientists—occupations that showed high concentrations of native-born white men.[116]

As can be seen in Table 12–2, Filipino Americans are now concentrated in white-collar jobs, although they are less heavily represented in managerial and professional positions and more heavily represented in technical, sales, and administrative support jobs than Chinese Americans. Unlike the Chinese American group, however, foreign-born Filipinos are more likely than their U.S.-born counterparts to be in the professional and managerial category. Like Chinese Americans, Filipino Americans are more likely to hold service sector jobs and less likely to hold skilled blue-collar jobs than are whites. Significantly, the 1990 unemployment rate for Filipino Americans was lower than that of the U.S. population as a whole.[117]

Filipino Americans have a relatively high median family income, which is one-third greater than the national average. The median family income for foreign-born Filipinos who arrived in the United States prior to 1980 is even higher—almost one and one-half times the national average. However, these figures are somewhat misleading because on average more family members work among Filipino Americans than among the general population, and most Filipino Americans work and live on the West Coast, where both wages and living costs are higher. Indeed, this is generally the case for most Asian American groups. Moreover, Filipino Americans have the lowest family poverty rate of any of these Asian American groups. In recent years the relative affluence of many Asian Americans, such as Filipino and Asian Indian Americans, has triggered specific marketing campaigns targeting them as consumers.

Filipino Americans have faced—and fought—serious job discrimination, including language discrimination. For example, a 1988 class action lawsuit filed with the Equal Employment Opportunity Commission charged that the San Francisco city government systematically discriminated against Filipino Americans. The suit cited statistical data indicating that Filipino Americans held only 1 percent of the city's administrative and supervisory positions although they made up 12 percent of the city's professional workers. The Filipino American organizations behind the lawsuit charged that Filipino professionals were stereotyped by many whites in the city government as incapable of leadership, and that they were penalized because of their accent.[118] In 1991, a federal judge upheld a Los Angeles area hospital's ban on speaking Tagalog, the native language of many Filipinos. The hospital prohibited its Filipino nurses from speaking Tagalog, even while on breaks. In Hawaii, a Filipino American unsuccessfully sued city officials who discriminated against him by turning him down for a white-collar job because of his heavy Filipino accent.[119]

Korean Americans

Language barriers and racial discrimination kept early Korean immigrants, most of whom were in Hawaii, from obtaining employment in accordance with their abilities. Like other Asian immigrants, the early-twentieth century Korean immigrants engaged in hard physical labor for extremely low wages. Many, including professionals, worked as agricultural laborers or as dishwashers, kitchen helpers, houseboys, or janitors in urban areas. During World War I a few Korean Americans began to open small, family-operated shops—laundries, shoe-repair shops, and used-furniture stores, mainly in Hawaii. By World War II, Korean Americans owned about fifty small and medium-sized businesses on the mainland. But among the total Korean population of ten thousand, only 5 percent were engaged in business.[120]

Koreans arriving after the 1965 immigration reforms have included mathematicians, scientists, and other professionals. A significant percentage of recent immigrants have become entrepreneurs, starting small grocery and other retail stores, often in low-income black and Latino areas. Korean Americans have filled an important small-business niche in cities, such as New York, Philadelphia, and Los Angeles. In the early 1990s, about 17 percent of Korean American workers nationwide were self-employed, compared with 7 percent in the general population. In the Los Angeles area the proportion was 24 percent.[121]

Earlier surveys of Korean American small-business owners have found that few had been small-business owners in Korea; most had held white-collar jobs in their homeland but had arrived in the United States with some capital. Korean American entrepreneurs tend to employ other Korean Americans. At one point in the late 1970s, fully 80 percent of employed Korean Americans in Los Angeles County either owned or worked in Korean-owned firms, mostly service and retail proprietorships.[122]

Many Korean immigrants have been forced into self-employment because of *exclusion* from the professions for which they were trained. Limited English proficiency is one factor, but anti-Asian discrimination in the U.S. labor market is more significant. Korean Americans who hold white-collar jobs are often passed over for promotions, especially to higher management ranks, regardless of their language skills. Indeed, several news reports in the late 1990s indicated that some Korean American managers and professionals have moved back to Korea, where their talents and skills do allow them to move up the corporate ladder.[123]

Given the situation of discrimination and language barriers, many Korean Americans prefer the freedom and dignity afforded by self-employment. Most recent Korean immigrants have arrived at a time when earlier white immigrant groups are moving out of the inner-city small-business niche into the professions and other white-collar jobs. Many Korean women have little knowledge of spoken English, and thus their main employment option is a family business where the entire family may work long hours for a modest income. Many first-generation Korean Americans say they accept the idea that "the first generation must be sacrificed" in order to provide education and a brighter future for the children. Many small businesses are highly profitable, although in order to succeed many proprietors have exploited other Korean immigrants, who are paid low wages because they have few options in the labor market.[124]

Researchers have found a high degree of geographic mobility among Korean immigrants in Los Angeles. Many live for only a short time in a heavily Korean inner-city area before moving to a suburb. Today, Korean American businesses are dispersed throughout Los Angeles county. There are an estimated 30,000 Korean American entrepreneurs in southern California.[125]

Many Korean immigrants have arrived with some capital, which may be grouped family assets. They often have the support of others in the Asian American community and of Asian American banks. A survey of the Los Angeles area found that Korean American merchants whose customers are primarily black or Latino earn more than those whose customers are primarily white. Many of these Korean American merchants take the money they earn in low-income black or Latino communities and move to middle-class areas. Black resentment over Korean merchants taking money out of the black community has contributed to the hostility many black urbanites feel toward Korean American busi-nesses.[126] We have already noted the conflict before and during the 1992 Los Angeles riot. Over the years since that uprising, many Korean American busi-nesses have not been rebuilt. Other businesses closed as their owners moved to more affluent areas of Los Angeles, and often into other types of businesses, including franchise operations seen as a safer type of business. The number of Korean American businesses in the general riot area had dropped by an estimat-ed 25–50 percent by the late 1990s.[127]

As can be seen in Table 12–2, Korean Americans are somewhat less likely to hold professional and managerial jobs and more likely to hold technical, sales, and administrative support jobs than white Americans. Korean Americans are also more likely to be in service occupations and less likely to hold skilled blue-collar jobs than white Americans. Moreover, in 1990 the unemployment rate for Korean Americans was well below that of the population as a whole. As can be seen in Table 12–3, the 1990 median family income for Korean Americans ($33,909) was below the white median ($37,628). Korean Americans also have the second-high-est poverty rate of the Asian groups considered in this chapter.[128]

Vietnamese Americans

Because the Vietnamese are such recent immigrants to this country, they do not have a long economic history. Most have arrived since the mid-1970s. Those who came immediately after the fall of Saigon in 1975 were often more affluent and bet-ter educated than those who came later. Many knew English and had adopted some aspects of Western culture. Some of these immigrants had been in business in their home country. Their contact with Western trade in Vietnam made it some-what easier to adjust to the business milieu in the United States. However, the information available for the late 1970s shows a pattern of downward occupa-tional mobility for many immigrants. One 1977 survey found that more than six in ten of those immigrants who had held white-collar jobs in Vietnam held blue-collar jobs at the time of the study. The remainder held white-collar jobs, primar-ily clerical or sales work. Professionals experienced downward mobility as well. Fewer than one in five of those who had been employed as professionals in Vietnam had been able to find similar work in the United States.[129]

Vietnamese Americans face overt discrimination in employment. In the early 1990s, one large convenience store chain settled a class action lawsuit charging that one of its managers had ordered discrimination against Vietnamese American employees. Two of the company's white supervisors reported that in the mid-1980s they had been told to fire Vietnamese workers and hire whites instead. In the settlement, the company agreed to hire more Vietnamese American managers. However, in the mid-1990s Vietnamese American employees of the chain were back in court protesting continuing discrimination in some of the company's stores.[130]

Most Vietnamese immigrants have come since the 1970s, and many have remained poor. They and their children have not been as economically successful as earlier arrivals.[131] As can be seen in Table 12–2, in the early 1990s Vietnamese Americans held professional or managerial positions at half the rate of Chinese Americans; they held about the same proportion of technical, sales, and administrative support positions as well as service-sector jobs as did Chinese Americans. Vietnamese Americans held the highest proportion of blue-collar jobs of any of the Asian groups considered in this chapter. More than half of all Vietnamese American workers held blue-collar or service jobs. This occupational situation was reflected in the median family income for Vietnamese Americans ($30,550), which was substantially below that of European Americans ($37,628) and of the other Asian groups considered in this chapter (see Table 12–3). Nearly one-fourth of Vietnamese American families fell below the poverty line. Moreover, in 1990 the unemployment rate for Vietnamese Americans was one-third higher than the national average and the highest of any Asian group considered in this chapter.[132] The economic status of many Vietnamese Americans is lower than it was before their immigration to the United States. As with other Asian Americans, discrimination in business circles and in the job market also remains a problem for Vietnamese Americans.

Asian-Indian Americans

Asian Indians are a relatively recent immigrant group, and many who came to the United States already had substantial monetary capital and "cultural capital" in the form of college educations or professional training. Today, the majority of employed Asian-Indian Americans are white-collar workers or business people. Like other Asian Americans, many Asian Indians have developed small businesses. (Today, the rate of creation of Asian American businesses is twice that for the nation as a whole.) In 1992 Asian-Indian Americans owned some 93,000 businesses in the United States, compared with 153,000 businesses owned by Chinese Americans and 68,000 by Japanese Americans. Most of these businesses are in the retail trade and services areas.[133]

In addition, Asian-Indian Americans have by far the largest proportion of college graduates and professional and managerial employees of all Asian–Pacific American groups (see Table 12–2). The proportions are much higher than for white Americans. In the early 1990s, they had the second-highest (after Japanese Americans) median family income among Asian Americans (see Table 12–3). Still, all in this group have not achieved economic success; in the same year 7 percent of Asian-Indian American families were below the poverty level.[134]

EDUCATION

Historically, Chinese, Japanese, and other Asian American children were often segregated in separate schools. A 1927 decision by the U.S. Supreme Court, for example, upheld the state of Mississippi's segregation of children of the "Mongolian race." This overt racist segregation began to break down after World

War II, but de facto school segregation persisted in many cities because discriminatory housing covenants kept Asian Americans out of white housing areas.[135] Still, this discrimination did not keep Asian Americans from pressing for better educational opportunities for their children.

High Achievement amid Persisting Problems

A stress on educational success has been a central part of most Asian American cultures. In 1993, four out of ten Westinghouse scholars (students with science projects) were Asian Americans, and in 1994 one of the ten scholars was Asian American. However welcome these prizes were to the student winners, they were a mixed blessing for Asian Americans as a group. Winning the national science competition has served to reinforce popular stereotypes of Asian Americans as "naturally" gifted in science and as "model minorities." Asian Americans have often criticized these stereotypes, in part because many Asian Americans excel in areas other than the natural sciences. Being stereotyped as especially high achievers also puts a great burden on those Asian American students who are not at the top of their class. In addition, many Asian American children, especially poorer immigrant children, are in great need of strong and well-funded educational environments. Yet the "model minorities" stereotype reduces the likelihood of government action to meet their educational and other needs.

Many Asian immigrant children, along with the American-born children of recent Asian immigrants, face problems of limited English proficiency and the

Asian American children make up a growing proportion of preschoolers in the western United States.

shock of an unfamiliar culture when they enter the public school system. Non-Asian teachers and administrators are often ignorant of Asian cultures and insensitive to the needs of these students. Some have been unwilling to protect Asian American students from mistreatment by non-Asian students. In addition, many recent arrivals from Southeast Asia have vivid memories of the horrors of war in their homeland; for many, a war-generated post-traumatic stress syndrome interferes with their success in school work.

In the early 1990s, the U.S. Civil Rights Commission reported that only a small proportion of limited-English-proficiency Asian American students had teachers who spoke their native languages, in spite of the legal obligation of the public schools to help these students develop English proficiency in supportive settings. In spite of media stories to the contrary, recent immigrants not proficient in English frequently have low grades and relatively high dropout rates. A study of San Diego high-school students found that Vietnamese, Cambodian, and Pacific Islander students had higher dropout rates than white students.[136]

A 1997 report of the non-profit organization Asian-American/Pacific Islanders in Philanthropy showed that 1.2 percent of the teachers in U.S. schools were Asian American. Yet 3.2 percent of the children in these same schools were Asian American. The report noted that these children have often faced school authorities who showed little concern for their language problems or for the hostility they receive from non-Asian children.[137]

Many public schools have been settings for substantial white hostility and violence against Asian Americans. One 1990s study quoted a female Chinese immigrant high-school student:

> Before I came to America I had a beautiful dream about this country. At that time I didn't know the first word I learned in this country would be a dirty word. American students always picked on us, frightened us, made fun of us, and laughed at our English. They broke our lockers, threw food on us in cafeteria, said dirty words to us, pushed us on the campus. Many times they shouted at me, "Get out of here, you Chink, go back to your country." Many times they pushed me and yell on me. I've been pushed, I had gum thrown on my hair. I've been hit by stones.[138]

Educational Attainment

As a group Asian Americans have a substantially higher educational level than the U.S. population as a whole. They are almost twice as likely to have a college degree as the average American.[139] This figure is misleading, however, because of the wide variations *between* the various Asian American groups as well as *within* each group. Using data from the 1990 census for persons over twenty-four years of age, we can compare the educational attainment of the five Asian American groups considered in this chapter with that of white Americans and with the total population (Table 12–4).[140]

Vietnamese Americans ranked the lowest among the Asian American groups in educational attainment. This was the only Asian American group to fall below the national percentage for college completion. While Chinese Americans fell

TABLE 12–4   Educational Attainment by Ethnic Group

	Chinese American	Filipino American	Korean American	Vietnamese American	Asian-Indian American	White American	Total Population
Less than 5 years of school completed	9.4%	4.2%	4.6%	11.4%	3.8%	1.3%	2.7%
High-school graduate or more	73.6%	82.6%	80.2%	61.2%	84.7%	79.1%	75.2%
Bachelor's degree or more	40.7%	39.3%	34.5%	17.4%	58.1%	22.0%	20.3%

slightly below the national percentage in terms of high-school graduation, the rate at which this group completed college was double the national rate. Asian-Indian and Filipino Americans are much more likely to have graduated from college than the general population. These data also show a wide variation *within* Asian American groups. The proportion with less than a fifth-grade education is higher for all Asian American groups than for the total population. Other research confirms this internal variation. One mid-1980s study in southern California found that Vietnamese Americans constituted a high proportion of the straight-A students, but a somewhat higher proportion of Vietnamese than of white students also dropped out of high school.[141]

The reasons for Asian American success in education have been the subject of considerable public discussion. Some observers say the success is rooted in a traditional reverence for learning in Asian cultures or the strong support of family. For example, one national poll of Asian-Indian high-school seniors conducted by the Educational Testing Service reported that every single student said their parents had pressed them to secure a college degree. Such high expectations are found among parents in other Asian American groups as well.[142] In assessing educational success, other analysts point to those Asian Americans who have learned English at a young age and argue that they have gained significant educational benefits from their bilingualism. In addition, the aggressive pursuit of education is used as a weapon against the prejudices of non-Asian Americans; the educational effort has become part of an oppositional culture in which education is seen as part of family rather than individual achievement.

Asian Americans often have access to educational institutions, such as those in California, that facilitate economic and educational mobility better than the schools attended by, for example, many black students in the southern states. Even though most Asian American students reside in large metropolitan areas, they are usually not segregated from the mainstream of the educational system like other students of color. Asian American students, unlike most black and Latino students, are often integrated into better-funded public schools with white student majorities.

Yet discrimination in the job market has kept Asian Americans from achieving the economic success that they might have expected based on their educational achievements. "Based on a fairness model, the success image of Asian Americans is a myth."[143]

Controversy in Higher Education

Asian Americans, who make up about 2 percent of the college-age population, today account for more than 10 percent of the first-year classes at the nation's top universities. In spite of this apparent success Asian American leaders have argued that discrimination against students persists. Some colleges have apparently imposed measures to reduce their numbers. For example, Ivy League universities began admitting a large percentage of Asian American applicants in the mid-1970s, but the acceptance rates often dropped as the number of Asian American applications increased. For example, at Yale, the acceptance rate for Asian Americans fell from 39 percent to 17 percent between 1977 and 1986.[144] Critics have accused some universities of using such nonacademic pretexts as lack of alumni parents and the necessity for a regional distribution to exclude some Asian American students.

The proportion of Asian Americans among the students admitted at Brown University rose from 2.6 percent for the class of 1979 to 14.8 percent for the class of 1993, although the proportion of Asian American applicants admitted fluctuated between 14 percent and 41 percent during this period. When the proportion of Asian applicants admitted dropped sharply between 1982 and 1983, Brown's Asian American Student Association voiced its concern to the administration. Investigators reported that the admissions staff had assigned comparatively low nonacademic ratings to Asian American applicants and had sought to hold steady the number of Asian American students admitted, even though their applicant pool had more than tripled between 1979 and 1983. As a result, the Brown administration took action to ensure that the percentage of qualified Asian American applicants admitted would not fall below the percentage of qualified non-Asian applicants admitted.[145]

Between 1983 and 1992, the proportion of Asian American students at Harvard University increased from 5.5 percent to 14.2 percent. However, in each of these years the admissions rate for Asian Americans, which fluctuated between 11 percent and 15 percent, was lower than Harvard's admissions rate for non-Asians. An investigation found the major cause of this disparity to be the special preference given to children of (mostly white) alumni and to recruited athletes. Alumni preferences are recognized as legal under Title VI of the Civil Rights Act of 1964. This practice puts Asian Americans and other groups without alumni parents at a disadvantage.[146]

ASSIMILATION FOR ASIAN AMERICANS?

Assimilation Views

Milton Gordon has argued that a theory of assimilation is applicable to a wide range of ethnic and racial groups. However, Gordon has not explicitly applied the stages of his assimilation scheme to Asian American groups, groups whom other assimilation-oriented analysts have viewed as well on their way to integration at the dominant-culture level in terms of language and at the secondary–structural level in terms of job placement. Yet most Asian American groups examined in this chapter appear to have achieved modest integration with whites at the primary-group and marriage levels. Substantial acculturation in language and dominant-culture values has taken place, but assimilation at the other levels has come slowly. Still, assimilation-oriented analysts tend to be optimistic about the full assimilation of Asian Americans, including the trend toward a large middle class among these groups.

Some optimistic assimilation-oriented analysts have underscored Asian American progress in terms of cultural and economic integration. Sociologist Talcott Parsons argued that racial and ethnic inclusion is a basic process in U.S. society; one aspect of this process is the increasing inclusion of various racial and ethnic groups in the institutions of the society. Analysts such as Thomas Sowell and Nathan Glazer have long argued that traditional discrimination is collapsing and that assimilation of non-European Americans, such as Asians, into the dominant institutions is well underway. Some recent media analysts of Asian Americans have argued in a similar vein: "with a command of English, light brown skin, and Spanish-sounding names, Filipinos have few problems assimilating into American society," asserted James T. Madore, a reporter for the *Christian Science Monitor*.[147] It is true that Filipino immigrants find the United States a reasonably comfortable point of destination because they have been influenced by the somewhat Americanized culture of their own country, which was a U.S. colony for a half-century. Even today English is the language used in most schools in the Philippines. Yet the ease of Filipino and other Asian adaptation can easily be exaggerated, as the discrimination we have discussed indicates.

Numerous assimilation scholars and other analysts see not only Japanese Americans but also other Asian Americans as "model minorities." In their view, a non-European group has succeeded when it attains certain economic privileges comparable to or superior to those of the dominant white group, attainments measured by quantitative socioeconomic indicators such as education, occupation, and income. This message is used by some white analysts to affirm that the United States is a just and fair society in which any subordinate group can succeed if its members are willing to work hard enough. As a result, some analysts argue that government programs such as affirmative action are counterproductive and should be eradicated.[148] The National Asian Pacific Bar Association (NAPBA) opposed Supreme Court nominee Clarence Thomas at the 1991 Senate confirmation hearings, challenging Thomas's publicly asserted image of Asian–Pacific Americans as model minorities. Judge Thomas had argued that Asian–Pacific Americans "transcended the ravages caused even by harsh legal and social discrimination" and should not be the beneficiaries of affirmative action because they are "overrepresented in key institutions." In contrast, the NAPBA pointed out the actual conditions of racial hostility and discrimination faced by Asian Americans. Affirmative action programs, particularly in states like California, have been critical to the employment of Asian American workers in historically white job categories.[149]

Kitano and Daniels have applied a version of the assimilation model to Asian Americans. They have developed a model of assimilation and "ethnic identity" that distinguishes three major types of adaptation: (1) high assimilation, low ethnic identity; (2) high assimilation, high ethnic identity; and (3) low assimilation, high ethnic identity. In their view Asian Americans who fall into the category of high assimilation and low ethnic identity are more "core American" than Asian. Their language, lifestyle, and expectations are more like those of white Americans, and their traditional culture and language are mostly forgotten. High rates of marriage to non-Asians occur in this group. While a significant proportion of Japanese Americans seem to fall into this category of assimilation, the proportions for the groups examined in this chapter appear to be smaller.

Those Asian Americans in the category of high assimilation and high group identity differ from those in the previous category by retaining a strong group identity. They move easily in and out of both cultures, and their friendship patterns and interests reflect a bicultural perspective. They tend to be comfortable with their group identity, and they question persisting prejudice and discrimination. A significant proportion of Filipino and Asian-Indian Americans appear to fall into this category of adaptation. For example, Marica Mogelonsky suggests that Asian-Indian children are "straddling two cultures." Most speak English well and are strongly influenced by American pop music and movies, yet also watch Indian movies and usually "follow the ways of their elders when it comes to such traditions as marriage and child-rearing." In the United States a number of Asian-Indian magazines feature and thus help perpetuate Indian culture. Most young people seem to have a strong sense of their racial-ethnic identity.[150]

Asian Americans in the third major category, low assimilation and high group identity, are often recent immigrants or those who have spent most of their lives in traditional enclaves in cities. Most have attained some level of adaptation to the dominant culture, but they prefer their own communities. These individuals tend to form friendship and marriage bonds within their own group.[151] An assimilation analyst might argue that most recent Korean and Vietnamese immigrants fall into this category. A significant proportion of recent Filipino and Chinese immigrants also appear to be modestly assimilated at the cultural level but firmly rooted culturally and socially in their own communities. Takaki has noted that Korean, Chinese, and Vietnamese immigrants over the last three decades "have concentrated their economic resources in their own ethnic communities."[152]

A 1989 survey of Vietnamese American adults in Orange County found that the Vietnamese language was still dominant in 83 percent of households. Two-thirds said that their families remained strongly Vietnamese in customs and traditions, and most of the rest said they were somewhat involved in Vietnamese culture. There is dependence on a type of oppositional culture in the face of white antagonism. Three-fourths reported regular contact with relatives and friends in Vietnam; six in ten reported spending their dollars in Vietnamese businesses.[153] But research by Alden Roberts and Paul Starr found "a slow change toward a more Americanized reference group and away from traditional Vietnamese beliefs and values" among Vietnamese refugees as a group. Still, these researchers also found that refugees with close Vietnamese friends were more likely to maintain Vietnamese customs and thus assimilate more slowly.[154]

Today, Vietnamese Americans are mostly first-generation immigrants, and what the future holds in terms of further assimilation is not clear. Among the respondents to the 1989 Orange County survey, one-third said that the greatest community need was more English classes—the largest percentage for any community need listed. These Vietnamese Americans express a strong desire for mastering English in order to acculturate and advance economically. Moreover, nearly half the adults interviewed did not expect their children to marry a Vietnamese American.[155]

Most Korean immigrants seem committed to their language, culture, and relatives and have built strong institutions within their own communities. For example, in the "Koreatown" area of Los Angeles, Korean Americans have created many important community institutions, including newspapers, schools, a symphony orchestra, and many Korean Christian churches.[156] Religion has sometimes facilitated the adjustment of Koreans in the United States. Korea has one of the largest Protestant populations of any Asian nation, and many Korean immigrants come to this country as Christians. These immigrants have established new churches here. For example, in Chicago in the early 1980s, Korean Americans supported as many as 100 Christian churches, which typically combined Western practices with Korean ceremonies and Korean-language services.[157]

Korean Americans who operate businesses in non-Korean areas of large cities such as Los Angeles come into contact with non-Asians on a daily basis. Their children are likely to have much contact with white children in public schools. Over time this interaction may facilitate greater assimilation to the dominant culture and institutions, as it has for Japanese Americans.

A recent study by Karen Pyke examined the views that seventy-three children of Korean and Vietnamese immigrants have of their family life. Most of these respondents accepted the dominant U.S. conception of the "normal" family as their framework for understanding their own families. For example, they criticized their parents as too strict or emotionally distant and thought they should be more like the "normal" family. In this sense, they were assimilating the dominant view of family styles. However, when they discussed plans for taking care of their parents in later life, they expressed strong traditional Korean and Vietnamese values, giving positive descriptions of their parents' family practices. In this sense, they held onto important filial values drawn from their parents' culture of origin. For these children of Asian immigrants the adaptation pattern is one that blends aspects of the culture of origin with aspects of the dominant U.S. culture, as might be predicted from Greeley's ethnogenesis perspective.[158]

Many Asian-Indian Americans are well integrated into the dominant culture. Families often reside in predominantly white neighborhoods, and children spend a lot of time with white teachers and students. The majority of Asian-Indian adults work in predominantly white work or business settings. Most Asian-Indian Americans have adopted certain aspects of the core culture. Still, most Asian-

Indian families also maintain essential aspects of their traditional Indian culture. For example, they have built numerous temples in U.S. cities, and the majority maintain traditional customs and marriages within the group. They are both highly assimilated and highly Indian, depending on the dimensions of assimilation that one accents.

One sign of the generally slower overall assimilation of several Asian–Pacific groups in this chapter, compared with the assimilation rate for Japanese Americans, may be their lower out-marriage rates. For Japanese Americans out-marriage rates are high—between 30 and 50 percent for the younger generations—with most of these marriages involving whites. Although the rates have been lower for the groups in this chapter, intermarriage between Asian and white Americans is increasing. In California in 1980, the rate of marriage to whites was 24 percent for Filipinos, 19 percent for Koreans, 15 percent for Vietnamese, and 14 percent for Chinese.[159] In 1991 the rate of marriage to whites for all Asian American groups taken together was estimated to be about 17 percent, well above the 3 percent rate for African Americans but still much lower than the rate for third-generation Japanese Americans.[160]

Recently, Nazli Kibria has used the ethnogenesis model in assessing the adaptations of certain Asian American groups to each other. In her research on second generation middle-class Chinese and Korean Americans she has found what she calls a Pan-Asian ethnogenesis. Members of each second generation group are developing a sense of a shared Asian American identity, in addition to their own group identities. The construction of this new Asian American identity is a "process that involves recognition of the shared personal experiences and orientations of Asian-origin persons, including that of being racially labelled as Asian by the dominant society, of growing up in an Asian home, and of adhering to the Asian values of an emphasis on family, education, hard work and respect for elders."[161] Note that Kibria's data reveal the important role that being defined as racially different plays in the shaping of this new Asian American identity.

Some Questions from a Power–Conflict Perspective

Power–conflict analysts of Asian Americans reject the optimistic assimilationist perspectives, including the model minorities image. They argue that the model minority view exaggerates Asian Americans' progress and downplays the problems of racist prejudice and discrimination.[162] As we noted in the chapter on Japanese Americans, the model minority image of Asian groups was created not by those groups but by outsiders. In response to black and Latino American protesting, some whites broadcast this image to suggest that non-European groups could achieve the American dream not by protesting discrimination but simply by working as hard as Asian Americans. For example, in the 1960s the term *model minority* was used in a speech by Democratic politician Hubert Humphrey at a Chinese American high school, during which Humphrey praised Chinese Americans for *not* rioting and demonstrating. An article in *U.S. News & World Report* entitled "Success Story of One Minority Group in U.S." compared Chinese and African Americans. The tone of the article was negative toward African Americans: In praising the hard work, thrift, and morality of Chinese Americans, the article clearly implied that if black Americans possessed these virtues it would not be necessary to spend "hundreds of billions [of dollars] to uplift" them. The article omitted any mention of the widespread discrimination still being suffered by African Americans. The model minority stereotype is pervasive today, but it obscures the problems and needs of many poor Asian Americans. Recent studies have shown that many Southeast Asian immigrants, especially those from rural backgrounds with little education, have experienced severe economic strain in the 1980s and 1990s.[163]

Given the variation in assimilation to U.S. society from one Asian group or subgroup to the next, the segmented assimilation view of analysts such as Min Zhou seems appropriate for this case. Asian groups with greater family and group resources, such as many Korean immigrants, generally have a different experience adapting to U.S. society than those with fewer resources, such as many Vietnamese or Mexican immigrants.[164]

Thus, a power–conflict analyst might point out that the secondary–structural integration of many Asian Americans into the U.S. economy is not as untroubled as some assimilation analysts suggest. Many still suffer discrimination in employment and educational institutions. We have noted the informal quotas used to reduce Asian American participation in some universities. Once in the universities many report an array of blatant and subtle barriers that are thrown in their paths by white students, faculty, or administrators. In addition, many Asian Americans who have excelled in the U.S. educational system are finding employment discrimination barriers once they finish school. For many, the only jobs available are not as good as what their credentials should have secured them. Asian Americans tend to excel in their college studies, but many receive a lower rate of return on their investment in higher education than whites do.[165] Moreover, although many Asian Americans are hired by major companies, most find that promotions to upper management are very unlikely.[166]

Assimilation analysts often do not discuss the problem of anti-Asian violence. Kitano and Daniels's approach to assimilation, for example, indicates the complexity in patterns of adaptation, which depend on length of stay in the United States and strength of group identity. But it does not pay sufficient attention to such external factors as continuing racial prejudice and discrimination, which handicap Asian Americans and affect long-term assimilation probabilities, particularly in powerful institutions. Many non-Asian Americans seem to view Asian Americans in racial terms or as non-American foreigners. We have seen that some Asian Americans have been the victims of vicious violence, such as the killing of Vincent Chin and the attack on Vietnamese Americans by whites in Texas and on Asian-Indian Americans by whites in New Jersey. Asian-bashing has increased in the 1990s. Asian Americans had to struggle to protect their civil rights and growing political power. In the spring of 1992, the Asian American Legal Defense Fund had to fight for an extension of the 1965 Voting Rights Act in order to protect the right of non-English speakers to bilingual election materials. Several white senators argued that Asian American voters did not need such protection, even though the Senate itself included no Asian Americans from mainland states. In addition, in 1997 the appointment of Bill Lann Lee, a brilliant Chinese American lawyer, as assistant attorney general was killed by white Republican senators who disagreed with his views on affirmative action. From the perspective of most Asian Americans, the struggle over power and resources goes on, and full inclusion in U.S. society is a long way from being realized. For that reason numerous Pan-Asian organizations fighting against anti-Asian racism and for Asian American rights have been formed in recent years.[167]

SUMMARY

Korean, Filipino, Asian-Indian, and Vietnamese Americans—and the newest Chinese Americans—are among the most recent of the immigrant additions to the bubbling cauldron. Yet, as with immigrants before them, they have been the targets of much prejudice and hostility, and not a little violence. In general, their educational success has been so dramatic that they have often been stereotyped, like the Japanese Americans, as "model minorities." Some whites who portray Asian Americans in this way have had the ulterior motive of criticizing certain non-Asian groups, such as African and Latino Americans, for their alleged deficiencies. Moreover, assimilation-oriented social scientists have been inclined to accent Asian American progress in the U.S. economy but to downplay the persisting problems of racial discrimination.

We have documented the problems that Asian Americans confront today. From a power–conflict perspective, an Asian American group has not achieved success until it can participate fully in the mainstream of the economy, politics, and society without paying higher material or psychological costs than the dominant group. No Asian American group has attained that comfortable equality with the oldest white immigrant groups, such as English Americans. As physically and racially distinguished groups, Asian Americans have remained disadvantaged and have experienced some economic problems, recurrent hostility and discrimination, and only modest gains in political power.[168]

During the 1980s and 1990s, as Daniels has emphasized, "immigration took up a central position on the American social agenda" and there was much talk about regaining "control of U.S. borders."[169] In 1981, Congress set up a Select Commission on Immigration and Refugee Policy to investigate the so-called "immigration crisis." The commission presented an ambiguous set of recommendations, including on the one hand a continuing liberal policy on immigration and on the other hand strict border control to reduce illegal immigration. In earlier chapters we have examined the restrictive immigration legislation that was passed in the 1980s and 1990s. Much of the current white opposition to immigration goes beyond the question of immigrants taking jobs to the issue of racial characteristics, since most recent immigrants have been Asian and Latin American. Recent Asian immigrants have often been the victims of anti-Asian stereotyping, much of it suggesting they are a new "yellow peril." They have also suffered from anti-Japan sentiment among some non-Asian Americans.

However, it is the hard work and vigor of these new immigrants, like those of earlier immigrants, that have helped to make the United States a great nation. Nathan Glazer has spoken of the United States as being "a permanently unfinished country."[170] It is the new-immigrant dimension of the "unfinishedness" that has made this nation capable time and again of surging out of economic or social stagnation into new development and enhanced creativity.

CHAPTER 13

The Future of Racial and Ethnic Relations in the United States

INTRODUCTION

U.S. society is currently undergoing important changes in its racial and ethnic composition. The challenges and conflicts brought about by these changes will continue for the next several decades. Among these are challenges to white American domination of U.S. society in terms of its population composition and also in terms of its power and resources. The proportion of whites in the U.S. population is decreasing. Whites currently are a numerical minority in four of the five largest cities, including New York, Los Angeles, and Chicago. In addition, whites are a minority of the population in larger areas such as the states of Hawaii and New Mexico and the southern parts of Florida, Texas, and California. If immigration and birth rates continue near current levels, around the year 2002 whites will be a minority of California's population; about 2010 they will constitute a minority of the Texas population. Between about 2015 and 2040, moreover, whites will become a minority of the populations of Arizona, New York, Nevada, Florida, New Jersey, Maryland, and probably other states as well. According to recent Census Bureau projections, in the year 2050 the U.S. population will be about 383 million; just under half will be Americans of color.[1]

Somewhere around the year 2060 it seems likely that white Americans will become a minority of the U.S. population. This demographic shift is distinctive and significant, for whites have not been a minority of the North American population since perhaps the 1700s. Unfortunately, however, much private and public discussion of these demographic changes, especially among Americans of European descent, has a fearful or alarmist tone. Many white Americans seem to have a deep concern about non-European challenges to the dominant Euro-American culture. For example, Patrick Buchanan, a recent contender for the Republican presidential nomination, has expressed the concerns of many whites about a nation no longer predominantly white or Western. Buchanan has asserted that "Our Judeo-Christian values are going to be preserved and our Western heritage is going to be handed down to future generations and not dumped on some landfill called multiculturalism."[2] Variations on this view have been expressed by liberal analysts as well. The distinguished historian Arthur Schlesinger, Jr., has written about a new multiculturalism that he sees as dominating all levels of U.S. education. This is not good in his view, for it involves "an astonishing repudiation" of the idea of "a unifying American identity." He fears the great "assault on the Western tradition" by multiculturalism, which he also terms "tribalism."[3] Many white analysts see aggressive efforts to create a multiracial democracy whose core culture is no longer predominantly European in its character as disturbing challenges to white European values and interests that they believe must be preserved.

A NATION OF IMMIGRANTS

The United States has always been a *nation of immigrants*. Recurring immigration is its uniqueness and its great strength. Many millions of immigrants have come to these shores from all corners of the globe, in numbers and diversity unparalleled in the rest of the world. Dozens of languages, scores of cultures, a great diversity of resources, and an array of physical characteristics have characterized these millions of immigrants. This diversity can be seen in something as simple as the array of Asian, African, European, Middle Eastern, Asian-Indian, and South American restaurants in large cities, or something as complex as voting patterns in California and debates over multicultural education in the public schools.

In the last U.S. Census, the following countries were checked off by at least 1 percent of Americans as countries of national origin:[4]

Canada	Italy	Poland
England and Wales	Mexico	Russia
France	Netherlands	Scotland
Germany	Norway	Sweden
Ireland		

Dozens of other countries of ancestry were represented in proportions of less than 1 percent. As this list shows, the greatest infusions of immigrants to this country originated in Mexico and certain areas of Europe, particularly Great Britain and the rest of northern Europe. Conspicuously absent from the list are countries in the Middle East and Asia. In addition, we should note that many Americans—far more than one percent—indicated that their ancestors originated in the continent of Africa. For most of these, however, the particular point of origin on that continent is not known because of the brutal conditions of the forced migration from Africa.

The countries of ancestry represented in the U.S. population, as well as the total number of immigrants from each, have been shaped by the distinctive economic and political conditions that characterized the United States and the sending countries in particular historical periods. The economic and political situations in the immigrants' homelands were often distressing or inhospitable to personal and family development. During boom times when many low-wage jobs were available, the U.S. economy attracted poor immigrants such as the Irish, the Jews, the Koreans, and the Italians—all studied in this book. Most came more or less voluntarily. Only the Africans came in chains.

In thinking about ancestry and migration patterns, one must keep in mind that numerous Native American nations were already present in what would later be named North America when the strangers from many distant shores arrived. The ancestors of contemporary Native Americans had migrated to these shores from Asia thousands of years before the first Europeans and Africans stepped off their boats. Immigration from Europe brought much oppression and loss to Native Americans.

Immigration must be analyzed within the relevant economic and political contexts. Political actions by the colonial and U.S. governments have helped determine immigration patterns. For example, European Americans, who have controlled the major institutions and the government, have had the power to launch military invasions overseas. These military interventions sometimes spurred immigration to the United States. Late-nineteenth-century U.S. imperialism in the Philippines and Puerto Rico shaped immigration to the United States. White Protestant leaders have also used restrictive, often discriminatory immigration laws to control migration according to their racial and ethnic prejudices. As an article in a major literary magazine noted in 1914: "Immigrants who came earlier and their descendants have always tried to keep this country for those who were already here and for their kinfolk."[5] The Chinese Exclusion Act (1882) and restrictive national-origin quotas in the 1924 Immigration Act guaranteed that by the late twentieth century the population mix of the United States would include fewer Americans from Asia or southern and eastern Europe than would otherwise have been the case. The 1924 law sharply reduced the number of Catholic immigrants from Italy and Poland and the number of Jews from eastern Europe. As a result, the United States is today overwhelmingly Protestant; only one-fourth of the population is Catholic or Jewish. Asian Americans constitute less than 3 percent of the total U.S. population.[6] It is ironic that the anti-immigrant "nativists" in one period have been the descendants of immigrants of a previous period. Only the Native Americans can accurately claim that they are the real natives and that all others are intruders.

Beginning in 1965 exclusionary racial or national-origin quotas in U.S. immigration laws were replaced with limits on the number of immigrants allowed to enter the United States from any one country. Still, both the 1986 Immigration Reform and Control Act and 1990 Immigration Act can be viewed as reflecting dominant-group concerns about immigration. The 1986 act was intended to limit the number of immigrants from south of the U.S. border, particularly from Mexico. As we have seen in Chapter 9, Latino and other Americans are troubled by several provisions of that act, including intrusive governmental documentation of legal work status and sanctions for businesses that employ undocumented aliens.

The 1990 Immigration Act set the annual limit of all immigrants at 700,000 for the early 1990s and 675,000 after 1994. This limit most affects immigrants from those countries, such as certain Asian countries, in which many people now wish to enter the United States and contrasts with the generally unlimited immigration allowed before about 1910, when most potential immigrants were European. The 1990 act established several visa categories, the largest of which is reserved for family members of legal U.S. residents in order to facilitate family reunification. The 140,000 employment-based visas are mostly reserved for highly skilled workers; visas for unskilled workers are virtually unavailable. The act designated a special category of 40,000 visas to provide legalization for certain illegal immigrants from 34 (mostly European) countries and set aside 10,000 visas for wealthy immigrants willing to invest at least $1 million to create jobs in the United States.[7]

In recent years, immigration and immigration laws have been widely debated in Congress and by the public. Many native-born (especially white) business leaders and politicians have questioned the character and values of the Latinos and Asians who constitute the majority of recent newcomers. Some native-born Americans today doubt that the United States can absorb, economically or politically, even the legally permitted number of new immigrants. Some also worry that current immigrants are a serious threat to the jobs of those already here, especially during recessions, and that they are likely to become public charges. (These arguments are similar to those made by opponents of immigration in the late nineteenth and early twentieth centuries against European immigrants.) The impact of immigrant children on public school systems is of concern to many in states—particularly California, New York, Florida, and Texas—that are receiving a large proportion of today's immigrants.

One nationwide poll found that three-fourths of adult Americans favor strict limitations on immigration to the United States. Although two-thirds believed that immigrants who have come in the past ten to fifteen years are hardworking and productive citizens, nearly two-thirds also felt that these immigrants "take jobs away from Americans."[8] Yet most research studies have shown that immigrants do not generally take away more jobs than they create. Indeed, immigrants' presence creates new demands for housing and other commodities, and they often take unpleasant or low-paid jobs that most native-born Americans will not do. Drawing on several studies showing that immigrants actually create more jobs than they take, a 1990 report of the Council of Economic Advisors concluded that the low-wage jobs "taken by immigrants in years past have . . . increased employment and income for the population as a whole."[9]

However, the impact of job competition from immigrants is not evenly felt. Native-born, lower-wage workers are hurt more than better-off Americans because immigrants are often hired for lower-wage jobs. (Numerous defenders of continuing immigration suggest that government should deal with the negative job consequences of immigration.) Surprisingly, perhaps, it is often those whites who are unlikely to suffer serious job competition from immigrants that are the strongest supporters of, if not the leaders of, anti-immigrant campaigns.[10]

In 1994, the U.S. Commission on Immigration Reform, which was established to advise Congress on immigration reforms, issued a report asking Congress to police the borders and worksites more vigorously and to establish a computerized citizen identification system for the purpose of decreasing the number of undocumented immigrants working in the United States. The Commission also asked that these immigrants be barred from public services except in emergencies, a provision that was part of California's Proposition 187.[11]

Over the last decade the growing misinformation about and hostility toward immigrants, both those who are legal and those who are not, have too seldom been countered by educators and public officials willing to speak out effectively on the truth about immigration. Contrary to public belief recent census data indicate that the new immigration from Asia and Latin America is not fueling a great population expansion in the United States. The 1980s saw a population increase of about 10 percent, the second-lowest rate of increase for any decade in U.S. history. Moreover, the ratio of immigrants to native-born population is much lower today than in earlier decades of the twentieth century. Today, the United States has not only a smaller percentage of foreign-born than it had in the 1920s but also a smaller percentage of foreign-born than several European nations. Given its long history of successful absorption of immigrants and its geographical size, the United States is not likely to be overwhelmed by the new non-European immigrants.

In contrast to opponents of current immigration levels, some social analysts and demographers have argued that immigrants make mostly positive contributions to this country: As a group immigrants are "upwardly mobile, ambitious, saving; they have traditional values, care about their children, all that sort of stuff. They've done something very dramatic to upgrade themselves."[12] Immigrants are generally hardworking and honest and seek to make a good life for themselves and their families. Data from the 1990 Census on immigrants' financial status underscore this point. Even though the median family income of the foreign-born Americans was well below that of native-born Americans, the per capita income of the foreign-born was higher than that of the native-born, reflecting in part a greater number of workers per family among the foreign born. In addition, incomes rise dramatically with length of residence in the United States. The foreign-born who entered the country prior to 1980 had more than twice the per capita income, a 45 percent higher median family income, and less than half the poverty rate of the newer arrivals. The median family income of pre-1980 immigrants was even slightly higher than that of the native born.[13]

Implicit in public discussions of restricting immigrants to the United States is a concern that the new immigrants—who are now mostly from Asia and Latin America—are not compatible with, or assimilable to, a culture and institutions that have been substantially European American in orientation. For more than a century many opponents of immigration have worried about new immigrants and their physical (and thus racial) characteristics. For a century the agenda of most anti-immigration groups has been the protection of the dominant European American culture and the structural domination of new immigrants by prior immigrant groups. Today, as in the past, many anti-immigrant groups believe that the U.S. experiment as a "nation of immigrants" should be stopped. Strong opposition to this view comes from Americans whose pro-immigration sentiments tap the pluralistic values that are also part of U.S. history.

The United States is still seen overseas as a "golden land"—a land of opportunity and freedom for the poor and oppressed peoples of the world. Recent immigrants, like their predecessors from Europe, generally bring intelligence, hard work, and cultural invigoration to the United States. A deeper understanding of these contributions and the recognition that most Americans are immigrants or the descendants of immigrants might make native-born Americans more accepting of subsequent streams of immigrants to U.S. shores.

THE MELTING POT: EARLY IMAGES
OF IMMIGRANT INCORPORATION

No consensus has yet been reached as to how immigrants, once ashore, are to be incorporated into the society. Pressures for assimilation are often matched by immigrants' desire to maintain their own cultures and values. For nearly a century the most prominent image of the incorporation of immigrants has been that of the "melting pot." In the early 1900s, playwright Israel Zangwill made an influential statement of this optimistic idea in *The Melting Pot*, in which a struggling Russian immigrant argued:

> America is God's Crucible, the great Melting-Pot where all races of Europe are melting and re-forming! Here you stand, good folks, think I, when I see them at Ellis Island, here you stand in your fifty groups, with your fifty languages and histories, and your fifty blood hatreds and rivalries. But you won't be long like that, brothers, for these are the fires of God. . . . A fig for your feuds and vendettas! Germans and Frenchmen, Irishmen and Englishmen, Jews and Russians—into the Crucible with you all! God is making the American.[14]

Zangwill's idealistic image of a crucible that melts fifty divergent groups to form a truly new "American blend" symbolizes a mutual adaptation process in which old and new groups freely blend together on a more or less equal basis. Yet actual intergroup adaptation has often involved more conflict than Zangwill envisioned. Also conspicuously absent from this melting pot image are Americans of color, such as African, Asian, Latino, and Native Americans.

Assimilation theorists such as Milton Gordon (see Chapter 2) argue that in practice the U.S. melting pot has diverged greatly from Zangwill's ideal. Immigrant adaptation has typically been in the direction of Anglo-conformity as those in each new stream have given up much of their cultural heritage for the dominant Anglo-Protestant culture. Recall Gordon's argument: "If there is anything in American life which can be described as an overall American culture which serves as a reference point for immigrants and their children, it can best be described, it seems to us, as the middle-class cultural patterns of, largely, white Protestant, Anglo-Saxon origins."[15]

CONTEMPORARY CULTURAL DIVERSITY ISSUES

In recent years the melting pot imagery has again become common. Modern-day assimilationists have expressed concern over the racial and ethnic groups formed by recent immigrants from Asia and Latin America. Popular and scholarly analysts debate the meaning of the melting pot image for the United States today. These debates have reached colleges and universities, corporate boardrooms, the U.S. Congress, and the White House. President Bill Clinton set up a White House advisory panel in 1997–1998 to hold hearings across the nation on how to preserve "One America." Recent discussions are centered in terms such as *multiculturalism* and *cultural diversity*—terms that stress the importance of respecting the many racial and ethnic groups and subcultures that have contributed to U.S. development, especially the contributions of non-European groups.

Multiculturalism is a variation of the cultural pluralism perspective. It emerged out of the racial and ethnic protest movements of the 1960s, and has spread across the United States. There are variations in multicultural perspectives. Some U.S. colleges and universities, as well as many public and private elementary and secondary schools, have developed a few multicultural courses and study programs in order to give voice to the people of color (and sometimes white women) who have done much of the hard work that built U.S. society. Since the late 1980s, colleges and universities from Stanford University and the University of California at Irvine to the University of Florida and Tufts University have implemented new B.A. requirements that have included a few courses that focus on some aspects of cultural diversity. Multicultural programs, usually modest in scope, have also been implemented at many public schools. Teachers at one high school in Brooklyn's predominantly white Bensonhurst section, where a black man shopping for a used car was brazenly killed in 1989 by a mob of whites, pioneered a successful multicultural class that was soon added to the curriculum in other high schools. Their goal was to shatter racial and ethnic stereotypes and provide students with an opportunity to discuss the causes of intergroup strife.[16] Publishers and voluntary organizations have made multicultural teaching materials more readily available to colleges and public schools. The Southern Poverty Law Center in Montgomery, Alabama, has developed a program for public schools that includes a high-quality magazine, called *Teaching Tolerance*, and other curriculum materials for multicultural programs.

A strong version of multiculturalism has been enthusiastically embraced by numerous scholars and other Americans with roots in Africa, Asia, and Latin America. However, some scholars and analysts, mostly white Americans, have

Colleges in the United States draw students from various racial and ethnic backgrounds, many of whom are calling for courses that focus on cultural diversity.

viewed the stronger variants of multiculturalism as an attack on the dominant Euro-American culture and institutions. As we noted in the opening, in several books and speeches historian Arthur Schlesinger, Jr., has called the multiculturalism perspective a repudiation of the idea of the melting pot: "The contemporary ideal is not assimilation but ethnicity. We used to say *e pluribus unum*. Now we glorify *pluribus* and belittle *unum*. The melting pot yields to the Tower of Babel."[17]

Social scientists and popular writers who make such arguments usually reflect the "order theory" framework. These critics of an assertive multiculturalism, seemingly fearful of losing the centripetal forces of the Euro-American culture, argue that some type of Anglo-conformity is still the best assimilation model for non-European groups in the United States. Their "melting pot" is not so much a mutual blending of diverse groups as a melting of newcomers (and some older groups) into the dominant Euro-American (or British American) culture. While they often recognize some of the contributions of non-Europeans to U.S. culture, many critics of multiculturalism emphasize a version of the Anglo-conformity assimilation theory when they assert, for example, that the United States is founded on the Eurocentric philosophy of individualism, not on a philosophy of ethnic and racial pluralism. A Eurocentric bias is evident in Schlesinger's argument: "It is not that the Western cultures are superior to other cultures as much as it is, for better or worse—our culture."[18] He adds that "our public schools, in particular, have been along with the workplace a great agency of assimilation, a great means of transforming newcomers into Americans."[19]

The Western cultural bias frequently found in many U.S. schools and other institutions is seen not as problematic but rather as essential for the integration of diverse racial and ethnic groups into one workable societal whole. Eurocentric observers are concerned that non-Europeans, including those in recent immigrant groups, assimilate rapidly to the dominant culture in order to prevent a cultural and structural "Balkanization" of the United States. They worry that this country will not survive with a vibrant pluralism of racial and ethnic groups. As a result, they usually oppose the teaching of multiculturalism and the creation of most multicultural courses and programs in public schools, colleges, and universities. For example, Dinesh D'Souza, himself a recent immigrant from India, argues that multiculturalism represents an "academic and cultural revolution" on college campuses that is "revising the rules by which students are admitted to college, and by which they pay for college. It is changing what students learn in the class-room, and how they are taught." In his view even modest programs of multicul-turalism, which he stigmatizes as "illiberal education," represent a serious threat to education in the United States.[20]

However, some former critics have recently come to recognize that the coun-try has changed and that pluralism or multiculturalism is, or will soon become, the reality in many U.S. institutions. In his book *We are All Multiculturalists Now,* Nathan Glazer, once a strong critic, concedes that multiculturalism has become the reality, especially in education. Cultural differences are significant, and notice must be paid to this reality. Moreover, Glazer is less optimistic now about society's ability to bring progressive change for groups like African Americans. While he once saw African Americans as gradually becoming fully integrated into U.S. soci-ety following the example of early white immigrants, he now recognizes the small amount of progress in residential and school desegregation that has occurred for Americans of color. Taken as a whole, his analysis represents an acceptance of the gradual end of white European dominance in the United States, although, as he has done since the 1970s, he continues to argue against new government action to end persisting racial discrimination.[21]

Other analysts have responded that multiculturalism and cultural diversity programs provide a necessary corrective to the dominance of Euro-American cul-ture and thus need to be expanded in number and scope. Such programs protect those subcultures and values repressed or excluded by Euro-Americans in control of educational, economic, and political institutions. Multicultural studies, University of Delaware sociologist Margaret Andersen suggests, "have encour-aged us to look at traditionally excluded cultures and study them on their own terms rather than seeing them through the eyes of the dominant class." From this point of view multiculturalism is not separatist but rather encourages "people to see in plural ways, so that they are not seeing through the lens of any single cul-ture, but understanding the relationships of cultures to each other."[22] Analyses such as that of Schlesinger miss the fact that multicultural education is in tune with the changing demographic reality of the United States.

For many, multiculturalism provides a needed challenge to white (or white male) dominance in most U.S. institutions. Harvard literary critic Henry Louis Gates, an African American, has argued for setting aside the "antebellum aesthetic position" articulated by such authors as Schlesinger, an approach "where men were men and men were white, when scholar-critics were white men, and when women and persons of color were voiceless, faceless servants and laborers, pouring tea and filling brandy snifters in the boardrooms of old boys' clubs."[23]

Debates over multiculturalism and cultural diversity programs often involve more than the creation of a few new courses on racial and ethnic issues. The debate becomes most heated when it encompasses issues of white privilege and power and thus racial and ethnic inequalities. Some see multicultural courses as simply exposing students to diverse racial and ethnic cultures, but others also want the courses to analyze the oppressive stratification at the heart of U.S. racial and ethnic relations. This has been called by some "revolutionary multiculturalism." The latter concern is an issue of power and resource inequality and leads to questions of major social change. Some power–conflict analysts argue that multiculturalism should mean not only including the perspectives of nondominant groups but also scrutinizing and changing the core curricula in all college disciplines so that they "fairly represent the variegated nature of American culture."[24] From this power–conflict viewpoint multiculturalism also means changing the hierarchies of colleges and universities so that people of color (and white women) are adequately represented at all levels of the administrative chain of command and are an empowered presence in policy making on such matters as the admission and funding of students, hiring of administrators and faculty, the drafting of curricula, and the makeup of college investments.[25] Moreover, multiculturalism is viewed as not just an issue for colleges and universities, for it also should entail an alteration of the hierarchies of all private and public organizations, including corporations and government agencies, so that people of color (and white women) are substantially represented at all levels of decision-making.

EQUALITY AND A PLURALISTIC DEMOCRACY

An Egalitarian Society?

The equality and justice sought by subordinated racial and ethnic groups have been viewed in changing ways since 1776. The philosophy that "all men are created equal" articulated by the founders of this nation initially meant equality of social and political participation for white, European, Protestant, male immigrants and their male descendants, especially those with property. This limited equality of access to political institutions was certainly a dramatic and democratic step forward in an autocratic and feudalistic era, but it excluded such groups as women, African Americans, Native Americans, and to some extent Jewish and Catholic Americans.

Over the next two centuries, conceptions of equality would become more inclusive, so much so that numerous commentators have seen equality as an ideal whose driving force has been extraordinarily great in U.S. history and society. From this perspective the historical process has been a progressive egalitarianization of the U.S. social, economic, and political systems. The concept of equality has evolved to include equality of worth among individuals, equality of opportunity for all individuals, equality before the law (civil rights), and even "equality of results." Many scholars and popular analysts, as well as politicians and business leaders, have praised the egalitarian trend they see over the course of U.S. history. Over time poor and subordinated ethnic and racial groups have achieved greater equality in some or all of these categories. Between the early 1800s and the early 1900s, economic development and prosperity came dramatically to the United States, giving substantial opportunity to the many millions of white immigrants from Europe. Although they suffered discrimination, white ethnic Americans or their children eventually succeeded. From this optimistic perspective, the white ethnics soon "made it." Many assimilation analysts view non-European groups from the same perspective, arguing that these groups too are moving, albeit more slowly, toward full equality in the social, economic, and political institutions of this society.

Yet the rosy view of a society committed to "liberty and justice for all" is problematical. Substantial movement up the economic and political ladders did indeed come for most white ethnic groups. But an overly optimistic view ignores the great misery and discrimination that white ethnics endured, for a generation at least, as poorly paid laborers, servants, or peddlers in an exploitative economic system. In this book we have documented the capitalistic exploitation of workers such as Italian, Irish, and Jewish Americans. The racist immigration law that existed until 1965, restricting the entry of allegedly inferior (white) "races" from southern and eastern Europe, presented serious obstacles for immigrant families trying to reunite. White ethnics faced racist stereotyping for several decades; for some, such as Jewish and Italian Americans, the stereotyping persists, sometimes resulting in discrimination. Thus, in assessing the present scene one should not overlook the significant discrimination that still takes place for some white ethnics, particularly for Jewish Americans, who are still the target of occasional violence and of institutionalized discrimination, such as in elite white-Protestant clubs and in the executive suites of some corporations.

The optimistic picture of equality and freedom in the United States also glosses over the continuing subordination and widespread discrimination faced by Americans with roots outside of Europe. Indeed, Asian, African, Latino, and Native Americans have helped to force an emphasis on reducing discrimination and on expanded equality. Significant changes have been made in regard to formal legal rights and opportunities since the 1960s. Nonetheless, today's problems of discrimination are centered in the *informal* operation of our economic, social, educational, and political institutions, where prejudiced whites frequently discriminate against people of color, usually without fear of punishment under the law. All too often, U.S. civil rights laws go unenforced.

Racial Discrimination: The 1990s and Beyond

The early 1990s marked the 500th anniversary of the landing of Christopher Columbus in the Americas. In the United States many celebrations were planned. But as we have seen, the Quincentenary celebrations generated protests from many Americans, especially Native Americans, who worked hard to counter the traditional images of brave and beneficent European explorers "discovering" America. They showed how arrogant it was of Europeans to claim to "discover" a land that had already been occupied by millions of people for thousands of years. The European invasion benefited Europe, but it created major new problems for Native Americans, who were forced into a long and continuing struggle to maintain their lands, cultures, and institutions in the face of land theft, attempted genocide, and omnipresent discrimination.

"Liberty and justice for all" has bypassed the *original* Americans, who remain the forgotten Americans. As Native American leader LaDonna Harris has put it, "How do our children feel when they read the textbooks and they're not included? What does it do to their psyche?" Harris has emphasized the vital pluralism of the Native American tribes that survived white attempts to destroy them. Respect for this pluralism could help white Americans prepare for a future of diversity that seems to frighten many. "The browning of America is coming whether or not we like it. It's coming and we're not prepared for it, because we haven't incorporated it into our thinking."[26]

Asian Americans too have provided lessons in cultural pluralism. In the broad category of Asian Americans one finds many diverse groups, including Japanese Americans, who today must struggle with anti-Japanese (and thus anti-Asian) sentiment among some whites and others concerned and confused about job losses and economic restructuring in the United States. Some observers have noted that Japan has replaced the former Soviet Union as the latest "enemy" of the United States, an enemy seen by many white workers as responsible for U.S. economic decline. Yet this "Japan loathing" has targeted not only the country but also the character and color of a people, a racist aspect of U.S. ethnocentrism that did not characterize, for example, fear of the former Soviet Union.[27]

Anti-Asian sentiment has recently generated violence by whites against Asian Americans in cities across the nation. We have noted the report of the U.S. Commission on Civil Rights citing the killing in Detroit of Vincent Chin by two white auto workers who thought him to be Japanese, and the murders of five Indochinese children at a Stockton, California, school in 1989 by a white man who harbored racial hatred.[28] "Liberty and justice" for Asian Americans is frustrated today by bias in the justice system. In the early 1990s a group of Asian Californians testified before a distinguished panel of state judges and lawyers about problems of punishing racial violence in the state justice system. Dennis Hayashi, director of the Japanese American Citizens League, testified before the panel that the courts must become tougher on hate criminals: "Hate violence is at an all-time high in America. But acts of racial violence are assigned a low priority [by the courts]."[29]

Latino Americans continue to face many problems in securing justice and equality. Reading through newspapers across the country, the authors have found much evidence that anti-Latino discrimination continues to be a serious problem. One newspaper story reported that the chief executive of a health insurance firm in the Southwest had publicly defended discrimination against Latinos by insurance companies, noting that people "who cannot speak, understand or read English are considered ineligible for coverage."[30] Other media stories reported Latino leaders protesting the absence of Latino actors in major roles on television and the portrayal of Latinos in the media as drug dealers, maids, and "Latin lovers." One article cited a recent research study that found discrimination by white employers against Latinos. Recent (1995–1997) research studies in Fresno, California and San Antonio, Texas have found high levels of discrimination against Latinos seeking rental housing. Today, numerous research reports show that Latinos continue to find their progress toward equality and justice limited by racial stereotyping and discrimination.[31]

African Americans too face major obstacles in securing the equality and justice promised by the American creed. Only a little more than a century ago Reconstruction, a period of progress in opportunities for African Americans (from about 1865 to 1885), was followed by a dramatic resurgence of white reaction and oppression, the so-called Redemption period. And in the twentieth century, only a few years after public policy shifted significantly in favor of expanded opportunities for blacks and other people of color in the 1960s and 1970s, this society and its governments again moved in a reactionary direction. From 1981 to 1992 powerful political leaders such as Ronald Reagan and George Bush cut back, eliminated, or kept ineffective, various affirmative action, equal opportunity, and other civil rights programs designed to redress discrimination against people of color. Beginning in 1993, the Clinton administration began to place greater emphasis on enforcing civil rights laws and expanding equal opportunity, but the election of more conservative Congresses in 1995 and 1997 brought a renewed emphasis on curtailing affirmative action and other anti-discrimination programs. In a recent book, *Turning Back: The Retreat from Racial Justice in American Thought and Policy,* Stephen Steinberg documents a movement backward on civil rights over the last two decades. He suggests that both conservatives and liberals have evaded "any reckoning with America's greatest crime—slavery—and its legacy in the present."[32] Decades after civil rights laws were passed, racial discrimination and ethnic discrimination are still widespread in most areas of the United States, and many of the nation's governments are found to be backing away from programs designed to counter discrimination, such as effective affirmative action and school desegregation programs.

Today, no fundamental or lasting changes have occurred at the top levels in most major institutions in the United States. White men still, overwhelmingly, dominate upper-level (and usually middle-level) positions in most major organizations, from the executive branch of the U.S. government to Fortune 1000 corporations, major universities, state legislatures, local banks, and supermarket chains.

As we explained in Chapter 8, discrimination against African Americans remains commonplace across the nation. Research in Washington, DC and Chicago using black and white testers applying for entry-level jobs uncovered significant discrimination in hiring.[33] In Los Angeles, about 60 percent of black employees in a recent survey reported experiencing job discrimination in the previous year, and those with the most education faced rates of discrimination approaching 100 percent. A majority of highly educated Asian and Latino American workers also reported job discrimination.[34] Just under half (45 percent) of the black respondents in a 1997 nationwide Gallup survey—and 70 percent of black men aged 18–34—reported experiencing discrimination in one of the following five areas in the previous thirty days: at work, dining out, shopping, with police, or in public transportation. Shopping had the highest reported rate (30 percent) of unfair treatment. Twenty-one percent also reported discrimination at work, and 15 percent (34 percent of young men) reported experiencing problems with the police. Gallup found that young men generally faced more discrimination than other groups of African Americans. Overall, those living in the South did not report more discrimination than those living elsewhere.[35]

Since the 1970s, the dominant white concern has shifted away from eradicating racial and ethnic discrimination in the United States. Indeed, in recent years a majority of whites have denied the reality of racism; they seem to feel that racial discrimination is not a major, widespread problem in this country. Yet the reality and pain of discrimination can be seen by any person who wishes to see it. For example, when asked what it is like being black in America, a retired professor who has lived in several regions of the country replied:

> I feel angry. I feel betrayed. Sometimes I feel very cynical. Most of the time I feel that I live in a country where I'm still not respected as a person. I lived at a time when I was told that if I got a good education, did all the right things, that I could be anything I wanted to be. I got a good education. I did all the right things, but even today I run into situations where my opportunity structure is limited because I am black. So I found that all along that no matter what I did, no matter how hard I tried, limitations were placed on me strictly because of the color of my skin. So I feel betrayed by the Constitution that guaranteed me certain rights. I feel betrayed by the Pledge of Allegiance to the flag, which says "liberty and justice for all."

When asked, on a scale from one to ten, how angry he gets at whites, he replied:

> Ten! I think that there are many blacks whose anger is at that level. Mine has had time to grow over the years more and more and more, until now I feel that my grasp on handling myself is tenuous. I think that now I would strike out to the point of killing, and not think anything about it. I really wouldn't care. Like many blacks you get tired, and you don't know which straw would break the camel's back. But you do know that there is a straw that might, and you don't try to prepare yourself not to do it any longer. You allow yourself the luxury of doing that. And I think that I'm at that point in my life where I avoid as many situations as I can, but if I'm forced and pushed into a corner, I'm going to strike out blindly. I will strike out blindly. I know that now, and I really don't care. Because it gets to a point where your life isn't worth it if you don't have some sense of respect and freedom. I don't mean license. I simply mean freedom to be like anybody else, to be treated

like anybody else. And I'm angry at what's happening to our young people. I call it impotent rage, because it's more than anger. It's a rage reaction, but something that you can't do something about and that makes it even more dangerous when you do strike out.[36]

These comments were made not long before the twentieth century's most severe racial riot—the explosion that rocked poverty-stricken South Central Los Angeles for several days in the spring of 1992. The acquittal of four police officers in the beating of a black man—an incident captured in a widely viewed videotape—sparked the rebellion. Angry at the verdict, many blacks and Latinos took to the streets and burned or looted thousands of local businesses. By the time the rebellion was over, more than fifty people had died. Los Angeles was not the only city to explode along its racial and ethnic fault lines. Other cities have experienced similar protests in the late 1980s and 1990s. The underlying conditions have included racism, poverty, unemployment, and poor housing conditions.[37]

In the aftermath of 1990s urban uprisings, many whites have asked why African Americans rebelled. As they did in earlier decades, some white officials have asserted that urban rebellions are not about protest, racism, or civil rights; instead they speak mostly of wild youngsters, criminal rioters, "deviants," and the need for more police and, sometimes, for one-shot economic programs of a modest sort for the troubled central cities. However, across the country African Americans (and other Americans of color) in all income groups have spoken of their great frustration, disillusionment, anger, and rage over persisting racial discrimination. Angry black reactions to discrimination signal that the equality-and-justice agenda remains substantially unfinished in the United States. Contrary to the conclusions of many white Americans, the black rebellions are substantially about protest, economic equality, and civil rights. They are usually about inequality in a justice system that winks at police officers who engage in excessive force against blacks and other people of color. They are usually about the persistence of racial discrimination that keeps many men and women of color from having jobs at decent wages. And they are usually about the discrimination that many black Americans and other Americans of color routinely encounter on the streets and in restaurants, department stores, workplaces, and historically white neighborhoods.

CONCLUSION: AN INCREASINGLY BALKANIZED NATION?

We began this chapter with a brief discussion of the major demographic changes now taking place in the United States. In the last two decades the U.S. has seen much urban growth. Moreover, the country is becoming more geographically segregated along racial–ethnic lines. Without immigration several major U.S. cities would have experienced serious population declines between 1985 and 2000. Internal or external migration was responsible for the growth that did occur during this period. However, the destinations for most internal migrants are different from the destinations of most new immigrants. Internal migrants, who are disproportionately white, are going primarily to cities in the Pacific, Mountain, and south Atlantic regions, such as Atlanta, Las Vegas, Phoenix, Portland, Denver, and Seattle. The states receiving the greatest interstate migration are Florida, Georgia, North Carolina, Virginia, Washington, and Arizona.[38]

In contrast, most new immigrants from overseas, who are mostly Asian and Latino, go to port-of-entry metropolitan areas on the coasts, particularly Los Angeles, New York City, San Francisco, Chicago, Miami, Baltimore, Houston, San Diego, and Boston. The ten highest-immigration metropolitan areas are becoming heavily populated by Americans of color (40 percent as of 1995), while the rest of the United States is more white.[39] The states with the highest levels of new immigration—California, New York, Texas, Illinois, Massachusetts, Florida, and New Jersey—have also seen a net outmigration of older whites and less-skilled whites. The latter movement has been characterized by some as a "white flight" from the large numbers of immigrants of color.[40]

About half the white population of the U.S. now lives in the Northeast or Midwest, but only one third of Americans of color live in those areas. Demographers project that by 2025 in the states of California, Texas, New Mexico, and Hawaii Americans of color will constitute the majority of these states' populations. In addition, New York, New Jersey, and Florida, along with five other states, are projected to be more than 40 percent people of color. In contrast, twelve states, including several in New England and in the Mountain and North Central areas, are projected to be overwhelmingly white (85 percent or more).[41]

These population trends will likely increase the separation and informal segregation of the nation's major racial and ethnic groups and will pose a further serious challenge not only for the lives of ordinary Americans of all backgrounds but also for the nation's ability to live up to the ideals of tolerance, pluralism, equality, freedom, and justice. This increasing separation strongly conflicts with these ideals.

The population shift from a predominantly white nation to one in which no racial or ethnic group has a majority has significant economic, social, and political implications. In our view much more thought needs to be given by American citizens, researchers, and policy makers to the possible or likely impact of these changes. For example, think for a moment about the educational system. No later than 2040 the U.S. educational system will be predominantly composed of students of color. Such a population change will provide major challenges to the traditional white domination of the structure and curriculum of the public schools. Students and teachers of color will likely press for more of a say in how schools are run. Discrimination against Americans of color is not likely to be tolerated when these groups have significant organizational and political power. Schools will likely become more concerned with issues of multiculturalism, whatever the views of the critics. In addition, by the 2050s, if not before, it seems likely that a majority of working Americans will no longer be white, while the older retired population will be majority white. One can wonder how workers of color will view paying taxes to support elderly whites on social security, when many of those whites were the ones who created and maintained the patterns of racial discrimination that oppressed these workers of color or their parents in prior decades.

Intergroup debate about and conflict over a range of diversity and equality issues—such as the dismantling of affirmative action or movements to make English the only official language—is likely to increase. Areas in which a majority of voters are people of color are not likely to elect white politicians who have a history of strong opposition to legal immigration and affirmative action. As voting constituencies change, the composition of juries and justice systems, educational systems, and other government agencies are likely to change as well.[42]

Is it possible to move in the direction of real racial-ethnic equality and justice? These ideals have long been part of an authentic American dream. The roots of that dream lie in Americans' aspirations for liberty and human rights and in the Declaration of Independence and the U.S. Constitution—both pathbreaking documents that reflect this nation's centuries-old (albeit erratic) movement in the direction of equality and justice. However, as we have seen, both of these documents were seriously marred by a capitulation to white supporters of the slavery system. After the Civil War, the Constitution was amended to abolish slavery and expand the liberties of African Americans. Later, in the mid- and late-twentieth century, Supreme Court decisions and civil rights laws brought formal equality and justice to Americans of all racial and ethnic backgrounds. Yet antidiscrimination decisions and laws have often gone unenforced, and civil rights laws do not encompass, and thus cannot eradicate, many informal types of racial and ethnic discrimination that persist as we move into the twenty-first century.

Whether equality and justice can ever be a reality in the sphere of racial and ethnic relations in the United States remains to be seen. In the recent and distant past the expansion of equality and justice has often resulted from the effective organization of people of color and their white allies against racial and ethnic oppression. The likelihood of a further expansion of equality and justice seems conditioned on successful political action and organization by Americans, of all colors and creeds, who are committed to the eradication of racial and ethnic oppression and to the ideals of equality and justice.

CHAPTER 14

*Colonialism and Post-Colonialism: The Global Expansion of Racism** *

In the spring of 1994, after the first elections in which blacks and whites voted together, South Africa's new black president, Nelson Mandela, commented: "Today is a day like no other before it. Today marks the dawn of our freedom. . . . We are starting a new era of hope, reconciliation and nation-building."[1] After casting his ballot in this historic election, Anglican Archbishop Desmond Tutu remarked, "I am about two inches taller than when I arrived."[2] A black worker stated that voting day was the best day of his life: "I don't have to carry a pass. I can work anywhere in the country I want. I am free."[3] Thirty million South Africans that day felt free of apartheid, the legally institutionalized system of racial segregation and social, economic, and political inequality that had long invaded every aspect of daily life. The newly elected South African government outlawed apartheid and promised to move toward equality in rights and in black access to everything whites had in South Africa. With this assurance, Nkosingthi Msesizwe, a black miner, believed he could now ride the same elevator with white miners in post-apartheid South Africa. But Msesizwe was beaten by white miners who shouted that "this hoist is for whites. It is not for you."[4] His experience suggests how difficult large-scale racial change can be.

South Africa's new government assured South Africans that equality would be achieved through constitutional changes. Realizing this goal is the new government's greatest challenge because racism and overt discrimination are still everyday reality in South African society. In a country with massive unemployment, direct and indirect institutional racism is commonplace in workplaces, be they offices, factories, or mines. For example, skilled miners, 85 percent of whom are white, earn *ten times* more than the mostly unskilled black miners. Black miner Kenneth Buda, acting chairperson of the National Union's Gold Fields Kloof mine, earns about $40 a week after twelve years as a miner. Organizers for the white miners' union responded to white miners' resistance to sharing lifts

---

* This chapter was written by Pinar Batur-VanderLippe of Vassar College.

with black miners, commenting, "Some of our members are racist. . . . That's also part of the atmosphere in a mine. . . . So why not keep things separate; it works so much better."[5] In order to face the problems of institutional racism throughout its society, the government will have to confront the foundations of racial apartheid—the social, economic, and political arrangements legitimated by a culture of white racism that began with the Western nations' seventeenth- and eighteenth-century colonial invasions of southern Africa. Apartheid's legality and rationality are rooted in a system of racial discrimination based on the "separate but equal" myth.

In this chapter, we move away from racial and ethnic relations in the United States to look at patterns of racial-ethnic discrimination and institutional racism around the world. We will briefly examine cases from South Africa, Brazil, France, Russia, and Bosnia to illustrate how colonialism and the global culture of racism and institutionalized discrimination have been implemented by and maintained by whites, both white Europeans and Euro-Americans. The case of South Africa demonstrates the major life-determining and life-threatening consequences of colonialism and the institutionalization of racism, whereas Brazil exhibits how a racist culture maintains racist institutions and cultural practices. Turning to France, we explore the legacy and impact of colonialism in one major colonizing society. Furthermore, through the examples of the ethnic dissolution of the Soviet Union and Yugoslavia, we examine unexpected racial–ethnic conflict in complex, large multiethnic societies in Europe. In our view students of contemporary racial–ethnic relations must know more than something about group relations in their own country. In order to understand the global realities of the twenty-first century, students must know something about the history and development of colonialism, imperialism, and racialized societies across the globe.

COLONIALISM AND RACISM

In F. Scott Fitzgerald's classic 1920s novel, *The Great Gatsby*, one discussion among wealthy Euro-American characters focuses on a racist book that argued that if not prevented "the white race will be . . . utterly submerged. It's all scientific stuff; it's been proved. . . . It is up to us, who are the dominant race, to watch out or these other races will have control of things." One of the white characters then whispers, "We've got to beat them down."[6] As revealed in novels as well as in policy decisions, ideological racism has long validated for the white public imperialist expansion and colonialism around the world. Economic and political racism has exploited people who are not of the "dominant" racial group, while the ideology of racism has rationalized this oppression. White racism has been the framework for rationalizing the subordination of people of color in many societies colonized by Europeans, including the United States, South Africa, Brazil, and the Muslim republics of the former Soviet Union.

Edward Said uses the term *orientalism* to name a broad Eurocentric perspective that has encompassed the economic and political interests of the West (the

Occident) in the East (the Orient) from the beginning of the expansion of capitalism to the present.[7] *Orientalism* is a racist construction of Eastern and Islamic societies as static, militaristic, nonrational, and despotic. Western society, in contrast, is portrayed as progressive, civil, rational, and individualistic. Orientalism sees societies outside the West as not only different from the West but inherently *inferior* to Western societies. As a racist dichotomy, orientalism became an ideological perspective justifying the oppression of non-Europeans from the early expansion of capitalism and imperialism to the present.

The division of people according to racial group, including the assignment of superior and inferior characteristics to the "races," has been fostered by the expansion of Western capitalism around the globe since the 1500s. As we noted in Chapter 2, the dynamics of this Western capitalistic expansion, which created colonies of subordinated peoples, made racial inequality a permanent part of global existence through the ideologies and discriminatory practices of institutionalized racism. The international development of Western capitalism fostered the advancement of ideological and "scientific" racism, integrating them into a global culture of systemic racism. The examination of racism as a *global* culture is important to the general study of racial and ethnic relations because racism's global culture superimposes itself on most other cultural institutions in the societies it invades, including the construction of the personal identities and the everyday experiences of the colonizers and the colonized.[8]

White racism is now a global mode of thought, a way to ask questions, a way to connect "not only words with objects, but more profoundly a way to connect words with images to create concepts."[9] Racism has become a process of defining and building communities and societies based on racialized privileges and a hierarchy of power. The global expansion of Western capitalism through colonialism gave white racism a new and global scope; by 1914 a majority of the earth's peoples were under the control of European colonizers.

THE HISTORY AND LEGACY OF COLONIALISM

Western colonialism began with the major overseas expansion of Spain and Portugal, whose rulers sought to enhance their treasuries with gold, silver, and other goods taken by force from the world's peoples. One goal of Spanish and Portuguese expansion was the ending of the Muslim control of the trade across the Indies and Africa. The legal and ideological rationale for this colonialism was provided by Roman Catholic popes in several papal bulls, declarations echoing earlier papal justifications for the Christian crusades against Muslims in earlier centuries. For example, a 1452 papal bull permitted the Portuguese to conquer the "Saracens" (Muslims) and other pagans and to take their lands and goods.[10] On May 3, 1493 Pope Alexander VI issued a bull of demarcation resolving Spanish and Portuguese disputes over colonization. As revised by the Treaty of Tordesillas in 1494, this bull put all the world's non-Christian ("pagan") peoples at the economic disposal of these growing colonial powers.[11]

The Christian justification for expansion was for a time in tension with the profit-making desire of European entrepreneurs for land and slave labor. For a short period, some Catholic theologians and priests, most notably the Spanish priest Las Casas, opposed the ruthless enslavement of the native populations. However, in a 1550 debate with Las Casas in Spain, theologian Gaines de Sepulveda carried the day with his arguments that it was lawful to make war on and enslave the native populations because of their heathen, sinful, and barbarous "natures," which obligated them to serve those (the Spanish) with the superior culture and virtues.[12] As Cox has noted, de Sepulveda was one of the first of the "great racists," a European theologian who argued that "Indians were inferior to the Spaniards."

By the 1500s, freewheeling capitalism was developing in several nations of northern and western Europe. Over the next few centuries a number of nations, especially the Netherlands, England, and France, spurred the global expansion of capitalism, in the process fostering economic and racial inequality between the colonizers and the colonized.[13] These nations generated many scholars, theologians, and politicians who developed theories of the superiority of Europeans and of the animal-like inferiority of peoples caught in the web of western colonialism. Europeans distinguished themselves from the "savages" overseas in many ways. Often, the colonized peoples of color were demonized and considered to have the vices Europeans feared in themselves: wildness, brutishness, cruelty, laziness, sexual promiscuity, and non-Christian heathenism. "Far from English civilization, [the Europeans] had to remind themselves constantly what it meant to be civilized—Christian, rational, sexually controlled, and white. And they tried to impute to peoples they called 'savages' the instinctual forces they had within themselves."[14] By the 1700s and 1800s, well-developed theories of the cultural and racial inferiority of the "savages" had been developed, as we have shown in Chapter 1. As the major racist scholar of the nineteenth century, Joseph de Gobineau, put it: "[White people] are gifted with reflective energy, or rather with an energetic intelligence. . . . They have a remarkable, even extreme love of liberty, and are openly hostile to the formalism under which the Chinese are glad to vegetate, as well as the strict despotism which is the only way of governing the Negro."[15]

At an early point in time, colonialism became a system of control based on a colonial political administration, an exploitative commercial trade, and a missionary zeal to convert native populations to Christianity and western "civilization." In Asian, African, and American societies this threefold domination fostered the colonial administrations' oppressive rule, unequal trade practices, and the imposition of Christianity and Western culture. For example, in the case of nineteenth-century Russian colonial expansion, the invasion of the Crimea, the Caucasus, and Central Asia not only was meant to extend power to challenge the strength of the Iranian and Ottoman Empires, it was also justified by the Orthodox Christian church as a legitimate objective of a Christian nation. Moreover, the Russian Minister of Finance defined the reason for expansion as having "a colony producing raw materials," such as cotton and tobacco, in a southern climate.[16]

Desire for raw materials motivated European colonial expansion, such as obtaining black pepper and lumber from Brazil or tea and spices from India. Securing raw materials required the use of military oppression and violence, which after conquest was carried out by the colonial administration. This oppression was supported directly and indirectly by the Christian churches. In India, British colonialism served as a vehicle for the spread of Christian missionary schools and activities, which were aimed at assimilating Hindus and Muslims to British culture and ideas and fostering their acceptance of British political and economic rule. The colonists must not resist, or they would be violently repressed. The North American colonists learned about British oppression in the 1700s. The people of India learned about this British oppression in the 1800s and 1900s. On April 13, 1919, fearing insurrection, a British-led army unit fired on an unarmed assembly celebrating the Hindu New Year, killing 379 people and wounding 1,200, an event still remembered as the Amritsar Massacre.[17]

Everyday life in the colonies was reshaped by the European oppressors, who controlled colonized societies not only politically but also economically and culturally. Exploitation of colonized peoples and their natural resources was accompanied by systematic violence. Moreover, the violence and exploitation were justified through an ideology of cultural and racial superiority that penetrated religious and political views and even language. This racism was not only an integral aspect of the dominant group's racial identity, it also seeped into the subordinate group's racialized construction of its self-conception. Pervasive material and ideological racism fostered the view of the colonized as subordinate and powerless.[18] Albert Memmi, a north African author educated in French colonial schools, has written about the impact of colonial rule: "I am ill at ease in my own land and I know of no other. My culture is borrowed and I speak my mother tongue haltingly. I have neither religious beliefs nor tradition and am ashamed of whatever particle of them has survived deep within me. . . . I am Tunisian, but of French culture."[19]

Since the sixteenth century European colonialism has also had a major impact on the colonizers and their home countries. The flow of raw materials from the colonies demanded a docile working class in both the colonized and the colonizing societies. For example, the British Empire not only subjugated India, but the system of subjugation and racism also permeated British society, thereby shaping conditions for the white working class in Great Britain. The white working class accepted colonialism and white racism, with its sense of racial superiority. British racism has long fostered a false sense of superiority and contributed to many British workers' uncritical acceptance of their own political and economic system. Today, the impact of this racism can be seen in white British workers' hostility to immigrants from various countries in the former Empire. Similarly, French colonialism oppressed Algerians, and in today's post-colonial period racist arguments still influence the political and economic positions of first and second generation Algerians residing in France.[20] In the United States, as we have documented previously, colonial oppression included African slavery, the extermination of Native Americans, the theft of Mexican lands, and the conquest of Puerto Rico and the Philippines. The scars of this colonial oppression continue to influence contemporary social and political events in the United States.

Drawing on the old racist ideologies and verbally and physically attacking people of color in their midst, neo-Nazi groups and racist political parties have recently reemerged in most of the former colonizer societies of Europe and North America. The ongoing relationships between colonizing and colonized societies firmly establish racism as a mode of global thinking—an ideology that shapes images of the colonized as well as institutionalized practices and everyday life in the framework of racial superiority and inferiority. Both the ideology of racism and the practices of institutional racism are global realities. Even though specific conditions differ in particular countries with different histories, there are important similarities.

We now turn to an exploration of the impact and the legacy of colonialism in the colonized societies of South Africa and Brazil and in the colonizing society of France. Later, we examine the complexities of racial–ethnic relations in the modern world using the examples of the former Soviet Union and Yugoslavia.

TO WHOM DOES SOUTHERN AFRICA BELONG?

In many countries those who occupy the land often ask, "To whom does this land really belong?" According to racist constructions of colonial history, the land is usually "discovered" by "civilized" white people who are the first to "use the land in a productive way." For the colonizers, the very history of a place begins with colonization.

An examination of land ownership in southern Africa reveals the following: The Khoisan, who were hunters and gatherers, were living in what is now South Africa when the ancestors of the current Bantu-speaking black majority began to settle there around A.D. 300.[21] The first European expedition to the area came much later in the form of Portuguese explorers in 1487. The first European settlement in southern Africa dates only to 1652, when Jan van Riebeeck established a station for the Dutch East India Company. As Dutch colonial settlements spread, Dutch confrontations with the Bantu peoples led to a series of what the Europeans call the "Kaffir Wars."

In Arabic, *kaffir* originally meant "infidel"; today it is a degrading term (like "nigger" in the United States) that white settlers have applied to black South Africans. The early European settlers saw their colonization in part as a religious and civilizing mission that justified the killing, subjugation, or enslavement of the indigenous Khoisan and Bantu peoples. The Europeans rated themselves as religiously and racially superior to Africans, whom they considered to be animal-like, and stereotyped them as heathens, "idolatrous and licentious, thieving and lying, lazy and dirty."[22] Europeans often rationalized what they saw as the inferiority of Africans through "scientific" racism, arguing that the tropical environment was responsible for producing immature, childish, and "beastlike" creatures who would be civilized only by the European work ethic and by Christian discipline.

Europeans legitimated the brutal enslavement of Africans as a vehicle to lift the latter from the "barbarism" of their own societies.[23] The view of native inferiority, a critical aspect of a colonizing, racist ideology, was well established among the first white settlers in southern Africa.

The Dutch colonial interest in southern Africa collided with British determination to control the route to India around the tip of Africa. Britain's conquest of southern Africa's Cape Colony in 1806 and British colonial settlement beginning in 1820 fueled the out-migration of 15,000 Dutch farmers (called "Boers") into the interior, a movement whites called the "Great Trek." The Great Trek became an important symbol for descendants of the Dutch settlers. The British imperialist colonizers abolished slavery and changed the regulations on black labor. The Boers interpreted British actions as putting the Khoisan and Bantus "on an equal footing with Christians, contrary to the laws of God and the natural distinction of race."[24] These views were supported by Christian ministers and also reflected the goals of the Dutch East India Company, which tried to create a racially divided society to buttress the slave trade and the extraction of raw materials.[25]

During this period, a white mythology about land ownership developed. Some Dutch settlers began calling themselves "Afrikaners," or the "white tribe of Africa."[26] Defending slavery, the white colonizers argued that "we make the people work for us in consideration of allowing them to live in our country."[27] According to the assumptions of the whites, there were "no native blacks" in southern Africa prior to the arrival of Europeans. This view persists today: "Basically we came here more or less at the same time. We both belong to South Africa. There is no one black man who can say that this is his country more so than a white. We belong here as much as they do."[28] From the beginning, European colonizers in southern Africa justified the subjugation of and violence against Africans in racist terms, and their descendants have often claimed the land as more or less for whites only.

Later on, the colonial subjugation of various indigenous peoples was also violent. In 1838, the Boer farmers defeated the once-powerful Zulu army. In 1848, British and local forces defeated the Xhosa, and in 1879, they conquered the remaining Zulu domains. In addition to this war, forced labor was imposed on indigenous peoples through slavery and the use of a tax system. Under growing colonial control, oppressive conditions in the European-controlled mines and on agricultural plantations contributed to the brutality of everyday life for Africans.

Formation of the State and Apartheid

European interest in southern Africa was further stimulated by the discovery of diamonds and gold in the late nineteenth century. In 1910, the Union of South Africa was created, which united British areas with Boer areas. The new white-controlled state imposed racial segregation on the politically defined population of "blacks" and "coloreds," the latter being of mixed racial ancestry. The 1913 Native Lands Act limited land ownership and settlement for blacks and coloreds, but not for whites, to certain restricted areas. Voting rights and political representation were reserved for whites. At the beginning of the twentieth century, whites were not homogeneous but did feel that they shared the common heritage of Christianity and a mission of "civilizing" Africa.

As gold and other mining expanded, the racial structure of the preindustrial colonial society became part of the new capitalist industry. The labor force was divided between white workers, who held skilled and supervisory positions with better wages and working conditions, and black unskilled workers, who worked under harsh conditions with little pay.[29]

The indigenous peoples drew on their cultures to resist apartheid. Organized opposition to the increasingly racist policies came from the African National Congress (ANC), which was founded in 1912 to demand voting rights, freedom of residence, and land ownership for black Africans. The ANC was resisting a growing white determination to create an openly racist state. White voters elected the National Party in 1948 on a platform of apartheid that mandated separate development and complete segregation. The supporters of apartheid drew on fascist ideas then dominant in Europe. Afrikaner whites, like Germans in the Nazi ideology, were constructed as a "special nation with a special mission: the Afrikaner believes that it is the will of God that there should be a diversity of races and nations and that obedience to the will of God therefore requires the acknowledgement and maintenance of that diversity."[30] Afrikaner nationalist defenders argued that "the preservation of the pure race tradition of the Boerevolk must be preserved at all costs. . . . Any movement, school, or individual who sins against this must by dealt with as a racial criminal by the effective authorities."[31] Church-sanctioned racism was a great buttress for apartheid; the Dutch Reform Church of South Africa became a citadel for the National Party.[32]

Apartheid had several interlocking aspects. One was the hierarchical structure in which whites, about 18 percent of the population, ruled over the 82 percent who were called "colored" or "black." This hierarchy was fostered by a white-controlled nation state that denied citizenship to black Africans. Another aspect of apartheid was widespread institutional discrimination, which took the form of racial segregation in everyday life.[33]

Apartheid was reinforced by racist laws. The 1950 Population Registration Act established legal registration by racial group; the Group Areas Act prohibited blacks from residing outside of racially zoned areas. In 1950, the government sought to control opposition to apartheid by passing security legislation against "Communist activities." Since the white Minister of Justice was empowered to decide just who were "Communists," this law permitted the state to silence blacks as well as whites who opposed government racial policies through the use of intimidation, imprisonment, and police violence. To control the transfer of knowledge, in 1953 the white government took control of education from the missionary schools, creating a separate and inferior educational system for black South Africans.[34] The government desired education that would produce unskilled laborers to meet the needs of South African industries.[35]

The Bantu Self-Government Act forced much of the black population into territorially fragmented areas, called "homelands," with limited resources.

Recognized only by white South Africans as "independent countries," the home-lands were another form of apartheid. Another example of the brutality of apartheid was the 1956 decision to order 100,000 non-Europeans to leave their homes in the city of Johannesburg within one year in order to make space available for whites. In 1964, new laws expanded apartheid by regulating black employment, giving the police power to hold suspects for six months without trial, and prohibiting mixed-race political organizations.

Some scholars have debated the role of South African capitalists in maintaining apartheid. Clearly, capitalists have benefited from apartheid, yet some have been opposed to its more extreme manifestations. A good example is Harry Oppenheimer, who in 1957 inherited the Anglo-American Corporation and DeBeers Consolidated Mines, which control 40 percent of South African gold, 80 percent of the world's diamonds, one-sixth of the world's copper, and almost all coal production in South Africa. After 1959, Oppenheimer supported the Progressive Party, which advocated incorporation of black Africans into the political system. In 1976, he established the Urban Foundation for social support projects in black urban areas. Yet Oppenheimer also took advantage of the racist labor structure by depressing wages for black workers. Even though some capitalists objected to apartheid because it was bad for the country's image, they played a role in prolonging apartheid because it kept their production costs down.[36]

Opposition to Apartheid

As apartheid intensified, so did the efforts of the African National Congress (ANC) and another resistance group called the Pan-African Congress (PAC), both of which had been banned by the government in 1960.[37] In 1964, after the infamous Sharpeville massacre, in which the police killed sixty-nine black demonstrators, Nelson Mandela and other ANC and PAC leaders were sentenced to life in prison. These imprisonments were followed by the torture and deaths of black leaders held in police custody. As the support of apartheid became more violent, the anti-apartheid movement in South Africa became stronger and more violent in response. A growing number of demonstrations, including student demonstrations, resulted in hundreds of deaths of black protestors at the hands of police forces.[38]

By the late 1970s, open opposition to apartheid in segregated black townships near the larger cities forced the government to search for new ways to legitimize white control. White leaders first tried co-optation. Beginning in 1978, the restrictions on labor union organization among black workers and on multiracial political parties were lifted. Meanwhile, the ANC enlarged its political base and changed its emphasis from armed struggle to mass political mobilization.[39]

In the most recent period, three critical issues have been "black on black violence," which reflected group differences among black South Africans; the political and economic problems plaguing the homelands, which began to receive attention from both the South African government and the ANC; and the question of who is South African, debated by black and white intellectuals.

For a time, the white government attempted to continue its control by exacerbating divisions among blacks and coloreds. Differences among black South Africans have also been used by whites to channel black anger away from white oppression. The South African government funded the Inkatha Zulu separatist movement and secretly provided it with military training in order to fuel Zulu hostility towards the ANC and its primary supporters, especially the Xhosa people.[40]

By providing for some limited political participation by Asian and colored people in the new 1984 constitution, the government tried to further divide the South African population, provoking widespread opposition among black Africans. Demonstrations in the townships were again met with brutal suppression. Declaring a state of emergency, the government tried to prevent the press from reporting clashes and detained thousands; 250,000 black mineworkers responded to these actions with a three-week strike.[41] For a few years, such divide-and-conquer strategies allowed the government to continue to impose its rule on black South Africans. By accentuating racial and ethnic divisions, these actions produced lasting problems for the development of a democratic South Africa.

White resistance to the anti-apartheid movement had its limits. Black protests, together with an international economic boycott, made life difficult for many whites in the country. The white elite, particularly the economic elite, was disturbed by the social chaos and loss of profits. In 1989, after becoming the head of the government, F. W. deKlerk began to dismantle the policies of racial apartheid under the pressure of blacks and white opponents of the old racist regime. After 12,000 deaths in political clashes over four years, the South African government moved to free elections. In April 1994, about two and one-half years after being freed from prison, Nelson Mandela, the head of the ANC, was elected to the presidency of South Africa.

The Future of South Africa

F. W. deKlerk, looking back into history, said on the anniversary of the Sharpeville massacre: "Let the memory of those who died at Sharpeville, and all others who died as a result of the conflicts of the past, be an inspiration for the new beginning—not as a reason for dwelling in the past."[42] Yet the racist past is integral to South Africa's present reality. Racism is still well institutionalized in everyday life, from Pretoria, which white Afrikaner separatists see as their spiritual capital, to the Zulu homelands, where many Zulus consider the ANC and Nelson Mandela as instruments of the continuation of white oppression.[43]

Frantz Fanon, a critic of colonialism, has asked: "What is South Africa? A boiler into which thirteen million blacks are clubbed and penned in by two and a half million whites."[44] Today, South Africa is changing, but many feel it is not changing fast enough. This is especially true for those in the poverty-stricken black townships. Throughout the 1990s, the income gap between rich and poor blacks has grown. The proportion of blacks in the poorest fifth of the population has increased from 34 percent to 38 percent, while the proportion of blacks in the richest fifth has grown from 2 percent to 6 percent. Contrary to expectations, the growth of black wealth has not resulted in investment in black townships. As the number of affluent black South Africans has increased, critics of Mandela's government have argued that it is too removed from the realities of the black townships. The younger generation expects speedy and radical changes, rather than moves calculated not to alienate white investors in South Africa. Indeed, many black youth and other critics see the innovative South African Truth and Reconciliation Commission's questioning of Winnie Madikizela-Mandela— Nelson Mandela's ex-wife and a critic of his government—for her role in a "reign of terror," while the Commission is also questioning white police officers who tortured and murdered blacks under apartheid, as very inappropriate and motivated to eliminate opponents of the existing government.[45]

Other problems for the black-led government have emerged as it seeks to correct the legacy of racist policies. For example, to combat an infant and child mortality rate of 72 per 1,000, the Health Department established a program of

Black and white South Africans stand in line waiting to vote in the first multiracial elections in South Africa in 1994.

free treatment for all children under six and for pregnant women. The unantici-
pated flood of patients strained the fragile structure of public hospitals and clinics, forcing them to overspend and face closure without immediate government
help. The government is planning to build 200 new clinics per year, but at this
point it has no money to run them.[46] Moreover, since the mid-1990s mixed-race
South Africans (the coloreds) have challenged what they consider favoritism in
government policies aimed at benefiting black South Africans in the courts and in
parliament. In addition, continuing violence in South Africa is being dismissed by
the Western media as "tribal skirmishes." Yet, the persisting intergroup violence
between various factions in the black, colored, and white communities reveals a
deep legacy of institutional racism yet to be confronted in South Africa despite the
elimination of legal apartheid.

The case of South Africa shows how European colonialism has historically
operated through a trilogy of domination—administration, trade, and religion—
to establish a system of white control and antiblack violence. Through this domination racism has become part of both major social institutions and white culture.
Racial discrimination has shaped the construction of racial and ethnic identities
and everyday experiences. The segregated patterns of housing, education, and
employment reveal persisting patterns of overt racist practices of white South
Africans targeting black South Africans. After three centuries of colonial exploitation, the lives of the black people of southern Africa have been changed fundamentally and irrevocably. These changes have made struggle against racism integral to the present and future of South Africa.

BRAZIL: THE LEGACY OF SLAVERY AND THE ILLUSION OF EQUALITY

The country of Brazil in South America is second in population only to the United
States in the Western Hemisphere. Brazil has the largest number of people of African
descent outside of Africa—about 60 million, almost half of its population. Slavery
was abolished in Brazil more than one hundred years ago, but a culture of racism and
institutional discrimination still impacts the black experience today. For example, in
a restaurant, black customers are often told that all empty tables are reserved. A television soap opera that showed a white man and black woman kissing received
numerous protests. Black women complain that in apartment buildings they are presumed to be maids and are shown the service elevator. Some 95 percent of the more
than 150,000 teenagers on whom the police reportedly have files are not white. Many
employers consistently choose white over black applicants for jobs.[47] Today, 40 percent of the black population works in minimum-wage jobs that pay about $50 per
month.[48] Black Brazilians constitute only 1 percent of the students enrolled in the universities. At the University of São Paulo, for instance, only five of the five thousand
faculty members are black. Overall, blacks in Brazil have the highest rate of illiteracy, unemployment, underemployment, and marginal housing.[49] Is this social, economic, and political situation the legacy of European colonization and slavery?

Brazil was colonized during the early period of the expansion of Spain and Portugal, when European knowledge of the world beyond Europe was sketchy. The Portuguese sought to establish a commercial empire, and explorer Pedro Alvarez Cabral claimed this land for the Portuguese crown. The Portuguese named the land after a dye extracted from native trees. The emerging European textile industry consumed so much of the dye that, by the end of the 1500s, one hundred ships oscillated regularly between Brazil and Portugal. The Portuguese established sugar cane plantations around small colonial settlements. Some original inhabitants of these lands were enslaved, although most were slaughtered during wars between the native groups and the European colonizers or in wars between Portuguese and other European powers in Brazil. Or, like Native Americans in the United States, these natives died from European diseases.[50]

By the nineteenth century, Brazil resembled the American South. Large numbers of slaves worked on plantations to produce sugar, coffee, and rubber for the capitalist world market.[51] Brazil's slave population numbered about five million—more than half its total population—just before the abolition of slavery in 1888. Brazil became independent in 1822, and in 1889 the military overthrew the monarch and declared a republic. Since that time, Brazilian history has been marked by recurring military intervention in politics and by continuous debates about the establishment of democracy.

A Racial Democracy?

Brazil's slave system was one of great racial inequality. This inequality was maintained by slavelike conditions for many Afro-Brazilians long after slavery's abolition. Nonetheless, a grand myth emerged that Brazil had "benign patterns" of racial relations and that Brazil was and is a "racial democracy." Many Brazilians, especially whites, have proclaimed their society to be a racial democracy.

Those who hold this view make the assumption that Portuguese colonialism was a benign form of colonial rule and that Roman Catholicism as a religion was oriented to black inclusion and assimilation. The Catholic church, they argue, encouraged the occasional freeing of slaves and thus more humane treatment of African slaves than existed in the North American colonies. Furthermore, the influence of the Muslim and probably darker-skinned North African Moors, who conquered and controlled Spain and Portugal from 711 to 1492, is seen as making the Spanish and Portuguese more accommodating than northern Europeans on matters of race.[52] However, this interpretation of the Portuguese and Spanish past overlooks the Catholic church's brutal inquisition and torture of Jews and Muslims in the fifteenth and sixteenth centuries, as well as the unyielding hostility of the Spanish and Portuguese to the Moors' rule.

The notion of Brazil's "racial democracy" does recognize the existence of some prejudice and discrimination, but, in an extension of the assumption of the benign nature of slavery, it claims that such occurrences are isolated aberrations and that in reality Afro-Brazilians are roughly equal in a multicultural society. The mainstream white ideology in Brazil argues that because of "Brazilian exceptionalism," meaning the allegedly equal treatment of the former slave population and the equal opportunities available to all, multicultural Brazil is not so starkly divided along racial lines as the United States and South Africa.[53] However, this view ignores Brazil's continuing patterns of institutional racism and its racist ideologies.

In the late nineteenth century, one aspect of Brazil's racist ideology was a focus on racial mixing. Many white Brazilians, including scholars and intellectuals, argued that people of mixed descent exhibit the worst characteristics of their parents' racial groups, and thus Brazilian society would degenerate with the "mixing" of the "races." This societal degeneration view was imported from the United States and Europe. Based on nineteenth-century assumptions about the origins and hierarchy of "races" (see Chapter 1), this racist notion fit in well with white fears of losing control to a growing Afro-Brazilian population. Opponents of racial mixing fortified their argument with what has been called the "whitening thesis," claiming that "stronger and better white genes" are essential to the positive evolution of the Brazilian population.

Even though these racist notions share an assumption about the superiority of the white race, they are in conflict. Fear of racial mixing would encourage racial segregation, while the whitening notion would favor interracial marriages to improve society's "gene pool."[54] Emerging together in the nineteenth century, these racist views still remain part of Brazil's popular "knowledge" and culture of racism and influence white Brazilians' thinking about the future. Today, this can be seen in immigration policies favoring white Europeans, in white attitudes to interracial marriages, and in many blacks' adherance to a color hierarchy that shows preference for lighter skin tones.

Many light-skinned Brazilians believe that differences between their racial groups are less important than such differences in South Africa or the United States. However, Brazilians use 125 words for racial identification; the word *black* does not have the same meaning in Brazil as in the United States or South Africa. In Brazil, *preto* (black) describes a person with mostly or all African ancestry. Yet a racially mixed person who would be called "black" in the United States is identified in Brazil as *moreno*. *Morenos* are further divided into light (*morenos claros*) and dark (*morenos escuros*). The term *mulatto* is used to refer specifically to a person of mixed African and Caucasian backgrounds. In addition, since the term *Negro* includes *pretos* and *morenos* it has provided a political term for black-power movements, as in Brazil's *Movimento Negro*.[55] The racial hierarchy is supported by white stereotypes that view blacks as "bad-smelling, dirty, unhygienic, ugly" and mulattoes as "pushy and envious of whites." According to one Brazilian ditty, "The white man goes to heaven, the mulatto stays on earth, the *caboclo* (mestizo) goes to purgatory, the black goes to hell."[56]

Whiteness remains a symbol of superiority and the key to power. In censuses, the number of people identifying themselves as *mulatto* has grown faster than is statistically possible, suggesting that the belief that "brownness" (*pardo*) is an escape hatch for Brazilians who are not white, allowing them to achieve greater upward mobility by acquiring an intermediate, whiter, racial status.[57]

By downplaying real racial differences, Brazil's white elites avoid addressing problems of racially based economic inequality as well as racial inequalities in education and mortality rates.[58] Brazil had an economic boom between 1950 and 1980, but the benefits flowed heavily to the upper class, the top 20 percent of Brazilian society, which was and remains almost exclusively white. The racial disparity in income increased during this period to a level similar to that in the United States.[59]

A Century of Lies?

The colonial histories of Brazil and the United States are different, but racial inequality is similar in both countries. The inequality between Brazil's racial groups sharpened between 1960 and 1990 during the nation's process of "modernization" as transnational corporations seeking lower wages and new markets invested heavily there; many of these firms are headquartered in the United States. Afro-Brazilians have confronted white elites and demanded equal-opportunity legislation to secure greater access to education and employment. They have developed a political movement resembling U.S. civil rights and black power movements. Conservative presidential administrations in the United States during the 1980s sought to reduce federal commitments to civil rights and affirmative action and to curtail government efforts to reduce racial inequality (see Chapter 8). Similar government actions occurred in Brazil. As in the United States, powerful whites rejected affirmative action for Afro-Brazilians as "reverse racism."[60]

May 13, 1988, marked the centennial of the abolition of slavery in Brazil. The Brazilian government organized a celebration, but Afro-Brazilian groups organized their own counterdemonstrations. The latter protested persisting racial inequality and institutionalized discrimination; labeling the celebration a "farce" and "100 years of lies," they called for a "march for the real liberation of the race." These demonstrations illustrated Afro-Brazilians' demands for the elimination of inequality in jobs and political power. They also addressed issues of racial categorization and the African influence in Brazilian culture. They advocated a strengthening of cultural and other ties between blacks in Brazil and in other parts of the African diaspora in order to challenge racism everywhere.[61]

Helio Santos, a black university professor, has underscored the contradictions in his country today: "Brazilian society discriminates against blacks at every point, but it is hidden, disguised. . . . There is an illusion of social democracy in Brazil. . . . Blacks internalize discrimination so often they can't see it."[62] Just as in the United States, the illusion of equality in Brazil serves white elites' political purposes while racial discrimination remains integral to society. As another black professor argues, "It is an illusion to think [their] situation will automatically get better as the [economic] situation of the country improves. Inequality will continue."[63] The promise of economic success frames the European colonizers' persisting myth that equality will come, along with prosperity, in the near future. This myth has been part of the political debate during

Brazil's elections in the 1990s. In this sense, Brazil differs little from the United States and South Africa. Institutional racism and a racist culture continue to shape the debates on equality and democracy.

Moreover, in Brazil one's racial group often coincides with class position, in both urban and rural areas. Since 5 percent of the Brazilian population, which is overwhelmingly white, controls 95 percent of the land, it is not surprising that more than 50,000 rural poor marched in 1997 to protest the slow pace of long-promised land reform. President Fernando Henrique Cardoso was criticized for not undertaking major reforms that would confront the traditional white elites. These include investing in national infrastructure and education and carrying out the much-needed land reform.[64]

The Brazilian case shows the impact of European colonialism not only on economic and political institutions but also on ideological racism's development and its permeation into popular culture. Afro-Brazilian slavery, although considered by whites to be a thing of the past, remains an integral part of Brazil's present and promises to continue to influence the nation's future through the dominance of ideological racism in elite thinking and in popular culture. The Brazilian case illustrates that colonialism not only enslaved colonized people and forced them into physical labor, it also tried to colonize their thoughts and imaginations, their relationships with each other, and the way in which they construct their identities.

COLONIALISM AND COLONIZER IN FRANCE: THE VIOLENCE OF EXCLUSION

Frantz Fanon has argued that European colonialism brought violence on the subordinated peoples in part through a construction of the colonial world in terms of good and evil. Through the "totalitarian character of colonial exploitation the settler paints the native as a sort of quintessence of evil."[65] This symbolism of good Europeans and evil colonials had religious roots and was part of the European culture of racism and helped to legitimate violence in colonized societies. The ideology was an integral aspect of racial subordination and conflict during the colonial period and also during the subsequent post-colonial period. While there are many examples of this point, contemporary France is an important case.

The Character of French Colonialism

French colonialism differed from British and Portuguese colonialism by claiming its colonized peoples as "citizens of France." To realize this ideal, French colonial administrators propagated French culture and language in a vigorous attempt to assimilate colonized peoples into the French culture and empire. However, at no point in its history has France itself been unified or monocultural. Subordinated racial–ethnic groups in France, especially the Jews, have long been targets of racial hostility and exclusion. In a famous case, Alfred Dreyfus, a Jewish captain in the

French army, was falsely accused by his superiors and convicted in 1898 of selling military secrets to the Germans. The trial became a major political issue in the elections of that year when many candidates adopted anti-Semitic platforms. Jews made up a tiny 0.2 percent of the French population at the time. Yet in the first two months of 1898 French Jews were the targets of no fewer than sixty-nine anti-Semitic riots in which 4,000 people participated; the rioters destroyed Jewish businesses and synagogues and attacked individual Jews.[66] France's anti-Semitic orientation emerged again during World War II in the pro-Nazi Vichy area of France. While the Vichy government opposed the exportation of French Jews to German extermination camps, it did not resist the deportation of foreign Jews in the region.[67] When former French President Francois Mitterand's association with the pro-Nazi Vichy government was revealed in the press, he only responded that at the time "I did not think about the anti-Semitism of Vichy."[68] Official and popular obliviousness to racism, even among "left" politicians, is integral to a culture of racism and its allied racist practices.

During and after the period of France's overseas colonialism, debates surrounding immigration to France have reflected racism in government policies. Today, it is estimated that one in every four French citizens has a non-French parent or grandparent.[69] Currently both popular and official analyses of the problems of immigration focus on those immigrants of color from north and west Africa, most of whom settled in France after the Algerian War of 1954–1962.

Algeria, a country in north Africa, became a French colony in the 1830s, although Algerians vigorously resisted the invasion. French colonial settlers confiscated land and stripped Algerians of all political and economic rights. In response some Algerians advocated complete assimilation of Algerians into French society; others demanded the total independence of Algeria through resistance. Interestingly, when France itself was controlled by the Germans during World War II, Algiers became the capital of Free France. Algerians fought in the French army against Germans in north Africa in expectation of Algerian independence from France after the war. This did not happen. Following the war, a growing Algerian nationalist movement led by the National Liberation Front met with violent suppression from the French colonial government. The war of independence did not end until 1962, when Algeria gained complete independence from France.

Immigrants and Racism

The migration of Algerians to France since 1962 has made Islam the nation's second major religion, after Roman Catholicism. The large number of Muslims in France has kept alive memories of the brutal colonial war and brought a hostile reaction from whites who fear the loss of the essence of French culture.[70] Many native-born French have argued that cultural differences between the native-born and the African immigrants are more important than the racial division. Intellectual and popular debates focus on individual assimilation into or conflict with existing French culture rather than a recognition of the racialized perceptions of different communities and the conflicts that develop between them, as is common in the United States.[71] When the native-born French view segregation in housing as a result of immigrants' individual choices, they miss the dynamics of institutional racism directed against African immigrant groups in the housing market.

Indeed, the term *immigrant* in French (as increasingly, in English) is popularly used to define only those of non-European origin, especially Africans. According to one social worker, "immigrant" is a pejorative word: "I am a foreigner. You and I are foreigners. We are not victims of racism. An immigrant is someone who is forced to leave his country, the poor bloke—Arabs and so on."[72] Officially, people in France are classified in terms of nationality as foreigner or national. Yet there is no popular recognition that those Africans who are naturalized are citizens of France. Unlike naturalized citizens from other parts of Europe, even naturalized Africans remain "undesirable immigrants."

The French far-right has engaged in a great deal of agitation against immigrants from Africa. Interestingly, the proportion of immigrants in the French population has not increased: Immigrants account for about the same proportion of the population today (7 percent) as in 1931. In addition, 80 percent of those popularly classified as immigrants have lived in France more than ten years; one-fourth were born in France. Seventy percent of those under fifteen have never lived in another country.[73]

Especially since 1980, the issue of African immigration has been pushed to the forefront of political debates, particularly by the reactionary Jean-Marie Le Pen and the French far right, which has received as much as 15 percent of the vote in recent French elections. Le Pen's support is greatest in urban areas with sizable numbers of Africans, and his xenophobic racism is especially popular among the Algerian-born French who came to France following Algerian independence. These far-right groups advocate ending African immigration, providing job priority only for native-born French whites, forcing Africans to return to Africa, and reimposing the death penalty for criminals.[74] The far-right particularly objects to the acquisition of French nationality by second-generation Africans, whose parents are often criticized for their attachment to their own cultural values and for teaching these values to their French-born children.[75] Some rightist politicians have even argued that the increasing numbers of Muslims in Europe are a threat to the supposedly Christian core of western civilization. Such arguments have roots going back to the Crusades.

In an effort to attract voters who support the racist right, the French government is pursuing repressive policies against African immigrants and their supporters. For example, in the summer of 1996, when three hundred African immigrants, as well as non-African intellectuals, staged a mass protest in a church, the government sent 1,000 police officers to break down the gates of the church "so that law and order be respected."[76]

Clearly, racism is dividing France politically. An antiracist association called SOS Racism, which includes native-born French and immigrants, is actively challenging the xenophobia, anti-Semitism, and racism of the French Right. SOS

Racism advocates equality of rights and favors giving immigrants the right to vote. SOS Racism had 350 local committees and fifty thousand followers at its inception and attracted media attention in the mid-1980s when it organized an antiracism demonstration that was attended by hundreds of thousands.[77]

Still, the attacks on African (Arab) immigrants continue. The most extreme form of discrimination is *Arabicide,* a term some use for the more than two hundred unsolved murders of Arab residents of France over the last two decades. Fausto Giudice argues that Arabs are killed because they are Arabs. French law includes no category for hate crimes, and the French police do not classify the killings in a way that shows the systematic violence against the French Arab community. These murders are often dismissed by whites as the settling of accounts between rival Arab factions. This official government attitude is similar to the French government's response to the 1961 Papon Massacre during the Algerian War. In that case a demonstration in Paris organized to protest the nightly curfew for Algerians in France was met with massive police violence. Protestors were clubbed, machine gunned, or driven into the Seine River by the police. At least 140 Algerians were killed, and 400 people were declared missing. According to the official government report these were all "gangland killings" between the

Algerian refugees stand in a cluster in Tunisia in 1959.

National Liberation Front and the Algerian National Movement. The police were thereby excused for their killings.[78]

In addition to the violence, anti-African discrimination in housing, the workplace, and education remains commonplace. Muslim communities also face attacks on their culture and traditions. One recent issue is the right of Muslim girls to wear traditional head scarves in French schools. Depending on the circumstances, the wearing of these head scarves has different meanings. Some Muslim feminists have argued that the traditional head scarves for women represent the oppression of patriarchy if forced on women by men. However, other feminists have argued the head scarves can represent an assertion of women's rights if they are worn by women of their own free will. They can thus represent a political statement.

The controversy began in 1989, when three Arab students wearing head scarves were excluded from school classes. In September 1994, the French government banned the wearing of head scarves in public schools, arguing that the practice violated the tradition of secular education. The Education Minister claimed, "We must respect the culture and faith of Muslims, but the history and will of our people was to build a united secular society specifically where schools were concerned." In this view, scarves divided Muslims from non-Muslims, therefore violating the separation of church and state.[79] The French government interprets the increasing number of students wearing head scarves in schools as an indication of the increasing appeal of Muslim fundamentalism in France, including French Muslim support for Algeria's Islamic Salvation Front, which is fighting to establish an Islamic government in Algeria. In fact, the Education Ministry's ban on head scarves coincided with police raids in which the residents of Arab neighborhoods in French cities were arrested on suspicion of being Muslim militants.[80]

During the 1990s, the French government has been deeply involved in the civil war between Islamic militants and the government in Algeria. The government, especially President Jacques Chirac, has supported the Algerian government. Chirac has also aroused the racist sentiments of whites by accusing Algerian immigrants in France of being "welfare cheats" who are alleged to produce many children in order to drain the French welfare system.[81]

Colonialism brings oppression and violence not only to the land of the colonized but also to the land of the colonizer, especially if the colonized migrate to the colonizing country. In the post-colonial era institutional discrimination and the culture of racism persist in countries like France. Immigrants to France experience the violent legacy of colonialism in the land of the colonizer. Their expressions of identity and culture are suppressed with racial hatred. Their social and political participation is restricted even though the French system claims to be democratic. Their economic participation is channeled mostly into low-wage jobs usually spurned by whites. Frantz Fanon, who participated in the Algerian struggle against the French, has noted that violence "has ruled over the colonial world, ... has ceaselessly drummed the rhythm for the destruction of native social forms and broken up without reserve the systems of reference of the economy, the customs of dress and external life."[82] This situation is not unique to France: The ordeals of the East and West Indians in Britain and of the Tatars in Russia are similar to those of North Africans in France.[83]

RACIAL–ETHNIC RELATIONS IN THE POST-SOVIET WORLD: THE CASE OF RUSSIA

Modern Russia is composed of many different racial and ethnic groups with many different cultures and languages. Overall, Russians make up 85 percent of the people in the Russian Republic and more than 85 percent of the population in the city of Moscow. The rest of the population consists of Ukrainians, Byelorussians, Muslims, and other nationalities.

Discriminatory practices are not aimed at the non-Russian ethnic groups that are considered Christian and Slavic, such as the Ukrainians and Byelorussians. However, the non-Slavic groups are often victims of discrimination. One of the non-Slavic groups is Muslims. They began settling around Moscow in the fifteenth century and are now the largest group after Russians in the capital area; in the early 1990s, about 1 million Muslims lived in the Moscow province. In 1994, when some Muslim Tatars (a major Muslim ethnic group) began building an Islamic cultural center in Moscow, the foundation stone was destroyed, and a nearby building was painted with graffiti, including the phrase "Blacks Out!" Some Russians see the Muslims as "mountain people" or even as "mafiosi." They see Russia as under attack from these hated Muslim "others." Father Gregory, a priest at the nearby Church of the Archangel Michael, denounced the construction: "Moscow is and will continue to be a holy city for the Orthodox [Christians]. . . . Moscow is the third Rome, not the second Mecca."[84]

In their thinking many Russians are merging "Muslims" with "blacks" and are thereby rationalizing the move to exclude Muslims from Russian society in a manner modeled after racial segregation in the United States. Recent surveys indicate that more than 60 percent of Russians in Moscow are anti-Muslim ("anti-black"). Since 1991 the Russian government and local authorities have been trying to "cleanse" Moscow of Muslims by legally expelling them, a policy that has received popular support from Russians. At an anti-Muslim rally organized by the Congress of Russian Communities, brutal racism was openly expressed against Muslim Muscovites, including hostile comments such as "Your children will be dismembered [by the Muslims] and roasted on skewers for shish kebab."[85] Nativist notions about Muslim cannibalism remind us of the wild anti-Semitic views held by neo-Nazis and Ku Klux Klan groups around the globe (See Chapter 6).

In addition to anti-Muslim views, anti-Semitism is on the rise in Russia. Since the mid 1980s, the Pamyat Society, an ultranationalist, anti-Semitic, paramilitary organization, has gained support by using openly racist slogans such as "End the power of the Jews over Christians." According to one Jewish Muscovite who attended a Pamyat Society meeting, people wearing black t-shirts and Nazi-style coats chanted poems against Jews: "For the vermin there will come a time. . . . We'll pulverize that filthy reptile slime." While a boy yelled at her about how he was dreaming of bashing in the head of a Jewish child, the Jewish observer heard a mother say to her daughter, "Let's go. . . . They are not telling us anything concrete about how to fight Zionism."[86] Anti-Semitism and anti-Muslim prejudices and discrimination are reaching new levels as Slavic Russians struggle to redefine their identity and Russian nationalism in a rapidly changing post-Soviet world.

The Soviet Union, which was established over the skeleton of the Russian Empire in 1917, maintained the empire's territorial spread and its ethnic and racial configuration of 130 distinct nationalities, including Russians, Jews, Estonians, Ukrainians, Kurds, and Azerbaijanis.[87] The nationalities have distinct languages and religious beliefs varying from Christian Orthodoxy to Buddhism.[88] Through this inheritance, the racial–ethnic problems of the colonial period have extended into the post-colonial period, establishing the terms of a new racial and ethnic colonialism.

Beginning in the seventeenth century, Russian expansionist policy targeted nearby lands on Russia's borders rather than establishing an overseas empire as the British, French, and Dutch had done. Nonetheless, Russian colonialism was similarly based on the trilogy of administration, trade and religion, and violence and destruction for the colonized.

When the Russian Empire first expanded to the nearby Ukraine and other Slavic lands, some local non-Russian elites were granted privileges to facilitate speedy assimilation and cooperation with the Russian colonial administration. However, the Russian Empire developed a more aggressive and violent "Russification" campaign as it moved into the Caucasus and Central Asia, which were populated mostly by Muslims. The Russian Empire began to forcibly convert the Christian populations to Russian Orthodoxy.[89]

Russian colonialism systematically discriminated against and devastated colonized peoples, their economies, and their cultures. For example, the commander of the Russian army in the Caucasus during the early nineteenth century, Paul Tsitsianov, was called the "Shedder of Blood" by the Muslims. He viewed himself as a superior Russian and an agent of change. Phrases such as "Persian scum" and "Asian treachery" in his writings reveal his contempt for Muslims.[90]

To a substantial degree, Russian identity and nationalism were products of this colonial expansion. Formulated around a belief in the superiority of Russian civilization, Russian nationalism had three assumptions: faithfulness to the Russian Orthodox church, an emphasis on the glory of the medieval Muscovite period (with its success against the Muslim Tatars), and faith in the Russian peasantry as a moral force for unity.[91] Russian nationalism overlapped with, and was reinforced by, the supra-nationalist movement of pan-Slavism, which advocated unification of all Slavic people, including the Russians, Ukrainians, Byelorussians, and Serbs, under Russian control. Originating in the late nineteenth century, pan-Slavism was attractive to Slavic intellectuals.[92]

Beginning in 1917, however, Soviet government policy rejected pan-Slavism and similar nationalist movements in favor of a real union of the many different nationalities. Officially the governmental policy was one of cultural autonomy for the many racial–ethnic groups coupled with political and economic unity. Nonetheless, Russian culture gradually came to be celebrated as the superior culture, and the cultures of the "nationalities" were measured against Russian standards.[93] From the earliest times anti-Semitism and other forms of prejudice were institutionalized in the Russian imperial system of education. This educational system became the basis for the new Soviet system, which also emphasized Russian culture and continued to teach non-Russians to view their own cultures as inferior.

Through the means of institutionalized prejudice and discrimination in education and other sectors, the Soviet system supported the advancement of Russians, and a culture of racism was integrated into Communist Party thinking and organization. The authoritarian regimes that followed Joseph Stalin tried to suppress non-Russian nationalism—through coercion or cooptation of the national elites and by the appointment of Russians to leadership positions at all levels of the Communist Party. Russification by the Communist Party was similar to the earlier Russification of the colonial administrations. Both Russian-dominated systems regulated the economy and politics and used ideology or religion to maintain Russian domination.

Since the Soviet Union began to break up in the 1980s, the new freedom not only has fostered a free exchange of ideas and the development of Western-style markets but also has generated strong expressions of nationalism. When the Soviet system collapsed in 1991, a "nationalities problem" emerged for the Russian leaders in regard to maintaining some unity in a territory with many different racial–ethnic groups. The issues included how to deal with the Russians returning from the non-Russian (former Soviet) republics, what to do with breakaway non-Russian groups such as the Chechens, and how to maintain ties to the non-Russian Republics. In addition, the status of the Russian immigrants who make up a significant proportion of the populations in all non-Russian republics of the old Soviet Union became an urgent "foreign" problem for the new Russian Republic. As colonizers in liberated colonial lands, how would these Russian immigrants be treated? Another major issue facing the new Russian Republic was the problem of nationalist separatist movements within Russia itself. The newly independent republics, including Azerbaijan, Georgia, Armenia, Ukraine, and the Baltic republics, are trying to control independence movements among nationalities within their own borders. Resettlement is yet another racial-ethnic problem. For example, about 500,000 Tatars were deported from Crimea to central Asia by Stalin during World War II because of accusations of collaboration with the Germans. Now they want to return to their former territory. Territorial rearrangements imposed by Soviet rule have emerged as critical issues for the new Russia and its former colonies.

Today, Russians and their new government face many problems that stem from the dissolution of the Soviet Union. These include the responsibility for the former Soviet Union's foreign debt and the costs of its industrial pollution and the economic dependency on the now-independent republics as well as rising inflation and unemployment. Often thinking in racist terms, many Russians believe that "alien" nationalities within the Russian federation, such as the Chechens, are the primary cause of their current difficulties and that the instability of the now-independent republics surrounding Russia is contributing to Russia's instability and restricting its advancement into the capitalist global economy.

When the Russian parliament has debated these growing problems, right-wing politicians have often advocated a popular solution: Bring back the Russian empire. In the 1990s, this position, supported by the openly racist rhetoric of Vladimir Zhirinovsky and his right-wing Liberal Democratic Party of Russia, has gathered widespread support among rank-and-file Russians. At a Liberal Democratic Party convention in 1994, Zhirinovsky was cheered by Russian crowds as he was escorted by his "falcons," young men in blue uniforms and black boots with sidearms. His special guests included German neo-fascists. Zhirinovsky and his associates advocate recapturing the past glory of Russia by uniting Slavs against Muslims and Jews and thus recreating Russia in the image of the old empire. General Alexander I. Lebed, a nationalist military leader, has argued: "I am not sure Russia can get used to its current borders—not because of aggression, but because of human ties and marriages. . . . It's impossible to cut these links. . . . It is like cutting flesh."[94] Even Alexander Solzhenitsyn, the anti-Soviet Nobel prize winning Russian author who spent years in exile in the United States advocating "freedom" against Communist authoritarianism, has advocated rebuilding Russia by uniting it with the now independent Slavic republics of Ukraine and Belarus and with Russian-populated territories in the now independent republic of Kazakhstan.[95] Such a reunification might well mean renewed colonial violence against Russia's neighbors.

Today, the possibility that such violence could emerge out of the rhetoric of the extreme nationalist leaders is dismissed by many Russian and Western intellectuals who see the nationalists as members of fringe groups. However, expansionist ideas and their accompanying racism are being integrated into popular culture. As support for these views grows and Zhirinovsky is hailed as "the last hope of cheated and humiliated people," memories of the Russian empire and of pan-Slavism are shaping the discontent of the Russian people.[96] Economic problems may lead Russian leaders to try to satisfy the Russian public through pro-Russian, racist policy proposals.

Indeed, in 1997, Russian president Boris Yeltsin and many other Russians supported a law creating a heirarchy of religious groups, with the Russian Orthodox church at the top followed by other Christian churches and the Jewish and Muslim faiths. While Russian Orthodox church officials maintained that this law "secures and defends the rights of Russian believers,"[97] many observers felt that this government-supported law would generate more hatred and discord between Russian religious and ethnic groups and thus distract attention away from the political and economic failures of the government.

One Russian historian has argued that "the history of Russia is the history of a country that colonizes itself." The new Russian government's policies reveal that recolonization, the building of a new empire, has already begun.[98] Besides remili-

tarizing Russia, the new nationalist position has led national and local governments to pass laws discriminating against non-Russian groups, including laws
that force the removal of Muslims from Moscow in order to "cleanse" the capital.
In addition, governments are allowing anti-Semitism to flourish along with discriminatory and segregative practices against non-Russians in housing, employment, and education. The new Russian nationalism stresses the commonality of
Slavic interests, a position that can be seen in Russian support for the Serbian
(anti-Muslim) position regarding the war in Bosnia and Croatia. The nationalist
right also takes credit for the anti-Western and anti-American tone in new Russian
foreign policy.

The old Soviet Union was an example of how the colonialism and racism of
the Russian imperial past were integrated into a new social and political system
theoretically based on equality for citizens of different racial–ethnic groups. Even
though the expressed aim of the new Soviet system created after 1917 was to eradicate the injustice and discrimination of the imperial past, it nonetheless evolved
to perpetuate and reinforce the old racism, primarily because the new system did
not confront the racism imbedded in Russian culture and society. Although the
Soviet Union's leaders vowed to start anew, the racist past lived on under a thin
veneer of cultural equality and autonomy. Since the destruction of the Soviet
Union in 1991, Russia's leaders and much of the Russian populace have become
open in their display of the racist baggage of their imperial past, as can be seen in
their many racist political debates and policies. The new Russian reality illustrates
how racism not only establishes itself through colonialism but leaves a legacy in
the post-colonial period even though the political-economic system undergoes a
total transformation. Racism has remained through all Russia's social changes; it
now dominates domestic politics and influences foreign policy in ever more fundamental ways.

"ETHNIC CLEANSING" IN BOSNIA, CROATIA, AND SERBIA

The dissolution of the former Soviet Union and the changes that led to the
interethnic war in the former Yugoslavia in the 1990s are closely related events.
Yugoslavia became a socialist federal republic in 1945 through the union of six
Slavic communities, including Serbs, Croats, and Bosnians. The union began to
dissolve in the 1980s when the Communist Party weakened, and its strong central control gave way to regional power structures organized primarily around
non-Communist, nationalist parties. In the 1990s, the conflict between several of
these communities led to a war involving Bosnia-Hercegovina, Croatia, and
Serbia. Yugoslavia's prewar population was about 23 million. The Serbs made
up about 40 percent; the Croats, 23 percent; and the Muslims of Bosnia-
Hercegovina, 9 percent. As a result of the war, at least 1 million Muslims have
become refugees, and in northern Bosnia, once home to 200,000 Muslims, 7,000
were left in late 1994.

Ties to Other European Powers

In the recent war in the former Yugoslavia we see actions once thought to be limited to the madness of the Nazis in Germany. Atrocities of this war included "ethnic cleansing," death by starvation in concentration camps, and the rape of more than 20,000 Bosnian Muslim women by Serbian soldiers. The Serbs carried out what some call "slow-motion genocide."[99] Some outsiders have been supportive of the Serbs. For instance, a senior French diplomat has been quoted as saying, "Our interests are closer to the Serbs than you think."[100] He added that the French have more to fear from the Muslims than from the Serbs. In addition, in the past the Germans have had ties to the Croatians, who were their allies during World War II. Only the Bosnian Muslims have no supporter among the major European states.

The governments of other European countries and of the United States have not responded in an effective way to the Serbs' fears of annihilation by Muslims or Croatians, or the Serbs' "ethnic cleansing" of Muslims and Croatians in what the Serbs claim as their territory. Most other Europeans seem uncomfortable about a Muslim-led state in Bosnia. A French parliament member said "what many in my party fear is the emergence of a kind of Gaza Strip in the midst of the Balkans."[101] United Nations officials have been cautious about the role of the U.N. peacekeeping force in the region.[102] The U.S. government has been understandably reluctant to intervene in Europe. In September 1994, the United States decided to abandon a push to end a weapons embargo on Bosnia, even though the Serbs were still violating negotiated ceasefires.[103] Thus, the strife in Yugoslavia is about more than local territorial control; it is also about old European politics and the present and future of ethnic and racial conflicts. The divisions that underlie the conflict have often been interpreted as "modern nationalism." However, in the view of Ivo Banac the constant references to nationalism, civil war, and "ancient hatreds" are only a way of accommodating aggression between communities and of rationalizing the violence that has claimed many lives.[104]

Based on similar Slavic ancestry and language and their Orthodox Christianity, Russia and Serbia have had a special relationship. Based on this relationship, the Russian army has intervened in Serbia many times over the last few centuries. Many Slavic politicians used the tools of Pan-Slavism and "Slavic Brotherhood" long before the birth of the present Serbian and Russian leaders. In the case of Bosnia, the Serbs have depended on Russia's support for their aggression. Russian leaders support the Serbs in part to create Russian unity around a popular cause and in part to advance Russia's influence in the region.[105] As one Russian politician stated, "Russia has . . . returned to the sources of its historical policy and role in the Balkans and defended the Serbs, who are close in faith, culture, and national spirit."[106] Some diplomats argue that Russians are not deeply committed to the Serbs, but rather that this conflict is more important in establishing "the parameters of [Russian] influence in Europe and the world."[107] While the Bosnian conflict may be a matter of politics for some, it is said to be a matter of "honor" for the Serbian army's Russian volunteers, who reportedly believe that "all the Slavs in Europe are being suppressed."[108] Russian soldiers, who have fought along with Serbian army regulars since 1992, were not the only volunteers. According to U.N. sources, in 1994 two French soldiers stationed with U.N. forces left their posts to join the Serbs. Serb military officials said that the French soldiers joined the Serbs to "fight the Muslims who have flooded France, which will soon also have to begin fighting against them."[109]

The war in the former Yugoslavia reveals how history can be used and reconstructed to justify ethnic violence. The former Yugoslavia stood at the crossroads of major historical events in the European past. Its history relative to the recent conflict began with the Ottoman conquest of Bosnia in 1463. Europe was uneasy about this Ottoman expansion, and at the time Europe's Christian leaders saw the confrontation as an extension of the Crusades—Islam versus Christianity. Croatia's Roman Catholic Slavs and Serbia's Orthodox Christian Slavs viewed the Bosnian Slavs who converted to Islam as agents of Ottoman colonial rule and carriers of a non-Christian Muslim religious identity. This view has lasted to the present. After 1918, when the Kingdom of the Serbs, Croats, and Slovenes governed the area, the Serbs emerged as the dominant group. The oppression of this Serbian rule generated widespread anti-Serbian sentiment, especially among Croats. When Germany invaded the area during World War II, the Croats collaborated with German Nazis in the killing of many Serbs and Muslims as well as Jews and Gypsies.

After World War II, the major task of the new Communist regime was to establish a nonantagonistic general Yugoslavian identity that enveloped all groups and promoted cooperative coexistence. Yet the supposedly "new" identity was no more than a cloak for the identities of the past that remained integrated in current politics and popular memory. As the Bosnian war has shown, aggression is perpetrated not only against people but against memory and the objects of civilization as well. For example, the library of Bosnia-Hercegovina, which contained manuscripts written over a period of a thousand years, was shelled and much of its collection consumed in a fire. The destruction of mosques and churches accompanied the torture and slaughter of civilians.[110] The Serbs' motivation apparently was to retaliate against Bosnian Muslims for their fifteenth century surrender to the Ottoman invaders and to avenge the Croatians' World War II genocidal actions against Serbs.[111] Serbian leaders said they are remembering that in 1941 Croatian leaders planned a thorough cleansing of "Serbian dirt" from Bosnia and Croatia.[112]

The events surrounding the breakup of Yugoslavia provide a window to the future of European racial–ethnic relations. Russian and European support for Serbs as well as Croatians is based on a shared past of Christian religion and culture, which reinforces a shared sense of Slavic roots. The possibility of a state dominated by Muslims in Bosnia is bringing back the centuries-old anti-Muslim language of the Crusades to Europe, arguments focusing on the conflict of interests between Muslims and Christians. The attacks on Bosnian Muslims illustrate how Christian religion and culture have become part of a culture of ethnic hostility and racism that is the heritage of colonialism common to white Christians throughout

Europe. Significantly, the Christian Serbs and their Russian allies are attacking fellow Slavs, who are not only Muslim but also "white" and European! Serbian leaders have long claimed that Serbian unity is based on bonds of blood, but in reality it is their Orthodox Christian culture that most unifies them. Muslims are viewed as enemies.

For a time it appeared that Bosnia-Hercegovina, the part of the former Yugoslavia that has been home to a mixture of Serbs, Croats, and Bosnian Muslims, might become a multiethnic state. Yet the idea of a state dominated by Muslims in Bosnia has elicited massive Serbian aggression legitimated in the centuries-old language that speaks of good Christians and infidel Muslims.

Today, as we also saw in the case of France, this view of the Muslims is an integral part of the modern European culture of post-colonial ethnic and racial hostility. Today, this anti-Muslim view forms the basis of neo-colonial policies for those white-Christian states emerging from the cold-war era as dominant European states. One example of this is the debate at the United Nations and elsewhere about whether the bloody killings of Muslims in Bosnia constitute *genocide*. Genocide, the systematic annihilation of members of a particular racial or ethnic group, was declared a crime against humanity by the UN General Assembly in 1948. According to the United Nations, a definition of events as genocide requires a multi-country reaction to these events. However, the United Nations' reluctance to define the Muslim killings in Bosnia as genocide is reminiscent of the similar reluctance on the part of the United States and its allies to recognize the reality of the Holocaust as it was being carried out by German Nazis during World War II. Even after bloody pictures of ethnic cleansing in Bosnia were seen nightly on television screens and in newspapers beginning in August 1992, the United Nations could not decide whether this mass killing was genocide.

In the late 1990s, the second international tribunal on war crimes, following the example of the post-World War II Nuremberg trials of Nazi war criminals, is examining the evidence of Bosnian genocide, such as concentration camps and graveyards, in order to establish responsibility for the mass killings. While some soldiers have been tried at the international tribunal in the Hague and in Germany, as of now (mid-1998) the top leaders who gave the orders for the mass killings are still free. The international human rights community and anti-racist intellectuals have questioned the reasons for not arresting the war criminals in Bosnia, Serbia, and Croatia, while the United Nations and the international tribunal drag their feet with excuses such as lack of financial support. Such ambivalence about genocide against Muslims and other racial–ethnic groups is evidence of the continuing impact of colonialism and racism in the post-colonial era.

THE FUTURE OF COLONIALISM AND POST-COLONIALISM

As we noted earlier, Edward Said uses the term *orientalism* to designate the Eurocentric perspective that has encompassed the economic and political interests of the West in other nations around the globe. Orientalism views African, Eastern, and Islamic societies as static and nonrational and defines European nations as progressive and rational. Societies outside Europe are seen as inherently *inferior*. Orientalism has legitimated the oppression of non-Europeans from the early days of capitalist expansion to the present. Orientalism ignores European colonizers' role in post-colonial interracial and interethnic conflicts as well as Europeans' continuing desires for the natural resources of post-colonial lands. And orientalism allows French schools to force Muslim female students to remove their head scarves, which are seen as backward symbols of fundamentalist Islam.

With the imperialistic expansion of capitalism, European racism became a global culture, tying the hatred and exclusion of peoples of African ancestry together with the hatred and exclusion of Jews and Muslims—from Moscow to Rio de Janiero to Paris to New York. Targeting populations considered physically, culturally, and religiously different, Europeans and Euro-Americans constantly create and re-create material and ideological racism. Through the expansion of European and Euro-American capitalism, racism has become a global mode of thought that has been integrated into the formation of many new communities and countries around the world. Through administration, trade, and religion, colonialism made racism part of many institutions and many cultures. Colonialism reinforced preexisting differences in colonized and colonizing societies, thereby creating racist hierarchies of superiority and inferiority, which became integrated into popular knowledge through the construction of the "self" and the "other." For the colonizing society, the "other" has always been stereotyped as inferior, ugly, dirty, lazy, or barbaric.[113]

During colonialism and the post-colonial era, Europeans and Euro-Americans have believed that the seeds of "westernization" and "modernization" will bring "civilization" to the colonies. Expecting a slow evolution, modernization theorists argue that Euro-colonialism spread Western culture and ideology to the inferior lands. Following westernization, conflict between the colonizers and the colonized was expected to eventually disappear as the colonized peoples assimilated into the dominant European culture.

However, this westernization view is not only racist but unrealistic. First, the westernization process requires colonized peoples to accept racist stereotypes of themselves as "inferior." Secondly, the westernization process demands that colonized peoples acquiesce to the continuation of global patterns of racial–ethnic inequality by accepting external European and American economic and political domination. These two aspects of westernization reinforce one another and re-create colonialism in the post-colonial era. One example can be seen in the maintenance of non-European countries as extractive economies that provide natural resources for Europeans; this arrangement perpetuates the colonial exploitation of human and natural resources and the destruction of cultures, bodies, and spirits.[114]

Some Western analysts argue that colonial control of "underdeveloped" countries established new economic development and strong state administrations and thus helped most colonized societies advance into the "modern world." One goal of Western colonization, however, was to create local elites that were assimilated to Western cultures. The well-educated indigenous elites created by the colonial administrations are offered as evidence of the success of this modernization process, even though most of the elites are considered by their own peoples to be as foreign as the European colonizers.[115]

Challenging this colonialism and racism, power–conflict analysts reject this assimilationist and westernizing perspective. They argue that today as in the past racism is a global epidemic, although it has not yet been globally confronted. From the power–conflict perspective, the awareness of global diversity should emphasize differences for the purpose of creating new terms of coexistence to establish peace. Current world conditions do not allow for the careful exploration of alternatives to external colonialism or its post-independence variants (for example, economic colonialism), in part because warring factions in many post-colonial countries continue to practice oppression and violence. In Bosnia interethnic violence continues to take human lives, while in the United States, South Africa, Brazil, and France institutionalized racial discrimination continues to destroy the lives and communities of people of color.

The human slavery, whether of indigenous or imported populations, that was a common aspect of colonialism had effects that have lasted to the present. As it destroyed human beings and their cultures, it became integrated into social institutions that still dominate post-colonial societies. For example, South Africa is today confronting the continuing effects of slavery under its slowly disintegrating apartheid system; African Americans and Afro-Brazilians are demanding an abolition of the contemporary effects of slavery in their lives and communities.

From a power–conflict perspective colonialism is an exploitative system that brought great racial and ethnic inequalities to many nations. Racial subordination integrated segregation and racial inequality into the everyday life of North Americans, South Africans, and Brazilians. In the post-colonial era the painful realities of Euro-colonialism are evident in the continuing racial inequality and segregation in education, housing, business, employment, and health care. Around the globe this inequality influences the life chances of all people of color who were (and are) racially, ethnically, and religiously oppressed. Although the modes of inequality and segregation may be different, oppression and violence have been perpetuated in the post-colonialist era in both the colonizing and colonized societies.

From the power–conflict perspective, a realistic assessment of the present and future of post-colonial societies requires a confrontation with the entrenched inequality and segregation and a major struggle against the practices and effects of institutionalized racism and the global culture of racism. After World War II, the conditions of the cold-war era defined the possibilities for the colonial societies as they revolted against their colonial masters. The cold war between the Soviet Union and the United States and its European allies shaped the economic dependency and cultural experiences of many post-colonial societies. *Neocolonialism*—the continuation of the economic and cultural dominance of the former colonial states—was an extension of the bipolar cold war. When the Soviet Union broke up in the late 1980s and early 1990s and the cold war ended, many people in the former Soviet Union and in its satellites pressed toward full independence with the expectation that colonialism and neocolonialism, including that of the former Soviet Union, would end. However, this has not been the case. In most of these countries Communism has been replaced by a form of capitalism that constitutes a new type of economic and political colonialism with ties to Western banks and corporations. As the capitalist system recreates itself in new colonial forms, it often creates new modes of inequality and segregation that remain imbedded in a culture of ethnic hostility and racism.[116]

SUMMARY

European racism became a global reality through colonialism, which operated through bureaucratic administrations, exploitative trade, and a missionary type of Christian culture. European, and later American, colonizers rationalized their colonial expansion and violence by defining themselves as superior civilizations whose duty it was to modernize the uncivilized. The construction of colonized peoples as racially inferior was a fundamental aspect of the legitimizing of exploitation. Colonialism was deadly in many ways. It destroyed local economies and political arrangements. It even shaped many colonized peoples' conceptions of themselves and of their future possibilities. Racist culture and racist institutions were integral to European colonialism, and Euro-racism has persisted in numerous ways into the post-colonial era. Everywhere, institutional racism can be seen in racial prejudices, emotions, practices, and institutions.

The colonization of black South Africans by European states began in the seventeenth century. Over a 300-year period a powerful racist ideology and culture evolved that has shaped every aspect of the existence of black South Africans from housing to education to employment. The racist system of apartheid created separate racial communities. Since the free election of 1994, white and black South Africans are attempting to reconcile differences in a post-apartheid system. They face major obstacles because of persisting overt racism and institutionalized discrimination.

In contrast to racism in South Africa, Brazilian racism is more subtle and is wrapped in the myth of "racial democracy." Brazil was colonized in the sixteenth century. Today, Brazilian politics, economy, and society reveal the impact of this European colonization and the slave system imposed by whites. Even though slavery was abolished more than 100 years ago, a culture of racism is evident in institutionalized racial discrimination, media and intellectual discussions, popular culture, and other aspects of everyday life. This white racism penetrates the images Brazilians have of who they are and works to divide Brazilians, including those with some African ancestry, according to shades of skin color. One hundred years after slavery's abolition, neocolonialism persists in the way that whites treat people of African ancestry and in the way that all Brazilians view themselves and their communities.

Colonialism left scars on colonized lands and also on colonizer countries. The post-colonial lives of colonized and colonizers have been plagued by disruption and violence. For example, France, a colonizer, has experienced continuing violence in the post-colonial era. Racialized thinking and practice are part of an institutionalized racism directed against French Muslims, who still experience verbal and physical violence, the destruction of property, and attacks on Muslim cultures.

During the 1990s, the breakup of the Soviet Union and the war in the former Yugoslavia offered a glimpse of the future of global ethnic and racial relations. In Russia the global racist culture penetrated pre-existing patterns of institutionalized discrimination and reinforced them. In Moscow some Russians refer to light-skinned Muslims from the Caucasus as "blacks," even though these Muslims' physical characteristics resemble the Russians themselves. It is clear that the Russian use of the term "black" does not refer to skin color but to "alien" cultural characteristics. Muslims are "black" regardless of coloring or origins. This Russian racism is very ironic. Johann Blumenbach, the German anatomist who originated the hierarchy of races from "Caucasians" to "Malays," thought that the people in the Caucasus were the "most beautiful" of all white Europeans. Russian racism can also be seen in the new emphasis on superior Russian national identity, which includes reinvigorated colonial dreams of Russian expansion into the inferior cultures on the Russian borders. In Bosnia, Serbs and Muslims have engaged in a violent struggle confronting the ghosts of the past and the ethnic differences of the present, thereby paving the way for a bitter ethnic future.

Yet the European community, the United States, and the United Nations have been hesitant to condemn the violent acts in Bosnia. They have also been reluctant to name and confront racism in other places around the globe. The world appears to be in the increasingly tight grip of a culture of ethnic hostility and racism long propagated by European colonialism and neocolonialism—a world in which ethnic and racial discrimination and violence are accepted as common, everyday occurrences.

Glossary

affirmative action programs—private and governmental programs that seek to improve the economic opportunities for formerly excluded racial, ethnic, and gender groups

Anglo-Protestant—a more accurate term for those often referred to as white Anglo-Saxon Protestant Americans

Anglo-Saxon—a term that originally referred to Germanic tribes, the Angles and the Saxons, that came to the area now called England in the fifth and sixth centuries A.D.; it was later applied to the inhabitants of England and to those English who came to North America

anti-Semitism—stereotyping of, prejudice toward, or discrimination against Jews

assimilation—an incoming group's adoption of the cultural traits and identity of the host group or integration into the primary networks and secondary organizations of the host group

attitude-receptional assimilation—Milton Gordon's term for the absence of prejudice and stereotyping

authoritarian personalities—personalities characterized by a high degree of submission to authority, a tendency to stereotype, great concern for status, a view of the world as threatening, and an intolerance of outgroups that occupy socially subordinate positions

behavior-receptional assimilation—Milton Gordon's term for the absence of intentional discrimination

bilingualism—the ability to speak two or more languages; school (and similar) programs for children speaking two languages

braceros—farm workers on seasonal contracts (for example, Mexican farm workers)

caste school of race relations—power-conflict theory that emphasizes institutionalized discrimination as the foundation of a caste-like system of U.S. apartheid

Chicano political movement—a militant political movement that began during the 1960s and that has sought increased power and respect for Mexican Americans

civic assimilation—Milton Gordon's term for the absence of value and power conflict between two racial or ethnic groups

civil rights movement—a collective movement to establish or improve the legal and political rights of a subordinate racial or ethnic group

color coding—social stratification based on skin color

competition theory—a view of ethnicity that emphasizes the stability of ethnic boundaries over time and the intergroup competition over resources that results from shifts in these boundaries that result from migration

competitive capitalism—an economic system dominated by competition between small and medium-sized for-profit businesses

conformity function of prejudice—prejudiced attitudes held in order to conform to the expectations of an important social reference group

506

covert discrimination—harmful treatment of members of subordinate racial and ethnic groups that is hidden and difficult to document

cultural assimilation—the change of one group's cultural patterns to those of the host group

cultural pluralism—the view that each racial or ethnic group has the democratic right to preserve and practice its own cultural heritage without being forced to assimilate to a dominant culture

direct institutionalized discrimination—organizationally prescribed or community-prescribed action that by intention has a differential and negative impact on members of subordinate racial and ethnic groups

discrimination—actions carried out by members of dominant groups, or their representatives, that have a differential and harmful impact on members of subordinate racial or ethnic groups

dominant group—a racial or ethnic group with the greatest power and resources in a society (also called a majority group)

ethnic enclave—the economic (often market) and social niche that certain racial and ethnic groups have developed as a way of surviving or prospering in U.S. cities

ethnic group—a group socially distinguished or set apart, by others or by itself, primarily on the basis of cultural or national-origin characteristics

ethnogenesis—the sociological theory that over time immigrant groups not only share cultural traits with the host group but also retain major nationality characteristics

ethnoviolence—violence directed at an individual or group because of their ethnic identity

external colonialism—the economic or political exploitation of overseas societies by powerful groups, such as aristocrats or capitalists, in another (imperial) society

externalization function of prejudice—the transfer of an individual's internal psychological problem to an external racial or ethnic group as an attempted solution to a personal psychological problem

gendered racism—the interaction of racial discrimination and sexual discrimination that affects women of color

genocide—the deliberate and systematic extermination of a nationality or racial group

hate crimes—crimes motivated by hatred of a racial or ethnic outgroup

identification assimilation—Milton Gordon's term for an incoming group's development of a sense of identity linked to that of the host group

ideological racism—an ideology that considers a group's unchangeable physical characteristics to be linked in a direct, causal way to psychological or intellectual characteristics, and that on this basis distinguishes between superior and inferior racial groups

illegals—undocumented immigrants

indigenous superordination—a societal condition in which immigrant groups are placed in a subordinate position to a host-dominant group

indirect institutionalized discrimination—dominant-group practices that have a harmful impact on members of subordinate race and ethnic groups even though the organizationally or community-prescribed norms guiding the actions were established with no intent to harm

individual racism—racially hostile acts of an individual directed at one or more members of another racial group

institutional racism—institutionalized practices that differentially and negatively affect members of a subordinate racial group

intermarriage—marriage between members of different racial or cultural groups

internal colonialism—the colony-like control and exploitation of subordinate groups by a dominant group within a given society

IQ tests—paper-and-pencil or object/symbol manipulation tests that advocates claim can measure a global human intelligence

isolate discrimination—harmful action taken intentionally by a member of a dominant racial or ethnic group against members of a subordinate group, without the support of the immediate social or community context

lynching—the illegal killing of a person by a mob, especially by hanging

Mafia myth—a stereotype of Italian Americans as substantially involved in organized crime and violence

marital assimilation—significant intermarriage between one racial or ethnic group and another racial or ethnic group

Marranos—Jews who were forced to publicly convert to Christianity during the Spanish Inquisition under threat of death but who privately maintained allegiance to Judaism

melting pot—the view that immigrants to the United States have lost or will lose their racial-ethnic identities as they mix together in one new American blend

middleman minority—a racial or ethnic group that occupies an in-between position in terms of societal power and resources

migrant superordination—a societal condition in which immigrants assume a dominant position over an indigenous population

millenarian movements—movements among native groups, such as Native Americans, that included the belief in a golden age in which supernatural events would change present oppressive conditions

minority group—a group that is singled out because of physical or cultural characteristics for differential and unequal treatment and whose members become objects of discrimination; it typically has less power and resources than the dominant group (also called a subordinate group)

model minority stereotype—the non-Asian stereotype that views certain Asian American groups as uniquely exemplary in socioeconomic and moral characteristics compared to other people of color

modern racism—symbolic racism

movements of forced labor—involuntary immigration, such as the forcible removal of Africans to North America

multiculturalism—cultural pluralism; the political or educational movement to respect the human rights of all Americans and to recognize the diverse cultural ways of the many racial and ethnic groups in the United States, particularly those groups that have suffered widespread racial-ethnic discrimination

multinational capitalism—an economic system dominated by large-scale, for-profit corporations that operate in many different countries, thereby creating an international market system

nativism—an anti-immigrant ideology that advocates the protection of the native inhabitants of a country from immigrants who are seen as threatening or dangerous

oppositional culture—the culture of resistance often found among subordinate groups; distinct from the dominant culture, it reflects the struggle with that dominant culture

order theories—racial-ethnic theories that accent group adaptation patterns involving the orderly and progressive assimilation of particular racial and ethnic groups to a dominant culture and its related institutions

patriarchal system—a social system in which men generally predominate in power and status over women and in which men maintain the subordinate social roles for women

power–conflict theories—racial-ethnic theories that accent the persisting and great inequality in the power and resource distributions associated with racial or ethnic subordination in a society

prejudice—an antipathy, felt or expressed, based upon a faulty generalization and directed toward a group as a whole or toward individual members of a group

race—a term developed in the 1700s by European analysts to refer to what is also called a racial group (see racial group)

race relations cycle—Robert E. Park's view of a progressive sequence of intergroup events that usually results from one group's migration into a host society: contact, competition, accommodation, and eventual assimilation

racial and ethnic hierarchy—stratification of, and substantial inequality among, a society's racial and ethnic groups

racial formation theory—the view that racial-ethnic relations and hierarchies in a society are substantially defined by the historical actions of governments

racial group—a social group that persons inside or outside the group have decided is important to single out as inferior or superior, typically on the basis of real or alleged physical characteristics subjectively selected

Reconstruction—the period in U.S. history following the Civil War during which an attempt was made by the federal government to disenfranchise the slaveholding oligarchy of the South and to improve the economic, educational, political, and human rights conditions for poor white and black Americans in the South

Scotch-Irish immigrants—immigrants from northern Ireland whose ancestors are said to have immigrated to Ireland from Scotland

slavery—the legal ownership of one human being by another; the system that makes the trade in and ownership of human beings possible

small-group discrimination—harmful action taken intentionally by a small number of dominant-group individuals acting in concert against members of subordinate racial and ethnic groups without the support of the immediate social or community context

split labor market view—a power-conflict perspective that argues that the white employer class and the white part of the working class both discriminate, to a substantial degree independently, against the racially subordinated part of the working class

stereotype—an image, usually negative, of a racial or ethnic outgroup that is false or that greatly distorts the real characteristics of the outgroup

structural assimilation—Milton Gordon's term for an incoming group's penetration of the primary social networks of the host group

subordinate group—a group that is singled out because of physical or cultural characteristics for differential and unequal treatment and whose members become objects of discrimination; it typically has less power and fewer resources than the dominant group

subtle discrimination—unequal and harmful treatment of members of subordinate racial and ethnic groups that is obvious to the victim but not as overt as traditional "doorslamming" varieties of discrimination

symbolic racism—beliefs held by some whites that serious antiblack discrimination does not exist today and that African Americans or other people of color are making illegitimate demands for social and racial change

systemic discrimination—institutionalized patterns of discrimination that cut across most political, economic, and social organizations in a society

undocumented immigrants—immigrants without legal immigration papers

voluntary migration—migration primarily by choice

white Anglo-Saxon protestant Americans—a label often applied to Protestant Americans whose ancestry is English or British

Zionism—a worldwide movement for the establishment in Palestine of a national homeland for the world's Jewish communities

Notes

PART I

1. Leonard Dinnerstein and Frederic C. Jaher, "Introduction," in *The Aliens*, eds. Leonard Dinnerstein and Frederic C. Jaher (New York: Appleton-Century-Crofts, 1970), p. 4.
2. Leonard Dinnerstein and Frederic C. Jaher, "The Colonial Era," in *The Aliens*, eds. Dinnerstein and Jahr, p. 17.
3. Quoted in Peter M. Bergman, *The Chronological History of the Negro in America* (New York: Harper & Row, 1969), p. 52.
4. John Hope Franklin, *From Slavery to Freedom*, 2nd ed. (New York: Knopf, 1963), pp. 141–43.
5. Ibid., p. 143.
6. Samuel E. Morison, *The Oxford History of the American People* (New York: Oxford University Press, 1965), p. 353.

CHAPTER 1

1. Frances F. Marcus, "Louisiana Repeals Black Blood Law," *The New York Times*, July 6, 1983, p. A10.
2. Wilton M. Krogman, "The Concept of Race," in *The Science of Man in the World Crisis*, ed. Ralph Linton (New York: Columbia University Press, 1945) p. 38.
3. Winthrop D. Jordan, *White over Black* (Baltimore, MD: Penguin, 1969), p. 217.
4. Stephen J. Gould, "The Geometer of Race," *Discover*, November 1994, pp. 65–66.
5. Audrey Smedley, *Race in North America* (Boulder, CO: Westview, 1993), pp. 303–305.
6. Ibid, p. 26.
7. Peter I. Rose, *The Subject Is Race* (New York: Oxford University Press, 1968), pp. 32–33; Thomas F. Gossett, *Race* (New York: Schocken Books, 1965), p. 3.
8. M. Annette Jaimes, "Liberating Race," in *The State of Asian America: Activism and Resistance in the 1990s*, ed. Karin Aguilar-San Juan (Boston, MA: South End Press, 1994), p. 369.
9. Ibid., p. 370.
10. See Pierre L. van den Berghe, *Race and Racism* (New York: Wiley, 1967), p. 11.
11. Robert Bennett Bean, *The Races of Man* (New York: University Society, 1935), pp. 94–96, quoted in *In Their Place: White America Defines Her Minorities, 1850–1950*, ed. Lewis H. Carlson and George A. Colburn (New York: Wiley, 1972), p. 106.
12. Eugenia Shanklin, *Anthropology and Race* (Belmont, CA: Wadsworth, 1994).
13. James Shreeve, "Terms of Estrangement," *Discover*, November 1994, p. 60; see also Paul Hoffman, "The Science of Race," *Discover*, November 1994, p. 4.
14. Jared Diamond, "Race without Color," *Discover*, November 1994, p. 84.
15. Michael Banton and Jonathan Harwood, *The Race Concept* (New York: Praeger, 1975), pp. 13–50.
16. See Nathan Rutstein, *Healing Racism in America* (Springfield, MA: Whitcomb, 1993), pp. 1–51, 121–129.
17. Ashley Montagu, *Race, Science and Humanity* (Princeton, NJ: D. Van Nostrand, 1963).
18. Oliver C. Cox, *Caste, Class, and Race* (Garden City, NY: Doubleday, 1948), p. 402.
19. Van den Berghe, *Race and Racism*, p. 9.
20. Michael Banton, *Race Relations* (New York: Basic Books, 1967), p. 57; see also p. 58.
21. Charles Wagley and Marvin Harris, *Minorities in the New World* (New York: Columbia University Press, 1958), p. 7.
22. Thomas F. Pettigrew, *A Profile of the Negro American* (Princeton, NJ: D. Van Nostrand, 1964), p. 69.
23. Bill Zimmerman and Bob Herzog, "Golf: From Sheep to Tiger," *Newsday*, August 13, 1997, p. A34.
24. Denene Millner, "In Creating a Word to Describe His Racial Makeup, Golfer Tiger Woods Has Also Stirred Up a Round of Controversy among Blacks," *New York Daily News*, June 8, 1997, p. 2.
25. Wire reports, *Newsday*, May 20, 1997, p. A57.
26. Joe Drape, "Woods Meets Zoeller for Lunch," *The New York Times*, May 21, 1997, p. B13.
27. Barbara Vobejda, "Hill Reassured on Racial Checkoff Plan for Census," *The Washington Post*, July 26, 1997, p. A4; Art Shriberg and Carol Lloyd, "Interracial Marriages Still Taboo," *Tampa Tribune*, June 5, 1997, p. 1.
28. Milton M. Gordon, *Assimilation in American Life* (New York: Oxford University Press, 1964), p. 27.
29. Nathan Glazer, "Blacks and Ethnic Groups: The Difference, and the Political Difference It Makes," *Social Problems* 18 (Spring 1971): 447. See also Nathan Glazer and Daniel P. Moynihan, "Introduction," in *Ethnicity*, ed. Nathan Glazer and Daniel P. Moynihan (Cambridge, MA: Harvard University Press, 1975), p. 4.
30. Werner Sollors, *The Invention of Ethnicity* (New York: Oxford University Press, 1989); Thomas Sowell, *Ethnic America* (New York: Basic Books, 1981).
31. William M. Newman, *American Pluralism* (New York: Harper & Row, 1973), p. 19.
32. W. Lloyd Warner and Leo Srole, *The Social Systems of American Ethnic Groups* (New Haven, CT: Yale University Press, 1945), pp. 284–286.
33. Van den Berghe, *Race and Racism*, p. 10.
34. See Glazer, "Blacks and Ethnic Groups."
35. D. John Grove, *The Race vs. Ethnic Debate: A Cross-National Analysis of Two Theoretical Approaches* (Denver, CO: Center on International Race Relations, University of Denver, 1974); Robert Blauner, *Racial Oppression in America* (New York: Harper & Row, 1972).
36. Philomena Essed, *Understanding Everyday Racism* (Newbury Park, CA: Sage Publications, Inc., 1991), p. 28.
37. Letter to authors from Edna Bonacich, October 1994.
38. St. Clair Drake, *Black Folk Here and There* (Los Angeles: UCLA Center for Afro-American Studies, 1987), 1: xxiii. See also vol. 2 of this work.
39. Frank Snowden, *Color Prejudice* (Cambridge, MA: Harvard University Press, 1983), pp. 3–4, 107–108.
40. Max Weber, "Ethnic Groups," in *Theories of Society*, ed. Talcott Parsons, et al. (Glencoe, IL: Free Press, 1961), vol. 1, p. 306.

41. Joane Nagel, "Constructing Ethnicity: Creating and Recreating Ethnic Identity and Culture," *Social Problems,* 43 (February 1994): 152.

42. Mary Waters, *Ethnic Options: Choosing Identities in America* (Berkeley, CA: University of California Press, 1990).

43. Mary Waters, "The Intersection of Race and Ethnicity." Paper presented at annual meeting of the American Sociological Association, Cincinnati, Ohio, 1991.

44. This term was suggested by Donald M. Young in *American Minority Peoples* (New York: Harper, 1932), p. xviii.

45. Louis Wirth, "The Problem of Minority Groups," in *The Science of Man in the World Crisis,* ed. Linton, p. 347.

46. Clifford Goertz, *The Interpretation of Cultures* (New York: Basic Books, 1973), p. 89.

47. Wendy Griswold, *Cultures and Societies in a Changing World* (Thousand Oaks, CA: PinForge Press, 1994), p. xiv.

48. Milton M. Gordon, *Assimilation in American Life* (New York: Oxford University Press, 1964), pp. 72–73.

49. William G. Sumner, *Folkways* (New York: Mentor Books, 1960), pp. 27–28.

50. Robin M. Williams, Jr., *Strangers Next Door* (Englewood Cliffs, NJ: Prentice Hall, 1964), pp. 22–25.

51. Gordon Allport, *The Nature of Prejudice,* abridged ed. (New York: Doubleday Anchor Books, 1958), p. 7 (italics omitted); see also pp. 6–7.

52. Ibid., p. 10 (italics added).

53. See Thomas F. Pettigrew, *Racially Separate or Together?* (New York: McGraw-Hill, 1971), pp. 134–135.

54. T. W. Adorno et al., *The Authoritarian Personality* (New York: Harper, 1950), pp. 248–279.

55. Williams, *Strangers Next Door,* pp. 110–113; Pettigrew, *Racially Separate or Together?,* p. 131.

56. R. A. Schermerhorn, *Comparative Ethnic Relations* (New York: Random House, 1970), p. 6.

57. Herbert Blumer, "Race Prejudice as a Sense of Group Position," *The Pacific Sociological Review,* 1 (Spring 1959): 3–7.

58. Cox, *Caste, Class, and Race,* p. 400.

59. See Charles R. Lawrence, "The Id, the Ego, and Equal Protection," *Stanford Law Review* 39 (January, 1987): 317–23; Gerald D. Jaynes and Robin Williams, Jr., eds. *A Common Destiny: Blacks and American Society* (Washington, DC: National Academy Press, 1989).

60. David M. Wellman, *Portraits of White Racism* (Cambridge: Cambridge University Press, 1977).

61. David O. Sears, "Symbolic Racism," in *Eliminating Racism,* eds. Phyllis A. Katz and Dalmas A. Taylor (New York: Plenum, 1988), pp. 55–58; John B. McConahay, "Modern Racism," in *Prejudice, Discrimination and Racism,* eds. John F. Dovidio and Samuel L. Gaertner (Orlando, FL: Academic Press, 1986).

62. Lawrence Bobo, "Group Conflict, Prejudice, and the Paradox of Contemporary Racial Attitudes," in *Eliminating Racism,* eds. Katz and Taylor, pp. 99–101.

63. Marylee Taylor and Thomas Pettigrew, "Prejudice," in *Encyclopedia of Sociology,* eds. Edgar F. Borgatta and Marie L. Borgatta (New York: Macmillan, 1992), p. 1538.

64. Figure 1–1 and portions of this discussion are adapted from Joe R. Feagin, "Affirmative Action in an Era of Reaction," in *Consultations on the Affirmative Action Statement of the U.S. Commission on Civil Rights* (Washington, DC: U.S. Government Printing Office, 1982), pp. 46–48.

65. Allport, *The Nature of Prejudice,* p. 14.

66. Gunnar Myrdal, *An American Dilemma* (New York: McGraw-Hill, 1964; originally published 1944), vol. 1, p. 52.

67. Robert K. Merton, "Discrimination and the American Creed," in *Discrimination and National Welfare,* ed. Robert MacIver (New York: Harper, 1949), p. 103. See also Graham C. Kinloch, *The Dynamics of Race Relations* (New York: McGraw-Hill, 1974), p. 54.

68. Faye Crosby, Stephanie Bromley, and Leonard Saxe, "Recent Unobtrusive Studies of Black and White Discrimination and Prejudice," *Psychological Bulletin* 87 (1980): 546–563. See also Lester Hill, "Prejudice and Discrimination" (Ph.D. dissertation, University of Texas, 1978). This paragraph also draws on Joe R. Feagin and Douglas L. Eckberg, "Discrimination: Motivation, Action, Effects, and Context," in *Annual Review of Sociology,* eds. Alex Inkeles, Neil J. Smelser, and Ralph H. Turner (Palo Alto, CA: Annual Reviews, 1980), pp. 3–4.

69. Charles Hamilton and Stokely Carmichael, *Black Power* (New York: Random House/Vintage Books, 1967), p. 4. See also *Institutional Racism in America,* eds. Louis L. Knowles and Kenneth Prewitt (Englewood Cliffs, NJ: Prentice Hall, 1969), p. 5.

70. Anthony Downs, *Racism in America and How to Combat It* (Washington, DC: U.S. Commission on Civil Rights, 1970), pp. 5, 7.

71. Thomas F. Pettigrew, "Racism and the Mental Health of White Americans: A Social Psychological View," in *Racism and Mental Health,* eds. Charles V. Willie, Bernard M. Kramer, and Bertram S. Brown (Pittsburgh, PA University of Pittsburgh Press, 1973), p. 271.

72. Essed, *Understanding Everyday Racism,* p. 39.

73. Joe R. Feagin, "Indirect Institutionalized Discrimination," *American Politics Quarterly* 5 (April 1977): 177–200.

74. Diana M. Pearce, "Black, White, and Many Shades of Gray: Real Estate Brokers and Their Racial Practices" (Ph.D. dissertation, University of Michigan, 1976); Diana Kendall, "Square Pegs in Round Holes: Nontraditional Students in Medical Schools" (Ph.D. dissertation, University of Texas, 1980).

75. Joe R. Feagin, "The Continuing Significance of Race: Antiblack Discrimination in Public Places, " *American Sociological Review* 56 (February 1991): 101–116.

76. Allport, *The Nature of Prejudice,* pp. 14–15.

77. Nijole V. Benokraitis and Joe R. Feagin, *Modern Sexism,* 2nd ed. (Englewood Cliffs, NJ: Prentice Hall, 1995), pp. 39–43.

78. Ed Jones, "What It's Like to Be a Black Manager," *Harvard Business Review* 64 (May/June 1986): 84–93; Thomas Pettigrew and Joanne Martin, "Shaping the Organizational Context for Black American Inclusion," *Journal of Social Issues* 43 (Spring 1987): 41–78; Joe R. Feagin and Melvin Sikes, *Living with Racism: The Black Middle Class Experience* (Boston, MA: Beacon Press, 1994).

79. Benokraitis and Feagin, *Modern Sexism*, p. 135.
80. Quoted in Itabari Njeri, "Words to Live or Die By," *The Los Angeles Times Magazine*, May 31, 1992, p. 23.
81. Quoted in Joe R. Feagin and Melvin P. Sikes, *Living with Racism* (Boston, MA: Beacon, 1994), pp. 145–147.
82. See Joe R. Feagin and Herna Vera, *White Racism: The Basics* (New York: Routledge, 1995), Chap. 8; Feagin and Sikes, *Living with Racism.*
83. See Joe R. Feagin and Aaron Porter, "Affirmative Action and African Americans: Rhetoric and Practice," *Humboldt Journal of Social Relations* 21 (1995): 81–104. Nijole Benokraitis and Joe R. Feagin, *Affirmative Action and Equal Opportunity: Action, Inaction, Reaction* (Boulder, CO: Westview, 1978).
84. The last two paragraphs draw on Feagin and Porter, "Affirmative Action and African Americans: Rhetoric and Practice."

CHAPTER 2

1. See Tamotsu Shibutani and Kian M. Kwan, *Ethnic Stratification* (The New York: Macmillan, 1965), pp. 28–33; and Donald L. Noel, "A Theory of the Origin of Ethnic Stratification," in *Majority and Minority*, eds. Norman R. Yetman and C. Hoy Steele (Boston, MA: Allyn & Bacon, 1971), p. 32.
2. William M. Newman, *American Pluralism* (New York: Harper & Row, 1973), pp. 30–38.
3. Ernest A. T. Barth and Donald L. Noel, "Conceptual Frameworks for the Analysis of Race Relations: An Evaluation," *Social Forces* 50 (March 1972): 336.
4. Charles Tilly, *Migration to an American City* (Wilmington, DE: University of Delaware Agricultural Experiment Station, 1965).
5. Barth and Noel, "Conceptual Frameworks," pp. 337–339.
6. R. A. Schermerhorn, *Comparative Ethnic Relations* (New York: Random House, 1970), p. 98.
7. Ibid., p. 99.
8. Stanley Lieberson, "A Societal Theory of Racial and Ethnic Relations," *American Sociological Review* 29 (December 1961): 902–910.
9. Charles Hirschman, "America's Melting Pot Reconsidered," *Annual Review of Sociology* 9 (1983): 397–423.
10. Robert E. Park, *Race and Culture* (Glencoe, IL: Free Press, 1950), p. 150 (italics added).
11. Robert E. Park and Ernest W. Burgess, *Introduction to the Science of Society* (Chicago: University of Chicago Press, 1924), p. 735.
12. Janice R. Hullum, "Robert E. Park's Theory of Race Relations." (Master's thesis, University of Texas, 1973), pp. 81–88; Park and Burgess, *Introduction to the Science of Society*, p. 760.
13. Milton M. Gordon, *Assimilation in American Life* (New York: Oxford University Press, 1964), pp. 72–73.
14. Ibid., p. 71.
15. Silvia Pedraza, *Political and Economic Migrants in America: Cubans and Mexicans* (Austin: University of Texas Press, 1985), pp. 5–7; Richard Alba, *Ethnic Identity: The Transformation of White America* (New Haven, CT: Yale University Press, 1990), p. 311; J. Allen Williams and Suzanne T. Ortega, "Dimensions of Assimilation," *Social Science Quarterly* 71 (1990): 697–709.
16. Milton M. Gordon, *Human Nature, Class, and Ethnicity* (New York: Oxford University Press, 1978), pp. 67–89.
17. Gordon, *Assimilation in American Life*, pp. 78–108.
18. See Will Herberg, *Protestant–Catholic–Jew*, rev. ed. (Garden City, NY: Doubleday/Anchor Books, 1960).
19. Milton M. Gordon, "Models of Pluralism: The New American Dilemma," *Annals of the American Academy of Political and Social Science* 454 (1981): 178–188.
20. Alba, *Ethnic Identity*, p. 3.
21. Stanley Lieberson and Mary Waters, "Ethnic Mixtures in the United States," *Sociology and Social Research* 70 (1985): 43–53; Cookie White Stephan and Walter Stephan, "After Intermarriage," *Journal of Marriage and the Family* 51 (May 1989): 507–519.
22. Milton R. Konvitz, "Horace Meyer Kallen (1882–1974)," in *American Jewish Yearbook, 1974–1975* (New York: American Jewish Committee, 1974), pp. 65–67; Milton Gordon, *Assimilation in American Life* (New York: Oxford University Press, 1964), pp. 142–159.
23. Nathan Glazer and Daniel P. Moynihan, *Beyond the Melting Pot* (Cambridge, MA: M.I.T. Press and Harvard University Press, 1963).
24. Andrew M. Greeley, *Ethnicity in the United States* (New York: Wiley, 1974), p. 293.
25. Ibid., pp. 295–309.
26. William L. Yancey, D. P. Ericksen, and R. N. Juliani, "Emergent Ethnicity: A Review and Reformulation," *American Sociological Review* 41 (June 1976): 391–393. See also Greeley, *Ethnicity in the United States*, pp. 290–317.
27. Gunnar Myrdal, *An American Dilemma* (New York: McGraw-Hill, 1964), vol. 2, p. 929.
28. Talcott Parsons, "Full Citizenship for the Negro American? A Sociological Problem," in *The Negro American*, eds. Talcott Parsons and Kenneth B. Clark (Boston, MA: Houghton Mifflin, 1965–1966), p. 740.
29. Ruben G. Rumbaut, "Paradoxes (and Orthodoxies) of Assimilation," *Sociological Perspectives* 40 (1997): 483.
30. Steven J. Gold, "Transnationalism and Vocabularies of Motive in International Migration: The Case of Israelis in the United States," *Sociological Perspectives* 40 (1997): 410–411.
31. Gordon, *Human Nature, Class, and Ethnicity*, pp. 73–78; See also Clifford Geertz, "The Integrative Revolution," in *Old Societies and New States*, ed. Clifford Geertz (New York: Free Press, 1963), p. 109.
32. Edna Bonacich, "Class Approaches to Ethnicity and Race," *Insurgent Sociologist* 10 (Fall 1980): 11.
33. Frederik Barth, "Introduction," in *Ethnic Groups and Boundaries: The Social Organization of Culture Difference* (Oslo: Universitets Forlaget, 1969), pp. 10–17.
34. Susan Olzak, "A Competition Model of Collective Action in American Cities," in *Competitive Ethnic Relations*, eds. Susan Olzak and Joane Nagel (Orlando, Fla.: Academic Press, 1986), pp. 17–46.
35. Susan Olzak, "Have the Causes of Ethnic Collective Action Changed over a Hundred Years?" (technical report, Department of Sociology, Cornell University, 1987), p. 18.
36. Susan Olzak, *The Dynamics of Ethnic Competition and Conflict* (Stanford, CA: Stanford University Press, 1992).
37. Joane Nagel, "Resource Competition Theories," *American Behavioral Scientist* 38 (January 1995): 442.
38. W. Lloyd Warner, "Introduction," in Allison Davis et al., *Deep South* (Chicago: University of Chicago Press, 1941), pp. 4–6; W. Lloyd Warner and Leo Srole, *The Social Systems of American Ethnic Groups* (New Haven, CT: Yale University Press, 1945), pp. 295–296.
39. Compare Robert Blauner, *Racial Oppression in America* (New York: Harper & Row, 1972), p. 7.
40. William E. B. Du Bois, "Is Man Free?" *Scientific Monthly* 66 (May 1948): 432–434. See also Manning

Marable, *How Capitalism Underdeveloped Black America* (Boston, MA: South End Press, 1983), pp. 3–15.

41. Oliver C. Cox, *Caste, Class, and Race* (Garden City, NY: Doubleday, 1948), p. 332.

42. Ronald Bailey and Guillermo Flores, "Internal Colonialism and Racial Minorities in the U.S.: An Overview," in *Structures of Dependency*, eds. Frank Bonilla and Robert Girling (Stanford, CA: privately published by a Stanford faculty–student seminar, 1973), pp. 151–53.

43. G. Balandier, "The Colonial Situation: A Theoretical Approach," in *Social Change*, ed. Immanuel Wallerstein (New York: Wiley, 1966), p. 35.

44. Pablo Gonzalez-Casanova, "Internal Colonialism and National Development," in *Latin American Radicalism*, ed. Irving L. Horowitz, et al. (New York: Random House, 1969), p. 130; Bailey and Flores, "Internal Colonialism," p. 156.

45. Bailey and Flores, "Internal Colonialism," p. 156.

46. Blauner, *Racial Oppression in America*, p. 55. Our analysis of internal colonialism draws throughout on Blauner's provocative discussion.

47. See Stokely Carmichael and Charles Hamilton, *Black Power* (New York: Random House/Vintage Books, 1967), pp. 2–7.

48. Mario Barrera, *Race and Class in the Southwest* (Notre Dame, IN: University of Notre Dame Press, 1979), pp. 214–217.

49. Guillermo B. Flores, "Race and Culture in the Internal Colony: Keeping the Chicano in His Place," in *Structures of Dependency*, eds. Bonilla and Girling, p. 192.

50. Bonnie Mitchell and Joe Feagin, "America's Racial-Ethnic Cultures: Opposition within a Mythical Melting Pot," In *Toward the Multicultural University*, eds. Benjamin Bowser, Gale Auletta, snd Terry Jones (Westport, CT: Praeger, 1995), pp. 65–86. See also Michael Hechter, Debra Friedman, and Malka Appelbaum, "A Theory of Ethnic Collective Action," *International Migration Review* 16 (1982): 412–434.

51. See Carol B. Stack, "Sex Roles and Survival Strategies in an Urban Black Community," in *Woman, Culture and Society*, eds. Michelle Zimbalist Rosaldo and Louise Lamphere (Stanford, CA: Stanford University Press, 1974), p. 128; Ronald Angel and Marta Tienda, "Determinants of Extended Household Structure: Cultural Pattern or Economic Need?" *American Journal of Sociology* 87 (1981–1982): 1360–1383.

52. James C. Scott, *Domination and the Arts of Resistance* (New Haven, CT: Yale University Press, 1990); John Gaventa, *Power and Powerlessness* (Urbana, IL: University of Illinois Press, 1980).

53. Scott, *Domination and the Arts of Resistance*, p. 116.

54. Sterling Stuckey, *Slave Culture* (New York: Oxford University Press, 1987), pp. 27, 42–46.

55. W. E. B. Du Bois, "The Future of Africa," *Advocate of Peace* 81 (January 1919): 12, as quoted in Manning Marable, *W. E. B. Du Bois: Black Radical Democrat* (Boston, MA: Twayne, 1986, p. 100.

56. Marable, *W. E. B. Du Bois*, p. 101.

57. Ibid., p. 107.

58. Michael Omi and Howard Winant, *Racial Formation in the United States*, 2nd ed. (New York: Routledge, 1994), p. 40.

59. Omi and Winant, *Racial Formation in the United States*, p. 41.

60. *The Afrocentric Idea* (Philadelphia: Temple, 1987); Molefi Kete Asante, *Afrocentricity* (Trenton, NJ: Africa World Press, 1988).

61. Marimba Ani, *Yurugu: An African-Centered Critique of European Cultural Thought and Behavior* (Trenton, NJ: Africa World Press, 1994), p. 567.

62. Ani, *Yurugu*, p. 570.

63. Joan W. Moore, "American Minorities and 'New Nation' Perspectives," *Pacific Sociological Review* 19 (October 1976): 448–455; Michael Omi and Howard Winant, *Racial Formation in the United States* (New York: Routledge, 1986), pp. 47–49.

64. Bonacich, "Class Approaches to Ethnicity and Race," p. 14.

65. Cox, *Caste, Class, and Race*; Al Szymanski, *Class Structure* (New York: Praeger, 1983), pp. 420–440; Al Szymanski, "Racial Discrimination and White Gain," *American Sociological Review* 41 (1976): 403–414.

66. Stanley B. Greenberg, *Race and State in Capitalist Development* (New Haven, CT: Yale University Press, 1980), p. 349.

67. Barrera, *Race and Class in the Southwest*, pp. 201–203; Bonacich, "Class Approaches to Ethnicity and Race," p. 14.

68. Bonacich, "Class Approaches to Ethnicity and Race," pp. 14–15.

69. Edna Bonacich and John Modell, *The Economic Basis of Ethnic Solidarity* (Berkeley, CA: University of California Press, 1980), pp. 1–37.

70. Alejandro Portes and Robert D. Manning, "The Immigrant Enclave: Theory and Empirical Examples," in *Competitive Ethnic Relations*, eds. Olzak and Nagel, pp. 47–68.

71. Rumbaut, "Paradoxes (and Orthodoxies) of Assimilation," p. 483; Alejandro Portes, "Segmented Assimilation among New Immigrant Youth: A Conceptual Framework," in *California's Immigrant Children*, eds. Ruben Rumbaut and Wayne Cornelius (La Jolla, CA: Center for Mexican American Studies, University of California, 1995), pp. 71–76; and Min Zhou, "Growing Up American: The Challenge Confronting Immigrant Children and Children of Immigrants," *Annual Review of Sociology*, 23 (1997): 63–95.

72. Quoted in Michael Albert et al., *Liberating Theory* (Boston, MA: South End Press, 1986), p. 35.

73. Philomena Essed, *Understanding Everyday Racism* (Newbury Park, CA: Sage, 1991), pp. 30–32.

74. Patricia Hill Collins, *Black Feminist Thought: Knowledge, Consciousness, and the Politics of Empowerment* (Boston, MA: Unwin Hyman, 1990), pp. 40–48.

75. Denise A. Segura, "Chicanas and Triple Oppression in the Labor Force," in *Chicana Voices: Intersections of Class, Race and Gender*, ed. Teresa Cordova, et al. (Austin, TX: Center for Mexican American Studies, 1986), p. 48.

76. Omi and Winant, *Racial Formation in the United States*, pp. 75–76.

77. William E. B. Du Bois, *The World and Africa* (New York: International Publishers, 1965 [1946]), p. 37.

78. Oliver C. Cox, *Caste, Class, and Race: A Study in Social Dynamics* (New York: Doubleday, 1948), p. 578.

79. Cox, *Caste, Class, and Race*, p 332.

80. Andrew Hacker, *Two Nations: Black and White, Separate, Hostile, Unequal* (New York: Scribner's, 1992).

81. Ian Craib, *Modern Social Theory: From Parsons to Habermas* (New York: St. Martin's Press, 1984), p. 53.

82. Iris Young, *Justice and the Politics of Difference* (Princeton, NJ: Princeton University Press, 1990), p. 52.

83. See Tomas Almaguer, *Racial Fault Lines* (Berkeley, CA: University of California Press, 1994), p. 7.

513

84. Aldon Morris, *The Origins of the Civil Rights Movement* (New York: Free Press, 1984).

PART II

1. Edna Bonacich, "United States Capitalist Development: A Background to Asian Immigration," in *Labor Immigration under Capitalism*, eds. Lucie Cheng and Edna Bonacich (Berkeley, CA: University of California Press, 1984), p. 82.
2. Ibid., p. 81.
3. Herbert Aptheker, lectures on American history, University of Minnesota, 1984.
4. Lucie Cheng and Edna Bonacich, "Imperialism, Distorted Development, and Asian Emigration to the United States," in *Labor Immigration under Capitalism*, eds. Cheng and Bonacich, pp. 214–217.
5. Bonacich, "United States Capitalist Development," pp. 99–110.
6. Coretta Scott King, "It's a Bit Late to Protest Preferential Treatment," *Detroit Free Press*, December 13, 1985, p. 9A.
7. Stephen Steinberg, *The Ethnic Myth* (New York: Atheneum, 1981), p. 36.
8. Bonacich, "United States Capitalist Development," pp. 112–115.
9. Irving Kristol, "The Negro Today Is Like the Immigrant of Yesterday," *The New York Times Magazine*, September 11, 1966, pp. 50–51, 124–142.
10. Theodore Hershberg et al., "A Tale of Three Cities: Blacks, Immigrants, and Opportunity in Philadelphia: 1850–1880, 1930, 1970," in *Philadelphia*, ed. Theodore Hershberg (New York: Oxford University Press, 1981), pp. 462–64.
11. William Yancey, E. P. Ericksen, and R. N. Juliani, "Emergent Ethnicity," *American Sociological Review* 41 (June 1976): 393.
12. Stanley Lieberson, *A Piece of the Pie* (Berkeley, CA: University of California Press, 1980), pp. 377–383.
13. Robert Blauner, *Racial Oppression in America* (New York: Harper & Row, 1972), p. 62.
14. H. Sitkoff, *A New Deal for Blacks* (New York: Oxford University Press, 1978), pp. 37–38; C. G. Wye, "The New Deal and the Negro Community," *Journal of American History* 59 (December 1972): 634.
15. Charles B. Keeley, "Population and Immigration Policy: State and Federal Roles," in *Mexican American and Central American Population Issues and U.S. Policy*, eds. Frank D. Bean, Jurgen Schmandt, and Sidney Weintraub (Austin, TX: Center for Mexican American Studies, 1988).

CHAPTER 3

1. Cleveland Amory, *The Proper Bostonians* (New York: Dutton, 1947), p. 11.
2. U.S. Bureau of the Census, *1990 Census of Population: Social and Economic Characteristics: United States*, CP-2-1 (Washington, DC: 1993), p. 166.
3. Carl Wittke, "Preface to the Revised Edition," in *We Who Built America*, rev. ed. (Cleveland, OH: Case Western Reserve University Press, 1967).
4. Milton M. Gordon, *Assimilation in American Life* (New York: Oxford University Press, 1964), p. 72.
5. Will Herberg, *Protestant—Catholic—Jew*, rev. ed. (Garden City, NY: Doubleday/Anchor Books, 1960), p. 21.

6. Rowland T. Berthoff, *British Immigrants in Industrial America* (Chicago: University of Chicago Press, 1953), p. 1.
7. John Jay, Alexander Hamilton, and James Madison, *The Federalist* (London: Penguin Classics, 1987 [1788]), p. 91.
8. Wilbur S. Shepperson, *British Emigration to North America* (Oxford: Basil Blackwell, 1957), p. 3.
9. Conrad Taeuber and Irene B. Taeuber, "Immigration to the United States," in *Population and Society*, ed. Charles B. Nam (Boston, MA: Houghton Mifflin, 1968), p. 316.
10. Immigration and Naturalization Service, *1975 Annual Report* (Washington, DC: 1975), pp. 62–64.
11. Alice Marriott and Carol K. Rachlin, *American Epic* (New York: Mentor Books, 1969), p. 105.
12. Samuel Eliot Morison, *The Oxford History of the American People* (New York: Oxford University Press, 1965), pp. 48–49.
13. Klaus E. Knorr, *British Colonial Theories, 1570–1850* (Toronto: University of Toronto Press, 1944), p. 126.
14. Marriott and Rachlin, *American Epic*, p. 106.
15. Ibid., pp. 104–106; Winthrop D. Jordan, *White over Black* (Baltimore, MD: Penguin, 1969), p. 89.
16. Quoted in John Collier, *Indians of the Americas*, abridged ed. (New York: Mentor Books, 1947), p. 115.
17. The remainder of this paragraph and the following paragraph draw on Morison, *Oxford History of the American People*, pp. 50–154; and Maldwyn A. Jones, *American Immigration* (Chicago: University of Chicago Press, 1960), pp. 10–38.
18. Morison, *Oxford History of the American People*, p. 74.
19. David Hackett Fischer, *Albion's Seed: Four British Folkways in America* (New York: Oxford University Press, 1989), pp. 6, 13–205, 785–786.
20. Ibid., pp. 207–418.
21. Ibid., pp. 419–603.
22. Ibid., pp. 605–782.
23. *Proceedings of the American Historical Association*, vol. 1 of *Annual Report of the American Historical Association* (Washington, DC: American Historical Association, 1932), p. 124.
24. Jones, *American Immigration*, pp. 34–35.
25. Berthoff, *British Immigrants in Industrial America*, p. vii.
26. Ibid., p. 5.
27. Shepperson, *British Emigration to North America*, p. 20.
28. Berthoff, *British Immigrants in Industrial America*, pp. 28–29; Charlotte Erickson, "English," in *Harvard Encyclopedia of American Ethnic Groups*, ed. Stephan Thernstrom (Cambridge, MA: Harvard University Press, 1980), pp. 324–332.
29. Shepperson, *British Emigration to North America*, pp. 27–32, 84; Berthoff, *British Immigrants in Industrial America*, pp. 46–87, 122; Charlotte Erickson, "Agrarian Myths of English Immigrants," in *In the Trek of the Immigrants*, ed. O. Fritiof Ander (Rock Island, IL: Augustana Library Publications, 1964), pp. 59–64.
30. Berthoff, *British Immigrants in Industrial America*, p. 125.
31. Ibid., p. 210; see also pp. 143–183.
32. Erickson, "English," pp. 335–336.
33. Stanley Lieberson and Mary C. Waters, *From Many Strands* (New York: Russell Sage, 1988), pp. 40–41.
34. Charles H. Anderson, *White Protestant Americans* (Englewood Cliffs, NJ: Prentice Hall, 1970), pp. 28–71, 79–87. See also Ian C. Graham, *Colonists from Scotland* (Ithaca, NY: Cornell University Press, 1956); and

Albert B. Faust, *The German Element in the United States* (New York: Steuben Society, 1927).

35. Ronald Takaki, *Iron Cages* (New York: Oxford University Press, 1990), pp. 12–14.

36. William E. B. Du Bois, *Black Reconstruction in America: An Essay Toward a History of the Part Which Black Folk Played in the Attempt to Reconstruct Democracy in America, 1860–1880* (New York: Atheneum, [1935] 1992). This and the following paragraph draw on Joe R. Feagin and Aaron Porter, "White Racism: Bibliographic Essay," *Choice*, 33 (February 1996): 903–914.

37. Theodore W. Allen, *The Invention of the White Race* (New York: Verso, 1994), pp. 21, 184; David Roediger, *Towards the Abolition of Whiteness: Essays on Race, Politics, and Working Class History* (New York: Verso, 1994).

38. John Higham, *Strangers in the Land* (New York: Atheneum, 1963), p. 4.

39. Henry P. Fairchild, *Immigration* (New York: Macmillan, 1920), p. 47; Jones, *American Immigration*, p. 44.

40. Jordan, *White over Black*, p. 86.

41. Ibid., p. 87.

42. Jones, *American Immigration*, pp. 41–46.

43. Fairchild, *Immigration*, pp. 57–58.

44. Michael Kammen, *People of Paradox* (New York: Knopf, 1972), p. 66.

45. Quoted in Nancy F. Conklin and Margaret A. Lourie, *A Host of Tongues* (New York: Free Press, 1983), p. 69.

46. Kammen, *People of Paradox*, p. 74; Jordan, *White over Black*, p. 339.

47. Higham, *Strangers in the Land*, p. 6; Marcus L. Hansen, *The Immigrant in American History* (New York: Harper Torchbooks, 1964), pp. 111–136; Wittke, *We Who Built America*, p. 505.

48. Quoted in Richard Hofstadter, *Social Darwinism in American Thought*, rev. ed. (Boston, MA: Beacon Press, 1955), pp. 171–172.

49. Higham, *Strangers in the Land*, p. 32; Hofstadter, *Social Darwinism in American Thought*, pp. 173–174.

50. Higham, *Strangers in the Land*, p. 33.

51. Hofstadter, *Social Darwinism in American Thought*, pp. 178–179; Lewis H. Carlson and George A. Colburn, *In Their Place* (New York: Wiley, 1972), pp. 305–308. Carlson and Colburn provide excerpts from the writings of Strong.

52. Higham, *Strangers in the Land*, pp. 96–152.

53. E. Digby Baltzell, *The Protestant Establishment* (New York: Random House/Vintage Books, 1966), pp. 96–98; Higham, *Strangers in the Land*, pp. 148–157.

54. See, for example, the excerpt from Roberts's *Why Europe Leaves Home* in *In Their Place*, eds. Carlson and Colburn, p. 312.

55. Richard Alba, *Ethnic Identity: The Transformation of White America* (New Haven, CT: Yale University Press, 1990), p. 365.

56. Jones, *American Immigration*, pp. 36–38.

57. W. Lloyd Warner and Leo Srole, *The Social Systems of American Ethnic Groups* (New Haven, CT: Yale University Press, 1945), p. 287.

58. Quoted in Juan F. Perea, "Demography and Distrust: An Essay on American Languages, Cultural Pluralism and Official English," *Minnesota Law Review* 77 (1992): 269.

59. Susanna McBee, "A War over Words," *U.S. News & World Report*, October 6, 1986, p. 64.

60. "National English Campaign Supports English as the Official Language of the United States," Business Wire, February 11, 1997.

61. "English for the Children—California English Campaign Endorses Initiative," Business Wire, August 28, 1997.

62. Clarence Petersen, "Tribune Books," *Chicago Tribune*, October 31, 1993, p. C8.

63. Bill Piatt, *Only English? Law and Language Policy in the United States* (Albuquerque: University of New Mexico Press, 1990), p. 159.

64. Amado Padilla et al., "The English-Only Movement," *American Psychologist* 46 (February 1991): 120–130; National Education Association, *Official English/ English Only* (Washington, DC: National Education Association, 1988), pp. 5–7.

65. Perea, "Demography and Distrust."

66. National Education Association, *Official English/ English Only*, p. 7; Carl J. Veltman, *Language Shift in the United States* (Berlin: Mouton, 1983).

67. Fischer, *Albion's Seed*, pp. 795–797.

68. Edwin S. Gaustad, *Historical Atlas of Religion in America* (New York: Harper & Row, 1962), pp. 1–20.

69. Herberg, *Protestant—Catholic—Jew*, p. 82.

70. Marshall Sklare, *Conservative Judaism* (Glencoe, IL: Free Press, 1955), pp. 31–117.

71. Takaki, *Iron Cages*, p. 7.

72. Cited in Max Weber, *The Protestant Ethic and the Spirit of Capitalism*, trans. Talcott Parsons (New York: Scribner's, 1958), pp. 158–160.

73. Joe R. Feagin, *Subordinating the Poor* (Englewood Cliffs, NJ: Prentice Hall, 1975), p. 22.

74. Weber, *The Protestant Ethic*, p. 17; see also p. 50.

75. David Ewen, *History of Popular Music* (New York: Barnes & Noble, 1961), pp. 1–10.

76. See Samuel Bowles and Herbert Gintis, *Schooling in Capitalist America* (New York: Basic Books, 1976).

77. Morison, *Oxford History of the American People*, p. 55.

78. Samuel P. Huntington, "Political Modernization: America versus Europe," *World Politics* 18 (April 1966): 147–148.

79. Jack P. Greene, *The Quest for Power* (Chapel Hill: University of North Carolina Press, 1963), pp. 1ff.

80. Roscoe Pound, *The Formative Era of American Law* (Boston, MA: Little, Brown, 1938), pp. 7–8.

81. Ibid., p. 12.

82. Elizabeth G. Brown and William W. Blume, *British Statutes in American Law, 1776–1836* (Ann Arbor: University of Michigan Law School, 1964), p. 44. See also Lawrence M. Friedman, *A History of American Law* (New York: Simon & Schuster, 1973), pp. 96–100.

83. Pound, *The Formative Era of American Law*, p. 81.

84. Maurice R. Davie, *World Immigration* (New York: Macmillan, 1939), p. 36.

85. Henry J. Ford, *The Scotch-Irish in America* (Princeton, NJ: Princeton University Press, 1915), p. 491.

86. Charles A. Beard, *An Economic Interpretation of the Constitution of the United States* (New York: Macmillan, 1947), p. 17.

87. Joseph N. Kane, *Facts about the Presidents*, 3rd ed. (New York: Wilson, 1974).

88. John R. Schmidhauser, "The Justices of the Supreme Court: A Collective Portrait," *Midwest Journal of Political Science* 3 (February 1959): 1–57.

89. William Miller, "American Historians and the Business Elite," *Journal of Economic History* 9 (November 1949): 202–203.

90. Baltzell, *The Protestant Establishment*, pp. 10–12.

91. On Protestant presidents before Kennedy, see ibid., p. 21.

92. Robert A. Dahl, *Who Governs?* (New Haven, CT: Yale University Press, 1961), pp. 15–16.

93. Matthew Holden, Jr., "Ethnic Accommodation in a Historical Case," *Comparative Studies in Society and History* 8 (January 1966): 172.

94. Rowland Berthoff, *An Unsettled People* (New York: Harper & Row, 1971), p. 13; Oliver C. Cox, *Caste, Class, and Race* (Garden City, NY: Doubleday, 1948), pp. 338–339; Barrington Moore, Jr., *Social Origins of Dictatorship and Democracy* (Boston, MA: Beacon Press, 1966), pp. 112–113.

95. Frank Thistlewaite, *The Anglo-American Connection in the Early Nineteenth Century* (Philadelphia: University of Pennsylvania Press, 1959), pp. 5–11.

96. Jesse Lemisch, "The American Revolution Seen from the Bottom Up," in *Toward a New Past*, ed. Barton J. Bernstein (New York: Random House, 1968), p. 8; J. O. Lindsay, ed., *The Old Regime*, vol. 7 of *The New Cambridge Modern History* (Cambridge: Cambridge University Press, 1957), pp. 509–511.

97. Morison, *Oxford History of the American People*, p. 89.

98. Abbot E. Smith, *Colonists in Bondage* (Chapel Hill: University of North Carolina Press, 1947), pp. 25, 336; Jordan, *White over Black*, p. 47; Howard Zinn, *The Politics of History* (Boston, MA: Beacon Press, 1970), p. 68.

99. Lee Soltow, *Men and Wealth in the United States, 1850–1870* (New Haven, CT: Yale University Press, 1975), p. 149.

100. Matthew Josephson, *The Robber Barons* (New York: Harcourt, Brace & World, 1934), pp. 32–35, 315–452.

101. John N. Ingham, *The Iron Barons* (Westport, CT: Greenwood Press, 1978), pp. 14–16.

102. Miller, "American Historians and the Business Elite," p. 202.

103. Elin L. Anderson, *We Americans* (Cambridge, MA: Harvard University Press, 1937), p. 137; see also pp. 21–247.

104. E. Digby Baltzell, *An American Business Aristocracy* (New York: Collier Books, 1962), p. 267.

105. Ibid., p. 431.

106. Baltzell, *The Protestant Establishment*, p. 321.

107. Thomas R. Dye, *Who's Running America?* (Englewood Cliffs, NJ: Prentice Hall, 1976), pp. 3–8, 150–153. See also Thomas R. Dye, *Who's Running America? The Carter Years* (Englewood Cliffs, NJ: Prentice Hall, 1979), pp. 171–177.

108. Thomas R. Dye, letter to author, April 11, 1977.

109. Julia Reed, "The New American Establishment," *U.S. News & World Report*, February 8, 1988, p. 38.

110. Richard D. Alba and Gwen Moore, "Ethnicity in the American Elite," *American Sociological Review* 47 (June 1982); see also Thomas R. Dye, *Who's Running America? The Clinton Years* (Upper Saddle River, NJ: Prentice Hall, 1995), pp. 170–173.

111. Michael Novak, "The Nordic Jungle: Inferiority in America," in *Divided Society*, ed. Colin Greer (New York: Basic Books, 1974), p. 134.

112. U.S. Bureau of the Census, *1990 Census of Population: Ancestry of the Population of the United States*, CP-3-2 (Washington, DC: 1993), p. 33; U.S. Bureau of the Census, *1990 Census of Population: Social and Economic Characteristics: United States*, p. 166.

113. Calculated from data in U.S. Bureau of the Census, *1990 Census of Population: Ancestry of the Population of the United States*, pp. 33, 237. U.S. Bureau of the Census, *1990 Census of Population: Social and Economic Characteristics: United States*, pp. 40, 42.

114. U.S. Bureau of the Census, *1990 Census of Population: Ancestry of the Population of the United States*, p. 441; U.S. Bureau of the Census, *1990 Census of Population: Social and Economic Characteristics: United States*, pp. 48, 49.

115. Calculated from data in U.S. Bureau of the Census, *1990 Census of Population: Ancestry of the Population of the United States*, p. 339; U.S. Bureau of the Census, *1990 Census of Population: Social and Economic Characteristics: United States*, p. 45.

116. U.S. Bureau of the Census, *1990 Census of Population: Ancestry of the Population of the United States*, p. 339; U.S. Bureau of the Census, *1990 Census of Population: Social and Economic Characteristics: United States*, pp. 44, 47.

117. The tabulation was done in 1997 by Joe R. Feagin using Mead Data Central's Nexis database.

118. Lieberson and Waters, *From Many Strands*, p. 173.

119. Alba, *Ethnic Identity*, pp. 49–82.

120. Fischer, *Albion's Seed*, pp. 199–205, 412, 597, 777–782, 897–898.

121. Ibid., pp. 887–897, quotation on p. 896.

122. Lieberson and Waters, *From Many Strands*, pp. 53–56.

123. Lewis M. Killian, *White Southerners* (New York: Random House, 1970), p. 16.

124. Peter Schrag, *The Decline of the WASP* (New York: Simon & Schuster, 1971), p. 164.

CHAPTER 4

1. U.S. Department of Justice, Immigration and Naturalization Service, *Annual Report* (Washington, DC, 1973), pp. 53–55. The figures for the period between 1820 and 1867 represent "alien passengers arrived"; for later periods they represent immigrants arrived or admitted.

2. Cited in William Peterson, *Population*, 2nd ed. (New York: Macmillan, 1969), p. 260.

3. U.S. Bureau of the Census, *Statistical Abstract of the United States 1991* (Washington, DC, 1991), p. 10; U.S. Bureau of the Census, *Statistical Abstract of the United States 1994* (Washington, DC, 1994), p. 11.

4. U.S. Bureau of the Census, *1990 Census of Population: Ancestry of the Population in the United States*, CP-3-2 (Washington, DC, 1993), pp. 50, 65.

5. U.S. Bureau of the Census, *1990 Census of Population: Social and Economic Characteristics: United States*, CP-2-1 (Washington, DC, 1993), p. 166.

6. Philip H. Bagenal, *The American Irish* (London: Kegan Paul, Trench, 1882), pp. 4–5.

7. Henry Jones Ford, *The Scotch-Irish in America* (Princeton, NJ: Princeton University Press, 1915), pp. 125–128.

8. James G. Leyburn, *The Scotch-Irish* (Chapel Hill: University of North Carolina Press, 1962), pp. 142–143.

9. Ford, *The Scotch-Irish in America*, pp. 183–186; Leyburn, *The Scotch-Irish*, pp. 160ff.

10. Michael J. O'Brien, *A Hidden Phase of American History* (New York: Devin-Adair, 1919), p. 249; see also pp. 287–288.

11. See Robert J. Dickson, *Ulster Immigration to Colonial America, 1718–1773* (London: Routledge, 1966), pp. 66–68; Grady McWhiney, *Cracker Culture* (Tuscaloosa: University of Alabama Press, 1988), pp. 3–4, 15–18; Andrew M. Greeley, "The Success and Assimilation of Irish Protestants and Irish Catholics in the United States," *Sociology and Social Research,* 72, no. 4 (July 1988): 231.

12. O'Brien, *A Hidden Phase of American History,* p. 267.

13. Quoted in ibid., p. 254.

14. McWhiney, *Cracker Culture,* pp. 5, 188; Emmet Larkin, "The Devotional Revolution in Ireland, 1850–1875," *American Historical Review,* 77 (1972): 623–652; S. J. Connolly, *Priest and People in Pre-Famine Ireland* (Dublin: Gill & Macmillan, 1982), cited in Greeley, "Success and Assimilation," pp. 229–230.

15. Thomas D'Arcy McGee, *A History of Irish Settlers in North America* (Boston, MA: Office of American Celt, 1851), pp. 25–34.

16. Leyburn, *The Scotch-Irish,* pp. 331–332.

17. Quoted in Ford, *The Scotch-Irish in America,* pp. 520–521.

18. Theodore Roosevelt, *The Winning of the West* (New York: Review of Reviews Co., 1904), 1:123–125.

19. Ford, *The Scotch-Irish in America,* pp. 522, 539.

20. John W. Dinsmore, *The Scotch-Irish in America* (Chicago: Winona Publishing Co., 1906), p. 7.

21. Winthrop D. Jordan, *White over Black* (Baltimore, MD: Penguin, 1969), pp. 86–88.

22. Edwin S. Gaustad, *Historical Atlas of Religion in America* (New York: Harper & Row, 1962), pp. 34–35; Dennis Clark, *The Irish in Philadelphia* (Philadelphia, PA: Temple University Press, 1973), p. 8.

23. Quoted in McGee, *A History of Irish Settlers in North America,* p. 79.

24. Ford, *The Scotch-Irish in America,* pp. 180–240; E. R. R. Green, "Ulster Immigrants' Letters," in *Essays in Scotch-Irish History,* ed. E. R. R. Green (London: Routledge, 1969), pp. 100–102.

25. Leyburn, *The Scotch-Irish,* pp. 262–269.

26. American Historical Association, *Annual Report* (Washington, DC: U.S. Government Printing Office, 1932), 1:255–270.

27. Arnold Shrier, *Ireland and the American Emigration, 1850–1900* (Minneapolis: University of Minnesota Press, 1958), pp. 13–16; T. A. Jackson, *Ireland Her Own* (New York: International Publishers, 1970), pp. 243–245; Kerby A. Miller, *Emigrants and Exiles* (New York: Oxford University Press, 1985), p. 556.

28. Carl Wittke, *The Irish in America* (Baton Rouge: Louisiana State University Press, 1956), pp. 24–27; Theodore Hershberg et al., "A Tale of Three Cities," in *Majority and Minority,* 3rd ed., eds. Norman Y. Yetman and C. Hoy Steele (Boston, MA: Allyn & Bacon, 1982), pp. 184–185.

29. Bagenal, *The American Irish,* p. 72 (the statistics on crime and poverty are found on pp. 70–71); Wittke, *The Irish in America,* p. 46.

30. Ronald Takaki, *A Different Mirror* (Boston, MA: Little, Brown, 1993), pp. 154–160; Hasia R. Diner, *Erin's Daughters in America* (Baltimore, MD: Johns Hopkins, 1983), pp. xiii–xv.

31. Dale T. Knobel, *Paddy and the Republic* (Middletown, CT: Wesleyan University Press, 1986), pp. 24–27; Bill Bryson, *The Mother Tongue: English and How It Got That Way* (New York: Morrow, 1990).

32. Lewis P. Curtis, Jr., *Apes and Angels: The Irish in Victorian Caricature* (Washington, DC: Smithsonian Institution Press, 1971), p. 59.

33. Ibid., p. 103.

34. Andrew M. Greeley, *That Most Distressful Nation* (Chicago: Quadrangle, 1972), pp. 119–120.

35. Quoted in Rita J. Simon and Susan H. Alexander, *The Ambivalent Welcome: Print Media, Public Opinion, and Immigration* (Westport, CT: Praeger, 1993), pp. 105–106.

36. Leonard Gordon, "Racial and Ethnic Stereotypes of American College Students over a Half Century" (paper presented at meetings of the Society for the Study of Social Problems, Washington, DC, August 1985), pp. 14–15.

37. American Institute of Public Opinion, *Roper Center,* 1982.

38. Richard D. Alba, *Ethnic Identity: The Transformation of White America* (New Haven, CT: Yale University Press, 1990), p. 156; Nick Carter, "In a Tip of the Hat to Tradition, Pubs Are Hubs of Festivities," *Milwaukee Journal Sentinel,* March 8, 1996, p. 17.

39. Andrew M. Greeley, *The Irish Americans* (New York: Harper & Row, 1981), p. 167.

40. Leonard Dinnerstein and Frederic C. Jaher, "Introduction," in *The Aliens,* eds. Leonard Dinnerstein and Frederic C. Jaher (New York: Appleton-Century-Crofts, 1970), p. 4.

41. Leyburn, *The Scotch-Irish,* pp. 234, 301–316.

42. Ford, *The Scotch-Irish in America,* pp. 291–324; Leyburn, *The Scotch-Irish,* pp. 225–230.

43. Nathan Glazer and Daniel P. Moynihan, *Beyond the Melting Pot* (Cambridge, MA: M.I.T. Press and Harvard University Press, 1963), p. 220; McGee, *A History of Irish Settlers in North America,* p. 88.

44. Wittke, *The Irish in America,* pp. 47ff, 119; Wayne G. Broehl, Jr., *The Molly Maguires* (Cambridge, MA: Harvard University Press, 1964), p. 75.

45. Clark, *The Irish in Philadelphia,* p. 21.

46. Wittke, *The Irish in America,* p. 120.

47. Rowland T. Berthoff, *British Immigrants in Industrial America* (Cambridge, MA: Harvard University Press, 1953), pp. 187, 190–193.

48. Broehl, *The Molly Maguires,* p. 85.

49. Leonard P. O. Wibberly, *The Coming of the Green* (New York: Henry Holt, 1958), pp. 101–103.

50. Takaki, *A Different Mirror,* pp. 150–152; Broehl, *The Molly Maguires,* pp. 87–90.

51. Broehl, *The Molly Maguires,* pp. 198–199.

52. Anthony Bimba, *The Molly Maguires* (New York: International Publishers, 1932), pp. 70–73.

53. Broehl, *The Molly Maguires,* pp. vi, 359–361.

54. Takaki, *A Different Mirror,* pp. 150–152; Oscar Handlin, *Boston's Immigrants, 1790–1865* (Cambridge, MA: Harvard University Press, 1941), p. 137.

55. See James McCague, *The Second Rebellion* (New York: Dial Press, 1968).

56. Theodore W. Allen, *The Invention of the White Race* (London: Verso, 1994), p. 21; David Roediger, *Towards the Abolition of Whiteness* (London: Verso, 1994), p. 12.

57. Allen, *The Invention of the White Race,* pp. 21–50. This paragraph draws on Joe R. Feagin and Hernan Vera, *White Racism: The Basics* (New York : Routledge, 1995), pp. 1–18.

58. Roediger, *Towards the Abolition of Whiteness,* p. 140.

59. Wittke, *The Irish in America,* pp. 191–192.

60. Richard Polenberg, *One Nation Divisible* (New York: Penguin, 1980), pp. 40–41.

61. Ford, *The Scotch-Irish in America*, pp. 246, 462, 491; McGee, *A History of Irish Settlers in North America*, p. 71; Shane Leslie, *The Irish Issue in Its American Aspect* (New York: Scribner's, 1919), p. 8.

62. Maldwyn A. Jones, "Ulster Emigration, 1783–1815," in *Essays in Scotch-Irish History*, ed. E.R.R. Green (London: Routledge, 1969), p. 67.

63. Paul Blanshard, *The Irish and Catholic Power* (Boston, MA: Beacon Press, 1953), p. 282.

64. William F. Adams, *Ireland and Irish Emigration to the New World* (New Haven, CT: Yale University Press, 1932), p. 377.

65. Wittke, *The Irish in America*, p. 104; Edward M. Levine, *The Irish and Irish Politicians* (Notre Dame, Ind.: University of Notre Dame Press, 1966), pp. 6–9.

66. Leo Hershkowitz, *Tweed's New York* (New York: Doubleday/Anchor Books, 1987), pp. xiii–xx.

67. Glazer and Moynihan, *Beyond the Melting Pot*, pp. 218–262; Robert A. Dahl, *Who Governs?* (New Haven, CT: Yale University Press, 1963), p. 41.

68. Levine, *The Irish and Irish Politicians*, p. 146.

69. Mike Royko, *Boss: Richard J. Daley of Chicago* (New York: Dutton, 1971); Sam Roberts, "In Search of Irish, or the Greening of the Suburbs," *The New York Times*, March 17, 1988, p. B1; Alba, *Ethnic Identity*, p. 156.

70. Levine, *The Irish and Irish Politicians*, pp. 145–155, quotation on p. 174.

71. Wittke, *The Irish in America*, pp. 110–112.

72. Greeley, *That Most Distressful Nation*, pp. 206–209.

73. Dennis J. Clark, "The Philadelphia Irish," in *The Peoples of Philadelphia*, eds. Allen F. Davis and Mark H. Haller (Philadelphia, PA: Temple University Press, 1973), p. 145.

74. Terry N. Clark, "The Irish Ethnic and the Spirit of Patronage," *Ethnicity* 2 (1975): 305–359; Mark R. Levy and Michael S. Kramer, *The Ethnic Factor* (New York: Simon & Schuster, 1972), pp. 130–135; Greeley, *The Irish Americans*, pp. 168–169.

75. Maldwyn Jones, *American Immigration* (Chicago: University of Chicago Press, 1960), p. 236.

76. William Miller, "American Historians and the Business Elite," *Journal of Economic History* 9 (November 1949): 202–203.

77. Quoted in Elmer Ellis, *Mr. Dooley's America* (New York: Knopf, 1941), p. 208.

78. John Aloysius Farrell, "Clinton Staff Alters Blair Brown's Status," *Boston Globe*, March 19, 1994, p. 3.

79. Donald H. Akenson, *The United States and Ireland* (Cambridge, MA: Harvard University Press, 1973), pp. 40–42.

80. Wittke, *The Irish in America*, pp. 281–91.

81. Linda Greenhouse, "Supreme Court Ruling Clears Way for Deportation of an I.R.A. Man," *The New York Times*, January 16, 1992, p. A1; "O'Connor Seeks Aid for I.R.A. Fugitive," *The New York Times*, February 1, 1992, sec. 1, p. 25; Cal McCrystal, "Notebook: A Tug-of-War for America's Irish Soul," *Independent*, February 2, 1992, p. 23.

82. Steve Fainaru, "Adams, in New York Limelight, Asks for U.S. Help on Peace," *Boston Globe*, February 2, 1994, p. 1; Gerald Renner, "Sinn Fein Leader Urges Peace Plan Support," *Hartford Courant*, September 26, 1994, p. A1; Kevin Cullen, "Loyalist Extremists Call Ulster Cease-Fire," *Boston Globe*, October 14, 1994, p. 1; "Northern Ireland Peace Talks," National Public Radio, Weekend Edition, Sept 21, 1997.

83. William V. Shannon, *The American Irish* (New York: Macmillan, 1963), pp. 151–181.

84. Ibid., pp. 332–352; Samuel Lubell, *The Future of American Politics*, 2nd rev. ed. (New York: Doubleday, Anchor Books, 1955), pp. 83–84.

85. Glazer and Moynihan, *Beyond the Melting Pot*, p. 287.

86. Ibid; Shannon, *The American Irish*, pp. 395–411; Levy and Kramer, *The Ethnic Factor*, pp. 126–127. Compare John R. Schmidhauser, "The Justices of the Supreme Court: A Collective Portrait," *Midwest Journal of Social Science* 3 (February 1950): 1–57.

87. *Reporting for the Russell Sage Foundation*, no. 6, May 1985, p. 6.

88. Leyburn, *The Scotch-Irish*, p. 322.

89. Stephen Steinberg, *The Ethnic Myth* (New York: Atheneum, 1981), pp. 160–164.

90. Bagenal, *The American Irish*, p. 69.

91. Handlin, *Boston's Immigrants*, p. 67.

92. Adams, *Ireland and Irish Emigration to the New World*, p. 358.

93. Stephan Thernstrom, *Poverty and Progress* (Cambridge, MA: Harvard University Press, 1964), pp. 154–158.

94. Ibid., p. 184; Clark, *The Irish in Philadelphia*, pp. 59, 167–175.

95. Greeley, *That Most Distressful Nation*, p. 120; Clark, "The Philadelphia Irish," p. 143; Wittke, *The Irish in America*, pp. 217–227.

96. Pitirim Sorokin, "American Millionaires and Multi-Millionaires," *Social Forces* 3 (May 1925): 634–635. Data are based on father's ancestry.

97. Stephan Thernstrom, *The Other Bostonians* (Cambridge, MA: Harvard University Press, 1973), p. 131; Berthoff, *British Immigrants in Industrial America*.

98. Hershberg et al., "A Tale of Three Cities," p. 190.

99. Lloyd Warner and Leo Srole, *The Social Systems of American Ethnic Groups* (New Haven, CT: Yale University Press, 1945), pp. 93–95; E. Digby Baltzell, *An American Business Aristocracy* (New York: Collier Books, 1962), pp. 267–431; E. Digby Baltzell, *The Protestant Establishment* (New York: Random House/Vintage Books, 1966), pp. 320–321.

100. Shannon, *The American Irish*, pp. 436–437.

101. Ronald P. Formisano, *Boston against Busing: Race, Class, and Ethnicity in the 1960s and 1970s* (Chapel Hill: University of North Carolina Press, 1991), p. 15.

102. Harold J. Abramson, *Ethnic Diversity in Catholic America* (New York: Wiley, 1973), pp. 41–44; Levy and Kramer, *The Ethnic Factor*, p. 125. See also Greeley, *The Irish Americans*, p. 111.

103. U.S. Bureau of the Census, *1990 Census of Population: Ancestry of the Population in the United States*, pp. 353, 371, 455, 473; U.S. Bureau of the Census, *1990 Census of Population: Social and Economic Characteristics: United States*, pp. 45, 48, 49; Andrew Hacker, *Money: Who Has How Much and Why* (New York: Scribner International, 1997).

104. Quoted in Roberts, "In Search of Irish," p. B1; Tim Unsworthy, "The Irish: Faith Persuasive as Metamucil in an Old Priest's Diet," *National Catholic Reporter*, March 15, 1996, p. 16.

105. John T. Ellis, *American Catholicism* (Garden City, NY: Doubleday/Image Books, 1965), p. 62; Clark, *The Irish in Philadelphia*, p. 123.

106. David O. Moberg, *The Church as a Social Institution* (Englewood Cliffs, NJ: Prentice Hall, 1962), p. 193.
107. Andrew M. Greeley, *Ethnicity, Denomination and Inequality* (Beverly Hills, CA: Sage, 1976), pp. 45–53.
108. U.S. Bureau of the Census, *1990 Census of Population: Ancestry of the Population in the United States*, pp. 251, 269; U.S. Bureau of the Census, *1990 Census of Population: Social and Economic Characteristics: United States*, p. 42; Andrew M. Greeley, review letter on chapter, September, 1997.
109. "Bill to Require Teaching of Irish Famine," United Press International, March 17, 1997.
110. Wittke, *The Irish in America*, pp. 52–61, 205.
111. Owen B. Corrigan, "Chronology of the Catholic Hierarchy of the United States," *Catholic Historical Review* 1 (January 1916): 267–389; Gaustad, *Historical Atlas of Religion in America*, p. 103; Ellis, *American Catholicism*, p. 56; Wittke, *The Irish in America*, p. 91; Greeley, *That Most Distressful Nation*, p. 93; correspondence between Andrew Greeley and the authors.
112. Greeley, *The Irish Americans*, p. 145.
113. National Opinion Research Center, 1990 General Social Survey. Tabulations by authors.
114. Greeley, *The Irish Americans*, pp. 130–132.
115. Ford, *The Scotch-Irish in America*, p. 538.
116. *Saturday Evening Post*, December 12, 1901; *Saturday Evening Post*, August 28, 1902. Quoted in Simon and Alexander, *The Ambivalent Welcome*, pp. 66–67.
117. Clark, *The Philadelphia Irish*, p. 178.
118. Thernstrom, *Poverty and Progress*, p. 179.
119. Abramson, *Ethnic Diversity in Catholic America*, p. 111; Greeley, *The Irish Americans*, pp. 149–151.
120. Glazer and Moynihan, *Beyond the Melting Pot*, p. 219.
121. Raymond E. Wolfinger, "The Development and Persistence of Ethnic Voting," *American Political Science Review* 60 (1965): 907; Greeley, "Success and Assimilation," p. 236.
122. Joseph P. O'Grady, *How the Irish Became American* (New York: Twayne, 1973), p. 141; Marjorie R. Fallows, *Irish Americans: Identity and Assimilation* (Englewood Cliffs, NJ: Prentice Hall, 1979), p. 147.
123. Abramson, *Ethnic Diversity in Catholic America*, p. 53; Alba, *Ethnic Identity*, p. 47; Nona Claren, "The Trouble with the Melting Pot," *Baltimore Sun*, June 24, 1997, p. 9a.
124. Fallows, *Irish Americans*, pp. 148–149. See also Richard D. Alba, "Social Assimilation among American Catholic National-Origin Groups," *American Sociological Review* 41 (December 1976): 1032.
125. Alba, *Ethnic Identity*, pp. 55, 61.
126. Formisano, *Boston Against Busing*, pp. 220–221.
127. Greeley, "Success and Assimilation," p. 233.
128. Greeley, *The Irish Americans*, p. 206.
129. Ibid. See also Andrew M. Greeley, *Ethnicity in the United States* (New York: Wiley, 1974), p. 311; S. L. Berry, "In Step with the Irish Heritage; Irish-Americans Struggle to Learn Ancestral Language," *Indianapolis Star*, March 17, 1997, p. E1.

CHAPTER 5

1. From *The New York Times*, June 17, 1970, p. 31. © 1970 by The New York Times Company. Reprinted by permission.
2. Richard Gambino, *Blood of My Blood* (Garden City, NY: Doubleday/Anchor Books, 1975), p. 344.
3. Giovanni Schiavo, *The Italians in America before the Civil War* (New York: Vigo Press, 1934), pp. 55–180.
4. Ibid., p. 135.
5. Philip di Franco, *The Italian American Experience* (New York: Tom Doherty Associates, 1988), pp. 45–47.
6. U.S. Department of Justice, Immigration and Naturalization Service, *Annual Report* (Washington, DC, 1973), pp. 52–54 (figures for 1820 to 1867 represent alien passengers arrived; for 1868–1891 and 1895–1897, immigrant aliens arrived; for 1892–1894 and 1898–1973, immigrant aliens admitted); Schiavo, *The Italians in America*, p. 204; Carl Wittke, *We Who Built America*, rev. ed. (Cleveland, OH: Case Western Reserve University Press, 1964), p. 441; Humbert S. Nelli, *The Italians in Chicago, 1880–1930* (New York: Oxford University Press, 1970), p. 5; Grazia Dore, "Some Social and Historical Aspects of Italian Emigration to America," in *The Italians*, eds. Francesco Cordasco and Eugene Bucchioni (Clifton, NJ: Augustus M. Kelley, 1974), p. 7.
7. Joseph Lopreato, *Italian Americans* (New York: Random House, 1970), pp. 23–27; John S. MacDonald, "Agricultural Organization, Migration, and Labor Militancy in Rural Italy," *Economic History Review*, 2d ser., 16 (1963–1964): 61–75. We are indebted to Phyllis Cancilla Martinelli for her useful suggestions concerning the sections that follow. We draw on her suggestions in this paragraph and in the rest of this chapter.
8. Luciano J. Iorizzo and Salvatore Mondello, *The Italian-Americans* (New York: Twayne, 1971), pp. 57–59; Michael La Sorte, *La Merica* (Philadelphia, PA: Temple University Press, 1985), pp. 1–13, 189–202.
9. Antonia Stella, *Some Aspects of Italian Immigration to the United States*, reprint ed. (San Francisco: R & E Associates, 1970), p. 33; Rudolph J. Vecoli, "Contadini in Chicago," in *Divided Society*, ed. Colin Greer (New York: Basic Books, 1974), p. 220.
10. William Petersen, *Population*, 2nd ed. (New York: Macmillan, 1969), p. 260; La Sorte, *La Merica*, pp. 189–202.
11. John Higham, *Strangers in the Land*, rev. ed. (New York: Atheneum, 1975), pp. 312–324.
12. U.S. Bureau of the Census, *Statistical Abstract of the United States 1994* (Washington, DC, 1994), p. 11.
13. U.S. Bureau of the Census, *1990 Census of Population: Ancestry of the Population in the United States*, CP-3–2 (Washington, DC, 1993), p. 50.
14. U.S. Bureau of the Census, *1990 Census of Population: Social and Economic Characteristics: United States*, CP-2–1 (Washington, DC, 1993), p. 166.
15. Stanley Lieberson, *Ethnic Patterns in American Cities* (Glencoe, IL: Free Press, 1963), pp. 209–218; La Sorte, *La Merica*, pp. 61–158.
16. William F. Whyte, *Street Corner Society*, 2nd ed. (Chicago: University of Chicago Press, 1955), pp. 272–273; Walter Firey, *Land Use in Central Boston* (Cambridge, MA: Harvard University Press, 1947), pp. 187–188; Wittke, *We Who Built America*, p. 446.
17. Firey, *Land Use in Central Boston*, p. 193; Paul J. Campisi, "Ethnic Family Patterns: The Italian Family in the United States," in *The Italians*, eds. Cordasco and Bucchioni, pp. 311–314; Lopreato, *Italian Americans*, pp. 51–53; Whyte, *Street Corner Society*, p. 274.
18. Eliot Lord, John J. D. Trenor, and Samuel J. Barrows, *The Italian in America*, reprint ed. (San Francisco: R & E Associates, 1970), pp. 17–18.
19. Quoted in Iorizzo and Mondello, *The Italian-Americans*, p. 64.

20. Rita J. Simon and Susan H. Alexander, *The Ambivalent Welcome: Print Media, Public Opinion, and Immigration* (Westport, CT: Praeger, 1993), pp. 84, 131.

21. *Scribner's*, April 1913. Quoted in ibid., p. 123.

22. Kenneth L. Roberts, *Why Europe Leaves Home*, excerpted in "Kenneth L. Roberts and the Threat of Mongrelization in America, 1922," in *In Their Place*, eds. Lewis H. Carlson and George A. Colburn (New York: Wiley, 1972), p. 312.

23. Mary F. Matthews, "The Role of the Public School in the Assimilation of the Italian Immigrant Child in New York City, 1900–1914," in *The Italian Experience in the United States*, eds. Silvano Tomasi and M. H. Engel (New York: Center for Migration Studies, 1970), p. 127; Stella, *Some Aspects of Italian Immigration*, pp. 38, 54.

24. Cited in Leon J. Kamin, *The Science and Politics of I.Q.* (New York: Wiley, 1974), pp. 15–16.

25. Ibid., pp. 16–19.

26. Carl C. Brigham, *A Study of American Intelligence* (Princeton, NJ: Princeton University Press, 1923), especially pp. 124–125 and 177–210. Later Brigham recanted.

27. See Roberts, *Why Europe Leaves Home*; for earlier views, see Woodrow Wilson, *A History of the American People* (New York: Harper, 1902), 5: 212–214.

28. See Kamin, *The Science and Politics of I.Q.*, p. 30.

29. Quoted in E. Digby Baltzell, *The Protestant Establishment* (New York: Random House/Vintage Books, 1966), p. 30.

30. Quoted in ibid.

31. Irving L. Allen, *Unkind Words* (New York: Bergin and Garvey, 1990), pp. 32, 60.

32. Iorizzo and Mondello, *The Italian-Americans*, pp. 35–36; quotation cited in Nelli, *The Italians in Chicago*, p. 126.

33. Stella, *Some Aspects of Italian Immigration*, pp. 60–61, 73.

34. di Franco, *The Italian American Experience*, pp. 84–86; Gambino, *Blood of My Blood*, pp. 293–298; Lopreato, *Italian Americans*, p. 126; Nelli, *The Italians in Chicago*, pp. 154–155.

35. Mary C. Waters, *Ethnic Options: Choosing Identities in America* (Berkeley, CA: University of California Press, 1990), pp. 142–143.

36. "Italian American Group Rips CBS for 'Mafia' Stereotypes," *Daily News* (New York), November 18, 1997, p. 96.

37. William F. Miller, "Lawyer Fights Italian American Stereotypes," *Plain Dealer*, June 15, 1996, p. 7B.

38. Gambino, *Blood of My Blood*, pp. 300–301; Selwyn Raab, "The Mob in Decline," *The New York Times*, October 22, 1990, p. A1.

39. Robert Lichter and Linda Lichter, "Italian-American Characters in Television Entertainment" (report prepared for the Commission for Social Justice, Order of Sons of Italy, May 1982).

40. Quotation cited in Micaela di Leonardo, *The Varieties of Ethnic Experience* (Ithaca, NY: Cornell University Press, 1984), pp. 160–161; Susanna Tardi, *Family and Society: The Case of the Italians in New Jersey* (Ann Arbor, MI: UMI Dissertation Service, 1991), p. 189.

41. Donna Haupt, Jan Mason, and Penny Ward Moser, "The Embattled Queen of Queens," *Time*, October 1, 1984, p. 34; Vivienne Walt, "Cuomo: Hurt by Prejudice toward Italians," *Newsday*, July 23, 1991, p. 19.

42. Richard D. Alba, *Ethnic Identity* (New Haven, CT: Yale University Press, 1990), pp. 141–142; Waters, *Ethnic Options*, pp. 142–43; see also Ross Harano and Jeryl

Levin, "Capone Image Hurts Italian-Americans," *Chicago Tribune*, August 3, 1993, p. N16.

43. William F. Whyte, "Race Conflicts in the North End of Boston," *New England Quarterly* 12 (December 1939): 626; Iorizzo and Mondello, *The Italian-Americans*, pp. 35, 66.

44. Luciano J. Iorizzo, "The Padrone and Immigrant Distribution," in *The Italian Experience in the United States*, eds. Tomasi and Engel, pp. 49–51; Gambino, *Blood of My Blood*, p. 119; Higham, *Strangers in the Land*, p. 169.

45. di Franco, *The Italian American Experience*, p. 85; Gambino, *Blood of My Blood*, pp. 118, 280–281; quotation cited in Gambino, *Blood of My Blood*, p. 118.

46. Gambino, *Blood of My Blood*, pp. 104, 119; Higham, *Strangers in the Land*, p. 90. See also Andrew F. Rolle, *The American Italian* (Belmont, CA: Wadsworth, 1972).

47. See, for example, William Young and David E. Kaiser, *Postmortem* (Amherst: University of Massachusetts Press, 1985). See also a work from the 1970s, Gambino, *Blood of My Blood*, pp. 120–21.

48. Iorizzo and Mondello, *The Italian-Americans*, p. 207; Gerald D. Suttles, *The Social Order of the Slum* (Chicago: University of Chicago Press, 1968), pp. 102–103; Richard Krickus, *Pursuing the American Dream* (Garden City, NY: Doubleday/Anchor Books, 1976), p. 280.

49. Curtis Rist, "Prosecutor: Race Riot in Bensonhurst," *Newsday*, April 17, 1990, p. 4.

50. Cited in Mark R. Levy and Michael S. Kramer, *The Ethnic Factor* (New York: Simon & Schuster, 1972), p. 174.

51. National Opinion Research Center, General Social Surveys, 1989 and 1990. Tabulations by authors.

52. Schiavo, *The Italians in America before the Civil War*, pp. 163–166.

53. Nelli, *The Italians in Chicago*, pp. 75–76; Wittke, *We Who Built America*, p. 447; Lopreato, *Italian Americans*, pp. 113–117; Giovanni Schiavo, *Italian American History* (New York: Vigo Press, 1947), 1: 499–504.

54. See Gambino, *Blood of My Blood*, p. 117.

55. Rolle, *The American Italian*, p. 85; William F. Whyte, *Street Corner Society*, p. 276; Samuel Lubell, *The Future of American Politics*, 2nd ed. (Garden City, NY: Doubleday, Anchor Books, 1955), p. 70; Lopreato, *Italian Americans*, p. 114; di Franco, *The Italian American Experience*, pp. 139–159.

56. Joel H. Spring, *Education and the Rise of the Corporate State* (Boston, MA: Beacon Press, 1972), pp. 86–87.

57. Herbert J. Gans, *The Urban Villagers* (Glencoe, IL: Free Press, 1962), pp. 285–287.

58. di Franco, *The Italian American Experience*, pp. 146–147. Salvatore J. LaGumina, "Case Studies of Ethnicity and Italo-American Politicians," in *The Italian Experience in the United States*, eds. Tomasi and Engel, p. 147; Krickus, *Pursuing the American Dream*, pp. 174–181.

59. "World War II Italian American Internment," Bill Ritter, Charles Gibson, ABC *Good Morning America*, October 30, 1997.

60. Wittke, *We Who Built America*, p. 450; Iorizzo and Mondello, *The Italian-Americans*, pp. 200–205, 208; Gambino, *Blood of My Blood*, p. 316.

61. Richard Alba, *Italian Americans* (Englewood Cliffs, NJ: Prentice Hall, 1985), pp. 78–81.

62. Lubell, *The Future of American Politics*, pp. 70, 83–84; LaGumina, "Case Studies of Ethnicity and Italo-American Politics," p. 145.

63. Alba, *Italian Americans*, p. 143; General Social Surveys, 1989 and 1990. See also Andrew M. Greeley, *Ethnicity in the United States* (New York: Wiley, 1974), pp. 94–101.
64. "Italian Americans: Big Swing?" *Campaigns & Elections*, August, 1996, p. 63.
65. Krickus, *Pursuing the American Dream*, p. 92; Sylvia Pellini Macphee, *Changing Perspectives of Italian Americans* (Cambridge, MA: Center for Community Economic Development, 1974), pp. 10–15.
66. John M. Goshko, "Italian Americans Lobbying UN for Their Motherland," *International Herald Tribune*, September 18, 1997, p. 10.
67. Iorizzo, "The Padrone and Immigrant Distribution," p. 43.
68. di Franco, *The Italian American Experience*, pp. 139–141. Nelli, *The Italians in Chicago*, pp. 56–60, 64–66; anonymous, "The Philanthropists' View of the Italian in America," in *The Italian in America: The Progressive View*, ed. Lydio F. Tomasi (New York: Center for Migration Studies, 1972), p. 79 (this article is reprinted by Tomasi from *Charities*, an early journal of social and settlement workers); Iorizzo and Mondello, *The Italian-Americans*, pp. 138–158.
69. Stella, *Some Aspects of Italian Immigration*, p. 94.
70. Nelli, *The Italians in Chicago*, pp. 13–14; Antonio Stella, "Tuberculosis and the Italians in the United States," in *The Italians*, eds. Cordasco and Bucchioni, pp. 449–452.
71. Gambino, *Blood of My Blood*, p. 85; Leonard Covello, "The Influence of Southern Italian Family Mores upon the School Situation in America," in *The Italians*, eds. Cordasco and Bucchioni, p. 513; Lord, Trenor, and Barrows, *The Italian in America*, pp. 16–19; E. P. Hutchinson, *Immigrants and Their Children, 1850–1950* (New York: Wiley, 1956), pp. 137–138.
72. Higham, *Strangers in the Land*, p. 48.
73. Gambino, *Blood of My Blood*, p. 77.
74. Stephan Thernstrom, *The Other Bostonians* (Cambridge, MA: Harvard University Press, 1973), p. 161.
75. Elizabeth Gurley Flynn, "The Lawrence Textile Strike," in *America's Working Women*, eds. R. Baxandall, L. Gordon, and S. Reverby (New York: Random House, Vintage Books, 1976), pp. 194–199; Nelli, *The Italians in Chicago*, pp. 78–85; Gambino, *Blood of My Blood*, pp. 115–117.
76. John J. d'Alesandre, "Occupational Trends of Italians in New York City," *Italy-America Monthly* 2 (February 1935): 11–21.
77. W. Lloyd Warner and Leo Srole, *The Social Systems of American Ethnic Groups* (New Haven, CT: Yale University Press, 1945), pp. 96–97; Gambino, *Blood of My Blood*, p. 101; Wittke, *We Who Built America*, p. 443.
78. Nelli, *The Italians in Chicago*, pp. 211–214; Smith, *The Mafia Mystique*, p. 322.
79. Ianni, *A Family Business*, p. 193.
80. Smith, *The Mafia Mystique*, p. 323.
81. Rolle, *The American Italians*, pp. 89–93.
82. Thernstrom, *The Other Bostonians*, p. 171.
83. U.S. Bureau of the Census, *U.S. Census of Population, 1970: Subject Reports–National Origin and Language*, PC(2)-1A (Washington, DC, 1973), p. 166.
84. U.S. Bureau of the Census, *1990 Census of Population: Ancestry of the Population in the United States*, p. 356; U.S. Bureau of the Census, *1990 Census of Population: Social and Economic Characteristics: United States*, p. 45.
85. Personal correspondence with Dr. Alfred Rotondaro, executive director of the National Italian American Foundation, June 12, 1991.
86. U.S. Bureau of the Census, *U.S. Census of Population, 1970: Subject Reports—National Origin and Language*, p. 167; U.S. Bureau of the Census, *U.S. Census of Population, 1970: General Social and Economic Characteristics*, PC(1)-C1 (Washington, DC, 1972), pp. 177, 368.
87. U.S. Bureau of the Census, *1990 Census of Population: Ancestry of the Population in the United States*, pp. 307, 356, 458; U.S. Bureau of the Census, *1990 Census of Population: Social and Economic Characteristics: United States*, pp. 48.
88. Gambino, *Blood of My Blood*, p. 89.
89. National Center for Urban Ethnic Affairs Newsletter 1, no. 5 (1976): 8.
90. Robert Viscusi, "Giving the Boot to Italians," *Newsday*, May 30, 1991, p. 74
91. "CUNY Settles Suit by Italian Institute," *The New York Times*, January 9, 1994, section 1, p. 22.
92. Congress of Italian-American Organizations, *A Portrait of the Italian-American Community in New York City* (New York, 1975), pp. 7–10, 49–51; "Ferraro's Mixed Blessing," *Newsweek*, October 1, 1984, p. 12.
93. Lawrence A. Cremin, *The Transformation of the School* (New York: Knopf, 1961), pp. 67–68; Colin Greer, *The Great School Legend* (New York: Basic Books, 1972), pp. 3–6.
94. U.S. Bureau of the Census, *U.S. Census of Population, 1950: Special Reports—Nativity and Parentage*, p. 155; U.S. Bureau of the Census, *U.S. Census of Population, 1950: Vol. II, Characteristics of the Population*, Part 1 (Washington, DC, 1953), p. 96; U.S. Bureau of the Census, *U.S. Census of Population, 1970: Subject Reports—National Origin and Language*, p. 165; U.S. Bureau of the Census, *U.S. Census of Population, 1970: General Social and Economic Characteristics*, p. 368.
95. U.S. Bureau of the Census, *1990 Census of Population: Ancestry of the Population in the United States*, p. 254; U.S. Bureau of the Census, *1990 Census of Population: Social and Economic Characteristics: United States*, p. 42.
96. Quoted in Silvano M. Tomasi, "The Ethnic Church and the Integration of Italian Immigrants in the United States," in *The Italian Experience in the United States*, eds. Tomasi and Engel, p. 168.
97. Rudolph J. Vecoli, "Contadini in Chicago: A Critique of The Uprooted," in *The Aliens*, eds. Leonard Dinnerstein and Frederic C. Jaher (New York: Appleton-Century-Crofts, 1970), p. 226; Harold J. Abramson, *Ethnic Diversity in Catholic America* (New York: Wiley, 1973), pp. 136–139.
98. Tomasi, "The Ethnic Church," p. 167.
99. Ibid., pp. 187–188; Nelli, *The Italians in Chicago*, p. 195; di Franco, *The Italian American Experience*, pp. 269–270.
100. Nicholas J. Russo, "Three Generations of Italians in New York City: Their Religious Acculturation," in *The Italian Experience in the United States*, eds. Tomasi and Engel, pp. 200–206; Tardi, *Family and Society*, pp. 145–153.
101. National Opinion Research Center, *A Profile of Italian Americans: 1972–1991*, March 1992; Stuart Vincent, "Devotion to Saints a Part of LI Life; Festivals Have an Italian Flavor," *Newsday*, May 1, 1996, p. A6.
102. Covello, "The Influence of Southern Italian Family Mores," p. 515.

103. Paul J. Campisi, "Ethnic Family Patterns: The Italian Family in the United States," *American Journal of Sociology* 53 (May 1948): 443–449; Covello, "The Influence of Southern Italian Family Mores," pp. 525–530.

104. Irvin L. Child, *Italian or American?* (New Haven, CT: Yale University Press, 1943) (an important excerpt from this book can be found in *The Italians*, eds. Cordasco and Bucchioni, pp. 321–336); Alba, *Italian Americans*, p. 114.

105. Alba, *Italian Americans*, p. 166.

106. See ibid.

107. Herbert Gans, *The Urban Villagers*, rev. ed. (New York: Free Press, 1982), pp. 412–413. Greeley, *Why Can't They Be Like Us?* (New York: Dalton, 1971), p. 77. See also Phyllis Cancilla Martinelli, "Beneath the Surface: Ethnic Communities in Phoenix, Arizona" (paper, Arizona State University, 1980); James A. Crispino, *The Assimilation of Ethnic Groups: The Italian Case* (New York: Center for Migration Studies, 1980), pp. 80–86.

108. Colleen L. Johnson, *Growing Up and Growing Old in Italian American Families* (New Brunswick, NJ: Rutgers University Press, 1985), pp. 221–228; Richard D. Alba, *Ethnic Identity* (New Haven, CT: Yale University Press, 1990), pp. 47–48, 59–61, 70–71, 224–226; Tardi, *Family and Society*, pp. 179–192.

109. Anthony L. LaRuffa, *Monte Carmelo: An Italian-American Community in the Bronx* (New York: Gordon & Breach, 1988), pp. 135–139.

110. Commentary from Richard Alba given to authors, May 1994 and June 1997.

111. Francis X. Femminella and Jill S. Quadagno, "The Italian American Family," in *Ethnic Families in America*, eds. Charles H. Mindel and Robert W. Habenstein (New York: Elsevier, 1976), pp. 74–75; Ruby Jo Reeves Kennedy, "Single or Triple Melting Pot? Intermarriage in New Haven, 1870–1950," *American Journal of Sociology* 58 (July 1952): 56–59; Nelli, *The Italians in Chicago*, p. 196; Crispino, *The Assimilation of Ethnic Groups*, p. 105; Alba, *Italian Americans*, pp. 146–147; Waters, *Ethnic Options*, p. 104; Nona Claren, "The Trouble with the Melting Pot," *Baltimore Sun*, June 24, 1997, p. 9a.

112. Alba, *Italian Americans*, pp. 159–162; Alba, *Ethnic Identity*, p. 47.

113. Alba, *Italian Americans*, p. 162.

114. LaRuffa, *Monte Carmelo*, pp. 17–28.

115. Phyllis Cancilla Martinelli, *Ethnicity in the Sunbelt* (New York: AMS Press, 1989), pp. 234–258; Alba, *Ethnic Identity*, pp. 59–60, 70.

116. Marcus Lee Hansen, "The Third Generation," in *Children of the Uprooted*, ed. Oscar Handlin (New York: Harper & Row, 1966), pp. 255–271; P. J. Gallo, *Ethnic Alienation* (Rutherford, NJ: Fairleigh Dickinson University Press, 1974), p. 194; John M. Goering, "The Emergence of Ethnic Interests," *Social Forces* 49 (March 1971): 381–382; Tardi, *Family and Society*, pp. 179–192.

117. di Leonardo, *The Varieties of Ethnic Experience*, p. 156.

118. Richard D. Alba, "Identity and Ethnicity among Italians and Other Americans of European Ancestry," in *The Columbus People: Perspectives in Italian Immigration to the Americas and Australia*, ed. Lydio Tomasi, Piero Gautaldo, and Thomas Row (Staten Island, NY: Center for Migration Studies, 1994), pp. 21–41.

CHAPTER 6

1. Alan Dershowitz, *Chutzpah* (Boston, MA: Little, Brown, 1991), p. 202.

2. Ibid., pp. 198–199, 206, 343–354; Arthur Hertzberg, *The Jews in America* (New York: Simon & Schuster, 1989), pp. 377–388.

3. Hertzberg, *The Jews in America*, pp. 13–28.

4. Charles E. Silberman, *A Certain People* (New York: Summit Books, 1985), pp. 40–42; Chaim I. Waxman, *America's Jews in Transition* (Philadelphia, PA: Temple University Press, 1983), pp. 5–6.

5. Silberman, *A Certain People*, pp. 42–45; Waxman, *America's Jews in Transition*, pp. 6–8.

6. Silberman, *A Certain People*, pp. 42–49; Hertzberg, *The Jews in America*, pp. 102–104.

7. Hertzberg, *The Jews in America*, pp. 152–154, 185; Silberman, *A Certain People*, p. 49; Waxman, *America's Jews in Transition*, p. 43.

8. Hertzberg, *The Jews in America*, pp. 160–176, 224; Silberman, *A Certain People*, pp. 49–51.

9. Milton Meltzer, *Never to Forget: The Jews of the Holocaust* (New York: Harper and Row, 1976), p. 45.

10. Maurice J. Karpf, *Jewish Community Organization in the United States* (New York: Arno, 1971), p. 33; Sidney Goldstein, "American Jewry: A Demographic Analysis," in *The Future of the Jewish Community in America*, ed. David Sidorsky (New York: Basic Books, 1973), p. 71; Alvin Chenkin, "Jewish Population in the United States," in *American Jewish Yearbook, 1973* (New York: American Jewish Committee, 1973), pp. 307–309; Arthur A. Goren, "Jews," in *Harvard Encyclopedia of American Ethnic Groups* (Cambridge, MA: Harvard University Press, 1980), pp. 591–592; Rita J. Simon and Julian L. Simon, "Social and Economic Adjustment," in *New Lives*, ed. Rita J. Simon (Lexington, MA: Heath/Lexington Books, 1985), pp. 26–41; Douglass Stanglin, Kenneth Walsh, Edward Pound, Charles Fenyvesi, Josh Chetwynd, "Quale's Newest Place in the Sun," *U.S. News and World Report*, August 26, 1996, pp. 16, 19.

11. Stanglin et al., "Quale's Newest Place in the Sun," pp. 16, 19.

12. Calvin Goldscheider and Sidney Goldstein, *The Jewish Community of Rhode Island* (Providence: Jewish Federation of Rhode Island, 1988), pp. 3–35.

13. "Religion in Brief," *Atlanta Journal and Constitution*, September 6, 1997, p. 6E.

14. Barry A. Kosmin, et al., *Highlights of the CJF 1990 National Jewish Population Survey* (New York: Council of Jewish Federations, 1991), pp. 3–6, 10, 20–22, 25–26; Nathan Glazer, *New Perspectives in American Jewish Sociology* (New York: American Jewish Committee, 1987), p. 8.

15. See David Sidorsky, "Introduction," in *The Future of the Jewish Community in America*, ed. Sidorsky, pp. xix–xxv; and Stephen D. Isaacs, *Jews and American Politics* (Garden City, NY: Doubleday, 1974), pp. ix–x.

16. Charles Y. Glock and Rodney Stark, *Christian Beliefs and Anti-Semitism* (New York: Harper & Row, 1966), p. 64 et passim.

17. Carey McWilliams, *A Mask for Privilege* (Boston, MA: Little, Brown, 1948), pp. 164–165, 170–173; John Higham, "Social Discrimination against Jews in America, 1830–1930," *Publication of the American Jewish Historical Society* 47 (September 1957): 5.

18. Silberman, *A Certain People*, p. 48; Hertzberg, *The Jews in America*, pp. 86–87, 188–189; Higham, "Social Discrimination against Jews in America," pp. 9–10.

19. Silberman, *A Certain People*, p. 47.

20. Leonard Dinnerstein, *Antisemitism in America* (New York: Oxford University Press, 1994), pp. 80–82.
21. Gustavus Meyers, *History of Bigotry in the United States*, rev. ed. (New York: Capricorn Books, 1960), pp. 277–313; McWilliams, *A Mask for Privilege*, pp. 110–111; T. W. Adorno et al., *The Authoritarian Personality* (New York: Harper, 1950), pp. 69–79; Isaacs, *Jews and American Politics*, pp. 51, 98.
22. Gary A. Tobin, *Jewish Perceptions of Anti-Semitism* (New York: Plenum, 1988), pp. 106–112.
23. Silberman, *A Certain People*, pp. 22–27, 335–337, 360–366; Dershowitz, *Chutzpah*, pp. 116–129.
24. Kosmin et al., *Highlights of the CJF 1990 National Jewish Population Survey*, p. 29.
25. "Anti-Semitism Concerns Surveyed," *San Diego Union-Tribune*, June 6, 1997, p. E5.
26. Henry L. Feingold, *Zion in America* (New York: Twayne, 1974), pp. 143–144; C. Vann Woodward, *Tom Watson* (New York: Oxford University Press, 1963), pp. 435–445.
27. Rufus Learski, *The Jews in America* (New York: KTAV Publishing House, 1972), pp. 290–291; John Higham, *Strangers in the Land* (New York: Atheneum, 1975), pp. 298–299; Woodward, *Tom Watson*.
28. Milton R. Konvitz, "Inter-group Relations," in *The American Jew*, ed. O. I. Janowsky (Philadelphia, PA: Jewish Publication Society of America, 1964), pp. 78–79; Donald S. Strong, *Organized Anti-Semitism in America* (Washington, DC: American Council on Public Affairs, 1941), pp. 14–20.
29. Strong, *Organized Anti-Semitism in America*, p. 67.
30. Lucy S. Dawidowicz, *The War against the Jews: 1933–1945* (New York: Holt, Rinehart & Winston), p. 148; see also pp. 164 and 403.
31. Lewis H. Carlson and George A. Colburn, "The Jewish Refugee Problem," in *In Their Place*, eds. Lewis H. Carlson and George A. Colburn (New York: Wiley, 1972), pp. 290–291; Stephanie Chavez, "Anti-Semitic Incidents Reported Rising," *Los Angeles Times*, February 7, 1992, p. A3.
32. "ADL Demands Full Investigation into Pike County Alabama School Practices," PR Newswire, August 6, 1997.
33. Lenni Brenner, *Jews in America Today* (Secaucus, NJ: Lyle Stuart, 1986), pp. 205–206, 209; Chavez, "Anti-Semitic Incidents Reported Rising," p. A3. See discussion of "hate crimes" in Chapter 12.
34. Konvitz, "Inter-group Relations," pp. 85–95.
35. Dershowitz, *Chutzpah*, p. 326; Linda Greenhouse, "Justices Affirm Ban on Prayers in Public School," *The New York Times*, June 25, 1992, p. A1.
36. Robert F. Drinan, "The Supreme Court, Religious Freedom and the Yarmulke," *America*, June 12, 1986, pp. 9–11.
37. Gerald S. Strober, *American Jews* (Garden City, NY: Doubleday, 1974), pp. 149–176.
38. Anti-Defamation League, *Extremism in the Name of Religion: The Violent Legacy of Meir Kahane* (Washington, DC: ADL, 1995).
39. Ronald Takaki, *A Different Mirror: A History of Multicultural America* (Boston, MA: Little, Brown, 1993), p. 406.
40. "Two Deaths Ignite Racial Clash in Tense Brooklyn Neighborhood," *The New York Times*, August 21, 1991, p. A1; Scott Minerbrook and Miriam Horn, "Side by Side, Apart," *U.S. News & World Report*, November 4, 1991, p. 44.

41. Silberman, *A Certain People*, p. 340.
42. Ibid., p. 41.
43. Ibid., pp. 333, 339–343; Dershowitz, *Chutzpah*, pp. 241, 301–302.
44. Letty Cottin Pogrebin, *Deborah, Golda, and Me: Being Female and Jewish in America* (New York: Crown, 1991).
45. Joe R. Feagin and Leslie Inniss, "Racial Attitudes in Four Socio-religious Groups" (research paper, University of Florida, Spring 1992).
46. *Highlights from an Anti-Defamation League Survey on Racial Attitudes in America* (New York: Anti-Defamation League, 1993), pp. 51, 55, 61, 80–86.
47. Tom Tugend, "L.A. Jews Step Up Aid to Riot-Hit Areas," *Jerusalem Post*, May 12, 1992, n.p.
48. Buddy Nevins, "Idea of Saving Bucks Doesn't Compute with School Officials," *Ft. Lauderdale Sun-Sentinel*, December 18, 1994, p. B4.
49. Gene Warner, "Black, Jewish Teens Team Up to Honor King Legacy," *Buffalo News*, January 21, 1997, p. 1B; and Judith Reitman, "Black, Jewish Teens Look to Past to Find New Understanding," *Times-Picayune*, March 9, 1997, p. A3.
50. Waxman, *America's Jews in Transition*, pp. 5–10, quotation from p. 10; Hertzberg, *The Jews in America*, pp. 62–69; Lawrence H. Fuchs, *The Political Behavior of American Jews* (Glencoe, IL: Free Press, 1956), pp. 23–25; Silberman, *A Certain People*, p. 44; Will Herberg, *Protestant–Catholic–Jew*, rev. ed. (New York: Doubleday/Anchor Books, 1960), pp. 98–99.
51. Hertzberg, *The Jews in America*, pp. 108–109; Mark R. Levy and Michael S. Kramer, *The Ethnic Factor* (New York: Simon & Schuster, 1972), p. 101; William R. Heitzmann, *American Jewish Voting Behavior* (San Francisco: R & E Research Associates, 1975), pp. 27–28.
52. Irving Howe, *World of Our Fathers* (New York: Simon & Schuster, 1976), pp. 362–364; Emanuel Hertz, "Politics: New York," in *The Russian Jew in the United States*, ed. Charles S. Bernheimer (Philadelphia, PA: John Winston, 1905), pp. 256–265.
53. Edward M. Levine, *The Irish and Irish Politicians* (Notre Dame, IN: University of Notre Dame Press, 1966); Isaacs, *Jews and American Politics*, pp. 23–24; Feingold, *Zion in America*, p. 321.
54. Hertz, "Politics," pp. 265–267; Heitzmann, *American Jewish Voting Behavior*, p. 37; Fuchs, *The Political Behavior of American Jews*, pp. 57–58.
55. Levy and Kramer, *The Ethnic Factor*, pp. 102–103; Howe, *World of Our Fathers*, pp. 381–388.
56. Hertzberg, *The Jews in America*, pp. 282–283.
57. Heitzmann, *American Jewish Voting Behavior*, p. 49; Fuchs, *The Political Behavior of American Jews*, pp. 99–100.
58. Isaacs, *Jews and American Politics*, pp. 6, 152; Heitzmann, *American Jewish Voting Behavior*, pp. 56–58; Strober, *American Jews*, pp. 186–188; Levy and Kramer, *The Ethnic Factor*, p. 103; Milton Plesur, *Jewish Life in Twentieth Century America* (Chicago: Nelson Hall, 1982), pp. 134–152; William Schneider, "The Jewish Vote in 1984," *Public Opinion* 7 (December/January 1985): 58; Brenner, *Jews in America Today*, pp. 37, 128–131.
59. Kosmin et al., *Highlights of the CJF 1990 National Jewish Population Survey*, pp. 30–35.
60. Isaacs, *Jews and American Politics*, pp. 23, 201; Levy and Kramer, *The Ethnic Factor*, p. 118; Plesur, *Jewish Life in Twentieth Century America*, pp. 143–145; Andrew

Herrmann, "Buddhists See Cup as Half Full," *Chicago Sun-Times*, January 21, 1995, p. 13.

61. Isaacs, *Jews and American Politics*, pp. 12, 118–119.

62. Bernard Cohen, *Sociocultural Changes in American Jewish Life as Reflected in Selected Jewish Literature* (Rutherford, NJ: Fairleigh Dickinson University Press, 1972), pp. 183–185; Learski, *The Jews in America*, pp. 158–159; Rudolf Glanz, *The Jewish Woman in America*, vol. 1, *The Eastern European Jewish Woman* (New York: KTAV Publishing House, 1976), pp. 48–57.

63. Nathan Reich, "Economic Status," in *The American Jew*, ed. Janowsky, pp. 70–71; Karpf, *Jewish Community Organization in the United States*, pp. 11–12; Howe, *World of Our Fathers*, pp. 391–393; Feingold, *Zion in America*, pp. 235–236.

64. Jonathan S. Woocher, *Sacred Survival* (Bloomington: Indiana University Press, 1986), pp. vii–viii.

65. Karpf, *Jewish Community Organization in the United States*, pp. 62–65; Naomi Cohen, *Not Free to Desist* (Philadelphia, PA: Jewish Publication Society of America, 1972), pp. 3–18, 37–80, 433–452.

66. Arnold Foster and Benjamin R. Epstein, *The New Anti-Semitism* (New York: McGraw-Hill, 1974), pp. 155–284; Strober, *American Jews*, pp. 7–42.

67. Wolfe Kelman, "The Synagogue in America," in *The Future of the Jewish Community in America*, ed. Sidorsky, pp. 171–173.

68. Dershowitz, *Chutzpah*, p. 49; see also Hertzberg, *The Jews in America*, pp. 350–351.

69. Brenner, *Jews in America Today*, p. 10.

70. Hertzberg, *The Jews in America*, pp. 17–28, 63.

71. Feingold, *Zion in America*, p. 12; McWilliams, *Brothers under the Skin*, pp. 305–306.

72. Wittke, *We Who Built America*, p. 325; George Cohen, *The Jews in the Making of America* (Boston, MA: Stratford, 1924), pp. 120–122; Silberman, *A Certain People*, pp. 44–45; Waxman, *America's Jews in Transition*, pp. 22–24.

73. Jacob Lestschinsky, "Economic and Social Development of American Jewry," in *The Jewish People* (New York: Jewish Encyclopedic Handbooks, 1955) 4:78.

74. Nathan Goldberg, *Occupational Patterns of American Jewry* (New York: Jewish Teachers Seminary Press, 1947), pp. 15–17; Marshall Sklare, *America's Jews* (New York: Random House, 1971), p. 61; Isaac M. Rubinow, "Economic and Industrial Conditions: New York," in *The Russian Jew in the United States*, ed. Bernheimer, pp. 110–111.

75. Lestschinsky, "Economic and Social Development of American Jewry," pp. 74–77; Rubinow, "Economic and Industrial Conditions," pp. 103–107; Waxman, *America's Jews in Transition*, p. 58; Hertzberg, *The Jews in America*, p. 198.

76. Charlotte Baum, Paula Hyman, and Sonya Michel, *The Jewish Woman in America* (New York: Dial Press, 1976), p. 98; Hertzberg, *The Jews in America*, pp. 198–201.

77. Karpf, *Jewish Community Organization in the United States*, pp. 9–14; Lestschinsky, "Economic and Social Development of American Jewry," pp. 91–92; W. Lloyd Warner and Leo Srole, *The Social Systems of American Ethnic Groups* (New Haven, CT: Yale University Press, 1945), p. 112; Silberman, *A Certain People*, pp. 127–130.

78. McWilliams, *A Mask for Privilege*, pp. 38, 40–41; Karpf, *Jewish Community Organization in the United States*, pp. 20–21; Higham, "Social Discrimination against Jews in America," pp. 18–19.

79. For the February 1936 *Fortune* survey, see Karpf, *Jewish Community Organization in the United States*, pp. 9–11.

80. McWilliams, *A Mask for Privilege*, pp. 143–150. See also Lestschinsky, "Economic and Social Development of American Jewry," p. 81.

81. Lestschinsky, "Economic and Social Development of American Jewry," pp. 71, 87; McWilliams, *A Mask for Privilege*, p. 159; Reich, "Economic Status," pp. 63–65; Dershowitz, *Chutzpah*, p. 74.

82. Cited in Barry R. Chiswick, "The Labor Market Status of American Jews," in *American Jewish Handbook*, eds. M. Himmelfarb and D. Singer (New York: American Jewish Committee, 1984), p. 137.

83. Mabel Newcomer, *The Big Business Executive* (New York: Columbia University Press, 1955), pp. 46–48.

84. Donald J. Bogue, *The Population of the United States* (Glencoe, IL: Free Press, 1959), p. 706; Silberman, *A Certain People*, pp. 117–118; Goldscheider and Goldstein, *The Jewish Community of Rhode Island*, p. 12.

85. Kosmin et al., *Highlights of the CJF 1990 National Jewish Population Survey*, p. 19; U.S. Bureau of the Census, *Statistical Abstract of the United States 1991* (Washington, DC, 1991), pp. 449, 450. Median household income is lower than median family income in census data.

86. Goren, "Jews," p. 593; Sklare, *America's Jews*, pp. 61–62; Goldscheider and Goldstein, *The Jewish Community of Rhode Island*, pp. 11–12; Kosmin et al., *Highlights of the CJF 1990 National Jewish Population Survey*, p. 12.

87. Abraham K. Korman, *The Outsiders: Jews and Corporate America* (Lexington, MA: Heath/Lexington Books, 1988), pp. 79–82.

88. Richard L. Zweigenhaft and G. William Domhoff, *Jews in the Protestant Establishment* (New York: Praeger, 1982), p. 46.

89. Korman, *The Outsiders*, pp. 66–88.

90. Ibid., pp. 35–41.

91. Dov B. Levy, "Top Jobs," *Jerusalem Post*, March 30, 1997, p. 6.

92. "Florida Legislature Passes Bill," PR Newswire, March 13, 1992; Sklare, *America's Jews*, p. 65; McWilliams, *Brothers under the Skin*, pp. 310–311.

93. Allen Myerson, "At Rental Counters, Are All Drives Created Equal? Avis Finds Itself at the Center of Discrimination Complaints," *The New York Times*, March 18, 1997, p. D1; Ellen Neuborne, "Car Renters Outline Charges at State Hearing," *USA Today*, April 1, 1997, p. 1B.

94. Hertzberg, *The Jews in America*, pp. 50, 273; Silberman, *A Certain People*, p. 51; Waxman, *America's Jews in Transition*, p. 53.

95. J. K. Paulding, "Educational Influences: New York," in *The Russian Jew in the United States*, ed. Bernheimer, pp. 186–197; Cohen, *The Jews in the Making of America*, pp. 140–141; Karpf, *Jewish Community Organization in the United States*, p. 57; Hertzberg, *The Jews in America*, p. 200; Waxman, *America's Jews in Transition*, p. 137.

96. Silberman, *A Certain People*, pp. 52–55; Hertzberg, *The Jews in America*, pp. 246–247; Higham, "Social Discrimination against Jews in America," p. 22; Karpf, *Jewish Community Organization in the United States*, p. 19; McWilliams, *A Mask for Privilege*, pp. 128–129.

97. Silberman, *A Certain People*, pp. 98–100; Hertzberg, *The Jews in America*, p. 309; Dershowitz, *Chutzpah*, pp. 73–74.

98. Strober, *American Jews*, pp. 120–130; Maurice R. Berube and Marilyn Gittell, "The Struggle for Community Control," in *Confrontation at Ocean Hill–Brownsville*, eds. Maurice R. Berube and Marilyn Gittell (New York: Praeger, 1969), pp. 3–12 et passim; Joe R. Feagin and Harlan Hahn, *Ghetto Revolts* (New York: Macmillan, 1973), pp. 327–328; Nathan Glazer, *Affirmative Discrimination* (New York: Basic Books, 1975), pp. 33–76, 196–221.

99. Dershowitz, *Chutzpah*, pp. 75–79, quotation from pp. 78–79.

100. Hertzberg, *The Jews in America*, p. 309; Kosmin et al., *Highlights of the CJF 1990 National Jewish Population Survey*, pp. 10–11; Holly J. Lebowitz, "High Holy Days Can Be Lonely for Students," *Plain Dealer*, September 7, 1996, p. 6E.

101. Silberman, *A Certain People*, pp. 171–172; Goldscheider and Goldstein, *The Jewish Community of Rhode Island*, pp. 11, 25–28; Kosmin et al., *Highlights of the CJF 1990 National Jewish Population Survey*, pp. 10–11; Robert Alter, "What Jewish Studies Can Do," *Commentary* 58 (October 1974): 71–74.

102. Waxman, *America's Jews in Transition*, p. 10; Hertzberg, *The Jews in America*, pp. 117–123, 146–147, 254–262, quotation from p. 120. See also Silberman, *A Certain People*, p. 46.

103. Waxman, *America's Jews in Transition*, p. 10; Hertzberg, *The Jews in America*, pp. 113–116.

104. Hertzberg, *The Jews in America*, pp. 159–161, 167–168, 195, 214–236.

105. Ibid., pp. 277–279; Waxman, *America's Jews in Transition*, p. 17.

106. Kelman, "The Synagogue in America," pp. 157–158; Louis Lipsky, "Religious Activity: New York," in *The Russian Jew in the United States*, ed. Bernheimer, pp. 152–154; Silberman, *A Certain People*, pp. 170–177; Hertzberg, *The Jews in America*, pp. 277–279.

107. Silberman, *A Certain People*, pp. 176–181, quotation from p. 179.

108. Goldscheider and Goldstein, *The Jewish Community of Rhode Island*, pp. 18–25.

109. Kosmin et al., *Highlights of the CJF 1990 National Jewish Population Survey*, pp. 6, 28, 32–33, 35–37.

110. J. L. Blau, *Judaism in America* (Chicago: University of Chicago Press, 1976), as summarized in Samuel C. Heilman, "The Sociology of American Jewry," in *Annual Review of Sociology*, ed. Ralph Turner, vol. 8 (Palo Alto, CA: Annual Reviews, 1982), p. 147.

111. Michael Greenstein, *The American Jew: A Contradiction in Terms* (New York: Gefen, 1990), pp. 1–5.

112. Dershowitz, *Chutzpah*, p. 209.

113. Goldscheider and Goldstein, *The Jewish Community of Rhode Island*, p. 22; Monty Noam Penkower, *At the Crossroads: American Jewry and the State of Israel* (Haifa, Israel: University of Haifa, 1990), p. 26; Kosmin et al., *Highlights of the CJF 1990 National Jewish Population Survey*, pp. 29, 35.

114. Penkower, *At the Crossroads*, p. 27.

115. Stanley Reed, "Will Palestine's Peace Dividend Buy Peace?" *Business Week*, May 16, 1994, p. 53.

116. "U.S. Jews Favor Palestinian State: Poll," Agence France Presse, September 29, 1997.

117. Howe, *World of Our Fathers*, p. 645; Karpf, *Jewish Community Organization in the United States*, pp. 37–39, 49–50; Tobin, *Jewish Perceptions of Anti-Semitism*, p. 84.

118. Milton R. Konvitz, "Horace Meyer Kallen (1882–1974)," in *American Jewish Yearbook, 1974–1975* (New York: American Jewish Committee, 1974), pp. 65–67; Milton Gordon, *Assimilation in American Life* (New York: Oxford University Press, 1964), pp. 142–159.

119. Hertzberg, *The Jews in America*, pp. 102–130, 167–176, 195.

120. Sidney Goldstein and Calvin Goldscheider, *Jewish Americans* (Englewood Cliffs, NJ: Prentice Hall, 1968), p. 226; Silberman, *A Certain People*, pp. 173–181.

121. Nathan Glazer, "The American Jew and the Attainment of Middle-class Rank: Some Trends and Explanations," in *The Jews*, ed. M. Sklare (Glencoe, IL: Free Press, 1958), p. 143, quoted in Stephen Steinberg, *The Ethnic Myth* (New York: Atheneum, 1981), p. 93.

122. Steinberg, *The Ethnic Myth*, pp. 94–102.

123. Hertzberg, *The Jews in America*, pp. 167–171, 195, 254–255, quotation from p. 171; Waxman, *America's Jews in Transition*, pp. 55–58.

124. Calvin Goldscheider, *Jewish Continuity and Change* (Atlanta, GA: Scholars Press, 1986), pp. 17–18, quotation from p. 17.

125. Quoted in Sidney Goldstein, "Jews in the United States: Perspectives from Demography," in *American Jewish Yearbook, 1981* (New York: American Jewish Committee, 1980–1981), p. 28.

126. Goldscheider and Goldstein, *The Jewish Community of Rhode Island*, p. 28.

127. Kosmin, et al., *Highlights of the CJF 1990 National Jewish Population Survey*, p. 35.

128. Gordon, *Assimilation in American Life*, pp. 76–77.

129. Paul R. Spickard, *Mixed Blood* (Madison: University of Wisconsin Press, 1989), pp. 180–228; Kosmin, et al., *Highlights of the CJF 1990 National Jewish Population Survey*, p. 14; Judith Dunford, "An Inside View of Interfaith Marriage," *Newsday*, September 28, 1997, p. B12.

130. Goldscheider and Goldstein, *The Jewish Community of Rhode Island*, pp. 13–15.

131. Kosmin, et al., *Highlights of the CJF 1990 National Jewish Population Survey*, p. 29.

132. Goldscheider, *Jewish Continuity and Change*, pp. 15–19, quotation from p. 16.

133. Alan Dershowitz, *The Vanishing American Jew: In Search of Jewish Identity for the Next Century* (New York: Little Brown, 1997).

134. "Anti-Semitism Concerns Surveyed," *San Diego Union-Tribune*, June 6, 1997, p. E5.

135. Marilyn Henry, "Israeli Immigrants to the United States Moving Up the Ladder," *Jerusalem Post*, August 13, 1996, p. 12; Henry summarizes a report in the 1996 *American Jewish Yearbook* by Steven Gold and Bruce Phillips.

136. Simon and Simon, "Social and Economic Adjustment," pp. 27–38.

137. Steven J. Gold, *Refugee Communities* (Newbury Park, CA: Sage, 1992), pp. 39–44, 67–89.

138. Kosmin, et al., *Highlights of the CJF 1990 National Jewish Population Survey*, p. 28.

139. Ibid., p. 29.

140. Ibid., pp. 3–6, 14–17.

141. Herbert J. Gans, "Symbolic Ethnicity," *Ethnic and Racial Studies* 2 (1979): 1–20; Richard Alba, *Ethnic Identity: The Transformation of White America* (New Haven, CT: Yale University Press, 1990), p. 306.

142. Hertzberg, *The Jews in America*, p. 386.
143. The report is cited in Ira Rifkin, "Jewish Social Agency Finds Support Eroding," *Sacramento Bee*, December 2, 1995, p. G5.
144. Alba, *Ethnic Identity*, p. 310.
145. Silberman, *A Certain People*, pp. 25, 159–324.

CHAPTER 7

1. "Counter-Quincentenary Protesters Encounter Celebrators at Kickoff of Quincentenary Year," *Indigenous Thought* 1, nos. 4 and 5 (October 1991): 1–3.
2. "We Have No Reason to Celebrate an Invasion," *Rethinking Columbus* (Milwaukee, WI: Rethinking Schools, 1991), p. 4.
3. For a discussion of the development of the designations *white* and *red*, see David R. Roediger, *The Wages of Whiteness* (New York: Verso, 1991), pp. 21–23.
4. Henry F. Dobyns, "Estimating Aboriginal American Population," *Current Anthropology* 7 (October 1960): 395–416; Kirkpatrick Sale, *The Conquest of Paradise* (New York: Knopf, 1990); Lenore A. Stiffarm and Phil Lane, Jr., "The Demography of Native North America," in *The State of Native America*, ed. M. Annette Jaimes (Boston, MA: South End Press, 1992), pp. 23–28; see also Russell Thornton, *American Indian Holocaust and Survival* (Norman: University of Oklahoma Press, 1987); C. Matthew Snipp, *American Indians: The First of This Land* (New York: Russell Sage Foundation, 1989).
5. U.S. Bureau of the Census, *1990 Census of Population: Social and Economic Characteristics: United States*, CP-2–1 (Washington, DC, 1993), p. 105; U.S. Bureau of the Census, *We the First Americans* (Washington, DC, 1993), pp. 2–3, 7–8.
6. Joane Nagel, *American Indian Ethnic Renewal: Red Power and the Resurgence of Indian Identity and Culture* (New York: Oxford University Press, forthcoming).
7. Edward H. Spicer, *Cycles of Conquest* (Tucson: University of Arizona Press, 1962), pp. 20–23; Clyde Kluckhohn and Dorothy Leighton, *The Navaho*, rev. ed. (Garden City, NY: Doubleday/Anchor Books, 1962), pp. 23–27 et passim.
8. Jack Weatherford, *Indian Givers: How the Indians of the Americas Transformed the World* (New York: Ballantine, 1988), pp. 39–133.
9. U.S. Bureau of Indian Affairs, *The American Indians: Answers to 101 Questions* (Washington, DC, 1974), pp. 2–3.
10. Howard M. Bahr, "An End to Invisibility," in *Native Americans Today*, eds. Howard M. Bahr, Bruce A. Chadwick, and Robert C. Day (New York: Harper & Row, 1972), pp. 407–409; James E. Officer, "The American Indian and Federal Policy," in *The American Indian in Urban Society*, ed. Jack O. Waddell and O. Michael Watson (Boston, MA: Little, Brown, 1971), pp. 45–60.
11. U.S. Bureau of the Census, *1990 Census of Population: General Population Characteristics: Urbanized Areas*, CP-1–1C (Washington, DC, 1992), p. 48.
12. Donald L. Fixico, *Termination and Relocation* (Albuquerque: University of New Mexico Press, 1986), pp. 7–10.
13. Spicer, *Cycles of Conquest*, pp. 5, 306–307; Murray L. Wax, Indian Americans (Englewood Cliffs, NJ: Prentice Hall, 1971), pp. 6–7; Lynn R. Bailey, *Indian Slave Trade in the Southwest* (Los Angeles: Westernlore Press, 1966), pp. 73–140.
14. Leo Grebler, Joan W. Moore, and Ralph C. Guzman, *The Mexican-American People* (New York: Free Press, 1970),

pp. 320–321; Spicer, *Cycles of Conquest*, pp. 4–5; Carey McWilliams, *North from Mexico* (New York: Greenwood Press, 1968), pp. 20–33; Herbert Blatchford, "Historical Survey of American Indians," Appendix H in Stan Steiner, *The New Indians* (New York: Harper & Row, 1968), pp. 314–315.
15. D'Arcy McNickle, *The Indian Tribes of the United States* (London: Oxford University Press, 1962), pp. 13–17; Alice Marriott and Carol K. Rachlin, *American Epic* (New York: Mentor Books, 1969), pp. 104–108; John Collier, *Indians of the Americas* (New York: Mentor Books, 1947), p. 115.
16. William T. Hagan, *American Indians* (Chicago: University of Chicago Press, 1961), p. 14. The discussion of these wars is taken from ibid., pp. 12–15.
17. Almon W. Lauber, *Indian Slavery in Colonial Times within the Present Limits of the United States* (New York: Columbia University Press, 1913), pp. 107–169.
18. McNickle, *The Indian Tribes of the United States*, pp. 23–28; Ruth M. Underhill, *Red Man's America* (Chicago: University of Chicago Press, 1953), pp. 321–322; Wax, *Indian Americans*, p. 13.
19. Quoted on the title page of Vine Deloria, Jr., *Of Utmost Good Faith* (New York: Bantam, 1972).
20. McNickle, *The Indian Tribes of the United States*, pp. 32–35; National Indian Youth Council, "Chronology of Indian History, 1492–1955," in Steiner, *The New Indians*, pp. 318–319; Ward Churchill, "Perversions of Justice: Examining U.S. Rights to Occupancy in North America," in *Struggle for Land: Indigenous Resistance to Genocide, Ecocide and Expropriation* (Monroe, ME: Common Courage Press, 1993), pp. 33–83.
21. Blatchford, "Historical Survey of American Indians," pp. 316–318; Hagan, *American Indians*, pp. 41–44.
22. Alexis de Tocqueville, *Democracy in America* (New York: Random House/Vintage Books, 1945), 1:364.
23. Virgil J. Vogel, "The Indian in American History, 1968," in *This Country Was Ours*, ed. Virgil J. Vogel (New York: Harper & Row, 1972), pp. 284–287; McNickle, *The Indian Tribes of the United States*, pp. 40–41.
24. Ralph K. Andrist, *The Long Death* (London: Collier-Macmillan, 1964), p. 3.
25. John D. Unruh, *The Plains Across* (Urbana: University of Illinois Press, 1979), p. 185 et passim.
26. Vogel, "The Indian in American History, 1968," p. 285; Wendell H. Oswalt, *This Land Was Theirs* (New York: Wiley, 1966), pp. 501–502.
27. Andrist, *The Long Death*, pp. 31–68, 78–91.
28. William Meyer, *Native Americans* (New York: International, 1971), p. 32. See also Thornton, *American Indian Holocaust and Survival*.
29. Andrist, *The Long Death*, pp. 140–148.
30. Ibid., pp. 240–250, 350–353; Alvin M. Josephy, *The Indian Heritage of America* (New York: Bantam, 1968), pp. 284–342; Theodora Kroeber and Robert F. Heizer, *Almost Ancestors* (San Francisco: Sierra Club, 1968), pp. 14–20.
31. Spicer, *Cycles of Conquest*, pp. 216–221, 247–270.
32. Robert F. Spencer, Jesse D. Jennings, et al., *The Native Americans* (New York: Harper & Row, 1965), pp. 495–496; David Miller, "The Fur Men and Explorers View the Indians," in *Red Men and Hat Wearers*, ed. Daniel Tyler (Fort Collins, CO: Pruett, 1976), pp. 26–28; Roediger, *The Wages of Whiteness*, pp. 21–23.
33. Peter Farb, *Man's Rise to Civilization as Shown by the Indians of North America from Primeval Times to the*

Coming of the Industrial State (New York: Dutton, 1968), pp. 246–249; Tyler, ed., *Red Men and Hat Wearers*, passim.

34. Lewis H. Carlson and George A. Colburn, "Introduction," in *In Their Place*, eds. Lewis H. Carlson and George A. Colburn (New York: Wiley, 1972), p. 44.

35. Vogel, "The Indian in American History, 1968," pp. 288–289; Tocqueville, *Democracy in America*, 1:355–357.

36. Rayna Green, "The Pocahontas Perplex: The Image of Indian Women in American Culture," in *Unequal Sisters*, ed. Ellen Carol DuBois and Vicki L. Ruiz (New York: Routledge, 1990), pp. 15–21, quotation from p. 17.

37. "Children's Secret Lessons," *Indigenous Thought* 1, nos. 4 and 5 (October 1991): 24.

38. U.S. Senate Subcommittee on Indian Education, *Hearings on Indian Education* (Washington, DC, 1969), passim; Jeanette Henry, "Text Book Distortion of the Indian," *Civil Rights Digest* 1 (Summer 1968): 4–8; Kathleen C. Houts and Rosemary S. Bahr, "Stereotyping of Indians and Blacks in Magazine Cartoons," in *Native Americans Today*, eds. Bahr, Chadwick, and Day, pp. 112–113; see also p. 49.

39. Snipp, *American Indians*, pp. 23–25; Jimmie Durham, "Cowboys and . . . ," in *The State of Native America*, ed. Jaimes, pp. 423–425.

40. Ward Churchill, *Fantasies of the Master Race* (Monroe, ME: Common Courage Press, 1992), pp. 243–247, quotation from p. 246.

41. Howard M. Bahr, Bruce A. Chadwick, and Robert C. Day, "Introduction: Patterns of Prejudice and Discrimination," in *Native Americans Today*, eds. Bahr, Chadwick, and Day, pp. 44–45; Emory S. Bogardus, *Immigration and Race Attitudes* (Boston, MA: Heath, 1928); Beverly Brandon Sweeney, "Native American: Stereotypes and Ideologies of an Adult Anglo Population in Texas" (M.A. thesis, University of Texas at Austin, 1976), pp. 125–133.

42. Gayle Pollard Terry, "Los Angeles Times Interview with Suzane Shown Harjo: Fighting to Preserve the Legacy and Future of Native Americans," *Los Angeles Times*, November 27, 1994, p. M3.

43. Jeff Cohen and Norman Solomon, "Using History, CNN Delivers Improved Coverage of Indians," *Star Tribune*, November 30, 1994, p. A17.

44. U.S. Bureau of Indian Affairs, *Federal Indian Policies* (Washington, DC, 1975), p. 6.

45. Ibid., p. 7; Spicer, *Cycles of Conquest*, p. 348.

46. *Elk* v. *Wilkins*, 112 U.S. 94 (1884); see also Deloria, *Of Utmost Good Faith*, pp. 130–132.

47. U.S. Bureau of Indian Affairs, *Federal Indian Policies*, p. 7; S. Lyman Tyler, *A History of Indian Policy* (Washington, DC, 1973), pp. 95–107 and elsewhere; Jack Forbes, *Native Americans of California and Nevada* (Berkeley, CA: Far West Laboratory for Educational Research and Development, 1968), pp. 79–80.

48. Spicer, *Cycles of Conquest*, pp. 351–353; McNickle, *The Indian Tribes of the United States*, p. 59; Alison R. Bernstein, *American Indians and World War II* (Norman: University of Oklahoma Press, 1991), pp. 4–10.

49. Virgil J. Vogel, "Introduction," in *This Country Was Ours*, ed. Vogel, pp. 196–197.

50. M. Annette Jaimes, "Federal Indian Identification Policy: A Usurpation of Indigenous Sovereignty in North America," in *The State of Native America*, ed. Jaimes, p. 124.

51. Ibid., pp. 95–98; U.S. Bureau of Indian Affairs, *Federal Indian Policy*, p. 9.

52. W. A. Brophy and S. D. Aberle, *The Indian* (Norman: University of Oklahoma Press, 1966), pp. 179–193; Rebecca L. Robbins, "Self-Determination and Subordination: The Past, Present, and Future of American Indian Governance," in *The State of Native America*, ed. Jaimes, pp. 98–100.

53. U.S. Bureau of Indian Affairs, *Federal Indian Policy*, p. 12.

54. Jaimes, "Federal Indian Identification Policy," pp. 123–137; Susan Campbell, "A Mohegan Family," *Hartford Courant*, March 1, 1992, p. 10; Anne Fullam, "Tribe Seeks U.S. Recognition," *Newsday*, February 11, 1992, p. 20.

55. Forbes, *Native Americans of California and Nevada*, pp. 80–82; Alan L. Sorkin, *American Indians and Federal Aid* (Washington, DC: Brookings Institution, 1971), pp. 48–65; Vogel, "Introduction," p. 205; James S. Olson and Raymond Wilson, *Native Americans in the Twentieth Century* (Provo, UT: Brigham Young University Press, 1984), p. 209; E. S. Cahn, *Our Brother's Keeper* (New York: World, 1969), pp. 157–158.

56. Robbins, "Self-Determination and Subordination," pp. 98–112, quotation from p. 109.

57. Dana Wilkie, "Two Centuries of Indian Sovereignty Under Attack," Copley News Service, September 8, 1997.

58. "Yet Another Reason to Reorganize BIA," *Albuquerque Journal*, September 5, 1997, p. A14.

59. Brophy and Aberle, *The Indian*, pp. 33–44; Olson and Wilson, *Native Americans in the Twentieth Century*, pp. 189, 191.

60. Virgil J. Vogel, "Famous Americans of Indian Descent," in *This Country Was Ours*, ed. Vogel, pp. 310–351.

61. Olson and Wilson, *Native Americans in the Twentieth Century*, p. 186.

62. "Indians Flashing Casino Profits in D.C.: The Mashantucket Pequot Tribe, for Example, Employs a Full-time Lobbyist in Washington," *Providence Journal-Bulletin*, July 13, 1997, p. 5A.

63. Hazel W. Hertzberg, *The Search for an American Indian Identity* (Syracuse, NY: Syracuse University Press, 1971), pp. 20–21, 42–76, 180–200.

64. Ibid., pp. 200–208, 291–293; Isabel Wilkerson, "Indignant Indians Seeking Changes," *The New York Times*, January 26, 1992, p. 14.

65. Robert C. Day, "The Emergence of Activism as a Social Movement," in *Native Americans Today*, eds. Bahr, Chadwick, and Day, pp. 516–517.

66. Vogel, "Famous Americans of Indian Descent," pp. 310–351.

67. Robbins, "Self-Determination and Subordination," p. 103.

68. Meyer, *Native Americans*, p. 88; "Pine Ridge after Wounded Knee: The Terror Goes on," *Akwesasne Notes* 7 (Summer 1975): 8–10.

69. Glenn T. Morris, "Resistance to Radioactive Colonialism: A Reply to the Churchill/La Duke Indictment," *Insurgent Sociologist* 13 (Spring 1986): 82.

70. Richard Meryhew, "Be It Redskins, Chiefs, or Lions, Indians to Protest," *St. Paul Star Tribune*, January 3, 1992, p. 1B; Wilkerson, "Indignant Indians Seeking Changes," p. 14.

71. "Doby's Best Pitch Comes at Playground," *Austin American-Statesman*, July 9, 1997, p. C4.

72. Laurel R. Davis, "Protest Against the Use of Native American Mascots: A Challenge to Traditional American Identity," *Journal of Sport and Social Issues,* 17 (April 1993): 9–22; quotation on pp. 13, 17.
73. Ibid., p. 19.
74. Ibid., p. 17.
75. Greg Toppo, "Group Wants a Peltier Pardon," *The Santa Fe New Mexican,* December 8, 1996, p. B1.
76. Quoted in "Newspaper Defends Dropping Native American Names from Teams," Reuters News Service, February 19, 1992.
77. Joe Olivera, "We Can All Change Attitudes," Gannett News Service, February 20, 1992.
78. Terry, "Los Angeles Times Interview with Suzane Shown Harjo"; "Indian Mascots Are Out, Says Vote in L.A.," *Los Angeles Times,* September 10, 1997, p. A6.
79. Rochelle L. Stanfield, "Cultural Collision," *National Journal,* January 25, 1992, p. 206.
80. U.S. Commission on Civil Rights, *Indian Tribes: A Continuing Quest for Survival* (Washington, DC, 1981), pp. 61–99; Institute for Natural Progress, "In Usual and Accustomed Places," in *The State of Native America,* ed. Jaimes, pp. 223–226.
81. Institute for Natural Progress, "In Usual and Accustomed Places," pp. 224–226.
82. Ibid., pp. 231–235.
83. U.S. Commission on Civil Rights, *Indian Tribes,* p. 103.
84. Olson and Wilson, *Native Americans in the Twentieth Century,* p. 195.
85. Ward Churchill, "The Earth Is Our Mother," in *The State of Native America,* ed. Jaimes, pp. 151–169.
86. Peter Carlson, "The Un-Fashionable: In the Year of 'Dances with Wolves,' Everybody Wanted to Be on the Senate Indian Affairs Committee. Nearly a Decade Later, It Can Hardly Get a Quorum," *Washington Post Magazine,* February 23, 1997, p. W6.
87. Cohen and Solomon, "Using History, CNN Delivers Improved Coverage of Indians."
88. U.S. Commission on Civil Rights, *Indian Tribes,* pp. 1–2 (Hatfield quotation from p. 1; quotation from tribal leader from p. 2); Institute for Natural Progress, "In Usual and Accustomed Places," pp. 223, 231, 233–234.
89. "Shattering the Myth of the Vanishing American," *Ford Foundation Letter* 22, no. 3 (Winter 1991): 1–5.
90. "The Hidden Victims: Hate Crimes Against American Indians Under-Reported, *Southern Poverty Law Center Intelligence Report,* October 1994, pp. 1–4; quotation on p. 4.
91. Churchill, *Fantasies of the Master Race,* pp. 5–7 (quotation from p. 5); Ward Churchill and Winona LaDuke, "Native North America: The Political Economy of Radioactive Colonialism," in *The State of Native America,* ed. Jaimes, pp. 241–262; Susan Campbell, "A Mohegan Family," *Hartford Courant,* March 1, 1992, p. 10. See also Sar A. Levitan, Garth L. Mangum, and Ray Marshall, *Human Resources and Labor Markets,* 2nd ed. (New York: Harper & Row, 1976), p. 441.
92. Joseph G. Jorgensen, "Indians and the Metropolis," in *The American Indian in Urban Society,* ed. Waddell and Watson, p. 85. This paragraph draws on Jorgensen's theory.
93. Quoted in Deloria, *Of Utmost Good Faith,* pp. 380–381.
94. Hagan, *American Indians,* pp. 126–127; Spicer, *Cycles of Conquest,* pp. 349–356.
95. Cahn, *Our Brother's Keeper,* pp. 69–110; Rupert Costo, "Speaking Freely," *Wassaja* 4 (November–December 1976): 2; Sorkin, *American Indians and Federal Aid,* pp.

70–71; Jorgensen, "Indians and the Metropolis," pp. 96–99.
96. Sorkin, *American Indians and Federal Aid,* pp. 105, 136–139, 201; Levitan, Mangum, and Marshall, *Human Resources and Labor Markets,* p. 443; Theodore D. Graves, "Drinking and Drunkenness among Urban Indians," in *The American Indian in Urban Society,* eds. Waddell and Watson, pp. 292–295.
97. Levitan, Mangum, and Marshall, *Human Resources and Labor Markets,* p. 443; Jorgensen, "Indians and the Metropolis," p. 83; Brophy and Aberle, *The Indian,* p. 99.
98. James Cook, "Help Wanted—Work, Not Handouts," *Forbes,* May 4, 1987, pp. 68–71.
99. Olson and Wilson, *Native Americans in the Twentieth Century,* p. 181; Robert Bryce, "Indians Seek Control of Tribal-Land Resources," *Christian Science Monitor,* September 14, 1994, p. 4.
100. Churchill and LaDuke, "Native North America," pp. 247–248.
101. Michael Parfit, "Keeping the Big Sky Pure," *Perspectives* 13 (Spring 1981): 44.
102. Bryce, "Indians Seek Control of Tribal-Land Resources."
103. U.S. Bureau of the Census, *Population, 1940: Characteristics of the Nonwhite Population by Race* (Washington, DC, 1943), pp. 83–84; U.S. Bureau of the Census, *Population, 1960: Nonwhite Population by Race* (Washington, DC, 1963), p. 104; U.S. Bureau of the Census, *1990 Census of Population: Social and Economic Characteristics: United States,* p. 45. Data for 1960 do not include states with less than 25,000 Native Americans.
104. U.S. Bureau of the Census, *1990 Census of Population: Social and Economic Characteristics: United States,* p. 45.
105. U.S. Bureau of the Census, *Sixteenth Census of the United States: The Labor Force, Part I: U.S. Summary* (Washington, DC, 1943), p. 39; U.S. Department of Health, Education and Welfare, *A Study of Selected Socio-economic Characteristics of Ethnic Minorities Based on the 1970 Census,* vol. 3, *American Indians* (Washington, DC, 1974), p. 49.
106. U.S. Bureau of the Census, *1990 Census of Population: Social and Economic Characteristics: United States,* p. 44.
107. U.S. Bureau of the Census, *1990 Census of Population: Social and Economic Characteristics: American Indian and Alaska Native Areas,* CP-2–1A (Washington, DC, 1993), p. 56.
108. U.S. Department of Health, Education and Welfare, *A Study of Selected Socio-economic Characteristics,* pp. 59–78; U.S. Bureau of the Census, *1990 Census of Population: Social and Economic Characteristics: United States,* pp. 48, 49; U.S. Bureau of the Census, *1990 Census of Population: Social and Economic Characteristics: American Indian and Alaska Native Areas,* p. 82.
109. Nagel, *American Indian Ethnic Renewal.*
110. U.S. Department of Health and Human Services, *Regional Differences in Indian Health* (Washington, DC, 1994), pp. 33, 45, 56–61, 90.
111. U.S. Bureau of the Census, *1990 Census of Population: General Population Characteristics: Urbanized Areas,* pp. 165, 192; U.S. Bureau of the Census, *1990 Census of Population: Social and Economic Characteristics: Urbanized Areas,* CP-2–1C (Washington, DC, 1993), pp. 1527, 1543, 2272, 2288, 3310, 3336, 4009, 4035, 4877, 4893.
112. "Reviving Native Economies," *Dollars and Sense,* no. 170 (October 1991): 18–20.

113. Peter Carlson, "The Un-Fashionable: In the Year of 'Dances with Wolves,' Everybody Wanted to Be on the Senate Indian Affairs Committee," *Washington Post*, February 23, 1997, p. W6.

114. Bill Lueders, "Casino Cowboys Take Indians for a Ride," *Progressive*, August 1994, pp. 30–33.

115. Quoted in Bob von Sternberg, "Tribe Fights Storage of Reactor's Spent Fuel," *St. Paul Star Tribune*, November 27, 1991, p. 2B. See also Dan Fagin, "Badlands in Demand," *Newsday*, October 21, 1991, p. 5; David Seals, "Sacred Ground Must Not Be Abused," *Newsday*, October 31, 1991, p. 129.

116. U.S. Bureau of Indian Affairs, *Federal Indian Policies*, p. 5; Jorge Noriega, "American Indian Education in the United States," in *The State of Native America*, ed. Jaimes, pp. 371–383.

117. U.S. Bureau of Indian Affairs, *Federal Indian Policies*, pp. 5–6; Spicer, *Cycles of Conquest*, p. 349; Noriega, "American Indian Education in the United States," pp. 381–383.

118. U.S. Bureau of Indian Affairs, *Federal Indian Policies*, p. 9.

119. Noriega, "American Indian Education in the United States," pp. 384–385.

120. Office of Indian Education Programs, *Fingertip Facts: 1994* (Washington, DC: U.S. Bureau of Indian Affairs, 1994), p. 10.

121. Interview with Phyllis Young, quoted in ibid., p. 387.

122. *Indian Nations at Risk: An Educational Strategy for Change*, report of U.S. Department of Education Task Force (Washington, DC, 1991), cited in Kenneth Cooper, "Multicultural Focus Recommended for Education of Native Americans," *Washington Post*, December 27, 1991, p. A19; U.S. Bureau of the Census, *1990 Census of Population: Social and Economic Characteristics: United States*, p. 42.

123. "Shattering the Myth of the Vanishing American," pp. 1–3.

124. U.S. Bureau of the Census, *1990 Census of Population: Social and Economic Characteristics: United States*, p. 107.

125. Noriega, "American Indian Education in the United States," pp. 391–392; Office of Indian Education Programs, *Fingertip Facts: 1994*, p. 16.

126. U.S. Bureau of the Census, *1990 Census of Population: Social and Economic Characteristics: United States*, p. 42.

127. U.S. Bureau of the Census, *1990 Census of Population: Social and Economic Characteristics: American Indian and Alaska Native Areas*, pp. 5–20.

128. "Indian Nations at Risk."

129. Stan Steiner, "Sacred Objects, Secular Laws," *Perspectives* 13 (Summer–Fall 1981): 13.

130. Quoted in Vine Deloria, Jr., *Custer Died for Your Sins* (London: Collier-Macmillan, 1969), p. 101.

131. Ibid., pp. 108–116.

132. Vittorio Lanternari, *The Religion of the Oppressed* (New York: Mentor Books, 1963), pp. 110–132; Spencer, Jennings, et al., *The Native Americans*, pp. 498–499; Wax, *Indian Americans*, p. 141.

133. Lanternari, *The Religions of the Oppressed*, pp. 99–100; Hertzberg, *The Search for an American Indian Identity*, pp. 239–240, 251, 280.

134. Hertzberg, *The Search for an American Indian Identity*, pp. 246, 257, 271–274, 280–284; Elaine G. Eastman, "Does Uncle Sam Foster Paganism?" in *In Their Place*, eds. Carlson and Colburn, pp. 29ff.

135. Deloria, *Of Utmost Good Faith*, pp. 177–180; idem, *Custer Died for Your Sins*, pp. 110–115.

136. Brad Knickerbocker, "Indians Fight for Religious Freedom," *Christian Science Monitor*, April 1, 1992, p. 14.

137. Quoted in Olson and Wilson, *Native Americans in the Twentieth Century*, p. 219. See also Deloria, *Custer Died for Your Sins*, pp. 122–124; and Cahn, *Our Brother's Keeper*, pp. 175–190.

138. For example, Lurie, as quoted in John A. Price, "Migration and Adaptation of American Indians to Los Angeles," *Human Organization* 27 (Summer 1968): 168–175.

139. Snipp, *American Indians*, pp. 23–25

140. Olson and Wilson, *Native Americans in the Twentieth Century*, p. 212; see also pp. 210–211.

141. Prodipto Roy, "The Measurement of Assimilation: The Spokane Indians," *American Journal of Sociology* 67 (March 1962): 541–551; Price, "Migration and Adaptation of American Indians to Los Angeles," pp. 169–174; U.S. Department of Health, Education and Welfare, *A Study of Selected Socio-economic Characteristics*, p. 35; Oswalt, *This Land Was Theirs*, pp. 513–514.

142. Lynn C. White and Bruce A. Chadwick, "Urban Residence, Assimilation, and Identity of the Spokane Indian," in *Native Americans Today*, eds. Bahr, Chadwick, and Day, p. 243; Brophy and Aberle, *The Indian*, p. 10; Spicer, *Cycles of Conquest*, p. 577.

143. Weibel-Orlando, *Indian Country, L.A.* (Urbana: University of Illinois Press, 1991), pp. 22–43.

144. Robert Blauner, *Racial Oppression in America* (New York: Harper & Row, 1972), p. 54; Spicer, *Cycles of Conquest*, pp. 573–574.

145. Quoted in Francis McKinley, Stephen Bayne, and Glen Nimnicht, *Who Should Control Indian Education?* (Berkeley, CA: Far West Laboratory for Educational Research and Development, 1969), p. 13 (italics added).

146. Quoted in Shirley Hill Witt, "Pressure Points in Growing Up Indian," *Perspectives* 12 (Spring 1980): 31.

147. Wilbur J. Scott, "Attachment to Indian Culture," *Youth and Society* 17 (June 1986): 392–394.

148. Witt, "Pressure Points in Growing Up Indian," pp. 28–31; Robert W. Blum, et al., "American Indian—Alaska Native Youth Health," *Journal of the American Medical Association* 267 (March 25, 1992): 1637–1644; see also U.S. Department of Health and Human Services, *Trends in Indian Health* (Washington, DC, 1993), pp. 60–61; U.S. Department of Health and Human Services, *Regional Differences in Indian Health* (Washington, DC, 1994), p. 56.

149. Albert l. Wahrhaftig and Robert K. Thomas, "Renaissance and Repression: The Oklahoma Cherokee," in *Native Americans Today*, eds. Bahr, Chadwick, and Day, p. 81.

150. Institute for Natural Progress, "In Usual and Accustomed Places," pp. 228–236.

CHAPTER 8

1. Bebe Moore Campbell, "To Be Black, Gifted, and Alone," *Savvy* 5 (December 1984): 69.

2. James H. Dorman and Robert R. Jones, *The Afro-American Experience* (New York: Wiley, 1974), pp. 72–74; Thomas R. Frazier, preface to Chapter 1, in *Afro-American History: Primary Sources*, ed. Thomas R. Frazier (New York: Harcourt, Brace, & World, 1970), pp. 3–5.

3. Olaudah Equiano, "The Interesting Narrative of the Life of Olaudah Equiano," in *Afro-American History,* ed. Frazier, pp. 18, 20.
4. Dorman and Jones, *The Afro-American Experience,* pp. 80–82.
5. Philip D. Curtin, *The Atlantic Slave Trade* (Madison: University of Wisconsin Press, 1969), pp. 87–93; U.S. Bureau of the Census, *Historical Statistics of the United States* (Washington, DC, 1960), p. 770.
6. Carl N. Degler, *Out of Our Past* (New York: Harper, 1959), pp. 161–163; John Hope Franklin, *From Slavery to Freedom,* 4th ed. (New York: Knopf, 1984), p. 88.
7. Franklin, *From Slavery to Freedom,* pp. 132–133.
8. U.S. Bureau of the Census, *Historical Statistics of the United States,* p. 11; Degler, *Out of Our Past,* pp. 163–164; Ulrich B. Phillips, *Life and Labor in the Old South* (Boston, MA: Little, Brown, 1929), pp. 339ff; Kenneth M. Stampp, *The Peculiar Institution* (New York: Random House/Vintage Books, 1956), pp. 383–418.
9. Ben Simpson, "Ben Simpson: Georgia and Texas," in *Lay My Burden Down,* ed. B. A. Botkin (Chicago: University of Chicago Press, 1945), p. 75.
10. John W. Blassingame, *The Slave Community* (New York: Oxford University Press, 1972), pp. 155–160.
11. Quoted in Jacqueline Jones, *Labor of Love, Labor of Sorrow: Black Women, Work, and the Family, from Slavery to the Present* (New York: Random House/Vintage Books, 1985), p.16. We have emended the quotation slightly for clarity.
12. Quoted in ibid., p.19.
13. Eugene G. Genovese, *Roll, Jordan, Roll* (New York: Random House, 1974), pp. 5, 362–364; Stanley M. Elkins, *Slavery* (Chicago: University of Chicago Press, 1959), pp. 72–127.
14. Herbert Gutman, *The Black Family in Slavery and Freedom, 1750–1925* (New York: Pantheon, 1976); Stanley Elkins, "The Slavery Debate," *Commentary* 46 (December 1975): 46–47.
15. Patricia Williams, "Alchemical Notes: Reconstructing Ideals from Deconstructed Rights," *Harvard Civil Rights and Civil Liberties Review* 22 (1987): 415.
16. Blassingame, *The Slave Community,* pp. 203–214; Genovese, *Roll, Jordan, Roll,* p. 588.
17. Genovese, *Roll, Jordan, Roll,* p. 650.
18. Herbert Aptheker, *American Negro Slave Revolts* (New York: International, 1943), pp. 12–18, 162.
19. Ibid., pp. 165, 220–225, 249–250, 267–273.
20. Herbert Aptheker, *Essays in the History of the American Negro* (New York: International, 1945), pp. 39, 49–51.
21. Sterling Stuckey, *Slave Culture* (New York: Oxford University Press, 1987), pp. 42–46.
22. Cited in *Bartlett's Familiar Quotations,* 15th ed., ed. Emily M. Beck (Boston, MA: Little, Brown, 1980), p. 556.
23. Benjamin B. Ringer, *"We the People" and Others* (New York: Tavistock, 1983), p. 533.
24. A. L. Higginbotham, *In the Matter of Color* (New York: Oxford University Press, 1978), pp. 144–149.
25. Cited in Thomas F. Gossett, *Race* (New York: Schocken Books, 1965), pp. 42–43.
26. See, for example, Samuel Cartwright's infamous 1850s article "The Prognathous Species of Mankind," in *Slavery Defended,* ed. Eric L. McKitrick (Englewood Cliffs, NJ: Prentice Hall, 1963).
27. Williams, "Alchemical Notes," pp. 401–434. See also Duncan J. MacLeod, *Slavery, Race, and the American Revolution* (London: Cambridge University Press, 1974), p. 158.
28. I. A. Newby, *Jim Crow's Defense* (Baton Rouge: Louisiana State University Press, 1965), pp. 19–23.
29. Thomas F. Pettigrew, *A Profile of the Negro American* (Princeton, NJ: D. Van Nostrand, 1964), pp. 100–104.
30. Richard J. Herrnstein, *IQ in the Meritocracy* (Boston, MA: Little, Brown, 1973); Arthur R. Jensen, "How Much Can We Boost IQ and Scholastic Achievement?" *Harvard Education Review* 39 (1969): 1–123; Tom Wilkie, "The American Association for the Advancement of Science: Research Revives Dispute over IQ," *Independent,* February 19, 1991, p. 7.
31. Richard J. Herrnstein and Charles Murray, *The Bell Curve: Intelligence and Class Structure in American Life* (New York: Free Press, 1994), p. 311; see also pp. 295–316.
32. Cited in Richard Brookhiser, "Fear and Loathing at City College," *National Review,* June 11, 1990, p. 20.
33. An unsigned editorial, "Buchanan Campaign Rhetoric," *Boston Globe,* January 12, 1992, p. 68. Samuel Francis, "Out of the Mouths of Japanese," *Washington Times,* February 11, 1992, p. F1.
34. See, for example, data gathered by Otto Klinberg as cited in I. A. Newby, *Challenge to the Court* (Baton Rouge: Louisiana State University Press, 1967), p. 74. See also Pettigrew, *A Profile of the Negro American,* pp. 123–126.
35. Leon J. Kamin, *The Science and Politics of IQ* (New York: Wiley, 1974), pp. 175–178.
36. N. J. Block and Gerald Dworkin, "IQ, Heritability, and Inequality," in *The IQ Controversy,* eds. N. J. Block and Gerald Dworkin (New York: Random House, 1976), pp. 410–540.
37. *Highlights from an Anti-Defamation League Survey on Racial Attitudes in America* (New York: Anti-Defamation League, 1993), pp. 3–33.
38. Doris Wilkinson, "Minority Women: Social-Cultural Issues," in *Women and Psychotherapy,* eds. Annette M. Brodsky and Rachel T. Hare-Mustin (New York: Guilford, 1980), pp. 295–297. See also A. Thomas and S. Sillen, *Racism and Psychiatry* (New York: Bruner-Mazel, 1972), pp. 57–58.
39. NORC, General Social Survey, 199?. Tabulation by author.
40. John B. McConahay and Joseph C. Hough, "Symbolic Racism," *Journal of Social Issues* 32 (1976): 38.
41. National Opinion Research Center (NORC), General Social Survey, 1994. Tabulations by authors. "Survey Finds Minorities Resent Whites And Each Other," *Jet,* March 28, 1994, p. 14.
42. Matthew P. Smith, "Bridging the Gulf Between Blacks and Whites," *Pittsburgh Post-Gazette,* April 7, 1996, p. A1.
43. Richard L. Berke, "The 1994 Campaign; Survey Finds Voters in U.S. Rootless and Self-Absorbed," *The New York Times,* September 21, 1994, p. A21.
44. Joe R. Feagin and Melvin P. Sikes, *Living with Racism: The Black Middle Class Experience* (Boston, MA: Beacon Press, 1994).
45. Howard Schuman, Charlotte Steeh, and Lawrence Bobo, *Racial Attitudes in America* (Cambridge, MA: Harvard University Press, 1985), pp. 86–125; National Opinion Research Center, *1994 General Social Survey.*
46. National Council of La Raza, "Distorted Reality: Hispanic Characters in TV Entertainment"; Gregory Freeman, "Television Can Change the Channel on Hispanic Roles," *Crisis,* October 1994, p. 5.

47. John F. Dovidio, John C. Brigham, Blair T. Johnson, and Samuel L. Gaertner, "Stereotyping, Prejudice, and Discrimination: Another Look," in *Stereotypes and Stereotyping,* eds. C. Neil Macrae, Miles Hewstone, and Charles Stangor (New York: Guilford, 1995), pp. 276–319.

48. U.S. Bureau of the Census, *Historical Statistics of the United States,* p. 218.

49. W. J. Cash, *The Mind of the South* (New York: Random House/Vintage Books, 1960), p. 125.

50. Note a 1940 pamphlet written by a white southerner for U.S. senators and congressmen, quoted in Gunnar Myrdal, *An America Dilemma* (New York: McGraw-Hill, 1964), 2:1198.

51. Gilbert Osofsky, *Harlem: The Making of a Ghetto* (New York: Harper & Row, 1963), pp. 45–51; Arthur I. Waskow, *From Race Riot to Sit-In, 1919 and the 1960s* (Garden City, NY: Doubleday, 1966), pp. 209–210 et passim; Elliot M. Rudwick, *Race Riot at East St. Louis* (Carbondale: Southern Illinois University Press, 1964), pp. 3–30.

52. "Active White Supremacist Groups in 1993," *Intelligence Report,* March 1994, pp. 15–17; "White Supremacist Movement Reels from Severe Setbacks in 1993," *Intelligence Report,* March 1994, p. 12.

53. Linda Diebel, "Darkest Iowa," *Toronto Star,* February 23, 1992, p. F1; John Turner, *The Ku Klux Klan: A History of Racism and Violence* (Montgomery, AL: Southern Poverty Law Center, 1982), pp. 48–56; "Going after the Klan," *Newsweek,* February 23, 1987, p. 29.

54. Diebel, "Darkest Iowa"; "White Supremacist Movement Reels from Severe Setbacks in 1993," p. 13.

55. "Weapons, Explosives Stockpiling by White Supremacists Rampant Across U.S. in 1993," *Intelligence Report,* March 1994, p. 1.

56. "Violent Hate Crime Remains at Record Levels Nationwide," *Intelligence Report,* March 1994, pp. 1, 4–5.

57. "Hate Crime Violence," *Race Relations Reporter,* August 15, 1994, p. 2; "Residential Terrorism," *Race Relations Reporter,* August 15, 1994, p. 4.

58. "U.S. Supreme Court Upholds Stiffer Sentences for Hate Crimes," *Intelligence Report,* September 1993, pp. 4–5.

59. Joe R. Feagin and Harlan Hahn, *Ghetto Revolts* (New York: Macmillan, 1973), p. 134.

60. "The Mood of Ghetto America," *Newsweek,* June 2, 1980, pp. 32–34.

61. Lara Parker, "Violence after Police Shooting Exposes Miami Racial Tensions," *Washington Post,* June 29, 1991, p. A2.

62. Kim Lersch, "Current Trends in Police Brutality: An Analysis of Recent Newspaper Accounts." (Master's thesis, University of Florida, 1993.)

63. "Accidents or Police Brutality?" *Time,* October 26, 1981, p. 70; Charles Leerhsen, "L.A.'s Violent New Video," *Newsweek,* March 18, 1991, pp. 33, 53.

64. *Reporting for the Russell Sage Foundation,* no. 6, May 1985, pp. 6–7.

65. Doris Y. Wilkinson, "The Segmented Labor Market and African American Women from 1890 to 1960," in *Research in Race and Ethnic Relations,* vol. 6, ed. Rutledge M. Dennis (Greenwich, CT: JAI Press, 1991), p. 88.

66. Wilkinson, "The Segmented Labor Market and African American Women from 1890 to 1960," p. 89. See also Ray Marshall, *The Negro Worker* (New York: Random House, 1967), pp. 7–12; MacLeod, *Slavery, Race, and the American Revolution,* pp. 151–153; Pete Daniel, *The Shadow of Slavery: Peonage in the South* (London: Oxford University Press, 1972); and Myrdal, *An American Dilemma,* 1:228.

67. Quoted in Jones, *Labor of Love, Labor of Sorrow,* p. 123.

68. Karl E. Taeuber and Alma F. Taeuber, *Negroes in Cities* (Chicago: Aldine, 1965), pp. 12–13.

69. Charles Tilly, "Race and Migration to the American City," in *The Urban Scene,* ed. Joe R. Feagin (New York: Random House, 1973), p. 35; Taeuber and Taeuber, *Negroes in Cities,* pp. 144–147.

70. Edna Bonacich, "Class Approaches to Ethnicity and Race," *Insurgent Sociologist* 10 (Fall 1980): 11. See also Bennett Harrison, *Education, Training, and the Urban Ghetto* (Baltimore, MD: Johns Hopkins, 1972).

71. Wilkinson, "The Segmented Labor Market and African American Women from 1890 to 1960," pp. 90–94.

72. U.S. Bureau of the Census, *Negroes in the United States, 1920–1932* (Washington, DC, 1935), p. 289.

73. Jones, *Labor of Love, Labor of Sorrow,* p. 179; Myrdal, *An American Dilemma,* 1:304–306.

74. Marshall, *The Negro Worker,* pp. 23–24, 56–57.

75. U.S. Bureau of the Census, *Population,* vol. 3, *The Labor Force* (Washington, DC, 1943). See also Sidney M. Wilhelm, *Who Needs the Negro?* (Cambridge, MA: Schenkman, 1970), p. 57.

76. Bureau of Labor Statistics, *Employment and Earnings,* March 1994, p. 37.

77. U.S. Bureau of the Census, *The Black Population in the United States: March 1994 and 1993,* Current Population Reports P20–480 (Washington, DC, 1995), p. 33.

78. Sam Fulwood, "Black-white Divide Appears to Be Widening," *Los Angeles Times,* October 11, 1994, p. A1.

79. Feagin and Sikes, *Living with Racism.*

80. Ibid.

81. Margery Austin Turner, Michael Fix, and Raymond J. Struyk, *Opportunities Denied: Discrimination in Hiring* (Washington, DC: Urban Institute, 1991).

82. Sharon M. Collins, "The Making of the Black Middle Class," *Social Problems* 30 (April 1983): 369–381.

83. Kenneth B. Clark, "The Role of Race," *The New York Times Magazine,* October 5, 1980, p. 30.

84. David Hatchett, "Corporate America and Affirmative Action: The Struggle Continues," *Crisis,* October 1994, pp. 8–9.

85. Kurt Eichenwald, "Texaco Executives, On Tape, Discussed Impeding a Bias Suit," *The New York Times,* November 4, 1996, p. A1.

86. Kurt Eichenwald, "The Two Faces Of Texaco," *The New York Times,* November 10, 1996, sec. 3, p. 1.

87. Ibid.

88. Glass Ceiling Commission, *Good for Business: Making Full Use of the Nation's Human Capital* (Washington, DC, 1995), pp. 12–60.

89. Ian Ayres, "Fair Driving: Gender and Race Discrimination in Retail Car Negotiations," *Harvard Law Review,* February 1991, 104 Harv. L. Rev. 817.

90. *Wards Cove Packing Co. v. Atonio* 109 S. Ct. 2115 (1989).

91. U.S. Bureau of the Census, *The Social and Economic Status of the Black Population in the United States, 1971* (Washington, DC, 1972), p. 52; U.S. Commission on Civil Rights, *Unemployment and Underemployment among Blacks, Hispanics, and Women* (Washington, DC, 1982), p. 5; U.S. Bureau of the Census, *Statistical Abstract of the United States: 1993* (Washington, DC, 1993), p. 395; Bureau of Labor Statistics, *Employment and Earnings,* January, 1997, p. 12.

92. U.S. Bureau of Labor Statistics, *Employment and Earnings*, March 1994, p. 35.

93. U.S. Bureau of the Census, *The Social and Economic Status of the Black Population in the United States, 1971* (Washington, DC, 1972), p. 29; U.S. Bureau of the Census, *Statistical Abstract of the United States: 1993*, p. 462; U.S. Bureau of the Census, *Statistical Abstract of the United States: 1997*, p. 49. The census category "non-white" consists mostly of blacks.

94. U.S. Bureau of the Census, *Statistical Abstract of the United States: 1997*, p. 474.

95. U.S. Bureau of the Census, *The Black Population in the United States: March 1994 and 1993*, p. 8.

96. Ibid., pp. 5, 26.

97. Robert B. Hill, "The Economic Status of Black Americans," in *The State of Black America, 1981*, ed. J. D. Williams (New York: Urban League, 1981), pp. 5–6, 33.

98. U.S. Bureau of the Census, *The Black Population in the United States: March 1994 and 1993*, pp. 5, 26.

99. U.S. Bureau of the Census, *Household Wealth and Asset Ownership: 1991*, Current Population Reports P70–34 (Washington, DC, 1994), pp. xiii.

100. U.S. Bureau of the Census, *Household Wealth and Asset Ownership: 1991*, p. xiv.

101. William J. Wilson, *The Declining Significance of Race* (Chicago: University of Chicago Press, 1978); Ken Auletta, *The Underclass* (New York: Random House, 1982); William J. Wilson, *The Truly Disadvantaged* (Chicago: University of Chicago Press, 1987).

102. See Joe R. Feagin *Subordinating the Poor: Welfare and American Beliefs* (Englewood Cliffs, NJ: Prentice Hall, 1975).

103. See Joe R. Feagin and Clairece B. Feagin, *Discrimination American Style*, 2nd ed. (Malabar, FL: Robert Krieger, 1986), pp. 207–234.

104. Douglas S. Massey and Nancy A. Denton, *American Apartheid: Segregation and the Making of the Underclass* (Cambridge, MA: Harvard University Press, 1993), p. 8.

105. William Julius Wilson, "The Political Economy and Urban Racial Tensions," *American Economist* 39 (March 1995): 3–6; quote on p. 3.

106. Isabel Wilkerson, "The Tallest Fence: Feelings on Race in a White Neighborhood," *The New York Times*, June 21, 1992, sec. 1, p. 18.

107. The discussion in this subsection draws on a course given by Thomas F. Pettigrew at Harvard University.

108. Franklin, *From Slavery to Freedom*, pp. 252–253; Chuck Stone, *Black Political Power in America*, rev. ed. (New York: Dell, 1970), pp. 30–31.

109. *Plessy* v. *Ferguson*, 163 U.S. 551–552.

110. Hanes Walton, Jr., *Black Politics* (Philadelphia, PA: Lippincott, 1972), pp. 100, 119.

111. Chandler Davidson and Bernard Grofman, "The Voting Rights Act and the Second Reconstruction," in *The Quiet Revolution in the South* (Princeton, NJ: Princeton University Press, 1994), p. 386.

112. Chandler Davidson, *Minority Vote Dilution: An Overview*, Reprint 85–1 (Houston, TX: Institute for Policy Analysis, Rice University, 1985), pp. 17–18; Frank R. Parker, *Black Votes Count* (Chapel Hill: University of North Carolina Press, 1990).

113. Davidson, *Minority Vote Dilution*, pp. 17–18.

114. Ibid.

115. David Garrow, "Lani Guinier," *The Progressive*, September 1993, p. 28; this section draws on Joe R.

116. William E. Forbath, "Civil Rights, Economic Justice, and the Meaning of the Guinier Affair," *Legal Times*, June 28, 1993, p. 21; Michael Isikoff, "Readings in Controversy: Guinier's Pivotal Articles," *Washington Post*, June 4, 1993, p. A10; Lani Guinier, *The Tyranny of the Majority: Fundamental Fairness and Representation Democracy* (New York: Free Press, 1994).

117. Quotes are from James W. Button, *Blacks and Social Change* (Princeton, NJ: Princeton University Press, 1989), pp. 226–227.

118. Data from the Joint Center for Political and Economic Studies, 1995.

119. Myrdal, *An American Dilemma*, 1:503; Raymond Wolters, *Negroes and the Great Depression* (Westport, CT: Greenwood Press, 1970), p. xi and elsewhere.

120. Congressional Black Caucus, *Directory of the 104th Congress* (Washington, DC, 1995).

121. Stone, *Black Political Power in America*, pp. 68–72.

122. Ibid., p. 47. Stone draws here on Henry L. Moon, *Balance of Power* (Garden City, NY: Doubleday, 1948).

123. Kevin Phillips, *The Emerging Republican Majority* (New Rochelle, NY: Arlington House, 1969).

124. Joe R. Feagin and Hernan Vera, *White Racism: Basic Principles* (New York: Routledge, 1995), pp. 114–122.

125. Joe R. Feagin, "White Elephant: Race and Electoral Politics in Texas," *Texas Observer*, August 23, 1991, pp. 15–16.

126. Feagin and Vera, *White Racism: Basic Principles*, pp. 124–134.

127. The discussions of oppositional culture in this chapter draw on Joe R. Feagin and Bonnie L. Mitchell, "America's Non-European Cultures: The Myth of the Melting Pot" (research paper, University of Florida, 1992).

128. Feagin and Hahn, *Ghetto Revolts*, pp. 81–85; Loren Miller, *The Petitioners* (New York: Random House, 1966), pp. 250–256.

129. Miller, *The Petitioners*, pp. 260–347.

130. Lerone Bennett, Jr., *Confrontation: Black and White* (Baltimore, MD: Penguin, 1966), pp. 164–169.

131. Ibid., pp. 223–234; Bryan T. Downes and Stephen W. Burks, "The Historical Development of the Black Protest Movement," in *Blacks in the United States*, eds. Norval D. Glenn and Charles Bonjean (San Francisco: Chandler, 1969), pp. 322–344.

132. Feagin and Hahn, *Ghetto Revolts*, pp. 92–94; Bennett, *Confrontation*, pp. 234–237; Inge P. Bell, *CORE and the Strategy of Nonviolence* (New York: Random House, 1968), pp. 13–16.

133. Aldon Morris, *The Origins of the Civil Rights Movement* (New York: Free Press, 1984).

134. U.S. Commission on Civil Rights, *The Federal Civil Rights Enforcement Effort: Fiscal Year 1983* (Washington, DC, 1982), pp. 5–7; Andrew Rosenthal, "Reagan Hints Rights Leaders Exaggerate Racism to Preserve Cause," *The New York Times*, January 14, 1989, p. 8.

135. Rupert Cornwell, "Rocketing Cost of Race Bias in the U.S.," *The Independent*, May 28, 1994, p. 8.

136. Feagin and Vera, *White Racism: Basic Principles*, pp. 52–57.

137. Sheila D. Collins, *The Rainbow Challenge* (New York: Monthly Review Press, 1986), pp. 128–143.

138. Michael Oreskes, "Voters and Jackson," *The New York Times*, August 13, 1988, p. 1.

Feagin and Hernan Vera, *White Racism: The Basics* (New York: Routledge, 1995), pp. 131–132.

139. Patricia Hill Collins, *Black Feminist Thought: Knowledge, Consciousness, and the Politics of Empowerment* (Boston, MA: Unwin Hyman, 1990).

140. Franklin, *From Slavery to Freedom*, pp. 280–281; Myrdal, *An American Dilemma*, 1:337–344; Henry A. Bullock, *A History of Negro Education in the South* (New York: Praeger, 1967), pp. 1–99.

141. Bullock, *A History of Negro Education in the South*, pp. 170–186; Franklin, *From Slavery to Freedom*, pp. 284–286.

142. U.S. Bureau of the Census, *Statistical Abstract of the United States 1993*, p. 152.

143. U.S. Bureau of the Census, *Statistical Abstract of the United States 1991* (Washington, DC, 1991), p. 138.

144. U.S. Bureau of the Census, *The Black Population in the United States: March 1994 and 1993*, p. 8.

145. Bullock, *A History of Negro Education in the South*, pp. 211–212, 225–230; Miller, *The Petitioners*, pp. 347–358.

146. U.S. Commission on Civil Rights, *Twenty Years after Brown* (Washington, DC, 1975), pp. 11–41; *Milliken v. Bradley*, 418 U.S. 717.

147. Nicolaus Mills, "Busing: Who's Being Taken for a Ride," in *The Great School Bus Controversy*, ed. Nicolaus Mills (New York: Teachers College Press, Columbia University, 1973), p. 7. See also U.S. Commission on Civil Rights, *Your Child and Busing* (Washington, DC, 1972).

148. See the numerous articles on innovative desegregation strategies in the 1966–1976 issues of the journal *Integrated Education*.

149. Russell W. Irvine and Jacqueline Jordan Irvine, "The Impact of the Desegregation Process on the Education of Black Students: Key Variables," *Journal of Negro Education* 53 (1983): 410–421.

150. R. Picott, *A Quarter Century of Elementary and Secondary Education* (Washington, DC: Association for the Study of Negro Life and History, 1976).

151. Quoted in William H. Freivogel, "Black, White, and Brown: Desegregation Ruling Established a Legal Landmark, Unkept Promises," *St. Louis Post-Dispatch*, May 15, 1994, p. 1B.

152. Patricia Edmonds, "Have Schools Really Changed?" *USA Today*, May 12, 1994, p. A1.

153. Gary Orfield, "The Growth of Segregation in American Schools: Changing Patterns of Separation and Poverty since 1968," Report of the Harvard Project on School Desegregation to the National School Boards Association, 1993, p. 7.

154. Ibid., pp. 7–9, 18–20.

155. Ibid., p. 22; U.S. Department of Education, *Prospects: The Congressionally Mandated Study of Educational Growth and Opportunity: The Interim Report* (Washington, DC, 1993), p. 25.

156. See Jonathan Kozol, "Romance of the Ghetto School", *Nation*, May 23, 1994, pp. 703–706; Jonathan Kozol, *Savage Inequalities: Children in America's Schools* (New York: Harper-Perennial, 1991); Nick Chiles, "Separate and Savagely Unequal," *Essence*, August 1992, pp. 61–62, 106–110.

157. Diana Pearce, "Breaking Down Barriers: New Evidence on the Impact of Metropolitan School Desegregation on Housing Patterns." Research report, School of Law, Catholic University, 1980, pp. 48–53.

158. New York ACORN Schools Office, *Secret Apartheid: A Report on Racial Discrimination against Black and Latino Parents and Children in the New York City Public Schools* (New York: ACORN, 1996).

159. Ibid., p. 2.

160. Amy Stuart Wells, Robert L. Crain, and Susan Uchitelle, *Stepping Over the Color Line: African American Students in White Suburban Schools* (New Haven, CT: Yale University Press, forthcoming, 1995).

161. Ibid.

162. Ibid.

163. Feagin and Feagin, *Discrimination American Style*, pp. 201–204.

164. Juan Williams, "The Seduction of Segregation, and Why King's Dream Still Matters," *Washington Post*, January 16, 1994, p. C1.

165. "Black Students and Educational Aspirations," *Race Relations Reporter*, August 15, 1994, p. 1

166. U.S. Department of Education, *The Condition of Education: 1994* (Washington, DC, 1994), p. 40.

167. U.S. Bureau of the Census, *The Black Population in the United States: March 1994 and 1993*, p. 8.

168. Mary Jordan, "Black College Enrollment Up," *Washington Post*, January 20, 1992, p. A14; "Is the Dream Over?" *Newsweek on Campus*, February 1987, pp. 10–14.

169. Komanduri S. Murty and Julian B. Roebuck, "The Case for Historically Black Colleges and Universities," *Journal of Social and Behavioral Sciences*, 36 (1992): 177–178.

170. Walter R. Allen, "Correlates of Black Student Adjustment, Achievement, and Aspirations at a Predominantly White Southern University," in *Black Students in Higher Education*, ed. Gail E. Thomas, (Westport, CT: Greenwood Press, 1981), pp. 128–137; Walter R. Allen, "Black and Blue: Black Students at the University of Michigan." Research report, University of Michigan, n.d., pp. 8–12.

171. See Joe R. Feagin, Hernan Vera, Nikitah Imani, *The Agony of Education*, forthcoming.

172. Stampp, *The Peculiar Institution*, pp. 156–162; Aptheker, *American Negro Slave Revolts*, pp. 56–60.

173. Stuckey, *Slave Culture*, p. 27.

174. James Scott, *Domination and the Arts of Resistance* (New Haven, CT: Yale University Press, 1990).

175. Richard C. Wade, *Slavery in the Cities* (New York: Oxford University Press, 1964), pp. 161–163; Winthrop Jordan, *White over Black* (Baltimore, MD: Penguin, 1969), pp. 422–425.

176. E. Franklin Frazier, *The Negro Church in America* (New York: Schocken Books, 1964), pp. 35–39; Myrdal, *An American Dilemma*, 2:938–939; E. U. Essien-Udom, *Black Nationalism* (New York: Dell, 1964).

177. Quoted in Michael Hirsley, "Churches Are Sources of Power," *Chicago Tribune*, February 5, 1992, p. C6.

178. Frazier, *The Negro Church in America*, p. 44; Joseph R. Washington, Jr., *Black Religion* (Boston, MA: Beacon Press, 1964), pp. 2–29.

179. David L. Lewis, *King* (Baltimore, MD: Penguin, 1970), p. 390.

180. This paragraph draws heavily on contributions by Bonnie Mitchell to Feagin and Mitchell, "America's Non-European Cultures."

181. Joe Klein, "Can Colin Powell Save America?" *Newsweek*, October 10, 1994, p. 26.

182. Jeffrey S. Passel and Barry Edmonston, "Immigrating and Race: Recent Trends in Immigration to the United States," in *Immigration and Ethnicity: The Integration of America's Newest Arrivals*, Barry Edmonston and Jeffrey S. Passel (Washington, DC: Urban Institute Press, 1994), pp. 52–53.

183. U.S. Bureau of the Census, *1990 Census of Population: Ancestry of the Population in the United States*, CP-3–2 (Washington, DC, 1993), p. 73; U.S. Bureau of the Census, *1990 Census of Population: Social and Economic Characteristics: United States*, CP-2–1 (Washington, DC, 1993), pp. 167–172.

184. Ibid., pp. 42, 44, 45, 48, 49; U.S. Bureau of the Census, *1990 Census of Population: Ancestry of the Population in the United States*, pp. 277, 379, 481.

185. U.S. Bureau of the Census, *1990 Census of Population: Ancestry of the Population in the United States*, pp. 87–88; U.S. Bureau of the Census, *1990 Census of Population: Social and Economic Characteristics: United States*, pp. 168, 170.

186. U.S. Bureau of the Census, *1990 Census of Population: Ancestry of the Population in the United States*, pp. 94–95.

187. Personal communication between authors and Haitian American professor Dr. Yanick St. Jean, September 1994.

188. Felix Robert Masud-Piloto, *With Open Arms: Cuban Migration to the U.S.* (Totowa, NJ: Rowman and Littlefield, 1988), pp. 111–125.

189. Ibid.; see also Paul Farmer, *The Uses of Haiti* (Monroe, ME: Common Courage Press, 1994); Amy Wilentz, *The Rainy Season: Haiti Since Duvalier* (New York: Simon & Schuster/Touchstone, 1989).

190. "757 Haitians Cleared to Seek Refuge in U.S.," *The New York Times*, December 10, 1991, p. A8.

191. Gwen Ifill, "President Names Black Democrat Advisor on Haiti," *The New York Times*, May 9, 1994, p. A1; Eric Schmitt, "Tents for Haitians Rise Again at Guantanamo," *The New York Times*, July 2, 1994, p. 1.

192. Eric Schmitt, "U.S. Ready to Declare Haiti 'Secure,'" *The New York Times*, January 15, 1995, p. 8.

193. U.S. Bureau of the Census, *1990 Census of Population: Social and Economic Characteristics: United States*, p. 45; U.S. Bureau of the Census, *1990 Census of Population: Ancestry of the Population in the United States*, p. 393.

194. U.S. Bureau of the Census, *1990 Census of Population: Ancestry of the Population in the United States*, p. 394.

195. Mary C. Waters, "Ethnic and Racial Identities of Second Generation Black Immigrants in New York City," *International Migration Review*, vol. 28, no. 2, Winter 1994.

196. U.S. Bureau of the Census, *1990 Census of Population: Social and Economic Characteristics: United States*, pp. 47, 48, 49; U.S. Bureau of the Census, *1990 Census of Population: Ancestry of the Population in the United States*, pp. 393, 495.

197. U.S. Bureau of the Census, *1990 Census of Population: Ancestry of the Population in the United States*, p. 496.

198. Elaine Sorensen and María E. Enchautegui, "Immigrant Male Earnings in the 1980s: Divergent Patterns by Race and Ethnicity," in *Immigration and Ethnicity: The Integration of America's Newest Arrivals*, pp. 144–146.

199. U.S. Bureau of the Census, *1990 Census of Population: Social and Economic Characteristics: United States*, p. 42; U.S. Bureau of the Census, *1990 Census of Population: Ancestry of the Population in the United States*, pp. 291–292.

200. U.S. Bureau of the Census, *1990 Census of Population: Ancestry of the Population in the United States*, p. 292.

201. Barbara J. Fields, "Ideology and Race in American History," in *Region, Race, and Reconstruction: Essays in Honor of C. Vann Woodward*, eds. J. Morgan Kousser and James M. McPherson (New York: Oxford University Press, 1982), p. 146.

202. Waters, "Ethnic and Racial Identities of Second Generation Black Immigrants in New York City."

203. Personal communication between authors and Yanick St. Jean, September 1994.

204. Waters, "Ethnic and Racial Identities of Second Generation Black Immigrants in New York City."

205. Personal communication between authors and Yanick St. Jean, September 1994.

206. Paul Farmer, *AIDS and Accusation* (Berkeley, CA: University of California Press, 1992), pp. 215–226.

207. Milton Gordon, *Assimilation in American Life* (New York: Oxford University Press, 1964), p. 78.

208. Talcott Parsons, "Full Citizenship for the Negro American? A Sociological Problem," in *The Negro American*, eds. Talcott Parsons and Kenneth B. Clark (Boston, MA: Houghton Mifflin, 1965), p. 740; see also pp. 714–715.

209. Nathan Glazer, *Affirmative Discrimination* (New York: Basic Books, 1975), pp. 40–76; Daniel P. Moynihan, *The Negro Family* (Washington, DC, 1965); Frazier, *The Negro Church in America*; Myrdal, *An American Dilemma*.

210. Robert Blauner, *Racial Oppression in America* (New York: Harper & Row, 1972), pp. 51–110.

211. Wade, *Slavery in the Cities*, pp. 273–275; Herman D. Bloch, *The Circle of Discrimination* (New York: New York University Press, 1969), pp. ix–xiii.

212. Wilhelm, *Who Needs the Negro?*; Robert L. Allen, *Black Awakening in Capitalist America* (Garden City, NY: Doubleday/Anchor Books, 1970), pp. 4–6; *Report of the National Advisory Commission on Civil Disorders* (New York: Bantam, 1968), pp. 278–279.

213. *Report of the National Advisory Commission on Civil Disorders*, pp. 279–280.

214. Marimba Ani, *Yurugu: An African-Centered Critique of European Cultural Thought and Behavior* (Trenton, NJ: Africa World Press, 1994), pp. 567–569.

215. Feagin and Sikes, *Living with Racism*, p. vii.

CHAPTER 9

1. Edward Múrguía, "On Latino/Hispanic Ethnic Identity," *Latino Studies Journal* 2, no. 3 (September 1991): 8–18.

2. Ibid.

3. Katharine Q. Seelye, "U.S. of Future: Grayer and More Hispanic," *The New York Times*, March 27, 1997, p. B16.

4. Strategy Research Corporation, *1991 U.S. Hispanic Market* (Miami, FL 1991), pp 78–129.

5. U.S. Bureau of the Census, *The Hispanic Population in the United States: March 1993*, Current Population Reports, P20–475 (Washington, DC, 1994), pp. 10–11.

6. Teresa L. Amott and Julie A. Matthaei, *Race, Gender, and Work* (Boston, MA: South End Press, 1991), pp. 64–67.

7. Américo Paredes, *With His Pistol in His Hand* (Austin: University of Texas Press, 1958), pp. 3–14; Roldolfo Acuña, *Occupied America* (San Francisco: Canfield Press, 1972), pp. 10–12.

8. Acuña, *Occupied America*, p. 15; S. Dale McLemore, "The Origin of Mexican American Subordination in Texas," *Social Science Quarterly* 53 (March 1973): 665–667; Rodolfo Alvarez, "The Psycho-historical and Socioeconomic Development of the Chicano Community in the United States," *Social Science*

Quarterly 53 (March 1973): 925; David Montejano, *Anglos and Mexicans in The Making of Texas, 1836–1986* (Austin: University of Texas Press, 1987).

9. William Lord, "Myths and Realities of the Alamo," *American West* 5 (May 1968): 20–25.

10. Carl N. Degler, *Out of Our Past* (New York: Harper, 1959), pp. 109–110; Acuña, *Occupied America*, pp. 23–29.

11. Joan Moore and Harry Pachon, *Hispanics in the United States* (Englewood Cliffs, NJ: Prentice Hall, 1985), pp. 18, 22–23; Leo Grebler, Joan W. Moore, and Ralph G. Guzmán, *The Mexican-American People* (New York: Free Press, 1970), pp. 43–44; Acuña, *Occupied America*, p. 105; Joan W. Moore, "Colonialism: The Case of the Mexican Americans," *Social Problems* 17 (Spring 1970): 468–469.

12. Moore and Pachon, *Hispanics in the United States*, p. 21; Ellwyn R. Stoddard, Mexican Americans (New York: Random House, 1973), pp. 9–13; Carey McWilliams, *North from Mexico* (New York: Greenwood Press, 1968), pp. 70–76; Acuña, *Occupied America*, pp. 60–62; Grebler, Moore, and Guzmán, *The Mexican American People*, pp. 43–44; Nancie L. Gonzales, *The Spanish-Americans of New Mexico* (Albuquerque: University of New Mexico Press, 1967), pp. 204–210.

13. Alvarez, "Psycho-historical and Socioeconomic Development," p. 925.

14. Oscar J. Martinez, "On the Size of the Chicano Population: New Estimates: 1850–1900," *Aztlán* 6 (Spring 1975): 55–56; U.S. Department of Justice, Immigration and Naturalization Service, *Annual Report* (Washington, DC, 1975), pp. 62–64; Julian Samora, *Los Mojados: The Wetback Story* (Notre Dame, IN: University of Notre Dame Press, 1971), pp. 7–8.

15. Leo Grebler, *Mexican Immigration to the United States: The Record and Its Implications* (Los Angeles: UCLA Mexican-American Study Project, 1965), pp. 20–21.

16. Mark Reisler, *By the Sweat of Their Brow: Mexican Immigrant Labor in the United States, 1900–1940* (Westport, CT: Greenwood, 1976); Grebler, *Mexican Immigration to the United States*, pp. 23–24; Manuel Gamio, *Mexican Immigration to the United States* (New York: Dover, 1971), pp. 171–174; Ronald Takaki, *A Different Mirror* (Boston, MA: Little, Brown, 1993), pp. 326–334.

17. Samora, *Los Mojados*, pp. 48–52.

18. Cardenas, "United States Immigration Policy toward Mexico," pp. 73–75; Grebler, *Mexican Immigration to the United States*, p. 26.

19. Samora, *Los Mojados*, pp. 18–19, 24–25, 44–46, 57; Joan Moore, *Mexican Americans*, 2nd ed. (Englewood Cliffs, NJ: Prentice Hall, 1976), pp. 49–51; Strategy Research Corporation, *1991 U.S. Hispanic Market*, pp. 39, 51.

20. Cardenas, "United States Immigration Policy toward Mexico," pp. 84–85; Cheryl Anderson, "Immigration Bill under Attack on Several Fronts," *Austin American-Statesman*, December 12, 1982, p. C1.

21. Luis Alberto Urrea, *By the Lake of Sleeping Children: The Secret Life of the Mexican Border* (New York: Anchor Books), 1996, p. 18.

22. Leo R. Chávez, *Shadowed Lives: Undocumented Immigrants in American Society* (Orlando, FL: Harcourt Brace Jovanovich, 1992), p. 39. See also Jorge A. Bustamante, "The Mexicans Are Coming," *International Migration Review* 17 (1983): 323–441.

23. Michael Fix and Jeffrey S. Passel, *Immigration and Immigrants: Setting the Record Straight* (Washington, DC: Urban Institute, 1994), p. 24.

24. Chávez, *Shadowed Lives*, pp. 19–20, 29–30, 39, 70, 79–80, 126–129, 148–151.

25. Fix and Passel, *Immigration and Immigrants*, pp. 24–25, 51, 60, 62, 71, 81; Chávez, *Shadowed Lives*, pp. 143, 151.

26. Stephen Koepp, "Rotten Shame: Who Will Pick the Crops?" *Time*, June 22, 1987, p. 49.

27. Jacqueline Maria Hagan and Susan González Baker, "Implementing the U.S. Legalization Program," *International Migration Review*, 27 (Fall 1993): 514; Susan González Baker and Frank Bean, "The Legalization Programs of the 1986 Immigration Reform and Control Act," in *In Defense of the Alien*, ed. Lydio F. Tomasi (New York: Center for Migration Studies, 1990), pp. 3–11; Susan González Baker, *The Cautious Welcome: The Legalization Programs of the Immigration Reform and Control Act* (Washington, DC: Urban Institute, 1990); data provided by Demographics Statistics Branch, Immigration and Naturalization Service, January 1995.

28. Jose A. Pagan and Alberto Davila, "On-the-job Training, Immigration Reform, and the True Wages of Native Male Workers," *Industrial Relations* 35 (January 1996): 45–58.

29. U.S. Bureau of the Census, *1990 Census of the Population: Ancestry of the Population in the United States*, CP-3–2 (Washington, DC, 1993), p. 1; Karen A. Woodrow and Jeffrey S. Passel, "Post-IRCA Undocumented Immigration to the United States" in *Undocumented Migration to the United States*, eds. Frank Bean, Barry Edmonston, and Jeffrey Passel (Santa Monica, CA: Rand Corporation, 1990), p. 42.

30. Lynda Gorov, "Poor Immigrants Face New Hurdles," *Boston Globe*, November 30, 1997, p. A1.

31. This research by David Hayes-Bautista is summarized in "Immigrants and Cohesion," *Orange County Register*, June 17, 1997, p. B8.

32. Montgomery, *The Hispanic Population in the United States 1993*, p. 11.

33. U.S. Bureau of the Census, *1990 Census of Population: The Foreign-Born Population in the United States*, CP-3–1 (Washington, DC, 1993), p. 38.

34. Jesus M. Garcia, *The Hispanic Population in the United States 1992*, U.S. Bureau of the Census, Current Population Reports, P20–465RV (Washington, DC, 1993), p. 19.

35. Quoted in Philip D. Ortego, "The Chicano Renaissance," in *Introduction to Chicano Studies*, eds. Livie I. Duran and H. Russell Bernard (New York: Macmillan, 1973), p. 337.

36. Ricardo Romo, *East Lost Angeles: History of a Barrio* (Austin: University of Texas Press, 1983), pp. 89–111.

37. Cardenas, "United States Immigration Policy toward Mexico," pp. 70–71.

38. Quoted in Ralph Guzmán, "The Function of Anglo-American Racism in the Political Development of Chicanos," in *La Causa Politica*, ed. F. Chris Garcia (South Bend, IN: University of Notre Dame Press, 1974), p. 22.

39. McWilliams, *North from Mexico*, p. 213.

40. William Sheldon, "Educational Research and Statistics: The Intelligence of Mexican-American Children," in *In Their Place*, ed. Lewis H. Carlson and George A. Colburn (New York: Wiley, 1972), pp. 149–151.

41. Ricardo Romo, "George I. Sanchez and the Civil Rights Movement: 1940–1960," *La Raza Law Journal* (Berkeley: University of California), 1 (Fall 1986): 342–362.

42. Quoted in Guillermo V. Flores, "Race and Culture in the Internal Colony: Keeping the Chicano in His Place," in "Structures of Dependency," eds. Frank Bonilla and Robert Girling. Manuscript, research seminar, Stanford, CA, 1973, p. 194.

43. Quoted in Armondo Morales, *Ando Sangrando* (Fair Lawn, NJ: R. E. Burdick, 1972), p. 43.

44. Octavio Ignacio Romano, "The Anthropology and Sociology of the Mexican-Americans," *El Grito* 2 (Fall 1968): 13–19; Oscar Lewis, *Five Families* (New York: Wiley, 1962); William Madsen, *Mexican Americans of South Texas* (New York: Holt, Rinehart & Winston, 1964).

45. Americo Paredes, *With His Pistol in His Hand* (Austin: University of Texas Press, 1958); Romano, "The Anthropology and Sociology of the Mexican Americans"; Stoddard, *Mexican Americans*, pp. 42–44; Lea Ybarra, "Empirical and Theoretical Developments in the Study of the Chicano Family," in *The State of Chicano Research on Family, Labor, and Migration*, eds. Armando Valdez, Albert Camarillo, and Tomás Almaguer (Stanford, CA: Stanford Center for Chicano Research, 1983), p. 96.

46. Edward E. Telles and Edward Múrguía, "Phenotypic Discrimination and Income Differences among Mexican Americans." (Typescript, University of Texas, 1987.)

47. American Institute of Public Opinion, *Roper Center*, 1982. Cited in Rita J. Simon and Susan H. Alexander, *The Ambivalent Welcome: Print Media, Public Opinion, and Immigration* (Westport, CT: Praeger, 1993), p. 45.

48. National Conference of Christians and Jews, *Taking America's Pulse: The National Conference Survey on Inter-Group Relations* (New York: National Conference, 1994).

49. Tomás Martinez, "Advertising and Racism: The Case of the Mexican American," *El Grito* 2 (Summer 1969): 3–13. See also Stoddard, *Mexican Americans*, p. 6.

50. Livie I. Duran and H. Russell Bernard, introduction to Part 2 of *Introduction to Chicano Studies*, eds. Duran and Bernard, p. 237. See also Stoddard, *Mexican Americans*, p. 6.

51. Ansel Martinez, "Study Shows Television Shows Stereotype Hispanics." Washington, DC: National Public Radio, *All Things Considered*, September 10, 1994.

52. National Council of La Raza, "Distorted Reality: Hispanic Characters in TV Entertainment," September 1994. See also Gregory Freeman, *Crisis*, October 1994, p. 5.

53. "Study: Latino TV Characters Often Negative Or Absent," *Newsday*, September 8, 1994, p. A7.

54. Jane H. Hill, "Mock Spanish: A Site for the Indexical Reproduction of Racism in American English," unpublished research paper, University of Arizona, 1995.

55. Ibid.

56. E. J. Hobsbawm, *Primitive Rebels* (New York: W. W. Norton, 1959), pp. 15–16.

57. Acuña, *Occupied America*, pp. 48–50; McWilliams, *North from Mexico*, pp. 110–112.

58. Paredes, *With His Pistol in His Hand*, pp. 27–32; McWilliams, *North from Mexico*, p. 127; Moore, "Colonialism," p. 466; Stoddard, *Mexican Americans*, p. 181.

59. Ralph H. Turner and Lewis M. Killian, *Collective Behavior* (Englewood Cliffs, NJ: Prentice Hall, 1957), pp. 125–128; McWilliams, *North from Mexico*, pp. 229–238.

60. Morales, *Ando Sangrando*, pp. 100–108.

61. U.S. Commission on Civil Rights, *Mexican Americans and the Administration of Justice in the Southwest* (Washington, DC, 1970), pp. 6–10; Robert Lee Maril, *Poorest of Americans* (South Bend, IN: University of Notre Dame Press, 1989), p. 52; Andrea Ford and Sheryl Stolberg, "Latinos Tell Panel of Anger at Police Conduct," *Los Angeles Times*, May 21, 1991, p. A1; Louis Sahagun, "Shooting Spurs Latinos to Reassess Law Enforcement," *Los Angeles Times*, August 8, 1991, p. A1; George Ramos, "Latinos Push Demand for Sheriff's Dept. Probe," *Los Angeles Times*, September 19, 1991, p. B3.

62. Raymond Smith, "The Chase and Beating Incident," *Press-Enterprise* (Riverside), March 30, 1997, p. B1.

63. Antonio H. Rodríguez and Carlos A. Chávez, "Latinos Unite in Self-Defense on Proposition 187," *Los Angeles Times*, October 21, 1994, p. B7; Beth Shuster and Chip Johnson, "Hundreds of Students Stage Walkouts to Protest Proposition 187," *Los Angeles Times*, October 21, 1994, p. B3.

64. Frank Trejo, "Thousands of Hispanics March in Washington; Texas Residents Join Call for End to Discrimation, Rights Abuses," *Dallas Morning News*, Oct 13, 1996, p. 1.

65. Abel G. Rubio, *Stolen Heritage* (Austin, TX: Eakin Press, 1986).

66. Clark Knowlton, "Recommendations for the Solution of Land Tenure Problems among the Spanish Americans," in *Chicano: The Evolution of a People*, eds. Renato Rosaldo, Robert A. Calvert, and Gustav L. Seligmann (San Francisco: Rinehart Press, 1973), pp. 334–335; George I. Sanchez, *Forgotten People* (Albuquerque: University of New Mexico Press, 1940), p. 61; Arnoldo Deleón, *The Tejano Community, 1836–1900* (Albuquerque: University of New Mexico Press, 1982), pp. 63–91.

67. Tomas Almaguer, "Historical Notes on Chicano Oppression: The Dialectics of Racial and Class Domination in North America," *Atzlán* 5 (Spring–Fall 1974): 38–39; Richard del Castillo, "Myth and Reality: Chicano Economic Mobility in Los Angeles, 1850–1880," *Atzlán* 6 (Summer 1975): 153–154; McWilliams, *North from Mexico*, pp. 127–128; Gamio, *Mexican Immigration to the United States*, pp. 39–40; Charles Wollenberg, "Huelga, 1928 Style: The Imperial Valley Canteloupe Workers' Strike," in *Chicano*, eds. Rosaldo, Calvert, and Seligmann, pp. 185–188; Amott and Matthaei, *Race, Gender, and Work*, pp. 76–77.

68. Samora, *Los Mojados*, p. 130; Grebler, Moore, and Guzmán, *The Mexican-American People*, p. 91.

69. McWilliams, *North from Mexico*, pp. 193, 220; Grebler, Moore, and Guzmán, *The Mexican-American People*, p. 526; Amott and Matthaei, *Race, Gender, and Work*, p. 77.

70. Ruth H. Tuck, *Not with the Fist* (New York: Harcourt, Brace, & World, 1946), pp. 173–183.

71. McWilliams, *North from Mexico*, pp. 217–218; U.S. Commission on Civil Rights, *Mexican American Education Study*, vol. 1, *Ethnic Isolation of Mexican Americans in the Public Schools of the Southwest* (Washington, DC, 1971), p. 11.

72. Anne Brunton, "The Chicano Migrants," in *Introduction to Chicano Studies*, eds. Duran and Bernard, pp. 489–492.

73. Jesus Luna, "Luna's Abe Lincoln Story," in *Chicano*, ed. Rosaldo, Calvert, and Selgmann, p. 348.

74. Roberto Suro, "Border Boom's Dirty Residue Imperils U.S.–Mexico Trade," *The New York Times*, March 31,

1991, p. 1; Patrick McDonnell, "Foreign-Owned Companies Add to Mexico's Pollution," *Los Angeles Times*, November 18, 1991, p. A1; Richard W. Stevenson, "Economic Scene: The Hidden Costs of Mexico Plants," *The New York Times*, July 19, 1991, p. D2; Judy Pasternak, "Firms Find a Haven from U.S. Environmental Rules," *Los Angeles Times*, November 19, 1991, p. A1; Patrick McDonnell, "Mexico: Progress and Promise," *Los Angeles Times*, October 22, 1991, p. 11.

75. Chávez, *Shadowed Lives*, pp. 19, 139–155.
76. Teresa Puente, "When Hope Turns into Slavery," *Chicago Tribune*, August 10, 1997, p. 1C.
77. H. Cross, G. Keeney, J. Mell, and W. Zimmerman, *Employer Hiring Practices: Differential Treatment of Hispanic and Anglo Job Seekers* (Washington, DC: Urban Institute, 1990).
78. Marc Bendick, Jr., Charles Jackson, Victor Reinoso, and Laura Hodges, "Discrimination against Latino Job Applicants: A Controlled Experiment," *Human Resource Management*, 30 (Winter 1991): 469–484.
79. Jim Doyle, "Court Curbs 'English-Only' Company Rules," *San Francisco Chronicle*, October 5, 1991, p. A12; Juan Perea, "English-Only Rules and the Right to Speak One's Primary Language in the Workplace," *University of Michigan Journal of Law Reform* 23, no. 2 (Winter 1990): 265–318.
80. 618 F.2d 264 (5th Cir. 1980), *cert. denied*, 449 U.S. 1113 (1981).
81. *Gutierrez v. Municipal Court*, 838 F.2d at 1039.
82. *Gutierrez v. Municipal Court*, 838 F.2d at 1040, quoted in Perea, "English-Only Rules," pp. 271–272.
83. *Gutierrez v. Municipal Court*, 838 F.2d 1031, *vacated as moot*, 109 S. Ct. 1736 (1989).
84. *Garcia v. Spun Steak Co.*, DC NCalif, No. C91–1949 RHS, October 14, 1991; Doyle, "Court Curbs 'English-Only' Company Rules."
85. Montgomery, *The Hispanic Population in the United States 1993*, pp. 12, 14.
86. Edward E. Telles and Edward Múrguía, "Phenotypic Discrimination and Income Differences among Mexican Americans," *Social Science Quarterly* 71, no. 4 (December 1990): 682–696.
87. Ibid., pp. 13, 15, 18–19.
88. Ibid., pp. 12, 14, 18, 19.
89. Ibid., pp. 15, 18, 19.
90. Steven A. Holmes, "For Hispanic Poor, No Silver Lining," *The New York Times*, October 13, 1996, sec. 4, p. 5.
91. The study was conducted by Eugene Turner and James P. Allen. It is summarized in Efrain Hernandez, Jr., "Growing Gap Seen Between Minority and White Income; Earnings: Study's Findings in Southland Run Counter to National Trend. Lag Is Most Apparent among Mexican Americans." *Los Angeles Times*, May 11, 1997, p. A3.
92. Joan Moore and Raquel Pinderhughes, *In the Barrios: Latinos and the Underclass Debate* (New York: Russell Sage, 1993).
93. Avelardo Valdez, "Persistent Poverty, Crime, and Drugs: U.S.–Mexican Border Region," in *In the Barrios: Latinos and the Underclass Debate*, eds. Joan Moore and Raquel Pinderhughes (New York: Sage, 1993), pp. 184–194.
94. Carlos Velez-Ibanez, "U.S. Mexicans in the Borderlands: Being Poor Without the Underclass," in *In the Barrios: Latinos and the Underclass Debate*, eds. Moore and Pinderhughes, pp. 195–214.

95. "Census Bureau Reports Number of Hispanic Businesses Up 26 Percent in Five Years," U.S. Newswire, July 11, 1996.
96. Nestor Rodríguez, "Economic Restructuring and Latino Growth in Houston," in *In the Barrios: Latinos and the Underclass Debate*, eds. Moore and Pinderhughes, pp. 101–126.
97. Joan Moore and James Diego Vigil, "Barrios in Transition," in *In the Barrios: Latinos and the Underclass Debate*, eds. Moore and Pinderhughes, pp. 27–47.
98. Charles Oliver, "Is American Culture Changing?" *Investor's Business Daily*, October 4, 1994, p. A1.
99. Moore, *Mexican Americans*, p. 33.
100. *Garza v. County of Los Angeles*, 918 F.2d 763; 1990 U.S. App.
101. *Williams v. City of Dallas*, 734 F. Supp. 1317; 1990 U.S. Dist.
102. U.S. Bureau of the Census, *1990 Census of Population: Social and Economic Characteristics: United States Summary*, CP-2–1 (Washington, DC, 1993), p. 123.
103. Information provided by Valerie Martinez, staff member for the Latino Legislative Caucus of the California State Legislature.
104. The data on Mexican American officials in this and the following paragraph come from Juan Gómez-Quiñones, *Chicano Politics: Reality and Promise, 1940–1990* (Albuquerque: University of New Mexico Press, 1990), pp. 167–169, 173; *National Association of Latino Elected and Appointed Officials, National Report* 11, no. 1 (Fourth Quarter 1991): 1, 3; and personal communications with Rodolfo de la Garza and Robert Brischetto.
105. Hector Tobar and Richard Simon, "Molina's First Goal Expand County Board," *Los Angeles Times*, February 21, 1991, p. A1; Carla Rivera, "Heated Meeting Marks Burke's Debut as Leader," *Los Angeles Times*, December 8, 1993, p. B3.
106. National Association of Latino Elected and Appointed Officials, *1994 National Roster of Latino Elected Officials*; Margarita Contin, "Hispanics Inch Up in Legislatures But Fear for Agendas," *Hispanic Link Weekly Report*, November 21, 1994, p. 2.
107. U.S. Bureau of the Census, *Voting and Registration in the Election of November 1992*, P20–466 (Washington, DC, 1993), p. 29.
108. Information provided by staff of Latino Legislative Caucus of the Texas State Legislature.
109. U.S. Bureau of the Census, *Voting and Registration in the Election of November 1992*, p. 23.
110. Information provided by Valerie Martinez, staff member for the Latino Legislative Caucus of the California State Legislature.
111. Southwest Voter Registration Project, *The Hispanic Electorates* (San Antonio, TX Hispanic Policy Development Project, 1984), pp. 145–149; Robert R. Brischetto, "Chicano Voting and Views in the 1986 Elections" (typescript, Southwest Voter Research Institute, San Antonio, 1987); U.S. Commission on Civil Rights, *Ethnic Isolation of Mexican Americans in the Public Schools of the Southwest*, p. 55; Gómez-Quiñones, *Chicano Politics*, p. 163; Marjorie Connelly, "The 1994 Elections," *The New York Times*, November 13, 1994, p. 24.
112. Ray Suarez, "Latinos Politics," National Public Radio, Talk of the Nation, August 5, 1997.
113. *Hernandez v. Texas*, 347 U.S. 482 (1954). Cited in Ricardo Romo, "Mexican Americans in the New West," in *The*

Twentieth-Century West, eds. Gerald D. Nash and Richard W. Etulian (Albuquerque: University of New Mexico Press, 1989), p. 135.

114. U.S. Commission on Civil Rights, *Mexican Americans and the Administration of Justice in the Southwest,* pp. 79–86.

115. Ibid., pp. 66–69.

116. Eric Lichtblau, "High Court Won't Hear Harvard Scholar's Plea," *Los Angeles Times,* November 14, 1991, p. B6.

117. *Hernandez* v. *New York,* 1991, 111 S. Ct. 1859; "*Hernandez* v. *New York*: Courts, Prosecutors, and the Fear of Spanish," *Hofstra Law Review,* 21 (Fall 1992): 1–61.

118. See Romo, "Mexican Americans in the New West," pp. 136–139.

119. Michael V. Miller and James D. Preston, "Vertical Ties and the Redistribution of Power in Crystal City," *Social Science Quarterly* 53 (March 1973): 772–782; John S. Shockley, *Chicano Revolt in a Texas Town* (Notre Dame, IN: University of Notre Dame Press, 1974), pp. 28–148, 162–177.

120. Maril, *Poorest of Americans,* p. 52.

121. Armando Gutiérrez and Herbert Hirsch, "The Militant Challenge to the American Ethos: 'Chicanos' and the 'Mexican Americans,'" *Social Science Quarterly* 53 (March 1973): 844–845; Carlos Muñoz, Jr., *Youth, Identity, Power: The Chicano Movement* (New York: Verso, 1989); Ignacio M. Garcia, *United We Win* (Tuscon: University of Arizona Press, 1989), pp. 228–231.

122. Marta Cotera, "Feminism, the Chicana and Anglo Versions," in *Twice a Minority,* ed. Margarita B. Melville (St. Louis: C. V. Mosby, 1980), p. 231.

123. Amott and Matthaei, *Race, Gender, and Work,* pp. 83–84; Cotera, *Feminism,* pp. 213–233.

124. Robert R. Brischetto, *The Mexican American Electorate: Political Opinions and Behavior across Cultures in San Antonio,* Occasional Paper No. 5, Southwest Voter Registration Education Project and the Center for Mexican American Studies at the University of Texas (San Antonio and Austin, TX, 1985).

125. McWilliams, *North from Mexico,* pp. 191–193; Grebler, Moore, and Guzmán, *The Mexican-American People,* pp. 91–92.

126. Stoddard, *Mexican Americans,* p. 180; Gamio, *Mexican Immigration to the United States,* pp. 135–138.

127. Grebler, Moore, and Guzmán, *The Mexican-American People,* pp. 543–545; Stoddard, *Mexican Americans,* p. 188; Moore, *Mexican Americans,* p. 152.

128. U.S. Commission on Civil Rights, *Mexican Americans and the Administration of Justice in the Southwest,* pp. 15–17; Rees Lloyd and Peter Montague, "Ford and La Raza: 'They Stole Our Land and Gave Us Powdered Milk,'" in *Introduction to Chicano Studies,* eds. Duran and Bernard, pp. 376–378; Frances L. Swadesh, "The Alianza Movement: Catalyst for Social Change in New Mexico," in *Chicano,* eds. Rosaldo, Calvert, and Seligmann, pp. 270–274.

129. Robert Pear, "U.S. Sues Houston to Block Election," *The New York Times,* October 22, 1991, p. A16; William Grady and Thomas Hardy, "Court Orders New Remap," *Chicago Tribune,* December 14, 1991, p. 1; Kenneth Weiss, "Latinos to Challenge Court Plan," *Los Angeles Times,* December 17, 1991, p. B1.

130. Mary Pardo, "Mexican American Women Grassroots Community Activists: 'Mothers of East Los Angeles,'" *Frontiers* XI, no. 1 (1990): 4.

131. Jacques E. Levy, *César Chávez* (New York: W. W. Norton, 1975), pp. 182–201; Peter Matthiessen, *Sal Si Puedes* (New York: Delta Books, 1969), pp. 59–216; John G. Dunne, *Delano* (New York: Farrar, Straus & Giroux, 1967), pp. 110–167.

132. Shockley, *Chicano Revolt in a Texas Town,* pp. 216–217.

133. Levy, *César Chávez,* pp. 495, 522–535.

134. J. Craig Jenkins, *The Politics of Insurgency* (New York: Columbia University Press, 1985), pp. x–xi; Robert Reinhold, "Environmental Agency Moves to End Most Uses of Deadly Agricultural Pesticide," *The New York Times,* September 6, 1991, p. A17.

135. Marla Cone, "EPA Accord Could Ban Up to 85 Pesticides," *Los Angeles Times,* October 13, 1994, p. A3.

136. Ann Bancroft, "10,000 at Rally for Farm Workers," *San Francisco Chronicle,* April 25, 1994, p. A1.

137. Mark Arax, "UFW Pledges New Activism as March Ends," *Los Angeles Times,* April 25, 1994, p. A3.

138. Gómez-Quiñones, *Chicano Politics,* p. 167; Muñoz, Jr., *Youth, Identity, Power,* p. 177.

139. Hector L. Delgado, *New Immigrants, Old Unions: Undocumented Workers in Los Angeles* (Philadelphia, PA: Temple University Press, 1993).

140. Thomas P. Carter, *Mexican Americans in School* (New York: College Entrance Examination Board, 1970), pp. 204–205.

141. George I. Sánchez, "History, Culture, and Education," in *La Raza,* ed. Julian Samora (Notre Dame, IN: University of Notre Dame Press, 1966), pp. 1–26; Paul Taylor, *An American-Mexican Frontier* (Chapel Hill: University of North Carolina Press, 1934), pp. 196–204; Guadalupe San Miguel, Jr., "Let All of Them Take Heed: Mexican Americans and the Campaign for Educational Equality" in *Texas, 1910–1981* (Austin: University of Texas Press, 1987), pp. 1–58.

142. Charles Wollenberg, *All Deliberate Speed: Segregation and Exclusion in California Schools, 1855–1975* (Berkeley: University of California Press, 1976), pp. 123–124.

143. Ibid., pp. 125–135.

144. San Miguel, Jr., "Let All of Them Take Heed," p. 217.

145. Carter, *Mexican Americans in School,* pp. 97–102; Thomas P. Carter, "The Negative Self-concept of Mexican-American Students," *School and Society* 96 (March 30, 1968): 217–220.

146. George I. Sanchez, "Bilingualism and Mental Measures, a Word of Caution," *Journal of Applied Psychology,* December 1934, pp. 767–769. See also Wollenberg, *All Deliberate Speed,* pp. 118–119; Ricardo Romo, "George I. Sanchez and the Civil Rights Movement: 1940–1960," *La Raza Law Journal,* 1 (Fall 1986): 342–362.

147. Jane Mercer, *Labelling the Mentally Retarded* (Berkeley, CA: University of California Press, 1973), pp. 96–189; U.S. Commission on Civil Rights, *Mexican American Education Study,* vol. 6, *Toward Quality Education for Mexican Americans* (Washington, DC, 1974), pp. 21–22.

148. Juan F. Perea, "Demography and Distrust: An Essay on American Languages, Cultural Pluralism, and Official English," *Minnesota Law Review* 77 (1992): 269.

149. Ibid.

150. See Kenji Hakuta and Eugene E. Garcia, "Bilingualism and Education," *American Psychologist* 44 (February 1989): 374–379; Dick Kirschten, "Speaking English," *National Review,* June 17, 1989, pp. 1556–1561; Manuel Ramirez and Alfredo Castaneda, *Cultural Democracy, Bicognitive Development, and Education* (New York: Academic Press, 1974); Guadalupe San Miguel, Jr., *Let*

All of Them Take Heed: Mexican Americans and the Campaign for Educational Equality in Texas, 1919–1981 (Austin: University of Texas Press, 1987).

151. U.S. Commission on Civil Rights, *Toward Quality Education for Mexican Americans*, pp. 6–8.

152. National Commission for Employment Policy, *Hispanics and Jobs: Barriers to Progress* (Washington, DC, 1982), pp. 60–62, 81–82; U.S. Bureau of the Census, *U.S. Census of Population, 1980: General Social and Economic Characteristics*, PC 80–1–C1 (Washington, DC, 1983), p. 163. The 1980 census was the last data set that reported median education level for the Mexican American population; Montgomery, "The Hispanic Population in the United States 1993," pp. 10–11.

153. Montgomery, "The Hispanic Population in the United States 1993," pp. 10–11.

154. Quoted in Beth Barrett, "College Disparity Costly: Mexican-Americans' Wage Gap Up, Study Says," *Daily News of Los Angeles*, May 27, 1997, p. N1.

155. Barbara Kantrowitz with Lourdes Rosado, "Falling Further Behind," *Newsweek*, August 19, 1991, p. 60; Maril, *Poorest of Americans*, pp. 117–118.

156. The research discussed in this and the following paragraph is reported in Harriett Romo and Toni Falbo, *Defying the Odds: Keeping Latino Youth in School* (Austin: University of Texas Press, 1995).

157. Ibid.

158. Concha Delgado-Gaitan and Henry Trueba, *Crossing Cultural Borders: Education for Immigrant Families in America* (Philadelphia, PA: The Falmer Press, 1991).

159. Catherine Walsh, *Pedagogy and the Struggle for Voice* (New York: Bergin and Garvey, 1991), pp. 95–113, quotation on p. 112.

160. Moore, *Mexican Americans*, pp. 67–69; Carter, *Mexican Americans in Schools*, pp. 30–31; National Commission for Employment Policy, *Hispanics and Jobs*, p. 11.

161. Edward H. Spicer, *Cycle of Conquest* (Tucson: University of Arizona Press, 1962), pp. 285–365; Patrick H. McNamara, "Bishops, Priests, and Prophecy: A Study in the Sociology of Religious Protest." (Ph.D. dissertation, UCLA, 1968.)

162. Moore, *Mexican Americans*, pp. 88–89.

163. Ibid., p. 91; Stoddard, *Mexican Americans*, p. 93; Grebler, Moore, and Guzmán, *The Mexican-American People*, pp. 459–460; Gómez-Quiñones, *Chicano Politics*, p. 179; "Latinos Shift Loyalties," *Christian Century*, April 6, 1994, p. 344.

164. Grebler, Moore, and Guzmán, *The Mexican-American People*, pp. 436–439, 473–477; Tuck, *Not with the Fist*, pp. 152–154. See also Jane M. Christian and Chester C. Christian, "Spanish Language and Loyalty in the Southwest," in *Language Loyalty in the United States*, ed. Joshua A. Fishman (London: Mouton, 1966), pp. 296–297.

165. Report by Allan F. Beck, as described in "Latinos Shift Loyalties," *Christian Century*, April 6, 1994, p. 344.

166. Jill Leovy, "More Hispanics Hear Call of Witnesses," *Seattle Times*, March 25, 1991, p. E1.

167. Jorge Casuso and Michael Hirsley, "Troubled Hispanics Find Haven within Strict Pentecostal Rules," *Chicago Tribune*, June 8, 1990, p. C1.

168. Tuck, *Not with the Fist*; Sanchez, *Forgotten People*; Madsen, *Mexican Americans of South Texas*; Grebler, Moore, and Guzmán, *The Mexican-American People*.

169. Edward Múrguía, *Assimilation, Colonialism, and the Mexican American People* (Austin: University of Texas Press, 1975), pp. 4–5.

170. Rodolfo Alvarez, "The Unique Psycho-historical Experience of the Mexican-American People," *Social Science Quarterly* 52 (June 1971): 15–29; Stoddard, *Mexican Americans*, p. 103; Benjamin S. Bradshaw and Frank Bean, "Trends in the Fertility of Mexican Americans, 1950–1970," *Social Science Quarterly* 53 (March 1973): 696–697.

171. Strategy Research Corporation, *1991 U.S. Hispanic Market*, pp. 107–108.

172. U.S. Bureau of the Census, *1990 Census of Population: Social and Economic Characteristics: Urbanized Areas*, CP-2–1C (Washington, DC, 1993), p. 2844.

173. Oliver, "Is American Culture Changing?" p. A1.

174. Strategy Research Corporation, *1991 U.S. Hispanic Market*, pp. 111–115.

175. Edward Múrguía, *Chicano Intermarriage: A Theoretical and Empirical Study* (San Antonio, TX: Trinity University Press, 1982), pp. 45–51; U.S. Department of Health, Education and Welfare, *Americans of Spanish Origin* (Washington, DC, 1984), p. 46.

176. Oliver, "Is American Culture Changing?" p. A1.

177. Linda Chávez, *Out of the Barrio: Toward a New Politics of Hispanic Assimilation* (New York: Basic Books, 1991).

178. Nathan Glazer, "The Political Distinctiveness of the Mexican Americans," in *Mexican-Americans in Comparative Perspective*, ed. Walter Connor (Washington, DC: Urban Institute, 1985), pp. 212–216.

179. Walter Connor, "Who Are the Mexican Americans? A Note on Comparability," in *Mexican-Americans in Comparative Perspective*, ed. Connor, pp. 4–28.

180. Grebler, Moore, and Guzmán, *The Mexican-American People*, pp. 385, 558; "Maintaining a Group Culture," *Institute for Survey Research Newsletter*, n.d., p. 8.

181. Peter Skerry, "Not Much Cooking," *Brookings Review*, June 22, 1993, p. 42.

182. Montejano, *Anglos and Mexicans in the Making of Texas, 1836–1986*.

183. Múrguía, *Assimilation, Colonialism, and the Mexican American People*, p. 112.

184. Strategy Research Corporation, *1991 U.S. Hispanic Market*, pp. 109–120. SRC's survey reported specific measures of assimilation by region; the majority of Latinos in the Southwest, West, and Central regions are Mexican American (89 percent, 72 percent, and 61 percent, respectively). In this survey, the Southwest region consisted of Texas, New Mexico, and Arizona; California and Colorado accounted for 93 percent of the Latinos in the eleven-state West region; 52 percent of the Latinos in the fourteen-state Central region resided in Illinois.

185. Ibid., pp. 78–120; Jim Loretta, "Latin Population Pressure Mounts," *Inside Strategy* 3, no. 2 (September 1990): 2.

186. Strategy Research Corporation, *1991 U.S. Hispanic Market*, pp. 80–94.

187. See Achy Obejas, "A Changing Nation: Shades of Future Seen in Census Report on Hispanics," *Chicago Tribune*, March 31, 1996, p. 1.

188. Rodolfo O. de la Garza, Nestor Rodríguez, and Harry Pachon, "The Domestic and Foreign Policy Consequences of Mexican and Central American Immigration: Mexican-American Perspectives," in *Immigration and International Relations*, ed. Georges Vernes (Santa Monica, CA: Rand Corporation, 1990), pp. 135–147.

189. Acuña, *Occupied America*, p. 3.

190. Alvarez, "Psycho-historical and Socioeconomic Development," pp. 928–930.
191. Múrguía, *Assimilation, Colonialism, and the Mexican American People*, pp. 8–9.
192. John U. Ogbu, *Minority Education and Caste* (New York: Academic Press, 1987), pp. 236–237; see also John Obgu, "Variability in Minority Responses to Schooling: Nonimmigrants vs. Immigrants," in *Interpretive Ethnography of Education*, eds. George Spindler and Louise Spinder (Hillsdale, NJ: Lawrence Erlbaum, 1987), pp. 255–275.
193. Barrera, *Race and Class in the Southwest*, p. 213.
194. Flores, "Race and Culture in the Internal Colony," p. 194.
195. Chandler Davidson and Charles M. Gaitz, "Ethnic Attitudes as a Basis for Minority Cooperation in a Southwestern Metropolis," *Social Science Quarterly* 53 (March 1973): 747–748.

CHAPTER 10

1. Enrique Fernandez, "Puerto Rican Independence: Is It a Dream?" *Newsday*, February 27, 1992, p. 94.
2. Daniel Adams, "Puerto Ricans Vote on Independence from U.S.," *The Independent*, December 9, 1991, p. 14.
3. U.S. Bureau of the Census, *The Hispanic Population in the United States: March 1993*, Current Population Reports P20–475 (Washington, DC, 1994), p. 11.
4. U.S. Bureau of the Census, *Statistical Abstract of the United States 1994* (Washington, DC, 1994), p. 832.
5. Manuel Maldonado-Denis, *Puerto Rico, A Socio-historic Interpretation*, trans. Elena Vialo (New York: Random House/Vintage Books, 1972), pp. 13–19; Luis Antonio Cardona, *A History of the Puerto Ricans in the U.S.A.* (Rockville, MD: Carreta Press, 1990), pp. 8–9; Eric Williams, *From Columbus to Castro: The History of the Caribbean 1492–1969* (London: André Deutsch: 1970), pp. 109, 291.
6. U.S. Commission on Civil Rights, *Puerto Ricans in the Continental United States: An Uncertain Future* (Washington, DC, 1976), pp. 11–12; Jorge Heine, "A People Apart," *Wilson Quarterly* 4, no. 2 (Spring 1980): 119–123.
7. Maldonado-Denis, *Puerto Rico*, p. 77.
8. U.S. Commission on Civil Rights, *Puerto Ricans in the Continental United States*, p. 12.
9. Maldonado-Denis, *Puerto Rico*, pp. 305–306; Heine, "A People Apart," p. 123.
10. Maldonado-Denis, *Puerto Rico*, pp. 311–312; Heine, "A People Apart," p. 125; Jaime Santiago, "One Step Forward," *Wilson Quarterly* 4, no. 2 (Spring 1980): 132–137; Frank Bonilla and Ricardo Campos, "A Wealth of Poor: Puerto Ricans in the New Economic Order," *Daedalus* 110 (Spring 1981): 135.
11. Piri Thomas, "Puerto Ricans in the Promised Land," *Civil Rights Digest* 6, no. 2 (n.d.): 19.
12. U.S. Bureau of the Census, *Statistical Abstract of the United States 1994*, Table 1342 (Washington, DC, 1994), p. 835.
13. Kristin S. Krause, "Post-incentive Puerto Rico; Island's Future as Manufacturing Center in Doubt as Congress Phases Out Income Tax Break," *Traffic World*, October 27, 1997, p. 20.
14. Adalberto Lopez, "The Puerto Rican Diaspora: A Survey," in *Puerto Rico and Puerto Ricans: Studies in History and Society*, eds. Adalberto Lopez and James Petras (New York: Wiley, 1974), p. 318; Clara E. Rodríguez, *Puerto Ricans: Born in the U.S.A.* (Boston, MA: Unwin Hyman, 1989), pp. 1–10.
15. Thomas, "Puerto Ricans in the Promised Land," p. 20.
16. Jack Agueros, "Halfway to Dick and Jane," in *The Immigrant Experience: The Anguish of Becoming American*, ed. Thomas C. Wheeler (New York: Dial Press, 1971), p. 93.
17. Rodríguez, *Puerto Ricans*, pp. 11–13.
18. Cardona, *A History of the Puerto Ricans in the U.S.A.*, pp. 95–96.
19. U.S. Commission on Civil Rights, *Puerto Ricans in the Continental United States*, p. 25; Rodríguez, *Puerto Ricans*, pp. 4–13; Cardona, *A History of the Puerto Ricans in the U.S.A.*, pp. 95–112; Felix M. Padilla, *Puerto Rican Chicago* (Notre Dame, IN: University of Notre Dame Press, 1987), pp. 66–72.
20. U.S. Commission on Civil Rights, *Puerto Ricans in the Continental United States*, pp. 19–25; Pedro A. Rivera, "Angel and Aurea," *Wilson Quarterly* 4, no. 2 (Spring 1980): 146–152; "The Spending Power of Puerto Ricans," *American Demographics*, April 1991, pp. 46–49; Rodríguez, *Puerto Ricans*, pp. 4–8, 28; correspondence with U.S. representative Jose Serrano's staff.
21. U.S. Bureau of the Census, *Hispanic Americans Today*, Current Population Reports, P23–183 (Washington, DC, 1993), pp. 3–4, 31.
22. Quoted in Frank Bonilla, "Beyond Survival: Porque Sequiremos Siendo Puertoriquenos," in *Puerto Rico and Puerto Ricans*, eds. Lopez and Petras, p. 439.
23. Alfredo Lopez, *The Puerto Rican Papers* (Indianapolis, IN: Bobbs-Merrill, 1973), p. 120.
24. Quoted in ibid., p. 211.
25. This pamphlet, entitled *What Is Prejudice?* is reprinted in *The Puerto Ricans: A Documentary History*, ed. Kal Wagenheim (Garden City, NY: Doubleday/Anchor Books, 1973), p. 291.
26. Migration Division, Department of Labor and Human Resources, Commonwealth of Puerto Rico, *Puerto Rican Voter Registration in New York City* (New York: Commonwealth of Puerto Rico, 1988), p. 9.
27. Nathan Glazer and Daniel P. Moynihan, *Beyond the Melting Pot* (Cambridge: M.I.T. Press and Harvard University Press, 1963), pp. 88–90.
28. Oscar Lewis, *La Vida* (New York: Random House, 1965).
29. Rose Marie Arce, "Crime, Drugs, and Stereotypes," *Newsday*, December 2, 1991, p. 5.
30. Mirta Ojito, "A Movement Is Born; New Britain Puerto Ricans React to Report Revealing Bias," *The New York Times*, June 28, 1997, p. 23.
31. Rodríguez, *Puerto Ricans*, pp. 51–56.
32. Piri Thomas, *Down These Mean Streets* (New York: Knopf, 1967), pp. 85–86.
33. Rodríguez, *Puerto Ricans*, pp. 56–59, 79.
34. Angel R. Martínez, "The Effects of Acculturation and Racial Identity on Self-Esteem and Psychological Well-Being among Young Puerto Ricans" (Ph.D. dissertation, City University of New York, 1988); cited in ibid., pp. 60–61.
35. Rodríguez, *Puerto Ricans*, pp. 61–68.
36. Jesús Colon, "The Early Days," in *The Puerto Ricans*, ed. Wagenheim, p. 286.
37. Thomas, *Down These Mean Streets*, pp. 102–104.
38. Rodríguez, *Puerto Ricans*, p. 2; U.S. Commission on Civil Rights, *Puerto Ricans in the Continental United States*, p. 54; Bonilla and Campos, "A Wealth of Poor," p. 158.
39. U.S. Bureau of the Census, *The Hispanic Population in the United States: March 1993*, pp. 12, 14.

40. Juan Gonzalez, "Puerto Ricans on the Mainland," *Perspectives* 13 (Winter 1982): 16; U.S. Commission on Civil Rights, *Puerto Ricans in the Continental United States,* p. 52; Bonilla and Campos, "A Wealth of Poor," p. 160.

41. U.S. Bureau of the Census, *The Hispanic Population in the United States: March 1993,* pp. 12, 14.

42. U.S. Commission on Civil Rights, *Puerto Ricans in the Continental United States,* pp. 59–62.

43. Western Regional Office, U.S. Commission on Civil Rights, *Puerto Ricans in California* (Washington, DC, 1980), p. 17.

44. Rodríguez, *Puerto Ricans,* pp. 92–93, quotation on p. 93. See also Herbert Hill, "Guardians of the Sweatshops: The Trade Unions, Racism, and the Garment Industry," in *Puerto Rico and Puerto Ricans,* eds. Lopez and Petras, pp. 386–388.

45. U.S. Commission on Civil Rights, *Puerto Ricans in the Continental United States,* p. 60; Vilma Ortiz, "Latinos and Industrial Change in New York and Los Angeles" (paper, 1990); Clara E. Rodríguez, "Economic Factors Affecting Puerto Ricans in New York," in *Labor Migration under Capitalism: The Puerto Rican Experience,* ed. History Task Force (New York: Center for Puerto Rican Studies, 1979), pp. 208–210; Rodríguez, *Puerto Ricans,* pp. 85–91.

46. Marta Tienda and William A. Diaz, "Puerto Ricans' Special Problems," *The New York Times,* August 28, 1987, p. A30; Marta Tienda and William Diaz, letter to *The New York Times,* October 10, 1987, p. A30.

47. Mercer L. Sullivan, "Puerto Ricans in Sunset Park, Brooklyn: Poverty Amidst Ethnic and Economic Diversity," in *In the Barrios,* eds. Joan Moore and Raquel Pinderhughes (New York: Russell Sage, 1993), pp. 1–25.

48. Felipe Luciano, "America Should Never Have Taught Us to Read, She Should Have Never Given Us Eyes to See," in *Puerto Rico and Puerto Ricans,* eds. Lopez and Petras, pp. 430–431.

49. Tienda and Diaz, "Puerto Ricans' Special Problems."

50. U.S. Bureau of the Census, *1990 Census of Population: Social and Economic Characteristics: United States Summary,* CP-2-1 (Washington, DC, 1993), pp. 135–136, 147.

51. U.S. Bureau of the Census, *The Hispanic Population in the United States: March 1993,* pp. 18–19.

52. Ibid., pp. 13, 15; Maria T. Padilla, "Hispanics Map Their Future," *Orlando Sentinel,* September 11, 1997, p. A1.

53. Agueros, "Halfway to Dick and Jane," pp. 96–102; Rivera, "Angel and Aurea," p. 148.

54. See Padilla, *Puerto Rican Chicago,* pp. 117–123.

55. U.S. Bureau of the Census, *The Hispanic Population in the United States: March 1993,* pp. 16–17.

56. Rodríguez, *Puerto Ricans,* pp. 106–116; quotation from pp. 109, 110.

57. Clay F. Richards, "Jobs Top Latinos' List of Concerns," *Newsday,* October 13, 1991, p. 27.

58. U.S. Bureau of the Census, *The Hispanic Population in the United States: March 1993,* pp. 10–11.

59. Rodríguez, *Puerto Ricans,* pp. 122–123, 127; George Borjas and Marta Tienda, eds. *Hispanics in the U.S. Economy* (New York: Academic Press, 1985), cited in Rodríguez, *Puerto Ricans,* p. 91.

60. Milga Morales-Nadal, "Puerto Rican/Latino(a) Vistas on Culture and Education" (paper, 1991), n.p.

61. Rodríguez, *Puerto Ricans,* pp. 139–140.

62. Ibid., pp. 122–123, 149–150.

63. Quoted in U.S. Commission on Civil Rights, *Puerto Ricans in the Continental United States,* p. 99.

64. Rodríguez, *Puerto Ricans,* pp. 126.

65. Henry A. Giroux, Series Introduction to Catherine E. Walsh, *Pedagogy and the Struggle for Voice* (New York: Bergin and Garvey, 1991), p. xx.

66. Quoted in U.S. Commission on Civil Rights, *Puerto Ricans in the Continental United States,* p. 103.

67. Rodríguez, *Puerto Ricans,* pp. 139–140.

68. Ibid., pp. 147–148; quotation from Gonzalez, "Puerto Ricans on the Mainland," p. 11.

69. Walsh, *Pedagogy and the Struggle for Voice,* pp. 101, 127.

70. Rusty Butler, *On Creating a Hispanic America: A Nation within a Nation?* (Washington, DC: Council for Interamerican Security, 1985), quoted in ibid., p. 100.

71. Walsh, *Pedagogy and the Struggle for Voice,* p. ix.

72. Ibid., pp. vii–xi, 1–27, 65–68, quotations from p. vii.

73. Migration Division, *Puerto Rican Voter Registration in New York City,* pp. 5–6.

74. Information provided by the Midwest–Northeast Voter Registration Education Project.

75. Garcia, letter to *The New York Times,* p. A34. In this section on politics and the following section on protest we draw on some insights provided by Maria Merrill-Ramirez in comments on this chapter.

76. Information provided by the Midwest–Northeast Voter Registration Education Project.

77. Ibid.

78. Lopez, "The Puerto Rican Diaspora," p. 329; Western Regional Office, U.S. Commission on Civil Rights, *Puerto Ricans in California,* p. 16.

79. Information provided by the Midwest–Northeast Voter Registration Education Project.

80. *Building a Road Towards Tomorrow,* Midwest–Northeast Voter Registration Education Project Newsbulletin (Chicago, 1991); David E. Pitt, "Puerto Rico Expands New York Voter Drive," *The New York Times,* October 14, 1987, p. A18; conversation with Carmen Ambert at the Department of Puerto Rican Community Affairs for the United States, New York City, December 23, 1991.

81. Lopez, *The Puerto Rican Papers,* pp. 55–58.

82. Bonilla and Campos, "A Wealth of Poor," pp. 166–167; Larry Rohter, "Puerto Rico Votes to Retain Status as Commonwealth," *The New York Times,* November 15, 1993, p. A1.

83. Ruben Berrios Martinez, "Puerto Rico's Decolonization," *Foreign Affairs,* November/December, 1997; "Puerto Rico Crosscurrents Likely to Wash over Florida," *Broward Daily Business Review,* March 21, 1997, p. A5.

84. Georgie Anne Geyer, "Puerto Rico Should Teach the Language That Binds," *Tulsa World,* September 5, 1997, p. A21.

85. Fitzpatrick, "Puerto Ricans," in *Harvard Encyclopedia of Ethnic Groups,* ed. Stephen Thernstrom (Cambridge, MA: Harvard University Press, 1981), p. 866; Padilla, *Puerto Rican Chicago,* pp. 54, 99–143.

86. John Adam Moreau, "My Parents, They Cry for Joy," in *The Puerto Ricans,* ed. Wagenheim, pp. 327–330.

87. Lopez, "The Puerto Rican Diaspora," p. 331.

88. Ibid., pp. 331–332.

89. Gonzalez, "Puerto Ricans on the Mainland," p. 17; Padilla, *Puerto Rican Chicago,* pp. 117–125; Steven A. Holmes, "Puerto Ricans' Alienation Is Cited in Miami Rampage," *The New York Times,* December 5, 1990, p. A24.

90. Lopez, "The Puerto Rican Diaspora," p. 332.
91. Joseph Torres, "Racism Mars Puerto Rican Parade," New America News Service, September 10, 1997.
92. Fitzpatrick, "Puerto Ricans," p. 865.
93. Paul Moses, "Church's Challenge," *Newsday*, October 14, 1991, p. 6.
94. Joseph P. Fitzpatrick, *Puerto Rican Americans: The Meaning of Migration to the Mainland* (Englewood Cliffs, NJ: Prentice Hall, 1971), pp. 22–43; Milton Gordon, *Assimilation in American Life* (New York: Oxford University Press, 1964), pp. 75–77; Elena Padilla, *Up from Puerto Rico* (New York: Columbia University Press, 1958); Walsh, *Pedagogy and the Struggle for Voice*, pp. 101–102.
95. Maldonado-Denis, *Puerto Rico*, p. 319.
96. Lloyd H. Rogler and Rosemary Santana Cooney, *Puerto Rican Families in New York City: Intergenerational Processes* (Maplewood, NJ: Waterfront Press, 1984), pp. 76–79; Strategy Research Corporation, *1991 U.S. Hispanic Market* (Miami, FL 1991), p. 78.
97. Fitzpatrick, *Puerto Rican Americans*, p. 43.
98. "Interview with Leonard Covello," *Urban Review*, 3 (January 1969): 53–61.
99. U.S. Commission on Civil Rights, *Puerto Ricans in the Continental United States*, p. 29; Rogler and Cooney, *Puerto Rican Families in New York City*, p. 204.
100. Rogler and Cooney, *Puerto Rican Families in New York City*, pp. 76–79.
101. Nancy Rivera Brooks, "Barbie's Online Critics See Guise in Dolls; Toys: Puerto Rican Incarnation Is at Center of Latest Mattel Brouhaha. First, the Hair . . . ," *Los Angeles Times*, November 21, 1997, p. D1.
102. See Lopez, "The Puerto Rican Diaspora," p. 343.
103. Bonilla and Campos, "A Wealth of Poor," p. 172.
104. Felix Robert Masud-Piloto, *With Open Arms: Cuban Migration to the U.S.* (Totowa, NJ: Rowman and Littlefield, 1988), pp. 7–11.
105. Ibid., pp. 11–16.
106. Ibid., pp. 13, 20.
107. Ibid., p. 11.
108. Ibid., pp. 20–35.
109. Ibid., pp. 1, 32–35, 39–41; "U.S. Hispanics: Who They Are, Whence They Came, and Why," in *The Hispanic Almanac* (Washington, DC: Hispanic Policy Development Project, 1984), pp. 17–18; Antonio Jorge and Raul Moncarz, *The Political Economy of Cubans in South Florida* (Miami, FL: Institute of Interamerican Studies, 1987), pp. 4, 18; Hugh Thomas, *Cuba: The Pursuit of Freedom* (New York: Harper & Row, 1971), p. 117; Silvia Pedraza-Bailey, "Cuba's Exiles: Portrait of a Refugee Migration," *International Migration Review* 19, no. 1 (Spring 1985): 9–11, 23; Silvia Pedraza, "Cubans in Exile (1959–1989): The State of the Research," *Scholarship on the Cuban Experience: A Dialogue Among Cubanists*, ed. Damian Fernandez (Gainesville: University of Florida, 1992).
110. Masud-Piloto, *With Open Arms*, pp. 1–5, 83–87.
111. Pedraza-Bailey, "Cuba's Exiles," pp. 15–17; Michael G. Wenk, "Adjustment and Assimilation: The Cuban Refugee Experience," *International Migration Review* 3, no. 1 (Fall 1968): 44, 48.
112. Pedraza-Bailey, "Cuba's Exiles," pp. 22–26; Masud-Piloto, *With Open Arms*, pp. 92–108.
113. Masud-Piloto, *With Open Arms*, pp. 83–87.
114. Tim Golden, "U.S.-Cuban Accord Sets Off a Surge of New Refugees," *The New York Times*, September 11, 1994, p. 1; "Prepared Statement of the Honorable Phylis E. Oakley, Assistant Secretary of State, Bureau of Population, Refugees and Migration, Before the Senate Committee on the Judiciary, Subcommittee on Immigration," Federal News Service, July 31, 1997.
115. U.S. Bureau of the Census, *The Hispanic Population in the United States: March 1993*, pp. 10–11.
116. Lisandro Perez, "Immigrant Economic Adjustment and Family Organization," *International Migration Review* 20, no. 1 (Spring 1986): 13.
117. "Trouble in Paradise," *Time*, November 23, 1981, pp. 24–32; Max J. Castro and Guillermo J. Grenier, "Black–Latino Relations under Conditions of Latino Empowerment: The Miami Case" (research proposal, Miami, 1991), pp. 3–4; Jeffrey Schmalz, "Miami Tensions Simmering 3 Months after Violence," *The New York Times*, April 10, 1989, p. A8; Holmes, "Puerto Ricans' Alienation Is Cited in Miami Rampage," p. A24.
118. Mike Clary, "Black, Cuban Racial Chasm Splits Miami," *Los Angeles Times*, March 23, 1997, p. A1.
119. "757 Haitians Cleared to Seek Refuge in U.S.," *The New York Times*, December 10, 1991, p. A8.
120. "A Million More Poor U.S. Hispanic Children in 1980s," *Reuter Library Report*, August 26, 1991.
121. Matt Spetalnick, "Florida Declares English Official Language," *Reuter Library Report*, November 9, 1988, n.p.
122. Neil A. Lewis, "Committee Rejects Bush Nominee to Key Appellate Court in South," *The New York Times*, April 12, 1991, pp. A1, A11.
123. Philip Shenon, "FBI Suspends Veteran Agent," *The New York Times*, March 5, 1990, p. A1.
124. Jorge and Moncarz, *The Political Economy of Cubans in South Florida*, pp. 16–19.
125. Ibid., p. 9.
126. Wenk, "Adjustment and Assimilation," pp. 39–42.
127. Lisandro Perez, "Immigrant Economic Adjustment and Family Organization: The Cuban Success Story Reexamined," *International Migration Review* 20, no. 1 (Spring 1986): 4–7; Silvia Pedraza-Bailey, "Cubans and Mexicans in the United States: The Functions of Political and Economic Migration," *Cuban Studies* 11, no. 2/12, no. 1 (July 1981–January 1982); Alejandro Portes and Robert L. Bach, *Latin American Journey* (Berkeley, CA: University of California Press, 1985), pp. 200–220.
128. Perez, "Immigrant Economic Adjustment and Family Organization," pp. 4–20, quotation on p. 18.
129. U.S. Bureau of the Census, *The Hispanic Population in the United States: March 1993*, pp. 10–11.
130. Ibid., pp. 18–19.
131. Ibid., pp. 13, 15.
132. Quoted in "Widespread Political Efforts Open New Era for Hispanics," *Congressional Quarterly*, October 23, 1982, p. 2709.
133. Jorge and Moncarz, *The Political Economy of Cubans in South Florida*, p. 30; Masud-Piloto, *With Open Arms*, p. 16.
134. Information provided by the Midwest–Northeast Voter Registration Education Project; Clary, "Black, Cuban Racial Chasm Splits Miami."
135. See Samuel P. Huntington, "The Erosion of American National Interests," *Foreign Affairs*, September/October, 1997, p. 28.
136. Richard Boudreaus, "Cuba Strikes Democracy Movement," *Los Angeles Times*, January 19, 1992, p. A1; Deborah Sharp, "Execution in Cuba," *USA Today*, January 22, 1992, p. 3A.

137. Peter Kornbluh and Jon Elliston, "Will Congress Kill TV Marti?" *Nation*, August 22/29, 1994, pp. 194–196.

138. Donald P. Baker, "Thousands Mourn Death of Anti-Castro Leader; Some Cuban American Moderates Look for an Easing of Mas Canosa's Hard-Line," *Washington Post*, November 26, 1997, p. A3.

139. "Protesters Disrupt 'Peace for Cuba' Rally," *Los Angeles Times*, January 26, 1992, p. A5; Arun Gupta, "5,000 Oppose Crunching Cuba at N.Y. Rally," *Guardian*, February 5, 1992, p. 13.

140. Jon Nordheimer, "Where Old Havana Plays," *The New York Times*, April 3, 1991, p. C1.

141. Deborah Sontag, "The Lasting Exile of Cuban Spirits," *The New York Times*, September 11, 1994, section 4, p. 1.

142. Portes and Bach, *Latin American Journey*, pp. 91–93, 193–199.

143. Ibid., pp. 246–247.

144. "Trouble in Paradise," pp. 30–31.

145. Data in this and the following paragraph are from Strategy Research Corporation, *1991 U.S. Hispanic Market*, pp. 78–130.

146. Matea Gold, "Cultural Celebration Sways to a Cuban Beat; Heritage: About 20,000 Attend L.A.'s Third Annual Cuban American Festival of Art, Music, and Food in Echo Park," *Los Angeles Times*, May 19, 1997, p. B1.

147. Private communication with Maria Merril-Ramirez, July 1982.

CHAPTER 11

1. Yen Le Espiritu, *Asian American Panethnicity: Bridging Institutions and Identities* (Philadelphia, PA: Temple University Press, 1992).

2. U.S. Bureau of the Census, *U.S. Census of Population, 1980: Asian and Pacific Islander Population in the United States*, PC80-2–1E (Washington, DC, 1988), p. 1; U.S. Bureau of the Census, *1990 Census of Population: Social and Economic Characteristics: United States*, CP-2–1 (Washington, DC, 1993), pp. 105–106.

3. U.S. Commission on Civil Rights, *Civil Rights Issues Facing Asian Americans in the 1990s*, p. 15; Robert Daniels, *Coming to America* (New York: HarperCollins, 1990), p. 350.

4. Kathryn Tolbert, "Pacific Grim," *Boston Globe Sunday Magazine*, March 29, 1992, p. 14.

5. Ronald Takaki, *Strangers from a Different Shore: A History of Asian Americans* (New York: Penguin, 1989), p. 7.

6. Alan T. Moriyama, *Imingaisha: Japanese Immigration Companies and Hawaii, 1894–1908* (Honolulu: University of Hawaii Press, 1985); Wayne Patterson, *The Korean Frontier in America: Immigration to Hawaii, 1896–1910* (Honolulu: University of Hawaii Press, 1988).

7. Roger Daniels, *The Politics of Prejudice* (New York: Atheneum, 1969), pp. 3–6; Hilary Conroy, *The Japanese Frontier in Hawaii, 1868–1898* (Berkeley, CA: University of California Press, 1953), passim; Moriyama, *Imingaisha*, pp. xvi–xix.

8. Takaki, *Strangers from a Different Shore*, p. 179.

9. U.S. Immigration and Naturalization Service, *1975 Annual Report* (Washington, DC, 1975), pp. 62–66.

10. Arinori Mori, *The Japanese in America* (Japan Advertiser Press, 1926), pp. 19–21; Kaizo Naka, *Social and Economic Conditions among Japanese Farmers in California* (San Francisco: R & E Research Associates, 1974), p. 6; John Modell, "On Being an Issei:

11. Sucheng Chan, *Asian Americans: An Interpretive History* (Boston, MA: Twayne, 1991), pp. 103–117; Roger Daniels, *Asian America: Chinese and Japanese in the United States Since 1850* (Seattle: University of Washington Press, 1988), pp. 100–154.

12. Jacobus tenBroek, Edward N. Barnhart, and Floyd W. Matson, *Prejudice, War, and the Constitution* (Berkeley, CA: University of California Press, 1968), pp. 42–43; *Takao Ozawa v. United States*, 260 U.S. 178 (1922); Takaki, *Strangers from a Distant Shore*, pp. 14–15.

13. Hillary Conroy and T. Scott Miyakawa, "Foreword," in *East across the Pacific*, eds. Conroy and Miyakawa, pp. xiv–xv.

14. The statistics are from U.S. Census Bureau publications.

15. Takaki, *Strangers from a Different Shore*, pp. 479–481.

16. E. Manchester-Boddy, *Japanese in America* (San Francisco: R & E Research Associates, 1970), pp. 25–30.

17. V. S. McClatchy, *Japanese Immigration and Colonization*, reprint ed. (San Francisco: R & E Research Associates, 1970), p. 42.

18. Quoted in Edward K. Strong, Jr., *The Second-Generation Japanese Problem* (Stanford, CA: Stanford University Press, 1934), p. 133.

19. tenBroek, Barnhart, and Matson, *Prejudice, War, and the Constitution*, p. 31.

20. Dennis M. Ogawa, *From Japs to Japanese* (Berkeley: McCutchan, 1971), p. 12; Carey McWilliams, *Brothers Under the Skin*, rev. eds. (Boston, MA: Little, Brown, 1964), pp. 148–149; Stanley Sue and Harry H. L. Kitano, "Stereotypes as a Measure of Success," *Journal of Social Issues* 29 (1973): 83–98.

21. C. N. Reynolds, "Oriental–White Race Relations in Santa Clara County, California" (Ph.D. dissertation, Stanford University, 1927); E. S. Bogardus, "Social Distance: A Measuring Stick," *Survey* 56 (1927); 169–171. Both are cited in Strong, *The Second-Generation Japanese Problem*, pp. 109, 128.

22. tenBroek, Barnhart, and Matson, *Prejudice, War, and the Constitution*, pp. 66–70.

23. Quoted in Ogawa, *From Japs to Japanese*, p. 11.

24. U.S. Department of the Interior, War Relocation Authority, *Myths and Facts about the Japanese American* (Washington, DC, 1945), pp. 7–8; Ogawa, *From Japs to Japanese*, pp. 35–54. Survey data document attitude changes in the period 1942–1961. See also Roger Daniels, "Why It Happened Here," in *The Social Reality of Ethnic America*, eds. R. Gomez et al. (Lexington, MA: D. C. Heath, 1971), p. 236.

25. Council on Interracial Books for Children, *Stereotypes, Distortions and Omissions in U.S. History Textbooks* (New York: Racism and Sexism Resource Center for Educators, 1977), pp. 42–46.

26. Letta Tayler, "Dateline: Washington," States News Service, May 8, 1987, n.p.; Takaki, *Strangers from a Different Shore*, p. 6.

27. Karl Taro Greenfield, "Return of the Yellow Peril," *Nation*, May 11, 1992, p. 636; Michael Crichton, *Rising Sun* (New York: Knopf, 1991).

28. Steven A. Chin, "KFRC Deejay Draws Suspension for On-Air Derogatory Remarks," *San Francisco Examiner*, December 6, 1994, p. A2.

29. Herbert B. Johnson, *Discrimination against the Japanese in California* (Berkeley, CA: Courier, 1907), pp. 73–74;

Daniels, *The Politics of Prejudice*, pp. 33–34; Howard H. Sugimoto, "The Vancouver Riots of 1907: A Canadian Episode," in *East across the Pacific*, eds. Conroy and Miyakawa, pp. 92–110.

30. Jean Pajus, *The Real Japanese California* (San Francisco: R & E Research Associates, 1971), pp. 164–166; Daniels, *The Politics of Prejudice*, p. 87; tenBroek, Barnhart, and Matson, *Prejudice, War, and the Constitution*, p. 73.

31. Lemuel F. Ignacio, *Asian Americans and Pacific Islanders* (San Jose, CA: Pilipino Development Associates, 1976), pp. 95–96; tenBroek, Barnhart, and Matson, *Prejudice, War, and the Constitution*, passim.

32. Dorothy Swaine Thomas and Richard S. Nishimoto, *The Spoilage* (Berkeley, CA: University of California Press, 1946), pp. 5–10; tenBroek, Barnhart, and Matson, *Prejudice, War, and the Constitution*, pp. 82–84.

33. Thomas and Nishimoto, *The Spoilage*, pp. 8–16; tenBroek, Barnhart, and Matson, *Prejudice, War, and the Constitution*, pp. 118–120.

34. tenBroek, Barnhart, and Matson, *Prejudice, War, and the Constitution*, pp. 120, 126–129, 130; Thomas and Nishimoto, *The Spoilage*, pp. 10–20; Edward H. Spicer et al., *Impounded People* (Tucson: University of Arizona Press, 1969), pp. 141–241.

35. Richard Drinnon, *Keeper of Concentration Camps* (Berkeley, CA: University of California Press, 1987), pp. 47, 153; quotation from Valerie Matsumoto, "Japanese American Women during World War II," in *Unequal Sisters*, eds. Ellen C. DuBois and Vicki L. Ruiz (New York: Routledge, 1990), p. 373.

36. Thomas and Nishimoto, *The Spoilage*, pp. 54–71; tenBroek, Barnhart, and Matson, *Prejudice, War, and the Constitution*, pp. 126–132, 149–155; Spicer et al., *Impounded People*, pp. 252–280.

37. Leonard Bloom and Ruth Riemer, *Removal and Return* (Berkeley; University of California Press, 1949), pp. 124–157, 198–204; tenBroek, Barnhart, and Matson, *Prejudice, War, and the Constitution*, pp. 155–177, 180–181.

38. Bradford Smith, *Americans from Japan* (New York; Lippincott, 1948), pp. 10–12, 202–276; Carey McWilliams, *Prejudice* (Boston; Little, Brown, 1944), p. 4; tenBroek, Barnhart, and Matson, *Prejudice, War, and the Constitution*, pp. 211–223; Harry H. L. Kitano, *Japanese Americans*, 2nd ed. (Englewood Cliffs, NJ: Prentice Hall, 1976), pp. 82–88; S. Frank Miyamoto, "The Forced Evacuation of the Japanese Minority during World War II," *Journal of Social Issues* 29 (1973): 11–29.

39. Drinnon, *Keeper of Concentration Camps*, pp. 255–256. See also Christopher Thorne, *Allies of a Kind* (New York: Oxford University Press, 1978).

40. Kitano, *Japanese Americans*, p. 73.

41. Gary Y. Okihiro, "Japanese Resistance in America's Concentration Camps: A Re-evaluation," *Amerasia Journal* 2 (Fall 1973): 20–34; Arthur A. Hansen and David A. Hacker, "The Manzanar Riot: An Ethnic Perspective," *Amerasia Journal* 3 (Fall 1974): 112–142. See also Roger Daniels, *Concentration Camps, U.S.A.* (New York: Holt, Rinehart & Winston, 1971).

42. See *Intelligence Report*, March 1994, pp. 17–29; *Intelligence Report*, October 1994, pp. 9–14.

43. Daniels, *The Politics of Prejudice*, pp. 104–105.

44. Ivan H. Light, *Ethnic Enterprise in America* (Berkeley, CA: University of California Press, 1972), pp. 174–179; Bill Hosokawa, *The Nisei* (New York: Morrow, 1969), pp. 199–200; Kitano, *Japanese Americans*, pp. 55–58.

45. Hosokawa, *The Nisei*, pp. 439–446; Kitano, *Japanese Americans*, pp. 89–90.

46. Nathaniel C. Nash, "House Votes Payments to Japanese Americans," *The New York Times*, September 18, 1987, p. A15.

47. Ken Miller, "U.S. Pays Japanese Internees $20,000—and Apologies," Gannett News Service, October 9, 1990, n.p.

48. Santiago O'Donnell and Psyche Pascual, "Kato Slaying Raises Fears of Hate Crime," *Los Angeles Times*, March 1, 1992, p. B1.

49. Rodolfo Acuña, *Occupied America* (San Francisco: Canfield Press, 1972), pp. 212–213.

50. Kitano, *Japanese Americans*, pp. 174–186; Daniel Inouye and Lawrence Elliot, *Journey to Washington* (Englewood Cliffs, NJ: Prentice Hall, 1967), pp. 248–250; Hosokawa, *The Nisei*, pp. 460–469.

51. Hosokawa, *The Nisei*, pp. 486–487.

52. Stanley Karnow, "Apathetic Asian Americans?" *Washington Post*, November 29, 1992, p. C1.

53. "Slur Stirs Party In-fighting," *Commercial Appeal*, May 4, 1994, p. 5A.

54. Sonni Effron, "Politics Are Changing for Asian Americans," *Los Angeles Times*, August 16, 1990, p. A3.

55. Rob Gurwitt, "Have Asian Americans Arrived Politically? Not Quite," *Governing*, November 1990, p. 38.

56. U.S. Commission on Civil Rights, *Recent Activities against Citizens and Residents of Asian Descent* (Washington, DC, 1986), pp. 3–6.

57. Kenneth Walsh, Gloria Borger, Susan Dentzer, and Carla A. Robbins, "The 'America First' Fallacies," *U.S. News & World Report*, February 3, 1992, p. 22.

58. O'Donnell and Pascual, "Kato Slaying Raises Fears of Hate Crime," p. B1.

59. Daniels, *The Politics of Prejudice*, pp. 23–24.

60. Yuji Ichioka, "A Buried Past," *Amerasia Journal* 1 (July 1971): 1–25; Karl Yoneda, "100 Years of Japanese Labor History in the U.S.A.," in *Roots*, eds. Amy Tachiki et al. (Los Angeles, CA: UCLA Asian American Studies Center, 1971), pp. 150–157; Takaki, *Strangers from a Different Shore*, p. 200.

61. See the various articles in *Roots*, ed. Tachiki et al.

62. Russell Endo and William Wei, "On the Development of Asian American Studies Programs," in *Reflections on Shattered Windows*, eds. Gary Y. Okihiro et al. (Pullman: Washington State University Press, 1988), pp. 6–12.

63. "Prepared Testimony of Karen Narasaki, Executive Director, National Asian Pacific American Legal Consortium, Before the House Judiciary Committee," Subcommittee on the Constitution, Subcommittee Hearing on H.R. 1909: The Civil Rights Act of 1997, Federal News Service, June 26, 1997; Randal C. Archibold, "UC Irvine Expected to Offer Asian Studies Major; Education: On a Campus Where More Than Half the Students Are of Asian Background, Absence of Such a Program Has Been a Concern and a Topic of Protests," *Los Angeles Times*, May 13, 1997, p. A3.

64. Cited in Sidney L. Gulick, *The American Japanese Problem* (New York: Scribner's, 1914), p. 11.

65. Japanese Association of the Pacific Northwest, *Japanese Immigration* (San Francisco: R & E Research Associates, 1972), pp. 22–25; Daniels, *The Politics of Prejudice*, pp. 7, 10–12.

66. Edna Bonacich and John Modell, *The Economic Basis of Ethnic Solidarity* (Berkeley, CA: University of California Press, 1980), pp. 38–47.

67. Kitano, *Japanese Americans*, pp. 19–21; Light, *Ethnic Enterprise in America*, pp. 27–29; S. Frank Miyamoto, "An Immigrant Community in America," in *East across the Pacific*, eds. Conroy and Miyakawa, pp. 223–225.

68. Gulick, *The American Japanese Problem*, pp. 11, 32–33; Light, *Ethnic Enterprise in America*, p. 71; Roger Daniels, "Japanese Immigrants on the Western Frontier: The Issei in California, 1890–1940," in *East across the Pacific*, eds. Hilary Conroy and T. Scott Miyakawa (Santa Barbara, CA: ABC-CLIO, 1972), p. 85.

69. Pajus, *The Real Japanese California*, pp. 147–151; Light, *Ethnic Enterprise in America*, p. 76.

70. Bloom and Riemer, *Removal and Return*, pp. 115–117; Strong, *The Second-Generation Japanese Problem*, pp. 209–211.

71. Bloom and Riemer, *Removal and Return*, pp. 17–20.

72. Evelyn Nakano Glenn, "The Dialectics of Wage Work: Japanese American Women and Domestic Service, 1905–1940," in *Unequal Sisters*, eds. DuBois and Ruiz, p. 345.

73. Ibid., p. 369.

74. Bloom and Riemer, *Removal and Return*, pp. 44, 144.

75. Bonacich and Modell, *The Economic Basis of Ethnic Solidarity*, pp. 256–259.

76. U.S. Bureau of the Census, *1990 Census of Population: Social and Economic Characteristics: United States*, CP-2-1 (Washington, DC, 1993), pp. 44, 45, 111, 115.

77. Ibid., pp. 48, 49, 105–106, 117, 119; U.S. Bureau of the Census, *1990 Census of Population: Social and Economic Characteristics: California*, CP-2-6 (Washington, DC, 1993), pp. 186, 252, 256, 286.

78. U.S. Commission on Civil Rights, *Success of Asian Americans: Fact or Fiction?* (Washington, DC, 1980), pp. 14–15.

79. Harry H. L. Kitano and Roger Daniels, *Asian Americans: Emerging Minorities* (Englewood Cliffs, NJ: Prentice Hall, 1988), p. 171.

80. Winfred Yu, "Asian Americans Charge Prejudice Slows Climb to Management Ranks," *Wall Street Journal*, September 11, 1985, n.p., quoted in Takaki, *Strangers from a Different Shore*, p. 476.

81. Takaki, *Strangers from a Different Shore*, pp. 475–477.

82. Art Pine, "Marines Pin Bars on Man They Dismissed," *Los Angeles Times*, March 19, 1994, p. A4; Judy Tachibana, "Triumph over Racism in the Marines," *Sacramento Bee*, April 20, 1994, p. B3.

83. K. K. Kawakami, *The Japanese Question* (New York: Macmillan, 1921), pp. 143–145; John Modell, "Tradition and Opportunity: The Japanese Immigrant in America," *Pacific Historical Review* 40 (May 1971): 163–182.

84. Johnson, *Discrimination against the Japanese in California*, pp. 3–20, 40–47; Franklin Hichborn, *The Story of the Session of the California Legislature of 1909* (San Francisco: James H. Barry Press, 1909), p. 207; Pajus, *The Real Japanese California*, pp. 170–178; Kawakami, *The Japanese Question*, pp. 168–169.

85. Pajus, *The Real Japanese California*, pp. 180–181; Kawakami, *The Japanese Question*, pp. 162–163.

86. William Petersen, *Japanese Americans* (New York: Random House, 1971), p. 183; Strong, *The Second-Generation Japanese Problem*, pp. 201–204; Kawakami, *The Japanese Question*, pp. 146–151; Pajus, *The Real Japanese California*, p. 181.

87. Pajus, *The Real Japanese California*, p. 183; Strong, *The Second-Generation Japanese Problem*, pp. 185–188.

88. U.S. Department of Health, Education and Welfare, *A Study of Selected Socio-economic Characteristics of Ethnic Minorities Based on the 1970 Census* (Washington, DC, 1974), pp. 70–72; U.S. Commission on Civil Rights, *Social Indicators of Equality for Minorities and Women* (Washington, DC, 1978), pp. 12–14; U.S. Bureau of the Census, *U.S. Census of Population, 1980: General Social and Economic Characteristics*, PC80–1–C1 (Washington, DC, 1983), p. 157.

89. U.S. Bureau of the Census, *1990 Census of Population: Social and Economic Characteristics: United States*, pp. 42, 107.

90. Kitano, *Japanese Americans*, pp. 93, 174–175; U.S. Commission on Civil Rights, *Social Indicators of Equality for Minorities and Women*, pp. 24–26; U.S. Bureau of the Census, *1990 Census of Population: Social and Economic Characteristics: California*, pp. 181, 246.

91. Manchester-Boddy, *Japanese in America*, p. 118.

92. Petersen, *Japanese Americans*, p. 177; Manchester-Boddy, *Japanese in America*, pp. 114–118.

93. Strong, *The Second-Generation Japanese Problem*, p. 229; Shotaro Frank Miyamoto, "Social Solidarity among the Japanese in Seattle," *University of Washington Publications in Social Sciences* 11 (December 1939): 99–102; Petersen, *Japanese Americans*, pp. 174–75.

94. Andrew W. Lind, *Hawaii's Japanese* (Princeton, NJ: Princeton University Press, 1946), pp. 212–257; Petersen, *Japanese Americans*, pp. 177–178, 185.

95. Hosokawa, *The Nisei*, p. 131; Kitano, *Japanese Americans*, p. 115; Christie Kiefer, *Changing Cultures, Changing Lives* (San Francisco: Jossey-Bass, 1974), pp. 34–38; Petersen, *Japanese Americans*, p. 187.

96. John Dart, "Military Opens Chaplain Ranks to Buddhists," *Los Angeles Times*, October 27, 1987, p. 1.

97. Modell, "On Being an Issei," pp. 1–2, 19–20.

98. John Modell, "The Japanese American Family: A Perspective for Future Investigations," *Pacific Historical Review* 37 (February 1968): 79; Joe R. Feagin and Nancy Fujitaki, "On the Assimilation of Japanese Americans," *Amerasia Journal* 1 (February 1972): 15–17; Abe Arkoff, "Need Patterns in Two Generations of Japanese Americans in Hawaii," *Journal of Social Psychology* 50 (1959): 75–79; Kitano and Daniels, *Asian Americans*, p. 179.

99. Peter Y. Hong, "Japanese American Newspaper's Layoffs Anger Community," *Los Angeles Times*, November 15, 1997, p. B1.

100. Petersen, *Japanese Americans*, pp. 6–7; Light, *Ethnic Enterprise in America*, passim; William Caudill, "Japanese American Personality and Acculturation," *Genetic Psychology Monographs* 45 (1952): 3–102; Kitano and Daniels, *Asian Americans*, p. 179.

101. Paul Spickard, *Mixed Blood* (Madison: University of Wisconsin Press, 1988), p. 347.

102. David J. O'Brien and Stephen S. Fugita, "Generational Differences in Japanese Americans' Perceptions and Feelings about Social Relationships between Themselves and Caucasian Americans," in *Culture, Ethnicity, and Identity*, ed. William McCready (New York: Academic Press, 1983), pp. 235–236.

103. Darrel Montero, *Japanese Americans: Changing Patterns of Ethnic Affiliation over Three Generations* (Boulder, CO: Westview Press, 1980), p. 80; Petersen, *Japanese Americans*, pp. 220–224; Modell, "The Japanese American Family," pp. 76–79; Kitano, *Japanese Americans*, pp. 189, 196; George Kagiwada, "Assimilation of Nisei in Los Angeles," in *East Across the Pacific*, eds. Conroy and Miyakawa, p. 273.

104. Feagin and Fujitaki, "On the Assimilation of Japanese Americans," p. 23.

105. Akemi Kikumura and Harry H. L. Kitano, "Interracial Marriage: A Picture of Japanese Americans," *Journal of Social Issues* 29 (1973): 67–81; John N. Tinker, "Intermarriage and Ethnic Boundaries: The Japanese American Case," *Journal of Social Issues* 29 (1973): 55; John W. Connor, *Tradition and Change in Three Generations of Japanese Americans* (Chicago: Nelson-Hall, 1977), p. 308; Gene N. Levine and Colbert Rhodes, *The Japanese American Community* (New York: Praeger, 1981), p. 145.

106. Sharon M. Lee and Keiko Yamanaka, "Intermarriage in the Asian American Population" (typescript, Cornell University, 1987); Kitano and Daniels, *Asian Americans*, pp. 176–178.

107. O'Brien and Fugita, "Generational Differences," pp. 231–235. See also Connor, *Tradition and Change in Three Generations of Japanese Americans*, pp. 304–308.

108. Kitano and Daniels, *Asian Americans*, pp. 191–192.

109. Petersen, *Japanese Americans*, pp. 214–221.

110. Greg Mayeda, "Japanese Americans Don't Lose Identity," *The New York Times*, December 28, 1995, p. A20.

111. Edna Bonacich, "United States Capitalist Development: A Background to Asian Immigration," in *Labor Immigration under Capitalism*, eds. Lucie Cheng and Edna Bonacich (Berkeley, CA: University of California Press, 1984), p. 82.

112. *U.S. v. Bhagat Singh Thind*, 261 U.S. 215 (1923).

113. For a list of media presentations, see Takaki, *Strangers from a Different Shore*, p. 474.

114. This section draws on Robert Blauner, *Racial Oppression in America* (New York: Harper & Row, 1972), pp. 54–55; Paul Takagi, "The Myth of 'Assimilation in American Life,'" *Amerasia Journal* 2 (Fall 1973): 149–158; Peter Uhlenberg, "Demographic Correlates of Group Achievement: Contrasting Patterns of Mexican-Americans and Japanese-Americans," *Demography* 9 (February 1972): 119–128.

115. B. Suzuki, "Education and the Socialization of Asian Americans," in *Asian Americans: Social and Psychological Perspectives*, eds. R. Endo, S. Sue, and N. Wagner (Palo Alto, CA: Science & Behavior Books, 1980), 2:155–178; William Petersen, "Success Story, Japanese-American Style," *The New York Times*, January 9, 1966, p. 21; "Success Story of One Minority Group in the U.S.," *U.S. News & World Report*, December 26, 1966, pp. 73–76; Thomas Sowell, Ethnic America (New York: Basic Books, 1981).

116. Amado Cabezas and Gary Kawaguchi, "Empirical Evidence for Continuing Asian American Inequality: The Human Capital Model and Labor Market Segmentation," in *Reflections on Shattered Windows*, ed. Okihiro et al.

117. Studies cited in Amado Cabezas, "Testimony to U.S. Commission on Civil Rights," in *Civil Rights Issues of Asian and Pacific Americans*, pp. 389–393. See also Takaki, *Strangers from a Different Shore*, p. 475.

118. Takagi, "The Myth of 'Assimilation in American Life,'" pp. 149–158; Ogawa, *From Jap to Japanese*, pp. 43ff.

119. Brad Knickerbocker, "U.S. Japanese Retain Cultural Ties," *Christian Science Monitor*, July 27, 1993, p. 11.

120. See the comments of a Japanese American woman in Miranda Ewell, "Japanese American Still Trying to Find a Way to Belong in U.S.; Asians Have Achieved Measurable Success but Continue to Face a Complex Racial and Ethnic Landscape," *Orange County Register*, August 19, 1996, p. A10.

121. U.S. Commission on Civil Rights, *Success of Asian Americans*, p. 21.

122. David Mura, "Whites: How to Face the Angry Racial Tribes," *Utne Reader*, July/August 1992, p. 80. See also David Mura, *Turning Japanese: Memoirs of a Sansei* (New York: Atlantic Monthly Press, 1991).

123. Charles Burress, "Looking to Hawaii for Harmony: Japanese American Panel Wants a Model for the New California," *San Francisco Chronicle*, October 21, 1997, p. A17.

CHAPTER 12

1. Elaine H. Kim, "They Armed in Self-Defense," *Newsweek*, May 18, 1992, p. 10.

2. Ibid.

3. Data provided by Statistics Division, U.S. Immigration and Naturalization Service, 1994.

4. Ronald Takaki, *A Different Mirror* (Boston, MA: Little, Brown, 1993), pp. 211–214; Roger Daniels, *Asian America: Chinese and Japanese in the United States Since 1850* (Seattle: University of Washington Press, 1988), pp. 16–17, 44; Bill Ong Hing, *Making and Remaking Asian America Through Immigration Policy: 1850–1990* (Stanford, CA: Stanford University Press, 1993), p. 23, 48–49, 80.

5. U.S. Commission on Civil Rights, *Recent Activities against Citizens and Residents of Asian Descent* (Washington, DC, 1986), p. 7.

6. Immigration and Naturalization Service, *1985 Statistical Yearbook*, pp. 2–5; Ronald Takaki, *Strangers from a Different Shore: A History of Asian Americans* (Boston, MA: Little, Brown, 1989), pp. 111–112.

7. U.S. Commission on Civil Rights, *Recent Activities against Citizens and Residents of Asian Descent*, p. 8.

8. U.S. Commission on Civil Rights, *The Tarnished Golden Door: Civil Rights Issues in Immigration* (Washington, DC, 1980), p. 10.

9. Immigration and Naturalization Service, *1985 Statistical Yearbook*, pp. 2–5; U.S. Bureau of the Census, *1990 Census of Population: Social and Economic Characteristics: United States Summary*, CP-2–1 (Washington, DC, 1993), p. 105.

10. U.S. Bureau of the Census, *1990 Census of Population: Asians and Pacific Islanders in the United States*, CP-3–5 (Washington, DC, 1993), pp. 5–6.

11. Stephan Thernstrom, ed., *Harvard Encyclopedia of American Ethnic Groups* (Cambridge, MA: Harvard University Press, 1981), pp. 357–359.

12. U.S. Commission on Civil Rights, *Recent Activities against Citizens and Residents of Asian Descent*, p. 9.

13. Vanessa Ho, "Filipinos' American Dream Comes True," *Seattle Times*, April 29, 1992, p. B1.

14. *Harvard Encyclopedia of American Ethnic Groups*, ed. Thernstrom, p. 359.

15. Tim Schreiner, "Philippine Brain Drain," *American Demographics* 8 (December 1986): 14.

16. U.S. Bureau of the Census, *1990 Census of Population: Asians and Pacific Islanders in the United States*, p. 10.

17. Frank Viviano, "Asian Population Booming in U.S.," *San Francisco Chronicle*, February 27, 1991, p. A7; L. A. Chung, "State's Asian Americans Push for Unity," *San Francisco Chronicle*, May 7, 1992, p. A1.

18. Wayne Patterson, *The Korean Frontier in America: Immigration to Hawaii, 1896–1910* (Honolulu: University of Hawaii Press, 1988), p. 177; Takaki, *Strangers from a Different Shore*, pp. 270–271; U.S. Commission on Civil Rights, *Recent Activities against Citizens and Residents of Asian Descent*, p. 9.

19. Warren Y. Kim, *Koreans in America* (Seoul: Po Chin Chai Printing Co., 1971), pp. 22–25.
20. Takaki, *Strangers from a Different Shore*, pp. 365–366.
21. David M. Reimers, *Still the Golden Door: The Third World Comes to America* (New York: Columbia University Press, 1985), pp. 110–111; data from the U.S. Immigration and Naturalization Service, 1994.
22. U.S. Bureau of the Census, *1990 Census of Population: Asians and Pacific Islanders in the United States*, p. 14.
23. Darrel Montero, *Vietnamese Americans: Patterns of Resettlement and Socioeconomic Adaptation in the United States* (Boulder, CO: Westview Press, 1979), pp. 1–3.
24. Morrison G. Wong and Charles Hirschman, "The New Asian Immigrants," in *Culture, Ethnicity, and Identity*, ed. William C. McCready (New York: Academic Press, 1983), p. 381.
25. U.S. Bureau of the Census, *1990 Census of Population: Asians and Pacific Islanders in the United States*, p. 15; U.S. Bureau of the Census, *1990 Census of Population: General Population Characteristics: United States Summary*, CP-1–1 (Washington, DC, 1992), p. 259; U.S. Bureau of the Census, *1990 Census of Population: General Population Characteristics: California*, CP-1–6 (Washington, DC, 1992), p. 29.
26. Data from the U.S. Immigration and Naturalization Service, 1995.
27. This paragraph draws on research of Arun Jain, as cited in Marcia Mogelonsky, "Asian-Indian Americans," *American Demographics*, August 1995, p. 36.
28. U.S. Bureau of the Census, *1990 Census of Population: Asians and Pacific Islanders in the United States*, p. 13; U.S. Bureau of the Census, *1990 Census of Population: General Population Characteristics: United States Summary*, CP-1–1 (Washington, DC, 1992), p. 259; U.S. Bureau of the Census, *1990 Census of Population: General Population Characteristics: Urbanized Areas*, CP-1–1C (Washington, DC, 1992), pp. 87, 188.
29. Harry H. L. Kitano and Roger Daniels, *Asian Americans: Emerging Minorities* (Englewood Cliffs, N. J.: Prentice Hall, 1988), p. 176.
30. Quoted in K. Connie Kang, "Building Bridges to Equality," *Los Angeles Times*, January 7, 1995, p. A1.
31. Cited in Mike Dorsher, "Speech Decries Asian American Stereotypes," *Wisconsin State Journal*, March 4, 1994, p. D1.
32. Quoted in "Prepared Testimony of Karen Narasaki, Executive Director, National Asian Pacific American Legal Consortium Before the House Judiciary Committee, Subcommittee on the Constitution," Subcommittee Hearing on H.R. 1909: The Civil Rights Act of 1997, Federal News Service, June 26, 1997.
33. Quoted in Takaki, *Strangers from a Different Shore*, p. 370.
34. Miriam Sharma, "Labor Migration and Class Formation among the Filipinos in Hawaii, 1940–1946," in *Labor Immigration under Capitalism*, eds. Lucie Cheng and Edna Bonacich (Berkeley, CA: University of California Press, 1984), pp. 583, 593.
35. Montero, *Vietnamese Americans*, pp. 3–4.
36. Paul Sweeney, "Tolerance in a Texas Town," *Texas Observer*, September 17, 1982, pp. 7–9.
37. Steve Emmons and David Reyes, "Gangs, Crime Top Fears of Vietnamese in Orange County," *Los Angeles Times*, February 5, 1989, p. 3.
38. Sonni Efron, " 'Saigon' Is Under Fire Once More," *Los Angeles Times*, September 7, 1990, p. F1.

39. Center for Integration and Improvement of Journalism, *News Watch: A Critical Look at Coverage of People of Color* (San Francisco: San Francisco State University, 1994), pp. 40–43.
40. Steven Rosenfeld, Liane Hansen, "Asian Americans," NPR Weekend Sunday, November 23, 1997; Andrea Stone and Robert Silvers, "Asian Americans See Rising Racism," *USA Today*, July 15, 1997, p. 8A.
41. "Daphne Kwok, Organization of Chinese Americans, and John O'Sullivan, *National Review*, Discuss Recent Cover Story for That Magazine That Asian Americans Are Saying Is Offensive and Racist," NBC News Transcripts, March 21, 1997; Mae M. Cheng, "Magazine Cover Ripped; Coalition Calls *National Review* Illustration Racist," *Newsday*, April 11, 1997, p. A4.
42. U.S. Commission on Civil Rights, *Civil Rights Issues Facing Asian Americans in the 1990s*, pp. 5–6; U.S. Commission on Civil Rights, *Recent Activities against Citizens and Residents of Asian Descent*, pp. 3–6.
43. U.S. Department of Justice, "Criminal Justice Information Services Uniform Crime Reports," press release for June 1994; Lena H. Sun, "Anti-Asian American Incidents Rising, Civil Rights Group Says; Organization Executives to Meet With Reno Today," *Washington Post*, September 9, 1997, p. A2; "Prepared Testimony of Karen Narasaki," Federal News Service, June 26, 1997.
44. U.S. Commission on Civil Rights, *Civil Rights Issues Facing Asian Americans in the 1990s*, pp. 22–48.
45. Information provided by Sergeant Flynn of the Boston Police Department, February 1995.
46. David Reyes, "Coalition Urges More Prosecutions of Hate Crimes," *Los Angeles Times*, September 9, 1994, p. B1; Mara Rose Williams, "Asian Americans Say Police Are Biased," *Atlanta Journal and Constitution*, September 9, 1994, p. C5; Sandy Coleman, "A Place to Turn for Victims of Hate," *Boston Globe*, June 26, 1994, p. 1.
47. U.S. Commission on Civil Rights, *Civil Rights Issues Facing Asian Americans in the 1990s*, pp. 49–69, quotation from p. 52.
48. Mimi Ko, "Forum to Examine Police Harassment," *Los Angeles Times*, June 11, 1994, p. B2.
49. U.S. Commission on Civil Rights, *Civil Rights Issues Facing Asian Americans in the 1990s*, pp. 5–6; U.S. Commission on Civil Rights, *Recent Activities against Citizens and Residents of Asian Descent*, pp. 3–6.
50. Ann Bancroft, "Jury Gets Racist Firebombings Case in Sacramento," *San Francisco Chronicle*, August 25, 1994, p. A20.
51. U.S. Commission on Civil Rights, *Recent Activities against Citizens and Residents of Asian Descent*, pp. 43–44; U.S. Commission on Civil Rights, *Civil Rights Issues Facing Asian Americans in the 1990s*, pp. 25–26; quotation from p. 28.
52. U.S. Commission on Civil Rights, *Civil Rights Issues Facing Asian Americans in the 1990s*, pp. 25–26.
53. Ibid., pp. 26–28, quotation from p. 28.
54. Julie Chao, "Berkeley students claim bias in D.C.; Asian Americans Offended by Guards," *San Francisco Examiner*, September 30, 1997, p. A1.
55. Howard A. DeWitt, *Anti-Filipino Movements in California: A History, Bibliography and Study Guide* (San Francisco: R & E Research Associates, 1976), pp. 27–66.
56. David Ibata, "Asians Seek Spot in America's Melting Pot," *Chicago Tribune*, April 26, 1992, p. 1.

57. Moon H. Jo, "Korean Merchants in the Black Community: Prejudice Among the Victims of Prejudice," *Ethnic and Racial Studies* 15 (1992): 395–411; Robert L. Bach, *Changing Relations: Newcomers and Established Residents in U.S. Communities* (New York: Ford Foundation, 1993).

58. U.S. Commission on Civil Rights, *Civil Rights Issues Facing Asian Americans in the 1990s*, pp. 34–40; Greg Krikorian, "Grocer Says He's Sorry," *Los Angeles Times*, December 20, 1991, p. B3.

59. Andrea Ford, "Slain Girl Was Not Stealing Juice, Police Say," *Los Angeles Times*, March 19, 1991, p. B1; Itabari Njeri, "Perspectives on Race Relations," *Los Angeles Times*, November 29, 1991, p. B5; Mike Davis, "In L.A., Burning All Illusions," *Nation* 254, no. 21 (June 1, 1992): 743–746.

60. Quoted in Njeri, "Perspectives on Race Relations," p. B5.

61. Davis, "In L.A., Burning All Illusions," p. 745.

62. Quoted in ibid., p. 746.

63. Kim, "They Armed in Self-Defense," p. 10.

64. Ku-Sup Chin, "New Immigrants, Industrial Flexibility, and Ethnic Conflicts: Korean and Hispanic Immigrants in the Los Angeles Garment Industry." (Paper presented at the American Sociological Association meetings, August 1994.)

65. U.S. Commission on Civil Rights, *Recent Activities against Citizens and Residents of Asian Descent*, pp. 50–52; Sweeney, "Tolerance in a Texas Town," pp. 7–10.

66. Michael McCabe, "U.S. Leaders Urged to Fight Hate Crimes," *San Francisco Chronicle*, February 29, 1992, p. A1.

67. Jonathan Schuppe and Aditi Kinkhabwala, "Education a Family Affair; Asian Indians Work Hard for Success in Classroom," *Asbury Park Press* (Neptune, NJ.), August 17, 1997, p. 27A.

68. Arlene Newman, "Festival Reflects Indians' Growth," *The New York Times*, August 18, 1991, sec. 12NJ, p. 1; Joel Kotkin, "Asian Indians in California Spotlight after Years in Shadows," *Washington Post*, May 6, 1990, p. H2.

69. Tim Schreiner, "Asians, Hispanics Upset about Reapportionment Boundaries," *San Francisco Chronicle*, December 4, 1991, p. A18.

70. U.S. Commission on Civil Rights, *Civil Rights Issues Facing Asian Americans in the 1990s*, pp.157–163.

71. Daniels, *Asian America*, p. 113.

72. Yen Le Espiritu, *Asian American Panethnicity* (Philadelphia; Temple University Press, 1992), pp. 19–49.

73. Lisa Lowe, "Heterogeneity, Hybridity, Multiplicity: Marking Asian American Differences," *Diaspora* 1 (1991): 31.

74. Espiritu, *Asian American Panethnicity*, pp. 47–49.

75. Ibid., 50–51.

76. Paul Sweeney, "Asian Americans Gain Clout," *American Demographics* 8 (February 1986): 18–19.

77. Kang, "Building Bridges to Equality."

78. Frank Wu, "Asian Americans Finally Organize the NCAPA," New America News Service, November 27, 1997.

79. Carla Rivera, "Orange County Focus," *Los Angeles Times*, April 28, 1992, p. B3; K. Connie Kang, "Korean Groups Back Union Fight for Jobs," *Los Angeles Times*, November 17, 1994, p. B1.

80. Peter Kwong, *Chinatown, N.Y.: Labor and Politics, 1930–1950* (New York: Monthly Review Press, 1979), pp. 45–67.

81. Judy Yung, "The Social Awakening of Chinese American Women," in *Unequal Sisters*, eds. Ellen Carol DuBois and Vicki L. Ruiz (New York: Routledge, 1990), p. 196.

82. Martin F. Nolan, "California Confronts the Politics of Growth," *Boston Globe*, October 23, 1991, p. 1.

83. Kitano and Daniels, *Asian Americans*, p. 49.

84. Nicholas Lemann, "Growing Pains," *Atlantic Monthly*, January 1988, pp. 57–62.

85. Frank Wu, "What Do Chinese Americans Think of China?" New America News Service, October 30, 1997.

86. John Gregory Dunne, *Delano: The Story of the California Grape Strike* (New York: Farrar, Straus & Giroux, 1967), p. 77.

87. Lemuel F. Ignacio, *Asian Americans and Pacific Islanders* (San Jose, CA: Pilipino Development Associates, 1976), pp. 11–56; Kitano and Daniels, *Asian Americans*, p. 86.

88. Michelle Mizal, "Filipino Americans Hope to Build Unity; Group also Hopes to Build Political Clout at D.C. Event," *Virginian-Pilot* (Norfolk, VA), August 21, 1997, p. B1.

89. James T. Madore, "Long-quiet Asian Group Starts to Mobilize," *Christian Science Monitor*, May 20, 1988, p. 7; "Filipino Americans Protest S.F. Memorial," United Press International, March 31, 1997.

90. Bong-youn Choy, *Koreans in America* (Chicago: Nelson-Hall, 1979), pp. 141–189.

91. Quoted in Greg La Motte, "Asian Americans: A Diverse Voting Block," Cable News Network, June 1, 1992, transcript no. 76–5.

92. Julie Ha, "Korean American Political Power," New America News Service, March 18, 1997.

93. "Korean Americans Send 100,000 Dollars in Aid to North Korea," Agence France Presse, April 3, 1997.

94. Steve Emmons and David Reyes, "The Orange County Poll," *Los Angeles Times*, February 5, 1989, p. 1.

95. Ibid.

96. Quyen Do, "Little Saigon Readies for Community Balloting; Vietnamese Americans Will Elect Their Unofficial Leaders," *Orange County Register*, January 13, 1996, p. B1.

97. Joel Kotkin, "Asian Indians in California Spotlight after Years in Shadows," *Washington Post*, May 6, 1990, p. H2.

98. Arlene Newman, "Festival Reflects Indians' Growth," *The New York Times*, August 18, 1991, sec. 12NJ, p. 1; Vindu P. Goel, "The Rise of Asian Indians," *Plain Dealer*, July 28, 1996, p. 8.

99. Norimitsu Onishi, "Merging Identity: New Sense of Race Arises Among Asian-Americans," *The New York Times*, May 30, 1996, p. A1.

100. U.S. Commission on Civil Rights, *Civil Rights Issues Facing Asian Americans in the 1990s*, pp. 131–136, 145–148.

101. Paul Ong, ed., *Economic Diversity: Issues and Policies* (Los Angeles: Leadership Education for Asian Pacifics, 1994); E. J. Park, "Asian Americans in Silicon Valley: Race and Ethnicity in the Postindustrial Economy," Unpublished doctoral dissertation, University of California, Berkeley, Department of Ethnic Studies, 1992; Cliff Cheng, "Are Asian American Employees a Model Minority or Just a Minority?" *Journal of Applied Behavioral Science*, 33, no. 3 (September 1997): 277–290.

102. U.S. Commission on Civil Rights, *Civil Rights Issues Facing Asian Americans in the 1990s*, pp. 131–136, 153–156, quotation from pp. 155–156.
103. Ibid., pp. 136–148.
104. *Harvard Encyclopedia of American Ethnic Groups*, ed. Thernstrom, pp. 218–220.
105. Takaki, *Strangers from a Different Shore*, pp. 374–375.
106. Reimers, *Still the Golden Door*, p. 107.
107. Ibid.
108. U.S. Bureau of the Census, *1990 Census of Population: Social and Economic Characteristics: United States Summary*, p. 45; U.S. Bureau of the Census, *1990 Census of Population: Asians and Pacific Islanders in the United States*, p. 111.
109. U.S. Bureau of the Census, *1990 Census of Population: Social and Economic Characteristics: United States Summary*, pp. 44, 111–112.
110. Roger Daniels, *Coming to America* (New York: HarperCollins, 1990), p. 355.
111. U.S. Bureau of the Census, *1990 Census of Population: Social and Economic Characteristics: United States Summary*, CP-2–1 (Washington, DC, 1993), pp. 48, 117; U.S. Bureau of the Census, *1990 Census of Population: Asians and Pacific Islanders in the United States*, p. 146.
112. U.S. Bureau of the Census, *1990 Census of Population: Asians and Pacific Islanders in the United States*, pp. 76, 111, 146.
113. Sharma, "Labor Migration and Class Formation among the Filipinos in Hawaii, 1906–1946," p. 589.
114. Takaki, *Strangers from a Different Shore*, pp. 322–323, quotation from p. 323.
115. Steve Lohr, "Filipinos Flocking to the U.S. as Manila's Troubles Grow," *The New York Times*, June 6, 1985, p. A14.
116. Amado Cabezas, Larry Hajime Shinagawa, and Gary Kawaguchi, "New Inquiries into the Socioeconomic Status of Pilipino Americans in California," *Amerasia Journal* 13 (1986–87): 3–7.
117. U.S. Bureau of the Census, *1990 Census of Population: Social and Economic Characteristics: United States Summary*, pp. 48, 111, 117; U.S. Bureau of the Census, *1990 Census of Population: Asians and Pacific Islanders in the United States*, p. 146.
118. United Press International, March 30, 1988.
119. Irene Chang, "Ruling on Foreign Language Ban Criticized," *Los Angeles Times*, October 26, 1991, p. B3.
120. Choy, *Koreans in America*, pp. 123–133.
121. U.S. Bureau of the Census, *1990 Census of Population: Social and Economic Characteristics: United States Summary*, pp. 47, 113; U.S. Bureau of the Census, *1990 Census of the Population: Social and Economic Characteristics: Urbanized Areas*, CP-2–1C (Washington, DC, 1993), p. 4759.
122. Takaki, *Strangers from a Different Shore*, pp. 441–444; Reimers, *Still the Golden Door*, pp. 111–112; Ivan Light, "Immigrant Entrepreneurs in America: Koreans in Los Angeles," in *Clamor at the Gates*, ed. Nathan Glazer (San Francisco: ICS Press, 1985), p. 162.
123. "Korean Americans Adjust to Life in Korea," New America News Service, February 3, 1997.
124. Takaki, *Strangers from a Different Shore*, pp. 441–442.
125. Ivan Light and Edna Bonacich, *Immigrant Entrepreneurs* (Berkeley, CA: University of California Press, 1988).
126. Survey by Eui-Young Yu, cited in MacFarquhar, "Fighting over the Dream," p. 34.
127. Keith Bradsher, "Flight From a Los Angeles Hotbed; Five Years After Riots, Exodus of Korean Americans Continues," *International Herald Tribune*, January 7, 1997, p. 7.
128. U.S. Bureau of the Census, *1990 Census of Population: Social and Economic Characteristics: United States Summary*, pp. 44, 48, 111, 117, 119.
129. Montero, *Vietnamese Americans*, p. 39.
130. "Prepared Testimony of Karen Narasaki," Federal News Service, June 26, 1997.
131. Dennis McLellan, "Writer Urges the U.S. to See 'A Hidden Treasure of Talents,'" *Los Angeles Times*, February 7, 1992, p. E3; Efron, "Few Viet Exiles Find U.S. Riches," p. A1.
132. U.S. Bureau of the Census, *1990 Census of Population: Social and Economic Characteristics: United States Summary*, pp. 44, 48, 112, 119.
133. "Asian, Indian Firms Growing," *Omaha World Herald*, August 5, 1996, p. 13.
134. U.S. Bureau of the Census, *1990 Census of Population: Social and Economic Characteristics: United States Summary*, pp. 107, 115, 117, 119.
135. "Prepared Testimony of Karen Narasaki," Federal News Service, June 26, 1997.
136. U.S. Commission on Civil Rights, *Civil Rights Issues Facing Asian Americans in the 1990s*, pp. 68–99.
137. Somini Sengupta, "Not All Asian Americans Prospering, Study Reports; Students' Academic Success Obscuring Needs," *Dallas Morning News*, November 14, 1997, p. 44A.
138. Laurie Olsen, *Crossing the Schoolhouse Border: Immigrant Students and the California Public Schools* (San Francisco: California Tomorrow, 1988), p. 90; see also p. 34.
139. U.S. Bureau of the Census, *Statistical Abstract of the United States 1994* (Washington, DC, 1994), pp. 49, 157.
140. U.S. Bureau of the Census, *1990 Census of Population: Social and Economic Characteristics: United States Summary*, pp. 44, 107–108.
141. Efron, "Few Viet Exiles Find U.S. Riches," p. A1.
142. Schuppe and Kinkhabwala, "Education a Family Affair."
143. Quoted in Melita Marie Garza, "Asians Feel Bias Built on Perceptions," *Chicago Tribune*, August 7, 1994, p. C1.
144. Eloise Salholz et al., "Do Colleges Set Asian Quotas?" *Newsweek*, February 9, 1987, p. 60.
145. U.S. Commission on Civil Rights, *Civil Rights Issues Facing Asian Americans in the 1990s*, pp. 109–112.
146. Ibid., pp. 120–129.
147. Madore, "Long-Quiet Asian Group Starts to Mobilize," p. 7.
148. Ronald Takaki, "Is Race Surmountable? Thomas Sowell's Celebration of Japanese-American 'Success,'" in *Ethnicity and the Work Force*, ed. Winston A. Van Horne (Madison: University of Wisconsin Press, 1985), pp. 218–220.
149. Senate Judiciary Committee, "Capitol Hill Hearings," September 20, 1991; "Prepared Testimony of Karen Narasaki," Federal News Service, June 26, 1997.
150. Takaki, *Strangers from a Different Shore*, p. 473; Marcia "Asian-Indian Americans," pp. 32–38.
151. Kitano and Daniels, *Asian Americans*, pp. 190–192.
152. Takaki, *Strangers from a Different Shore*, p. 473.
153. Emmons and Reyes, "Gangs, Crime Top Fears of Vietnamese in Orange County," p. 3.
154. Alden E. Roberts and Paul D. Starr, "Differential Reference Group Assimilation among Vietnamese

Refugees," in *Refugees as Immigrants: Cambodians, Laotians, and Vietnamese in America*, ed. David W. Haines (Totowa, NJ: Rowman & Littlefield, 1989), p. 51.

155. Emmons and Reyes, "The Orange County Poll," p. 1.

156. Daniels, *Coming to America*, p. 367.

157. Reimers, *Still the Golden Door*, p. 111.

158. Karen Pyke, "'The Normal American Family' as an Interpretive Structure of Family Life among Adult Children of Korean and Vietnamese Immigrants," unpublished paper, Gainesville, University of Florida, 1997.

159. Takaki, *Strangers from a Different Shore*, p. 473.

160. John Dillin, "More Blacks Enter Middle Class," *Christian Science Monitor*, August 9, 1991, p. 7.

161. Nazli Kibria, "The Construction of 'Asian American': Reflections on Intermarriage and Ethnic Identity among Second-Generation Chinese and Korean Americans," *Ethnic and Racial Studies*, 20 (July 1997): 523–544.

162. B. Suzuki, "Education and the Socialization of Asian Americans," in *Asian Americans: Social and Psychological Perspectives*, eds. R. Endo, S. Sue, and N. Wagner (Palo Alto, CA: Science & Behavior Books, 1980), 2:155–178.

163. Ishmael Reed, "America's Color Bind: The Modeling of Minorities," *San Francisco Examiner*, November 19, 1987, p. A20; "Success Story of One Minority Group in the U.S.," *U.S. News & World Report*, December 26, 1966, pp. 73–76.

164. Min Zhou, "Growing Up American: The Challenge Confronting Immigrant Children and Children of Immigrants," *Annual Review of Sociology* 23 (1997): 63–95.

165. Gloria Luz R. Martinez and Wayne J. Villemez, "Assimilation in the United States: Occupational Attainment of Asian Americans, 1980" (paper presented at the American Sociological Association meetings, Chicago, 1987), pp. 31–32.

166. U.S. Commission on Civil Rights, *Civil Rights Issues Facing Asian Americans in the 1990s*, pp. 103–136.

167. Wendy Lin, "Asians, Latinos Rip Voting Plan," *Newsday*, May 29, 1992, p. 4.

168. Kwang Chung Kim and Won Moo Hurh, "Korean Americans and the 'Success' Image: A Critique," *Amerasia* 10 (Fall/Winter 1983): 15.

169. Daniels, *Coming to America*, pp. 388–389.

170. Nathan Glazer, "Introduction," in *Clamor at the Gates*, ed. Nathan Glazer, p. 3.

CHAPTER 13

1. S. H. Murdock, *An America Challenged: Population Change and the Future of the United States* (Boulder, CO: Westview, 1995), pp. 33–47.

2. Quoted in Clarence Page, "U.S. Media Should Stop Abetting Intolerance," *Toronto Star*, December 27, 1991, p. A27.

3. Arthur Schlesinger, *The Disuniting of America: Reflections on a Multicultural Society* (New York: Norton, 1991), pp. 13, 124–125.

4. U.S. Bureau of the Census, *1990 Census of Population: Social and Economic Characteristics: United States*, CP-2–1 (Washington, DC, 1993), p. 166; U.S. Bureau of the Census, *Hispanic Americans Today*, Current Population Reports P23–183 (Washington, DC, 1993), p. 4; U.S. Bureau of the Census, *We the American Blacks* (Washington, DC, 1993), p. 2.

5. U.S. Bureau of the Census, *We the American Asians* (Washington, DC, 1993), p. 2.

6. Andrew Piatt, "The Crux of the Immigration Question," *North American Review*, 199 (June 1914): 866, quoted in Rita J. Simon and Susan H. Alexander, *The Ambivalent Welcome: Print Media, Public Opinion, and Immigration* (Westport, CT: Praeger, 1993), p. 59.

7. Wendy Lin, "Stakes Are High in Lottery for U.S. Green Cards," *Newsday*, October 13, 1991, p. 19.

8. Bruce W. Nelan, "Not Quite So Welcome Anymore," *Time*, Special Issue, Fall 1993, pp. 10–12.

9. Cited in Shawn Foster, "Immigrants: Blessing or Curse for Utah?" *Salt Lake Tribune*, November 10, 1994, p. A1.

10. See David Cole, "Five Myths about Immigration," *Nation*, October 7, 1994, p. 410.

11. Josh Friedman, "Experts Tell of Boom among Immigrants," *Newsday*, November 3, 1994, p. A34.

12. Quoted in Keith Henderson, "Immigration as an Economic Engine," *Christian Science Monitor*, March 27, 1992, p. 9. See also Ben Wattenberg, *The First Universal Nation* (New York: Free Press, 1990).

13. U.S. Bureau of the Census, *1990 Census of Population: Ancestry of the Population in the United States*, CP-3–2 (Washington, DC, 1990), pp. 307, 409.

14. Israel Zangwill, *The Melting Pot* (New York: Macmillan, 1925), p. 33.

15. Milton M. Gordon, *Assimilation in American Life* (New York: Oxford University Press, 1964), pp. 72–73.

16. Terry Lefton, "Building Bridges in the Big Apple," *Teaching Tolerance* 1, no. 1 (Spring 1992): 8–13; Ralph Blumenthal, "Black Youth Is Killed by Whites; Brooklyn Attack Is Called Racial," *The New York Times*, August 25, 1989, p. A1.

17. Quoted in Njeri, "Beyond the Melting Pot," p. E1.

18. Arthur Schlesinger, Jr., "Speaking Up: A Look at Noteworthy Addresses in the Southland," *Los Angeles Times*, February 7, 1992, p. B2.

19. Ibid. See also Arthur Schlesinger, Jr., *The Disuniting of America: Reflections on a Multicultural Society* (New York: W. W. Norton, 1991).

20. Dinesh D'Souza, *Illiberal Education* (New York: Random House/Vintage Books, 1991), p. 13.

21. Nathan Glazer, *We are All Multiculturalists Now* (Cambridge, MA: Harvard University Press, 1997).

22. Quoted in Njeri, "Beyond the Melting Pot," p. E1.

23. Henry Louis Gates, Jr., "Whose Canon Is It Anyway?" in *Debating P.C.*, ed. Paul Berman (New York: Bantam, 1992), pp. 190–191.

24. Ted Gordon and Wahneema Lubiano, "The Statement of the Black Faculty Caucus," in *Debating P.C.*, ed. Berman, p. 251.

25. Ibid., pp. 251–253.

26. LaDonna Harris, "Rediscovering Native Americans," *Forum*, Spring 1992, p. 8.

27. Robert J. Samuelson, "The Loathing of Japan," *Washington Post*, February 19, 1992, p. A19.

28. "Asian-Americans: Growing Racism; Major New Report Warns against the Vile Danger," *Los Angeles Times*, March 3, 1992, p. B6.

29. Quoted in Reynolds Holding, "Panel of Judges, Lawyers Chided for Courts' Toleration of Racism," *San Francisco Chronicle*, May 9, 1992, p. A15.

30. Scott Rothschild and Debra Beachy, "Insurance Bias Probe Requested," *Houston Chronicle*, February 14, 1992, p. 1.

31. Reuben Blades, "The Politics behind the Latino's Legacy," *The New York Times*, April 19, 1992, sec. 2, p. 31;

Fair Housing Council of Fresno County, "Audit Uncovers Blatant Discrimination against Hispanics, African Americans, and Families with Children in Fresno County," press release, October 6, 1995.

32. Stephen Steinberg, *Turning Back: The Retreat from Racial Justice in American Thought and Policy* (Boston, MA: Beacon, 1995), p. 136.

33. M. A. Turner, M. Fix, and R. J. Struyk, *Opportunities Denied: Discrimination in Hiring*, Urban Institute Report 91–9, Washington, D.C., August 1991.

34. Larry Bobo and S. A. Suh, "Surveying Racial Discrimination: Analyses from a Multiethnic Labor Market," unpublished research report, Department of Sociology, University of California, Los Angeles, 1995.

35. Gallup, *Black/White Relations in the United States* (Princeton, NJ: The Gallup Organization, 1997), pp. 29–30, 108–110.

36. Joe R. Feagin and Melvin P. Sikes, *Living with Racism* (Boston, MA: Beacon, 1994).

37. See Tom Mathews et al., "Fire and Fury," *Newsweek*, May 11, 1992, pp. 30–37.

38. William H. Frey, "Immigration, Domestic Migration, and Demographic Balkanization in America: New Evidence from the 1990s," *Population and Development Review* 22 (December 1996): 741–763.

39. Ibid.; see also William H. Frey, "Immigrant and Native Migrant Magnets," *American Demographics* (November 1996), pp. 1–4.

40. William H. Frey, "The New White Flight," *American Demographics* (April 1994), pp. 1–6.

41. William H. Frey, "Immigration, Domestic Migration, and Demographic Balkanization in America: New Evidence from the 1990s," *Population and Development Review* 22 (December 1996), p. 758.

42. See Joe R. Feagin, "The Future of U.S. Society in an Era of Racism, Group Segregation, and Demographic Revolution," paper presented to International Sociology Association conference on The Heritage and Future of Sociology, Toronto, Canada, August 1997.

CHAPTER 14

1. Peter Turnley, et. al., "Graceland," *Newsweek*, May 9, 1994, pp. 30–33.

2. Russell Watson, et. al., "Black Power!," *Newsweek*, May 9, 1994, pp. 34–39.

3. Ibid.

4. Paul Taylor, "In New South Africa, Pace of Change Has Race Tensions Simmering," *Washington Post*, July 21, 1994, p. A20.

5. Ibid.

6. F. Scott Fitzgerald, *The Great Gatsby* (New York: Penguin Books, 1983), p. 19.

7. Edward Said, *Orientalism* (New York: Random House/Vintage Books, 1978); "Orientalism Reconsidered," *Race and Class* 27 (1985): 1–15; *Covering Islam: How the Media and the Experts Determine How We See the Rest of the World* (New York: Pantheon Books, 1981); *Culture and Imperialism* (New York: Knopf, 1993).

8. For a fuller discussion of issues raised in this chapter, see Pinar Batur-VanderLippe, *Broken Mirrors: Colonialism and Identity Formation* (forthcoming).

9. Etienne Balibar, *Masses, Classes, Ideas: Studies on Politics and Philosophy Before and After Marx*, trans. James Swanson (New York: Routledge, 1994), p. 200.

10. Zia Sardar, Ashis Nandy, and Merryl Wyn Davies, *Barbaric Others: A Manifesto on Western Racism* (London: Pluto Press, 1993), pp. 8–9.

11. Oliver C. Cox, *Caste, Class and Race: A Study in Social Dynamics* (Garden City, NY: Doubleday, 1948), pp. 331–332.

12. Ibid., p. 334.

13. Albert Memmi, *The Colonizer and the Colonized* (New York: Orion Press, 1965).

14. Ronald Takaki, *Iron Cages* (New York: Oxford University Press, 1990), p. 12.

15. Joseph Arthur de Gobineau, *Selected Political Writings*, ed. M. D. Biddiss (New York: Harper & Row, 1970), p. 136.

16. Tadeusz Swietochowski, *Russian Azerbaijan, 1905–1920: The Shaping of National Identity in a Muslim Community* (Cambridge: Cambridge University Press, 1985), p. 17.

17. Pinar Batur-VanderLippe, *Broken Mirrors*.

18. Frantz Fanon, "The Pitfalls of National Consciousness" and "On National Culture," in *The Wretched of the Earth*, trans. Constance Farrington (New York: Grove Press, 1963); Anthony Brewer, *Marxist Theories of Imperialism* (New York: Routledge, 1986).

19. Albert Memmi, *The Pillar of Salt* (Boston, MA: Beacon Press, 1992), p. 331.

20. Pinar Batur-VanderLippe, *Broken Mirrors*.

21. Leonard Thompson, *A History of South Africa* (New Haven, CT: Yale University Press, 1990); Nigel Worden, *The Making of Modern South Africa: Conquest, Segregation and Apartheid* (Oxford: Blackwell, 1994), Basil Davidson, *Africa in History* (New York: Collier Books, 1991); Roland Oliver and Anthony Atmore, *Africa Since 1800*, 3rd ed. (Cambridge: Cambridge University Press, 1989); Joseph Harris, *Africans and Their History* (New York: Mentor, 1987).

22. Leonard Thompson, *Political Mythology of Apartheid* (New Haven, CT: Yale University Press, 1985), p. 71.

23. Thompson, *Political Mythology of Apartheid*, pp. 72–73.

24. Worden, *Making of Modern South Africa*, pp. 11–12.

25. Thompson, *Political Mythology of Apartheid*, p. 75.

26. Ibid., p. 76.

27. Davidson, *Africa in History*, p. 269.

28. Thompson, *Political Mythology of Apartheid*, p. 70.

29. Thompson, *History of South Africa*, pp. 111–112.

30. Allister Sparks, *The Mind of South Africa* (New York: Knopf, 1990), pp. 148–149.

31. Thompson, *History of South Africa*, p. 184.

32. Sparks, *Mind of South Africa*, p. 153.

33. Merle Lipton, *Capitalism and Apartheid: South Africa, 1910–1984* (Totowa, NJ: Rowman & Allenheld, 1985), pp. 14–15.

34. Thompson, *History of South Africa*.

35. Oliver and Atmore, *Africa Since 1800*, p. 295.

36. Thompson, *History of South Africa*, p. 206; Lipton, *Capitalism and Apartheid*.

37. Francis Meli, *South Africa Belongs to Us: A History of the ANC* (Bloomington: Indiana University Press, 1988).

38. Nozipho Diseko, "The Origins and Development of the South African Student's Movement (SASM): 1968–1976," *Journal of South African Studies* 18 (March 1991): 40–62.

39. Howard Barrell, "The Turn to the Masses: the African National Congress' Strategic Review of 1978–1979," *Journal of South African Studies* 18 (March 1991): 64–92.

40. Bill Keller, "In South Africa, A White 'Third Force' of Violence Is Confirmed," *The New York Times*, March 20, 1994, section 4, p. 5.

41. Thompson, *History of South Africa*.

42. Bill Keller, "Where Blood Ran and a Tide Turned," *The New York Times*, March 27, 1994, section 4, p. 5.

43. Bill Keller, "Rival Visions of a Post-Apartheid Future Divide South Africa's Zulus," *The New York Times*, April 4, 1994, p. A1; Tom Masland and Joseph Conteras, "Ballots or Bullets," *Newsweek*, April 11, 1994, pp. 34–37.
44. Frantz Fanon, *Black Skin, White Masks*, translated by Charles Markmann (New York: Grove Weidenfeld, 1967), p. 87.
45. Stephen Greenhouse, "Mandela Bids U.S. Assist in New Fight," *The New York Times*, October 5, 1994, p. A11; "Even Less Equal in South Africa," *The Economist*, October 25, 1997, p. 5; Stephen Greenhouse, "Mandela Bids U.S. Assist in New Fight," *The New York Times*, October 5, 1994, p. A11.
46. Bill Keller, "A Post-Apartheid Nightmare: Hospitals Swamped," *The New York Times*, August 29, 1994, p. A4.
47. "The Colours of Brazil," *Economist*, May 10, 1986, p. 42.
48. Charles Whitaker, "Blacks in Brazil: the Myth and the Reality," *Ebony*, February, 1991, pp. 41, 60–64.
49. Daniela Hart, "Racial Bias Entrenched," *Chronicle of Higher Education*, July 20, 1988, p. A31–32.
50. E. Bradford Burns, *A History of Brazil*, 3rd ed. (New York: Cornell Press, 1993), pp. 23–27.
51. Thomas Skidmore and Peter Smith, *Modern Latin America*, 2nd ed. (Oxford: Oxford University Press, 1994), p. 140; Burns, *History of Brazil*, pp. 216–217.
52. Michael Hanchard, *Orpheus and Power: The Movimento Negro of Rio de Janeiro and São Paulo, Brazil, 1945–1988* (Princeton, NJ: Princeton University Press, 1994). p. 45.
53. Hanchard, *Orpheus and Power*, p. 43.
54. Thomas Skidmore, *Black Into White: Race and Nationality in Brazilian Thought* (Oxford: Oxford University Press, 1974), pp. 48–69; Dain Borges, "Puffy, Ugly, Slothful and Inert: Degeneration in Brazilian Social Thought, 1880–1940," *Journal of Latin American Studies* 25 (1993): 235–256.
55. Thomas Sanders, "Racial Discrimination and Black Consciousness in Brazil," *American Universities Field Staff Reports* 42 (1981); Hanchard, *Orpheus and Power*.
56. Sanders, "Racial Discrimination and Black Consciousness in Brazil," p. 2.
57. George Andrews, "Racial Inequality in Brazil and the United States: A Statistical Comparison," *Journal of Social History* 26 (1992): 234.
58. Peggy Webster and Jeffrey Dwyer, "The Cost of Being Nonwhite in Brazil," *Sociology and Social Research* 72 (1988): 136–142.
59. Andrews, "Racial Inequality in Brazil and the United States," pp. 247–254.
60. Ibid., pp. 256–257.
61. Howard Winant, "Rethinking Race in Brazil," *Journal of Latin American Studies* 24 (1992): 173–192.
62. Quoted in Whitaker, "Racial Bias Entrenched."
63. Ibid.
64. Anthony Faiola, "Yet Another Fresh Start for Brazil," *Washington Post National Weekly Edition*, October 20, 1997, p. 19.
65. Fanon, *Wretched of the Earth*, p. 41.
66. Pierre Birnbaum, *Anti-Semitism in France: A Political History from Leon Blum to the Present*, trans. Miriam Kochan (Oxford: Blackwell, 1992), p. 1.
67. Stephen Wilson, *Ideology and Experience: Antisemitism in France at the Time of the Dreyfus Affair* (Rutherford, NJ: Fairleigh Dickinson University Press, 1982).
68. Alan Riding, "Mitterand's Mistakes: Vichy Past is Unveiled," *The New York Times*, September 9, 1994. p. A4.
69. Maxim Silverman, *Deconstructing the Nation: Immigration, Racism and Citizenship in Modern France* (London: Routledge, 1992), p. 10.
70. Douglas Johnson, "The Making of the French Nation," in *The National Question in Europe in Historical Context*, eds. Mikulas Teich and Roy Porter (Cambridge: Cambridge University Press, 1993), p. 59.
71. Silverman, *Deconstructing the Nation*, pp. 3–4.
72. R. D. Grillo, *Ideologies and Institutions in Urban France* (Cambridge: Cambridge University Press, 1985), p. 65.
73. Silverman, *Deconstructing the Nation*, p. 3.
74. Julia Kristeva, *Nations Without Nationalism* (New York: Columbia University Press, 1993), pp. 97–98.
75. Catherine Wihtol De Wenden, "North African Immigration and the French Political Imaginary," in *Race, Discourse and Power in France*, ed. Maxim Silverman (Brookfield, VT: Gower, 1991), p. 108.
76. Daniel Singer, "Liberte, Egalite, Racisme?, *Nation*, October 21, 1996, p. 19.
77. Kristeva, *Nations Without Nationalism*, pp. 13–14.
78. Chris Woodall, "Arabicide in France: an Interview with Fausto Giudice," *Race and Class* 35 (1993): 21–33.
79. Youssef Ibrahim, "France Bans Muslim Scarf in Its Schools," *The New York Times*, September 11, 1994, p. 4.
80. Ibid.
81. Lœtitia Creamean, "Membership of Foreigners: Algerians in France," *Arab Studies Quarterly* 16 (1996): 49–67.
82. Fanon, *Wretched of the Earth*, p. 40.
83. Pinar Batur-VanderLippe, *Broken Mirrors*.
84. "Planned Muslim Center Disturbs Muscovites," *The Current Digest of the Post-Soviet Press*, September 7, 1994. pp. 1–2.
85. Ibid.
86. "How Fascism Starts," letter by Sasha Kalner, in *Small Fires: Letters from the Soviet People to OGONYOK Magazine, 1987–1990*, eds. Christopher Cerf and Marina Albee (New York: Simon & Schuster, 1990), pp. 212–213.
87. Roman Szporluk, "The Imperial Legacy and the Soviet Nationalities Problem," in *The Nationalities Factor in Soviet Politics and Society*, eds. Lubomyr Hajda and Mark Beissinger (Boulder, CO: Westview Press, 1990), pp. 1–2.
88. Hans Knippenberg, "The 'Nationalities Question' in the Soviet Union," in *States and Nations: The Rebirth of the 'Nationalities Question' in Europe*, eds. Hans van Amersfoort and Hans Knippenberg (Amsterdam: KNAG, 1991), p. 44.
89. Simon Dixon, "The Russians: The Dominant Nationality," in *The Nationalities Question in the Soviet Union*, ed. Graham Smith (London: Longman, 1990), p. 23.
90. Muriel Atkin, *Russia and Iran, 1780–1828* (Minneapolis: University of Minnesota Press, 1980), p. 75.
91. Dixon, "The Russians: The Dominant Nationality," pp. 23–24.
92. Hans Kohn, *Pan-Slavism: Its History and Ideology* (New York: Vintage Books, 1960).
93. Rachel Denber, "Introduction," in *The Soviet Nationality Reader: The Disintegration in Context*, ed. Rachel Denber (Boulder, CO: Westview Press, 1992), pp. 4–5.
94. Steven Erlanger, "Russia's Nationalists Love a Man in Uniform," *The New York Times*, October 9, 1994, section 4, p. 5.
95. Dorinda Elliott, "Solzhenitsyn Goes Home," *Newsweek*, June 6, 1994, p. 41.

96. Celestine Bohlen, "Zhirinovsky Cult Grows: All Power to the Leader," *The New York Times*, April 5, 1994, p. A1.

97. Michael Gordon, "Irking U.S., Yeltsin Signs Law Protecting Orthodox Church," *The New York Times*, September 27, 1997, p. A1, A5.

98. Steve LeVine, "Revival of the Empire?" *Newsweek*, June 27, 1994, pp. 26–29.

99. Rabia Ali and Lawrence Lifschultz, "In Plain View," in *Why Bosnia?* eds. Rabia Ali and Lawrence Lifschultz (Stony Creek, Conn.: Pamphleteer's Press, 1993), p. xvii.

100. Ibid., p. xlvii.

101. Roger Cohen, "West's Fears in Bosnia: 1) Chaos, 2) Islam," *The New York Times*, March 13, 1994, section 4, p. 3.

102. John Pomfret, "U.N., Western Officials Doubt Bosnian Serbs Will Be Punished, *Washington Post*, July, 22, 1994, p. A19.

103. Elaine Sciolino, "U.S. Abandons Push to End Bosnian Weapons Embargo," *The New York Times*, September 30, 1994, p. A8.

104. Ibid., p. xx.

105. Charles Lane, "Slav Story," *New Republic*, March 14, 1994.

106. Laurie Laird, "Shared History: Serbia's Ties to Russia," *Europe: the Magazine of the European Community*, June, 1994.

107. Ibid.

108. "Russian Volunteers—Not Diplomats—Help Serbs," *Current Digest of the Post-Soviet Press XLIV* 49 (1992): 18; see also p. 17.

109. "Two French Soldiers Go Over to Serbs," Reuters, July 26, 1994.

110. Ivan Lovrenovic, "The Hatred of Memory," *The New York Times*, May 28, 1994, section 4, p. 19; Charles Lane, "A Muslim Town's Long Nightmare," *Newsweek*, September 6, 1993, pp. 26–27; John Kifner, "Through the Serbian Mind's Eye," *The New York Times*, April 10, 1994, section 4, p. 1.

111. Aleksa Djilas, "The Nation That Wasn't," *The New Republic*, September 21, 1992, pp. 25–31.

112. Andrew Bell-Fialkoff, "A Brief History of Ethnic Cleansing," *Foreign Affairs* (Summer 1993): 116.

113. Batur-VanderLippe, *Broken Mirrors*.

114. Pinar Batur-VanderLippe, "The Discourse of Counterattack: Ethnic Movements and the Formation of Ethnic Identity." (Unpublished Ph.D. dissertation, University of Texas, 1992.)

115. Fanon, *Wretched of the Earth*.

116. Batur-VanderLippe, *Broken Mirrors*.

Photo Credits

Index